CO-AWS-315

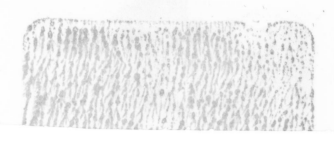

THE GREAT HISTORIES

A series under the general editorship of

Hugh R. Trevor-Roper,

REGIUS PROFESSOR OF MODERN HISTORY, OXFORD UNIVERSITY

THE ANNALS and
THE HISTORIES

The first ten titles in

THE GREAT HISTORIES *series are:*

HERODOTUS, *edited by W. G. Forrest, Fellow of Wadham College, Oxford University.*

THUCYDIDES, *edited by P. A. Brunt, Fellow of Oriel College, Oxford University.*

POLYBIUS, *edited by E. Badian, Lecturer of Ancient History, Durham University.*

JOSEPHUS, *edited by M. I. Finley, Fellow of Jesus College, Cambridge University.*

TACITUS, *edited by Hugh Lloyd-Jones, Regius Professor of Greek, Oxford University.*

MACHIAVELLI, *edited by Myron P. Gilmore, Professor of History, Harvard University.*

GUICCIARDINI, *edited by J. R. Hale, Fellow of Jesus College, Oxford University.*

VOLTAIRE, *edited by J. H. Brumfitt, Senior Lecturer in French, St. Andrews University.*

GIBBON, *edited by H. R. Trevor-Roper, Regius Professor of Modern History, Oxford University.*

HENRY ADAMS, *edited by E. N. Saveth, Professor of History, The New School.*

TACITUS

THE ANNALS
and
THE HISTORIES

Translated by A. J. Church and W. J. Brodribb

Edited and Abridged with an Introduction by

HUGH LLOYD-JONES

REGIUS PROFESSOR OF GREEK, OXFORD UNIVERSITY

TWAYNE PUBLISHERS, INC.
31 Union Square, N. Y. 3

Contents

*Tacitus: The Annals
and The Histories*

Introduction

For more than a century before the birth of Cornelius Tacitus, the Roman Republic had been nothing but a name and a memory. It had been not a democracy, but an aristocracy; the fierce rivalry of the Roman nobles for office and prestige had found its outlet first in a long series of foreign wars, but later, after the subjugation of the whole civilized western world, in civil strife. The end of the third century before Christ had seen the decisive defeat of Carthage, Rome's chief rival for world dominion; and during the next hundred years the kingdoms of the eastern Mediterranean fell one after another to Roman arms. Rome had already conquered Spain from Carthage; now she secured the land route to Spain by the acquisition of a strip of southern France. With the tribunate of Tiberius Gracchus in 133 B.C., the long sequence of Roman civil wars began. A powerful faction of nobles, united by jealousy of the younger Scipio, then the leading citizen, exploited the agrarian problem to launch a bid for power. Rome still obstinately refused the franchise to her Italian allies; and soon their grievances too became a factor in the clash of rival groups. Late in the century, the victories of a great general, Gaius Marius, saved Rome from the threat of annihilation by Teutonic invaders. Then Marius became a tool in the hands of unscrupulous demagogues, and their excesses provoked a violent reassertion of the Senate's power by means of the dictatorship of Lucius Cornelius Sulla. But Sulla's constitutional settlement did not last; it was rapidly undermined by many factors, chiefly by the vast prestige won by the brilliant young general Cnæus Pompeius Magnus. For a time Pompeius combined with two other political dynasts, Marcus Licinius Crassus and Gaius Julius Cæsar; then after Crassus' death Pompeius and Cæsar quarreled. Cæsar had conquered Gaul for Rome, and in doing so had trained a model army. Forced into an unnatural alliance with the main body of aristocrats, Pompeius fought this army and was defeated. So Cæsar got supreme power. He did not hold it long. His murder in the name of the Republic failed to restore republican government; his murderers were quickly crushed by the combination of three military dynasts—Marcus Antonius, Marcus Lepidus, and Cæsar's great-nephew and adopted son, later called Augustus. Lepidus was soon eliminated, and Antonius and the young Cæsar divided the western world between them; Antonius took the eastern, Cæsar the western half. When the inevitable conflict came, Cæsar was triumphant. With an efficiency greater than that of any of his predecessors and with a ruthlessness not less than theirs, he established a new order in the Roman state. The legal forms of republican government were superficially respected; Augustus claimed to have restored the Republic by his actions. The Senate's prejudices were patiently humored; Augustus needed its collaboration. But the subtly contrived structure of republican forms that was designed to hide the facts of power is not of prime importance; what matters is that the entire armed forces of the Empire were now under one man's absolute control.

With unrivaled cunning and relentlessness, Augustus firmly laid the foundations of the new monarchy. What remained of the old aristocracy combined peacefully with the generals and administrators who had risen under Augustus to form a new governing class; and so great was Augustus' discretion that only rarely did its members feel the iron hand within his velvet glove. The government of the provinces, now freed from the extortion and oppression practiced by so many governors under the Republic, was now vastly improved; the danger from Germany in the west and from Parthia in the east was guarded against by an active and intelligent frontier policy which used force or diplomacy as the case

required. The later Empire was to look back to the long
reign of Augustus as a golden age.

Augustus' plans to found a dynasty were wrecked by
the premature deaths of the nephew and later the two
grandsons whom he had marked out as his successors.
When he died in 14 A.D., he was succeeded by his stepson, Tiberius Claudius Nero, now fifty-six years old and
an experienced statesman and general. Tiberius' administration of the provinces was successful; in his relations with the governing class at Rome he was less
happy. Augustus had obliged Tiberius to adopt as his
heir not his son, Drusus, but his nephew, Germanicus,
an affable young man whose popularity won him a reputation which his known achievements hardly justify.
After conducting military operations in Germany whose
importance Tacitus has much exaggerated, Germanicus
was sent on a special mission to the East. There he
quarreled with the governor of Syria, Cnæus Piso, a
hot-tempered Roman nobleman and a friend of Tiberius.
When Germanicus died in suspicious circumstances,
Piso was tried on a charge of having poisoned him, and
anticipated condemnation by committing suicide. Germanicus' widow, Agrippina, herself a granddaughter of
Augustus, carried on a feud against the Emperor; her
imprudence was artfully exploited by the prefect of the
prætorian guard, Sejanus, who had become Tiberius'
chief adviser and secretly aspired to be chosen as his
successor. From early in the reign, there had been a
series of trials for the new and indeterminate offense
known as *maiestas;* this properly meant "diminishing
the majesty of the Roman people," but could be stretched
to cover not only actual conspiracy, but even the vaguest
indications of hostility or disrespect toward the Emperor. Agrippina's elder son, Nero, was executed and
she herself and her son Drusus were imprisoned through
the scheming of Sejanus, who, while Tiberius remained
in the seclusion of Capri, seemed to direct affairs at
Rome. Finally Tiberius received a warning that his minister was plotting against his life. Acting with great
speed and secrecy to ensure success, he sent orders for
the immediate execution of Sejanus; there followed a

massacre of Sejanus' family and many of his associates. Tiberius did not relent toward the family of Germanicus; after the death of Sejanus, Agrippina and Drusus died in prison.

Soon after this, in 37 A.D., Tiberius died at the age of seventy-nine. His son Drusus had predeceased him, poisoned, it was believed, by Sejanus; and the next emperor was his nephew, Gaius, the third son of Germanicus and Agrippina, nicknamed Caligula. The happenings of his reign are little known, since the part of Tacitus' work in which they were described is missing; but though some historians have labored to defend him, it seems clear that Gaius was a tyrant of the worst sort, probably a homicidal maniac. After four years he was assassinated, and was succeeded by his uncle Claudius, a brother of Germanicus who had so far taken little part in public life, owing to the supposed feebleness of his understanding.

How far Claudius deserved this reputation is disputed. He was intelligent enough to have written several learned, though pedantic, histories; and he was certainly conscientious in the discharge of his imperial duties. But he was far too easily influenced by others, partly by the able but unscrupulous Greek freedmen whom he used to form a substitute for a civil service, and still more by two successive wives, each equally disastrous. The first, Messallina, stopped at nothing to satisfy her lust and greed; in the end she went too far even for Claudius. After her execution Claudius married his niece, daughter of Germanicus and Agrippina and called after her mother, whose pride and ambition she inherited. Agrippina persuaded Claudius to pass over Britannicus, his son by Messallina, and to appoint as his successor her own son by a previous marriage, Lucius Domitius Ahenobarbus, whom he adopted under the imperial name of Nero. Under Claudius the imperial administration maintained its high quality; but like Tiberius, the Emperor was unhappy in his relations with the ruling class, and the succession of treason trials and executions of men of note continued.

In 54 A.D. Claudius died, poisoned, it was thought, by

Agrippina, and Nero at seventeen succeeded to the Empire. The first five years that followed were a period of model government, while Nero relied on the advice of Seneca, the greatest writer of the time, and Burrus, prefect of the prætorian guard. The imperial government did all it could to conciliate the Senate; the provinces continued to be well administered; and when Rome quarreled with Parthia over the buffer kingdom of Armenia, the command was given to a great general, Corbulo, who was to win important victories.

Then Nero's real character asserted itself. In 59 he had Agrippina murdered and in 62 Burrus died and was replaced by two successors, one of whom was the evil Tigellinus. Under his influence and that of his second wife, Poppæa Sabina, Nero threw off Seneca's restraining hand and began a reign of terror. A formidable conspiracy, designed to replace him by a distinguished senator called Gaius Piso, was detected and the conspirators, including Seneca and his nephew, the poet Lucan, wiped out with savage fury; then Corbulo was charged with plotting against the Emperor and was forced to commit suicide. In 68 a serious rebellion broke out: Gaius Julius Vindex, governor of the central Gallic province whose capital was at Lugdunum (Lyons), marched against Nero, while another proconsul rebelled in Africa and at Rome the prætorian prefect, Nymphidius Şabinus, schemed to get the Empire for himself. Resolute action might have saved the situation, but Nero panicked, fled from the palace, and committed suicide.

After Nero's reign of terror the Julio-Claudian family was extinct, and in Tacitus' words the secret became known that emperors could be made at other places besides Rome. The army of Vindex was crushed by the able but lowborn governor of Upper Germany, Verginius Rufus, who then refused the offer of his troops to make him emperor. But Vindex had been joined in his revolt by the legions in Spain under Servius Sulpicius Galba, an elderly and respected member of a great Roman family. Galba marched on Rome, supported by the governor of Lusitania (Portugal), Marcus Salvius Otho, the former favorite of Nero, and soon occupied the city, suppressed Nymphidius, and before the end of 68 established himself as Emperor.

But Galba's refusal to bribe them angered the troops; and his choice of a respectable young nobleman, Lucius Piso, as his successor provoked the jealousy of Otho. The prætorian guard rose against him; he perished miserably, and Otho was declared Emperor. But almost at once Otho was confronted with a new candidate for power, Aulus Vitellius, governor of Lower Germany. The German legions crossed the Alps and defeated Otho in a great battle at Bedriacum, near Cremona. Otho might have carried on resistance but preferred suicide, and his conqueror replaced him on his precarious throne.

Vitellius now had to reckon with the large forces stationed in the East, who chose as their candidate for emperor Titus Flavius Vespasianus. Vespasian, as we call him, was then in Palestine, besieging Jerusalem with a large army. It was the last stage of the great Jewish revolt made famous by the historian Josephus. Vespasian left the siege to his son Titus and himself prepared to march on Italy. His advance guard, led by the military adventurer and convicted forger Antonius Primus, defeated Vitellius' generals in a great battle near Cremona and marched on Rome. There Vespasian's brother, Flavius Sabinus, who happened to be prefect of the city, had failed in an attempt at negotiation and had had to take refuge in the Capitol. Vitellius' supporters had besieged and finally massacred him and his companions, so that the temple of Capitoline Jupiter, the most sacred monument of the state religion, had been burned to ashes. Long before the new claimant to the Empire reached the scene, Antonius' troops had occupied the city and Vitellius and his chief supporters had been cut to pieces.

Vespasian was a sensible and unpretentious military man of humble origins; he governed the Empire successfully for ten years before his death in 79. Abroad, his son Titus finished off the Jewish war; Julius Agricola began his successful career as governor of Britain; and on the German and Parthian frontiers peace was preserved. The Empire benefited from Vespasian's strict economy in money matters. At home, he handled the

Senate with discretion, although he came into sharp
conflict with the small family group of strict Stoics
which had already suffered under Nero for its republican sympathies.

Vespasian's elder son Titus succeeded him, but survived him by only two years. He was succeeded in his
turn by his far less able and popular brother, Domitian,
who reigned from 81 to 96. At first Domitian continued
the good government of his father and brother; but after
an unsuccessful rebellion in Upper Germany in 89, he
launched out on a reign of terror, culminating in 93 with
a small massacre of leading senators. Again the strict
Stoics were the chief sufferers.

When Domitian perished, not at the hands of indignant senators but at those of his wife and some of his
freedmen, Marcus Cocceius Nerva, a respectable and
cautious senator of advanced years, was chosen to succeed him. In 97, for part of which year Tacitus was
consul, Nerva's feeble government led to a crisis, making it urgent for him to choose without delay an heir
who would be strong enough to rule effectively. He
found one in the governor of Upper Germany, Marcus
Ulpius Traianus, who on Nerva's death in 98 succeeded
to the Empire. Trajan proved a successful ruler, able
to keep on good terms with the Senate as well as with
the armies while he embarked on a forward policy on
the frontiers. The Dacians (in modern Romania), with
whom Domitian had made a treaty, were reduced and
incorporated in the Empire; and after a successful war
against the Parthians, Armenia and Mesopotamia were
made Roman provinces. While Trajan was on his death-
bed in Cilicia in 117, it was announced that he had
adopted as his heir Publius Ælius Hadrianus, the husband of his great-niece. The circumstances were suspicious. Trajan's wife, Plotina, was accused of having
managed the adoption; and with very little delay Hadrian
reversed his predecessor's policy by giving up Armenia
and Mesopotamia. During the first year of the new
reign four men who had held high office under Trajan
were executed for alleged conspiracy. But Hadrian proved
a successful ruler, assiduous in organizing frontier de-

fense, prudent in financial matters, and tactful with the Senate. Only his marked partiality for everything Greek incurred some disapproval, and the increasing importance of the informal council that advised the Emperor, together with the growth of an imperial civil service staffed for the most part by Roman knights, presaged a further decline in senatorial power. After Hadrian's death in 138, the Antonine dynasty, founded by his successor, ensured good government until 180 when Marcus Aurelius was succeeded by his son Commodus.

THE LIFE OF CORNELIUS TACITUS

Like several earlier historians of Rome, Tacitus had a distinguished career in the service of the Roman state. Cornelius Tacitus—whether his first name was Gaius or Publius is uncertain—was born in 56 or 57 A.D., when Claudius had been Emperor for five years. At about this time a certain Cornelius Tacitus held the not unimportant post of financial agent of the government in Gallia Belgica, and he may have been the father of the great historian. Definite evidence is lacking, but it is likely that Tacitus was one of the many distinguished Romans of the time to come from a provincial family. Several facts seem to indicate that the place of his origin was Gallia Narbonensis, the southern strip of France, which had been acquired by Rome long before Cæsar's conquest of the main part of Gaul. But by the time of the historian's adolescence, his family must have moved to Rome.

As a young man Tacitus received the elaborate training in oratory that was necessary for all who aspired to high office in the Roman state. We learn something of his early years from his *Dialogue on Orators,* a work of uncertain date but perhaps published in 102 A.D., when the friend to whom it is dedicated held the consulship. The dialogue is supposed to take place during Vespasian's reign, in 75; and among its characters are two of the leading orators of that time, to whom Tacitus, according to the usual Roman custom, attached himself to serve a kind of apprenticeship. The subject of the work is one much discussed at that time—the decline of Roman eloquence. It reveals a dissatisfaction with the superficial training in declamation on imaginary and sometimes ridiculous subjects with which many of Tacitus' contemporaries were content, and expounds the same exalted conception of the orator that had been held by Cicero and was revived by the leading teacher of rhetoric in Tacitus' own time, Quintilian. Poetry, history, and philosophy must be studied by the aspiring orator; he should learn his trade not by performing artificial exercises under a professional teacher, but by attaching himself to some eminent advocate and politician whom he can accompany to the scenes of his activity and observe in action. Tacitus was to become the leading orator of his time, and must have distinguished himself from the first in this capacity.

At about the age of twenty, an aspirant for office like the young Tacitus would normally serve for a year with a legion as military tribune. Tacitus may have done this in 76 or 77. In the latter year he was betrothed to the daughter of one of the most eminent Romans of the time, Cnæus Julius Agricola. Agricola's father originated from Forum Julii (now Fréjus) in Gallia Narbonensis (Narbonese Gaul), and had reached the prætorship. As a young man Agricola took part in the suppression of Boudicca's revolt in Britain, and after holding the prætorship he commanded a legion there. Under Vespasian he successfully governed Aquitania, in Gaul, and during the year of his daughter's betrothal he held the consulship. At its conclusion he became governor of Britain, where he remained for seven years. Agricola's model governorship was marked both by military victories and by notable success in promoting civilization among the Britons; but it was rewarded by no further promotion. The Emperor Domitian looked on him with fear and jealousy, and when the time came at which Agricola might have taken part in the ballot for the two most coveted provinces, Africa and Asia, he was advised not to compete. This neglect did not provoke Agricola to any show of dissatisfaction; and when he died at the early age of fifty-three he had been prudent enough to name the Emperor among his heirs.

Passing through the normal stages of the official career, Tacitus was probably quæstor in 81 or 82, and then ædile or military tribune two or three years later. In 88 he held the office of prætor, and was also accorded an important priesthood, being made one of the fifteen members of the priestly college concerned with the administration of the secular games held in that year (see *Annals* XI, 11). After his prætorship he left for an appointment in the provinces and when his father-in-law died in 93 he had been out of Rome for four years. For the last year of this period he may have been governor of a minor province.

Tacitus held the consulship during part of the year 97, the year after Domitian's murder and the succession of the admirable Nerva. It is not safe to guess that he owed his consulship to the change of emperor. Instances are not wanting of consuls, who had been designated in advance, holding the office even after the death of the emperor by whom they had been chosen and the official condemnation of his memory; and the succession of offices held by Tacitus under Domitian shows that the hatred for that Emperor's tyranny which he revealed after Domitian's death found no open expression while he was alive. As consul he pronounced with dignity and eloquence the funeral oration of the eminent Verginius Rufus, three times consul, who after Nero's death in 68 had refused the offer of his troops to make him emperor. Three years later, under Trajan, Tacitus joined another famous writer, his friend the younger Pliny, in prosecuting a former governor of Africa, Marius Priscus, on charges of extortion and oppression. Priscus was condemned and exiled, though as Juvenal comments dryly, the unfortunate provincials were no better off for that. Doubtless Tacitus held other offices, probably abroad; and we know from an inscription that in 112-13 he held the appointment that above all others set the seal on a distinguished public career—the proconsulate of Asia. How long he survived after that is not certain; but it seems likely that he lived some years into the reign of Hadrian.

THE WORKS OF TACITUS

The earliest of Tacitus' works was probably the short biography of his father-in-law, Agricola, which seems to have been published either not long before or not long after the death of Nerva and the accession of Trajan, on January 28, 98 A.D. The panegyric on a famous man was at this time an accepted literary genre; so was the historical excursus on a particular country or a particular campaign; and the *Agricola* is something between the two. Soon afterward, perhaps in 99, while the new Emperor was still absent on the Rhine, Tacitus published the *Germania,* a monograph on the country and people of Germany. The subject could not have been more topical, nor the treatment more acceptable to authority; for the warning against the danger to Rome presented by the Germans must have been welcome to an emperor then actively engaged in guarding against this threat. Much of the information in the book was already out of date at the time of publication; no doubt it came from written sources. The author characteristically contrasts the primitive virtues of the barbarians with the civilized vices of his countrymen. In modern times the work has supplied material to believers in the noble savage and to writers on the German character, for and against.

Although the *Histories* begin where the *Annals,* when complete, finished, they were written earlier. Part of them seems to have circulated in 105, and in 106 Tacitus asked his friend Pliny for information about the eruption of Vesuvius in 79, in which his uncle, the elder Pliny, had lost his life. The *Histories* begin with the first day of 69 A.D., the Year of the Four Emperors. They were in twelve books. Only the first four books and the first twenty-six chapters of Book V are extant. Book I describes the murder of Galba, the accession of Otho, and the march of Vitellius' armies from Germany across the Alps. Book II contains the war between Otho and Vitel-

lius, Otho's suicide, and the proclamation of Vespasian
as emperor by the eastern armies. Book III begins with
Antonius Primus' invasion of Italy and describes the defeat of Vitellius' generals at Cremona, the burning of
the Capitol, the occupation of Rome, and the death of
Vitellius. Book IV is mainly occupied with the revolt of
the Batavi under Julius Civilis which followed the march
from Germany of Vitellius' legions. The surviving fragment of Book V begins with Titus' siege of Jerusalem
and finishes off with Civilis' rebellion. The book probably contained the whole story of the siege, and may
have gone on well into Vespasian's reign, perhaps as far
as 73 A.D. Book VI probably ended with the death of
Vespasian in 79; if so, Books VII-XII will have contained the fifteen years of Domitian's reign.

Tacitus probably went straight on to write the *Annals,*
which were in eighteen books. Book II, Chapter 61 can
hardly have been written after 117 A.D.; that is the most
positive indication we have of the date of the work's
composition. Book I begins with the death of Augustus
and the accession of Tiberius in 14 A.D. The first six
books contained Tiberius' reign and ended with his
death; but our single manuscript breaks off soon after
the beginning of Book V, just before the imprisonment
of Germanicus' widow and her elder son. All the rest of
Book V and some thirty chapters of Book VI are missing; the narrative starts again just after the execution
of Sejanus. Books VII-XII covered the reigns of Gaius and
Claudius; but Books VII-X are entirely lost, and only
about half (the second half) of Book XI survives. What
we have of Book XI describes the final episodes in the
career of Messallina, and Book XII carries the narrative
to the death of Claudius. Books XIII-XVIII were devoted
to the reign of Nero; but about halfway through Book
XVI the manuscript finally breaks off.

TACITUS IN LATER TIMES

The younger Pliny predicted that his friend's historical
works would be immortal; but they rapidly went out of
fashion in the archaizing and mannered second century;

nor did the rise of Christianity, of which Tacitus speaks so scathingly, assist his reputation to recover. But in 275 the Emperor Tacitus, who claimed to be a descendant of the historian, took measures to ensure the survival of his works; and during the fourth century they seem to have enjoyed some esteem. They influenced several writers of imperial biography at that time; and Ammianus Marcellinus, a Greek of Antioch, continued Tacitus' *Histories* from the death of Nerva down to the death of the Emperor Valens in 378, in a Latin history which is not unworthy of its model. During the fifth century, an age of disaster for the Empire, Tacitus could still be censured by the Christian historian Orosius and praised by the poet Sidonius Apollinaris. But with the eclipse of polite letters his works must have been scarce; for in the sixth century we find the learned Cassiodorus referring to him as "a certain Cornelius."

During the dark centuries that follow, we hear nothing of Tacitus. Petrarch, surprisingly, says nothing of him. The first Humanist to show acquaintance with his writings is Boccaccio, who seems to have acquired his knowledge about 1370. During the fifteenth century several writers show a knowledge of his work (except the first six books of the *Annals*). But these early humanists were too intoxicated with Cicero to relish an author who systematically rejected the Ciceronian symmetry in sentence construction; and they were too obsessed with style to value Tacitus for his content.

The first printed text of Tacitus was published by John of Spires at Venice in 1470. It contained *Annals* XI-XVI and all that survives of the *Histories,* together with the three minor works. What was published of the *Annals* and the *Histories* had been preserved by a single manuscript copied at Monte Cassino during the eleventh century; the minor works had survived in a manuscript at Hersfeld in Germany. The former is now at Florence and is known as Codex Mediceus II; the latter disappeared, and has had to be reconstructed laboriously from a number of descendants. Early in the present century part of it was discovered in the library of an Italian nobleman; the owner obstinately refused to allow scholars to make use of it until 1939, when a learned German achieved access, using the powerful persuasion of Heinrich Himmler, to whom he later dedicated his edition. *Annals* I-VI also survived the Middle Ages in a single manuscript, copied at Corvey in Germany during the ninth century, and first edited by the younger Beroaldus under the auspices of the cultivated Pope Leo X (Giovanni de' Medici) in 1515. It is known as Codex Mediceus I, and is also in Florence.

One might have expected that Niccolò Machiavelli would recognize Tacitus as a kindred spirit; and in fact he quotes him more often and with more approval than any previous writer since the printing of his works. But Tacitus meant less to Machiavelli than did Livy, and his main political work, the *Discorsi*, centers on the discussion of Livy and not of Tacitus. Had Machiavelli known the first six books of the *Annals* he might have reacted differently. But he wrote *The Prince* two years before and the *Discorsi* only a year after their first printing. In the *Discorsi* he does not quote them, and it is not likely that he had read them when he wrote it. Livy, whose style is so much more like that of Cicero, was at that time much the more famous author; and Livy's history dealt with a time when Rome was a republic, as Florence was for most of Machiavelli's lifetime.

Yet in the second half of the sixteenth century Tacitus was to acquire astonishing popularity. A reaction against Ciceronianism made it easier to appreciate his style. As early as 1532, Beatus Rhenanus, the friend and biographer of Erasmus, proclaimed Tacitus superior to Livy. But Tacitus did not owe his rise to favor to his style alone. Humanists were becoming less interested in style and more in content; and with the rise of absolute monarchies all over Europe, his content acquired a special interest. Although Machiavelli had failed to champion Tacitus in the way we might have expected, Tacitus owed no small part of the fame he enjoyed during the sixteenth and seventeenth centuries to the Florentine. For at the time of the Council of Trent, the Pope placed Machiavelli on the Index. He could not safely be discussed; but what was to hinder writers interested in political theory from commenting upon the work of a long dead classical historian, a work well calculated to promote the discussion of many burning topics of the age? Scholarly guidance was given to these "Tacitisti" by the great humanist of the Low Countries Justus Lipsius, whose commentary first appeared in 1574, to be followed seven years later by his first edition of the text. Soon afterward Charles Paschal in France, Annibale Scoti in Italy, and Alamos de Barrientes in Spain wrote political commentaries on Tacitus. From this time until the end of the seventeenth century Tacitus served as a peg on which to hang all kinds of political discussion. There flowed from the presses of France, Italy, Spain, Germany, and Holland a stream of collections of aphorisms, treatises, and "discourses" in the Machiavellian manner that used Tacitus as a pretext for the airing of all kinds of contemporary issues. These writers adopted the most diverse attitudes toward their chosen author. In the conflicts between Christianity and *Realpolitik,* between kingship and liberty, both sides might claim him as an ally and both sides might denounce him as an enemy. The learned Lipsius made out Tacitus almost as a Christian; the acute Jesuit Firmiano Strada attacked him as a Machiavellian. To Scipione Ammirato and Filippo Cavriana, who dedicated their works on Tacitus to the Grand Duke of Tuscany, Tacitus was the friend of kings; to Bacon he was the enemy of tyrants. Bacon's view was shared by the most distinguished of the "Tacitisti," Traiano Boccalini, who in a book published at about the time of his death, in 1613, amusingly describes how the author of a panegyric on the present age is cured by Apollo, who makes him the present of a pair of Tacitean spectacles. Boccalini's own *Observations on Tacitus* remained unpublished until 1677. The Senate of Venice referred a request for permission to print them to a commission of five senators, who reported that it was Tacitus' teaching that had produced Machiavelli "and other evil authors."

We must not imagine that at this time Tacitus was valued only as a substitute for Machiavelli. Many read and esteemed him for his own sake. His influence may be seen in the work of every important French moralist from Montaigne to La Rochefoucauld; and the most splendid literary monument to Tacitus, eclipsing Ben Jonson's *Sejanus* (1603), Corneille's *Othon* (1665), and Alfieri's *Ottavia* (1780), is Racine's *Britannicus* (1669).

England was less concerned with Tacitus than the Continent during the sixteenth and seventeenth centuries, perhaps because of the singularity of its political development. But in 1622 a Dutch refugee, who had begun to lecture on the *Annals* at Cambridge, was stopped before he had got to the end of the first chapter. Four years later Sir John Eliot in the House of Commons enraged Charles I by comparing Strafford to Sejanus; and in 1657 Piero Negesch, who had lived in England, published in his native Italian a comparison between Tiberius and Cromwell, much to the advantage of the former. The first important English writer on Tacitus, Thomas Gordon (1684-1750), true to the native empiricism, pours scorn on the dull commonplaces and lifeless paraphrases which he finds typical of the "Tacitisti." Not that his own commentary is closer than theirs to its ostensible subject; it is a political pamphlet against monarchy.

Tacitus was considered an apostle of liberty by a number of eighteenth-century writers: Rousseau, d'Alembert, and Diderot saw him in this light. He was a hero to the apologists of the French Revolution, especially to Camille Desmoulins; and not surprisingly Napoleon pursued him with a deadly hatred. The Emperor planned to write a commentary to refute Tacitus, attacked him in two articles in the *Journal des Débats,* and wanted to have him removed from the syllabus at the Ecole Normale.

> *Tacite en train de flamme accuse nos Séjans*
> *Et son nom prononcé fait pâlir les tyrans*

wrote Joseph-Marie Chénier. The lines cost him his post as an inspector of schools.

Tacitus profoundly influenced Vico and Montesquieu,

who both understood him far better than most of their
predecessors and contemporaries; but in general the
eighteenth century admired him less than the preceding
age. To a severe classicism his style is uncongenial;
and to doubts about his style were added doubts about
his matter. Fénelon and Bayle had both made reser-
vations with regard to Tacitus, and Voltaire looked upon
him with a cold eye. To him Tacitus seemed *"un fana-
tique pétillant d'esprit";* he found it hard to believe in
the excesses of Tiberius on Capri or the atrocities of
Nero. *"Je conçois,"* he wrote, *"que tout Romain avait
l'âme républicain dans son cabinet, et que Tacite se
venge quelque fois, la plume à la main, sur l'usurpation
de l'empereur."* But if Tacitus was not greatly admired
by those eighteenth-century writers who did most to win
for the period its title of the Age of Reason, a notable
exception is Edward Gibbon. Gibbon explicitly refuted
Voltaire's arguments against Tacitus, for whom he expressed the greatest admiration. "I know of no one except Tacitus," he once wrote, "who has quite come up
to my ideas of a philosophic historian."*

The rise of new historical methods together with the
vast increase in the amount of detailed study of the
past caused Tacitus to be subjected to a detailed scrutiny during the nineteenth century. The period covered
by his writings has been the subject of minute re-
searches; his handling of his sources and his credibility
as a witness have been carefully examined; he has become the center of a vast literature. Judged by the
canons of historical method that came into vogue during
the century of Burckhardt, Ranke, and Mommsen, Tacitus must appear deficient. From nineteenth-century Germany came much adverse criticism of a historian whose
methods outraged its scholarly requirements and whose
attitude contrasted lamentably with its cherished principle of trust in rulers. Ranke offered a fair and balanced
judgment, but even his admiration is mixed with disapproval; and at the close of the century Friedrich Leo

* See H. R. Trevor-Roper, *Gibbon* (New York: Washington Square
Press, 1963), p. xvi.

tried to excuse Tacitus' deficiencies on the ground that he was no historian, but a poet.

In our own time the climate of opinion has become more favorable to Tacitus. One can hardly deny that he, like other ancient writers, fails to conform to our principles of historiography. But the growth of a historical sense has made us less prone to pronounce judgment on writers of the past according to our own standards without bearing in mind the nature of their own. Further, we have had good opportunities to study despotism at close quarters and our experience has confirmed that Tacitus' depiction of its workings is less lacking in verisimilitude than many of our more comfortably situated predecessors have supposed. In recent years a reaction in Tacitus' favor has taken place. One of the most eminent historians of our own day broke new ground with a study of the Augustan Principate, so much idealized during the nineteenth century, from a Tacitean point of view, thereby throwing a brilliant new light on every corner of the subject.* Since then he has presented Tacitus himself, in a work of the greatest learning and intelligence, with sympathetic understanding. His Tacitus is shrewd, skeptical, unbiased, and wholly different from the sour, malignant slanderer others have depicted.

In the past Tacitus appeared to some as a cynic, to others as an idealist; to some as the counselor of tyrants, to others as their enemy; to some as a judicious historian, to others as a malicious rhetorician. Since the rise of objective historical studies in the nineteenth century, we have been less prone to force ancient writers into taking sides in the controversies of our own time. But even nowadays Tacitus still provokes the most varying assessments and arouses the most diverse emotions. In the pages that follow we will inquire into the reasons.

TACITUS AS A HISTORIAN

The place of Tacitus among the world's greatest historians has been disputed, but few will challenge his

---

* Sir Ronald Syme, *The Roman Revolution* (Oxford University Press, 1939); paperback edition, 1960.

claim to rank among its greatest writers. First, he is the creator of a style of unique power, dignity, and appropriateness to the subject matter. Strict classicists will deplore it as they did in fifteenth-century Italy and in eighteenth-century France; for like his master, Sallust, Tacitus deliberately rejected the flowing, balanced periods of Ciceronian prose in favor of a harsh and abrupt structure suited to the severity of his matter. No way of writing could be more remote from that of common speech; his language and vocabulary are to a large degree archaic and poetical. Tacitus was the leading orator of his time, trained from boyhood to persuade an audience. His style is nothing if not rhetorical, deliberate, and artificial in the extreme. Tacitus' manner varies with his matter. Sometimes he is flowing, ornate, and eloquent, notably in the *Agricola,* a work belonging to a genre halfway between oratory and history, and in the *Dialogue on Orators,* where the style approaches that of the inventor of this kind of dialogue in Latin, Cicero. More often he is brief, swift, concise, concentrated to the utmost. He takes over from his predecessors the traditional methods of annalistic history. Each year's events are grouped under the names of its two consuls; speeches —in most cases free compositions of the historian, skillfully varied according to speaker and occasion—are put into the mouths of characters at suitable moments; elaborate descriptive set pieces are frequently inserted. Yet Tacitus never degenerates into empty rhetoric; he is preserved from doing so by a truly Roman flair for the actual and the concrete, which fastens unerringly on the salient characteristics of a person or an episode. No historian draws more striking brief sketches of his characters—for instance, those of Poppæa Sabina (*Annals* XIII, 45) and Petronius (*Annals* XVI, 18); none has painted more impressively elaborate portraits than those of Nero, Agrippina, and above all Tiberius. No historian has surpassed him in descriptive power. Take for instance his narrations of the deaths of Galba and Vitellius—the latter all the better to be appreciated if one contrasts it with the matter-of-fact telling of the same story in Suetonius' Life of that Emperor (Ch. 16 f.); the

Bacchanalian festival of Messallina; the suppression of Piso's conspiracy against Nero. No historian has equaled him in the power to coin epigrammatic sayings that are at once concise, striking, and profound. Galba was *"omnium consensu capax imperii nisi imperasset"* ("by universal consent worthy of empire, till he ruled"); the brutal camp prefect Aufidienus Rufus, risen from the ranks, was *"eo immitior quia toleraverat"* ("all the more savage for having gone through the mill"); Domitian could not forgive Agricola because *"proprium humani ingenii est odisse quem læseris"* ("it is part of human nature to hate those whom you have injured"). The list could be protracted indefinitely.

Tacitus' reputation as a writer needs no defense. But must we agree with the eminent German Latinist who at the close of the last century excused Tacitus' failings on the ground that he was not a historian, but a poet? To assess his qualities as a historian, we must consider first his principles and methods. First, it is necessary to understand his attitude to facts. The ancient world did not demand that a historian should himself labor to establish his facts with all possible certainty. If he was writing of his own times, he was obliged to undertake some measure of research; but otherwise he would closely follow written sources. Tacitus used the works of several predecessors, whom he sometimes mentions. We see from the first chapter of the *Annals* that he held them in no high esteem. Their works are lost; but we can get some notion of how Tacitus used them by comparing his work with that of other writers who used the same material: with the Roman history written in Greek by the consul Cassius Dio during the third century and with the lives of emperors written by Plutarch in Tacitus' own time and by Suetonius a little later. When Tacitus finds different stories of the same event he sometimes gives both, quoting the source for each by name; but on the whole he seems to have followed his predecessors in factual matters very closely. In some cases he made use of published speeches. The original of the speech of Claudius at Lyons given by Tacitus in his own version in *Annals* XI, 24 has been preserved in an inscription, and shows that while condensing and improving it, Tacitus was faithful to its general sense. Once only Tacitus quotes the archives of the Senate. How often he made use of them is a controversial question, but it seems unlikely that he did so frequently. Sometimes we can convict him of actual error. Some of his mistakes are trifling, like his confusion between the two daughters of Mark Antony or the two tribunes called Livius Drusus; more serious is the topographical mistake in the account of Otho's defeat at Bedriacum (*Histories* II, 40) and the apparent error in a point of constitutional history which a recently found inscription has exposed (*Annals* I, 15).

Tacitus cannot be accused of having taken no trouble to find out the truth; he took as much pains as most ancient historians. Like them, he was not a researcher in the modern sense; had he been so he would have run counter to the whole conception of history current in his time, and we cannot reasonably reproach him for his failure. Nor can we blame him for not having been interested in the same kind of facts that interest most modern historians. Tacitus shows very little concern and not much respect for the common man. He contributes little to our knowledge of the economic history of the period; and he tells us little of the provinces, except when war or rebellion breaks out in one of them. The mention of some Greek city with a famous past or of a nation with a curious history, like the Jews, stimulates him to antiquarian digression. His interests are the traditional interests of Roman annalists—the wars and victories of Rome and the history of her governing class. To many modern critics this point of view will seem narrow; and he omits much that to a modern historian would seem essential to his purpose. His conception of history was not the same as ours. It follows, not that he was necessarily a bad historian, but that he was a historian of a different kind from that which is now fashionable.

The charge of indifference to truth that is leveled against Tacitus gains more substance from his subtle and pervasive use of innuendo to present facts in such a manner that the reader puts the worst construction on the motives of certain of his characters. A person who has read the *Annals* casually or long ago would very likely believe that Tacitus actually stated that Germanicus was poisoned by Piso on the orders of Tiberius. That is not the case; but the narrative is artfully constructed so as to leave one with that impression. Again, the reader might well think that Tacitus actually reported that the great fire at Rome in Nero's reign was started by the Emperor. In fact Tacitus denies this allegation; but he has presented the episode in such a way that the reader is left with the impression that Nero's guilt is probable. Above all, Tacitus' whole presentation of Tiberius is colored by this technique of innuendo. His considered view is that Tiberius became a tyrant only after the death of his son Drusus (*Annals* VI, 51). Yet like most ancient writers he ignores the possibility of change or development in character, and so must insist that the evil characteristics Tiberius showed in later life must have been latent in his nature from the start. In keeping with this belief, he puts the worst possible construction on every act and saying of the Emperor, even when these acts and sayings are, to all appearance, exactly those of which we might expect the historian to approve. For the sake of contrast with his black portrait of Tiberius, Tacitus has idealized his adopted son, Germanicus, whose victories in Germany were clearly far less important than the narrative would lead us to suppose.

To judge Tacitus' attitude fairly, we must examine the reasons that led him to adopt it. Like his predecessors in writing Roman history, he avows an aim that is first and foremost moral. He will put on record good actions to be admired and bad actions to be despised, thus encouraging the former and discouraging the latter. Tacitus did not take this duty lightly. Livy had been unusual among Roman historians in being a private person outside politics. Most of the others held office in the Roman state; and Tacitus had been consul and had held the most important of Rome's provincial governorships. Tradition demanded that the historian should

survey the actions he recorded from the standpoint of
the austere antique *virtus*—the word means something
between "courage," "manliness," and "excellence"—supposed to have been universal among noble Romans in
the early ages of the Republic's history. The golden age
of Rome was located in the remote past. Recent history
had for centuries been held to show a degeneration from
this legendary ideal. We find this attitude in the enthusiastic Livy, strongly though he maintains that Augustus by his "restoration of the Republic" and by
his moral legislation has to a large extent revived the
ancient virtues; we find it in the disillusioned Sallust,
although what we know of Sallust's private character
hardly suggests that he came nearer to the pattern of
antique morality than did most Roman nobles of his
day.

Tacitus' insistence on judging the men and actions of
his own period by this exacting and somewhat super-
annuated standard must often strike an artificial note.
In a year that had contained some of the most hideous
cruelties perpetrated by Tiberius, one of the most grievous events, according to Tacitus, was the marriage of
Julia, great-granddaughter of Augustus, to a man who
though wealthy and respectable happened not to be a
member of the Senate (*Annals* VI, 27). Livia, great-
niece of Augustus and wife of Tiberius' son Drusus,
"polluted herself and her ancestors by adultery with a
man from an Italian municipality." The man in question was the prefect of the prætorian guard, Sejanus, at
that time the most influential adviser of Tiberius. Nero's
worst atrocities, including the murder of his mother, do
not shock Tacitus more than his public appearances as
a charioteer or a musician. Yet it is unlikely that Tacitus was himself a Roman of ancient lineage. Since his
family probably came from Gallia Narbonensis, he was
therefore further removed from the ancient aristocracy
than either Rubellius Blandus, from Latium, or Ælius
Sejanus, from Etruria.

One may make allowances for this attitude by suggesting that the holders of high office at all periods felt
themselves to be members of a select body. But it is more

relevant to observe that Tacitus is here expressing an
attitude that was part of the tradition taken over from
his predecessors. In the same way he will enumerate
prodigies that have been thought to portend sinister
events, and he will use the special knowledge gained
as the holder of an important priesthood to expound
the niceties of the official cult—niceties for which Tiberius and Domitian also had a special relish. A writer
who continued the Roman tradition of annalistic history would almost inevitably approach his matter from
the standpoint of the ancient aristocracy with its traditional attitudes and prejudices; and a writer of provincial origins—as, in all likelihood, Tacitus was—who
had reached a high position in the Roman state would
have been especially unlikely to form an exception to
this rule.

This prejudice helps to determine an attitude to the
Principate that is far from simple. The reader who
starts from the beginning of the *Annals* will at first
suppose that it is altogether hostile; but as he reads on
he will revise his judgment. First, he will be surprised
to find that Tacitus explicitly acknowledges that in the
present state of the Empire and the world there is no
alternative to monarchic government. What would happen without it can be inferred from the memory of the
long period of civil war before Augustus, or from the
events of 69 A.D., the Year of the Four Emperors, after
the extinction of the dynasty founded by Augustus had
left the succession open, teaching the army commanders
the "secret of the Empire is that emperors could be made
elsewhere than at Rome" (*Histories* I, 4).

It might be argued that in thus acknowledging the
necessity of the Principate, Tacitus was only paying lip
service to the government which he was obliged to serve.
We may therefore assess the sincerity of his profession
by applying to it a test that is often useful in discovering the standpoint of a historian who gives no ex-
plicit statement of his own views and sympathies. Thucydides is notoriously such a case. Some have thought
him a relentless enemy of the Athenian democracy from
the start, others have supposed him a partisan of Peri-

cles, and others have believed him first a friend and later
an enemy of the demos. If we inquire which particular
men and which forms of government Thucydides admires, we find that the Athenian whom, after Pericles,
he especially praises is the moderate oligarch Antiphon,
and that the government he thinks the best at Athens
in his time is that of the Four Hundred, established by
Antiphon and his friends in 411. Starting from this
point of reference we find that Thucydides' other utterances are not hard to reconcile with the viewpoint which
this explicitly stated attitude seems to presuppose.

Let us now apply the same test to Tacitus. Under
Nero and the Flavian emperors an attitude of extreme
opposition was bravely kept up by a small family group
of senators, led first by Thrasea Pætus, then by his son-
in-law, Helvidius Priscus, and lastly by Helvidius' son
and namesake. They were sustained partly by their
strict adherence to the dogmas of the Stoic sect, but
even more by the example of heroes of the last phase
of the Republic, like Brutus, Cassius, and the younger
Cato, men who had chosen death rather than submission
to the dictatorship of Julius Cæsar. Tacitus handles
these martyrs of republicanism with real sympathy and
admiration, but by no means with unqualified approval.
We first meet Thrasea protesting in the Senate about
a trivial matter, the affair of a gladiatorial show at Syracuse. Protests of this nature do no good, says Tacitus
(*Annals* XIII, 49). Next, while the Senate is justifying
Nero's murder of his mother by its sycophantic resolutions, Thrasea walks out, "thereby imperiling himself,"
says Tacitus, "without communicating to the other senators any impulse toward freedom" (*Annals* XIV, 12).
Later, by a gallant effort, Thrasea saves from condemnation a man whose conduct would afterward show that
he had much better have been left to his fate (*Annals*
XIV, 48-9; cf. XVI, 14). Similarly, in his character
sketch of the elder Helvidius (*Histories* IV, 6), Tacitus
records that some found that he cared too much for
reputation.

The men Tacitus most admires are not these brave but
ineffective martyrs of republicanism; they are the men

who quietly carried on the business of the state, ignoring the injustices of a tyrannical emperor. The most obvious example is that of Tacitus' own father-in-law, Julius Agricola, who did not allow the disappointment of his hopes of employment to tempt him into treasonable activity against Domitian. "Those who habitually admire illegal activity," Tacitus writes, "should know that even under bad emperors there can be great men, and that obedience and discretion, if combined with application and activity, can raise a man to no less exalted heights than are reached by perilous paths, with no advantage to the commonwealth beyond the fame won by an ambitious death" (*Agricola*, Ch. 42). In earlier times also it is men like this whom Tacitus admires. Under Tiberius he singles out for special praise two distinguished members of the ancient nobility, Marcus Lepidus and Lucius Piso (*Annals* IV, 20; VI, 10). "Lepidus," writes Tacitus, accentuating with an echo of Sallust the archaic solemnity of his language, "was for that age a wise and high-principled man. Many a cruel suggestion made by the flattery of others he changed for the better, and yet he did not want tact, seeing that he always enjoyed a uniform prestige, and also the favor of Tiberius." Piso, he says, "never proposed a servile motion, and, whenever necessity was too strong for him, he would suggest judicious compromises." So too he commends Lucius Volusius, who died at ninety-three under Nero, "having used his great wealth to do good, and having enjoyed the friendship of so many emperors without having used it to do harm to others." In Nero's reign he praises the conduct of Memmius Regulus, whose "prestige, loyalty, and reputation made him, as far as the Emperor's overshadowing pre-eminence allowed, truly distinguished." Regulus had quietly resigned his wife, Lollia Paulina, to the Emperor Gaius, had conveyed her to him at Rome and presided over their betrothal. He, like others, was notable for "obedience and discretion."

Above all, Tacitus is markedly sympathetic in his attitude to the great writer and statesman whose career, more than any other, illustrates the dilemma that confronted the leading Romans of those times and whose character has since then been endlessly debated—Marcus Annæus Seneca. The son of a wealthy rhetorician who had come to Rome from Corduba in Spain, Seneca early made his mark as orator and man of letters. Under Claudius his career suffered a setback: indiscreet familiarity with an imperial princess led to his banishment to Corsica. But the Emperor's marriage with Agrippina, the sister of Seneca's alleged mistress, more than restored his fortunes. Agrippina chose him as Nero's tutor, and with his pupil's accession he became, for the first few years of the new reign, the most influential man in Rome. He accumulated vast wealth, often the subject of hostile comment. According to one story, the revolt of Boudicca in Britain was partly occasioned by his relentless usury. Yet for the most part he used his influence over Nero to promote good government and to resist evil influences. For that Tacitus gives him full credit. His account of Seneca's last hours, when, ousted from the Emperor's favor by the intrigues of Tigellinus and Poppæa, he became implicated in Piso's conspiracy and received orders to commit suicide, is one of his most moving passages.

A final example serves perhaps best of all to illustrate the attitude of Tacitus. After the period of chaos that followed Nero's fall, some senators hoped that they might bring to book the notorious informers and prosecutors who had grown rich on the proceeds of Nero's reign of terror. Helvidius Priscus made the first move. The Senate was to send a congratulatory mission to the new Emperor, Vespasian, still absent in the East. The composition of such an embassy would normally be settled by drawing lots, but Helvidius proposed that on this occasion the magistrates should make a special selection. He calculated that the Neronian prosecutors would be excluded from the embassy and that their omission would be widely held to show that they were now discredited (*Histories* IV, 6 ff.). The proposal of Helvidius was opposed by one of the ablest and most unscrupulous of the informers, Eprius Marcellus. Why, Tacitus makes him argue, should the Senate depart from prece-

dent? Any of its members will be able to attest its deference. The obstinacy of certain persons must not be allowed to provoke an emperor who would begin by carefully scrutinizing each senator's looks and words. He,
Marcellus, always remembered the nature of the times,
the character of the constitution; he admired the institutions of the past, but followed those of the present; he
prayed for good emperors, but put up with whatever
emperors they had. It was not his speech, but the judgment of the Senate that had destroyed Thrasea. Nero's
friendship toward him had brought him no less anxiety
than exile had to others. In loyalty and courage Helvidius might be a second Cato. He, Marcellus, was simply one member of the Senate which like him had been
enslaved to Nero. The historian's pervasive irony is directed against Marcellus, but not only against him. Can
we really feel certain that the attitude ascribed to Helvidius is in all ways closer to Tacitus' own than that
which he attributes to the archinformer?

Nothing that Tacitus said about the Julio-Claudian or
the Flavian dynasty was likely to offend the regime under which he wrote. When he began his historical activity, the Julio-Claudian house had been extinct for thirty
years; and the Flavian had lately ended with Domitian's
murder, followed by the official condemnation of his
memory. The new regime of Nerva and his successor,
Trajan, did not in its actions depart so far from the
policies of its predecessors as its words might lead
one to suppose; but by its official propaganda it tried to
dissociate itself from them as much as possible. We can
see this most easily from the panegyric on Trajan and
the published correspondence of Tacitus' friend and
collaborator, the younger Pliny. But we see it also from
other monuments of the time, and especially from the
satiric poetry of Martial and Juvenal. Some critics still
regard Juvenal as a courageous denouncer of contemporary abuses; but in his first satire he announces that
he will attack the dead, and he keeps strictly to his
program.

Tacitus' tone of hostility toward earlier emperors is
wholly in keeping with this general tendency of the age

in which he wrote; nor is it inconsistent with his expressed belief that monarchic government is in his time a necessity. In the *Agricola* (Ch. 3) he warmly praises Nerva and Trajan. Nerva, he says, has combined two things formerly thought irreconcilable, liberty and the Principate. It has been maintained that this praise is not sincere, that we cannot know Tacitus' real sentiments toward these emperors since if they had been hostile he could not have expressed them openly. It has even been contended that his works convey a cryptic comment on the happenings of the time after Domitian; that the account of Piso's adoption by Galba in the first book of the *Histories* glances at Trajan's adoption by Nerva; that the description of Nero's degrading indulgence in Greek practices is meant as a warning to another admirer of the Greeks, the Emperor Hadrian; and that Hadrian is obliquely reproached for his abandonment of Trajan's policy of conquest. But theories like these are mere speculations. Nothing in the text compels belief in them, and we have seen that a study of the men marked out by Tacitus for special admiration is decidedly opposed to them. In his own public life he seems to have followed the course laid down by Agricola: under Vespasian, Titus, and Domitian his career prospered. A remarkable passage in the *Agricola* suggests that he was driven to assert his principles all the more fervently by a secret sense of guilt. Agricola was fortunate, he writes, in dying before Domitian's reign of terror in 93, when a group of Stoic martyrs suffered death or exile; he thereby escaped the guilt that attached to those who stood helplessly by while the younger Helvidius and his friends met their fate. "*Our* hands dragged Helvidius to prison; *we* were polluted by looking on while Mauricus and Rusticus went to their ordeal; *we* were stained with Senecio's innocent blood" (*Agricola*, Ch. 45). Seen in the light of these revealing words, Tacitus' repeated implication that men like Agricola are more deserving of imitation than men like Thrasea seems significant.

The profound ambiguity of Tacitus' attitude toward the Principate lends to his writing an element of insincerity, with which his training as an advocate stands in close connection. But this very ambiguity helps him to throw light in innumerable ways upon the tensions and contradictions of his period. Throughout that time the government of the Empire was on the whole good and successful. The personal character of the emperor did not greatly affect the welfare of the provinces, which were in general much better off than they had been under the governors of the republican period, unaccountable to any emperor. No one can deny that Tacitus fails to give the Principate full credit for these achievements; for not only his prejudice against the emperors of whom he writes, but also the restriction of his interests prevent him from doing them justice. But though a modern reader may deplore Tacitus' preoccupation with the relation of the emperors to the governing class at Rome, he can hardly contend that it is either uninteresting or unimportant. All ancient history—perhaps all history— is the history of a ruling oligarchy. To grasp its nature we must follow the changes in the composition of the governing class and the extent and distribution of its powers; and this Tacitus helps us to do. His conception of the history of the period as a personal drama played out between the emperors and the governing class does, in a sense, limit his sphere and narrow his sympathies. But at the same time it not only helps to invest his writing with its immense dramatic power, but gives him the opportunity to display an acute, if in some ways restricted, historical insight.

Many writers suppose that all great historians depend upon some particular philosophy or set of general principles. Some of these have reproached Tacitus with his deficiency in this respect, and others have been at pains to fill the gap with a set of principles of their own manufacture. Stoic elements in his thought may be discovered, as they may be discovered in the thought of any writer of his time. But his work yields no evidence whatever of an adherence to the tenets of any systematic philosophy, whether Stoic, Epicurean, or incipient Neoplatonist. Tacitus is wholly Roman in his lack of interest in general ideas. The nearest thing to a philosophy that can

be discovered in his work is a somewhat vague belief
in fate and destiny. Whether, like most educated as well
as uneducated people in his time, he believed that what
fate held in store for the future could be predicted has
been a matter of dispute. In a famous passage (*Annals*
VI, 22) he notices the Epicurean and Stoic attitudes
toward prediction, and then declares that most men
hold firmly that the future can be predicted, but that
many of them fail to profit by accurate predictions
through the false constructions placed upon them by
those who make them. The belief ascribed by Tacitus
to most men is not necessarily his own; but it must be
noted that in two places he happens to report cases of
just such misconstructions as this belief supposes. When
Tiberius left Rome for Capri in 26 A.D. the prediction
that he would never return was widely reported. Some
inferred that he would die soon and based their plans
upon the inference. These people were disappointed, for
the Emperor lived another eleven years without returning to the city (*Annals* IV, 58). The Jews were encouraged in their rash resistance to overwhelming power
by a prophecy that people setting out from their country
would gain the Empire of the world. This prophecy, Tacitus tells us (*Histories* V, 13), referred not to the Jews,
but to Vespasian and his son Titus. When Tacitus
speaks disparagingly of Otho's reliance on his court
astrologer or dryly observes that the predictions of Vespasian's future greatness were believed after the event,
we cannot safely infer that he was exempt from a belief that in his time was almost universal. He speaks
without disrespect for Tiberius' astrologer, Thrasyllus,
who was also a philosopher of some distinction. And
would the ultraskeptical Tacitus of some historians have
found it necessary to observe that at the time of Otho's
death people near Reggio di Emilia noted the appearance
of a strange and peculiar-looking bird?

Tacitus may be reproached with bias and unfairness;
with an indifference to truth, which he has in common
with most ancient historians; with an element of insincerity closely bound up with his attitude to the Principate,
and with his lack of philosophical and religious princi-

ples. As an artist and as a historian he seizes the advantages that correspond to all these limitations. The very ambiguity of his attitude to Roman politics, together with his typically Roman feeling for the concrete and actual in any fact or situation, helps him again and again to do justice to the infinite complications and inconsistencies of real life. He can record a discreditable action of the virtuous Barea Soranus (*Annals* XXII, 53); he can give full credit to the excellence as a provincial governor of the infamous Lucius Vitellius (*Annals* VI, 32); he can keep in mind the weak points of Thrasea, Helvidius, and Seneca and the strong points of Suillius Rufus, Eprius Marcellus, and Vibius Crispus. Above all, he can achieve the marvelous chiaroscuro of his portrait of Tiberius. Despite the monstrous unfairness of many of the constructions which he puts upon this emperor's motives, despite the horror and disgust with which he describes his hideous cruelties, the reader cannot help suspecting that of all the characters in his history this is the one with whom Tacitus secretly has most in common. He sees the early period of imperial history as a tragic struggle between the emperors and the senatorial aristocracy, inevitable from the start and destined to prove fatal to both. A modern historian surveying the same field would not find this manner of approach congenial. Yet to Tacitus it offered unlimited opportunities not simply for the exercise of supreme literary art but for the attainment of profound though partial insight both into the history of the time that he recorded and into many permanent features of the human situation.

—Hugh Lloyd-Jones

Christ Church, Oxford

NOTE ON THE TEXT

Tacitus' minor works are omitted from this selection. I have preferred to present as much as possible of the *Annals* and the *Histories*. I have excluded much that relates to military operations on the frontiers that Rome shared with her two principal enemies, the Germans and the Parthians. Thus I have sacrificed Germanicus' wars in Germany, Corbulo's victories in Armenia, and Civilis' rebellion. I have also left out the chapters that describe how certain Greek cities of Asia Minor petitioned the Emperor for rights of asylum for their temples or other privileges, supporting their claims by historical or mythological evidence. Otherwise, the two main works of Tacitus appear virtually complete. The translation of A. J. Church and W. J. Brodribb (*Histories*, Macmillan & Co., 1873; *Annals*, Macmillan & Co., 1906) has been reproduced, with minor alterations.

Here is a list of passages omitted: *Annals* I, 16-52, 54-71, 95-99; II, 1-26, 47-61, 68; III, 20-21, 32, 60-63, 73-74; IV, 23-30, 43, 46-51, 55-56, 62-65, 72-75; VI, 31-37, 41-44; XI, 8-10, 16-21; XII, 10-21; 29-30, 44-51, 61-63; XIII, 6-9, part of 34, 35-41, 53-58; XIV, 23-26; XV, 1-17, 24-31. *Histories* I, 51-90; II, 51-78; IV, 12-37, 46-86; V, 14-26.

BIBLIOGRAPHICAL NOTE

BOOKS ON TACITUS

By far the most valuable modern study of Tacitus is Sir Ronald Syme, *Tacitus* (2 vols.), Oxford University Press, 1958. Its immense learning does not prevent it from being highly readable and its excellent indexes will help the reader from losing his way. If this great book has a weakness it is that of being too sympathetic to its subject. For an intelligent study of the *Annals* from a somewhat different point of view, see B. Walker, *The Annals of Tacitus*, 2nd ed., Manchester University Press, 1960. We eagerly await A. Momigliano's forthcoming book on *The Political Ideas of Tacitus*, in which the author will no doubt not only discuss these ideas themselves, but will make use of his unrivaled knowledge of the influence of Tacitus since the Renaissance.

GENERAL HISTORY

A good general account of most of the period dealt with by Tacitus is contained in the *Cambridge Ancient History*, Vol. X: *The Augustan Empire:* B.C. 44-A.D. 70, Cambridge University Press, 1934.

TEXTS

Annals, ed. C. D. Fisher, Oxford Classical Texts, 1906.
Histories, ed. C. D. Fisher, Oxford Classical Texts, 1910.
Minor Works, ed. H. Furneaux (*Germania* and *Agricola* revised by J. G. C. Anderson), Oxford Classical Texts, 1938.

CHRONOLOGICAL TABLE

B.C.	133	Tribunate of Tiberius Gracchus
	123-2	Tribunates of Gaius Gracchus
	105-100	Successive consulships of Gaius Marius
	91	Tribunate of Marcus Livius Drusus
	90-88	War against Italian allies claiming citizenship
	87-4	Cinna in power
	82-79	Sulla in power
	70	Pompeius and Crassus consuls together for first time; Sulla's settlement collapses
	56	Combination of Cæsar, Pompeius, and Crassus
	48	Cæsar defeats Pompeius at Pharsalus
	44	Cæsar murdered
	42	Brutus and Cassius defeated at Philippi
	31	Antony defeated by Augustus at Actium
A.D.	14	Death of Augustus; succession of Tiberius
	19	Death of Germanicus
	23	Death of Drusus, son of Tiberius
	26	Tiberius withdraws to Capri
	31	Death of Sejanus
	37	Death of Tiberius; succession of Gaius
	39	Execution of Gætulicus and Lepidus
	41	Death of Gaius; succession of Claudius
	42	Rebellion of Camillus Scribonianus
	44	Triumph of Claudius through victories in Britain
	48	Death of Messallina; Claudius marries Agrippina
	50	Adoption of Nero by Claudius
	54	Death of Claudius; succession of Nero
	56 or 57	Birth of Tacitus
	59	Death of Agrippina

62	Death of Burrus
64	Great fire; persecution of Christians
65	Conspiracy of Piso
68	Revolt of Vindex; death of Nero; succession of Galba
69	Murder of Galba by Otho; battle of Bedriacum and death of Otho; succession of Vitellius; battle of Cremona and death of Vitellius; succession of Vespasianus
70	Suppression of Civilis' revolt; destruction of Jerusalem
74	Execution of Helvidius Priscus the elder
76	Tacitus military tribune (?)
77	Tacitus betrothed to daughter of Agricola; Agricola consul
79	Earthquake in Campania; death of Vespasianus and succession of Titus
81	Death of Titus; Tacitus quæstor (?); succession of Domitian
83	Domitian's campaign against the Chatti
84	Recall of Agricola
85-9	Domitian's campaign in Dacia
88	Tacitus prætor and quindecemvir
92	Domitian's campaign in Pannonia
93	Death of Agricola; Domitian's reign of terror
96	Death of Domitian and succession of Nerva
97	Adoption of Trajan; Tacitus suffect consul
98	Death of Nerva and succession of Trajan; *Agricola* published about this time
99	*Germania* published about this time
100	Prosecution of Marius Priscus by Tacitus and Pliny
101-2	Trajan's first Dacian campaign; *Dialogue on Orators* published (?)
105-6	Tacitus known to be working on *Histories;* Trajan's second Dacian campaign
112-3	Tacitus governor of Asia

THE ROMAN EMPIRE
IN THE TIME
OF THE ANTONINES

SARMATIA

Mare
Caspium

Pontus Euxinus

Sinope

ARMENIA
MAGNA

CIA

ESIA
INE

RACIA

Byzantium

BITHYNIA & PONTUS

Nicomedia
Nicaea

ssalonica

ASIA

GALATIA

CAPPADOCIA

CILICIA

Antioch

MESOPOTAMIA

Athens
AEA

LYCIA

CYPRUS

SYRIA

PHOENICIA

•Palmyra

•Damascus

ARABIA
DESERTA

CRETA

editerraneum

•Jerusalem

ARABIA
FELIX

Alexandria

PALESTINA

ARABIA
PETRAEA

ENAICA

AEGYPTUS

TABLE A. AUGUSTUS AND HIS DIRECT DESCENDANTS

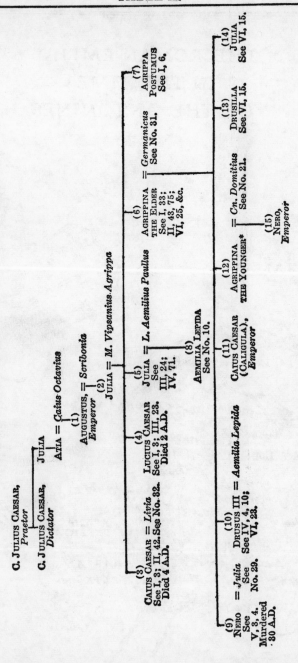

*Agrippina the Younger became the fourth wife of the Emperor Claudius.

TABLE B. THE COLLATERALS OF THE FAMILY OF AUGUSTUS

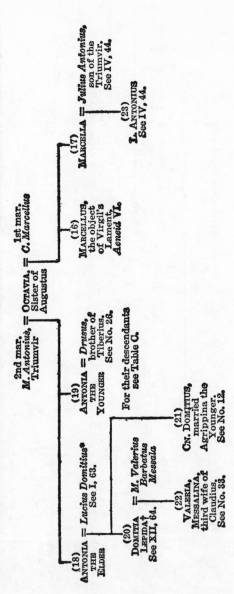

2nd mar. M. Antonius, Triumvir = OCTAVIA, Sister of Augustus = 1st mar. C. Marcellus

(18) ANTONIA THE ELDER = Lucius Domitius* See I, 63.

(19) ANTONIA THE YOUNGER = Drusus, brother of Tiberius, See No. 26. For their descendants see Table C.

(16) MARCELLUS, the object of Virgil's Lament, Aeneid VI.

(17) MARCELLA = Julius Antonius, son of the Triumvir, See IV, 44.

(23) L. ANTONIUS See IV, 44.

(20) DOMITIA LEPIDA† See XII, 64. = M. Valerius Barbatus Messala

(21) CN. DOMITIUS, married Agrippina the Younger, See No. 12.

(22) VALERIA MESSALINA, third wife of Claudius, See No. 33.

*Tacitus (See IV, 44) makes L. Domitius the husband of Antonia the Younger; but the authority of Suetonius, who says that he was married to the elder Antonia, is supposed to be preferable.

†Another Domitia is mentioned (See XIII, 19) and was evidently the sister of Domitia Lepida.

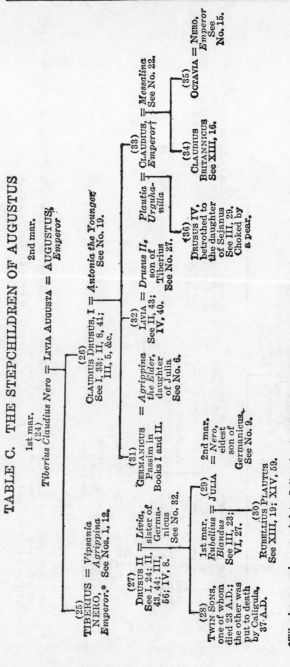

TABLE C. THE STEPCHILDREN OF AUGUSTUS

1st mar.
(24)
Tiberius Claudius Nero = Livia Augusta = Augustus, Emperor
2nd mar.

(25) TIBERIUS NERO, Emperor.* = Vipsania Agrippina See Nos. 1, 12.

(26) Claudius Drusus, I See I, 33; II, 8, 41; III, 5, &c. = Antonia the Younger, See No. 19.

(27) DRUSUS II = Livia, sister of Germanicus See No. 32. See I, 24; II, 43, 44; III, 56; IV, 8.

(28) TWIN SONS, one of whom died 23 A.D.; the other was put to death by Caligula, 37 A.D.

(29) JULIA 1st mar., Rubellius Blandus See III, 23; VI, 27. 2nd mar. = Nero, eldest son of Germanicus, See No. 9.

(30) RUBELLIUS PLAUTUS See XIII, 19; XIV, 59.

(31) GERMANICUS Passim in Books I and II. = Agrippina the Elder, daughter of Julia See No. 6.

(32) LIVIA = Drusus II, son of Tiberius See No. 27. See II, 43; IV, 40.

(33) Plautia Urgulanilla = Claudius, Emperor† = Messalina See No. 22.

(36) DRUSUS IV, betrothed to the daughter of Sejanus See III, 29. Choked by a pear.

(34) CLAUDIUS BRITANNICUS See XIII, 16.

(35) OCTAVIA = Nero, Emperor See No. 15.

*Tiberius was also married to Julia, the daughter of Augustus (See No. 2).

†Claudius was also married to Aelia Paetina (See XII, 2) and to his niece Agrippina the Younger, daughter of his brother Germanicus (See XII, 3-5). See No. 12.

The Annals

1. Rome at the beginning was ruled by kings. Freedom
and the consulship were established by Lucius Brutus.[1]
Dictatorships were held for a temporary crisis. The
power of the decemvirs[2] did not last beyond two years,
nor was the consular jurisdiction of the military tribunes
of long duration. The despotisms of Cinna and Sulla
were brief;[3] the rule of Pompeius and of Crassus soon
yielded before Cæsar; the arms of Lepidus and Antonius
before Augustus; who, when the world was wearied by
civil strife, subjected it to empire under the title of
Princeps. But the successes and reverses of the old
Roman people have been recorded by famous historians;
and fine intellects were not wanting to describe the times
of Augustus, till growing sycophancy scared them away.
The histories of Tiberius, Gaius, Claudius, and Nero,
while they were in power, were falsified through fear,
and after their death were written under the irritation
of a recent hatred. Hence my purpose is to relate a
few facts about Augustus—more particularly his last
acts, then the reign of Tiberius, and all which follows,
without either bitterness or partiality, from any motives
to which I am far removed.

2. When after the destruction of Brutus and Cassius[4]
there was no longer any army of the commonwealth,
when Pompeius was crushed in Sicily,[5] and when, with
Lepidus pushed aside and Antonius slain, even the
Julian faction had only Cæsar left to lead it, then, dropping the title of triumvir, and giving out that he was a
consul, and was satisfied with a tribune's authority for
the protection of the people,[6] Augustus won over the soldiers with gifts, the populace with cheap corn, and all
men with the sweets of repose, and so grew greater by
degrees, while he concentrated in himself the functions
of the Senate, the magistrates, and the laws. He was
wholly unopposed, for the boldest spirits had fallen in
battle, or in the proscription, while the remaining nobles,
the readier they were to be slaves, were raised the higher

by wealth and promotion, so that, aggrandized by revolution, they preferred the safety of the present to the dangerous past. Nor did the provinces dislike that condition of affairs, for they distrusted the government of the Senate and the people, because of the rivalries between the leading men and the rapacity of the officials, while the protection of the laws was unavailing, as they were continually deranged by violence, intrigue, and finally by corruption.

3. Augustus meanwhile, as supports to his despotism, raised to the pontificate and curule ædileship Claudius Marcellus,[7] his sister's son, while a mere boy, and Marcus Agrippa,[8] of humble birth, a good soldier, and one who had shared his victory, to consulships, and as Marcellus soon afterward died, he also accepted him as his son-in-law. Tiberius Nero and Claudius Drusus,[9] his stepsons, he honored with imperial titles, although his own family was as yet undiminished. For he had admitted the children of Agrippa, Gaius and Lucius,[10] into the house of the Cæsars; and before they had yet laid aside the dress of boyhood he had most fervently desired, with an outward show of reluctance, that they should be entitled "princes of the youth," and be consuls-elect. When Agrippa died, and Lucius Cæsar as he was on his way to our armies in Spain, and Gaius while returning from Armenia, still suffering from a wound, were prematurely cut off by destiny, or by their stepmother Livia's treachery, Drusus too having long been dead, Nero remained alone of the stepsons, and in him everything tended to center. He was adopted as a son, as a colleague in empire and a partner in the tribunician power, and paraded through all the armies, no longer through his mother's secret intrigues, but at her open suggestion. For she had gained such a hold on the aged Augustus that he drove out as an exile into the island of Planasia,[11] his only grandson, Agrippa Postumus, who, though devoid of worthy qualities, and having only the brute courage of physical strength, had not been convicted of any gross offense. And yet Augustus had appointed Germanicus, Drusus' offspring, to the command of eight legions on the Rhine,[12] and required

4

Tiberius to adopt him, although Tiberius had a son, now a young man, in his house;[13] but he did it that he might have several safeguards to rest on. He had no war at the time on his hands except against the Germans, which was rather to wipe out the disgrace of the loss of Quintilius Varus and his army[14] than out of an ambition to extend the empire, or for any adequate recompense. At home all was tranquil, and there were magistrates with the same titles; there was a younger generation, sprung up since the victory of Actium, and even many of the older men had been born during the civil wars. How few were left who had seen the Republic!

4. Thus the state had been revolutionized, and there was not a vestige left of the old sound morality. Stripped of equality, all looked up to the commands of a sovereign without the least apprehension for the present, while Augustus, in the vigor of life, could maintain his own position, that of his house, and the general tranquillity. When in advanced old age, he was worn out by a sickly frame, and the end was near and new prospects opened, a few spoke in vain of the blessings of freedom, but most people dreaded and some longed for war. The popular gossip of the large majority fastened itself variously on their future masters. "Agrippa was savage, and had been exasperated by insult, and neither from age nor experience in affairs was equal to so great a burden. Tiberius Nero was of mature years, and had established his fame in war,[15] but he had the old arrogance inbred in the Claudian family, and many symptoms of a cruel temper, though they were repressed, now and then broke out. He had also from earliest infancy been reared in an imperial house; consulships and triumphs had been heaped on him in his younger days; even in the years which, on the pretext of seclusion, he spent in exile at Rhodes,[16] he had had no thoughts but of wrath, hypocrisy, and secret sensuality. There was his mother too, with a woman's caprice. They must, it seemed, be subject to a female and to two boys besides, who for a while would burden and someday rend asunder the state."

5. While these and like topics were discussed, the in-

firmities of Augustus increased, and some suspected guilt
on his wife's part. For a rumor had gone abroad that a
few months before he had sailed to Planasia on a visit to
Agrippa, with the knowledge of some chosen friends, and
with one companion, Fabius Maximus;[17] that many tears
were shed on both sides, with expressions of affection,
and that thus there was a hope of the young man being
restored to the home of his grandfather. This, it was
said, Maximus had divulged to his wife Marcia, she again
to Livia. All was known to Cæsar, and when Maximus
soon afterward died, by a death some thought to be self-
inflicted, there were heard at his funeral wailings from
Marcia, in which she reproached herself for having been
the cause of her husband's destruction. Whatever the
fact was, Tiberius as he was just entering Illyria was
summoned home by an urgent letter from his mother,
and it has not been thoroughly ascertained whether at the
city of Nola[18] he found Augustus still breathing or quite
lifeless. For Livia had surrounded the house and its approaches with a strict watch, and favorable bulletins were
published from time to time, till, provision having been
made for the demands of the crisis, one and the same
report told men that Augustus was dead and that Tiberius
Nero was master of the state.

6. The first crime of the new reign was the murder of
Agrippa Postumus. Though he was surprised and unarmed, a centurion of the firmest resolution dispatched
him with difficulty. Tiberius gave no explanation of the
matter to the Senate; he pretended that there were directions from his father ordering the tribune in charge
of the prisoner not to delay the slaughter of Agrippa,
whenever he should himself have breathed his last. Beyond a doubt, Augustus had often complained of the
young man's character, and had thus succeeded in obtaining the sanction of a decree of the Senate for his
banishment. But he never was hardhearted enough to
destroy any of his kinsfolk, nor was it credible that death
was to be the sentence of the grandson in order that the
stepson might feel secure. It was more probable that
Tiberius and Livia, the one from fear, the other from a
stepmother's enmity, hurried on the destruction of a

youth whom they suspected and hated. When the centurion reported, according to military custom, that he
had executed the command, Tiberius replied that he had
not given the command, and that the act must be justified to the Senate.

As soon as Sallustius Crispus,[19] who shared the secret
(he had, in fact, sent the written order to the tribune),
knew this, fearing that the charge would be shifted on
himself, and that his peril would be the same whether he
uttered fiction or truth, he advised Livia not to divulge
the secrets of her house or the counsels of friends, or any
services performed by the soldiers, nor to let Tiberius
weaken the strength of imperial power by referring everything to the Senate, for "the condition," he said, "of holding empire is that an account cannot be balanced unless
it be rendered to one person."

7. Meanwhile at Rome people plunged into slavery—
consuls, senators, knights. The higher a man's rank, the
more eager his hypocrisy, and his looks the more carefully studied, so as neither to betray joy at the decease of
one emperor nor sorrow at the rise of another, while he
mingled delight and lamentations with his flattery. Sextus
Pompeius and Sextus Apuleius,[20] the consuls, were the
first to swear allegiance to Tiberius Cæsar, and in their
presence the oath was taken by Seius Strabo and Gaius
Turranius, respectively the commander of the prætorian
cohorts and the superintendent of the corn supplies. Then
the Senate, the soldiers, and the people did the same. For
Tiberius would inaugurate everything with the consuls,
as though the ancient constitution remained and he were
uncertain of his power. Even the proclamation by which
he summoned the senators to their chamber, he issued
merely with the title of the tribunician power, which he
had received under Augustus. The wording of the proclamation was brief, and in a very modest tone. "He
would," it said, "provide for the honors due to his father,
and not abandon the lifeless body, and this was the only
public duty he now claimed."

As soon, however, as Augustus was dead, he had given
the watchword to the prætorian cohorts, as commander-
in-chief. He had the guard under arms, with all the other

7

adjuncts of a court; soldiers attended him to the forum; soldiers went with him to the Senate House. He sent letters to the different armies, as though supreme power was now his, and showed hesitation only when he spoke in the Senate. His chief motive was fear that Germanicus, who had at his disposal so many legions, such vast auxiliary forces of the allies, and such wonderful popularity, might prefer the possession to the expectation of empire. He looked also at public opinion, wishing to have the credit of having been called and elected by the state rather than of having crept into power through the intrigues of a wife and a dotard's adoption. It was subsequently understood that he assumed a wavering attitude, to test likewise the temper of the nobles. For he would twist a word or a look into a crime and treasure it up in his memory.

8. On the first day of the Senate he allowed nothing to be discussed but the funeral of Augustus, whose will, which was brought in by the Vestal Virgins, named as his heirs Tiberius and Livia. The latter was to be admitted into the Julian family with the name of Augusta; next in expectation were the grandchildren and great-grandchildren. In the third place, he had named the chief men of the state, most of whom he hated, simply out of ostentation and to win credit with posterity. His legacies were not beyond the scale of a private citizen, except a bequest of forty-three million five hundred thousand sesterces "to the people and populace of Rome," of one thousand to every prætorian soldier, and of three hundred to every man in the legionary cohorts composed of Roman citizens.

Next followed a deliberation about funeral honors. Of these the most imposing were thought fitting. The procession was to be conducted through the "gate of triumph," on the motion of Asinius Gallus;[21] the titles of the laws passed, the names of the nations conquered by Augustus were to be borne in front, on that of Lucius Arruntius.[22] Valerius Messalla[23] further proposed that the oath of allegiance to Tiberius should be yearly renewed, and when Tiberius asked him whether it was at *his* bidding that he had brought forward this motion, he replied that he had proposed it spontaneously, and that in whatever concerned the state he would use only his own discretion, even at the risk of offending. This was the only style of adulation which yet remained. The senators unanimously exclaimed that the body ought to be borne on their shoulders to the funeral pile. The Emperor left the point to them with disdainful moderation, and he then admonished the people by a proclamation not to indulge in that tumultuous enthusiasm which had distracted the funeral of the divine Julius, or express a wish that Augustus should be burned in the Forum instead of in his appointed resting place in the Campus Martius.

On the day of the funeral soldiers stood round as a guard, amid much ridicule from those who had either themselves witnessed or who had heard from their parents of the famous day when slavery was still something fresh, and freedom had been resought in vain, when the slaying of Cæsar the dictator seemed to some the vilest, to others, the most glorious of deeds. "Now," they said, "an aged sovereign, whose power had lasted long, who had provided his heirs with abundant means to coerce the state, requires the defense of soldiers for his burial to remain undisturbed."

9. Then followed much talk about Augustus himself, and many expressed an idle wonder that the same day marked the beginning of his assumption of empire and the close of his life, and, again, that he had ended his days at Nola in the same house and room as his father Octavius. People extolled too the number of his consulships, in which he had equaled Valerius Corvus and Gaius Marius combined,[24] the continuance for thirty-seven years of the tribunician power,[25] the title of Imperator twenty-one times earned, and his other honors which had been either frequently repeated or were wholly new. Sensible men, however, spoke variously of his life with praise and censure. Some said that "dutiful feeling toward a father, and the necessities of the state in which laws had then no place, drove him into civil war, which can neither be planned nor conducted on any right principles. He had often yielded to Antonius, while he was taking vengeance on his father's murderers, often

also to Lepidus. When the latter sank into feeble dotage and the former had been ruined by his profligacy, the only remedy for his distracted country was the rule of a single man. Yet the state had been organized under the name neither of a kingdom nor a dictatorship, but under that of a prince. The ocean and remote rivers were the boundaries of the Empire; the legions, provinces, fleets, all things were linked together; there was law for the citizens; there was respect shown to the allies. The capital had been embellished on a grand scale; only in a few instances had he resorted to force, simply to secure general tranquillity."

10. It was said, on the other hand, that "filial duty and state necessity were merely assumed as a mask. It was really from a lust of sovereignty that he had excited the veterans by bribery, had, when a young man and a subject, raised an army, tampered with the consul's legions, and feigned an attachment to the faction of Pompeius. Then, when by a decree of the Senate he had usurped the high functions and authority of prætor, when Hirtius and Pansa were slain—whether they were destroyed by the enemy, or Pansa by poison infused into a wound, Hirtius by his own soldiers and Cæsar's treacherous machinations—he at once possessed himself of both their armies, wrested the consulate from a reluctant Senate, and turned against the state the arms with which he had been entrusted against Antonius. Citizens were proscribed, lands divided, without so much as the approval of those who executed these deeds.[26] Even granting that the deaths of Cassius and of the Bruti were sacrifices to a hereditary enmity (though duty requires us to waive private feuds for the sake of the public welfare), still Pompeius had been deluded by the phantom of peace, and Lepidus by the mask of friendship.[27] Subsequently, Antonius had been lured on by the treaties of Tarentum and Brundisium, and by his marriage with the sister of Augustus, and paid by his death the penalty of a treacherous alliance. No doubt, there was peace after all this, but it was a peace stained with blood; there were the disasters of Lollius and Varus,[28]

the murders at Rome of such men as Varro, Egnatius, and Iullus.[29]

The domestic life too of Augustus was not spared. Nero's wife had been taken from him, and there had been the farce of consulting the pontiffs, whether, with a child conceived and not yet born, she could properly marry.[30] There were the excesses of Vedius Pollio;[31] last of all, there was Livia, terrible to the state as a mother, terrible to the house of the Cæsars as a stepmother. No honor was left for the gods, when Augustus chose to be himself worshiped with temples and statues, like those of the deities, and with flamens and priests. He had not even adopted Tiberius as his successor out of affection or any regard to the state, but, having thoroughly seen his arrogant and savage temper, he had sought glory for himself by a contrast of extreme wickedness." For, in fact, Augustus, a few years before, when he was a second time asking from the Senate the tribunician power for Tiberius, though his speech was complimentary, had thrown out certain hints as to his manners, style, and habits of life, which he meant as reproaches, while he seemed to excuse. However, when his obsequies had been duly performed, a temple with a religious ritual was decreed him.

11. After this all prayers were addressed to Tiberius. He, on his part, urged various considerations, the greatness of the Empire, his distrust of himself. "Only," he said, "the intellect of the divine Augustus was equal to such a burden. Called as he had been by him to share his anxieties, he had learned by experience how exposed to fortune's caprices was the task of universal rule. Consequently, in a state which had the support of so many great men, they should not put everything on one man, as many, by uniting their efforts, would more easily discharge public functions." There was more grand sentiment than good faith in such words. Tiberius' language, even in matters which he did not care to conceal, either from nature or habit, was always hesitating and obscure, and now that he was struggling to hide his feelings completely, it was all the more involved in uncertainty and doubt. The senators, however, whose only

11

fear was lest they might seem to understand him, burst into complaints, tears, and prayers. They raised their hands to the gods, to the statue of Augustus, and to the knees of Tiberius, when he ordered a document to be produced and read. This contained a description of the resources of the state, of the number of citizens and allies under arms, of the fleets, subject kingdoms, provinces, taxes, direct and indirect, necessary expenses and customary bounties. All these details Augustus had written with his own hand, and had added a counsel, that the Empire should be confined to its present limits, either from fear or out of jealousy.

12. Meantime, while the Senate stooped to the most abject supplication, Tiberius happened to say that although he was not equal to the whole burden of the state, yet he would undertake the charge of whatever part of it might be entrusted to him. Thereupon Asinius Gallus said, "I ask you, Cæsar, what part of the state you wish to have entrusted to you?" Confounded by the sudden inquiry, he was silent for a few moments; then, recovering his presence of mind, he replied that it would by no means become his modesty to choose or to avoid in a case where he would prefer to be wholly excused. Then again Gallus, who had inferred anger from his looks, said that the question had not been asked with the intention of dividing what could not be separated, but to convince him by his own admission that the body of the state was one, and must be directed by a single mind. He further spoke in praise of Augustus, and reminded Tiberius himself of his victories, and of his admirable deeds for many years as a civilian. Still, he did not thereby soften the Emperor's resentment, for he had long been detested from an impression that, as he had married Vipsania, daughter of Marcus Agrippa, who had once been the wife of Tiberius,[32] he aspired to be more than a citizen, and kept up the arrogant tone of his father, Asinius Pollio.

13. Next, Lucius Arruntius, who differed but little from the speech of Gallus, gave like offense, though Tiberius had no old grudge against him, but simply mistrusted him, because he was rich and daring, had bril-

liant accomplishments, and corresponding popularity. For Augustus, when in his last conversations he was discussing who would refuse the highest place, though sufficiently capable, who would aspire to it without being equal to it, and who would unite both the ability and ambition, had described Marcus Lepidus[33] as able but contemptuously indifferent, Gallus Asinius as ambitious and incapable, Lucius Arruntius as not unworthy of it, and, should the chance be given him, sure to make the venture. About the two first there is a general agreement, but instead of Arruntius some have mentioned Cnæus Piso,[34] and all these men, except Lepidus, were soon afterward destroyed by various charges through the contrivance of Tiberius. Quintus Haterius[35] too and Mamercus Scaurus[36] ruffled his suspicious temper, Haterius by having said, "How long, Cæsar, will you suffer the state to be without a head?" Scaurus by the remark that there was a hope that the Senate's prayers would not be fruitless, seeing that he had not used his right as tribune to negative the motion of the consuls. Tiberius instantly broke out into invective against Haterius; Scaurus, with whom he was far more deeply displeased, he passed over in silence. Wearied at last by the assembly's clamorous importunity and the urgent demands of individual senators, he gave way by degrees, not admitting that he undertook empire, but yet ceasing to refuse it and to be entreated. It is known that Haterius, having entered the palace to ask pardon, and thrown himself at the knees of Tiberius as he was walking, was almost killed by the soldiers, because Tiberius fell forward, accidentally or from being entangled by the suppliant's hands. Yet the peril of so great a man did not make him relent, till Haterius went with entreaties to Augusta, and was saved by her very earnest intercessions.

14. Great too was the Senate's sycophancy to Augusta. Some would have her styled "parent"; others "mother of the country," and a majority proposed that to the name of Cæsar should be added "son of Julia." The Emperor repeatedly asserted that there must be a limit to the honors paid to women, and that he would observe similar

moderation in those bestowed on himself, but annoyed
at the invidious proposal, and indeed regarding a woman's elevation as a slight to himself, he would not allow
so much as a lictor to be assigned her, and forbade the
erection of an altar in memory of her adoption, and
any like distinction. But for Germanicus Cæsar he asked
proconsular powers, and envoys were dispatched to confer them on him, and also to express sympathy with his
grief at the death of Augustus. The same request was
not made for Drusus, because he was consul-elect and
present at Rome. Twelve candidates were named for
the prætorship, the number which Augustus had handed
down, and when the Senate urged Tiberius to increase it,
he bound himself by an oath not to exceed it.

15. It was then for the first time that the elections
were transferred from the Campus Martius to the Senate.
For up to that day, though the most important rested
with the Emperor's choice, some were settled by the
partialities of the tribes. Nor did the people complain
of having the right taken from them, except in mere idle
talk, and the Senate, being now released from the necessity of bribery and of degrading solicitations, gladly upheld the change, Tiberius confining himself to the recommendation of only four candidates who were to be
nominated without rejection or canvass.[37] Meanwhile
the tribunes of the people asked leave to exhibit at their
own expense games to be named after Augustus and
added to the calendar as the Augustales. Money was,
however, voted from the exchequer, and though the use
of the triumphal robe in the circus was prescribed, they
were not allowed to ride in a chariot.[38] Soon the annual
celebration was transferred to the prætors, to whose lot
fell the administration of justice between citizens and
foreigners.

[Chapters 16 to 52 are omitted. A mutiny of the legions
in Pannonia was dealt with by Tiberius' son, Drusus,
with a judicious mixture of firmness and liberality; a
similar outbreak among the legions on the Rhine also
came to nothing, though it is clear even from Tacitus'
partial narrative that Germanicus, to whom it fell to

deal with the situation, did so with an emotionalism that contrasted most unfavorably with the resolution of his cousin. After the revolt Germanicus launched a surprise attack on the Marsi, inflicting severe casualties.]

53. That same year Julia ended her days. For her profligacy she had formerly been confined by her father Augustus in the island of Pandataria,[39] and then in the town of the Regini[40] on the shores of the straits of Sicily. She had been the wife of Tiberius while Gaius and Lucius Cæsar were in their glory, and had disdained him as an unequal match. This was Tiberius' special reason for retiring to Rhodes. When he obtained the Empire, he left her in banishment and disgrace, deprived of all hope after the murder of Postumus Agrippa, and let her perish by a lingering death of destitution, with the idea that an obscurity would hang over her end from the length of her exile. He had a like motive for cruel vengeance on Sempronius Gracchus, a man of noble family, of shrewd understanding, and a perverse eloquence, who had seduced this same Julia when she was the wife of Marcus Agrippa. And this was not the end of the intrigue. When she had been handed over to Tiberius, her persistent paramour inflamed her with disobedience and hatred toward her husband; and a letter which Julia wrote to her father, Augustus, inveighing against Tiberius, was supposed to be the composition of Gracchus.[41] He was accordingly banished to Cercina, where he endured an exile of fourteen years. Then the soldiers who were sent to slay him found him on a promontory, expecting no good. On their arrival, he begged a brief interval in which to give by letter his last instructions to his wife Alliaria, and then offered his neck to the executioners, dying with a courage not unworthy of the Sempronian name, which his degenerate life had dishonored. Some have related that these soldiers were not sent from Rome, but by Lucius Asprenas,[42] proconsul of Africa, on the authority of Tiberius, who had vainly hoped that the infamy of the murder might be shifted on Asprenas.

[Chapters 54 to 71 are omitted. They describe further operations of Germanicus in support of Segestes, the father-in-law and enemy of Arminius, leader of the Cherusci, on the middle Weser, and the conqueror of Varus. Germanicus now had the theatrical idea of visiting the site of Varus' disaster on the Teutoburger Wald; on the way back, Arminius attacked him, and he made his way back with some difficulty.]

72. That year triumphal honors were decreed to Aulus Cæcina, Lucius Apronius, Gaius Silius for their achievements under Germanicus. The title "father of his country,"[43] which the people had so often thrust on him, Tiberius refused, nor would he allow obedience to be sworn to his enactments,[44] though the Senate voted it, for he said repeatedly that all human things were uncertain, and that the more he had obtained, the more precarious was his position. But he did not thereby create a belief in his willingness to be a citizen among citizens, for he had revived the law of treason,[45] the name of which indeed was known in ancient times, though other matters came under its jurisdiction, such as the betrayal of an army, or seditious stirring up of the people, or, in short, any corrupt act by which a man had "impaired the majesty of the people of Rome." Deeds only were liable to accusation; words went unpunished. It was Augustus who first, under color of this law, applied legal inquiry to libelous writings, provoked, as he had been, by the licentious freedom with which Cassius Severus[46] had defamed men and women of distinction in his insulting satires. Soon afterward, Tiberius, when consulted by Pompeius Macer, the prætor, as to whether prosecutions for treason should be revived, replied that the laws must be enforced. He too had been exasperated by the publication of verses of uncertain authorship, pointed at his cruelty, his arrogance, and his dissensions with his mother.

73. It will not be uninteresting if I relate in the cases of Falanius and Rubrius, Roman knights of moderate fortune, the first experiments at such accusations, in order to explain the origin of a most terrible scourge,

how by Tiberius' cunning it crept in among us; how subsequently it was checked; finally, how it burst into flame and consumed everything. Against Falanius it was alleged by his accuser that he had admitted among the votaries of Augustus, who in every great house were associated into a kind of brotherhood, one Cassius, a buffoon of infamous life, and that he had also in selling his gardens included in the sale a statue of Augustus. Against Rubrius the charge was that he had violated by perjury the divinity of Augustus. When this was known to Tiberius, he wrote to the consuls "that his father had not had a place in heaven decreed to him, that the honor might be turned to the destruction of the citizens. Cassius, the actor, with men of the same profession, used to take part in the games which had been consecrated by his mother to the memory of Augustus. Nor was it contrary to the religion of the state for the Emperor's image, like those of other deities, to be added to a sale of gardens and houses. As to the oath, the thing ought to be considered as if the man had deceived Jupiter. Wrongs done to the gods were the gods' concern."

74. Not long afterward, Granius Marcellus, proconsul of Bithynia, was accused of treason by his quæstor, Crispinus Cæpio, and the charge was supported by Romanius Hispo. Crispinus then entered on a line of life afterward rendered notorious by the miseries of the age and men's shamelessness. Needy, obscure, and restless, he wormed himself by stealthy informations into the confidence of a vindictive prince, and soon imperiled all the most distinguished citizens; and having thus gained influence with one, hatred from all besides, he left an example in following which beggars became wealthy, the insignificant, formidable, and brought ruin first on others, finally on themselves. He alleged against Marcellus that he had made some disrespectful remarks about Tiberius, a charge not to be evaded, inasmuch as the accuser selected the worst features of the Emperor's character and grounded his case on them. The things were true, and so were believed to have been said.

Hispo added that Marcellus had placed his own statue above those of the Cæsars, and had set the bust of Tiberius on another statue from which he had struck off the head of Augustus. At this the Emperor's wrath blazed forth, and, breaking through his habitual silence, he exclaimed that in such a case he would himself too give his vote openly on oath, that the rest might be under the same obligation. There lingered even then a few signs of expiring freedom. And so Cnæus Piso asked, "In what order will you vote, Cæsar? If first, I shall know what to follow; if last, I fear that I may differ from you unwillingly." Tiberius was deeply moved, and repenting of the outburst, all the more because of its thoughtlessness, he quietly allowed the accused to be acquitted of the charges of treason. As for the question of extortion, it was referred to a special commission. . . .

[*Chapters 75-79 are omitted.*]

80. Poppæus Sabinus[47] was continued in his government of the province of Mœsia[48] with the addition of Achæa and Macedonia. It was part of Tiberius' character to prolong indefinitely military commands and to keep many men to the end of their life with the same armies and in the same administrations. Various motives have been assigned for this. Some say that, out of aversion to any fresh anxiety, he retained what he had once approved as a permanent arrangement; others, that he grudged to see many enjoying promotion. Some, again, think that though he had an acute intellect, his judgment was irresolute, for he did not seek out eminent merit, and yet he detested vice. From the best men he apprehended danger to himself, from the worst, disgrace to the state. He went so far at last in this irresolution, that he appointed to provinces men whom he did not mean to allow to leave Rome.

81. I can hardly venture on any positive statement about the consular elections, now held for the first time under this Emperor, or, indeed, subsequently, so conflicting are the accounts we find not only in historians but in Tiberius' own speeches. Sometimes he kept back the names of the candidates, describing their origin, their life and military career, so that it might be under-

stood who they were. Occasionally even these hints were withheld, and, after urging them not to disturb the elections by canvassing, he would promise his own help toward the result. Generally he declared that only those had offered themselves to him as candidates whose names he had given to the consuls, and that others might offer themselves if they had confidence in their influence or merit. A plausible profession this in words, but really unmeaning and delusive, and the greater the disguise of freedom which marked it, the more cruel the enslavement into which it was soon to plunge us.[49]

BOOK II   *16-19 A.D.*

[*Chapters 1-26 are omitted. After a preliminary expedition against the Chatti, on the Lippe, Germanicus sailed with a great fleet through the lakes of Holland to the mouth of the Ems; from there, he somehow made his way to Minden, on the Weser, where he won a victory over Arminius which despite all the advocacy of Tacitus was clearly not decisive. At this moment the expulsion from Parthia of the pro-Roman king Vonones gave Tiberius the pretext to recall Germanicus to be his colleague in the consulship of 18 A.D. and to undertake a special mission to order affairs in the East.*]

27. About the same time Libo Drusus, of the family of Scribonii, was accused of revolutionary schemes. I will explain, somewhat minutely, the beginning, progress, and end of this affair, since then first were originated those practices which for so many years have eaten into the heart of the state. Firmius Catus, a senator, an intimate friend of Libo's, prompted the young man, who was thoughtless and an easy prey to delusions, to resort to astrologers' promises, magical rites, and interpreters of dreams, dwelling ostentatiously on his great-grandfather Pompeius, his aunt Scribonia,[1] who had formerly been wife of Augustus, his imperial cousins, his house crowded

with ancestral busts, and urging him to extravagance and debt, himself the companion of his profligacy and desperate embarrassments, thereby to entangle him in all the more proofs of guilt.

28. As soon as he found enough witnesses, with some slaves who knew the facts, he begged an audience of the Emperor, after first indicating the crime and the criminal through Vescularius Flaccus, a Roman knight, who was more intimate with Tiberius than himself. Cæsar, without disregarding the information, declined an interview, for the communication, he said, might be conveyed to him through the same messenger, Flaccus. Meanwhile he conferred the prætorship on Libo and often invited him to his table, showing no unfriendliness in his looks or anger in his words (so thoroughly had he concealed his resentment); and he wished to know all his sayings and doings, though it was in his power to stop them, till one Junius, who had been tampered with by Libo for the purpose of evoking by incantations the spirits of the dead, gave information to Fulcinius Trio.[2] Trio's ability was conspicuous among informers, as well as his eagerness for an evil notoriety. He at once pounced on the accused, went to the consuls, and demanded an inquiry before the Senate. The senators were summoned, with a special notice that they must consult on a momentous and terrible matter.

29. Libo meanwhile, in mourning apparel and accompanied by ladies of the highest rank, went to house after house, entreating his relatives, and imploring some eloquent voice to ward off his perils; which all refused, on different pretexts, but from the same apprehension. On the day the Senate met, jaded with fear and mental anguish, or, as some have related, feigning illness, he was carried in a litter to the doors of the Senate House, and leaning on his brother he raised his hands and voice in supplication to Tiberius, who received him with unmoved countenance. The Emperor then read out the charges and the accusers' names, with such calmness as not to seem to soften or aggravate the accusations.

30. Besides Trio and Catus, Fonteius Agrippa and Gaius Vibius were among his accusers, and claimed with

eager rivalry the privilege of conducting the case for the prosecution, till Vibius, as they would not yield one to the other, and Libo had entered without counsel, offered to state the charges against him singly, and produced an extravagantly absurd accusation, according to which Libo had consulted persons whether he would have such wealth as to be able to cover the Appian Way as far as Brundisium[3] with money. There were other questions of the same sort, quite senseless and idle; if leniently regarded, pitiable. But there was one paper in Libo's handwriting, so the prosecutor alleged, with the names of Cæsars and of senators, to which marks were affixed of dreadful or mysterious significance. When the accused denied this, it was decided that his slaves who recognized the writing should be examined by torture. As an ancient statute of the Senate forbade such inquiry in a case affecting a master's life, Tiberius, with his cleverness in devising new law, ordered Libo's slaves to be sold singly to the state agent, so that without an infringement of the Senate's decree, Libo might be tried on their evidence. As a consequence, the defendant asked an adjournment till next day, and having gone home he charged his kinsman Publius Quirinius[4] with his last prayer to the Emperor.

31. The answer was that he should address himself to the Senate. Meanwhile his house was surrounded with soldiers; they crowded noisily even about the entrance, so that they could be heard and seen, when Libo, whose anguish drove him from the very banquet he had prepared as his last gratification, called for a minister of death, grasped the hands of his slaves, and thrust a sword into them. In their confusion, as they shrank back, they overturned the lamp on the table at his side, and in the darkness, now to him the gloom of death, he aimed two blows at a vital part. At the groans of the falling man his freedmen hurried up, and the soldiers, seeing the bloody deed, stood aloof. Yet the prosecution was continued in the Senate with the same persistency, and Tiberius declared on oath that he would have interceded for his life, guilty though he was, but for his hasty suicide.

32. His property was divided among his accusers, and prætorships out of the usual order were conferred on those who were of senators' rank. Cotta Messalinus[5] then proposed that Libo's bust should not be carried in the funeral procession of any of his descendants; and Cnæus Lentulus that no Scribonius should assume the surname of Drusus. Days of public thanksgiving were appointed on the suggestion of Pomponius Flaccus.[6] Offerings were given to Jupiter, Mars, and Concord, and the 13th day of September, on which Libo had killed himself, was to be observed as a festival, on the motion of Asinius Gallus, Papius Mutilus,[7] and Lucius Apronius.[8] I have mentioned the proposals and sycophancy of these men in order to bring to light this old-standing evil in the state.

Decrees of the Senate were also passed to expel from Italy astrologers and magicians. One of their number, Lucius Pituanius, was hurled from the Tarpeian Rock. Another, Publius Marcius, was executed, according to ancient custom, by the consuls outside the Esquiline Gate, after the trumpets had been ordered to sound.

33. On the next day of the Senate's meeting much was said against the luxury of the country by Quintus Haterius, an ex-consul,[9] and by Octavius Fronto, an ex-prætor. It was decided that vessels of solid gold should not be made for the serving of food, and that men should not disgrace themselves with silken clothing from the East. Fronto went further, and insisted on restrictions being put on plate, furniture, and household establishments. It was indeed still usual with the senators, when it was their turn to vote, to suggest anything they thought for the state's advantage. Asinius Gallus argued on the other side. "With the growth of the Empire private wealth too," he said, "had increased, and there was nothing new in this, but it accorded with the fashions of the earliest antiquity. Riches were one thing in the time of Fabricius, quite another in the time of Scipio.[10] The state was the standard of everything; when it was poor, the homes of the citizens were humble; when it reached such magnificence, private grandeur increased. In household establishments, and plate, and

in whatever was provided for use, there was neither excess nor parsimony except in relation to the fortune of the possessor. A distinction had been made in the assessments of senators and knights, not because they differed naturally, but that the superiority of the one class in places in the theater, in rank and in honor, might be also maintained in everything else which ensured mental repose and bodily recreation, unless indeed men in the highest position were to undergo more anxieties and more dangers, and to be at the same time deprived of all solace under those anxieties and dangers." Gallus gained a ready assent, under these specious phrases, by a confession of failings with which his audience sympathized. And Tiberius too had added that this was not a time for censorship, and that if there were any decline in manners, a promoter of reform would not be wanting.

34. During this debate Lucius Piso,[11] after exclaiming against the corruption of the courts, the bribery of judges, the cruel threats of accusations from hired orators, declared that he would depart and quit the capital, and that he meant to live in some obscure and distant rural retreat. At the same moment he rose to leave the Senate House. Tiberius was much excited, and though he pacified Piso with gentle words, he also strongly urged his relatives to stop his departure by their influence or their entreaties.

Soon afterward this same Piso gave an equal proof of a fearless sense of wrong by suing Urgulania,[12] whom Augusta's friendship had raised above the law. Neither did Urgulania obey the summons, for in defiance of Piso she went in her litter to the Emperor's house; nor did Piso give way, though Augusta complained that she was insulted and her majesty slighted. Tiberius, thinking to win popularity by so far humoring his mother as to say that he would go to the prætor's court and support Urgulania, went forth from the palace, having ordered soldiers to follow him at a distance. He was seen, as the people thronged about him, to wear a calm face, while he prolonged his time on the way with various conversations, till at last when Piso's relatives tried in vain to restrain him, Augusta ordered the money which was claimed to be handed to him. This ended the affair, and Piso, in consequence, was not dishonored, and the Emperor rose in reputation. Urgulania's influence, however, was so formidable to the state that in a certain cause which was tried by the Senate she would not condescend to appear as a witness. The prætor was sent to question her at her own house, although the Vestal Virgins, according to ancient custom, were heard in the courts, before judges, whenever they gave evidence.

35. I should say nothing of the adjournment of public business in this year, if it were not worthwhile to notice the conflicting opinions of Cnæus Piso[13] and Asinius Gallus on the subject. Piso, although the Emperor had said that he would be absent, held that all the more ought the business to be transacted, that the state might have the honor of its Senate and knights being able to perform their duties in the sovereign's absence. Gallus, as Piso had forestalled him in the display of freedom, maintained that nothing was sufficiently impressive or suitable to the majesty of the Roman people, unless done before Cæsar and under his very eyes, and that therefore the gathering from all Italy and the influx from the provinces ought to be reserved for his presence. Tiberius listened to this in silence, and the matter was debated on both sides in a sharp controversy. The business, however, was adjourned.

36. A dispute then arose between Gallus and the Emperor. Gallus proposed that the elections of magistrates should be held every five years, and that the commanders of the legions who before receiving a prætorship discharged this military service should at once become prætors-elect, the Emperor nominating twelve candidates every year. It was quite evident that this motion had a deeper meaning and was an attempt to explore the secrets of imperial policy. Tiberius, however, argued as if his power would be thus increased. "It would," he said, "be trying to his moderation to have to elect so many and to put off so many. He scarcely avoided giving offense from year to year, even though a candidate's rejection was solaced by the near prospect of office. What

hatred would be incurred from those whose election was deferred for five years! How could he foresee through so long an interval what would be a man's temper, or domestic relations, or estate? Men became arrogant even with this annual appointment. What would happen if their thoughts were fixed on promotion for five years? It was in fact a multiplying of the magistrates fivefold, and a subversion of the laws which had prescribed proper periods for the exercise of the candidate's activity and the seeking or securing office." With this seemingly conciliatory speech he retained the substance of power.

37. He also increased the incomes of some of the senators. Hence it was the more surprising that he listened somewhat disdainfully to the request of Marcus Hortalus, a youth of noble rank in conspicuous poverty. He was the grandson of the orator Hortensius,[14] and had been induced by Augustus, on the strength of a gift of a million sesterces, to marry and rear children, that one of our most illustrious families might not become extinct. Accordingly, with his four sons standing at the doors of the Senate House, the Senate then sitting in the palace, when it was his turn to speak he began to address them as follows, his eyes fixed now on the statue of Hortensius which stood among those of the orators, now on that of Augustus:—"Senators, these whose numbers and boyish years you behold I have reared, not by my own choice, but because the Emperor advised me. At the same time, my ancestors deserved to have descendants. For myself, not having been able in these altered times to receive or acquire wealth or popular favor, or that eloquence which has been the hereditary possession of our house, I was satisfied if my narrow means were neither a disgrace to myself nor a burden to others. At the Emperor's bidding I married. Behold the offspring and progeny of a succession of consuls and dictators. Not to excite odium do I recall such facts, but to win compassion. While you prosper, Cæsar, they will attain such promotion as you shall bestow. Meanwhile save from penury the great-grandsons of Quintus Hortensius, the foster children of Augustus."

38. The Senate's favorable bias was an incitement to

Tiberius to offer prompt opposition, which he did in
nearly these words: "If all poor men begin to come here
and to beg money for their children, individuals will
never be satisfied, and the state will be bankrupt. Certainly our ancestors did not grant the privilege of occasionally proposing amendments or of suggesting, in
our turn for speaking, something for the general advantage in order that we might in this house increase our
private business and property, thereby bringing odium
on the Senate and on emperors whether they concede or
refuse their bounty. In fact, it is not a request, but an
importunity, as utterly unreasonable as it is unforeseen, for a senator, when the house has met on other
matters, to rise from his place and, pleading the number and age of his children, put a pressure on the delicacy of the Senate, then transfer the same constraint
to myself, and, as it were, try to break open the exchequer, which, if we exhaust it by improper favoritism,
will have to be replenished by crimes. Money was given
you, Hortalus, by Augustus, but without solicitation, and
not on the condition of its being always given. Otherwise industry will languish and idleness be encouraged,
if a man has nothing to fear, nothing to hope from himself, and everyone, in utter recklessness, will expect relief from others, thus becoming useless to himself and
a burden to me."

These and like remarks, though listened to with assent
by those who make it a practice to eulogize everything
coming from sovereigns, both good and bad, were received by the majority in silence or with suppressed
murmurs. Tiberius perceived it, and having paused
awhile, said that he had given Hortalus his answer, but
that if the senators thought it right, he would bestow
two hundred thousand sesterces on each of his children
of the male sex. The others thanked him; Hortalus said
nothing, either from alarm or because even in his reduced fortunes he clung to his hereditary nobility. Nor
did Tiberius afterward show any pity, though the house
of Hortensius sank into shameful poverty.

39. That same year the daring of a single slave, had
it not been promptly checked, would have ruined the

state by discord and civil war. A servant of Postumus
Agrippa, Clemens by name, having ascertained that Augustus was dead, formed a design beyond a slave's conception, of going to the island of Planasia and seizing
Agrippa by craft or force and bringing him to the armies
of Germany. The slowness of a merchant vessel thwarted
his bold venture. Meanwhile the murder of Agrippa had
been perpetrated, and then turning his thoughts to a
greater and more hazardous enterprise, he stole the
ashes of the deceased, sailed to Cosa,[15] a promontory of
Etruria, and there hid himself in obscure places till his
hair and beard were long. In age and figure he was not
unlike his master. Then through suitable emissaries who
shared his secret, it was rumored that Agrippa was alive,
first in whispered gossip, soon, as is usual with forbidden topics, in vague talk which found its way to the
credulous ears of the most ignorant people or of restless
and revolutionary schemers. He himself went to the
towns, as the day grew dark, without letting himself be
seen publicly or remaining long in the same places, but,
as he knew that truth gains strength by notoriety and
time, falsehood by precipitancy and vagueness, he would
either withdraw himself from publicity or else forestall it.

40. It was rumored meanwhile throughout Italy, and
was believed at Rome, that Agrippa had been saved by
the blessing of heaven. Already at Ostia, where he had
arrived, he was the center of interest to a vast concourse
as well as to secret gatherings in the capital, while Tiberius was distracted by the doubt whether he should
crush this slave of his by military force or allow time to
dissipate a silly credulity. Sometimes he thought that
he must overlook nothing, sometimes that he need not
be afraid of everything, his mind fluctuating between
shame and terror. At last he entrusted the affair to
Sallustius Crispus,[16] who chose two of his dependants
(some say they were soldiers) and urged them to go to
him as pretended accomplices, offering money and promising faithful companionship in danger. They did as
they were bidden; then, waiting for an unguarded hour
of night, they took with them a sufficient force, and

having bound and gagged him, dragged him to the palace. When Tiberius asked him how he had become Agrippa, he is said to have replied, "As you became Cæsar." He could not be forced to divulge his accomplices. Tiberius did not venture on a public execution, but ordered him to be slain in a private part of the palace and his body to be secretly removed. And although many of the Emperor's household and knights and senators were said to have supported him with their wealth and helped him with their counsels, no inquiry was made.

41. At the close of the year was consecrated an arch near the temple of Saturn to commemorate the recovery of the standards lost with Varus, under the leadership of Germanicus and the auspices of Tiberius; a temple of Fors Fortuna, by the Tiber, in the gardens which Cæsar the dictator bequeathed, to the Roman people;[17] a chapel to the Julian family, and statues at Bovillæ[18] to the divine Augustus.

In the consulship of Gaius Cæcilius and Lucius Pomponius,[19] Germanicus Cæsar, on the 26th day of May, celebrated his triumph over the Cherusci, Chatti, and Angrivarii, and the other tribes which extend as far as the Elbe. There were borne in procession spoils, prisoners, representations of the mountains, the rivers and battles; and the war, seeing that he had been forbidden to finish it, was taken as finished. The admiration of the beholders was heightened by the striking comeliness of the general and the chariot which bore his five children. Still, there was a latent dread when they remembered how unfortunate in the case of Drusus, his father, had been the favor of the crowd; how his uncle Marcellus,[20] regarded by the city populace with passionate enthusiasm, had been snatched from them while yet a youth, and how short-lived and ill-starred were the attachments of the Roman people.

42. Tiberius meanwhile in the name of Germanicus gave everyone of the city populace three hundred sesterces, and himself nominated his colleague in the consulship. Still, failing to obtain credit for sincere affection, he resolved to get the young prince out of the way, under pretense of conferring distinction, and for this he

invented reasons, or eagerly fastened on such as chance presented.

King Archelaus had been in possession of Cappadocia for fifty years, and Tiberius hated him because he had not shown him any mark of respect while he was at Rhodes. This neglect of Archelaus was not due to pride, but was suggested by the intimate friends of Augustus, because, when Gaius Cæsar was in his prime, and had charge of the affairs of the East, Tiberius' friendship was thought to be dangerous. When, after the extinction of the family of the Cæsars, Tiberius acquired the Empire, he enticed Archelaus by a letter from his mother, who without concealing her son's displeasure promised mercy if he would come to beg for it. Archelaus, either quite unsuspicious of treachery, or dreading compulsion, should it be thought that he saw through it, hastened to Rome. There he was received by a pitiless Emperor, and soon afterward was arraigned before the Senate. In his anguish and in the weariness of old age, and from being unused, as a king, to equality, much less to degradation, not, certainly, from fear of the charges fabricated against him, he ended his life, by his own act or by a natural death. His kingdom was reduced into a province, and Cæsar declared that, with its revenues, the one per cent tax could be lightened, which for the future, he fixed at one-half per cent.

During the same time, on the deaths of Antiochus and Philopator, kings respectively of Commagene and Cilicia, these nations became excited, a majority desiring the Roman rule, some, that of their kings. The provinces too of Syria and Judæa, exhausted by their burdens, implored a reduction of tribute.

43. Tiberius accordingly discussed these matters and the affairs of Armenia, which I have already related, before the Senate. "The commotions in the East," he said, "could be quieted only by the wisdom of Germanicus; his own life was on the decline, and Drusus had not yet reached his maturity." Thereupon, by a decree of the Senate, the provinces beyond the sea were entrusted to Germanicus, with greater powers wherever he

TACITUS

went than were given to those who obtained their provinces by lot or by the Emperor's appointment.

Tiberius had, however, removed from Syria Creticus Silanus,[21] who was connected by a close tie with Germanicus, his daughter being betrothed to Nero, the eldest of Germanicus' children. He appointed to it Cnæus Piso,[22] a man of violent temper, without an idea of obedience, with indeed a natural arrogance inherited from his father Piso, who in the civil war supported with the most energetic aid against Cæsar the reviving faction in Africa, then embraced the cause of Brutus and Cassius, and, when suffered to return, refrained from seeking promotion till he was actually solicited to accept a consulship offered by Augustus. But beside the father's haughty temper there was also the noble rank and wealth of his wife, Plancina,[23] to inflame his ambition. He would hardly be the inferior of Tiberius, and as for Tiberius' children, he looked down on them as far beneath him. He thought it a certainty that he had been chosen to govern Syria in order to thwart the aspirations of Germanicus. Some believed that he had even received secret instructions from Tiberius, and it was beyond a question that Augusta, with feminine jealousy, had suggested to Plancina calumnious insinuations against Agrippina. For there was division and discord in the court, with unexpressed partialities toward either Drusus or Germanicus. Tiberius favored Drusus, as his own son and born of his own blood.[24] As for Germanicus, his uncle's estrangement had increased the affection which all others felt for him, and there was the fact too that he had an advantage in the illustrious rank of his mother's family, among whom he could point to his grandfather Marcus Antonius and to his great-uncle Augustus.[25] Drusus, on the other hand, had for his great-grandfather a Roman knight, Pomponius Atticus, who seemed to disgrace the ancestral images of the Claudii.[26] Again, the consort of Germanicus, Agrippina, in number of children and in character, was superior to Livia, the wife of Drusus. Yet the brothers were singularly united, and were wholly unaffected by the rivalries of their kinsfolk.

30

44. Soon afterward Drusus was sent into Illyricum
to be familiarized with military service, and to win the
goodwill of the army. Tiberius also thought that it was
better for the young prince, who was being demoralized
by the luxury of the capital, to serve in a camp, while
he felt himself the safer with both his sons in command
of legions. However, he made a pretext of the Suebi,
who were imploring help against the Cherusci. For when
the Romans had departed and they were free from the
fear of an invader, these tribes, according to the custom
of the race, and then specially as rivals in fame, had
turned their arms against each other. The strength of
the two nations, the valor of their chiefs were equal.
But the title of king rendered Maroboduus hated among
his countrymen, while Arminius was regarded with
favor, as the champion of freedom.

45. Thus it was not only the Cherusci and their allies,
the old soldiers of Arminius, who took up arms, but even
the Semnones and Langobardi[27] from the kingdom of
Maroboduus revolted to that chief. With this addition
he must have had an overwhelming superiority, had not
Inguiomerus deserted with a troop of his dependents to
Maroboduus, simply for the reason that the aged uncle
scorned to obey a brother's youthful son. The armies
were drawn up, with equal confidence on both sides,
and there were not those desultory attacks or irregular
bands, formerly so common with the Germans. Prolonged warfare against us had accustomed them to keep
close to their standards, to have the support of reserves,
and to take the word of command from their generals.
On this occasion Arminius, who reviewed the whole
field on horseback, as he rode up to each band boasted
of regained freedom, of slaughtered legions, of spoils
and weapons wrested from the Romans, and still in the
hands of many of his men. As for Maroboduus, he called
him a fugitive, who had no experience of battles, who
had sheltered himself in the recesses of the Hercynian
Forest[28] and then with presents and embassies sued for
a treaty; a traitor to his country, a satellite of Cæsar,
who deserved to be driven out, with rage as furious as

31

that with which they had slain Quintilius Varus. They should simply remember their many battles, the result of which, with the final expulsion of the Romans, sufficiently showed who could claim the crowning success in war.

46. Nor did Maroboduus abstain from vaunts about himself or from revilings of the foe. Clasping the hand of Inguiomerus, he protested that "in the person before them centered all the renown of the Cherusci, that to his counsels was due whatever had ended successfully. Arminius in his infatuation and ignorance was taking to himself the glory which belonged to another, for he had treacherously surprised three unofficered legions and a general who had not an idea of perfidy, to the great hurt of Germany and to his own disgrace, since his wife and his son were still enduring slavery. As for himself, he had been attacked by twelve legions led by Tiberius, and had preserved untarnished the glory of the Germans, and then on equal terms the armies had parted. He was by no means sorry that they had the matter in their own hands, whether they preferred to war with all their might against Rome, or to accept a bloodless peace."

To these words, which roused the two armies, was added the stimulus of special motives of their own. The Cherusci and Langobardi were fighting for ancient renown or newly won freedom; the other side for the increase of their dominion. Never at any time was the shock of battle more tremendous or the issue more doubtful, as the right wings of both armies were routed. Further fighting was expected, when Maroboduus withdrew his camp to the hills. This was a sign of discomfiture. He was gradually stripped of his strength by desertions, and, having fled to the Marcomanni,[29] he sent envoys to Tiberius with entreaties for help. The answer was that he had no right to invoke the aid of Roman arms against the Cherusci, when he had rendered no assistance to the Romans in their conflict with the same enemy. Drusus, however, was sent as I have related, to establish peace.

[*Chapters 47-61 are omitted.*]

62. While Germanicus was spending the summer in visits to several provinces, Drusus gained no little glory by sowing discord among the Germans and urging them to complete the destruction of the now broken power of Maroboduus. Among the Gotones[30] was a youth of noble birth, Catualda by name, who had formerly been driven into exile by the might of Maroboduus, and who now, when the king's fortunes were declining, ventured on revenge. He entered the territory of the Marcomanni with a strong force, and, having corruptly won over the nobles to join him, burst into the palace and into an adjacent fortress. There he found the long-accumulated plunder of the Suebi and camp followers and traders from our provinces who had been attracted to an enemy's land, each from their various homes, first by the freedom of commerce, next by the desire of amassing wealth, finally by forgetfulness of their fatherland.

63. Maroboduus, now utterly deserted, had no resource but in the mercy of Cæsar. Having crossed the Danube where it flows by the province of Noricum,[31] he wrote to Tiberius, not like a fugitive or a suppliant, but as one who remembered his past greatness. When as a most famous king in former days he received invitations from many nations, he had still, he said, preferred the friendship of Rome. Cæsar replied that he should have a safe and honorable home in Italy, if he would remain there, or, if his interests required something different, he might leave it under the same protection under which he had come. But in the Senate he maintained that Philip[32] had not been so formidable to the Athenians, or Pyrrhus[33] or Antiochus[34] to the Roman people, as was Maroboduus. The speech is extant, and in it he magnifies the man's power, the ferocity of the tribes under his sway, his proximity to Italy as a foe, finally his own measures for his overthrow. The result was that Maroboduus was kept at Ravenna, where his possible return was a menace to the Suebi, should they ever disdain obedience. But he never left Italy for eighteen years, living to old age

and losing much of his renown through an excessive clinging to life.

Catualda had a like downfall and no better refuge. Driven out soon afterward by the overwhelming strength of the Hermunduri,[35] led by Vibilius, he was received and sent to Forum Julii,[36] a colony of Narbonese Gaul. The barbarians who followed the two kings, lest they might disturb the peace of the provinces by mingling with the population, were settled beyond the Danube between the rivers Marus and Cusus,[37] under a king, Vannius, of the nation of the Quadi.[38]

64. Tidings having also arrived of Artaxias being made king of Armenia by Germanicus, the Senate decreed that both he and Drusus should enter the city with an ovation. Arches too were raised round the sides of the temple of Mars the Avenger,[39] with statues of the two Cæsars. Tiberius was the more delighted at having established peace by wise policy than if he had finished a war by battle. And so next he planned a crafty scheme against Rhescuporis, king of Thrace. That entire country had been in the possession of Rhœmetalces, after whose death Augustus assigned half to the king's brother Rhescuporis, half to his son Cotys. In this division the cultivated lands, the towns, and what bordered on Greek territories fell to Cotys; the wild and barbarous portion, with enemies on its frontier, to Rhescuporis. The kings too themselves differed, Cotys having a gentle and kindly temper, the other a fierce and ambitious spirit, which could not brook a partner. Still at first they lived in a hollow friendship, but soon Rhescuporis overstepped his bounds and appropriated to himself what had been given to Cotys, using force when he was resisted, though somewhat timidly under Augustus, who having created both kingdoms would, he feared, avenge any contempt of his arrangement. When, however, he heard of the change of emperor, he let loose bands of freebooters and razed the fortresses, as a provocation to war.

65. Nothing made Tiberius so uneasy as an apprehension of the disturbance of any settlement. He commissioned a centurion to tell the kings not to decide their dispute by arms. Cotys at once dismissed the forces

which he had prepared. Rhescuporis, with assumed modesty, asked for a place of meeting where, he said, they might settle their differences by an interview. There was little hesitation in fixing on a time, a place, finally on terms, as every point was mutually conceded and accepted, by the one out of good nature, by the other with a treacherous intent. Rhescuporis, to ratify the treaty, as he said, further proposed a banquet; and when their mirth had been prolonged far into the night, and Cotys amid the feasting and the wine was unsuspicious of danger, he loaded him with chains, though he appealed, on perceiving the perfidy, to the sacred character of a king, to the gods of their common house, and to the hospitable board. Having possessed himself of all Thrace, he wrote word to Tiberius that a plot had been formed against him, and that he had forestalled the plotter. Meanwhile, under pretext of a war against the Bastarnian[40] and Scythian[41] tribes, he was strengthening himself with fresh forces of infantry and cavalry.

He received a conciliatory answer. If there was no treachery in his conduct, he could rely on his innocence, but neither the Emperor nor the Senate would decide on the right or wrong of his cause without hearing it. He was therefore to surrender Cotys, come in person and transfer from himself the odium of the charge.

66. This letter Latinius Pandusa, proprætor of Mœsia, sent to Thrace, with soldiers to whose custody Cotys was to be delivered. Rhescuporis, hesitating between fear and rage, preferred to be charged with an accomplished rather than with an attempted crime. He ordered Cotys to be murdered and falsely represented his death as self-inflicted. Still the Emperor did not change the policy which he had once for all adopted. On the death of Pandusa, whom Rhescuporis accused of being his personal enemy, he appointed to the government of Mœsia Pomponius Flaccus,[42] a veteran soldier, specially because of his close intimacy with the king and his consequent ability to entrap him.

67. Flaccus, on arriving in Thrace, induced the king by great promises, though he hesitated and thought of his guilty deeds, to enter the Roman lines. He then sur-

rounded him with a strong force under pretense of showing him honor, and the tribunes and centurions, by
counsel, by persuasion, and by a more undisguised captivity the further he went, brought him, aware at last
of his desperate plight, to Rome. He was accused before the Senate by the wife of Cotys, and was condemned
to be kept a prisoner far away from his kingdom. Thrace
was divided between his son Rhœmetalces, who, it was
proved, had opposed his father's designs, and the sons
of Cotys. As these were still minors, Trebellenus Rufus,
an ex-prætor, was appointed to govern the kingdom in
the meantime, after the precedent of our ancestors who
sent Marcus Lepidus[43] into Egypt as guardian to Ptolemy's children. Rhescuporis was removed to Alexandria,
and there attempting or falsely charged with attempting
escape, was put to death.

[*Chapter 68 is omitted.*]

69. Germanicus meanwhile, as he was returning from
Egypt, found that all his directions to the legions and
to the various cities had been repealed or reversed. This
led to grievous insults to Piso, while he as savagely assailed the prince. Piso then resolved to quit Syria. Soon he
was detained there by the failing health of Germanicus,
but when he heard of his recovery, while people were paying the vows they had offered for his safety, he went attended by his lictors, drove away the victims placed by
the altars with all the preparations for sacrifice, and the
festal gathering of the populace of Antioch. Then he left
for Seleucia[44] and awaited the result of the illness, which
had again attacked Germanicus. The terrible intensity of
the malady was increased by the belief that he had been
poisoned by Piso. And certainly there were found hidden
in the floor and in the walls disinterred remains of human bodies, incantations and spells, and the name of
Germanicus inscribed on leaden tablets, half-burned cin-
ders smeared with blood, and other horrors by which
in popular belief souls are devoted to the infernal deities.
Piso was also accused of sending emissaries to note curi-
ously every unfavorable symptom of the illness.

70. Germanicus heard of all this with anger, no less than with fear. "If my doors," he said, "are to be besieged, if I must gasp out my last breath under my enemies' eyes, what will then be the lot of my most unhappy wife, of my infant children? Poisoning seems tedious; he is in eager haste to have the sole control of the province and the legions. But Germanicus is not yet fallen so low, nor will the murderer long retain the reward of the fatal deed."

He then addressed a letter to Piso, renouncing his friendship, and, as many also state, ordered him to quit the province. Piso without further delay weighed anchor, slackening his course that he might not have a long way to return should Germanicus' death leave Syria open to him.

71. For a brief space the prince's hopes rose; then his frame became exhausted, and, as his end drew near, he spoke as follows to the friends by his side:

"Were I succumbing to nature, I should have just ground of complaint even against the gods for thus tearing me away in my youth by an untimely death from parents, children, country. Now, cut off by the wickedness of Piso and Plancina, I leave to your hearts my last entreaties. Describe to my father and brother, torn by what persecutions, entangled by what plots, I have ended by the worst of deaths the most miserable of lives. If any were touched by my bright prospects, by ties of blood, or even by envy toward me while I lived, they will weep that the once prosperous survivor of so many wars has perished by a woman's treachery. You will have the opportunity of complaint before the Senate, of an appeal to the laws. It is not the chief duty of friends to follow the dead with unprofitable laments, but to remember his wishes, to fulfill his commands. Tears for Germanicus even strangers will shed; vengeance must come from *you*, if you loved the man more than his fortune. Show the people of Rome her who is the granddaughter of the divine Augustus, as well as my consort; set before them my six children. Sympathy will be on the side of the accusers, and to those who screen themselves under infamous orders belief or pardon will be refused."

His friends clasped the dying man's right hand, and swore that they would sooner lose life than revenge.

72.   He then turned to his wife and implored her by the memory of her husband and by their common off-spring to lay aside her high spirit, to submit herself to the cruel blows of fortune, and not, when she returned to Rome, to enrage by political rivalry those who were stronger than herself. This was said openly; other words were whispered, pointing, it was supposed, to his fears from Tiberius. Soon afterward he expired, to the intense sorrow of the province and of the neighboring peoples. Foreign nations and kings grieved over him, so great was his courtesy to allies, his humanity to enemies. He inspired reverence alike by look and voice, and while he maintained the greatness and dignity of the highest rank, he had escaped the hatred that waits on arrogance.

73. His funeral, though it lacked the family statues and procession, was honored by panegyrics and a commemoration of his virtues. Some there were who, as they thought of his beauty, his age, and the manner of his death, the vicinity too of the country where he died, likened his end to that of Alexander the Great. Both had a graceful person and were of royal birth; neither had much exceeded thirty years of age, and both fell by the treachery of their own people in strange lands. But Germanicus was gracious to his friends, temperate in his pleasures, the husband of one wife, with only legitimate children. He was, too, no less a warrior, though rashness he had none, and, though after having cowed Germany by his many victories, he was hindered from crushing it into subjection. Had he had the sole control of affairs, had he possessed the power and title of a king, he would have attained military glory as much more easily as he had excelled Alexander in clemency, in self-restraint, and in all other virtues.

As to the body which, before it was burned, lay bare in the forum at Antioch, its destined place of burial, it is doubtful whether it exhibited the marks of poisoning.

For men, according as they pitied Germanicus and were prepossessed with suspicion or were biased by partiality toward Piso, gave conflicting accounts.

74. Then followed a deliberation among the generals and other senators present about the appointment of a governor to Syria. The contest was slight among all but Vibius Marsus[45] and Cnæus Santius,[46] between whom there was a long dispute. Finally Marsus yielded to Sentius as an older and keener competitor. Sentius at once sent to Rome a woman infamous for poisonings in the province and a special favorite of Plancina, Martina by name, on the demand of Vitellius and Veranius and others, who were preparing the charges and the indictment as if a prosecution had already been commenced.

75. Agrippina meantime, worn out though she was with sorrow and bodily weakness, yet still impatient of everything which might delay her vengeance, embarked with the ashes of Germanicus and with her children, pitied by all. Here indeed was a woman of the highest nobility, and but lately because of her splendid union wont to be seen amid an admiring and sympathizing throng, now bearing in her bosom the mournful relics of death, with an uncertain hope of revenge, with apprehensions for herself, repeatedly at fortune's mercy by reason of the ill-starred fruitfulness of her marriage. Piso was at the island of Cos[47] when tidings reached him that Germanicus was dead. He received the news with extravagant joy, slew victims, visited the temples, with no moderation in his transports; while Plancina's insolence increased, and she then for the first time exchanged for the gayest attire the mourning she had worn for her lost sister.

76. Centurions streamed in, and hinted to Piso that he had the sympathy of the legions at his command. "Go back," they said, "to the province which has not been rightfully taken from you, and is still vacant." While he deliberated what he was to do, his son, Marcus Piso, advised speedy return to Rome. "As yet," he said, "you have not contracted any inexpiable guilt, and you need not dread feeble suspicions or vague rumors. Your strife with Germanicus deserved hatred perhaps, but

not punishment, and by your having been deprived of the province, your enemies have been fully satisfied. But if you return, should Sentius resist you, civil war is begun, and you will not retain on your side the centurions and soldiers, who are powerfully swayed by the yet recent memory of their general and by a deep-rooted affection for the Cæsars."

77. Against this view Domitius Celer, one of Piso's intimate friends, argued that he ought to profit by the opportunity. "It was Piso, not Sentius, who had been appointed to Syria. It was to Piso that the symbols of power and a prætor's jurisdiction and the legions had been given. In case of a hostile menace, who would more rightfully confront it by arms than the man who had received the authority and special commission of a governor? And as for rumors, it is best to leave time in which they may die away. Often the innocent cannot stand against the first burst of unpopularity. But if Piso possesses himself of the army, and increases his resources, much which cannot be foreseen will haply turn out in his favor. Are we hastening to reach Italy along with the ashes of Germanicus, that, unheard and undefended, you may be hurried to ruin by the wailings of Agrippina and the first gossip of an ignorant mob? You have on your side the complicity of Augusta and the Emperor's favor, though in secret, and none mourn more ostentatiously over the death of Germanicus than those who most rejoice at it."

78. Without much difficulty Piso, who was ever ready for violent action, was led into this view. He sent a letter to Tiberius accusing Germanicus of luxury and arrogance, and asserting that, having been driven away to make room for revolution, he had resumed the command of the army in the same loyal spirit in which he had before held it. At the same time he put Domitius on board a trireme, with an order to avoid the coast and to push on to Syria through the open sea away from the islands. He formed into regular companies the deserters who flocked to him, armed the camp followers, crossed with his ships to the mainland, intercepted a detachment of new levies on their way to Syria, and wrote

word to the petty kings of Cilicia that they were to help him with auxiliaries, the young Piso actively assisting in all the business of war, though he had advised against undertaking it.

79. And so they coasted along Lycia and Pamphylia, and on meeting the fleet which conveyed Agrippina, both sides in hot anger at first armed for battle, and then in mutual fear confined themselves to revilings, Vibius Marsus telling Piso that he was to go to Rome to defend himself. Piso mockingly replied that he would be there as soon as the prætor who had to try poisoning cases had fixed a day for the accused and his prosecutors.

Meanwhile Domitius, having landed at Laodicea,[48] a city of Syria, as he was on his way to the winter quarters of the sixth legion, which was, he believed, particularly open to revolutionary schemes, was anticipated by its commander, Pacuvius. Of this Sentius informed Piso in a letter, and warned him not to disturb the armies by agents of corruption or the province by war. He gathered round him all whom he knew to cherish the memory of Germanicus, and to be opposed to his enemies, dwelling repeatedly on the greatness of the general, with hints that the state was being threatened with an armed attack, and he put himself at the head of a strong force, prepared for battle.

80. Piso too, though his first attempts were unsuccessful, did not omit the safest precautions under present circumstances, but occupied a very strongly fortified position in Cilicia, named Celenderis.[49] He had raised to the strength of a legion the Cilician auxiliaries which the petty kings had sent, by mixing with them some deserters, and the lately intercepted recruits with his own and Plancina's slaves. And he protested that he, though Cæsar's legate, was kept out of the province which Cæsar had given him, not by the legions (for he had come at their invitation) but by Sentius, who was veiling private animosity under lying charges. "Only," he said, "stand in battle array, and the soldiers will not fight when they see that Piso, whom they themselves once called 'father,' is the stronger, if right is to decide; if arms, is far from powerless."

He then deployed his companies before the lines of the fortress on a high and precipitous hill, with the sea surrounding him on every other side. Against him were the veteran troops drawn up in ranks and with reserves, a formidable soldiery on one side, a formidable position on the other. But his men had neither heart nor hope, and only rustic weapons, extemporized for sudden use. When they came to fighting, the result was doubtful only while the Roman cohorts were struggling up to level ground; then, the Cilicians turned their backs and shut themselves up within the fortress.

81. Meanwhile Piso vainly attempted an attack on the fleet which waited at a distance; he then went back, and as he stood before the walls, now smiting his breast, now calling on individual soldiers by name, and luring them on by rewards, sought to excite a mutiny. He had so far roused them that a standard bearer of the sixth legion went over to him with his standard. Thereupon Sentius ordered the horns and trumpets to be sounded, the rampart to be assaulted, the scaling ladders to be raised, all the bravest men to mount on them, while others were to discharge from the engines spears, stones, and brands. At last Piso's obstinacy was overcome, and he begged that he might remain in the fortress on surrendering his arms, while the Emperor was being consulted about the appointment of a governor to Syria. The proposed terms were refused, and all that was granted him were some ships and a safe return to Rome.

82. There meantime, when the illness of Germanicus was universally known, and all news, coming, as it did, from a distance, exaggerated the danger, there was grief and indignation. There was too an outburst of complaint. "Of course this was the meaning," they said, "of banishing him to the ends of the earth, of giving Piso the province; this was the drift of Augusta's secret interviews with Plancina. What elderly men had said of Drusus was perfectly true, that rulers disliked a citizen-like temper in their sons, and the young princes had been put out of the way because they had the idea of

comprehending in a restored era of freedom the Roman people under equal laws."

This popular talk was so stimulated by the news of Germanicus' death that even before the magistrates' proclamation or the Senate's resolution, there was a voluntary suspension of business, the public courts were deserted, and private houses closed. Everywhere there was a silence broken only by groans; nothing was arranged for mere effect. And though they did not refrain from the emblems of the mourner, they sorrowed yet the more deeply in their hearts.

It chanced that some merchants who left Syria while Germanicus was still alive brought more cheering tidings about his health. These were instantly believed, instantly published. Everyone passed on to others whom he met the intelligence, ill-authenticated as it was, and they again to many more, with joyous exaggeration. They ran to and fro through the city and broke open the doors of the temples. Night assisted their credulity, and amid the darkness confident assertion was comparatively easy. Nor did Tiberius check the false reports till by lapse of time they died away.

83. And so the people grieved the more bitterly as though Germanicus was again lost to them. New honors were devised and decreed, as men were inspired by affection for him or by genius. His name was to be celebrated in the song of the Salii;[50] chairs of state with oaken garlands over them were to be set up in the places assigned to the priesthood of the Augustales;[51] his image in ivory was to head the procession in the games of the circus; no flamen[52] or augur,[53] except from the Julian family, was to be chosen in the room of Germanicus. Triumphal arches were erected at Rome, on the banks of the Rhine, and on Mount Amanus[54] in Syria, with an inscription recording his achievements, and how he had died in the public service. A cenotaph was raised at Antioch, where the body was burned, a lofty mound at Epidaphna,[55] where he had ended his life. The number of his statues, or of the places in which they were honored, could not easily be computed. When a golden shield of remarkable size was voted him as a leader

among orators, Tiberius declared that he would dedicate to him one of the usual kind, similar to the rest, for in eloquence, he said, there was no distinction of rank, and it was a sufficient glory for him to be classed among ancient writers. The knights called the seats in the theater known as "the juniors'" Germanicus' benches, and arranged that their squadrons were to ride in procession behind his effigy on the 15th of July. Many of these honors still remain; some were at once dropped, or became obsolete with time.

84. While men's sorrow was yet fresh, Germanicus' sister Livia, who was married to Drusus, gave birth to twin sons. This, as a rare event, causing joy even in humble homes, so delighted the Emperor that he did not refrain from boasting before the senators that to no Roman of the same rank had twin offspring ever before been born. In fact, he would turn to his own glory every incident, however casual. But at such a time, even this brought grief to the people, who thought that the increase of Drusus' family still further depressed the house of Germanicus.

85. That same year the profligacy of women was checked by stringent enactments, and it was provided that no woman whose grandfather, father, or husband had been a Roman knight should get money by prostitution. Vistilia,[56] born of a prætorian family, had actually published her name with this object on the ædile's list, according to a recognized custom of our ancestors, who considered it a sufficient punishment on unchaste women to have to profess their shame. Titidius Labeo, Vistilia's husband, was judicially called on to say why with a wife whose guilt was manifest he had neglected to inflict the legal penalty. When he pleaded that the sixty days given for deliberation had not yet expired, it was thought sufficient to decide Vistilia's case, and she was banished out of sight to the island of Seriphus.[57]

There was a debate too about expelling the Egyptian and Jewish worship,[58] and a resolution of the Senate was passed that four thousand of the freedman class who were infected with those superstitions and were of military age should be transported to the island of Sar-

44

dinia, to quell the brigandage of the place, a cheap sacrifice should they die from the pestilential climate. The rest were to quit Italy, unless before a certain day they repudiated their impious rites.

86. Next the Emperor brought forward a motion for the election of a Vestal Virgin[59] in the room of Occia, who for fifty-seven years had presided with the most immaculate virtue over the Vestal worship. He formally thanked Fonteius Agrippa and Domitius Pollio for offering their daughters and so vying with one another in zeal for the commonwealth. Pollio's daughter was preferred, only because her mother had lived with one and the same husband, while Agrippa had impaired the honor of his house by a divorce. The Emperor consoled his daughter, passed over though she was, with a dowry of a million sesterces.

87. As the city populace complained of the cruel dearness of corn, he fixed a price for grain to be paid by the purchaser, promising himself to add two sesterces on every peck for the traders. But he would not therefore accept the title of "father of the country" which once before too had been offered him, and he sharply rebuked those who called his work "divine" and himself "lord." Consequently, speech was restricted and perilous under an Emperor who feared freedom while he hated sycophancy.

88. I find it stated by some writers and senators of the period that a letter from Adgandestrius, chief of the Chatti, was read in the Senate, promising the death of Arminius, if poison were sent for the perpetration of the murder, and that the reply was that it was not by secret treachery but openly and by arms that the people of Rome avenged themselves on their enemies. A noble answer, by which Tiberius sought to liken himself to those generals of old who had forbidden and even denounced the poisoning of King Pyrrhus.[60]

Arminius, meanwhile, when the Romans retired and Maroboduus was expelled, found himself opposed in aiming at the throne by his countrymen's independent spirit. He was assailed by armed force, and while fighting with various success, fell by the treachery of his

kinsmen. Assuredly he was the deliverer of Germany,
one too who had defied Rome, not in her early rise, as
other kings and generals, but in the height of her Empire's glory, had fought, indeed, indecisive battles, yet
in war remained unconquered. He completed thirty-seven
years of life, twelve years of power, and he is still a
theme of song among barbarous nations, though to Greek
historians, who admire only their own achievements, he
is unknown, and to Romans not as famous as he should
be, while we extoll the past and are indifferent to our
own times.

BOOK III   *20-22 A.D.*

1. WITHOUT pausing in her winter voyage, Agrippina
arrived at the island of Corcyra,[1] facing the shores of
Calabria. There she spent a few days to compose her
mind, for she was wild with grief and knew not how to
endure. Meanwhile, on hearing of her arrival, all her
intimate friends and several officers, everyone indeed
who had served under Germanicus, many strangers too
from the neighboring towns, some thinking it respectful
to the Emperor, and still more following their example,
thronged eagerly to Brundisium,[2] the nearest and safest
landing place for a voyager.

As soon as the fleet was seen on the horizon, not only
the harbor and the adjacent shores, but the city walls too
and the roofs and every place which commanded the
most distant prospect were filled with crowds of mourners, who incessantly asked one another whether, when
she landed, they were to receive her in silence or with
some utterance of emotion. They were not agreed on
what befitted the occasion when the fleet slowly approached, its crew not joyous as is usual, but wearing all
a studied expression of grief. When Agrippina descended
from the vessel with her two children, clasping the
funeral urn, with eyes riveted to the earth, there was
one universal groan. You could not distinguish kinsfolk
from strangers, or the laments of men from those of
women; only the attendants of Agrippina, worn out as

they were by long sorrow, were surpassed by the mourners who now met them, fresh in their grief.

2. The Emperor had dispatched two prætorian cohorts with instructions that the magistrates of Calabria, Apulia, and Campania were to pay the last honors to his son's memory. Accordingly tribunes and centurions bore Germanicus' ashes on their shoulders. They were preceded by the standards unadorned and the fasces reversed. As they passed colony after colony, the populace in black, the knights in their state robes, burned vestments and perfumes with other usual funeral adjuncts, in proportion to the wealth of the place. Even those whose towns were out of the route met the mourners, offered victims and built altars to the dead, testifying their grief by tears and wailings. Drusus went as far as Tarracina[3] with Claudius, brother of Germanicus, and the children who had been at Rome. Marcus Valerius and Gaius Aurelius, the consuls,[4] who had already entered on office, and a great number of the people thronged the road in scattered groups, everyone weeping as he felt inclined. Flattery there was none, for all knew that Tiberius could scarcely dissemble his joy at the death of Germanicus.

3. Tiberius and Augusta refrained from showing themselves, thinking it below their dignity to shed tears in public, or else fearing that, if all eyes scrutinized their faces, their hypocrisy would be revealed. I do not find in any historian or in the daily register, that Antonia, Germanicus' mother, rendered any conspicuous honor to the deceased, though besides Agrippina, Drusus, and Claudius, all his other kinsfolk are mentioned by name. She may either have been hindered by illness, or with a spirit overpowered by grief she may not have had the heart to endure the sight of so great an affliction. But I can more easily believe that Tiberius and Augusta, who did not leave the palace, kept her within, that their sorrow might seem equal to hers, and that the grandmother and uncle might be thought to follow the mother's example in staying at home.

4. The day on which the remains were consigned to the tomb of Augustus was now desolate in its silence,

47

now distracted by lamentations. The streets of the city were crowded; torches were blazing throughout the Campus Martius. There the soldiers under arms, the magistrates without their symbols of office, the people in the tribes, were all incessantly exclaiming that the commonwealth was ruined, that not a hope remained, too boldly and openly to let one think that they remembered their rulers. But nothing impressed Tiberius more deeply than the enthusiasm kindled in favor of Agrippina, whom men spoke of as the glory of the country, the sole surviving offspring of Augustus, the solitary example of the old times, while looking up to heaven and the gods they prayed for the safety of her children and that they might outlive their oppressors.

5. Some there were who missed the grandeur of a state funeral, and contrasted the splendid honors conferred by Augustus on Drusus, the father of Germanicus. "Then the Emperor himself," they said, "went in the extreme rigor of winter as far as Ticinum,[5] and never leaving the corpse entered Rome with it. Round the funeral bier were ranged the images of the Claudii and the Julii; there was weeping in the forum, and a panegyric before the Rostra; every honor devised by our ancestors or invented by their descendants was heaped on him. But as for Germanicus, even the customary distinctions due to any noble had not fallen to his lot. Granting that his body, because of the distance of the journey, was burned in any fashion in foreign lands, still all the more honors ought to have been afterward paid him, because at first chance had denied them. His brother had gone but one day's journey to meet him; his uncle, not even to the city gates. Where were all those usages of the past, the image at the head of the bier, the lays composed in commemoration of worth, the eulogies and laments, or at least the semblance of grief?"

6. All this was known to Tiberius, and, to silence popular talk, he reminded the people in a proclamation that many eminent Romans had died for their country and that none had been honored with such passionate regret. This regret was a glory both to himself and to all, provided only a due mean were observed; for what

48

was becoming in humble homes and communities did not befit princely personages and an imperial people. Tears and the solace found in mourning were suitable enough for the first burst of grief; but now they must brace their hearts to endurance, as in former days the divine Julius after the loss of his only daughter,[6] and the divine Augustus when he was bereft of his grand-children, had thrust away their sorrow. There was no need of examples from the past, showing how often the Roman people had patiently endured the defeats of armies, the destruction of generals, the total extinction of noble families. Princes were mortal; the state was everlasting. Let them then return to their usual pursuits, and, as the shows of the festival of the Great Goddess[7] were at hand, even resume their amusements.

7. The suspension of business then ceased, and men went back to their occupations. Drusus was sent to the armies of Illyricum, amidst a universal eagerness to exact vengeance on Piso, and the ceaseless complaints that he was meantime roaming through the delightful regions of Asia and Achæa, and was weakening the proofs of his guilt by an insolent and artful procrastination. It was indeed widely rumored that the notorious poisoner Martina, who, as I have related, had been dispatched to Rome by Cnæus Sentius, had died suddenly at Brundisium; that poison was concealed in a knot of her hair, and that no symptoms of suicide were discovered on her person.

8. Piso meanwhile sent his son on to Rome with a message intended to pacify the Emperor, and then made his way to Drusus, who would, he hoped, be not so much infuriated at his brother's death as kindly disposed toward himself to consequence of a rival's removal. Tiberius, to show his impartiality, received the youth courteously, and enriched him with the liberality he usually bestowed on the sons of noble families. Drusus replied to Piso that if certain insinuations were true, he must be foremost in his resentment, but he preferred to believe that they were false and groundless, and that Germanicus' death need be the ruin of no one. This he said openly, avoiding anything like secrecy. Men did not

doubt that his answer was prescribed him by Tiberius, inasmuch as one who had generally all the simplicity and candor of youth now had recourse to the artifices of old age.

9. Piso, after crossing the Adriatic Sea and leaving his ships at Ancona, went through Picenum[8] and along the Flaminian Way,[9] where he overtook a legion which was marching from Pannonia to Rome and was then to garrison Africa. It was a matter of common talk how he had repeatedly displayed himself to the soldiers on the road during the march. From Narnia,[10] to avoid suspicion or because the plans of fear are uncertain, he sailed down the Nar, then down the Tiber, and increased the fury of the populace by bringing his vessel to shore at the tomb of the Cæsars. In broad daylight, when the river bank was thronged, he himself with a numerous following of dependents, and Plancina with a retinue of women, moved onward with joy in their countenances. Among other things which provoked men's anger was his house towering above the forum, gay with festal decorations, his banquets and his feasts, about which there was no secrecy, because the place was so public.

10. Next day, Fulcinius Trio[11] asked the consuls' leave to prosecute Piso. It was contended against him by Vitellius and Veranius and the others who had been the companions of Germanicus that this was not Trio's proper part, and that they themselves meant to report their instructions from Germanicus, not as accusers, but as deponents and witnesses to facts. Trio, abandoning the prosecution on this count, obtained leave to accuse Piso's previous career, and the Emperor was requested to undertake the inquiry. This even the accused did not refuse, fearing as he did the bias of the people and of the Senate; while Tiberius, he knew, was resolute enough to despise report, and was also entangled in his mother's complicity. Truth too would be more easily distinguished from perverse misrepresentation by a single judge, where a number would be swayed by hatred and ill will.

Tiberius was not unaware of the formidable difficulty of the inquiry and of the rumors by which he was himself assailed. Having therefore summoned a few intimate friends, he listened to the threatening speeches of the prosecutors and to the pleadings of the accused, and finally referred the whole case to the Senate.

11. Drusus meanwhile, on his return from Illyricum, though the Senate had voted him an ovation for the submission of Maroboduus and the successes of the previous summer, postponed the honor and entered Rome. Then the defendant sought the advocacy of Lucius Arruntius,[12] Publius Vinicius,[13] Asinius Gallus, Æserninus Marcellus,[14] and Sextus Pompeius,[15] and on their declining for different reasons, Marcus Lepidus,[16] Lucius Piso,[17] and Livineius Regulus[18] became his counsel, amid the excitement of the whole country, which wondered how much fidelity would be shown by the friends of Germanicus, on what the accused rested his hopes, and how far Tiberius would repress and hide his feelings. Never were the people more keenly interested; never did they indulge themselves more freely in secret whispers against the Emperor or in the silence of suspicion.

12. On the day the Senate met, Tiberius delivered a speech of studied moderation. "Piso," he said, "was my father's representative and friend, and was appointed by myself, on the advice of the Senate, to assist Germanicus in the administration of the East. Whether he there had provoked the young prince by willful opposition and rivalry, and had rejoiced at his death or wickedly destroyed him, is for you to determine with minds unbiased. Certainly if a subordinate oversteps the bounds of duty and of obedience to his commander, and has exulted in his death and in my affliction, I shall hate him and exclude him from my house, and I shall avenge a personal quarrel without resorting to my power as Emperor. If, however, a crime is discovered which ought to be punished, whoever the murdered man may be, it is for you to give just reparation both to the children of Germanicus and to us, his parents.

"Consider this too, whether Piso dealt with the armies in a revolutionary and seditious spirit; whether he sought by intrigue popularity with the soldiers; whether he attempted to repossess himself of the province by arms, or whether these are falsehoods which his accusers have published with exaggeration. As for them, I am justly angry with their intemperate zeal. For to what purpose did they strip the corpse and expose it to the pollution of the vulgar gaze, and circulate a story among foreigners that he was destroyed by poison, if all this is still doubtful and requires investigation? For my part, I sorrow for my son and shall always sorrow for him; still I would not hinder the accused from producing all the evidence which can relieve his innocence or convict Germanicus of any unfairness, if such there was. And I implore you not to take as proven charges alleged, merely because the case is intimately bound up with my affliction. Do you, whom ties of blood or your own trueheartedness have made his advocates, help him in his peril, every one of you, as far as each man's eloquence and diligence can do so. To like exertions ànd like persistency I would urge the prosecutors. In this, and in this only, will we place Germanicus above the laws, by conducting the inquiry into his death in this house instead of in the forum, and before the Senate instead of before a bench of judges. In all else let the case be tried as simply as others. Let no one heed the tears of Drusus or my own sorrow, or any stories invented to our discredit."

13. Two days were then assigned for the bringing forward of the charges, and after six days' interval, the prisoner's defense was to occupy three days. Thereupon Fulcinius Trio began with some old and irrelevant accusations about intrigues and extortion during Piso's government of Spain. This, if proved, would not have been fatal to the defendant, if he cleared himself as to his late conduct, and, if refuted, would not have secured his acquittal, if he were convicted of the greater crimes. Next, Servæus, Veranius, and Vitellius, all with equal earnestness, Vitellius with striking eloquence, alleged against Piso that out of hatred of Germanicus and a desire of revolution he had so corrupted the common soldiers by license and oppression of the allies that he was called by the vilest of them "father of the legions," while on the other hand to all the best men, especially to the companions and friends of Germanicus, he had been savagely cruel. Lastly, he had, they said, destroyed

52

Germanicus himself by sorceries and poison, and hence came those ceremonies and horrible sacrifices made by himself and Plancina; then he had threatened the state with war, and had been defeated in battle, before he could be tried as a prisoner.

14. On all points but one the defense broke down. That he had tampered with the soldiers, that his province had been at the mercy of the vilest of them, that he had even insulted his chief, he could not deny. It was only the charge of poisoning from which he seemed to have cleared himself. This indeed the prosecutors did not adequately sustain by merely alleging that at a banquet given by Germanicus, his food had been tainted with poison by the hands of Piso, who sat next above him. It seemed absurd to suppose that he would have dared such an attempt among strange servants, in the sight of so many bystanders, and under Germanicus' own eyes. And, besides, the defendant offered his slaves to the torture, and insisted on its application to the attendants on that occasion. But the judges for different reasons were merciless, the Emperor because war had been made on a province, the Senate because they could not be sufficiently convinced that there had been no treachery about the death of Germanicus.

At the same time shouts were heard from the people in front of the Senate House, threatening violence if he escaped the verdict of the senators. They had actually dragged Piso's statues to the Gemonian Stairs,[19] and were breaking them in pieces, when by the Emperor's order they were rescued and replaced. Piso was then put in a litter and attended by a tribune of one of the prætorian cohorts, who followed him, so it was variously rumored, to guard his person or to be his executioner.

15. Plancina was equally detested, but had stronger interest. Consequently it was considered a question how far the Emperor would be allowed to go against her. While Piso's hopes were in suspense, she offered to share his lot, whatever it might be, and, in the worst event, to be his companion in death. But as soon as she had secured her pardon through the secret intercessions of Augusta, she gradually withdrew from her husband

and separated her defense from his. When the prisoner
saw that this was fatal to him, he hesitated whether he
should still persist, but at the urgent request of his sons
braced his courage and once more entered the Senate.
There he bore patiently the renewal of the accusation,
the furious voices of the senators, savage opposition
indeed from every quarter, but nothing daunted him so
much as to see Tiberius, without pity and without anger,
resolutely closing himself against any inroad of emotion.
He was conveyed back to his house, where, seemingly
by way of preparing his defense for the next day, he
wrote a few words, sealed the paper, and handed it to
a freedman. Then he bestowed the usual attention on
his person; after a while, late at night, his wife having
left his chamber, he ordered the doors to be closed, and
at daybreak was found with his throat cut and a sword
lying on the ground.

16. I remember to have heard old men say that a
document was often seen in Piso's hands, the substance
of which he never himself divulged, but which his
friends repeatedly declared contained a letter from Tiberius with instructions referring to Germanicus, and that
it was his intention to produce it before the Senate and
upbraid the Emperor, had he not been deluded by vain
promises from Sejanus. Nor did he perish, they said, by
his own hand, but by that of one sent to be his executioner. Neither of these statements would I positively
affirm; still it would not have been right for me to conceal what was related by those who lived up to the time
of my youth.

The Emperor, assuming an air of sadness, complained
in the Senate that the purpose of such a death was to
bring odium on himself, and he asked with repeated
questionings how Piso had spent his last day and night.
Receiving answers which were mostly judicious, though
in part somewhat incautious, he read out a note written
by Piso, nearly to the following effect:

"Crushed by a conspiracy of my foes and the odium
excited by a lying charge, since my truth and innocence find no place here, I call the immortal gods to
witness that toward you, Cæsar, I have lived loyally,

and with like dutiful respect toward your mother. And
I implore you to think of my children, one of whom,
Cnæus Piso, is in no way implicated in my career, whatever it may have been, seeing that all this time he has
been at Rome, while the other, Marcus Piso, dissuaded
me from returning to Syria. Would that I had yielded to
my young son rather than he to his aged father! And
therefore I pray the more earnestly that the innocent may
not pay the penalty of my wickedness. By forty-five years
of obedience, by my association with you in the consulate, as one who formerly won the esteem of the divine
Augustus, your father, as one who is your friend and
will never hereafter ask a favor, I implore you to save
my unhappy son." About Plancina he added not a word.

17. Tiberius after this acquitted the young Piso of the
charge of civil war on the ground that a son could not
have refused a father's orders, compassionating at the
same time the high rank of the family and the terrible
downfall even of Piso himself, however he might have
deserved it. For Plancina he spoke with shame and conscious disgrace, alleging in excuse the intercession of
his mother, secret complaints against whom from all
good men were growing more and more vehement. "So
it was the duty of a grandmother," people said, "to look
a grandson's murderess in the face, to converse with her
and rescue her from the Senate. What the laws secure
on behalf of every citizen had to Germanicus alone been
denied. The voices of a Vitellius and Veranius had be-
wailed a Cæsar, while the Emperor and Augusta had
defended Plancina. She might as well now turn her
poisonings, and her devices which had proved so successful, against Agrippina and her children, and thus
sate this exemplary grandmother and uncle with the
blood of a most unhappy house."

Two days were frittered away over this mockery of a
trial, Tiberius urging Piso's children to defend their
mother. While the accusers and their witnesses pressed
the prosecution with rival zeal, and there was no reply,
pity rather than anger was on the increase. Aurelius
Cotta, the consul, who was first called on for his vote
(for when the Emperor put the question, even those in

55

office went through the duty of voting), held that Piso's name ought to be erased from the public register, half of his property confiscated, half given up to his son Cnæus Piso, who was to change his first name; that Marcus Piso, stripped of his rank, with an allowance of five million sesterces, should be banished for ten years, Plancina's life being spared in consideration of Augusta's intercession.

18. Much of the sentence was mitigated by the Emperor. The name of Piso was not to be struck out of the public register, since that of Marcus Antonius, who had made war on his country, and that of Iullus[20] Antonius, who had dishonored the house of Augustus, still remained. Marcus Piso too he saved from degradation, and gave him his father's property, for he was firm enough, as I have often related, against the temptation of money, and now for very shame at Plancina's acquittal, he was more than usually merciful. Again, when Valerius Messallinus[21] and Cæcina Severus proposed respectively the erection of a golden statue in the temple of Mars the Avenger[22] and of an altar to Vengeance, he interposed, protesting that victories over the foreigner were commemorated with such monuments, but that domestic woes ought to be shrouded in silent grief.

There was a further proposal of Messallinus, that Tiberius, Augusta, Antonia, Agrippina, and Drusus ought to be publicly thanked for having avenged Germanicus. He omitted all mention of Claudius. Thereupon he was pointedly asked by Lucius Asprenas before the Senate whether the omission had been intentional, and it was only then that the name of Claudius was added. For my part, the wider the scope of my reflection on the happenings of the present and the past, the more am I impressed by their mockery of human plans in every transaction. Clearly, the very last man marked out for empire by public opinion, expectation and general respect was· he whom fortune was holding in reserve as the Emperor of the future.

19. A few days afterward the Emperor proposed to the Senate to confer the priesthood on Vitellius, Veranius, and Servæus. To Fulcinius he promised his support

in seeking promotion, but warned him not to ruin his eloquence by rancor. This was the end of avenging the death of Germanicus, a subject of conflicting rumors not only among the people then living but also in after times. So obscure are the greatest events that some take for granted any hearsay, whatever its source, while others turn truth into falsehood, and both errors find encouragement with posterity.

Drusus meanwhile quitted Rome to resume his command and soon afterward re-entered the city with an ovation. In the course of a few days his mother, Vipsania,[23] died, the only one of all Agrippina's children whose death was without violence. As for the rest, they perished, some it is certain by the sword, others it was believed by poison or starvation.[24]

[*Chapters 20-21 are omitted.*]

22. At Rome meanwhile, Lepida,[25] who besides the glory of being one of the Æmilii, was the great-granddaughter of Lucius Sulla and Cnæus Pompeius, was accused of pretending to be a mother by Publius Quirinius,[26] a rich and childless man. Then, too, there were charges of adulteries, of poisonings, and of inquiries made through astrologers concerning the imperial house. The accused was defended by her brother, Marcus Lepidus.[27] Quirinius, by his relentless enmity even after his divorce, had procured for her some sympathy, infamous and guilty as she was. One could not easily perceive the Emperor's feelings at her trial, so effectually did he interchange and blend the outward signs of resentment and compassion. He first begged the Senate not to deal with the charges of treason, and subsequently induced Marcus Servilius, an ex-consul,[28] to divulge what he had seemingly wished to suppress. He also handed over to the consuls Lepida's slaves, who were in military custody, but would not allow them to be examined by torture on matters referring to his own family. Drusus too, the consul-elect, he released from the necessity of having to speak first to the question. Some thought this a gracious act, done to save the rest

of the senators from a compulsory assent, while others
ascribed it to malignity, on the ground that he would
have yielded only where there was a necessity of condemning.

23. On the days of the games which interrupted the
trial, Lepida went into the theater with some ladies of
rank, and as she appealed with piteous wailings to her
ancestors and to that very Pompeius the public buildings
and statues of whom stood there before their eyes,[29] she
roused such sympathy that people burst into tears and
shouted, without ceasing, savage curses on Quirinius,
"to whose childless old age and miserably obscure family, one once destined to be the wife of Lucius Cæsar
and the daughter-in-law of the divine Augustus was being sacrificed." Then, by the torture of the slaves, her
infamies were brought to light, and a motion of Rubellius Blandus[30] was carried which outlawed her. Drusus
supported him, though others had proposed a milder
sentence. Subsequently Scaurus,[31] who had had a daughter by her, obtained as a concession that her property
should not be confiscated. Then at last Tiberius declared
that he had himself too ascertained from the slaves of
Publius Quirinius that Lepida had attempted their master's life by poison.

24. It was some compensation for the misfortunes of
great houses (for within a short interval the Calpurnii
had lost Piso and the Æmilii Lepida) that Decimus
Silanus[32] was now restored to the Junian family. I will
briefly relate his downfall.

Though the divine Augustus in his public life enjoyed
unshaken prosperity, he was unfortunate at home from
the profligacy of his daughter[33] and granddaughter,[34]
both of whom he banished from Rome, and punished
their paramours with death or exile. Calling, as he did,
a vice so habitual among men and women by the awful
name of sacrilege and treason, he went far beyond the
indulgent spirit of our ancestors, beyond indeed his own
legislation. But I will relate the deaths of others with
the remaining events of that time, if after finishing the
work I have now proposed to myself, I prolong my life
for further labors.

Decimus Silanus, the paramour of the granddaughter of Augustus, though the only severity he experienced was exclusion from the Emperor's friendship, saw clearly that it meant exile; and it was not till Tiberius' reign that he ventured to appeal to the Senate and to the prince, in reliance on the influence of his brother Marcus Silanus,[35] who was conspicuous for both his distinguished rank and his eloquence. But Tiberius, when Silanus thanked him, replied in the Senate's presence, "that he too rejoiced at the brother's return from his long foreign tour, and that this was justly allowable, inasmuch as he had been banished not by a decree of the Senate or under any law. Still," he said, "he felt toward him his father's resentment in all its force, and the return of Silanus had not canceled the intentions of Augustus." Silanus after this lived at Rome without attaining office.

25. It was next proposed to relax the Lex Papia Poppæa,[36] which Augustus in his old age had passed subsequently to the Julian statutes, for yet further enforcing the penalties on celibacy and for enriching the exchequer. And yet marriages and the rearing of children did not become more frequent, so powerful were the attractions of a childless state. Meanwhile there was an increase in the number of persons imperiled, for every household was undermined by the insinuations of informers; and now the country suffered from its laws, as it had hitherto suffered from its vices. This suggests to me a fuller discussion of the origin of law and of the methods by which we have arrived at the present endless multiplicity and variety of our statutes.

26. Mankind in the earliest age lived for a time without a single vicious impulse, without shame or guilt, and, consequently, without punishment and restraints. Rewards were not needed when everything right was pursued on its own merits; and as men desired nothing against morality, they were debarred from nothing by fear. When, however, they began to throw off equality, and ambition and violence usurped the place of self-control and modesty, despotisms grew up and became perpetual among many nations. Some from the begin-

ning, or when tired of kings, preferred codes of laws.
These were at first simple, while men's minds were un-
sophisticated. The most famous of them were those of
the Cretans, framed by Minos,[37] those of the Spartans,
by Lycurgus, and, subsequently, those which Solon[38]
drew up for the Athenians on a more elaborate and
extensive scale. Romulus[39] governed us as he pleased;
then Numa[40] united our people by religious ties and a
constitution of divine origin, to which some additions
were made by Tullus and Ancus.[41] But Servius Tullius
was our chief legislator, to whose laws even kings were
to be subject.[42]

27. After Tarquin's expulsion,[43] the people, to check
cabals among the senators, devised many safeguards for
freedom and for the establishment of unity. Decemvirs
were appointed;[44] everything ·specially admirable elsewhere was adopted, and the Twelve Tables drawn up,
the last specimen of equitable legislation.[45] For subsequent enactments, though occasionally directed against
evildoers for some crime, were oftener carried by violence amid class dissensions, with a view to obtain
honors not as yet conceded, or to banish distinguished
citizens, or for other base ends. Hence popular agitators,
like the Gracchi[46] and Saturninus, and Drusus too, as
flagrant a corrupter in the Senate's name; hence, the
bribing of our allies by alluring promises and the cheat-
ing them by tribunes' vetoes. Even the Italian and then
the civil war did not pass without the enactment of
many conflicting laws, till Lucius Sulla, the dictator, by
the repeal or alteration of past legislation and by many
additions, gave us a brief lull in this process, to be
instantly followed by the seditious proposals of Lepidus,[47] and soon afterward by the tribunes recovering
their license to excite the people just as they chose.[48]
And now bills were passed, not only for national objects
but for individual cases, and laws were most numerous
when the commonwealth was most corrupt.

28. Cnæus Pompeius was then for the third time
elected consul to reform the public morals,[49] but in applying remedies more terrible than the evils and repeal-
ing the legislation of which he had himself been the

author, he lost by arms what by arms he had been maintaining. Then followed twenty years of continuous strife; custom or law there was none; the vilest deeds went unpunished, while many noble acts brought ruin. At last, in his sixth consulship, Cæsar Augustus, feeling his power secure, annulled the decrees of his triumvirate,[50] and gave us a constitution which might serve us in peace under a monarchy. Henceforth our chains became more galling, and spies were set over us, stimulated by rewards under the Lex Papia Poppæa, so that if men shrank from the privileges of fatherhood, the state, as universal parent, might possess their ownerless properties. But this espionage became too searching, and Rome and Italy and Roman citizens everywhere fell into its clutches. Many men's fortunes were ruined, and over all there hung a terror, till Tiberius, to provide a remedy, selected by lot five ex-consuls, five ex-prætors, and five senators, by whom most of the legal knots were disentangled and some slight temporary relief afforded.

29. About this same time he commended to the Senate's favor Nero, Germanicus' son, who was just entering on manhood, and asked them, not without smiles of ridicule from his audience, to exempt him from serving as one of the Twenty Commissioners, and let him be a candidate for the quæstorship five years earlier than the law allowed. His excuse was that a similar decree had been made for himself and his brother at the request of Augustus. But I cannot doubt that even then there were some who secretly laughed at such a petition, though the Cæsars were but in the beginning of their grandeur, and ancient usage was more constantly before men's eyes, while also the tie between stepfather and stepson was weaker than that between grandfather and grandchild. A priesthood was likewise conferred on Nero, and on the day on which he first entered the forum, a gratuity was given to the city populace, who greatly rejoiced at seeing a son of Germanicus now grown to manhood. Their joy was further increased by Nero's marriage to Julia, Drusus' daughter. This news was met with favorable comments, but it was heard with disgust that Sejanus was to be the father-in-law

of the son of Claudius.[51] The Emperor was thought to have polluted the nobility of his house and to have yet further elevated Sejanus, whom they already suspected of overweening ambition.

30. Two remarkable men died at the end of the year, Lucius Volusius[52] and Sallustius Crispus.[53] Volusius was of an old family, which had however never risen beyond the prætorship. He brought into it the consulship; he also held the office of censor for arranging the classes of the knights, and was the first to pile up the wealth which that house enjoyed to a boundless extent.

Crispus was of equestrian descent and grandson of a sister of Gaius Sallustius, that most admirable Roman historian,[54] by whom he was adopted and whose name he took. Though his road to preferment was easy, he chose to emulate Mæcenas, and without rising to a senator's rank, he surpassed in power many who had won triumphs and consulships. He was a contrast to the manners of antiquity in his elegance and refinement, and in the sumptuousness of his wealth he was almost a voluptuary. But beneath all this was a vigorous mind, equal to the greatest labors, the more active in proportion as he made a show of sloth and apathy. And so while Mæcenas lived, he stood next in favor to him, and was afterward the chief depository of imperial secrets, and accessory to the murder of Postumus Agrippa, till in advanced age he retained the shadow rather than the substance of the Emperor's friendship. The same too had happened to Mæcenas, so rarely is it the destiny of power to be lasting, or perhaps a sense of weariness steals over princes when they have bestowed everything, or over favorites, when there is nothing left them to desire.

31. Next followed Tiberius' fourth, Drusus' second consulship,[55] memorable from the fact that father and son were colleagues. Two years previously the association of Germanicus and Tiberius in the same honor had not been agreeable to the uncle, nor had it the link of so close a natural tie.

At the beginning of this year Tiberius, avowedly to recruit his health, retired to Campania, either as a gradual preparation for a long and uninterrupted seclusion, or in order that Drusus alone in his father's absence might discharge the duties of the consulship. It happened that a mere trifle which grew into a sharp contest gave the young prince the means of acquiring popularity. Domitius Corbulo,[56] an ex-prætor, complained to the Senate that Lucius Sulla,[57] a young noble, had not given place to him at a gladiatorial show. Corbulo had age, national usage, and the feelings of the older senators in his favor. Against him Mamercus Scaurus, Lucius Arruntius, and other kinsmen of Sulla strenuously exerted themselves. There was a keen debate, and appeal was made to the precedents of our ancestors, as having censured in severe decrees disrespect on the part of the young, till Drusus argued in a strain calculated to calm their feelings. Corbulo too received an apology from Mamercus, who was Sulla's uncle and stepfather, and the most fluent speaker of that day.

It was this same Corbulo, who, after raising a cry that most of the roads in Italy were obstructed or impassable through the dishonesty of contractors and the negligence of officials, himself willingly undertook the complete management of the business. This proved not so beneficial to the state as ruinous to many persons, whose property and credit he mercilessly attacked by convictions and confiscations.

[*Chapter 32 is omitted.*]

33. During this debate Cæcina Severus proposed that no magistrate who had obtained a province should be accompanied by his wife. He began by recounting at length how harmoniously he had lived with his wife, who had borne him six children, and how in his own home he had observed what he was proposing for the public, by having kept her in Italy, though he had himself served forty campaigns in various provinces. "With good reason," he said, "had it been formerly decided that women were not to be taken among our allies or into foreign countries. A train of women involves delays through luxury in peace and through panic in

war, and converts a Roman army on the march into the likeness of a barbarian progress. Not only is the sex feeble and unequal to hardship, but, when it has liberty, it is spiteful, intriguing, and greedy of power. They show themselves off among the soldiers and have the centurions at their beck. Lately a woman had presided at the drill of the cohorts and the evolutions of the legions. You should yourselves bear in mind that, whenever men are accused of extortion, most of the charges are directed against the wives. It is to these that the vilest of the provincials instantly attach themselves; it is they who undertake and settle business; two persons receive homage when they appear; there are two centers of government, and the women's orders are the more despotic and intemperate. Formerly they were restrained by the Oppian and other laws; now, loosed from every bond, they rule our houses, our tribunals, even our armies."

34. A few heard this speech with approval, but the majority clamorously objected that there was no proper motion on the subject, and that Cæcina was no fit censor on so grave an issue. Presently Valerius Messallinus, Messalla's son, in whom the father's eloquence was reproduced,[58] replied that much of the sternness of antiquity had been changed into a better and more genial system. "Rome," he said, "is not now, as formerly, beset with wars, nor are the provinces hostile. A few concessions are made to the wants of women, but such as are not even a burden to their husband's homes, much less to the allies. In all other respects man and wife share alike, and this arrangement involves no trouble in peace. War of course requires that men should be unencumbered, but when they return what worthier solace can they have after their hardships than a wife's society? But some wives have abandoned themselves to scheming and rapacity. Well, even among our magistrates, are not many subject to various passions? Still, that is not a reason for sending no one into a province. Husbands have often been corrupted by the vices of their wives. Are then all unmarried men blameless? The Oppian laws were formerly adopted to meet the political

necessities of the time, and subsequently there was some remission and mitigation of them on grounds of expediency. It is idle to shelter our own weakness under other names; for it is the husband's fault if the wife transgresses propriety. Besides, it is wrong that because of the imbecility of one or two men, all husbands should be cut off from their partners in prosperity and adversity. And further, a sex naturally weak will be thus left to itself and be at the mercy of its own voluptuousness and the passions of others. Even with the husband's personal vigilance the marriage tie is scarcely preserved inviolate. What would happen were it for a number of years to be forgotten, just as in a divorce? You must not check vices abroad without remembering the scandals of the capital."

Drusus added a few words on his own experience as a husband. "Princes," he said, "must often visit the extremities of their Empire. How often had the divine Augustus traveled to the West and to the East accompanied by Livia? He had himself gone to Illyricum and, should it be expedient, he would go to other countries, not always, however, with a contented mind, if he had to tear himself from a much loved wife, the mother of his many children."[59]

35. Cæcina's motion was thus defeated. At the Senate's next meeting came a letter from Tiberius, which indirectly censured them for throwing on the Emperor every political care, and named Marcus Lepidus and Junius Blæsus, one of whom was to be chosen proconsul of Africa. Both spoke on the subject, and Lepidus begged earnestly to be excused. He alleged ill health, his children's tender age, his having a daughter to marry, and something more of which he said nothing was well understood, the fact that Blæsus was uncle of Sejanus and so had very powerful interest. Blæsus replied with an affectation of refusal, but not with the same persistency, nor was he backed up by the acquiescence of flatterers.

36. Next was exposed an abuse, hitherto the subject of many a whispered complaint. The vilest wretches used a growing freedom in exciting insult and obloquy against respectable citizens, and escaped punishment

by clasping some statue of the Emperor. The very freedman or slave was often an actual terror to his patron or master, whom he would menace by word and gesture. Accordingly Gaius Cestius,[60] a senator, argued that "though princes were like deities, yet even the gods listened only to righteous prayers from their suppliants, and that no one fled to the Capitol or any other temple in Rome to use it as an auxiliary in crime. There was an end and utter subversion of all law when, in the forum and on the threshold of the Senate House, Annia Rufilla, whom he had convicted of fraud before a judge, assailed him with insults and threats, while he did not himself dare to try legal proceedings, because he was confronted by her with the Emperor's image." There rose other clamorous voices, with even more flagrant complaints, and all implored Drusus to inflict exemplary vengeance, till he ordered Rufilla to be summoned, and on her conviction to be confined in the common prison.

37. Considius Æquus too and Cælius Cursor, Roman knights, were punished on the Emperor's proposal, by a decree of the Senate, for having attacked the prætor Magius Cæcilianus with false charges of treason. Both these results were represented as an honor to Drusus. By his moving in society at Rome, amid popular talk, his father's dark policy, it was thought, was mitigated. Even voluptuousness in one so young gave little offense. Better that he should incline that way, spend his days in architecture, his nights in banquets, than that he should live in solitude, cut off from every pleasure, and absorbed in a gloomy vigilance and mischievous schemes.

[*Chapters 38 to 47 are omitted. A revolt in Gaul among the Ædui and the Treveri, led by the Romanized Gauls Julius Sacrovir and Julius Florus, was suppressed without much difficulty.*]

48. About the same time Tiberius requested the Senate to let the death of Sulpicius Quirinius[61] be celebrated with a public funeral. With the old patrician family of the Sulpicii this Quirinius, who was born in the town of

Lanuvium,[62] was quite unconnected. An indefatigable soldier, he had by his zealous services won the consulship under the divine Augustus, and subsequently the honors of a triumph for having stormed some fortresses of the Homonadenses in Cilicia. He was also appointed adviser to Gaius Cæsar in the government of Armenia, and had likewise paid court to Tiberius, who was then at Rhodes. The Emperor now made all this known to the Senate, and extolled the good offices of Quirinius to himself, while he censured Marcus Lollius,[63] whom he charged with encouraging Gaius Cæsar in his perverse and quarrelsome behavior. But people generally had no pleasure in the memory of Quirinius, because of the perils he had brought, as I have related, on Lepida,[64] and the meanness and dangerous power of his last years.

49. At the close of the year, Gaius Clutorius Priscus, a Roman knight, who, after writing a popular poem bewailing the death of Germanicus, had received a reward in money from the Emperor, was fastened on by an informer, and charged with having composed another during the illness of Drusus, which, in the event of the prince's death, might be published with even greater profit to himself. He had in his vanity read it in the house of Publius Petronius[65] before Vitellia, Petronius' mother-in-law, and several ladies of rank. As soon as the accuser appeared, all but Vitellia were frightened into giving evidence. She alone swore that she had heard not a word. But those who incriminated him fatally were rather believed, and on the motion of Haterius Agrippa, the consul-elect, the last penalty was invoked on the accused.

50. Marcus Lepidus spoke against the sentence as follows: "Senators, if we look to the single fact of the infamous utterance with which Clutorius has polluted his own mind and the ears of the public, neither dungeon nor halter nor tortures fit for a slave would be punishment enough for him. But though vice and wicked deeds have no limit, penalties and correctives are moderated by the clemency of the sovereign and by the precedents of your ancestors and yourselves. Folly differs from wickedness; evil words from evil deeds, and thus there

is room for a sentence by which this offense may not go unpunished, while we shall have no cause to regret either leniency or severity. Often have I heard our Emperor complain when anyone has anticipated his mercy by a self-inflicted death. Clutorius' life is still safe; if spared, he will be no danger to the state; if put to death, he will be no warning to others. His productions are as empty and ephemeral as they are replete with folly. Nothing serious or alarming is to be apprehended from the man who is the betrayer of his own shame and works on the imaginations not of men but of silly women. However, let him leave Rome, lose his property, and be outlawed. That is my proposal, just as though he were convicted under the law of treason."

51. Only one of the ex-consuls, Rubellius Blandus, supported Lepidus. The rest voted with Agrippa. Priscus was dragged off to prison and instantly put to death. Of this Tiberius complained to the Senate with his usual ambiguity, extolling their loyalty in so sharply avenging the very slightest insults to the sovereign, though he deprecated such hasty punishment of mere words, praising Lepidus and not censuring Agrippa. So the Senate passed a resolution that their decrees should not be registered in the treasury till nine days had expired, and so much respite was to be given to condemned persons. Still the Senate had not liberty to alter their purpose, and lapse of time never softened Tiberius.

52. Gaius Sulpicius[66] and Didius Haterius were the next consuls. It was a year free from commotions abroad, while at home stringent legislation was apprehended against the luxury which had reached boundless excess in everything on which wealth is lavished. Some expenses, though very serious, were generally kept secret by a concealment of the real prices; but the costly preparations for gluttony and dissipation were the theme of incessant talk, and had suggested a fear that a prince who clung to old-fashioned frugality would be too stern in his reforms. In fact, when the ædile Gaius Bibulus broached the topic, all his colleagues had pointed out that the sumptuary laws were disregarded, that prohibited prices for household articles were every day on

the increase, and that moderate measures could not stop the evil.

The Senate on being consulted had, without handling the matter, referred it to the Emperor. Tiberius, after long considering whether such reckless tastes could be repressed, whether the repression of them would not be still more hurtful to the state, also how undignified it would be to meddle with what he could not succeed in, or what, if effected, would necessitate the disgrace and infamy of men of distinction, at last addressed a letter to the Senate to the following purport:

53. "Perhaps in any other matter, senators, it would be more convenient that I should be consulted in your presence, and then state what I think to be for the public good. In this debate it was better that my eyes should not be on you, for while you were noting the anxious faces of individual senators charged with shameful luxury, I too myself might observe them and, as it were, detect them. Had those energetic men, our ædiles, first taken counsel with me, I do not know whether I should not have advised them to let alone vices so strong and so matured, rather than merely attain the result of publishing what are the corruptions with which we cannot cope. They, however, have certainly done their duty, as I would wish all other officials likewise to fulfill their parts. For myself, it is neither seemly to keep silence nor is it easy to speak my mind, as I do not hold the office of ædile, prætor, or consul. Something greater and loftier is expected of a princeps, and while everybody takes to himself the credit of right policy, one alone has to bear the odium of every person's failures. For what am I first to begin with restraining and cutting down to the old standard? The vast dimensions of country houses? The number of slaves of every nationality? The masses of silver and gold? The marvels in bronze and painting? The apparel worn indiscriminately by both sexes, or that peculiar luxury of women which, for the sake of jewels, diverts our wealth to strange or hostile nations?

54. "I am not unaware that people at entertainments and social gatherings condemn all this and demand some restriction. But if a law were to be passed and a

penalty imposed, those very same persons will cry out
that the state is revolutionized, that ruin is plotted
against all our most brilliant fashion, that not a citizen
is safe from incrimination. Yet as even bodily disorders
of long standing and growth can be checked only by
sharp and painful treatment, so the fever of a diseased
mind, itself polluted and a pollution to others, can be
quenched only by remedies as strong as the passions
which inflame it. Of the many laws devised by our ancestors, of the many passed by the divine Augustus, the
first have been forgotten, while his (all the more to our
disgrace) have become obsolete through contempt, and
this has made luxury bolder than ever. The truth is that
when one craves something not yet forbidden, there is
a fear that it may be forbidden; but when people once
transgress prohibitions with impunity, there is no longer
any fear or any shame.

"Why then in old times was economy in the ascendant? Because everyone practiced self-control; because we
were all members of one city. Nor even afterward had
we the same temptations, while our dominion was confined to Italy. Victories over the foreigner taught us how
to waste the substance of others; victories over ourselves,
how to squander our own. What a paltry matter is this
of which the ædiles are reminding us! What a mere
trifle if you look at everything else! No one represents
to the Senate that Italy requires supplies from abroad,
and that the very existence of the people of Rome is
daily at the mercy of uncertain waves and storms. And
unless masters, slaves, and estates have the resources of
the provinces as their mainstay, our woods, presumably,
and our country houses will have to support us.

"Such, senators, are the anxieties which the princeps
has to sustain, and the neglect of them will be utter
ruin to the state. The cure for other evils must be sought
in our own hearts. Let us be led to amendment, the poor
by constraint, the rich by satiety. Or if any of our officials give promise of such energy and strictness as can
stem the corruption, I praise the man, and I confess that
I am relieved of a portion of my burdens. But if they
wish to denounce vice, and when they have gained

credit for so doing they arouse resentments and leave them to me, be assured, senators, that I too am by no means eager to incur enmities, and though for the public good I encounter formidable and often unjust enmities, yet I have a right to decline such as are unmeaning and purposeless and will be of use neither to myself nor to you."

55. When they had heard the Emperor's letter, the ædiles were excused from so anxious a task, and that luxury of the table which from the close of the war ended at Actium to the armed revolution in which Servius Galba rose to empire,[67] had been practiced with profuse expenditure, gradually went out of fashion. It is as well that I should trace the causes of this change.

Formerly rich or highly distinguished noble families often sank into ruin from a passion for splendor. Even then men were still at liberty to court and be courted by the city populace, by our allies and by foreign princes, and everyone who from his wealth, his mansion, and his establishment was conspicuously grand, gained too proportionate luster by his name and his numerous clientele. After the savage massacres in which greatness of renown was fatal, the survivors turned to wiser ways. The new men who were often admitted into the Senate from the towns, colonies, and even the provinces, introduced their household thrift, and though many of them by good luck or energy attained an old age of wealth, still their former tastes remained. But the chief encourager of strict manners was Vespasian,[68] himself old-fashioned both in his dress and diet. Henceforth a respectful feeling toward the prince and a love of emulation proved more efficacious than legal penalties or terrors. Or possibly there is in all things a kind of cycle, and there may be moral revolutions just as there are changes of seasons. Nor was everything better in the past, but our own age too has produced many specimens of excellence and culture for posterity to imitate. May we still keep up with our ancestors a rivalry in all that is honorable!

56. Tiberius, having gained credit for forbearance by the check he had given to the growing terror of the in-

formers, wrote a letter to the Senate, requesting the tribunician power for Drusus.[69] This was a phrase which Augustus devised as a designation of supremacy, so that without assuming the name of king or dictator he might have some title to mark his elevation above all other authority. He then chose Marcus Agrippa to be his associate in this power, and on Agrippa's death, Tiberius Nero, that there might be no uncertainty as to the succession. In this manner he thought to check the perverse ambition of others, while he had confidence in Nero's moderation and in his own greatness.

Following this precedent, Tiberius now placed Drusus next to the throne, though while Germanicus was alive he had maintained an impartial attitude toward the two princes. However, in the beginning of his letter he implored heaven to prosper his plans on behalf of the state, and then added a few remarks, without falsehood or exaggeration, on the character of the young prince. He had, he reminded them, a wife and three children, and his age was the same as that at which he had himself been formerly summoned by the divine Augustus to undertake this duty. Nor was it a precipitate step; it was only after an experience of eight years, after having quelled mutinies and settled wars, after a triumph and two consulships, that he was adopted as a partner in trials already familiar to him.

57. The senators had anticipated this message and hence their flattery was the more elaborate. But they could devise nothing but voting statues of the two princes, shrines to certain deities, temples, arches, and the usual routine, except that Marcus Silanus sought to honor the princes by a slur on the consulate, and proposed that on all monuments, public or private, should be inscribed, to mark the date, the names, not of the consuls, but of those who were holding the tribunician power. Quintus Haterius, when he brought forward a motion that the decrees passed that day should be set up in the Senate House in letters of gold, was laughed at as an old dotard, who would get nothing but infamy out of such utterly loathsome sycophancy.

58. Meantime Junius Blæsus received an extension of

his government of Africa, and Servius Maluginensis,[70] the priest of Jupiter, demanded to have Asia allotted to him. "It was," he asserted, "a popular error that it was not lawful for the priests of Jupiter to leave Italy; in fact, his own legal position differed not from that of the priests of Mars and of Quirinus.[71] If these latter had provinces allotted to them, why was it forbidden to the priests of Jupiter? There were no resolutions of the people or anything to be found in the books of ceremonies on the subject. Pontiffs had often performed the rites to Jupiter when his priest was hindered by illness or by public duty. For seventy-five years after the suicide of Cornelius Merula[72] no successor to his office had been appointed; yet religious rites had not ceased. If during so many years it was possible for there to be no appointment without any prejudice to religion, with what comparative ease might he be absent for one year's proconsulate? That these priests in former days were prohibited by the pontiffs from going into the provinces, was the result of private feuds. Now, thank heaven, the supreme pontiff was also the supreme man, and was influenced by no rivalry, hatred, or personal feeling."

59. As the augur Lentulus and others argued on various grounds against this view, the result was that they awaited the decision of the supreme pontiff.[73] Tiberius deferred any investigation into the priest's legal position, but he modified the ceremonies which had been decreed in honor of Drusus' tribunician power with special censure on the extravagance of the proposed inscription in gold, so contrary to national usage. Letters also from Drusus were read, which, though studiously modest in expression, were taken to be extremely supercilious. "We have fallen so low," people said, "that even a mere youth who has received so high an honor does not go as a worshiper to the city's gods, does not enter the Senate, does not so much as take the auspices on his country's soil. There is a war, we are told, or he is kept from us in some remote part of the world. Why, at this very moment, he is on a tour amid the shores and lakes of Campania. Such is the training of the future ruler of mankind; such the lesson he first learns from his father's

counsels. An aged Emperor may indeed shrink from the citizen's gaze, and plead the weariness of declining years and the toils of the past. But, as for Drusus, what can be his hindrance but pride?"

[*Chapters 60-63 are omitted.*]

64. About this time Julia Augusta had an alarming illness, which compelled the Emperor to hasten his return to Rome, for hitherto there had been a genuine harmony between the mother and son, or a hatred well concealed. Not long before, for instance, Julia in dedicating a statue to the divine Augustus near the theater of Marcellus[74] had inscribed the name of Tiberius below her own, and it was surmised that the Emperor, regarding this as a slight on a sovereign's dignity, had brooded over it with deep and disguised resentment. However, the Senate now decreed supplications to the gods and the celebration of the Great Games, which were to be exhibited by the pontiffs, augurs, the colleges of the Fifteen[75] and of the Seven,[76] with the Augustal brotherhood.[77] Lucius Apronius moved that the Fetials[78] too should preside over these Games. This the Emperor opposed, distinguishing the peculiar privileges of the sacred guilds, and quoting precedents. Never, he argued, had the Fetials had this dignity. The Augustal priests, he said, were included expressly because their sacred office was specially attached to the family for which vows were being performed.

65. My purpose is not to relate at length every motion, but only such as were conspicuous for excellence or notorious for infamy. This I regard as history's highest function, to let no worthy action be uncommemorated, and to hold out the reprobation of posterity as a terror to evil words and deeds. So corrupted indeed and debased was that age by sycophancy that not only the foremost citizens who were forced to save their grandeur by servility, but every ex-consul, most of the ex-prætors, and a host of inferior senators would rise in eager rivalry to propose shameful and preposterous motions. Tradition says that Tiberius as often as he left the Senate

House used to exclaim in Greek, "How ready these men are to be slaves." Clearly, even, he, with his dislike of public freedom, was disgusted at the abject abasement of his creatures.

66. From unseemly flatteries they passed by degrees to savage acts. Gaius Silanus,[79] proconsul of Asia, was accused by our allies of extortion; whereupon Mamercus Scaurus, an ex-consul, Junius Otho, a prætor, Bruttedius Niger, an ædile, simultaneously fastened on him and charged him with sacrilege to the divinity of Augustus, and contempt of the majesty of Tiberius, while Mamercus Scaurus quoted old precedents—the prosecutions of Lucius Cotta by Scipio Africanus,[80] of Servius Galba by Cato the Censor,[81] and of Publius Rutilius by Scaurus.[82] As if indeed Scipio's and Cato's vengeance fell on such offenses, or that of the famous Scaurus, whom his great-grandson, a blot on his ancestry, this Mamercus was now disgracing by his infamous occupation. Junius Otho's old employment had been the keeping of a preparatory school. Subsequently, becoming a senator by the influence of Sejanus, he shamed his origin, low as it was, by his unblushing effronteries. Bruttedius,[83] who was rich in excellent accomplishments, and was sure, had he pursued a path of virtue, to reach the most brilliant distinction, was goaded on by an eager impatience, while he strove to outstrip his equals, then his superiors, and at last even his own aspirations. Many have thus perished, even good men, despising slow and safe success and hurrying on even at the cost of ruin to premature greatness.

67. Gellius Publicola[84] and Marcus Paconius, respectively quæstor and legate of Silanus, swelled the number of the accusers. No doubt was felt as to the defendant's conviction for oppression and extortion, but there was a combination against him that must have been perilous even to an innocent man. Besides a host of adverse senators there were the most accomplished orators of all Asia, who, as such, had been retained for the prosecution, and to these he had to reply alone, without any experience in pleading, and under that personal apprehension which is enough to paralyze even the most

practiced eloquence. For Tiberius did not refrain from pressing him with angry voice and look, himself putting incessant questions, without allowing him to rebut or evade them, and he had often even to make admissions, that the questions might not have been asked in vain. His slaves too were sold by auction to the state agent, to be examined by torture. And that not a friend might help him in his danger, charges of treason were added, a binding guarantee of sealed lips. Accordingly he begged a few days' respite, and at last abandoned his defense, after venturing on a memorial to the Emperor, in which he mingled reproach and entreaty.

68. Tiberius, that his proceedings against Silanus might find some justification in precedent, ordered the divine Augustus' indictment of Volesus Messalla, also a proconsul of Asia,[85] and the Senate's sentence on him to be read. He then asked Lucius Piso his opinion. After a long preliminary eulogy on the prince's clemency, Piso pronounced that Silanus ought to be outlawed and banished to the island of Gyarus.[86] The rest concurred, with the exception of Cnæus Lentulus, who, with the assent of Tiberius, proposed that the property of Silanus' mother, as she had been an Atia,[87] should be exempted from confiscation, and given to the son.

69. Cornelius Dolabella, however, by way of carrying flattery yet further, sharply censured the morals of Silanus, and then moved that no one of disgraceful life and notorious infamy should be eligible for a province, and that of this the Emperor should be judge. "Laws, indeed," he said, "punish crimes committed; but how much more merciful would it be to individuals, how much better for our allies, to provide against their commission."

The Emperor opposed the motion. "Although," he said, "I am not ignorant of the reports about Silanus, still we must decide nothing by hearsay. Many a man has behaved in a province quite otherwise than was hoped or feared of him. Some are roused to higher things by great responsibility; others are paralyzed by it. It is not possible for a prince's knowledge to embrace everything, and it is not expedient that he should be exposed to the ambitious schemings of others. Laws are ordained to meet facts, inasmuch as the future is uncertain. It was the rule of our ancestors that, whenever there was first an offense, some penalty should follow. Let us not revolutionize a wisely devised and ever approved system. Princes have enough burdens, and also enough power. Rights are invariably abridged, as despotism increases; nor ought we to fall back on imperial authority, when we can have recourse to the laws."

Such constitutional sentiments were so rare with Tiberius that they were welcomed with all the heartier joy. Knowing, as he did, how to be forbearing, when he was not under the stimulus of personal resentment, he further said that Gyarus was a dreary and uninhabited island, and that, as a concession to the Junian family and to a man of the same order as themselves, they might let him retire by preference to Cythnus.[88] This, he added, was also the request of Torquata, Silanus' sister, a Vestal of primitive purity. The motion was carried after a division.

70. Audience was next given to the people of Cyrene, and on the prosecution of Ancharius Priscus, Cæsius Cordus was convicted of extortion. Lucius Ennius, a Roman knight, was accused of treason, for having converted a statue of the Emperor to the common use of silver plate; but the Emperor forbade his being put upon his trial, though Ateius Capito openly remonstrated, with a show of independence. "The Senate," he said, "ought not to have wrested from it the power of deciding a question, and such a crime must not go unpunished. Granted that the Emperor might be indifferent to a personal grievance, still he should not be generous in the case of wrongs to the commonwealth." Tiberius interpreted the remark according to its drift rather than its mere expression, and persisted in his veto. Capito's disgrace was the more conspicuous, for, versed as he was in the science of law, human and divine, he had now dishonored a brilliant public career as well as a virtuous private life.[89]

71. Next came a religious question, as to the temple in which ought to be deposited the offering which the

Roman knights had vowed to Fortune of the Knights for the recovery of Augusta. Although that goddess had several shrines in Rome, there was none with this special designation. It was ascertained that there was a temple so called at Antium,[90] and that all sacred rites in the towns of Italy as well as temples and images of deities were under the jurisdiction and authority of Rome. Accordingly the offering was placed at Antium.

As religious questions were under discussion, the Emperor now produced his answer to Servius Maluginensis, Jupiter's priest, which he had recently deferred, and read the pontifical decree, prescribing that whenever illness attacked a priest of Jupiter, he might, with the supreme pontiff's permission, be absent more than two nights, provided it was not during the days of public sacrifice or more than twice in the same year. This regulation of the Emperor Augustus sufficiently proved that a year's absence and a provincial government were not permitted to the priests of Jupiter. There was also cited the precedent of Lucius Metellus, supreme pontiff,[91] who had detained at Rome the priest Aulus Postumius. And so Asia was allotted to the ex-consul next in seniority to Maluginensis.

72. About the same time Lepidus asked the Senate's leave to restore and embellish, at his own expense, the basilica of Paullus,[92] that monument of the Æmilian family. Public-spirited munificence was still in fashion, and Augustus had not hindered Taurus, Philippus, or Balbus[93] from applying the spoils of war or their superfluous wealth to adorn the capital and to win the admiration of posterity. Following these examples, Lepidus, though possessed of a moderate fortune, now revived the glory of his ancestors.

Pompeius' theater[94] which had been destroyed by an accidental fire, the Emperor promised to rebuild, simply because no member of the family was equal to restoring it, but Pompeius' name was to be retained. At the same time he highly extolled Sejanus on the ground that it was through his exertions and vigilance that such fury of the flames had been confined to the destruction of a single building. The Senate voted Sejanus a statue, which was to be placed in Pompeius' theater. And soon afterward the Emperor, in honoring Junius Blæsus, proconsul of Africa, with triumphal distinctions, said that he granted them as a compliment to Sejanus, whose uncle Blæsus was.

[*Chapters 73-74 are omitted.*]

75. Two illustrious men died that year. One was Asinius Salonius,[95] distinguished as the grandson of Marcus Agrippa and Asinius Pollio, as the brother of Drusus and the intended husband of the Emperor's granddaughter. The other was Ateius Capito,[96] already mentioned, who had won a foremost position in the state by his legal attainments, though his grandfather was but a centurion in Sulla's army, his father having been a prætor. He was prematurely advanced to the consulship by Augustus, so that he might be raised by the honor of this promotion above Antistius Labeo, a conspicuous member of the same profession. That age indeed produced at one time two brilliant ornaments of peace. But while Labeo was a man of sturdy independence and consequently of wider fame, Capito's obsequiousness was more acceptable to those in power. Labeo, because his promotion was confined to the prætorship, gained in public favor through the wrong; Capito, in obtaining the consulship, incurred the hatred which grows out of envy.

76. Junia[97] too, the niece of Cato, wife of Gaius Cassius and sister of Marcus Brutus, died this year, the sixty-fourth after the battle of Philippi.[98] Her will was the theme of much popular criticism, for, with her vast wealth, after having honorably mentioned almost every nobleman by name, she passed over the Emperor. Tiberius took the omission graciously, and did not forbid a panegyric before the rostra with the other customary funeral honors. The busts of twenty most illustrious families were borne in the procession, with the names of Manlius, Quinctius, and others of equal rank. But Cassius and Brutus outshone them all, from the very fact that their likenesses were not to be seen.

BOOK IV   *23-28 A.D.*

1. The year when Gaius Asinius and Gaius Antistius were consuls[1] was the ninth of Tiberius' reign, a period of tranquillity for the state and prosperity for his own house, for he counted Germanicus' death a happy incident. Suddenly fortune deranged everything; the Emperor became a cruel tyrant, as well as an abettor of cruelty in others. Of this the cause and origin was Ælius Sejanus, commander of the prætorian cohorts, of whose influence I have already spoken. I will now fully describe his extraction, his character, and the daring wickedness by which he grasped at power.

Born at Vulsinii,[2] the son of Seius Strabo,[3] a Roman knight, he attached himself in his early youth to Gaius Cæsar, grandson of the divine Augustus,[4] and the story went that he had sold his person to Apicius,[5] a rich debauchee. Soon afterward he won the heart of Tiberius so effectually by various artifices that the Emperor, ever dark and mysterious toward others, was with Sejanus alone careless and freespoken. It was not through his craft, for it was by this very weapon that he was overthrown; it was rather from heaven's wrath against Rome, to whose welfare his elevation and his fall were alike disastrous. He had a body which could endure hardships, and a daring spirit. He was one who screened himself, while he was attacking others; he was as cringing as he was imperious; before the world he affected humility; in his heart he lusted after supremacy, for the sake of which he was sometimes lavish and luxurious, but oftener energetic and watchful, qualities quite as mischievous when hypocritically assumed for the attainment of sovereignty.

2. He strengthened the hitherto moderate powers of his office by concentrating the cohorts scattered throughout the capital into one camp, so that they might all receive orders at the same moment, and that the sight of their numbers and strength might give confidence to themselves, while it would strike terror into the citizens.

His pretexts were the demoralization incident to a dispersed soldiery, the greater effectiveness of simultaneous action in the event of a sudden peril, and the stricter discipline which would be ensured by the establishment of an encampment at a distance from the temptations of the city. As soon as the camp was completed, he crept gradually into the affections of the soldiers by mixing with them and addressing them by name, himself selecting the centurions and tribunes. With the Senate too he sought to ingratiate himself, distinguishing his partisans with offices and provinces, Tiberius readily yielding, and being so biased that not only in private conversation but before the senators and the people he spoke highly of him as the partner of his toils, and allowed his statues to be honored in theaters, in forums, and at the headquarters of our legions.

3. There were, however, obstacles to his ambition in the imperial house with its many princes, a son in youthful manhood and grown-up grandsons. As it would be unsafe to sweep off such a number at once by violence, while craft would necessitate successive intervals in crime, he chose, on the whole, the stealthier way, and to begin with Drusus, against whom he had the stimulus of a recent resentment. Drusus, who could not brook a rival and was somewhat irascible, had, in a casual dispute, raised his fist at Sejanus, and, when he defended himself, had struck him in the face. On considering every plan, Sejanus thought his easiest revenge was to turn his attention to Livia, Drusus' wife.[6] She was a sister of Germanicus, and though she was not handsome as a girl, she became a woman of surpassing beauty. Pretending an ardent passion for her, he seduced her, and having won his first infamous triumph, and assured that a woman after having parted with her virtue will hesitate at nothing, he lured her on to thoughts of marriage, of a share in sovereignty, and of her husband's destruction. And she, the niece of Augustus, the daughter-in-law of Tiberius, the mother of children by Drusus, for a provincial paramour foully disgraced herself, her ancestors, and her descendants,[7] giving up honor and a sure position for prospects as base as they were uncer-

tain. They took into their confidence Eudemus, Livia's friend and physician, whose profession was a pretext for frequent secret interviews. Sejanus, to avert his mistress' jealousy, divorced his wife, Apicata, by whom he had had three children. Still the magnitude of the crime caused fear and delay, and sometimes a conflict of plans.

4. Meanwhile, at the beginning of this year, Drusus, one of the children of Germanicus, assumed the dress of manhood, with a repetition of the honors decreed by the Senate to his brother Nero. The Emperor added a speech, with warm praise of his son for sharing a father's affection to his brother's children. Drusus indeed, difficult as it is for power and mutual harmony to exist side by side, had the character of being kindly disposed or at least not unfriendly toward the lads. And now the old plan, so often insincerely broached, of a progress through the provinces was again discussed. The Emperor's pretext was the number of veterans on the eve of discharge and the necessity of fresh levies for the army. Volunteers were not forthcoming, and even if they were sufficiently numerous, they had not the same bravery and discipline, as it is chiefly the needy and the homeless who adopt by their own choice a soldier's life. Tiberius also rapidly enumerated the legions and the provinces which they had to garrison. I too ought, I think, to go through these details, and thus show what forces Rome then had under arms, what kings were our allies, and how much narrower then were the limits of our Empire.

5. Italy on both seas was guarded by fleets, at Misenum[8] and at Ravenna, and the contiguous coast of Gaul by ships of war captured in the victory of Actium, and sent by Augustus powerfully manned to the town of Forum Julii.[9] But our chief strength was on the Rhine, as a defense alike against Germans and Gauls, and numbered eight legions. Spain, lately subjugated, was held by three. Mauretania was King Juba's, who had received it as a gift from the Roman people.[10] The rest of Africa was garrisoned by two legions, and Egypt by the same number. Next, beginning with Syria, all within the entire tract of country stretching as far as the Euphrates

was kept in restraint by four legions, and on this frontier were Iberian,[11] Albanian,[12] and other kings, to whom our greatness was a protection against any foreign power. Thrace was held by Rhœmetalces and the children of Cotys;[13] the bank of the Danube by two legions in Pannonia,[14] two in Mœsia,[15] and two also were stationed in Dalmatia,[16] which, from the situation of the country, were in the rear of the other four, and, should Italy suddenly require aid, not too distant to be summoned. But the capital was garrisoned by its own special soldiery— three city, nine prætorian cohorts—levied for the most part in Etruria and Umbria, or ancient Latium and the old Roman colonies. There were besides, in commanding positions in the provinces, allied fleets, cavalry, and light infantry, of but little inferior strength. But any detailed account of them would be misleading, since they moved from place to place as circumstances required, and had their numbers increased and sometimes diminished.

6. It is, however, I think, a convenient opportunity for me to review the hitherto prevailing methods of administration in the other departments of the state, inasmuch as that year brought with it the beginning of a change for the worse in Tiberius' policy. In the first place, public business and the most important private matters were managed by the Senate; the leading men were allowed freedom of discussion, and when they stooped to flattery, the Emperor himself checked them. He bestowed honors with regard to noble ancestry, military renown, or brilliant accomplishments as a civilian, letting it be clearly seen that there were no better men to choose. The consul and the prætor retained their prestige; inferior magistrates exercised their authority; the laws too, with the single exception of cases of treason, were properly enforced.

As to the duties on corn, the indirect taxes, and other branches of the public revenue, they were in the hands of companies of Roman knights.[17] The Emperor entrusted his own property to men of the most tried integrity or to persons known only by their general reputation, and once appointed they were retained without any limitation, so that most of them grew old in the same employments. The city populace indeed suffered much from high prices, but this was no fault of the Emperor, who actually endeavored to counteract barren soils and stormy seas with every resource of wealth and foresight. And he was also careful not to distress the provinces by new burdens, and to see that in bearing the old they were safe from any rapacity or oppression on the part of governors. Corporal punishments and confiscations of property were unknown. The Emperor had only a few estates in Italy, slaves on a moderate scale, and his household was confined to a few freedmen. If ever he had a dispute with a private person, it was decided in the law courts.

7. All this, not indeed with any graciousness, but in a blunt fashion which often alarmed, he still kept up, until the death of Drusus changed everything. While he lived, the system continued, because Sejanus, as yet only in the beginning of his power, wished to be known as an upright counselor, and there was one whose vengeance he dreaded, who did not conceal his 'hatred and incessantly complained that "a stranger was invited to assist in the government while the Emperor's son was alive. How near was the step of declaring the stranger a colleague! Ambition at first had a steep path before it; when once the way had been entered, zealous adherents were forthcoming. Already, at the pleasure of the commander of the guards, a camp had been established; the soldiers were given into his hands; his statues were to be seen among the monuments of Cnæus Pompeius; his grandsons would be of the same blood as the family of the Drusi. Henceforth they must pray that he might have self-control, and so be contented." So would Drusus talk, not unfrequently, or only in the hearing of a few persons. Even his confidences, now that his wife had been corrupted, were betrayed.

8. Sejanus accordingly thought that he must be prompt, and chose a poison the gradual working of which might be mistaken for a natural disorder. It was given to Drusus by Lygdus, a eunuch, as was ascertained eight years later. As for Tiberius, he went to the Senate House during the whole time of the prince's illness,

either because he was not afraid, or to show his strength of mind, and even in the interval between his death and funeral. Seeing the consuls, in token of their grief, sitting on the ordinary benches, he reminded them of their high office and of their proper place; and when the Senate burst into tears, suppressing a groan, he revived their spirits with a fluent speech. "He knew indeed that he might be reproached for thus encountering the gaze of the Senate after so recent an affliction. Most mourners could hardly bear even the soothing words of kinsfolk or to look on the light of day. And such were not to be condemned as weak. But he had sought a more manly consolation in the bosom of the commonwealth."

Then deploring the extreme age of Augusta, the childhood of his grandsons, and his own declining years, he begged the Senate to summon Germanicus' children, the only comfort under their present misery. The consuls went out, and having encouraged the young princes with kind words, brought them in and presented them to the Emperor. Taking them by the hand, he said: "Senators, when these boys lost their father, I committed them to their uncle, and begged him, though he had children of his own, to cherish and rear them as his own offspring, and train them for himself and for posterity. Drusus is now lost to us, and I turn my prayers to you, and before heaven and your country I adjure you to receive into your care and guidance the great-grandsons of Augustus, descendants of a most noble ancestry. So fulfill your duty and mine. To you, Nero and Drusus, these senators are as fathers. Such is your birth that your prosperity and adversity must alike affect the state."

9. There was great weeping at these words, and then many a benediction. Had the Emperor set bounds to his speech, he must have filled the hearts of his hearers with sympathy and admiration. But he now fell back on those idle and often ridiculed professions about restoring the republic, and the wish that the consuls or someone else might undertake the government, and thus destroyed belief even in what was genuine and noble.

The same honors were decreed to the memory of Drusus as to that of Germanicus, and many more were added. Such is the way with flattery, when repeated. The funeral with its procession of statues was singularly grand. Æneas, the father of the Julian house,[18] all the Alban kings,[19] Romulus, Rome's founder, then the Sabine nobility, Attus Clausus,[20] and the busts of all the other Claudii were displayed in a long train.

10. In relating the death of Drusus I have followed the narrative of most of the best historians. But I would not pass over a rumor of the time, the strength of which is not even yet exhausted. Sejanus, it is said, having seduced Livia into crime, next secured, by the foulest means, the consent of Lygdus, the eunuch, as from his youth and beauty he was his master's favorite, and one of his principal attendants. When those who were in on the secret had decided on the time and place of the poisoning, Sejanus, with the most consummate daring, reversed his plan, and, whispering an accusation against Drusus of intending to poison his father, warned Tiberius to avoid the first draught offered him as he was dining at his son's house. Thus deceived, the old Emperor, on sitting down to the banquet took the cup and handed it to Drusus. His suspicions were increased when Drusus, in perfect unconsciousness, drank it off with youthful eagerness, apparently, out of fear and shame, bringing on himself the death which he had plotted against his father.

11. These popular rumors, over and above the fact that they are not vouched for by any good writer, may be instantly refuted. For who, with moderate prudence, far less Tiberius with his great experience, would have thrust destruction on a son, without even hearing him, with his own hand too, and with an impossibility of returning to better thoughts? Surely he would rather have had the slave who handed the poison tortured, have sought to discover the traitor, in short, would have been as hesitating and tardy in the case of an only son hitherto unconvicted of any crime, as he was naturally even with strangers. But as Sejanus had the credit of contriving every sort of wickedness, the fact that he was the Emperor's special favorite, and that both were hated by the rest of the world, procured belief for any monstrous

fiction, and rumor too always has a dreadful side in regard to the deaths of men in power. Besides, the whole process of the crime was betrayed by Apicata, Sejanus' wife, and fully divulged, under torture, by Eudemus and Lygdus. No writer has been found sufficiently malignant to fix the guilt on Tiberius, though every circumstance was scrutinized and exaggerated. My object in mentioning and refuting this story is, by a conspicuous example, to put down hearsay, and to request all into whose hands my work shall come not to catch eagerly at wild and improbable rumors in preference to genuine history which has not been perverted into romance.

12. Tiberius pronounced a panegyric on his son before the Rostra, during which the Senate and people, in appearance rather than in heart, put on the expression and accents of sorrow, while they inwardly rejoiced at the brightening future of the family of Germanicus. This beginning of popularity and the ill-concealed ambition of their mother, Agrippina, hastened its downfall. Sejanus, when he saw that the death of Drusus was not avenged on the murderers and was no grief to the people, grew bold in wickedness, and, now that his first attempt had succeeded, speculated on the possibility of destroying the children of Germanicus, whose succession to the throne was a certainty. There were three, and poison could not be distributed among them, because of the singular fidelity of their guardians and the unassailable virtue of Agrippina. So Sejanus inveighed against Agrippina's arrogance, and worked powerfully on Augusta's old hatred of her and on Livia's consciousness of recent guilt, and urged both these women to represent to the Emperor that her pride as a mother and her reliance on popular enthusiasm were leading her to dream of empire. Livia availed herself of the cunning of accusers, among whom she had selected Julius Postumus, a man well suited to her purpose, as he had an intrigue with Mutilia Prisca,[21] and was consequently in the confidence of Augusta, over whose mind Prisca had great influence. She thus made her aged grandmother, whose nature it was to tremble for her power, irreconcilably hostile to her grandson's widow. Agrippina's

friends too were induced to be always inciting her proud spirit by mischievous talk.

13. Tiberius meanwhile, who did not relax his attention to business, and found solace in his work, occupied himself with the causes of citizens at Rome and with petitions from allies. Decrees of the Senate were passed at his proposal for relieving the cities of Cibyra²² and Ægium²³ in Asia and Achæa, which had suffered from earthquakes, by a remission of three years' tribute. Vibius Serenus²⁴ too, proconsul of Further Spain,²⁵ was condemned for violence in his official capacity, and was banished to the island of Amorgus²⁶ for his savage temper. Carsidius Sacerdos, accused of having helped our enemy Tacfarinas with supplies of grain, was acquitted, as was also Gaius Gracchus on the same charge. Gracchus' father, Sempronius, had taken him when a mere child to the island of Cercina²⁷ to be his companion in exile. There he grew up among outcasts who knew nothing of a liberal education, and after a while supported himself in Africa and Sicily by petty trade. But he did not escape the dangers of high rank. Had not his innocence been protected by Ælius Lamia and Lucius Apronius, successive governors of Africa, the splendid fame of that ill-starred family and the downfall of his father would have dragged him to ruin.

14. This year too brought embassies from the Greek communities. The people of Samos and Cos petitioned for the confirmation of the ancient right of sanctuary for the respective temples of Hera²⁸ and Asclepius.²⁹ The Samians relied on a decree of the Amphictyonic Council, which had the supreme decision of all questions when the Greeks, through the cities they had founded in Asia, had possession of the seacoast.³⁰ Cos could boast equal antiquity, and it had an additional claim connected with the place. Roman citizens had been admitted to the temple of Asclepius, when King Mithridates ordered a general massacre of them throughout all the islands and cities of Asia.

Next, after various and usually fruitless complaints from the prætors, the Emperor finally brought forward a motion about the licentious behavior of the players.

"They had often," he said, "sought to disturb the public peace, and to bring disgrace on private families, and the old Oscan farce,[31] once a wretched amusement for the vulgar, had become at once so indecent and so popular that it must be checked by the Senate's authority." The players, upon this, were banished from Italy.

15. That same year also brought fresh sorrow to the Emperor by being fatal to one of the twin sons of Drusus, equally too by the death of an intimate friend. This was Lucilius Longus,[32] the partner of all his griefs and joys, the only senator who had been the companion of his retirement in Rhodes. And so, though he was a man of humble origin, the Senate decreed him a censor's funeral[33] and a statue in the forum of Augustus at the public expense. Everything indeed was as yet in the hands of the Senate, and consequently Lucilius Capito, a procurator of Asia, who was impeached by his province, was tried by them, the Emperor vehemently asserting "that he had merely given the man authority over the slaves and property of the imperial establishments; that if he had taken upon himself the powers of a prætor and used military force, he had disregarded his instructions; therefore they must hear the provincials." So the case was heard and the accused condemned.[34] The cities of Asia, gratified by this retribution and the punishment inflicted in the previous year on Gaius Silanus, voted a temple to Tiberius, his mother, and the Senate, and were permitted to build it. Nero thanked the senators and his grandfather on their behalf, and carried with him the joyful sympathies of his audience, who, with the memory of Germanicus fresh in their minds, imagined that it was his face they saw, his voice they heard. The youth too had a modesty and a grace of person worthy of a prince, the more charming because of his peril from the notorious enmity of Sejanus.

16. About the same time the Emperor spoke on the subject of electing a priest of Jupiter in place of Servius Maluginensis, deceased, and of the enactment of a new law. "It was," he said, "the old custom to nominate together three patricians, sons of parents wedded according to the primitive ceremony, and of these one was to

be chosen. Now, however, there was not the same choice
as formerly, the primitive form of marriage having been
given up or being observed only by a few persons." For
this he assigned several reasons, the chief being men's
and women's indifference;[35] then, again, the ceremony
itself had its difficulties, which were purposely avoided;
and there was the objection that the man who obtained
this priesthood was emancipated from the father's authority, as also was his wife, as passing into the husband's
control. So the Senate, Tiberius argued, ought to apply
some remedy by a decree or a law, as Augustus had
accommodated certain relics of a rude antiquity to the
modern spirit.

It was then decided, after a discussion of religious
questions, that the institution of the priests of Jupiter
should remain unchanged. A law, however, was passed
that the priestess, in regard to her sacred functions,
was to be under the husband's control, but in other respects to retain the ordinary legal position of women.
Maluginensis, the son, was chosen successor to his father. To raise the dignity of the priesthood and to inspire the priests with more zeal in attending to the ceremonial, a gift of two million sesterces was decreed to
the Vestal Cornelia, chosen in place of Scantia; and,
whenever Augusta entered the theater, she was to have
a place among the seats of the Vestals.

17. In the consulship of Cornelius Cethegus and Visel-
lius Varro,[36] the pontiffs, whose example was followed
by the other priests in offering prayers for the Emperor's
health, commended also Nero and Drusus to the same
deities, not so much out of love for the young princes
as out of sycophancy, the absence and excess of which
in a corrupt age are alike dangerous. Tiberius indeed,
who was never friendly to the house of Germanicus,
was then vexed beyond endurance at their youth being
honored equally with his declining years. He summoned
the pontiffs, and asked them whether it was to the entreaties or the threats of Agrippina that they had made
this concession. And though they gave a flat denial, he
rebuked them but gently, for many of them were her
own relatives or were leading men in the state. However,

he addressed a warning to the Senate against encouraging pride in their young and excitable minds by premature honors. For Sejanus spoke vehemently, and charged them with rending the state almost by civil war. "There were those," he said, "who called themselves the party of Agrippina, and, unless they were checked, there would be more; the only remedy for the increasing discord was the overthrow of one or two of the most enterprising leaders."

18. Accordingly he attacked Gaius Silius and Titius Sabinus. The friendship of Germanicus was fatal to both. As for Silius, his having commanded a great army for seven years, and won in Germany the distinctions of a triumph for his success in the war with Sacrovir, would make his downfall all the more tremendous and so spread greater terror among others. Many thought that he had provoked further displeasure by his own presumption and his extravagant boasts that his troops had been steadfastly loyal, while other armies were falling into mutiny, and that Tiberius' throne could not have lasted had his legions too been bent on revolution. All this the Emperor regarded as undermining his own power, which seemed to be unequal to the burden of such an obligation. For benefits received are a delight to us as long as we think we can requite them; when that possibility is far exceeded, they are repaid with hatred instead of gratitude.

19. Silius had a wife, Sosia Galla, whose love of Agrippina made her hateful to the Emperor. The two, it was decided, were to be attacked, but Sabinus was to be put off for a time. Varro, the consul, was let loose on them, who, under color of a hereditary feud, humored the malignity of Sejanus to his own disgrace. The accused begged a brief respite, until the prosecutor's consulship expired, but the Emperor opposed the request. "It was usual," he argued, "for magistrates to bring a private citizen to trial, and a consul's authority ought not to be impaired, seeing that it rested with his vigilance to see that the state came to no harm." It was characteristic of Tiberius to veil new devices in wickedness under ancient names. And so, with a solemn appeal, he sum-

moned the Senate, as if there were any laws by which
Silius was being tried, as if Varro were a real consul,
or Rome a commonwealth. The accused either said nothing, or, if he attempted to defend himself, hinted, not
obscurely, at the person whose resentment was crushing
him. A long concealed complicity in Sacrovir's rebellion,
a rapacity which sullied his victory, and his wife Sosia's
conduct, were alleged against him. Unquestionably, they
could not extricate themselves from the charge of extortion. The whole affair, however, was conducted as a
trial for treason, and Silius forestalled impending doom
by a self-inflicted death.

20. Yet there was a merciless confiscation of his property, though not to refund their money to the provincials,
none of whom pressed any demand. But Augustus' bounty was wrested from him, and the claims of the imperial
exchequer were computed in detail. This was the first
instance on Tiberius' part of sharp dealing with the
wealth of others. Sosia was banished on the motion of
Asinius Gallus, who had proposed that half her estate
should be confiscated, half left to the children. Marcus
Lepidus, on the contrary, was for giving a fourth to the
prosecutors, as the law required, and the remainder to
the children.

This Lepidus,[37] I am satisfied, was for that age a wise
and high-principled man. Many a cruel suggestion made
by the flattery of others he changed for the better, and
yet he did not want tact, seeing that he always enjoyed
a uniform prestige, and also the favor of Tiberius. This
makes me wonder whether the liking of princes for
some men and their antipathy to others depend, like
other contingencies, on a fate and destiny to which we
are born, or, to some degree, on our own plans; so that
it is possible to pursue a course between a defiant independence and a debasing servility, free from ambition
and its perils. Cotta Messallinus,[38] of equally illustrious
ancestry to that of Lepidus, but wholly different in disposition, proposed that the Senate should pass a decree
providing that even innocent governors who knew nothing of the delinquencies of others should be punished

for their wives' offenses in the provinces as much as for their own.

21. Proceedings were then taken against Calpurnius Piso,[39] a high-spirited nobleman. He it was, as I have related, who had exclaimed more than once in the Senate that he would quit Rome because of the combinations of the informers, and had dared, in defiance of Augusta's power, to sue Urgulania and summon her from the Emperor's palace. Tiberius submitted to this at the time not ungraciously, but the remembrance of it was vividly impressed on a mind which brooded over its resentments, even though the first impulse of his displeasure had subsided.

Quintus Granius[40] accused Piso of secret treasonable conversation, and added that he kept poison in his house and wore a dagger whenever he came into the Senate. This was passed over as too atrocious to be true. He was to be tried on the other charges, a multitude of which were heaped on him, but his timely death cut short the trial.

Next was taken the case of Cassius Severus,[41] an exile. A man of mean origin and a life of crime, but a powerful pleader, he had brought on himself, by his persistent quarrelsomeness, a decision of the Senate, under oath, which banished him to Crete. There by the same practices he drew on himself fresh odium and revived the old; stripped of his property and outlawed, he wore out his old age on the rock of Seriphus.[42]

22. About the same time Plautius Silvanus, the prætor, for unknown reasons, threw his wife Apronia out of a window. When summoned before the Emperor by Lucius Apronius, his father-in-law, he replied incoherently, representing that he was in a sound sleep and consequently knew nothing, and that his wife had chosen to destroy herself. Without a moment's delay Tiberius went to the house and inspected the chamber, where were seen the marks of her struggling and of her forcible ejection. He reported this to the Senate, and as soon as judges had been appointed, Urgulania,[43] the grandmother of Silvanus, sent her grandson a dagger. This was thought equivalent to a hint from the Emperor,

because of the known intimacy between Augusta and Urgulania. The accused tried the steel in vain, and then allowed his veins to be opened. Shortly afterward Numantina, his former wife, was charged with having caused her husband's insanity by magical incantations and potions, but she was acquitted.

[*Chapters 23 to 30 are omitted. The Numidian rebel Tacfarinas, who had been triumphed over by no less than three Roman generals, was at length defeated and killed by Publius Cornelius Dolabella.*]

31. Some little joy broke this long succession of horrors. Gaius Cominius, a Roman knight, was spared by the Emperor, against whom he was convicted of having written libelous verses, at the intercession of his brother, who was a senator. Hence it seemed the more amazing that one who knew better things and the glory which waits on mercy should prefer harsher courses. He did not indeed err from lack of intelligence, and it is easy to see when the acts of a sovereign meet with genuine, and when with fictitious popularity. And even he himself, though usually artificial in manner, and though his words escaped him with a seeming struggle, spoke out freely and fluently whenever he came to a man's rescue.

In another case, that of Publius Suillius,[44] formerly quæstor to Germanicus, who was to be expelled from Italy on a conviction of having received money for a judicial decision, he held that the man ought to be banished to an island, and so intensely strong was his feeling that he bound the Senate by an oath that this was a state necessity. The act was thought cruel at the moment, but subsequently it redounded to his honor when Suillius returned from exile. The next age saw him in tremendous power and a venal creature of the Emperor Claudius, whose friendship he long used, with success, never for good.

The same punishment was adjudged to Firmius Catus, a senator, for having (it was alleged) assailed his sister with a false charge of treason. Catus, as I have related, had drawn Libo into a snare[45] and then destroyed him by some information. Tiberius, remembering this service, while he alleged other reasons, deprecated a sentence of exile, but did not oppose his expulsion from the Senate.

32. Much of what I have related and shall have to relate may perhaps, I am aware, seem petty trifles to record. But no one must compare my annals with the writings of those who have described Rome in old days. They told of great wars, of the storming of cities, of the defeat and capture of kings, or whenever they turned by preference to home affairs, they related, with a free scope for digression, the strifes of consuls with tribunes, land, and corn laws, and the struggles between the commons and the aristocracy. My labors are circumscribed and inglorious; peace wholly unbroken or but slightly disturbed, dismal misery in the capital, an Emperor careless about the enlargement of the Empire, such is my theme. Still it will not be useless to study those at first sight trifling events out of which the movements of vast changes often take their rise.

33. All nations and cities are ruled by the people, the nobility, or by one man. A constitution, formed by selection out of these elements, is easy to commend but not to produce; or, if it is produced, it cannot be lasting. Formerly, when the people had power or when the patricians were in the ascendant, the popular temper and the methods of controlling it had to be studied, and those who knew most accurately the spirit of the Senate and aristocracy had the credit of understanding the age and of being wise men. So now, after a revolution, when Rome is nothing but the realm of a single despot, there must be good in carefully noting and recording this period, for it is but few who have the foresight to distinguish right from wrong or what is sound from what is hurtful, while most men learn wisdom from the fortunes of others. Still, though this is instructive, it gives very little pleasure. Descriptions of countries, the various incidents of battles, glorious deaths of great generals, enchain and refresh a reader's mind. I have to present in succession the merciless biddings of a tyrant, incessant prosecutions, faithless friendships, the ruin of

innocence, the same causes issuing in the same results, and I am everywhere confronted by a wearisome monotony in my subject matter. Then, again, an ancient historian has but few disparagers, and no one cares whether you praise more heartily the armies of Carthage or Rome. But of many who endured punishment or disgrace under Tiberius, the descendants yet survive; or even though the families themselves may be now extinct, you will find those who, from a resemblance of character, imagine that the evil deeds of others are a reproach to themselves. Again, even honor and virtue make enemies, condemning, as they do, their opposites by too close a contrast. But I return to my work.

34. In the year of the consulship of Cornelius Cossus and Asinius Agrippa,[46] Cremutius Cordus was arraigned on a new charge, now for the first time heard. He had published a history in which he had praised Marcus Brutus and called Gaius Cassius the last of the Romans.[47] His accusers were Satrius Secundus and Pinarius Natta, creatures of Sejanus. This was enough to ruin the accused; and then too the Emperor listened with an angry frown to his defense, which Cremutius, resolved to give up his life, began thus:

"It is my words, senators, which are condemned, so innocent am I of any guilty act; yet these do not touch the Emperor or the Emperor's mother, who are alone comprehended under the law of treason. I am said to have praised Brutus and Cassius, whose careers many have described and no one mentioned without eulogy. Thus Livius,[48] pre-eminently famous for eloquence and truthfulness, extolled Cnæus Pompeius in such a panegyric that Augustus called him a Pomplian and yet this was no obstacle to their friendship. Scipio,[49] Afranius,[50] this very Cassius, this same Brutus, he nowhere describes as brigands and traitors, terms now applied to them, but repeatedly as illustrious men. Asinius Pollio's writings too hand down a glorious memory of them, and Messalla Corvinus[51] used to speak with pride of Cassius as his general. Yet both these men prospered to the end with wealth and preferment. Again, that book of Marcus Cicero, in which he lauded Cato to the skies—

how else was it answered by Cæsar the dictator, than by
a written oration in reply, as if he was pleading in
court?[52] The letters of Antonius,[53] the harangues of
Brutus contain reproaches against Augustus, false indeed, but urged with powerful sarcasm; the poems which
we read of Bibaculus[54] and Catullus[55] are crammed
with invectives on the Cæsars. Yet the divine Julius, the
divine Augustus themselves bore all this and let it pass,
whether in forbearance or in wisdom I cannot easily
say. Assuredly what is despised is soon forgotten; when
you resent a thing, you seem to recognize it.

35. "Of the Greeks I say nothing; with them not only
liberty but even license went unpunished, or if a person
aimed at chastising, he retaliated on satire by satire.
It has, however, always been perfectly open to us, without anyone to censure, to speak freely of those whom
death has withdrawn alike from the partialities of
hatred or esteem. Are Cassius and Brutus now in arms
on the fields of Philippi, and am I with them rousing
the people by harangues to stir up civil war? Did they
not fall more than seventy years ago, and as they are
known to us by statues which even the conqueror did
not destroy, so too is not some portion of their memory
preserved for us by historians? To every man posterity
gives his due honor, and, if a fatal sentence hangs
over me, there will be those who will remember me as
well as Cassius and Brutus."

He then left the Senate and ended his life by starvation. His books, so the senators decreed, were to be
burned by the ædiles; but some copies were left which
were concealed and afterward published. And so one
is all the more inclined to laugh at the stupidity of men
who suppose that the despotism of the present can actually efface the remembrances of the next generation. On
the contrary, the persecution of genius fosters its influence; foreign tyrants, and all who have imitated their
oppression, have merely procured infamy for themselves
and glory for their victims.

36. That year was such a continuous succession of
prosecutions that on the days of the Latin festival[56]
when Drusus, as city prefect, had ascended his tribunal

for the inauguration of his office, Calpurnius Salvianus appeared before him against Sextus Marius.[57] This the Emperor openly censured, and it caused the banishment of Salvianus. Next, the people of Cyzicus[58] were accused of publicly neglecting the established worship of the divine Augustus, and also of acts of violence to Roman citizens. They were deprived of the franchise which they had earned during the war with Mithridates, when their city was besieged, and when they repulsed the king as much by their own bravery as by the aid of Lucullus. Then followed the acquittal of Fonteius Capito,[59] the late proconsul of Asia, on proof that charges brought against him by Vibius Serenus were fictitious. Still this did not injure Serenus, to whom public hatred was actually a protection. Indeed any conspicuously restless informer was, so to say, inviolable; only the insignificant and undistinguished were punished.

37. About the same time Further Spain sent a deputation to the Senate, with a request to be allowed, after the example of Asia, to erect a temple to Tiberius and his mother. On this occasion, the Emperor, who had generally a strong contempt for honors, and now thought it right to reply to the rumor which reproached him with having yielded to vanity, delivered the following speech:

"I am aware, senators, that many deplore my want of firmness in not having opposed a similar recent petition from the cities of Asia. I will therefore explain both the grounds of my previous silence and my intentions for the future. Inasmuch as the divine Augustus did not forbid the founding of a temple at Pergamum[60] to himself and to the city of Rome, I, who respect as law all his actions and sayings, have the more readily followed a precedent once approved, seeing that with the worship of myself was linked an expression of reverence toward the Senate. But though it may be pardonable to have allowed this once, it would be a vain and arrogant thing to receive the sacred honor of images representing the divine throughout all the provinces, and the homage paid to Augustus will disappear if it is vulgarized by indiscriminate flattery.

38. "For myself, senators, I am mortal and limited to

the functions of humanity, content if I can adequately fill the highest place; of this I solemnly assure you, and would have posterity remember it. They will more than sufficiently honor my memory by believing me to have been worthy of my ancestry, watchful over your interests, courageous in danger, fearless of enmity, when the state required it. These sentiments of your hearts are my temples, these my most glorious and abiding monuments. Those built of stone are despised as mere tombs, if the judgment of posterity passes into hatred. And therefore this is my prayer to our allies, our citizens, and to heaven itself: to the last, that, to my life's close, it grant me a tranquil mind, which can discern alike human and divine claims; to the first, that, when I die, they honor my career and the reputation of my name with praise and kindly remembrance."

Henceforth Tiberius even in private conversations persisted in showing contempt for such homage to himself. Some attributed this to modesty; many to self-distrust; a few to a mean spirit. "The noblest men," it was said, "have the loftiest aspirations, and so Hercules and Bacchus among the Greeks and Quirinus among us were enrolled in the number of the gods.[61] Augustus did better, seeing that he had aspired. All other things princes have as a matter of course; one thing they ought insatiably to pursue, that their memory may be glorious. For to despise fame is to despise merit."

39. Sejanus meanwhile, dazed by his extravagant prosperity and urged on too by a woman's passion, Livia now insisting on his promise of marriage, addressed a memorial to the Emperor. For it was then the custom to apply to him by writing, even though he was at Rome. This petition was to the following effect: The kindness of Augustus, the father, and then the many favorable testimonies of Tiberius, the son, had engendered the habit of confiding his hopes and wishes to the ears of emperors as readily as to those of the gods. The splendor of high distinctions he had never craved; he had rather chosen watchings and hardships, like one of the common soldiers, for the Emperor's safety. But there was one most glorious honor he had won, the reputation of

being worthy of an alliance with a Cæsar. This was the first motive of his ambition. As he had heard that Augustus, in marrying his daughter, had even entertained some thoughts of Roman knights,[62] so if a husband were sought for Livia, he hoped Tiberius would bear in mind a friend who would find his reward simply in the glory of the alliance. He did not wish to rid himself of the duties imposed on him; he thought it enough for his family to be secured against the unjust displeasure of Agrippina, and this for the sake of his children. For, as for himself, enough and more than enough for him would be a life completed while such a sovereign still reigned.

40. Tiberius, in reply, after praising the loyal sentiments of Sejanus and briefly enumerating the favors he had bestowed on him, asked time for impartial consideration, adding that while other men's plans depended on their ideas of their own interest, princes, who had to regulate their chief actions by public opinion, were in a different position. "Hence," he said, "I do not take refuge in an answer which it would be easy to return, that Livia can herself decide whether she considers that, after Drusus, she ought again to marry or rather to endure life in the same home, and that she has in her mother and grandmother counselors nearer and dearer to her. I will deal more frankly. First, as to the enmity of Agrippina, I maintain that it will blaze out more fiercely if Livia's marriage rends, so to say, the house of the Cæsars into two factions. Even as it is, feminine jealousies break out, and my grandsons are torn asunder by the strife. What will happen if the rivalry is rendered more intense by such a marriage? For you are mistaken, Sejanus, if you think that you will then remain in the same position, and that Livia, who has been the wife of Gaius Cæsar[63] and afterward of Drusus, will have the inclination to pass her old age with a mere Roman knight. Though I might allow it, do you imagine it would be tolerated by those who have seen her brother, her father, and our ancestors in the highest offices of state? You indeed desire to keep within your station; but those magistrates and nobles who intrude on you against your wishes and consult you on all matters openly give out

that you have long overstepped the rank of a knight and gone far beyond my father's friendships, and from their dislike of you they also condemn me. But, you say, Augustus had thoughts of giving his daughter to a Roman knight. Is it surprising that, with so many distracting cares, foreseeing too the immense elevation to which a man would be raised above others by such an alliance, he talked of Gaius Proculeius and certain persons of singularly quiet life, wholly free from political entanglements? Still, if the hesitation of Augustus is to influence us, how much stronger is the fact that he bestowed his daughter on Marcus Agrippa, then on myself! All this, as a friend, I have stated without reserve, but I will not oppose your plans or those of Livia. My own earnest thoughts and the ties with which I am still purposing to unite you to myself, I shall for the present forbear to explain. This only I will declare, that nothing is too grand to be deserved by your merits and your goodwill toward me. When an opportunity presents itself, either in the Senate, or in a popular assembly, I shall not be silent."

41. Sejanus, no longer thinking of his marriage but filled with a deeper alarm, rejoined by deprecating the whispers of suspicion, popular rumor, and the gathering storm of odium. That he might not impair his influence by closing his doors on the throngs of his many visitors or strengthen the hands of accusers by admitting them, he made it his aim to induce Tiberius to live in some charming spot at a distance from Rome. In this he foresaw several advantages. Access to the Emperor would be under his own control, and letters, for the most part being conveyed by soldiers, would pass through his hands. Cæsar too, who was already in the decline of life, would soon, when enervated by retirement, more readily transfer to him the functions of empire; envy toward himself would be lessened when there was an end to his crowded levees and the reality of power would be increased by the removal of its empty show. So he began to declaim against the laborious life of the capital, the bustling crowds and streaming multitudes, while he praised repose and solitude, with their freedom from

vexations and misunderstandings, and their special opportunities for the study of the highest questions.

42. It happened that the trial at this time of Votienus Montanus, a popular wit, convinced the hesitating Tiberius that he ought to shun all assemblies of the Senate, where speeches, often true and offensive, were flung in his very face. Votienus was charged with insulting expressions toward the Emperor, and while the witness, Æmilius, a military man, in his eagerness to prove the case, repeated the whole story and amid angry clamor struggled on with loud assertion, Tiberius heard the reproaches by which he was assailed in secret, and was so deeply impressed that he exclaimed that he would clear himself either at once or on a legal inquiry, and the entreaties of friends, with the flattery of the whole assembly, hardly restored his composure. As for Votienus, he suffered the penalty of treason; but the Emperor, clinging all the more obstinately to the harshness with which he had been reproached in regard to accused persons, punished Aquilia with exile for the crime of adultery with Varius Ligur, although Lentulus Gætulicus,[64] the consul-elect, had proposed that she should be sentenced under the Julian Law. He next struck off Apidius Merula from the register of the Senate for not having sworn obedience to the legislation of the divine Augustus.

[*Chapter 43 is omitted.*]

44. Two men of noble rank died in that year, Cnæus Lentulus and Lucius Domitius.[65] It had been the glory of Lentulus, to say nothing of his consulship and his triumphal distinctions over the Gætuli, to have borne poverty with a good grace, then to have attained great wealth, which had been blamelessly acquired and was modestly enjoyed. Domitius derived luster from a father who during the civil war had been master of the sea, till he united himself to the party of Antonius and afterward to that of Cæsar. His grandfather had fallen in the battle of Pharsalia, fighting for the aristocracy. He had himself been chosen to be the husband of the

younger Antonia, daughter of Octavia, and subsequently led an army across the Elbe, penetrating further into Germany than any Roman before him. For this achievement he gained triumphal honors.

Lucius Antonius too then died, of a most illustrious but unfortunate family. His father, Iullus Antonius, was capitally punished for adultery with Julia,[66] and the son, when a mere youth, was banished by Augustus, whose sister's grandson he was, to the city of Massilia,[67] where the name of exile might be masked under that of student. Yet honor was paid him in death, and his bones, by the Senate's decree, were consigned to the sepulcher of the Octavii.[68]

45. While the same consuls were in office, an atrocious crime was committed in Nearer Spain by a peasant of the Termestine[69] tribe. Suddenly attacking the prætor of the province, Lucius Piso, as he was traveling in all the carelessness of peace, he killed him with a single wound. He then fled on a swift horse, and reached a wooded country, where he parted with his steed and eluded pursuit amid rocky and pathless wilds. But he was soon discovered. The horse was caught and led through the neighboring villages, and its owner ascertained. Being found and put to the torture that he might be forced to reveal his accomplices, he exclaimed in a loud voice, in the language of his country, that it was in vain to question him; his comrades might stand by and look on, but that the most intense agony would not wring the truth from him. Next day, when he was dragged back to torture, he broke loose from his guards and dashed his head against a stone with such violence that he instantly fell dead. It was, however, believed that Piso was treacherously murdered by the Termestini. Some public money had been embezzled, and he was pressing for its payment too rigorously for the patience of barbarians.

[*Chapters 46 to 51 are omitted.*]

52. At Rome meanwhile, besides the shocks already sustained by the imperial house, came the first step

toward the destruction of Agrippina, Claudia Pulchra,[70] her cousin, being prosecuted by Domitius Afer.[71] Lately a prætor, a man of but moderate position and eager to become notorious by any sort of deed, Afer charged her with unchastity, with having Furnius for her paramour, and with attempts on the Emperor by poison and sorcery. Agrippina, always impetuous, and now kindled into fury by the peril of her kinswoman, went straight to Tiberius and found him, as it happened, offering a sacrifice to his father. This provoked an indignant outburst. "It is not," she exclaimed, "for the same man to slay victims to the divine Augustus and to persecute his posterity. The celestial spirit has not transferred itself to the mute statue; here is the true image, sprung of heavenly blood, and she perceives her danger, and assumes its mournful emblems. Pulchra's name is a mere blind; the only reason for her destruction is that she has, in utter folly, selected Agrippina for her admiration, forgetting that Sosia[72] was thereby ruined." These words wrung from the Emperor one of the rare utterances of that inscrutable breast; he rebuked Agrippina with a Greek verse, and reminded her that "she was not wronged because she was not a queen." Pulchra and Furnius were condemned. Afer was ranked with the foremost orators, for the ability which he displayed, and which won strong praise from Tiberius, who pronounced him a speaker of natural genius. Henceforward as a counsel for the defense or the prosecution he enjoyed the fame of eloquence rather than of virtue, but old age robbed him of much of his speaking power, while, with a failing intellect, he was yet unwilling to remain silent.

53. Agrippina, in stubborn rage, with the grasp of disease yet on her, when the Emperor came to see her wept long and silently, and then began to mingle reproach and supplication. She begged him "to relieve her loneliness and provide her with a husband; her youth still fitted her for marriage, which was a virtuous woman's only solace, and there were citizens in Rome who would not disdain to receive the wife of Germanicus and his children." But the Emperor, who perceived the political aims of her request, but did not wish to show displeasure

or apprehension, left her, notwithstanding her urgency, without an answer. This incident, not mentioned by any historian, I have found in the memoirs of the younger Agrippina, the mother of the Emperor Nero, who handed down to posterity the story of her life and of the misfortunes of her family.

54. Sejanus meanwhile yet more deeply alarmed the sorrowing and unsuspecting woman by sending his agents, under the guise of friendship, with warnings that poison was prepared for her, and that she ought to avoid her father-in-law's table. Knowing not how to dissemble, she relaxed neither her features nor tone of voice as she sat by him at dinner, nor did she touch a single dish, till at last Tiberius, noticed her conduct, either casually or because he was told of it. To test her more closely, he praised some fruit as it was set on the table and passed it with his own hand to his daughter-in-law. This increased the suspicions of Agrippina, and without putting the fruit to her lips she gave it to the slaves. Still no remark fell from Tiberius before the company, but he turned to his mother and whispered that it was not surprising if he had decided on harsh treatment against one who implied that he was a poisoner. Then there was a rumor that a plan was laid for her destruction, that the Emperor did not dare to attempt it openly, and was seeking to veil the deed in secrecy.

[*Chapters 55-56 are omitted.*]

57. Meanwhile, after long reflection on his purpose and frequent deferment of it, the Emperor retired into Campania to dedicate, as he pretended, a temple to Jupiter at Capua and another to Augustus at Nola, but really resolved to live at a distance from Rome. Although I have followed most historians in attributing the cause of his retirement to the arts of Sejanus, still, as he passed six consecutive years in the same solitude after that minister's destruction, I am often in doubt whether it is not to be more truly ascribed to himself, and his wish to hide by the place of his retreat the cruelty and licentiousness which he betrayed by his actions. Some thought

that in his old age he was ashamed of his personal appearance. He had indeed a tall, singularly slender and stooping figure, a bald head, a face full of eruptions, and covered here and there with plasters. In the seclusion of Rhodes he had habituated himself to shun society and to hide his voluptuous life. According to one account his mother's domineering temper drove him away; he was weary of having her as his partner in power, and he could not thrust her aside, because he had received this very power as her gift. For Augustus had had thoughts of putting the Roman state under Germanicus, his sister's grandson, whom all men esteemed, but yielding to his wife's entreaties he left Germanicus to be adopted by Tiberius and adopted Tiberius himself. With this Augusta would taunt her son, and claim back what she had given.

58. His departure was attended by a small retinue: one senator, who was an ex-consul, Cocceius Nerva,[73] learned in the laws; one Roman knight, besides Sejanus, of the highest order, Curtius Atticus; the rest being men of liberal culture, for the most part Greeks, in whose conversation he might find amusement. It was said by men who knew the stars that the motions of the heavenly bodies when Tiberius left Rome were such as to forbid the possibility of his return. This caused ruin to many who conjectured that his end was near and spread the rumor; for they never foresaw the very improbable contingency of his voluntary exile from his home for eleven years. Soon afterward it was clearly seen what a narrow margin there is between such science and delusion and in what obscurity truth is veiled. That he would not return to Rome was not a mere random assertion; as to the rest, they were wholly in the dark, seeing that he lived to extreme old age in the country or on the coast near Rome and often close to the very walls of the city.

59. It happened at this time that a perilous accident which occurred to the Emperor strengthened vague rumors and gave him grounds for trusting more fully in the friendship and fidelity of Sejanus. They were dining in a country house called "The Caves" between the gulf of Amunclæ[74] and the hills of Fundi,[75] in a natural grotto.

The rocks at its entrance suddenly fell in and crushed some of the attendants; thereupon panic seized the whole company and there was a general flight of the guests. Sejanus hung over the Emperor, and with knee, face, and hand encountered the falling stones; and was found in this attitude by the soldiers who came to their rescue. After this he was greater than ever, and though his counsels were ruinous, he was listened to with confidence, as a man who had no care for himself. He pretended to act as a judge toward the children of Germanicus, after having suborned persons to assume the part of prosecutors and to inveigh specially against Nero, next in succession to the throne, who, though he had proper youthful modesty, often forgot present expediency, while freedmen and clients, eager to get power, incited him to display vigor and self-confidence. "This," they said, "was what the Roman people wished, what the armies desired, and Sejanus would not dare to oppose it, though now he insulted alike the tame spirit of the old Emperor and the timidity of the young prince."

60. Nero, while he listened to this and like talk, was not indeed inspired with any guilty ambition, but still occasionally there would break from him willful and thoughtless expressions which spies about his person caught up and reported with exaggeration, and this he had no opportunity of rebutting. Then again alarms under various forms were continually arising. One man would avoid meeting him; another after returning his salutation would instantly turn away; many after beginning a conversation would stand their ground and laugh at him. Tiberius indeed wore an angry frown or a treacherous smile. Whether the young prince spoke or held his tongue, silence and speech were alike criminal. Every night had its anxieties, for his sleepless hours, his dreams and sighs were all made known by his wife to her mother Livia and by Livia to Sejanus. Nero's brother Drusus Sejanus actually drew into his scheme by holding out to him the prospect of becoming Emperor through the removal of an elder brother, already all but fallen. The savage temper of Drusus, to say nothing of lust of power and the usual hatreds between brothers,

was inflamed with envy by the partiality of the mother, Agrippina, toward Nero. And yet Sejanus, while he favored Drusus, was not without thoughts of sowing the seeds of his future ruin, well knowing how very impetuous he was and therefore the more exposed to treachery.

61. Toward the close of the year died two distinguished men, Asinius Agrippa and Quintus Haterius. Agrippa was of illustrious rather than ancient ancestry, which his career did not disgrace; Haterius was of a senatorian family and famous for his eloquence while he lived, though the monuments which remain of his genius are not admired as of old. The truth is, he succeeded more by vehemence than by finish of style. While the research and labors of other authors are valued by an after age, the harmonious fluency of Haterius died with him.

[*Chapters 62 to 65 are omitted.*]

66. But though the zeal of the nobles and the bounty of the prince brought relief to suffering, yet every day a stronger and fiercer host of informers pursued its victims, without one alleviating circumstance. Quintilius Varus, a rich man and related to the Emperor, was suddenly attacked by Domitius Afer, the successful prosecutor of Claudia Pulchra, his mother,[76] and no one wondered that the needy adventurer of many years who had squandered his lately gotten recompense was now preparing himself for fresh iniquities. That Publius Dolabella should have associated himself in the prosecution was a marvel, for he was of illustrious ancestry, was allied to Varus, and was now himself seeking to destroy his own noble race, his own kindred. The Senate, however, stopped the proceeding, and decided to wait for the Emperor, this being the only means of escaping for a time impending horrors.

67. Cæsar, meanwhile, after dedicating the temples in Campania, warned the public by an edict not to disturb his retirement and posted soldiers here and there to keep off the throngs of townsfolk. But he so loathed the towns and colonies and, in short, every place on the mainland,

that he buried himself in the island of Capreæ,[77] which is separated by three miles of strait from the extreme point of the promontory of Sorrentum.[78] The solitude of the place was, I believe, its chief attraction, for a harborless sea surrounds it and even for a small vessel it has but few safe retreats, nor can anyone land unknown to the sentries. Its air in winter is soft, as it is screened by a mountain which is a protection against cutting winds. In summer it catches the western breezes, and the open sea round it renders it most delightful. It commanded too a prospect of the most lovely bay, till Vesuvius,[79] bursting into flames, changed the face of the country. Greeks, so tradition says, occupied those parts and Capreæ was inhabited by the Teleboi.[80] Tiberius had by this time filled the island with twelve country houses, each with a grand name and a vast structure of its own. Intent as he had once been on the cares of state, he was now for thoroughly unbending himself in secret profligacy and a leisure of malignant schemes. For he still retained that rash proneness to suspect and to believe which even at Rome Sejanus used to foster, and which he here excited more keenly, no longer concealing his machinations against Agrippina and Nero. Soldiers hung about them, and every message, every visit, their public and their private life were I may say regularly chronicled. And persons were actually suborned to advise them to flee to the armies of Germany, or when the forum was most crowded, to clasp the statue of the divine Augustus and appeal to the protection of the people and Senate. These counsels they disdained, but they were charged with having had thoughts of acting on them.

68. The year of the consulship of Silanus and Silius Nerva[81] opened with a foul beginning. A Roman knight of the highest rank, Titius Sabinus,[82] was dragged to prison because he had been a friend of Germanicus. He had indeed persisted in showing marked respect toward his wife and children, as their visitor at home, their companion in public, the solitary survivor of so many clients, and he was consequently esteemed by the good, as he was a terror to the evil-minded. Latinius Latiaris,

Porcius Cato, Petilius Rufus, and Marcus Opsius, ex-prætors, conspired to attack him, with an eye to the consulship, to which there was access only through Sejanus, and the goodwill of Sejanus was to be gained only by a crime. They arranged amongst themselves that Latiaris, who had some slight acquaintance with Sabinus, should devise the plot, that the rest should be present as witnesses, and that then they should begin the prosecution. Accordingly Latiaris, after first dropping some casual remarks, went on to praise the fidelity of Sabinus in not having, like others, forsaken after its fall the house of which he had been the friend in its prosperity. He also spoke highly of Germanicus and compassionately of Agrippina. Sabinus, with the natural softness of the human heart under calamity, burst into tears, which he followed up with complaints, and soon with yet more daring invective against Sejanus, against his cruelty, pride, and ambition. He did not spare even Tiberius in his reproaches. That conversation, having united them, as it were, in an unlawful secret, led to a semblance of close intimacy. Henceforward Sabinus himself sought Latiaris, went continually to his house, and imparted to him his griefs, as to a most faithful friend.

69. The men whom I have named now consulted how these conversations might fall within the hearing of more persons. It was necessary that the place of meeting should preserve the appearance of secrecy, and, if witnesses were to stand behind the doors, there was a fear of their being seen or heard, or of suspicion casually arising. Three senators thrust themselves into the space between the roof and ceiling, a hiding place as shameful as the treachery was execrable. They applied their ears to apertures and crevices. Latiaris meanwhile, having met Sabinus in the streets, drew him to his house and to the room, as if he was going to communicate some fresh discoveries. There he talked much about past and impending troubles, a copious topic indeed, and about fresh horrors. Sabinus spoke as before and at greater length, as sorrow, when once it has broken into utterance, is the harder to restrain. Instantly they hastened to accuse

him, and having dispatched a letter to the Emperor, they informed him of the order of the plot and of their own infamy. Never was Rome more distracted and terror-stricken. Meetings, conversations, the ear of friend and stranger were alike shunned; even things mute and lifeless, the very roofs and walls, were eyed with suspicion.

70. The Emperor in his letter on the first of January, after offering the usual prayers for the new year, referred to Sabinus, whom he reproached with having corrupted some of his freedmen and having attempted his life, and he claimed vengeance in no obscure language. It was decreed without hesitation, and the condemned man was dragged off, exclaiming as loudly as he could, with head covered and throat tightly bound, "that this was inaugurating the year; these were the victims slain to Sejanus." Wherever he turned his eyes, wherever his words fell, there was flight and solitude; the streets and public places were forsaken. A few retraced their steps and again showed themselves, shuddering at the mere fact that they had betrayed alarm. "What day," they asked, "will be without some execution, when amid sacrifices and prayers, a time when it is usual to refrain even from a profane word, the chain and halter are introduced? Tiberius has not incurred such odium blindly; this is a studied device to make us believe that there is no reason why the new magistrates should not open the dungeons as well as the temple and the altars." Thereupon there came a letter of thanks to them for having punished a bitter foe to the state, and the Emperor further added that he had an anxious life, that he apprehended treachery from enemies, but he mentioned no one by name. Still there was no question that this was aimed at Nero and Agrippina.

71. But for my plan of referring each event to its own year, I should feel a strong impulse to anticipate matters and at once relate the deaths by which Latinius and Opsius and the other authors of this atrocious deed perished, some after Gaius became Emperor, some even while Tiberius yet ruled. For although he would not have the instruments of his wickedness destroyed by

others, he frequently, when he was tired of them, and fresh ones offered themselves for the same services, flung off the old, now become a mere incubus. But these and other punishments of guilty men I shall describe in due course.[83]

Asinius Gallus, to whose children Agrippina was aunt, then moved that the Emperor should be requested to disclose his apprehensions to the Senate and allow their removal. Of all his virtues, as he counted them, there was none on which Tiberius so prided himself as his ability to dissemble, and he was therefore the more irritated at an attempt to expose what he was hiding. Sejanus, however, pacified him, not out of love for Gallus, but rather to wait the result of the Emperor's wavering mood, knowing, as he did, that, though slow in forming his purpose, yet having once broken through his reserve, he would follow up harsh words with terrible deeds.

About the same time, Julia died, the granddaughter of Augustus. He had condemned her on a conviction of adultery and had banished her to the island of Trimerus, not far from the shores of Apulia.[84] There she endured twenty years' exile, in which she was supported by relief from Augusta, who having overthrown the prosperity of her stepchildren by secret machinations, made open display of her compassion to the fallen family.

[Chapters 72 to 75 are omitted. A revolt of the Frisians was suppressed by Lucius Apronius, governor of Lower Germany.]

BOOK V 29-31 A.D.

1. IN the consulship of Rubellius and Fufius,[1] both of whom had the surname Geminus, died in an advanced old age Julia Augusta. A Claudia by birth and by adoption a Livia and a Julia, she united the noblest blood of Rome.[2] Her first marriage, by which she had children, was with Tiberius Nero, who, an exile during the Perusine war, returned to Rome when peace had been con-

cluded between Sextus Pompeius and the triumvirs.[3]
After this Cæsar, enamored of her beauty, took her away
from her husband, whether against her wish is uncertain. So impatient was he that he brought her to his
house actually pregnant, not allowing time for her confinement. She had no subsequent issue, but allied as
she was through the marriage of Agrippina and Germanicus to the blood of Augustus, her great-grandchildren were also his. In the purity of her home life
she was of the ancient type, but was more affable than
was thought fitting in ladies of former days. An imperious mother and an amiable wife, she was a match for
the diplomacy of her husband and the dissimulation of
her son. Her funeral was simple, and her will long remained unexecuted. Her panegyric was pronounced from
the Rostra by her great-grandson, Gaius Cæsar, who
afterward succeeded to power.

2. Tiberius, however, making no change in his voluptuous life, excused himself by letter for his absence from
his last duty to his mother on the ground of the pressure
of business. He even abridged, out of moderation, as it
seemed, the honors which the Senate had voted on a
lavish scale to her memory, allowing only a very few,
and adding that no religious worship was to be decreed,
this having been her own wish. In a part of the same
letter he sneered at female friendships, with an indirect
censure on the consul Fufius,[4] who had risen to distinction through Augusta's partiality. Fufius was indeed a
man well fitted to win the affection of a woman; he
was witty too, and used to ridicule Tiberius with those
bitter jests which the powerful remember so long.

3. This at all events was the beginning of an un-
mitigated and grinding despotism. As long indeed as
Augusta lived, there yet remained a refuge, for with
Tiberius obedience to his mother was the habit of a life,
and Sejanus did not dare to set himself above a parent's
authority. Now, so to say, they threw off the reins and
let loose their fury. A letter was sent, directed against
Agrippina and Nero, which was popularly believed to
have been kept back by Augusta, as it was publicly read
soon after her death. It contained expressions of studied

harshness, yet it was not armed rebellion or a longing for revolution, but unnatural passions and profligacy which the Emperor imputed to his grandson. Against his daughter-in-law he did not dare to invent this much; he merely censured her insolent tongue and defiant spirit, amid the panic-stricken silence of the Senate, till a few who had no hope from merit (and public calamities are ever used by individuals for interested purposes) demanded that the question should be debated. The most eager was Cotta Messallinus, who made a savage speech. Still, the other principal senators, and especially the magistrates, were perplexed, for Tiberius, notwithstanding his furious invective, had left everything else in doubt.

4. There was in the Senate one Junius Rusticus, who, having been appointed by the Emperor to record its debates, was therefore supposed to have an insight into his secret purposes. This man, whether through some fatal impulse (he had indeed never before given any evidence of courage) or a misdirected acuteness which made him tremble at the uncertain future, while he forgot impending perils, attached himself to the waverers, and warned the consuls not to enter on the debate. He argued that the highest issues turned on trivial causes, and that the old man might one day regret the fall of the house of Germanicus. At the same moment the people, bearing the images of Agrippina and Nero, thronged round the Senate House, and, with words of blessing on the Emperor, kept shouting that the letter was a forgery and that it was not by the prince's will that ruin was being plotted against his house. And so that day passed without any dreadful result.

Fictitious speeches too against Sejanus were published under the names of ex-consuls, for several persons indulged, all the more recklessly because anonymously, the caprice of their imaginations. Consequently the wrath of Sejanus was the more furious, and he had ground for alleging that the Senate disregarded the Emperor's trouble; that the people were in revolt; that speeches in a new style and new resolutions were being heard and read. What remained but to take the sword and choose for their generals and emperors those whose images they had followed as standards?

5. Upon this the Emperor, after repeating his invectives against his grandson and his daughter-in-law and reprimanding the populace in an edict, complained to the Senate that by the trick of one senator the imperial dignity had been publicly flouted, and he insisted that, after all, the whole matter should be left to his exclusive decision. Without further deliberation, they proceeded, not indeed to pronounce the final sentence (for this was forbidden), but to declare that they were prepared for vengeance, and were restrained only by the strong hand of the sovereign.

[*At this point the narrative breaks off; all the rest of Book V and the beginning of Book VI is lost; the missing portion covered the events of two and a half years. For this period we have to rely on other sources, principally Suetonius'* Life of Tiberius *and the history of Cassius Dio.*

During the year 29 Agrippina and her elder son, Nero, were both arrested and imprisoned on small islands. Nero went to Pontia, now Ponza, his mother to Pandateria (see I, 53). There she was treated with great brutality; Suetonius says that she underwent forcible feeding, and lost an eye as the result of a blow from a centurion. The charges must have been serious; probably they were accused of having planned to flee to the German armies and overthrow the Emperor (see IV, 67). Cotta Messallinus and Domitius Afer seem to have been prominent in accusation. At some time in the year 30, Nero killed himself. The same year saw the condemnation of Asinius Gallus, whom Tiberius had not forgiven for his marriage with Vipsania (see I, 12; VI, 23). Sejanus was nominated as consul for 31, with the Emperor himself as colleague.

Early in 31 Sejanus seemed more powerful than ever. Fufius Geminus, the consul of 29, and Curtius Rufus, at one time a close friend of Tiberius, were condemned at his instigation; he was given special proconsular power. But at about this time Tiberius received a warn-

ing of Sejanus' plotting from Antonia, Germanicus' mother. For a time he took no action; but an attempt by Sejanus to prosecute for treason the eminent consular Lucius Arruntius was frustrated. Then on October 18 a long and verbose letter from Tiberius was read out in the Senate. Sejanus seems to have expected that it would end with a request for him to be given tribunician power, which would have marked him out as the Emperor's colleague and eventual successor; instead it ended by charging him with conspiracy and gave orders for his arrest. The Senate House had meanwhile been surrounded by the city watch, a force Tiberius could trust; and the loyalty of the prætorian guard was assured by a large payment to Nævius Sertorius Macro, the officer chosen by Tiberius to succeed Sejanus as its prefect. The same evening Sejanus was strangled, and soon after his elder son and many of his associates were tried and executed. His former wife, Apicata, killed herself, leaving a letter to the Emperor in which she charged Sejanus and Livia with the poisoning of Drusus. Livia too committed suicide.

The peculiar numbering of the chapters is due to a mistake in the manuscript; six chapters that really belong to Book VI were thought, before Lipsius, to belong to Book V. The narrative begins again in the middle of a speech made by a man who had been friendly with Sejanus and was accused of taking part in his conspiracy; his name is not known.]

[BOOK VI   *32-37 A.D.*]

[V, 6.] There has now been a change of fortune, and even he who chose Sejanus to be his colleague and his son-in-law[1] excuses his error. As for the rest, the man whom they encouraged by shameful baseness, they now wickedly revile. Which is the most pitiable, to be accused for friendship's sake or to have to accuse a friend, I cannot decide. I will not put any man's cruelty or compassion to the test, but, while I am free and have a clear conscience, I will anticipate peril. I implore you to cherish my memory with joy rather than with sorrow, numbering me too with those who by a noble death have fled from the miseries of our country."

[V, 7.] Then detaining those of his friends who were minded to stay with him and converse, or, if otherwise, dismissing them, he thus spent part of the day, and with a numerous circle yet round him, all gazing on his fearless face, and imagining that there was still time to elapse before the last scene, he fell on a sword which he had concealed in his robe. The Emperor did not pursue him after his death with either accusation or reproach, although he had heaped a number of foul charges on Blæsus.[2]

[V, 8.] Next were discussed the cases of Publius Vitellius[3] and Pomponius Secundus.[4] The first was charged by his accusers with having offered the keys of the treasury, of which he was prefect, and the military chest in aid of a revolution. Against the latter, Considius, an ex-prætor, alleged intimacy with Ælius Gallus, who, after the punishment of Sejanus, had fled to the gardens of Pomponius, as his safest refuge. They had no resource in their peril but in the courageous firmness of their brothers, who became their sureties. Soon, after several adjournments, Vitellius, weary alike of hope and fear, asked for a penknife, avowedly for his literary pursuits, and inflicted a slight wound in his veins, and died at last of a broken heart. Pomponius, a man of refined manners and literary gifts, bore his adverse fortune with resignation, and outlived Tiberius.

[V, 9.] It was next decided to punish the remaining children of Sejanus, though the fury of the populace was subsiding, and people generally had been appeased by the previous executions. Accordingly they were carried off to prison, the boy, aware of his impending doom, and the little girl, who was so unconscious that she continually asked what was her offense, and whither she was being dragged, saying that she would do so no more, and a childish chastisement was enough for her correction. Historians of the time tell us that, as there was no precedent for the capital punishment of a virgin,

117

she was violated by the executioner, with the rope on her neck. Then they were strangled and their bodies, mere children as they were, were flung down the Gemonian stairs.

[V. 10.] About the same time Asia and Achæa were alarmed by a prevalent but short-lived rumor that Drusus, the son of Germanicus, had been seen in the Cyclades and subsequently on the mainland. There was indeed a young man of much the same age, whom some of the Emperor's freedmen pretended to recognize, and to whom they attached themselves with a treacherous intent. The renown of the name attracted the ignorant, and the Greek mind eagerly fastens on what is new and marvelous. The story indeed, which they no sooner invented than believed, was that Drusus had escaped from custody, and was on his way to the armies of his father, with the design of invading Egypt or Syria. And he was now drawing to himself a multitude of young men and much popular enthusiasm, enjoying the present and cherishing idle hopes of the future, when Poppæus Sabinus heard of the affair. At the time he was chiefly occupied with Macedonia, but he also had the charge of Achæa. So, to forestall the danger, let the story be true or false, he hurried by the bays of Torone and Thermæ,[5] then passed on to Eubœa, an island of the Ægæan, to Piræus[6] on the coast of Attica, thence to the shores of Corinth and the narrow Isthmus, and having arrived by the other sea at Nicopolis, a Roman colony, he there at last ascertained that the man, when skillfully questioned, had said that he was the son of Marcus Silanus,[7] and that, after the dispersion of a number of his followers, he had embarked on a vessel, intending, it seemed, to go to Italy. Sabinus sent this account to Tiberius, and of the origin and issue of the affair nothing more is known to me.

[V, 11.] At the close of the year a long growing feud between the consuls broke out. Trio,[8] a reckless man in incurring enmities and a practiced lawyer, had indirectly censured Regulus as having been halfhearted in crushing the satellites of Sejanus. Regulus, who, unless he was provoked, loved quietness, not only repulsed his

118

colleague's attack, but was for dragging him to trial as a guilty accomplice in the conspiracy. And though many of the senators implored them to compose a quarrel likely to end fatally, they continued their enmity and their mutual menaces till they retired from office.

BOOK VI   *32-37 A.D.*

1. Cnæus Domitius and Camillus Scribonianus had entered on the consulship[1] when the Emperor, after crossing the channel which divides Capreæ from Surrentum, sailed along the coast of Campania, in doubt whether he should enter Rome, or, possibly, simulating the intention of going thither, because he had resolved otherwise. He often landed at points in the neighborhood, visited the gardens by the Tiber, but went back again to the cliffs and to the solitude of the seashores, in shame at the vices and profligacies into which he had plunged so unrestrainedly that in the fashion of a despot he debauched the children of freeborn citizens. It was not merely beauty and a handsome person which he felt as an incentive to his lust, but the modesty of childhood in some, and noble ancestry in others. Hitherto unknown terms were then for the first time invented, derived from the abominations of the place and the endless phases of sensuality. Slaves too were set over the work of seeking out and procuring, with rewards for the willing and threats to the reluctant, and if there was resistance from a relative or a parent, they used violence and force, and actually indulged their own passions as if dealing with captives.

2. At Rome meanwhile, in the beginning of the year, as if Livia's crimes had just been discovered and not also long ago punished, terrible decrees were proposed against her very statues and memory, and the property of Sejanus was to be taken from the exchequer and transferred to the imperial treasury, as if there was any difference. The motion was being urged with extreme persistency, in almost the same or with but slightly changed language, by such men as Scipio,[2] Silanus,[3]

and Cassius[4] when suddenly Togonius Gallus, intruding his own obscurity among illustrious names, was heard with ridicule. He begged the Emperor to select a number of senators, twenty out of whom should be chosen by lot to wear swords and to defend his person, whenever he entered the Senate House. The man had actually believed a letter from him in which he asked the protection of one of the consuls, so that he might go in safety from Capreæ to Rome. Tiberius, however, who usually combined jesting and seriousness, thanked the senators for their goodwill, but asked who could be rejected, who could be chosen? "Were they always to be the same, or was there to be a succession? Were they to be men who had held office or youths, private citizens or officials? Then again, what a scene would be presented by persons grasping their swords on the threshold of the Senate House? His life was not of so much worth if it had to be defended by arms." This was his answer to Togonius, guarded in its expression, and he urged nothing beyond the rejection of the motion.

3. Junius Gallio, however, who had proposed that the prætorian soldiers, after having served their campaigns, should acquire the privilege of sitting in the fourteen rows of the theater, received a savage censure. Tiberius, just as if he were face to face with him, asked what *he* had to do with the soldiers, who ought not to receive the Emperor's orders or his rewards except from the Emperor himself? He had really discovered something which the divine Augustus had not foreseen. Or was not one of Sejanus' satellites rather seeking to sow discord and sedition, as a means of prompting ignorant minds, under the pretense of compliment, to ruin military discipline? This was Gallio's recompense for his carefully prepared flattery, with immediate expulsion from the Senate, and then from Italy. And as men complained that he would endure his exile with equanimity, since he had chosen the famous and lovely island of Lesbos, he was dragged back to Rome, and confined in the houses of different officials.

The Emperor in the same letter crushed Sextius Paconianus, an ex-prætor, to the great joy of the senators, as he was a daring, mischievous man, who pried into every person's secrets, and had been the chosen instrument of Sejanus in his treacherous designs against Gaius Cæsar. When this fact was divulged, there came an outburst of long-concealed hatreds, and there must have been a sentence of capital punishment, had he not himself volunteered a disclosure.

4. As soon as he named Latinius Latiaris,[5] accuser and accused, both alike objects of execration, presented a most welcome spectacle. Latiaris, as I have related, had been foremost in contriving the ruin of Titius Sabinus, and was now the first to pay the penalty. By way of episode, Haterius Agrippa inveighed against the consuls of the previous year for now sitting silent after their threats of impeaching one another. "It must be fear," he said, "and a guilty conscience which are acting as a bond of union. But the senators must not keep back what they have heard." Regulus replied that he was awaiting the opportunity for vengeance, and meant to press it in the Emperor's presence. Trio's answer was that it was best to efface the memory of rivalries between colleagues, and of any words uttered in quarrels. When Agrippa still persisted, Sanquinius Maximus,[6] one of the ex-consuls, implored the Senate not to increase the Emperor's anxieties by seeking further occasions of bitterness, as he was himself competent to provide remedies. This secured the safety of Regulus and the postponement of Trio's ruin. Haterius was hated all the more. Wan with untimely slumbers and nights of riot, and not fearing in his indolence even the cruelest of princes, he yet plotted amid his gluttony and lust the destruction of illustrious men.

5. Several charges were next brought, as soon as the opportunity offered, against Cotta Messallinus, the author of every unusually cruel proposal, and, consequently, regarded with inveterate hatred. He had made imputations, it was said, as to the virility of Gaius Cæsar,[7] and of an entertainment at which he was present on Augusta's birthday with the priests, as a funeral banquet. In remonstrating too against the influence of Marcus Lepidus and Lucius Arruntius, with whom he had dis-

putes on many matters, he had added the remark, "They will have the Senate's support; I shall have that of my Tiberius."[8] But the leading men of the state failed to convict him on all the charges. When they pressed the case, he appealed to the Emperor. Soon afterward, a letter arrived, in which Tiberius traced the origin of a friendship between himself and Cotta, enumerated his frequent services, and then requested that words perversely misrepresented and the freedom of table talk might not be construed into a crime.

6. The beginning of the Emperor's letter seemed very striking. It opened thus: "May all the gods and goddesses destroy me more miserably than I feel myself to be daily perishing, if I know at this moment what to write to you, senators, how to write it, or what, in short, not to write."[9] So completely had his crimes and infamies recoiled, as a penalty, on himself. With profound meaning was it often affirmed by the greatest teacher of philosophy that, could the minds of tyrants be laid bare, there would be seen gashes and wounds; for, as the body is lacerated by scourging, so is the spirit by brutality, by lust, and by evil thoughts. Assuredly Tiberius was not saved by his elevation or his solitude from having to confess the anguish of his heart and his self-inflicted punishment.

7. Authority was then given to the Senate to decide the case of Cæcilianus, one of its members, the chief witness against Cotta, and it was agreed that the same penalty should be inflicted as on Aruscius and Sanquinius, the accusers of Lucius Arruntius. Nothing ever happened to Cotta more to his distinction. Of noble birth, but beggared by extravagance and infamous for his excesses, he was now by the dignity of his revenge raised to a level with the stainless virtues of Arruntius.

Quintus Servæus and Minucius Thermus were next arraigned. Servæus was an ex-prætor, and had formerly been a companion of Germanicus; Minucius was of equestrian rank, and both had made a moderate use of the friendship of Sejanus. Hence they were the more pitied. Tiberius, on the contrary, denounced them as foremost in crime, and bade Gaius Cestius[10] the elder to tell the Senate what he had communicated to the Emperor by letter. Cestius undertook the prosecution. And this was the most dreadful feature of the age, that leading members of the Senate, some openly, some secretly, employed themselves in the very lowest work of the informer. One could not distinguish between aliens and kinsfolk, between friends and strangers, or say what was quite recent, or what half-forgotten from lapse of time. People were incriminated for some casual remark in the forum or at the dinner table, for everyone was impatient to be the first to mark his victim, some to screen themselves, most from being, as it were, infected with the contagion of the malady.

Minucius and Servæus, on being condemned, went over to the prosecution, and then Julius Africanus with Seius Quadratus were dragged into the same ruin. Africanus was from the Santones, one of the states of Gaul;[11] the origin of Quadratus I have not ascertained. Many authors, I am well aware, have passed over the perils and punishments of a host of persons, sickened by the multiplicity of them, or fearing that what they had themselves found wearisome and saddening, would be equally fatiguing to their readers. For myself, I have lighted on many facts worth knowing, though other writers have not recorded them.

8. A Roman knight, Marcus Terentius, at the crisis when all others had hypocritically repudiated the friendship of Sejanus, dared, when impeached on that ground, to cling to it by the following avowal to the Senate: "In my position it is perhaps less to my advantage to acknowledge than to deny the charge. Still, whatever is to be the issue of the matter, I shall admit that I was the friend of Sejanus, that I anxiously sought to be such, and was delighted when I was successful. I had seen him his father's colleague in the command of the prætorian cohorts, and subsequently combining the duties of civil and military life. His kinsfolk and connections were loaded with honors; intimacy with Sejanus was in every case a powerful recommendation to the Emperor's friendship. Those, on the contrary, whom he hated had to struggle with danger and humiliation. I take no individual as an instance. All of us who had no part in his last design, I

mean to defend at the peril of myself alone. It was really not Sejanus of Vulsinii, it was a member of the Claudian and Julian houses, in which he had taken a position by his marriage alliance, it was your son-in-law, Cæsar, your partner in the consulship, the man who administered your political functions, whom we courted. It is not for us to criticize one whom you may raise above all others, or your motives for so doing. Heaven has entrusted you with the supreme decision of affairs, and for us is left the glory of obedience. And, again, we see what takes place before our eyes, who it is on whom you bestow riches and honors, who are the most powerful to help or to injure. That Sejanus was such, no one will deny. To explore the prince's secret thought, or any of his hidden plans, is a forbidden, a dangerous thing, nor does it follow that one could reach them.

"Do not, senators, think only of Sejanus' last day, but of his sixteen years of power. We actually adored a Satrius[12] and a Pomponius. To be known even to his freedmen and hall porters was thought something very grand. What then is my meaning? Is this apology meant to be offered for all without difference and discrimination? No; it is to be restricted within proper limits. Let plots against the state, murderous designs against the Emperor be punished. As for friendship and its obligations, the same principle must acquit both you, Cæsar, and us."

9. The courage of this speech and the fact that there had been found a man to speak out what was in all people's thoughts had such an effect that the accusers of Terentius were sentenced to banishment or death, their previous offenses being taken into account. Then came a letter from Tiberius against Sextus Vistilius, an ex-prætor, whom, as a special favorite of his brother Drusus, the Emperor had admitted into his own select circle. His reason for being displeased with Vistilius was that he had either written an attack on Gaius Cæsar as a profligate, or that Tiberius believed a false charge that he had. For this Vistilius was excluded from the prince's table. He then tried the knife with his aged hand, but again bound up his veins, opening them once more, however, on hav-

ing begged for pardon by letter and received a pitiless answer. After him a host of persons were charged with treason: Annius Pollio, Appius Silanus Mamercus Scaurus, Sabinus Calvisius, Vinicianus too, coupled with Pollio, his father—men all of illustrious descent, some too of the highest political distinction.[13] The senators were panic-stricken, for how few of their number were not connected by alliance or by friendship with this multitude of men of rank! Celsus, however, tribune of a city cohort, and now one of the prosecutors, saved Appius and Calvisius from the peril. The Emperor postponed the cases of Pollio, Vinicianus, and Scaurus, intending to try them himself with the Senate, not, however, without affixing some ominous marks to the name of Scaurus.

10. Even women were not exempt from danger. Where they could not be accused of grasping at political power, their tears were made a crime. Vitia, an aged woman, mother of Fufius Geminus, was executed for bewailing the death of her son. Such were the proceedings in the Senate. It was the same with the Emperor. Vescularius Atticus and Julius Marinus were hurried off to execution, two of his oldest friends, men who had followed him to Rhodes and been his inseparable companions at Capreæ. Vescularius was his agent in the plot against Libo,[14] and it was with the cooperation of Marinus that Sejanus had ruined Curtius Atticus. Hence there was all the more joy at the recoil of these precedents on their authors.

About the same time Lucius Piso,[15] the pontiff, died a natural death, a rare incident in so high a rank. Never had he by choice proposed a servile motion, and, whenever necessity was too strong for him, he would suggest judicious compromises. His father, as I have related, had been a censor. He lived to the advanced age of eighty, and had won in Thrace the honor of a triumph. But his chief glory rested on the wonderful tact with which as city prefect he handled an authority recently made perpetual and all the more galling to men unaccustomed to obey it.

11. In former days, when the kings and subsequently the chief magistrates went from Rome, an official was temporarily chosen to administer justice and provide for

emergencies, so that the capital might not be left without government. It is said that Romulius Denter was appointed by Romulus,[16] then Marcius Numa by Tullus Hostilius, and Spurius Lucretius by Tarquinius Superbus. Afterward, the consuls made the appointment. The shadow of the old practice still survives, whenever in consequence of the Latin festival someone is deputed to exercise the consul's functions.[17] And Augustus too during the civil wars gave Cilnius Mæcenas, a Roman knight, charge of everything in Rome and Italy.[18] When he rose to supreme power, in consideration of the magnitude of the state and the slowness of legal remedies, he selected one of the ex-consuls to overawe the slaves and that part of the population which, unless it fears a strong hand, is disorderly and reckless. Messalla Corvinus[19] was the first to obtain the office, which he gave up within a few days, as not knowing how to discharge it. After him Statilius Taurus,[20] though in advanced years, sustained it admirably; and then Piso, after twenty years of similar credit, was, by the Senate's decree, honored with a public funeral.

12. A motion was next brought forward in the Senate by Quintilianus, a tribune of the people, respecting an alleged Book of the Sibyl. Caninius Gallus, a member of the college of the Fifteen,[21] had asked that it might be received among the other volumes of the same prophetess by a decree on the subject. This having been carried by a division, the Emperor sent a letter in which he gently censured the tribune, as ignorant of ancient usage because of his youth. Gallus he scolded for having introduced the matter in a thin Senate, notwithstanding his long experience in the science of religious ceremonies, without taking the opinion of the college or having the verses read and criticized, as was usual, by its presidents, though their authenticity was very doubtful. He also reminded him that, as many spurious productions were current under a celebrated name, Augustus had prescribed a day within which they should be deposited with the city prætor, and after which it should not be lawful for any private person to hold them. The same regulations too had been made by our ancestors after the burn-

ing of the Capitol in the social war, when there was a search throughout Samos, Ilium, Erythræ, and even in Africa, Sicily, and the Italian colonies for the verses of the Sibyl (whether there were but one or more)[22] and the priests were charged with the business of distinguishing, as far as they could by human means, what were genuine. Accordingly the book in question was now also submitted to the scrutiny of the college of the Fifteen.

13. During the same consulship a high price of corn almost brought on an insurrection. For several days there were many clamorous demands made in the theater with an unusual freedom of language toward the Emperor. This provoked him to censure the magistrates and the Senate for not having used the authority of the state to put down the people. He named too the corn-supplying provinces, and dwelt on the far larger amount of grain imported by himself than by Augustus. So the Senate drew up a decree in the severe spirit of antiquity, and the consuls issued a not less stringent proclamation. The Emperor's silence was not, as he had hoped, taken as a proof of patriotism, but of pride.

14. At the year's close Geminius, Celsus, and Pompeius, Roman knights, fell beneath a charge of conspiracy. Of these Gaius Geminius, a man of lavish expenditure and a luxurious life, had been a friend of Sejanus, but with no serious result. Julius Celsus, a tribune, while in confinement, loosened his chain, and having twisted it around him, broke his neck by throwing himself in an opposite direction. Rubrius Fabatus was put under surveillance, on a suspicion that, in despair of the fortunes of Rome, he meant to throw himself on the mercy of the Parthians. He was, at any rate, found near the Straits of Sicily, and, when dragged back by a centurion, he assigned no adequate reason for his long journey. Still, he lived on in safety, thanks to forgetfulness rather than to mercy.

15. In the consulship of Servius Galba and Lucius Sulla,[23] the Emperor, after having long considered whom he was to choose to be husbands for his granddaughters, now that the maidens were of marriageable age, selected Lucius Cassius[24] and Marcus Vinicius.[25] Vinicius was of

provincial descent; he was born at Cales, his father and grandfather having been consuls, and his family, on the other side, being of the rank of knights. He was a man of amiable temper and of cultivated eloquence. Cassius was of an ancient and honorable, though plebeian, house at Rome. Though he was brought up by his father under a severe training, he won esteem more frequently by his good nature than by his diligence. To him and to Vinicius the Emperor married respectively Drusilla and Julia, Germanicus' daughters, and addressed a letter on the subject to the Senate, with a slightly complimentary mention of the young men. He next assigned some very vague reasons for his absence, then passed to more important matters, the ill will against him originating in his state policy, and requested that Macro, who commanded the prætorians, with a few tribunes and centurions, might accompany him whenever he entered the Senate House. But though a decree was voted by the Senate on a liberal scale and without any restriction as to rank or numbers, he never so much as went near the walls of Rome, much less the state council, for he would often go round and avoid his native city by circuitous routes.

16. Meanwhile a powerful host of accusers fell with sudden fury on the class which systematically increased its wealth by usury in defiance of a law passed by Cæsar the dictator[26] defining the terms of lending money and of holding estates in Italy, a law long obsolete because the public good is sacrificed to private interest. The curse of usury was indeed of old standing in Rome and a most frequent cause of sedition and discord, and it was therefore repressed even in the early days of a less corrupt morality. First, the Twelve Tables[27] prohibited anyone from exacting more than 10 per cent, when, previously, the rate had depended on the caprice of the wealthy. Subsequently, by a bill brought in by the tribunes, interest was reduced to half that amount, and finally compound interest was wholly forbidden. A check too was put by several enactments of the people on evasions which, though continually put down, still, through strange artifices, reappeared. On this occasion, however, Gracchus the prætor, to whose jurisdiction the inquiry

had fallen, felt himself compelled by the number of persons endangered to refer the matter to the Senate. In their dismay the senators, not one of whom was free from similar guilt, threw themselves on the Emperor's indulgence. He yielded, and a year and six months were granted, within which everyone was to settle his private accounts conformably to the requirements of the law.

17. Hence followed a scarcity of money, a great shock being given to all credit, the current coin too, in consequence of the conviction of so many persons and the sale of their property, being locked up in the imperial treasury or the public exchequer. To meet this, the Senate had directed that every creditor should have two-thirds of his capital secured on estates in Italy. Creditors, however, were suing for payment in full, and it was not respectable for persons when sued to break faith. So, at first, there were clamorous meetings and importunate entreaties; then noisy applications to the prætor's court. And the very device intended as a remedy, the sale and purchase of estates, proved the contrary, as the usurers had hoarded up all their money for buying land. The facilities for selling were followed by a fall of prices, and the deeper a man was in debt, the more reluctantly did he part with his property, and many were utterly ruined. The destruction of private wealth precipitated the fall of rank and reputation, till at last the Emperor interposed his aid by distributing throughout the banks a hundred million sesterces, and allowing freedom to borrow without interest for three years, provided the borrower gave security to the state in land to double the amount. Credit was thus restored, and gradually private lenders were found. The purchase too of estates was not carried out according to the letter of the Senate's decree, rigor at the outset, as usual with such matters, becoming negligence in the end.

18. Former alarms then returned, as there was a charge of treason against Considius Proculus. While he was celebrating his birthday without a fear, he was hurried before the Senate, condemned, and instantly put to death. His sister Sancia was outlawed, on the accusation of Quintus Pomponius, a restless spirit, who pretended

that he employed himself in this and like practices to win favor with the sovereign, and thereby alleviate the perils hanging over his brother Pomponius Secundus.[28]

Pompeia Macrina too was sentenced to banishment. Her husband, Argolicus, and her father-in-law, Laco, leading men of Achæa, had been ruined by the Emperor. Her father likewise, an illustrious Roman knight, and her brother, an ex-prætor, seeing their doom was near, destroyed themselves. It was imputed to them as a crime that their great-grandfather Theophanes of Mitylene[29] had been one of the intimate friends of Pompeius the Great, and that after his death Greek flattery had paid him divine honors.

19. Sextus Marius,[30] the richest man in Spain, was next accused of incest with his daughter, and thrown headlong from the Tarpeian Rock. To remove any doubt that the vastness of his wealth had proved the man's ruin, Tiberius kept his gold mines for himself, though they were forfeited to the state. Executions were now a stimulus to his fury, and he ordered the death of all who were lying in prison under accusation of complicity with Sejanus. There lay, singly or in heaps, the unnumbered dead, of every age and sex, the illustrious with the obscure. Kinsfolk and friends were not allowed to be near them, to weep over them, or even to gaze on them too long. Spies were set round them, who noted the sorrow of each mourner and followed the rotting corpses, till they were dragged to the Tiber, where, floating or driven on the bank, no one dared to burn or to touch them. The force of terror had utterly extinguished the sense of human fellowship, and, with the growth of cruelty, pity was thrust aside.

20. About this time Gaius Cæsar, who became his grandfather's companion on his retirement to Capreæ, married Claudia, daughter of Marcus Silanus.[31] He was a man who masked a savage temper under an artful guise of self-restraint, and neither his mother's doom nor the banishment of his brothers extorted from him a single utterance. Whatever the humor of the day with Tiberius, he would assume the like, and his language differed as little. Hence the fame of a clever remark from the orator

Passienus,[32] that "there never was a better slave or a worse master."

I must not pass over a prognostication of Tiberius respecting Servius Galba, then consul. Having sent for him and sounded him on various topics, he at last addressed him in Greek to this effect: "You too, Galba, will someday have a taste of empire." He thus hinted at a brief span of power late in life, on the strength of his acquaintance with the art of astrologers, leisure for acquiring which he had had at Rhodes, with Thrasyllus for instructor. This man's skill he tested in the following manner.

21. Whenever he sought counsel on such matters, he would make use of the top of the house and of the confidence of one freedman, quite illiterate and of great physical strength. The man always walked in front of the person whose science Tiberius had determined to test, through an unfrequented and precipitous path (for the house stood on rocks), and then, if any suspicion had arisen of imposture or of trickery, he hurled the astrologer, as he returned, into the sea beneath, that no one might live to betray the secret. Thrasyllus accordingly was led up the same cliffs, and when he had deeply impressed his questioner by cleverly revealing his imperial destiny and future career, he was asked whether he had also thoroughly ascertained his own horoscope, and the character of that particular year and day. After surveying the positions and relative distances of the stars, he first paused, then trembled, and the longer he gazed, the more was he agitated by amazement and terror, till at last he exclaimed that a perilous and well-nigh fatal crisis impended over him. Tiberius then embraced him and congratulated him on foreseeing his dangers and on being quite safe. Taking what he had said as an oracle, he retained him in the number of his intimate friends.[33]

22. When I hear of these and like occurrences, I suspend my judgment on the question whether it is fate and unchangeable necessity or chance which govern the revolutions of human affairs. Indeed, among the wisest of the ancients and among their disciples you will find conflicting theories, many holding the conviction that heaven

does not concern itself with the beginning or the end of our life, or, in short, with mankind at all; and that therefore sorrows are continually the lot of the good, happiness of the wicked;[34] while others, on the contrary, believe that, though there is a harmony between fate and events, yet it is not dependent on wandering stars, but on primary elements, and on a combination of natural causes.[35] Still, they leave us the capacity of choosing our life, maintaining that, the choice once made, there is a fixed sequence of events. Good and evil, again, are not what vulgar opinion accounts them; many who seem to be struggling with adversity are happy; many, amid great affluence, are utterly miserable, if only the first bear their hard lot with patience, and the latter make a foolish use of their prosperity.

Most men, however, cannot part with the belief that each person's future is fixed from his very birth, but that some things happen differently from what has been foretold through the impostures of those who describe what they do not know, and that this destroys the credit of a science, clear testimonies to which have been given both by past ages and by our own.[36] In fact, how the son of this same Thrasyllus predicted Nero's reign I shall relate when the time comes,[37] not to digress too far from my subject.

23. That same year the death of Asinius Gallus became known. That he died of starvation, there was not a doubt; whether of his own choice or by compulsion was a question. The Emperor was asked whether he would allow him to be buried, and he blushed not to grant the favor, and actually blamed the accident which had proved fatal to the accused before he could be convicted in his presence. Just as if in a three years' interval an opportunity was wanting for the trial of an old ex-consul and the father of a number of ex-consuls.

Next Drusus perished, after having prolonged life for eight days on the most wretched of food, even chewing the stuffing of his bed. According to some writers, Macro had been instructed that, in case of Sejanus attempting an armed revolt, he was to hurry the young prince out of the confinement in which he was detained in the palace and put him at the head of the people. Subsequently the Emperor, as a rumor was gaining ground that he was on the point of a reconciliation with his daughter-in-law and his grandson, chose to be merciless rather than to relent.

24. He even bitterly reviled him after his death, taunting him with nameless abominations and with a spirit bent on his family's ruin and hostile to the state. And, what seemed most horrible of all, he ordered a daily journal of all that he said and did to be read in public. That there had been spies by his side for so many years, to note his looks, his sighs, and even his whispered thoughts, and that his grandfather[38] could have heard read, and published all, was scarce credible. But letters of Attius, a centurion, and Didymus, a freedman, openly exhibited the names of slave after slave who had respectively struck or scared Drusus as he was quitting his chamber. The centurion had actually added, as something highly meritorious, his own language in all its brutality, and some utterances of the dying man in which, at first feigning loss of reason, he imprecated in seeming madness fearful things on Tiberius, and then, when hope of life was gone, denounced him with a studied and elaborate curse. "As he had slain a daughter-in-law, a brother's son, and son's sons, and filled his whole house with bloodshed, so might he pay the full penalty due to the name and race of his ancestors as well as to future generations."

The Senate clamorously interrupted, with an affectation of horror, but they were penetrated by alarm and amazement at seeing that a hitherto cunning prince, who had shrouded his wickedness in mystery, had waxed so bold as to remove, so to speak, the walls of his house and display his grandson under a centurion's lash, amid the buffetings of slaves, craving in vain the last sustenance of life.

25. Men's grief at all this had not died away when news was heard of Agrippina. She had lived on, sustained by hope, I suppose, after the destruction of Sejanus, and, when she found no abatement of horrors, had voluntarily perished, though possibly nourishment was refused her and a fiction concocted of a death that might seem self-

chosen. Tiberius, it is certain, vented his wrath in the foulest charges. He reproached her with unchastity, with having had Asinius Gallus as a paramour and being driven by his death to loathe existence. But Agrippina, who could not endure equality and loved to domineer, was with her masculine aspirations far removed from the frailties of women. The Emperor further observed that she died on the same day on which Sejanus had paid the penalty of his crime two years before, a fact, he said, to be recorded; and he made it a boast that she had not been strangled by the halter and flung down the Gemonian Steps. He received a vote of thanks, and it was decreed that on the 17th of October, the day on which both perished, through all future years, an offering should be consecrated to Jupiter.

26. Soon afterward Cocceius Nerva,[39] a man always at the Emperor's side, a master of law both divine and human, whose position was secure and health sound, resolved to die. Tiberius, as soon as he knew it, sat by him and asked his reasons, adding entreaties, and finally protesting that it would be a burden on his conscience and a blot on his reputation if the most intimate of his friends were to fly from life without any cause for death. Nerva turned away from his expostulations and persisted in his abstinence from all food. Those who knew his thoughts said that as he saw more closely into the miseries of the state, he chose, in anger and alarm, an honorable death, while he was yet safe and unassailed.

Meanwhile Agrippina's ruin, strange to say, dragged Plancina with it. Formerly the wife of Cnæus Piso, and one who had openly exulted at the death of Germanicus, she had been saved, when Piso fell, by the entreaties of Augusta, and not less by the enmity of Agrippina. When hatred and favor had alike passed away, justice asserted itself. Pursued by charges universally notorious, she suffered by her own hand a penalty tardy rather than undeserved.

27. Amid the many sorrows which saddened Rome, one cause of grief[40] was the marriage of Julia, Drusus' daughter and Nero's late wife, into the humbler family of Rubellius Blandus,[41] whose grandfather many remem-

bered as a Roman knight from Tibur. At the end of the
year the death of Ælius Lamia,[42] who, after being at last
released from the farce of governing Syria, had become
city prefect, was celebrated with the honors of a censor's
funeral. He was a man of illustrious descent, and in a
hale old age; and the fact of the province having been
withheld gained him additional esteem. Subsequently, on
the death of Pomponius Flaccus, proprætor of Syria, a
letter from the Emperor was read, in which he complained that all the best men who were fit to command
armies declined the service, and that he was thus necessarily driven to entreaties, by which some of the ex-
consuls might be prevailed on to take provinces. He forgot
that Arruntius had been kept at home now for ten years,
that he might not go to Spain.

That same year Marcus Lepidus also died. I have
dwelled at sufficient length on his moderation and wisdom
in my earlier books,[43] and I need not further enlarge on
his noble descent. Assuredly the family of the Æmilii has
been rich in good citizens, and even the members of that
house whose morals were corrupt still lived with a certain
splendor.

28. During the consulship of Fabius Paulus and Lucius Vitellius,[44] the bird called the phœnix,[45] after a long
succession of ages, appeared in Egypt and furnished the
most learned men of that country and of Greece with
abundant matter for the discusion of the marvelous phe-
nomenon. It is my wish to make known all on which they
agree with several things, questionable enough indeed,
but not too absurd to be noticed.

That it is a creature sacred to the sun, differing from
all other birds in its beak and in the tints of its plumage,
is held unanimously by those who have described its
nature. As to the number of years it lives, there are
various accounts. The general tradition says five hundred years. Some maintain that it is seen at intervals of
1,461 years, and that the former birds flew into the city
called Heliopolis successively in the reigns of Sesosis,
Amasis, and Ptolemy,[46] the third king of the Macedonian
dynasty, with a multitude of companion birds marveling
at the novelty of the appearance. But all antiquity is of

course obscure. From Ptolemy to Tiberius was a period of less than five hundred years. Consequently some have supposed that this was a spurious phœnix, not from the regions of Arabia, and with none of the instincts which ancient tradition has attributed to the bird. For when the number of years is completed and death is near, the phœnix, it is said, builds a nest in the land of its birth and infuses into it a germ of life from which an offspring arises, whose first care, when fledged, is to bury its father. This is not rashly done, but taking up a load of myrrh and having tried its strength by a long flight, as soon as it is equal to the burden and to the journey, it carries its father's body, bears it to the altar of the Sun, and leaves it to the flames. All this is full of doubt and legendary exaggeration. Still, there is no question that the bird is occasionally seen in Egypt.

29. Rome meanwhile being a scene of ceaseless bloodshed, Pomponius Labeo, who was, as I have related, governor of Mœsia, severed his veins and let his life ebb from him. His wife, Paxæa, emulated her husband. What made such deaths eagerly sought was dread of the executioner, and the fact too that the condemned, besides forfeiture of their property, were deprived of burial, while those who decided their fate themselves had their bodies interred, and their wills remained valid, a recompense this for their dispatch. The Emperor, however, argued in a letter to the Senate that it had been the practice of our ancestors, whenever they broke off an intimacy, to forbid the person their house, and so put an end to friendship. "This usage he had himself revived in Labeo's case, but Labeo, being pressed by charges of maladministration in his province and other crimes, had screened his guilt by bringing odium on another, and had groundlessly alarmed his wife, who, though criminal, was still free from danger."

Mamercus Scaurus was then for the second time impeached, a man of distinguished rank and ability as an advocate, but of infamous life.[47] He fell, not through the friendship of Sejanus, but through what was no less powerful to destroy, the enmity of Macro, who practiced the same arts more secretly. Macro's information was grounded on the subject of a tragedy written by Scaurus, from which he cited some verses which might be twisted into allusions to Tiberius. But Servilius and Cornelius, his accusers, alleged adultery with Livia and the practice of magical rites. Scaurus, as befitted the old house of the Æmilii, forestalled the fatal sentence at the persuasion of his wife, Sextia, who urged him to die and shared his death.

30. Still the informers were punished whenever an opportunity occurred. Servilius and Cornelius, for example, whom the destruction of Scaurus had made notorious, were outlawed and transported to some islands for having taken money from Varius Ligur[48] for dropping a prosecution. Abudius Ruso too, who had been an ædile, in seeking to imperil Lentulus Gætulicus, under whom he had commanded a legion, by alleging that he had fixed on a son of Sejanus for his son-in-law, was himself actually condemned and banished from Rome. Gætulicus at this time was in charge of the legions of Upper Germany, and had won from them singular affection, as a man of unbounded kindliness, moderate in his strictness, and popular even with the neighboring army through his father-in-law, Lucius Apronius. Hence rumor persistently affirmed that he had ventured to send the Emperor a letter, reminding him that his alliance with Sejanus had not originated in his own choice but in the advice of Tiberius; that he was himself as liable to be deceived as Tiberius, and that the same mistake ought not to be held innocent in the prince and be a source of ruin to others. His loyalty was still untainted and would so remain, if he was not assailed by any plot. A successor he should accept as an announcement of his doom. A compact, so to say, ought to be sealed between them, by which he should retain his province and the Emperor be master of all else. Strange as this story was, it derived credibility from the fact that Gætulicus alone of all connected with Sejanus lived in safety and in high favor, Tiberius bearing in mind the people's hatred, his own extreme age, and how his government rested more on prestige than on power.

[*Chapters 31 to 37 are omitted. In 35* A.D. *Claudius' favorite, Lucius Vitellius, later infamous for servility but in the government of his province capable of acting, according to Tacitus, with the virtue of an ancient Roman, succeeded first in replacing the pro-Parthian king of Armenia by the Roman candidate, Mithridates, and then in ousting Artabanus himself and replacing him on the Parthian throne by the pro-Roman Tiridates.*]

38. I have related in sequence the events of two summer campaigns, as a relief to the reader's mind from our miseries at home. Though three years had elapsed since the destruction of Sejanus, neither time, entreaties, nor sated gratification, all which have a soothing effect on others, softened Tiberius, or kept him from punishing doubtful or forgotten offenses as most flagrant and recent crimes. Under this dread, Fulcinius Trio, unwilling to face an onslaught of accusers, inserted in his will several terrible imputations on Macro and on the Emperor's principal freedmen, while he taunted the Emperor himself with the mental decay of old age, and the virtual exile of continuous retirement. Tiberius ordered these insults, which Trio's heirs had suppressed, to be publicly read, thus showing his tolerance of free speech in others and his contempt for what was said against him, or, possibly, because he had long been ignorant of the villainies of Sejanus, and now wished any remarks, however reckless, to be published, and so to ascertain, through invective, if it must be so, the truth, which flattery obscures. About the same time Granius Marcianus, a senator, who was accused of treason by Gaius Gracchus,[49] laid hands on himself. Tarius Gratianus too, an ex-prætor, was condemned under the same law to capital punishment.

39. A similar fate befell Trebellenus Rufus[50] and Sextius Paconianus.[51] Trebellenus perished by his own hand; Paconianus was strangled in prison for having there written some lampoons on the Emperor. Tiberius received the news, no longer parted by the sea, as he had been once, or through messengers from a distance, but in close proximity to Rome, so that on the same day, or

after the interval of a single night, he could reply to the dispatches of the consuls, and almost behold the bloodshed as it streamed from house to house, and the strokes of the executioner.

At the year's close Poppæus Sabinus died, a man of somewhat humble extraction, who had risen by his friendship with two emperors to the consulship and the honors of a triumph. During twenty-four years he had the charge of the most important provinces, not for any remarkable ability, but because he was equal to business and was not too good for it.[52]

40. Quintus Plautius and Sextus Papinius were the next consuls.[53] The fact that that year Lucius Aruseius[54] was put to death did not strike men as anything horrible, from their familiarity with evil deeds. But there was a panic when Vibulenus Agrippa, a Roman knight, as soon as his accusers had finished their case, took from his robe, in the very Senate House, a dose of poison, drank it off, and, as he fell expiring, was hurried away to prison by the prompt hands of lictors, where the neck of the now lifeless man was crushed with the halter. Even Tigranes, who had once ruled Armenia and was now impeached, did not escape the punishment of an ordinary citizen on the strength of his royal title.

Gaius Galba[55] meanwhile and the Blæsi[56] perished by a voluntary death; Galba, because a harsh letter from the Emperor forbade him to have a province allotted to him; while, as for the Blæsi, the priesthoods intended for them during the prosperity of their house Tiberius had withheld when that prosperity was shaken, and now conferred, as vacant offices, on others. This they understood as a signal of their doom, and acted on it.

Æmilia Lepida too, whose marriage with the younger Drusus I have already related,[57] who, though she had pursued her husband with ceaseless accusations, remained unpunished, infamous as she was, as long as her father Lepidus lived, subsequently fell a victim to the informers for adultery with a slave. There was no question about her guilt, and so without an attempt at defense she put an end to her life.

[Chapters 41 to 44 are omitted. Tiridates occupied the important city of Seleuceia, on the Orontes, and was crowned at Ctesiphon. But he made the mistake of not quickly completing the occupation of the country; and Artabanus, who had fled to Hyrcania, was able to return and turn the tables on his rival.]

45. That same year Rome suffered from a terrible fire, and part of the circus near the Aventine Hill[58] was burned, as well as the Aventine quarter itself. This calamity the Emperor turned to his own glory by paying the values of the houses and blocks of tenements. A hundred million sesterces was expended in this munificence, a boon all the more acceptable to the populace as Tiberius was rather sparing in building at his private expense. He raised only two structures even at the public cost, the temple of Augustus and the stage of Pompeius theater, and when these were completed, he did not dedicate them, either out of contempt for popularity or from his extreme age. Four commissioners, all husbands of the Emperor's granddaughters—Cnæus Domitius,[59] Cassius Longinus,[60] Marcus Vinicius, Rubellius Blandus[61]—were appointed to assess the damage in each case, and Publius Petronius[62] was added to their number on the nomination of the consuls. Various honors were devised and decreed to the Emperor such as each man's ingenuity suggested. It is a question which of these he rejected or accepted, as the end of his life was so near.

For soon afterward Tiberius' last consuls, Cnæus Aceronius and Gaius Pontius, entered on office,[63] Macro's power being now excessive. Every day the man cultivated more assiduously than ever the favor of Gaius Cæsar, which, indeed, he had never neglected, and after the death of Claudia, who had, as I have related, been married to Gaius,[64] he had prompted his wife, Ennia,[65] to inveigle the young prince by a pretense of love, and to bind him by an engagement of marriage, and the lad, provided he could secure the throne, shrank from no conditions. For though he was of an excitable temper, he had thoroughly learned the falsehoods of hypocrisy under the loving care of his grandfather.

140

46. This the Emperor knew, and he therefore hesitated about bequeathing the Empire, first, between his grandsons. Of these, the son of Drusus was nearest in blood and natural affection, but he was still in his childhood.[66] Germanicus' son was in the vigor of youth and enjoyed the people's favor, a reason for having his grandfather's hatred. Tiberius had even thought of Claudius,[67] as he was of sedate age and had a taste for liberal culture, but a weak intellect was against him. If, however, he were to seek a successor outside of his house, he feared that the memory of Augustus and the name of the Cæsars would become a laughingstock and a scorn. It was, in fact, not so much popularity in the present for which he cared as for glory in the future.

Perplexed in mind, exhausted in body, he soon left to destiny a question to which he was unequal, though he threw out some hints from which it might be inferred that he foresaw what was to come. He taunted Macro, in no obscure terms, with forsaking the setting and looking to the rising sun. Once too when Gaius Cæsar in a casual conversation ridiculed Lucius Sulla, he predicted to him that he would have all Sulla's vices and none of his virtues. At the same moment he embraced the younger of his two grandsons with a flood of tears, and, noting the savage face of the other, said, "You will slay this boy, and will be yourself slain by another." But even while his strength was fast failing, he gave up none of his debaucheries. In his sufferings he would simulate health, and was wont to jest at the arts of the physician and at all who, after the age of thirty, require another man's advice to distinguish between what is beneficial or hurtful to their constitutions.

47. At Rome meanwhile were being sown the seeds of bloodshed to come even after Tiberius' death. Acutia, formerly the wife of Publius Vitellius, had been accused of treason by Lælius Balbus. When on her condemnation a reward was being voted to her prosecutor, Junius Otho,[68] tribune of the people, interposed his veto. Hence a feud between Vitellius and Otho, ending in Otho's banishment. Then Albucilla, notorious for the number of her lovers, who had been married to Satrius Secundus,[69]

the betrayer of the late conspiracy, was charged with ir-
reverence toward the Emperor. With her were involved
as her accomplices and paramours Cnæus Domitius,[70]
Vibius Marsus,[71] and Lucius Arruntius.[72] I have already
spoken of the illustrious rank of Domitius. Marsus too
was distinguished by the honors of his ancestors and by
his own attainments. It was, however, stated in the notes
of the proceedings furnished to the Senate that Macro
had superintended the examination of the witnesses and
the torture of the slaves, and the fact that there was no
letter from the Emperor against the defendants caused
a suspicion that, while he was very feeble and possibly
ignorant of the matter, the charge was to a great extent
invented to gratify Macro's well-known enmity against
Arruntius.

48. And so Domitius and Marsus prolonged their lives,
Domitius preparing his defense, Marsus having apparently resolved on starvation. Arruntius, when his friends
advised delay and temporizing, replied that "the same
conduct was not becoming in all persons. He had had
enough of life, and all he regretted was that he had endured amid scorn and peril an old age of anxious fears,
long detested by Sejanus, now by Macro, always, indeed,
by some powerful minister, not for any fault, but as a
man who could not tolerate gross iniquities. Granted the
possibility of passing safely through the few last days
of Tiberius, how was he to be secure under the youth
of the coming sovereign? Was it probable that, when
Tiberius with his long experience of affairs was, under
the influence of absolute power, wholly perverted and
changed, Gaius Cæsar, who had hardly completed his
boyhood, was thoroughly ignorant, and bred under the
vilest training, would enter on a better course, with
Macro for his guide, who having been selected for his
superior wickedness, to crush Sejanus had by yet more
numerous crimes been the scourge of the state? He
now foresaw a still more galling slavery, and therefore
sought to flee alike from the past and from the impending future."

While he thus spoke like a prophet, he opened his
veins. What followed will be a proof that Arruntius

rightly chose death. Albucilla, having stabbed herself with an ineffectual wound, was by the Senate's order carried off to prison. Those who had ministered to her profligacy, Carsidius Sacerdos, an ex-prætor, and Pontius Fregellanus, were sentenced, respectively, to transportation to an island and to loss of a senator's rank. A like punishment was adjudged in the case of Lælius Balbus, and, indeed, with intense satisfaction, as Balbus was noted for his savage eloquence and his eagerness to assail the innocent.

49. About the same time Sextus Papinius, who belonged to a family of consular rank,[73] chose a sudden and shocking death, by throwing himself from a height. The cause was ascribed to his mother, who, having been repeatedly repulsed in her overtures, had at last by her arts and seductions driven him to an extremity from which he could find no escape but death. She was accordingly put on her trial before the Senate, and, although she groveled at the knees of the senators and long urged a parent's grief, the greater weakness of a woman's mind under such an affliction and other sad and pitiful pleas of the same painful kind, she was after all banished from Rome for ten years, till her younger son would have passed the frail period of youth.

50. Tiberius' bodily powers were now leaving him, but not his skill in dissembling. There was the same stern spirit; he had his words and looks under strict control, and occasionally would try to hide his weakness, evident as it was, by a forced politeness. After frequent changes of place, he at last settled down on the promontory of Misenum[74] in a country house once owned by Lucius Lucullus.[75] It was there discovered that he was drawing near his end, as follows. There was a physician, distinguished in his profession, of the name of Charicles, usually employed, not indeed to have the direction of the Emperor's varying health, but to put his advice at immediate disposal. This man, as if he were leaving on business of his own, clasped his hand, with a show of homage, and touched his pulse. Tiberius noticed it. Whether he was displeased and strove the more to hide his anger is a question; at any rate, he ordered the ban-

quet to be renewed, and sat at the table longer than usual, by way, apparently, of showing honor to his departing friend. Charicles, however, assured Macro that his breath was failing and that he would not last more than two days. All was at once hurry; there were conferences among those on the spot and dispatches to the generals and armies. On the 15th of March, his breath failing, he was believed to have expired, and Gaius Cæsar was going forth with a numerous throng of congratulating followers to take the first possession of the Empire, when suddenly news came that Tiberius was recovering his voice and sight, and calling for persons to bring him food to revive him from his faintness. Then ensued a universal panic, and while the rest fled hither and thither, everyone feigning grief or ignorance, Gaius Cæsar, in silent stupor, passed from the highest hopes to the extremity of apprehension. Macro, nothing daunted, ordered the old Emperor to be smothered under a huge heap of clothes, and all to quit the entrance hall.

51. And so died Tiberius, in his seventy-eighth year. Nero was his father, and he was on both sides descended from the Claudian house, though his mother passed, by adoption, first into the Livian, then into the Julian family. From earliest infancy, perilous vicissitudes were his lot. Himself an exile, he was the companion of a proscribed father,[75] and on being admitted as a stepson into the house of Augustus, he had to struggle with many rivals, so long as Marcellus and Agrippa and, subsequently, Gaius and Lucius Cæsar were in their glory.[77] Again, his brother Drusus enjoyed in a greater degree the affection of the citizens. But he was more than ever on dangerous ground after his marriage with Julia, whether he tolerated or escaped from his wife's profligacy. On his return from Rhodes[78] he ruled the Emperor's now heirless house for twelve years, and the Roman world, with absolute sway, for about twenty-three. His character too had its distinct periods. It was a bright time in his life and reputation while under Augustus he was a private citizen or held high offices; a time of reserve and crafty assumption of virtue, as long as Germanicus and Drusus were alive. Again, while his mother

lived, he was a compound of good and evil; he was infamous for his cruelty, though he veiled his debaucheries, while he loved or feared Sejanus. Finally, he plunged into every wickedness and disgrace when, fear and shame being cast off, he simply indulged his own inclinations.

[*Books VII to X and the first part of Book XI are missing; they contained the whole reign of Gaius (37-41 A.D.) and the first years of the reign of Claudius (41-47).*

Gaius began—as Nero was to do later—with a period of model rule, taking great care to avoid the actions that had done most to make his predecessor unpopular. But after a short time he seems to have developed acute megalomania, insisting on an absurd degree of homage, irresponsibly transferring thrones and altering boundaries in the East and persecuting noble families. In 39, Cnæus Cornelius Lentulus Gætulicus, governor of Upper Germany (Annals VI, 30) and Marcus Æmilius Lepidus, who had been married to the Emperor's deceased sister, Drusilla, were executed for alleged conspiracy. In 41 Gaius was murdered; military officers were the leading figures in the plot, but the two prætorian prefects, the freedman Callistus (Annals XI, 29 ff.), and certain senators were also involved.

After Gaius' murder the consuls proposed the restoration of the Republic. But the prætorian guard insisted on the elevation of Gaius' uncle, Claudius. Claudius was too much influenced by his wife, Valeria Messallina, and by his Greek freedman; but under him much of Gaius' mistaken policy was reversed, and the administration of the Empire was on the whole admirable. In 43 an expeditionary force under Aulus Plautius (Annals XIII, 32) conquered a great part of Britain; Claudius went there for the last stages of the campaign, and the following year celebrated a triumph. But to the leading senators his rule was not acceptable. In 42 Camillus Scribonianus revolted in Dalmatia, only to be quickly crushed; and this was not the only plot against the Emperor. Several important persons fell victims to the intrigues of Messallina; they included Julia, the daughter of Tiberius' son

*Drusus and wife of Rubellius Blandus (Annals VI, 27;
XIII, 32); Catonius Justus, the prætorian_ prefect; and
two great nobles, Cnæus Pompeius Magnus and Marcus
Licinius Crassus Frugi.*

Book XI of the Annals *begins with the description of
Messallina's plot against a rival of whose wealth and
beauty she was jealous. This was Poppæa Sabina, daugh-
ter of the consul and governor of Mœsia, Achæa, and
Macedonia (Annals I, 80), at some time married to Titus
Ollius, but now, it appears, the mistress of the wealthy
Valerius Asiaticus.]*

BOOK XI *47-48 A.D.*

1. Messallina believed that Valerius Asiaticus,[1] who
had been twice consul, was one of Poppæa's old lovers.
At the same time she was looking greedily at the gardens
which Lucullus[2] had begun and which Asiaticus was
now adorning with singular magnificence, and so she
suborned Suillius[3] to accuse both him and Poppæa. With
Suillius was associated Sosibius,[4] tutor to Britannicus,
who was to give Claudius an apparently friendly warning to beware of a power and wealth which threatened
the throne. Asiaticus, he said, had been the ringleader
in the murder of a Cæsar, and then had not feared to
face an assembly of the Roman people, to own the deed,
and challenge its glory for his own. Thus grown famous
in the capital, and with a renown widely spread through
the provinces, he was planning a journey to the armies
of Germany. Born at Vienna, and supported by numerous and powerful connections, he would find it easy to
rouse nations allied to his house. Claudius made no further inquiry, but sent Crispinus,[5] commander of the
prætorians, with troops in hot haste, as though to put
down a revolt. Crispinus found him at Baiæ,[6] loaded him
with chains, and hurried him to Rome.

2. No hearing before the Senate was granted him. It
was in the Emperor's chamber, in the presence of Messallina, that he was heard. There Suillius accused him of
corrupting the troops, of binding them by bribes and in-

146

dulgences to share in every crime, of adultery with Poppæa, and finally of unmanly vice. It was at this last that the accused broke silence, and burst out with the words, "Question your own sons, Suillius; they will certify that I am a man." Then he entered on his defense. Claudius he moved profoundly, and he even drew tears from Messallina. But as she left the chamber to wipe them away, she warned Vitellius[7] not to let the man escape. She hastened herself to effect Poppæa's destruction, and hired agents to drive her to suicide by threatening the terrors of prison. Cæsar meanwhile was so unconscious that a few days afterward he asked her husband Scipio,[8] who was dining with him, why he sat down to table without his wife, and was told in reply that she had paid the debt of nature.

3. When Claudius began to deliberate about the acquittal of Asiaticus, Vitellius, with tears in his eyes, spoke of his old friendship with the accused, and of how they had both frequented the house of the Emperor's mother, Antonia. He then briefly reviewed the services of Asiaticus to the state, his recent part in the invasion of Britain, and everything else which seemed likely to win compassion, and suggested that he should be free to choose his death. Claudius' reply was in the same tone of mercy. Some friends urged on Asiaticus the quiet death of self-starvation, but he declined it with thanks. He took his usual exercise, then bathed and dined cheerfully, and saying that he had better have fallen by the craft of Tiberius or the fury of Gaius Cæsar than by the treachery of a woman and the shameless mouth of Vitellius, he opened his veins, but not till he had inspected his funeral pyre, and directed its removal to another spot, lest the smoke should hurt the thick foliage of the trees. So complete was his calmness even to the last.

4. The senators were then convoked, and Suillius proceeded to find new victims in two knights of the first rank who bore the surname of Petra. The real cause of their destruction was that they had lent their house for the meetings of Mnester and Poppæa. But it was a vision of the night that was the actual charge against one of them. He had, it was alleged, beheld Claudius crowned

with a garland of wheat, the ears of which were turned downward, and, from this appearance, he foretold scanty harvests. Some have said that it was a vine wreath, of which the leaves were white, which he saw, and that he interpreted it to signify the death of the Emperor after the turn of autumn. It is, however, beyond dispute that in consequence of some dream, whatever it was, both the man and his brother perished.

Fifteen hundred thousand sesterces and the insignia of the prætorship were voted to Crispinus.[9] Vitellius bestowed a million on Sosibius, for giving Britannicus the benefit of his teaching and Claudius that of his counsels. I may add that when Scipio was called on for his opinion, he replied, "As I think what all men think about the deeds of Poppæa, suppose me to say what all men say." A graceful compromise this between the affection of the husband and the necessities of the senator.

5. Suillius after this plied his accusations without cessation or pity, and his audacity had many rivals. By assuming to himself all the functions of laws and magistrates, the Emperor had left exposed everything which invited plunder, and of all articles of public merchandise nothing was more venal than the treachery of advocates. Thus it happened that one Samius, a Roman knight of the first rank, who had paid four hundred thousand sesterces to Suillius, stabbed himself in the advocate's house, on learning of his double dealing.[10] Upon this, following the lead of Silius, consul-elect, whose elevation and fall I shall in due course relate, the senators rose in a body, and demanded the enforcement of the Cincian Law, an old enactment, which forbade anyone to receive a fee or a gift for pleading a cause.[11]

6. When the men at whom this strong censure was leveled loudly protested, Silius,[12] who had a quarrel with Suillius, attacked them with savage energy. He cited as examples the orators of old who had thought fame with posterity the fairest recompense of eloquence. And, "apart from this," he said, "the first of noble accomplishments was debased by sordid services, and even good faith could not be upheld in its integrity, when men looked only to the greatness of their gains. If lawsuits

turned to no one's profit, there would be fewer of them. As it was, quarrels, accusations, hatreds, and wrongs were encouraged, in order that, as the violence of disease brings fees to the physician, so the corruption of the forum might enrich the advocate. They should remember Asinius Pollio and Messalla,[13] and, in later days, Arruntius and Æserninus,[14] men raised by a blameless life and by eloquence to the highest honors."

So spoke the consul-elect, and others agreed with him. A resolution was being framed to bring the guilty under the law of extortion, when Suillius and Cossutianus[15] and the rest, who saw themselves threatened with punishment rather than trial, for their guilt was manifest, gathered round the Emperor, and prayed forgiveness for the past.

7. When he had nodded assent, they began to plead their cause. "Who," they asked, "can be so arrogant as to anticipate in hope an eternity of renown? It is for the needs and the business of life that the resource of eloquence is acquired, thanks to which no one, for want of an advocate, is at the mercy of the powerful. But eloquence cannot be obtained for nothing; private affairs are neglected, in order that a man may devote himself to the business of others. Some support life by the profession of arms, some by cultivating land. No work is expected from anyone of which he has not before calculated the profits. It was easy for Asinius and Messalla, enriched with the prizes of the conflict between Antonius and Augustus, it was easy for Arruntius and Æserninus, the heirs of wealthy families, to assume grand airs. We have examples at hand. How great were the fees for which Publius Clodius and Gaius Curio[16] were wont to speak! We are ordinary senators, seeking in the tranquillity of the state for none but peaceful gains. You must consider humble people who gain distinction in the legal profession. Take away the rewards of a profession, and the profession must perish." The Emperor thought that these arguments, though less noble, were not without force. He limited the fee which might be taken to ten thousand sesterces, and those who exceeded this limit were to be liable to the penalties of extortion.

[*Chapters 8-10, which deal with events in Parthia and Armenia, are omitted.*]

11. It was during this consulship, in the eight hundredth year after the foundation of Rome and the sixty-fourth after their celebration by Augustus that the secular games were exhibited.[17] I say nothing of the calculations of the two princes, which I have sufficiently discussed in my history of the Emperor Domitian;[18] for he also exhibited secular games, at which indeed, being one of the priesthood of the Fifteen[19] and prætor at the time, I specially assisted. It is in no boastful spirit that I mention this, but because this duty has immemorially belonged to the college of the Fifteen, and the prætors have performed the chief functions in these ceremonies. While Claudius sat to witness the games of the circus, some of the young nobility acted on horseback the battle of Troy.[20] Among them was Britannicus, the Emperor's son, and Lucius Domitius,[21] who became soon afterward by adoption heir to the Empire with the surname of Nero. The stronger popular enthusiasm which greeted him was taken to presage his greatness. It was commonly reported that snakes had been seen by his cradle, which they seemed to guard, a fabulous tale invented to match the marvels of other lands.[22] Nero, never a disparager of himself, used to say that but one snake, at most, had been seen in his chamber.

12. Something, however, of popular favor was bequeathed to him from the remembrance of Germanicus, whose only male descendant he was, and the pity felt for his mother, Agrippina,[23] was increased by the cruelty of Messallina, who, always her enemy, and then more furious than ever, was only kept from planning an accusation and suborning informers by a new and almost insane passion. She had grown so frantically enamored of Gaius Silius, the handsomest of the young nobility of Rome, that she drove from his bed Junia Silana, a highborn lady, and had her lover wholly to herself. Silius was not unconscious of his wickedness and his peril; but a refusal would have ensured destruction, and he had some hope of escaping exposure; the prize too

150

was great, and so he consoled himself by awaiting the future and enjoying the present. As for her, careless of concealment, she went continually with a numerous retinue to his house, she haunted his steps, showered on him wealth and honors, and, at last, as though empire had passed to another, the slaves, the freedmen, the very furniture of the Emperor were to be seen in the possession of the paramour.

13. Claudius meanwhile, who knew nothing about his wife, and was busy with his functions as censor, published edicts severely rebuking the lawlessness of the people in the theater; because they had insulted Gaius Pomponius,[24] an ex-consul, who furnished verses for the stage, and certain ladies of rank. He introduced too a law restraining the cruel greed of the usurers, and forbidding them to lend at interest sums repayable on a father's death. He also conveyed by an aqueduct[25] into Rome the waters which flow from the hills of Simbrua. And he likewise invented and published for use some new letters,[26] having discovered, as he said, that even the Greek alphabet had not been completed at once.[27]

14. It was the Egyptians who first symbolized ideas, and that by the figures of animals. These records, the most ancient of all human history, are still seen engraved on stone. The Egyptians also claim to have invented the alphabet, which the Phœnicians, they say, by means of their superior seamanship, introduced into Greece, and of which they appropriated the glory, giving out that they had discovered what they had really been taught. Tradition indeed says that Cadmus,[28] visiting Greece with a Phœnician fleet, was the teacher of this art to its yet barbarous tribes. According to one account, it was Cecrops[29] of Athens, or Linus[30] of Thebes, or Palamedes[31] of Argos in Trojan times who invented the shapes of sixteen letters, and others, chiefly Simonides,[32] added the rest. In Italy the Etruscans learned them from Demaratus of Corinth,[33] and the Aborigines[34] from the Arcadian Evander.[35] And so the Latin letters have the same form as the oldest Greek characters. At first too our alphabet was scanty, and additions were afterward made. Following this precedent Claudius added three

letters, which were employed during his reign and subsequently disused. These may still be seen on the tablets of brass set up in the squares and temples, on which new statutes are published.

15. Claudius then brought before the Senate the subject of the college of haruspices, that, as he said, "the oldest of Italian sciences might not be lost through negligence.[36] It had often happened in evil days for the state that advisers had been summoned at whose suggestion ceremonies had been restored and observed more duly for the future. The nobles of Etruria, whether of their own accord or at the instigation of the Roman Senate, had retained this science, making it the inheritance of distinct families. It was now less zealously studied through the general indifference to all sound learning and to the growth of foreign superstitions. At present all is well, but we must show gratitude to the favor of heaven, by taking care that the rites observed during times of peril may not be forgotten in prosperity." A resolution of the Senate was accordingly passed, charging the pontiffs to see what should be retained or reformed with respect to the haruspices.

[Chapters 6 to 21 are omitted. The Cherusci asked Rome for a king and were sent Italicus, son of Arminius, who had been captured as a child and had been brought up in Italy; he made a good beginning, but later became a tyrant and was expelled. A rebellion of the Chauci was suppressed by Corbulo, later famous for his victories in the East.]

22. At Rome meanwhile, without any motive then known or subsequently ascertained, Cnæus Nonius, a Roman knight, was found wearing a sword amid a crowd who were paying their respects to the Emperor. The man confessed his own guilt when he was being torn in pieces by torture, but gave up no accomplices, perhaps having none to hide.

During the same consulship, Publius Dolabella proposed that a spectacle of gladiators should be annually exhibited at the cost of those who obtained the quæstorship.[37] In our ancestors' days such honors had been a reward of virtue, and every citizen, with good qualities to support him, was allowed to compete for office. At first there were no distinctions even of age, which prevented a man in his early youth from becoming a consul or a dictator.[38] The quæstors indeed were appointed while the kings still ruled, and this the revival by Brutus of the Lex Curiata[39] plainly shows. The consuls retained the power of selecting them, till the people bestowed this office as well as others. The first so created were Valerius Potitus and Mamercus Æmilius[40] sixty-three years after the expulsion of the Tarquins, and they were to attend to military affairs. As the public business increased, two more were appointed to attend to affairs at Rome. This number was again doubled, when to the contributions of Italy was added the tribute of the provinces. Subsequently Sulla, by one of his laws, provided that twenty should be elected to fill up the Senate, to which he had entrusted judicial functions. These functions the knights afterward recovered, but the quæstorship was obtained, without expense, by merit in the candidates or by the good nature of the electors, till at Dolabella's suggestion it was, so to speak, put up to sale.

23. In the consulship of Aulus Vitellius and Lucius Vipstanus[41] the question of filling up the Senate was discussed, and the chief men of Gallia Comata, as it was called,[42] who had long possessed the rights of allies and of Roman citizens, sought the privilege of obtaining public offices at Rome. There was much talk of every kind on the subject, and it was argued before the Emperor with vehement opposition. "Italy," it was asserted, "is not so feeble as to be unable to furnish its own capital with a senate. Once our native-born citizens sufficed for peoples of our own kin, and we are by no means dissatisfied with the Rome of the past. To this day we cite examples, which under our old customs the Roman character exhibited as to valor and renown. Is it a small thing that Veneti[43] and Insubres have already burst into the Senate House, unless a mob of foreigners, a troop of captives, so to say, is now forced upon us? What distinctions will be left for the remnants of our

noble houses, or for any impoverished senators from Latium? Every place will be crowded with these millionaires, whose ancestors of the second and third generations at the head of hostile tribes destroyed our armies with fire and sword, and actually besieged the divine Julius at Alesia.[44] These are recent memories. What if there were to rise up the remembrance of those who fell in Rome's citadel and at her altar by the hands of these same barbarians![45] Let them enjoy indeed the title of citizens, but let them not vulgarize the distinctions of the Senate and the honors of office."

24. These and like arguments failed to impress the Emperor. He at once addressed himself to answer them, and thus harangued the assembled Senate. "My ancestors, the most ancient of whom was made at once a citizen and a noble of Rome, encourage me to govern by the same policy of transferring to this city all conspicuous merit, wherever found. And indeed I know, as facts, that the Julii came from Alba,[46] the Coruncanii from Camerium,[47] the Porcii from Tusculum,[48] and not to inquire too minutely into the past, that new members have been brought into the Senate from Etruria and Lucania and the whole of Italy, that Italy itself was at last extended to the Alps, to the end that not only single persons but entire countries and tribes might be united under our name. We had unshaken peace at home; we prospered in all our foreign relations, in the days when Italy beyond the Po was admitted to share our citizenship, and when, enrolling in our ranks the most vigorous of the provincials, under color of settling our legions throughout the world, we recruited our exhausted Empire. Are we sorry that the Balbi came to us from Spain,[49] and other men not less illustrious from Narbonese Gaul?[50] Their descendants are still among us, and do not yield to us in patriotism.

"What was the ruin of Sparta and Athens but this, that mighty as they were in war, they spurned from them as aliens those whom they had conquered? Our founder, Romulus, on the other hand, was so wise that he fought as enemies and then hailed as fellow citizens several nations on the very same day. Strangers have reigned over us,[51] That freedmen's sons should be entrusted with public offices is not, as many wrongly think, a sudden innovation, but was a common practice in the old commonwealth. But, it will be said, we have fought with the Senones. I suppose then that the Volsci and Ædui[52] never stood in array against us! Our city was taken by the Gauls. Well, we also gave hostages to the Etruscans,[53] and passed under the yoke of the Samnites. On the whole, if you review all our wars, never has one been finished in a shorter time than that with the Gauls. Thenceforth they have preserved an unbroken and loyal peace. United as they now are with us by manners, education, and intermarriage, let them bring us their gold and their wealth rather than enjoy it in isolation. Everything, senators, which we now hold to be of the highest antiquity, was once new. Plebeian magistrates came after patrician,[54] Latin magistrates after plebeian; magistrates of other Italian peoples after Latin. This practice too will establish itself, and what we are this day justifying by precedents, will be itself a precedent."

25. The Emperor's speech was followed by a decree of the Senate, and the Ædui were the first to obtain the right of becoming senators at Rome. This compliment was paid to their ancient alliance, and to the fact that they alone of the Gauls cling to the name of brothers of the Roman people.

About the same time the Emperor enrolled in the ranks of the patricians such senators as were of the oldest families, and such as had had distinguished ancestors. There were now but scanty relics of the greater houses of Romulus and of the lesser houses of Lucius Brutus,[55] as they had been called, and those too were exhausted which the dictator Cæsar by the Cassian[56] and the Emperor Augustus by the Sænian Law had chosen into their place. These acts, as being welcome to the state, were undertaken with hearty gladness by the imperial censor. Anxiously considering how he was to rid the Senate of men of notorious infamy, he preferred a gentle method, recently devised, to one which accorded with the sternness of antiquity, and advised each to examine his own case and seek the privilege of laying aside his rank. Per-

155

mission, he said, would be readily obtained. He would publish in the same list those who had -been expelled and those who had been allowed to retire, that by this confounding together of the decision of the censors and the modesty of voluntary resignation the disgrace might be softened.

For this, the consul Vipstanus moved that Claudius should be called "father of the senate." The title "father of the country" had, he argued, been indiscriminately bestowed;[57] new services ought to be recognized by unusual titles. The Emperor, however, himself stopped the consul's flattery, as extravagant. He closed the lustrum,[58] the census for which gave a total of 5,984,072 citizens. Then too ended his blindness as to his domestic affairs. He was soon compelled to notice and punish his wife's infamies; afterward, his passion involved him in an incestuous union.

26. Messallina, now grown weary of the very facility of her adulteries, was rushing into strange excesses, when even Silius, either through some fatal infatuation or because he imagined that, amid the dangers which hung over him, danger itself was the best safety, urged the breaking off of all concealment. "They were not," he said, "in such an extremity as to have to wait for the Emperor's old age. Harmless measures were for the innocent. Crime once exposed had no refuge but in audacity. They had accomplices in all who feared the same fate. For himself, as he had neither wife nor child, he was ready to marry and to adopt Britannicus. Messallina would have the same power as before, with the additional advantage of a quiet mind, if only they took Claudius by surprise, who, though unsuspicious of treachery, was hasty in his wrath."

The suggestion was coldly received, not because the lady loved her husband, but from a fear that Silius, after attaining his highest hopes, would spurn an adulteress, and soon estimate at its true value the crime which in the midst of peril he had approved. But she craved the name of wife, for the sake of the monstrous infamy, that last source of delight to the reckless. She waited only till Claudius set out for Ostia[59] to perform

156

a sacrifice, and then celebrated all the solemnities of marriage.

27. I am well aware that it will seem a fable that any persons in the world could have been so obtuse in a city which knows everything and hides nothing, much more, that these persons should have been a consul-elect and the Emperor's wife; that, on an appointed day, before witnesses duly summoned, they should have come together as if for the purpose of legitimate marriage; that she should have listened to the words of the bridegroom's friends, should have sacrificed to the gods, have taken her place among a company of guests, have lavished her kisses and caresses, and passed the night in the freedom which marriage permits. But this is no story invented to excite wonder; I only relate what I have heard and what our fathers have recorded.

28. The Emperor's court indeed shuddered, especially its powerful personages, the men who had much to fear from a revolution. From secret whisperings they passed to loud complaints. "When an actor," they said, "impudently thrust himself into the imperial chamber,[60] it certainly brought scandal to the state, but we were a long way from ruin. Now a young noble of stately beauty, of vigorous intellect, with the near prospect of the consulship, is preparing himself for a loftier ambition. There can be no secret about what is to follow such a marriage." Doubtless there was a thrill of alarm when they thought of the apathy of Claudius, of his devotion to his wife and of the many murders perpetrated at Messallina's bidding. On the other hand, the very pliability of the Emperor inspired confident hope that if they could overpower him by the enormity of the charge, she might be condemned and crushed before she was accused. The critical point was this, that he should not hear her defense, and that his ears should be shut even against her confession.

29. At first Callistus,[61] of whom I have already spoken in connection with the assassination of Gaius Cæsar, Narcissus, who had contrived the death of Appius, and Pallas, who was then in the height of favor, debated whether they might not by secret threats turn Messallina

from her passion for Silius, while they concealed all else. Then fearing that they would be themselves involved in ruin, they abandoned the idea, Pallas out of cowardice, and Callistus, from his experience of a former court, remembering that prudent rather than vigorous counsels ensure the maintenance of power. Narcissus persevered, only so far changing his plan as not to make her aware beforehand by a single word what was the charge or who was the accuser. Then he eagerly watched his opportunity, and, as the Emperor lingered long at Ostia, he sought two of the concubines to whose society Claudius was especially partial, and, by gifts, by promises, by dwelling on power increased by the wife's fall, he induced them to undertake the work of the informer.

30. On this, Calpurnia (that was the woman's name), as soon as she was allowed a private interview, threw herself at the Emperor's knees, crying out that Messallina was married to Silius. At the same time she asked Cleopatra, who was standing near and waiting for the question, whether she knew it. Cleopatra nodding assent, she begged that Narcissus might be summoned. Narcissus entreated pardon for the past, for having concealed the scandal while confined to a Vettius or a Plautius.[62] Even now, he said, he would not make charges of adultery, and seem to be asking back the palace, the slaves, and the other belongings of imperial rank. These Silius might enjoy; only, he must give back the wife and annul the act of marriage. "Do you know," he said, "of your divorce? The people, the army, the Senate saw the marriage of Silius. Act at once, or the new husband is master of Rome."

31. Claudius then summoned all his most powerful friends. First he questioned Turranius, superintendent of the corn market,[63] next, Lusius Geta, who commanded the prætorians. When they confessed the truth, the whole company clamored in concert that he must go to the camp, must assure himself of the prætorian cohorts, must think of safety before he thought of vengeance. It is quite certain that Claudius was so overwhelmed by terror that he repeatedly asked whether he was indeed

in possession of the Empire, whether Silius was still a subject.

Messallina meanwhile, more wildly profligate than ever, was celebrating in mid-autumn a representation of the vintage in her new home. The presses were being trodden; the vats were overflowing; women girt with skins were dancing, as Bacchanals dance in their worship or their frenzy. Messallina with flowing hair shook the thyrsus, and Silius at her side, crowned with ivy and wearing the buskin, moved his head to some lascivious chorus. It is said that one Vettius Valens[64] climbed a very lofty tree in sport, and when they asked him what he saw, replied, "A terrible storm from Ostia." Possibly some such appearance had begun; perhaps a word dropped by chance became a prophecy.

32. Meanwhile no mere rumor but messengers from all parts brought the news that everything was known to Claudius, and that he was coming, bent on vengeance. Messallina upon this went to the gardens of Lucullus,[65] Silius, to conceal his fear, to his business in the forum. The other guests were flying in all directions when the centurions appeared and put everyone in irons where they found them, either in the public streets or in hiding. Messallina, though her peril took away all power of thought, promptly resolved to meet and face her husband, a course in which she had often found safety; while she bade Britannicus and Octavia[66] hasten to embrace their father. She besought Vibidia, the eldest of the Vestal Virgins, to demand audience of the supreme pontiff and to beg for mercy. Meanwhile, with only three companions, so lonely did she find herself in a moment, she traversed the whole length of the city, and, mounting on a cart used to remove garden refuse, proceeded along the road to Ostia; not pitied, so overpoweringly hideous were her crimes, by a single person.

33. There was equal alarm on the Emperor's side. They put but little trust in Geta, who commanded the prætorians, a man swayed with equal ease to good or evil. Narcissus, in concert with others who dreaded the same fate, declared that the only hope of safety for the Emperor lay in his transferring for that one day the

159

command of the soldiers to one of the freedmen, and he offered to undertake it himself. And that Claudius might not be induced by Lucius Vitellius and Largus Cæcina[67] to repent, while he was riding into Rome, he asked and took a seat in the Emperor's carriage.

34. It was currently reported in after times that while the Emperor broke into contradictory exclamations, now inveighing against the infamies of his wife, and now returning in thought to the remembrance of his love and of his infant children, Vitellius said nothing but "What audacity! What wickedness!" Narcissus indeed kept pressing him to clear up his ambiguities and let the truth be known, but still he could not prevail upon him to utter anything that was not vague and susceptible of any meaning which might be put on it, or upon Largus Cæcina to do anything but follow his example. And now Messallina had presented herself, and was insisting that the Emperor should listen to the mother of Octavia and Britannicus, when the accuser roared out at her the story of Silius and her marriage. At the same moment, to draw Cæsar's eyes away from her, he handed him some papers which detailed her debaucheries. Soon afterward, as he was entering Rome, his children by Messallina were to have shown themselves, had not Narcissus ordered their removal. Vibidia he could not repel, when, with a vehemently indignant appeal, she demanded that a wife should not be given up to death without a hearing. So Narcissus replied that the Emperor would hear her, and that she should have an opportunity of disproving the charge. Meanwhile the holy virgin was to go and discharge her sacred duties.

35. All throughout, Claudius preserved a strange silence; Vitellius seemed unconscious. Everything was under the freedman's control. By his order, the paramour's house was thrown open and the Emperor conducted thither. First, on the threshold, he pointed out the statue of Silius' father, which a decree of the Senate had directed to be destroyed; next, how the heirlooms of the Neros and the Drusi had been degraded into the price of infamy. Then he led the Emperor, furious and bursting out in menace, into the camp, where the sol-

diers were purposely assembled. Claudius spoke to them a few words at the dictation of Narcissus. Shame indeed checked the utterance even of a righteous anger. Instantly there came a shout from the cohorts, demanding the names of the culprits and their punishment. Brought before the tribunal, Silius sought neither defense nor delay, but begged that his death might be hastened. A like courage made several Roman knights of the first rank desirous of a speedy doom. Titius Proculus, who had been appointed to watch Messallina and was now offering his evidence, Vettius Valens, who confessed his guilt, together with Pompeius Urbicus and Saufeius Trogus from among her accomplices, were ordered to execution. Decius Calpurnianus too, commander of the watch, Sulpicius Rufus, who had the charge of the games, and Juncus Virgilianus, a senator, were similarly punished.

36. Mnester alone occasioned a pause. Rending off his clothes, he insisted on Claudius looking at the scars of his stripes and remembering his words when he surrendered himself, without reserve, to Messallina's bidding. The guilt of others had been the result of presents or of large promises; his, of necessity. He must have been the first victim had Silius obtained empire.

Cæsar was touched by his appeal and inclined to mercy, but his freedmen prevailed on him not to let any indulgence be shown to a player when so many illustrious citizens had fallen. "It mattered not whether he had sinned so greatly from choice or compulsion." Even the defense of Traulus Montanus, a Roman knight, was not admitted. A young man of pure life, yet a singular beauty, he had been summoned and dismissed within the space of one night by Messallina, who was equally capricious in her passions and dislikes. In the cases of Suillius[68] Cæsoninus and Plautius Lateranus,[69] the extreme penalty was remitted. The latter was saved by the distinguished services of his uncle; the former by his very vices, having amid that abominable throng submitted to the worst degradation.

37. Messallina meanwhile, in the gardens of Lucullus, was struggling for life, and writing letters of entreaty,

161

as she alternated between hope and fury. In her extremity, it was her pride alone which forsook her. Had not Narcissus hurried on her death, ruin would have recoiled on her accuser. Claudius had returned home to an early banquet; then, in softened mood, when the wine had warmed him, he bade someone go and tell the "poor creature" (this is the word which they say he used) to come on the morrow and plead her cause. Hearing this, seeing too that his wrath was subsiding and his passion returning, and fearing, in the event of delay, the effect of approaching night and conjugal recollections, Narcissus rushed out and ordered the centurions and the tribunes, who were on guard, to accomplish the deed of blood. Such, he said, was the Emperor's bidding. Evodus, one of the freedmen, was appointed to watch and complete the affair. Hurrying on before with all speed to the gardens, he found Messallina stretched upon the ground, while by her side sat Lepida, her mother,[70] who, though estranged from her daughter in prosperity, was now melted to pity by her inevitable doom, and urged her not to wait for the executioner. "Life," she said, "was over; all that could be looked for was honor in death." But in that heart, utterly corrupted by profligacy, nothing noble remained. She still prolonged her tears and idle complaints, till the gates were forced open by the rush of the newcomers, and there stood at her side the tribune, sternly silent, and the freedman, overwhelming her with the copious insults of a servile tongue.

38. Then for the first time she understood her fate and put her hand to a dagger. In her terror she was applying it ineffectually to her throat and breast, when a blow from the tribune drove it through her. Her body was given up to her mother. Claudius was still at the banquet when they told him that Messallina was dead, without mentioning whether it was by her own or another's hand. Nor did he ask the question, but called for the cup and finished his repast as usual. During the days which followed he showed no sign of hatred or joy or anger or sadness, in a word, of any human emotion, either when he looked on her triumphant accusers

or on her weeping children. The Senate assisted his forgetfulness by decreeing that her name and her statues should be removed from all places, public or private. To Narcissus were voted the decorations of the quæstorship, a mere trifle to the pride of one who rose in the height of his power above Pallas or Callistus.

BOOK XII *48-54 A.D.*

1. THE destruction of Messallina shook the imperial house; for a strife arose among the freedmen, who should choose a wife for Claudius, impatient as he was of a single life and submissive to the rule of wives. The ladies were fired with no less jealousy. Each insisted on her rank, beauty, and fortune, and pointed to her claims to such a marriage. But the keenest competition was between Lollia Paulina, the daughter,[1] of Marcus Lollius, an ex-consul, and Julia Agrippina,[2] the daughter of Germanicus. Callistus favored the first, Pallas the second. Ælia Pætina,[3] however, of the family of the Tuberones, had the support of Narcissus. The Emperor, who inclined now one way, now another, as he listened to this or that adviser, summoned the disputants to a conference and bade them express their opinions and give their reasons.

2. Narcissus dwelt on the marriage of years gone by, on the tie of offspring, for Pætina was the mother of Claudius' daughter Antonia, and on the advantage of excluding a new element from his household, by the return of a wife to whom he was accustomed, and who would assuredly not look with a stepmother's animosity on Britannicus and Octavia, who were next in her affections to her own children. Callistus argued that she was compromised by her long separation, and that were she to be taken back, she would be supercilious on the strength of it. It would be far better to introduce Lollia, for, as she had no children of her own, she would be free from jealousy, and would take the place of a mother toward her stepchildren.

Pallas again selected Agrippina for special commendation because she would bring with her Germanicus' grandson, who was thoroughly worthy of imperial rank, the scion of a noble house and a link to unite the descendants of the Claudian family. He hoped that a woman who was the mother of many children and still in the freshness of youth would not carry off the grandeur of the Cæsars to some other house.

3. This advice prevailed, backed up as it was by Agrippina's charms. On the pretext of her relationship, she paid frequent visits to her uncle, and so won his heart that she was preferred to the others, and, though not yet his wife, already possessed a wife's power. For as soon as she was sure of her marriage, she began to aim at greater things, and planned an alliance between Domitius, her son by Cnæus Ahenobarbus, and Octavia, the Emperor's daughter. This could not be accomplished without a crime, for the Emperor had betrothed Octavia to Lucius Silanus,[4] a young man otherwise famous, whom he had brought forward as a candidate for popular favor by the honor of triumphal distinctions and by a magnificent gladiatorial show. But no difficulty seemed to be presented by the temper of a sovereign who had neither partialities nor dislikes, but such as were suggested and dictated to him.

4. Accordingly Vitellius, who used the name of censor to screen a slave's trickeries, and looked forward to new despotisms, already impending, associated himself in Agrippina's plans, with a view to her favor, and began to bring charges against Silanus, whose sister, Junia Calvina, a handsome and lively girl,[5] had shortly before become his daughter-in-law. Here was a starting point for an accuser. Vitellius put an infamous construction on the somewhat incautious though not criminal love between the brother and sister. The Emperor listened, for his affection for his daughter inclined him the more to admit suspicions against his son-in-law. Silanus meanwhile, who knew nothing of the plot, and happened that year to be prætor, was suddenly expelled from the Senate by an edict of Vitellius, though the roll of senators had been recently reviewed and the lustrum closed.[6] Claudius at the same time broke off the connec-

tion; Silanus was forced to resign his office, and the one remaining day of his prætorship was conferred on Eprius Marcellus.[7]

5. In the year of the consulship of Gaius Pompeius and Quintus Veranius,[8] the marriage arranged between Claudius and Agrippina was confirmed both by popular rumor and by their own illicit love. Still, they did not yet dare to celebrate the nuptials in due form, for there was no precedent for the introduction of a niece into an uncle's house. It was positively incest, and if disregarded, it would, people feared, issue in calamity to the state. These scruples ceased not till Vitellius undertook the management of the matter in his own way. He asked the Emperor whether he would yield to the recommendations of the people and to the authority of the Senate. When Claudius replied that he was one among the citizens and could not resist their unanimous voice, Vitellius requested him to wait in the palace, while he himself went to the Senate. Protesting that the supreme interest of the commonwealth was at stake, he begged to be allowed to speak first, and then began to urge that the very burdensome labors of the Emperor in a world-wide administration required assistance, so that, free from domestic cares, he might consult the public welfare. How again could there be a more virtuous relief for the mind of an imperial censor than the taking of a wife to share his prosperity and his troubles, to whom he might entrust his inmost thoughts and the care of his young children, unused as he was to luxury and pleasure, and wont from his earliest youth to obey the laws?

6. Vitellius, having first put forward these arguments in a conciliatory speech, and met with decided acquiescence from the Senate, began afresh to point out that, as they all recommended the Emperor's marriage, they ought to select a lady conspicuous for noble rank and purity, herself too the mother of children. "It cannot," he said, "be long a question that Agrippina stands first in nobility of birth. She has given proof, too, that she is not barren, and she has suitable moral qualities. It is indeed a singular advantage to us, due to divine providence, that

she is a widow, ready to be united to an Emperor who has only such experience of matrimony as he has had.[9] We have heard from our fathers, we have ourselves seen that married women were seized at the caprice of the Cæsars. This is quite alien to the propriety of our day. Rather let a precedent be now set for the taking of a wife by an emperor. But, it will be said, marriage with a brother's daughter is with us a novelty. True; but it is common in other countries, and there is no law to forbid it. Marriages of cousins were long unknown, but after a time they became frequent. Custom adapts itself to expediency, and this novelty will hereafter take its place among recognized usages."[10]

7. There were some who rushed out of the Senate, passionately protesting that if the Emperor hesitated, they would use violence. A promiscuous throng assembled, and kept exclaiming that the same too was the prayer of the Roman people. Claudius without further delay presented himself in the forum to their congratulations; then, entering the Senate, he asked from them a decree which should decide that for the future marriages between uncles and brothers' daughters should be legal. There was, however, found only one person who desired such a marriage, Alledius Severus, a Roman knight, who, as many said, was swayed by the influence of Agrippina. Then came a revolution in the state, and everything was under the control of a woman, who did not, like Messallina, insult Rome by loose manners. It was a stringent and, so to say, masculine despotism; there was sternness and generally arrogance in public, no sort of immodesty at home, unless it conduced to power. A boundless greed of wealth was veiled under the pretext that riches were being accumulated as a prop to the throne.

8. On the day of the marriage Silanus committed suicide, having up to that time prolonged his hope of life, or else choosing that day to heighten the popular indignation. His sister, Calvina, was banished from Italy.[11] Claudius further added that sacrifices after the ordinances of King Tullius[12] and atonements were to be offered by the pontiffs in the grove of Diana, amid gen-

eral ridicule at the idea of devising penalties and propitiations for incest at such a time. Agrippina, that she
might not be conspicuous only by her evil deeds, procured for Annæus Seneca[13] a remission of his exile, and
with it the prætorship. She thought this would be universally welcome, from the celebrity of his attainments,
and it was her wish too for the boyhood of Domitius to
be trained under so excellent an instructor, and for
them to have the benefit of his counsels in their designs
on the throne. For Seneca, it was believed, was devoted
to Agrippina from a remembrance of her kindness, and
an enemy to Claudius from a bitter sense of wrong.

9. It was then resolved to delay no longer. Memmius
Pollio, the consul-elect, was induced by great promises to
deliver a speech, praying Claudius to betroth Octavia
to Domitius.[14] The match was not unsuitable to the age
of either, and was likely to develop still more important
results. Pollio introduced the motion in much the same
language as Vitellius had lately used. So Octavia was
betrothed, and Domitius, besides his previous relationship, became now the Emperor's designate son-in-law,
and an equal of Britannicus, through the exertions of his
mother and the cunning of those who had been the
accusers of Messallina, and feared the vengeance of
her son.

[*Chapters 10-21 are omitted; they describe events in Parthia and Pontus.*]

22. In the same consulship, Agrippina, who was terrible in her hatred and detested Lollia,[15] for having
competed with her for the Emperor's hand, planned an
accusation, through an informer who was to tax her
with having consulted astrologers and magicians and
the image of the Clarian Apollo, about the imperial marriage. Upon this, Claudius, without hearing the accused,
first reminded the Senate of her illustrious rank, that
the sister of Lucius Volusius[16] was her mother, Cotta
Messallinus[17] her granduncle, Memmius Regulus formerly her husband (for of her marriage to Gaius Cæsar
he purposely said nothing), and then added that she

had mischievous designs on the state, and must have the means of crime taken from her. Consequently, her property should be confiscated, and she herself banished from Italy. Thus out of immense wealth only five million sesterces were left to the exile. Calpurnia too, a lady of high rank, was ruined, simply because the Emperor had praised her beauty in a casual remark, without any passion for her. And so Agrippina's resentment stopped short of extreme vengeance. A tribune was dispatched to Lollia, who was to force her to suicide. Next, on the prosecution of the Bithynians, Cadius Rufus was condemned under the law against extortion.

23. Narbonese Gaul,[18] for its special reverence of the Senate, received a privilege. Senators belonging to the province, without seeking the Emperor's approval, were to be allowed to visit their estates, a right enjoyed by Sicily. Ituræa[19] and Judæa, on the death of their kings, Sohæmus and Agrippa,[20] were annexed to the province of Syria.

It was also decided that the augury of the public safety,[21] which for seventy-five years had been neglected, should be revived and henceforth observed. The Emperor likewise widened the sacred precincts of the capital, in conformity with the ancient usage according to which those who had enlarged the Empire were permitted also to extend the boundaries of Rome. But Roman generals, even after the conquest of great nations, had never exercised this right, except Lucius Sulla and the divine Augustus.[22]

24. There are various popular accounts of the ambitious and vainglorious efforts of our kings in this matter. Still, I think, it is interesting to know accurately the original plan of the precinct, as it was fixed by Romulus. From the Ox Market,[23] where we see the brazen statue of a bull, because that animal is yoked to the plow, a furrow was drawn to mark out the town, so as to embrace the great altar of Hercules;[24] then, at regular intervals, stones were placed along the foot of the Palatine Hill to the altar of Consus,[25] soon afterward, to the old assembly places, and then to the chapel of the Lares.[26] The Roman forum and the Capitol were not, it

was supposed, added to the city by Romulus, but by Titus Tatius. In time, the precinct was enlarged with the growth of Rome's fortunes. The boundaries now fixed by Claudius may be easily recognized, as they are specified in the public records.

25. In the consulship of Gaius Antistius and Marcus Suillius,[27] the adoption of Domitius was hastened on by the influence of Pallas. Bound to Agrippina, first as the promoter of her marriage, then as her paramour, he urged Claudius to think of the interests of the state, and to provide some support for the tender years of Britannicus. "So," he said, "it had been with the divine Augustus, whose stepsons, though he had grandsons to be his stay, had been promoted; Tiberius too, though he had offspring of his own, had adopted Germanicus. Claudius also would do well to strengthen himself with a young prince who could share his cares with him."

Overcome by these arguments, the Emperor preferred Domitius to his own son, though he was but two years older,[28] and made a speech in the Senate, the same in substance as the representations of his freedman. It was noted by learned men that no previous example of adoption into the patrician family of the Claudii was to be found; and that from Attus Clausus[29] there had been one unbroken line.

26. However, the Emperor received formal thanks, and still more elaborate flattery was paid to Domitius. A law was passed, adopting him into the Claudian family with the name of Nero.[30] Agrippina too was honored, with the title of Augusta. When this had been done, there was not a person so void of pity as not to feel keen sorrow at the position of Britannicus. Gradually forsaken by the very slaves who waited on him, he turned into ridicule the ill-timed attentions of his stepmother, perceiving their insincerity. For he is said to have had by no means a dull understanding; either this is a fact, or perhaps his perils won him sympathy, and so he possessed the credit of it, without actual evidence.

27. Agrippina, to show her power even to the allied nations, procured the dispatch of a colony of veterans to

the chief town of the Ubii, where she was born. The place was named after her.[31] Agrippa, her grandfather, had, as it happened, received this tribe, when they crossed the Rhine, under our protection.[32]

During the same time, there was a panic in Upper Germany through an irruption of plundering bands of Chatti. Thereupon Publius Pomponius,[33] who was in command, directed the Vangiones and Nemetes, with the allied cavalry, to anticipate the raid, and suddenly to fall upon them from every quarter while they were dispersed. The general's plan was backed up by the energy of the troops. These were divided into two columns; and those who marched to the left cut off the plunderers, just on their return, after a riotous enjoyment of their spoil, when they were heavy with sleep. It added to the men's joy that they had rescued from slavery after forty years some survivors of the defeat of Varus.

28. The column which took the right-hand, and the shorter, route, inflicted greater loss on the enemy who met them, and ventured on a battle. With much spoil and glory they returned to Mount Taunus,[34] where Pomponius was waiting with the legions, to see whether the Chatti, in their eagerness for vengeance, would give him a chance of fighting. However, fearing to be hemmed in on one side by the Romans, on the other by the Cherusci, with whom they are perpetually at feud, they sent envoys and hostages to Rome. To Pomponius was decreed the honor of a triumph, a mere fraction of his renown with the next generation, with whom his poems constitute his chief glory.

[Chapters 29-30 are omitted; they deal with the affairs of the Suebi and the Iazyges.]

31. Meanwhile, in Britain, Publius Ostorius,[35] the proprætor, found himself confronted by disturbances. The enemy had burst into the territories of our allies with all the more fury, as they imagined that a new general would not march against them with winter beginning and with an army of which he knew nothing.

Ostorius, well aware that first events are those which produce alarm or confidence, by a rapid movement of his light cohorts cut down all who opposed him, pursued those who fled, and lest they should rally, and so an unquiet and treacherous peace might allow no rest to the general and his troops, he prepared to disarm all whom he suspected, and to occupy with encampments the whole country that side of the Trent and Severn. The Iceni,[36] a powerful tribe, which war had not weakened, as they had voluntarily joined our alliance, were the first to resist. At their instigation the surrounding nations chose as a battlefield a spot walled in by a rude barrier, with a narrow approach, impenetrable to cavalry. Through these defenses the Roman general, though he had with him only the allied troops, without the strength of the legions, attempted to break, and having assigned their positions to his cohorts, he equipped even his cavalry for the work of infantry. Then at a given signal they forced the barrier, routing the enemy, who were entangled in their own defenses. The rebels, conscious of their guilt, and finding escape barred, performed many noble feats. In this battle, Marcus Ostorius, the general's son, won the reward for saving a citizen's life.

32. The defeat of the Iceni quieted those who were hesitating between war and peace. Then the army was marched against the Decangi;[37] their territory was ravaged, spoil taken everywhere without the enemy venturing on an engagement, or if they attempted to harass our march by stealthy attacks, their cunning was always punished. And now Ostorius had advanced within a little distance of the sea, facing the island Hibernia,[38] when feuds broke out among the Brigantes and compelled the general's return, for it was his fixed purpose not to undertake any fresh enterprise till he had consolidated his previous successes. The Brigantes indeed, when a few who were beginning hostilities had been slain and the rest pardoned, settled down quietly; but on the Silures[39] neither terror nor mercy had the least effect; they persisted in war and could be quelled only by legions encamped in their country. That this might be

the more promptly effected, a colony of a strong body of veterans was established at Camulodunum[40] on the conquered lands, as a defense against the rebels, and as a means of imbuing the allies with respect for our laws.

33. The army then marched against the Silures, a naturally fierce people and now full of confidence in the might of Caratacus, who by many an indecisive and many a successful battle had raised himself far above all the other generals of the Britons. Inferior in military strength, but deriving an advantage from the deceptiveness of the country, he at once shifted the war by a stratagem into the territory of the Ordovices,[41] where, joined by all who dreaded peace with us, he resolved on a final struggle. He selected a position for the engagement in which advance and retreat alike would be difficult for our men and comparatively easy for his own, and then on some lofty hills, wherever their sides could be approached by a gentle slope, he piled up stones to serve as a rampart. A river too of varying depth was in his front, and his armed bands were drawn up before his defenses.

34. Then too the chieftains of the several tribes went from rank to rank, encouraging and confirming the spirit of their men by making light of their fears, kindling their hopes, and by every other warlike incitement. As for Caratacus, he flew hither and thither, protesting that that day and that battle would be the beginning of the recovery of their freedom, or of everlasting bondage. He appealed, by name, to their forefathers, who had driven back the dictator Cæsar[42] by whose valor they were free from the Roman axe and tribute, and still preserved inviolate the persons of their wives and of their children. While he was thus speaking, the host shouted applause; every warrior bound himself by his national oath not to shrink from weapons or wounds.

35. Such enthusiasm confounded the Roman general. The river too in his face, the rampart they had added to it, the frowning hilltops, the stern resistance and masses of fighting men everywhere apparent, daunted him. But his soldiers insisted on battle, exclaiming that

valor could overcome all things; and the prefects and tribunes, with similar language, stimulated the ardor of the troops. Ostorius, having ascertained by a survey the inaccessible and the assailable points of the position, led on his furious men, and crossed the river without difficulty. When he reached the barrier, as long as it was a fight with missiles, the wounds and the slaughter fell chiefly on our soldiers; but when we had formed the military *testudo*, and the rude, ill-compacted fence of stones was torn down, and it was an equal hand-to-hand engagement, the barbarians retired to the heights. Yet even there, both light- and heavy-armed soldiers rushed to the attack; the first harassed the foe with missiles, while the latter closed with them, and the opposing ranks of the Britons were broken, destitute as they were of the defense of breastplates or helmets. When they faced the auxiliaries, they were felled by the swords and javelins of our legionaries; if they wheeled round, they were again met by the sabers and spears of the auxiliaries. It was a glorious victory; the wife and daughter of Caratacus were captured, and his brothers too were admitted to surrender.

36. There is seldom safety for the unfortunate, and Caratacus, seeking the protection of Cartimandua, queen of the Brigantes, was put in chains and delivered up to the conquerors nine years after the beginning of the war in Britain. His fame had spread thence, and traveled to the neighboring islands and provinces, and was actually celebrated in Italy. All were eager to see the great man, who for so many years had defied our power. Even at Rome the name of Caratacus was no obscure one; and the Emperor, while he exalted his own glory, enhanced the renown of the vanquished. The people were summoned as to a grand spectacle; the prætorian cohorts were drawn up under arms in the plain in front of their camp; then came a procession of the royal vassals, and the ornaments and neck chains and the spoils which the king had won in wars with other tribes were displayed. Next were to be seen his brothers, his wife and daughter; last of all, Caratacus himself. All the rest stooped in their fear to abject supplication; not so the

king, who neither by humble look nor speech sought compassion.

37. When he was set before the Emperor's tribunal, he spoke as follows: "Had my moderation in prosperity been equal to my noble birth and fortune, I should have entered this city as your friend rather than as your captive; and you would not have disdained to receive, under a treaty of peace, a king descended from illustrious ancestors and ruling many nations. My present lot is as glorious to you as it is degrading to myself. I had men and horses, arms and wealth. What wonder if I parted with them reluctantly? If you Romans choose to lord it over the world, does it follow that the world is to accept slavery? Were I to have been at once delivered up as a prisoner, neither my fall nor your triumph would have become famous. My punishment would be followed by oblivion, whereas, if you save my life, I shall be an everlasting memorial of your clemency."

Upon this the Emperor granted pardon to Caratacus, to his wife, and to his brothers. Released from their bonds, they did homage also to Agrippina, who sat near, conspicuous on another throne, in the same language of praise and gratitude. It was indeed a novelty, quite alien to ancient manners, for a woman to sit in front of Roman standards. In fact, Agrippina boasted that she was herself a partner in the Empire which her ancestors had won.

38. The Senate was then assembled, and speeches were delivered full of pompous eulogy on the capture of Caratacus. It was as glorious, they said, as the display of Syphax by Scipio,[43] or of Perseus by Æmilius Paullus[44] or indeed of any captive prince by any of our generals to the people of Rome. Triumphal distinctions were voted to Ostorius, who thus far had been successful, but soon afterward met with reverses; either because, when Caratacus was out of the way, our discipline was relaxed under an impression that the war was ended, or because the enemy, out of compassion for so great a king, was more ardent in his thirst for vengeance. Instantly they rushed from all parts on the camp prefect, and legionary cohorts left to establish

fortified positions among the Silures, and had not speedy succor arrived from towns and fortresses in the neighborhood, our forces would then have been totally destroyed. Even as it was, the camp prefect, with eight centurions, and the bravest of the soldiers, were slain; and shortly afterward, a foraging party of our men, with some cavalry squadrons sent to their support, was utterly routed.

39. Ostorius then deployed his light cohorts, but even thus he did not stop the flight, till our legions sustained the brunt of the battle. Their strength equalized the conflict, which after a while was in our favor. The enemy fled with trifling loss, as the day was on the decline. Now began a series of skirmishes, for the most part like raids, in woods and morasses, with encounters due to chance or to courage, to mere heedlessness or to calculation, to fury or to lust of plunder, under directions from the officers, or sometimes even without their knowledge. Conspicuous above all in stubborn resistance were the Silures, whose rage was fired by words rumored to have been spoken by the Roman general, to the effect that as the Sugambri had been formerly destroyed or transplanted into Gaul, so the name of the Silures ought to be blotted out. Accordingly they cut off two of our auxiliary cohorts, the rapacity of whose officers let them make incautious forays; and by liberal gifts of spoil and prisoners to the other tribes, they were luring them too into revolt, when Ostorius, worn out by the burden of his anxieties, died, to the joy of the enemy, who thought that a campaign at least, though not a single battle, had proved fatal to a general whom none could despise.

40. The Emperor, on hearing of the death of his representative, appointed Aulus Didius[45] in his place, that the province might not be left without a governor. Didius, though he quickly arrived, found matters far from prosperous, for the legion under the command of Manlius Valens had meanwhile been defeated, and the disaster had been exaggerated by the enemy to alarm the new general, while he again magnified it, that he might win the more glory by quelling the movement or have a fairer excuse if it lasted. This loss too had been inflicted on us

175

TACITUS

by the Silures, and they were scouring the country far
and wide, till Didius hurried up and dispersed them.
After the capture of Caratacus, Venutius of the Brigantes,
as I have already mentioned, was pre-eminent in military
skill; he had long been loyal to Rome and had been defended by our arms while he was united in marriage to
the queen Cartimandua. Subsequently a quarrel broke out
between them, followed instantly by war, and he then
assumed a hostile attitude also toward us. At first, however, they simply fought against each other, and Cartimandua by cunning stratagems captured the brothers and
kinsfolk of Venutius. This enraged the enemy, who were
stung with shame at the prospect of falling under the
dominion of a woman. The flower of their youth, picked
out for war, invaded her kingdom. This we had foreseen;
some cohorts were sent to her aid and a sharp contest
followed, which was at first doubtful but had a satisfac-
tory termination.

The legion under the command of Cæsius Nasica
fought with a similar result. For Didius, burdened with
years and covered with honors, was content with acting
through his officers and merely holding back the enemy.
These transactions, though occurring under two pro-
prætors, and occupying several years, I have closely connected, lest, if related separately, they might be less
easily remembered. I now return to the chronological
order.

41. In the fifth consulship of Tiberius Claudius, with
Sextius Cornelius Orfitus[46] for his colleague, Nero was
prematurely invested with the dress of manhood, that he
might be thought qualified for political life. The Emperor
willingly complied with the flatteries of the Senate, who
wished Nero to enter on the consulship in his twentieth
year, and meanwhile, as consul-elect, to have proconsular
authority beyond the limits of the capital with the title
of "prince of the youth." A donative was also given to the
soldiery in Nero's name, and a largess to the city populace. At the games of the circus, which were then being
celebrated to win for him popular favor, Britannicus wore
the dress of boyhood, Nero the triumphal robe, as they
rode in the procession. The people would thus behold the

176

one with the decorations of a general, the other in a boy's habit, and would accordingly anticipate their respective destinies. At the same time those of the centurions and tribunes who pitied the lot of Britannicus were removed, some on false pretexts, others by way of a seeming compliment. Even of the freedmen, all who were of incorruptible fidelity were discarded on the following provocation. Once when they met, Nero greeted Britannicus by that name and was greeted in return as Domitius. Agrippina reported this to her husband, with bitter complaint, as the beginning of a quarrel, as implying, in fact, contempt of Nero's adoption and a canceling at home of the Senate's decree and the people's vote. She said, too, that if the perversity of such malignant suggestions were not checked, it would issue in the ruin of the state. Claudius, enraged by what he took as a grave charge, punished with banishment or death all his son's best instructors, and set persons appointed by his stepmother to have the care of him.

42. Still Agrippina did not yet dare to attempt her greatest scheme, unless Lusius Geta and Rufrius Crispinus were removed from the command of the prætorian cohorts; for she thought that they cherished Messallina's memory and were devoted to her children. Accordingly, as the Emperor's wife persistently affirmed that faction was rife among these cohorts through the rivalry of the two officers, and that there would be stricter discipline under one commander, the appointment was transferred to Afranius Burrus, who had a brilliant reputation as a soldier, but knew well to whose wish he owed his promotion.[47] Agrippina, too, continued to exalt her own dignity; she would enter the Capitol in a chariot, a practice which, being allowed of old only to the priests and sacred images, increased the popular reverence for a woman who up to this time was the only recorded instance of one who, a prince's daughter, was sister, wife, and mother of a sovereign. Meanwhile her foremost champion, Vitellius, in the full tide of his power and in extreme age (so uncertain are the fortunes of the great), was attacked by an accusation of which Junius Lupus, a senator, was the author. He was charged with treason

and designs on the throne. The Emperor would have lent a ready ear, had not Agrippina, by threats rather than entreaties, induced him to sentence the accuser to outlawry. This was all that Vitellius desired.

43. Several prodigies occurred in that year.[48] Birds of evil omen perched on the Capitol; houses were thrown down by frequent shocks of earthquake, and as the panic spread, all the weak were trodden down in the hurry and confusion of the crowd. Scanty crops, too, and consequent famine were regarded as a token of calamity. Nor were there merely whispered complaints; while Claudius was administering justice, the populace crowded round him with a boisterous clamor and drove him to a corner of the forum, where they violently pressed on him till he broke through the furious mob with a body of soldiers. It was ascertained that Rome had provisions for no more than fifteen days, and it was through the signal bounty of heaven and the mildness of the winter that its desperate plight was relieved. And yet in past days Italy used to send supplies for the legions into distant provinces, and even now it is not a barren soil which causes distress. But we prefer to cultivate Africa and Egypt, and trust the life of the Roman people to ships and all their risks.

[*Chapters 44-51 are omitted; they concern events in Parthia and Armenia.*]

52. In the consulship of Faustus Sulla and Salvius Otho,[49] Furius Scribonianus[50] was banished on the ground that he was consulting the astrologers about the Emperor's death. His mother, Junia, was included in the accusation, as one who still resented the misfortune of exile which she had suffered in the past. His father, Camillus, had raised an armed insurrection in Dalmatia, and the Emperor in again sparing a hostile family sought the credit of clemency. But the exile did not live long after this; whether he was cut off by a natural death, or by poison, was matter of conflicting rumors, according to people's belief.

A decree of the Senate was then passed for the expulsicn of the astrologers from Italy, stringent but ineffectual. Next the Emperor, in a speech, commended all who, from their limited means, voluntarily retired from the senatorial order, while those were degraded from it who, by retaining their seats, added effrontery to poverty.

53. During these proceedings he proposed to the Senate a penalty on women who united themselves in marriage to slaves, and it was decided that those who had thus degraded themselves, without the knowledge of the slave's master, should be reduced to slavery; if with his consent, should be ranked as free women. To Pallas, who, as the Emperor declared, was the author of this proposal, were offered, on the motion of Barea Soranus,[51] consul-elect, the decorations of the prætorship and fifteen million sesterces. Cornelius Scipio[52] added that he deserved public thanks for thinking less of his ancient nobility, as a descendant from the kings of Arcadia, than of the welfare of the state, and allowing himself to be numbered among the Emperor's ministers. Claudius assured them that Pallas was content with the honor, and that he limited himself to his former poverty. A decree of the Senate was publicly inscribed on a bronze tablet, heaping the praises of primitive frugality on a freedman, the possessor of three hundred million sesterces.

54. Not equally moderate was his brother, surnamed Felix,[53] who had for some time been governor of Judæa, and thought that he could do any evil act with impunity, backed up as he was by such power. It is true that the Jews had shown symptoms of commotion in a seditious outbreak, and when they had heard of the assassination of Gaius, there was no hearty submission, as a fear still lingered that any of the emperors might impose the same orders.[54] Felix meanwhile, by ill-timed remedies, stimulated disloyal acts; while he had, as a rival in the worst wickedness, Ventidius Cumanus, who held a part of the province, which was so divided that Galilee was governed by Cumanus, Samaria by Felix. The two peoples had long been at feud, and now less than ever restrained their enmity, from contempt of their rulers. And accordingly they plundered each other, letting loose bands of robbers, forming ambuscades, and occasionally fighting battles,

and carrying the spoil and booty to the two procurators, who at first rejoiced at all this, but, as the mischief grew, they interposed with an armed force, which was cut to pieces. The flame of war would have spread through the province, but it was saved by Quadratus,[55] governor of Syria. In dealing with the Jews, who had been daring enough to slay our soldiers, there was little hesitation about their being capitally punished. Some delay indeed was occasioned by Cumanus and Felix; for Claudius, on hearing the causes of the rebellion, had given authority for deciding also the case of these procurators. Quadratus, however, exhibited Felix as one of the judges, admitting him to the bench with the view of cowing the ardor of the prosecutors. And so Cumanus was condemned for the crimes which the two had committed, and tranquillity was restored to the province.

55. Not long afterward, some tribes of the wild population of Cilicia, known as the Clitae,[56] which had often been in commotion, established a camp, under their leader Troxobor, on their rocky mountains, whence, rushing down on the coast, and on the towns, they dared to do violence to the farmers and townsfolk, frequently even to the merchants and ship owners. They besieged the city Anemurium, and routed some troopers sent from Syria to its rescue under the command of Curtius Severus; for the rough country in the neighborhood, suited as it is for the fighting of infantry, did not allow of cavalry operations. After a time, Antiochus, king of that coast, having broken the unity of the barbarian forces, by cajolery of the people and treachery to their leader, slew Troxobor and a few chiefs, and pacified the rest by gentle measures.

56. About the same time, the mountain between Lake Fucinus[57] and the river Liris[58] was bored through, and that this grand work might be seen by a multitude of visitors, preparations were made for a naval battle on the lake, just as formerly Augustus exhibited such a spectacle in a basin he had made on this side the Tiber, though with light vessels, and on a smaller scale. Claudius equipped galleys with three and four banks of oars, and nineteen thousand men; he lined the circumference of the lake with rafts, that there might be no means of

escape at various points, but he still left full space for the strength of the crews, the skill of the pilots, the impact of the vessels, and the usual operations of a sea fight. On the rafts stood companies of the prætorian cohorts and cavalry, with a breastwork in front of them, from which catapults and ballistas might be worked. The rest of the lake was occupied by marines on decked vessels. An immense multitude from the neighboring towns, others from Rome itself, eager to see the sight or to show respect to the Emperor, crowded the banks, the hills, and mountain tops, which thus resembled a theater. The Emperor, with Agrippina seated near him, presided; he wore a splendid military cloak, she, a mantle of cloth of gold. A battle was fought with all the courage of brave men, though it was between condemned criminals. After much bloodshed they were released from the necessity of mutual slaughter.

57. When the sight was over, the outlet of the water was opened. The careless execution of the work was apparent, the tunnel not having been bored down so low as the bottom, or middle of the lake. Consequently, after an interval the excavations were deepened, and to attract a crowd once more, a show of gladiators was exhibited, with floating pontoons for an infantry engagement. A banquet too was prepared close to the outflow of the lake, and it was the means of greatly alarming the whole company, for the water, in the violence of its outburst, swept away the adjoining parts, shook the more remote, and spread terror with the tremendous crash. At the same time, Agrippina availed herself of the Emperor's fright to charge Narcissus,[59] who had been the agent of the work, with avarice and peculation. He too was not silent, but inveighed against the domineering temper of her sex, and her extravagant ambition.

58. In the consulship of Decimus Junius and Quintus Haterius,[60] Nero, now sixteen years of age, married Octavia, the Emperor's daughter. Anxious to distinguish himself by noble pursuits, and the reputation of an orator, he advocated the cause of the people of Ilium, and having eloquently recounted how Rome was the offspring of Troy, and Æneas the founder of the Julian line,[61] with

other old traditions akin to myths, he gained for his
clients exemption from all public burdens. His pleading
too procured for the colony of Bononia,[62] which had been
ruined by a fire, a subvention of ten million sesterces.
The Rhodians also had their freedom restored to them,
which had often been taken away, or confirmed, according to their services to us in our foreign wars, or their
seditious misdeeds at home.[63] Apamea,[64] too, which had
been shaken by an earthquake, had its tribute remitted
for five years.

59. Claudius, on the other hand, was being prompted
to exhibit the worst cruelty by the artifices of the same
Agrippina. On the accusation of Tarquitius Priscus, she
ruined Statilius Taurus,[65] who was famous for his wealth,
and at whose gardens she cast a greedy eye. Priscus had
served under Taurus in his proconsular government of
Africa, and after their return charged him with a few
acts of extortion, but particularly with magical and superstitious practices. Taurus, no longer able to endure a
false accusation and an undeserved humiliation, put a
violent end to his life before the Senate's decision was
pronounced. Tarquitius was, however, expelled from the
Senate, a point which the senators carried, out of hatred
for the accuser, notwithstanding the intrigues of Agrippina.[66]

60. That same year the Emperor was often heard to
say that the legal decisions of the commissioners of the
imperial treasury ought to have the same force as if
pronounced by himself. Lest it might be supposed that he
had stumbled inadvertently into this opinion, its principle
was also secured by a decree of the Senate on a more
complete and ample scale than before. It had indeed
already been arranged by the divine Augustus that the
Roman knights who governed Egypt should hear causes,
and that their decisions were to be as binding as those of
Roman magistrates, and after a time most of the cases
formerly tried by the prætors were submitted to the
knights.[67] Claudius handed over to them the whole administration of justice, for which there had been, by sedition or war, so many struggles; the Sempronian Laws,
vesting judicial power in the equestrian order, and those

of Servilius, restoring it to the Senate, while it was for this above everything else that Marius and Sulla fought of old.[68] But those were days of political conflict between classes, and the results of victory were binding on the state. Gaius Oppius[69] and Cornelius Balbus were the first who were able, with Cæsar's support, to settle conditions of peace and terms of war. To mention after them men like Matius,[70] Vedius, and other too influential Roman knights would be superfluous, when Claudius, we know, raised freedmen whom he had set over his household to equality with himself and with the laws.

[*Chapters 61-63 are omitted.*]

64. In the year of the consulship of Marcus Asinius and Manius Acilius[71] it was seen to be portended by a succession of prodigies that there were to be political changes for the worse. The soldiers' standards and tents were set in a blaze by lightning. A swarm of bees settled on the summit of the Capitol; births of monsters, half man, half beast, and of a pig with a hawk's talons, were reported. It was accounted a portent that every order of magistrates had had its number reduced, a quæstor, an ædile, a tribune, a prætor, and a consul having died within a few months. But Agrippina's terror was the most conspicuous. Alarmed by some words dropped by Claudius when half intoxicated, that it was his destiny to have to endure his wives' infamy and at last punish it, she determined to act without a moment's delay. First she destroyed Lepida from motives of feminine jealousy. Lepida,[72] indeed, as the daughter of the younger Antonia, as the grandniece of Augustus, the cousin of Agrippina, and sister of her husband, Cnæus Domitius, thought herself of equally high rank. In beauty, age, and wealth they differed but slightly. Both were shameless, infamous, and intractable, and were rivals in vice as much as in the advantages they had derived from fortune. It was indeed a desperate contest whether the aunt or the mother should have the most power over Nero. Lepida tried to win the young prince's heart by flattery and lavish liberality, while Agrippina, on the other hand, who could

183

give her son empire but not endure that he should rule, was fierce and full of menace.

65. It was charged on Lepida that she had made attempts on the Emperor's consort by magical incantations, and was disturbing the peace of Italy by an imperfect control of her troops of slaves in Calabria. For this she was sentenced to death, notwithstanding the vehement opposition of Narcissus, who, as he more and more suspected Agrippina, was said to have plainly told his intimate friends that "his destruction was certain, whether Britannicus or Nero were to be Emperor, but that he was under such obligations to Claudius that he would sacrifice life to his welfare. Messallina and Silius had been convicted, and now again there were similar grounds for accusation. If Nero were to rule, or Britannicus succeed to the throne, he would himself have no claim on the then reigning sovereign. Meanwhile, a stepmother's treacherous schemes were convulsing the whole imperial house, with far greater disgrace than would have resulted from his concealment of the profligacy of the Emperor's former wife. Even as it was, there was shamelessness enough, seeing that Pallas was her paramour, so that no one could doubt that she held honor, modesty, and her very person, everything, in short, cheaper than sovereignty."

This, and the like, he was always saying, and he would embrace Britannicus, expressing earnest wishes for his speedy arrival at a mature age, and would raise his hand, now to heaven, now to the young prince, with entreaty that as he grew up, he would drive out his father's enemies and also take vengeance on the murderers of his mother.

66. Under this great burden of anxiety, he had an attack of illness, and went to Sinuessa[73] to recruit his strength with its balmy climate and salubrious waters. Thereupon, Agrippina, who had long decided on the crime and eagerly grasped at the opportunity thus offered, and did not lack instruments, deliberated on the nature of the poison to be used. The deed would be betrayed by one that was sudden and instantaneous, while if she chose a slow and lingering poison, there was a fear that Claudius,

184

when near his end, might, on detecting the treachery,
return to his love for his son. She decided on some rare
compound which might derange his mind and delay
death. A person skilled in such matters was selected,
Locusta[74] by name, who had lately been condemned for
poisoning, and had long been retained as one of the tools
of despotism. By this woman's art the poison was prepared, and it was to be administered by a eunuch, Halo-
tus, who was accustomed to bring in and taste the dishes.

67. All the circumstances were subsequently so well
known that writers of the time have declared that the
poison was infused into some mushrooms, a favorite
delicacy, and its effect not at the instant perceived, from
the Emperor's lethargic, or intoxicated, condition. His
bowels too were relieved, and this seemed to have saved
him. Agrippina was thoroughly dismayed. Fearing the
worst, and defying the immediate obloquy of the deed,
she availed herself of the complicity of Xenophon, the
physician, which she had already secured. Under pretense of helping the Emperor's efforts to vomit, this man,
it is supposed, introduced into his throat a feather
smeared with some rapid poison; for he knew that the
greatest crimes are perilous in their inception, but well
rewarded after their consummation.

68. Meanwhile the Senate was summoned, and prayers
rehearsed by the consuls and priests for the Emperor's
recovery, though the lifeless body was being wrapped in
blankets with warm applications, while all was being
arranged to establish Nero on the throne. At first Agrippina, seemingly overwhelmed by grief and seeking comfort, clasped Britannicus in her embraces, called him the
very image of his father, and hindered him by every
possible device from leaving the chamber. She also detained his sisters, Antonia and Octavia, closed every
approach to the palace with a military guard, and repeatedly gave out that the Emperor's health was better,
so that the soldiers might be encouraged to hope, and
that the fortunate moment foretold by the astrologers
might arrive.

69. At last, at noon on the 13th of October, the gates
of the palace were suddenly thrown open, and Nero,

accompanied by Burrus, went forth to the cohort which was on guard after military custom. There, at the suggestion of the commanding officer, he was hailed with joyful shouts, and set in a litter. Some, it is said, hesitated, and looked round and asked where Britannicus was; then, when there was no one to lead a resistance, they yielded to what was offered them. Nero was conveyed into the camp, and having first spoken suitably to the occasion and promised a donative after the example of his father's bounty, he was unanimously greeted as Emperor. The decrees of the Senate followed the voice of the soldiers, and there was no hesitation in the provinces. Divine honors were decreed to Claudius, and his funeral rites were solemnized on the same scale as those of Augustus; for Agrippina strove to emulate the magnificence of her great-grandmother, Livia. But his will was not publicly read, as the preference of the stepson to the son might provoke a sense of wrong and angry feeling in the popular mind.

BOOK XIII   54-58 A.D.

1. THE first death under the new Emperor, that of Junius Silanus,[1] proconsul of Asia, was, without Nero's knowledge, planned by the treachery of Agrippina. Not that Silanus had provoked destruction by any violence of temper, apathetic as he was, and so utterly despised under former despotisms that Gaius Cæsar used to call him the golden sheep. The truth was that Agrippina, having contrived the murder of his brother Lucius Silanus, dreaded his vengeance; for it was the incessant popular talk that preference ought to be given over Nero, who was scarcely out of his boyhood and had gained the Empire by crime, to a man of mature age, of blameless life, of noble birth, and, as a point then much regarded, of the line of the Cæsars. Silanus in fact was the son of a great-grandson of Augustus. This was the cause of his destruction. The agents of the deed were Publius Celer, a Roman knight, and Helius,[2] a freedman, men who had the charge of the Emperor's domains in Asia. They gave

the proconsul poison at a banquet, too openly to escape discovery.

With no less precipitation, Narcissus, Claudius' freedman, whose quarrels with Agrippina I have mentioned, was driven to suicide by his cruel imprisonment and hopeless plight, even against the wishes of Nero, with whose yet concealed vices he was wonderfully in sympathy from his rapacity and extravagance.

2. And now they would have proceeded to further murders but for the opposition of Afranius Burrus and Annæus Seneca. These two men guided the Emperor's youth with a unity of purpose seldom found where authority is shared, and though their accomplishments were wholly different, they had equal influence. Burrus, with his soldier's discipline and severe manners, Seneca, with lessons of eloquence and a dignified courtesy, strove alike to confine the frailty of the prince's youth, should he loathe virtue, within allowable indulgences. They had both alike to struggle against the domineering spirit of Agrippina, who, inflamed with all the passions of an evil ascendancy, had Pallas on her side, at whose suggestion Claudius had ruined himself by an incestuous marriage and a fatal adoption of a son. Nero's temper, however, was not one to submit to slaves, and Pallas, by a surly arrogance quite beyond a freedman, had provoked disgust. Still every honor was openly heaped on Agrippina, and to a tribune who according to military custom asked the watchword, Nero gave "the best of mothers.' The Senate also decreed her two lictors, with the office of priestess to Claudius, and voted to the late Emperor a censor's funeral,[3] which was soon followed by deification.

3. On the day of the funeral the prince pronounced Claudius' panegyric, and while he dwelled on the antiquity of his family and on the consulships and triumphs of his ancestors, there was enthusiasm both in himself and in his audience. The praise of his graceful accomplishments, and the remark that during his reign no disaster had befallen Rome from the foreigner, were heard with favor. When the speaker passed on to his foresight and wisdom, no one could refrain from laughter, though the speech, which was composed by Seneca,

187

exhibited much elegance, as indeed that famous man had an attractive genius which suited the popular ear of the time. Elderly men who amuse their leisure with comparing the past and the present observed that Nero was the first Emperor who needed another man's eloquence. The dictator Cæsar rivaled the greatest orators, and Augustus had an easy and fluent way of speaking, such as became a sovereign. Tiberius too thoroughly understood the art of balancing words, and was sometimes forcible in the expression of his thoughts, or else intentionally obscure. Even Gaius Cæsar's disordered intellect did not wholly mar his faculty of speech. Nor did Claudius, when he spoke with preparation, lack elegance. Nero from early boyhood turned his lively genius in other directions; he carved, painted, sang, or practiced the management of horses, occasionally composing verses which showed that he had the rudiments of learning.

4. When he had done with his mimicries of sorrow, he entered the Senate, and having first referred to the authority of the senators and the concurrence of the soldiery, he then dwelled on the counsels and examples which he had to guide him in the right administration of empire. "His boyhood," he said, "had not had the taint of civil wars or domestic feuds, and he brought with him no hatreds, no sense of wrong, no desire of vengeance." He then sketched the plan of his future government, carefully avoiding anything which had kindled recent odium. "He would not," he said, "be judge in all cases, or, by confining the accuser and the accused within the same walls, let the power of a few favorites grow dangerously formidable.[4] In his house there should be nothing venal, nothing open to intrigue;[5] his private establishment and the state should be kept entirely distinct. The Senate should retain its ancient powers; Italy and the public provinces should plead their causes before the tribunals of the consuls, who would give them a hearing from the senators. Of the armies he would himself take charge, as specially entrusted to him."

5. He was true to his word and several arrangements were made on the Senate's authority. No one was to receive a fee or a present for pleading a cause;[6] the quæs-

tors-elect were not to be under the necessity of exhibiting gladiatorial shows.[7] This was opposed by Agrippina, as a reversal of the legislation of Claudius, but it was carried by the senators, who used to be summoned to the palace, in order that she might stand close to a hidden door behind them, screened by a curtain which was enough to shut her out of sight, but not out of hearing. When envoys from Armenia were pleading their nation's cause before Nero, she was actually on the point of mounting the Emperor's tribunal and of presiding with him; but Seneca, when everyone else was paralyzed with alarm, motioned to the prince to go and meet his mother. Thus, by an apparently dutiful act, a scandalous scene was prevented.

[*Chapters 6-9 are omitted.*]

10. The Emperor in the same year asked the Senate for a statue to his father, Domitius, and also that the consular decorations might be conferred on Asconius Labeo, who had been his guardian. Statues to himself of solid gold and silver he forbade, in opposition to offers made, and although the Senate passed a vote that the year should begin with the month of December, in which he was born, he retained for its commencement the old sacred associations of the first of January. Nor would he allow the prosecution of Carrinas Celer, a senator, whom a slave accused, or of Julius Densus, a knight, whose partiality for Britannicus was construed into a crime.

11. In the year of his consulship with Lucius Antistius,[8] when the magistrates were swearing obedience to imperial legislation, he forbade his colleague to extend the oath to his own enactments, for which he was warmly praised by the senators, in the hope that his youthful spirit, elated with the glory won by trifles, would follow on to nobler aspirations. Then came an act of mercy to Plautius Lateranus, who had been degraded from his rank for adultery with Messallina, and whom he now restored, assuring them of his clemency in a number of speeches which Seneca, to show the purity of

189

his teaching or to display his genius, published to the world by the Emperor's mouth.[9]

12. Meanwhile the mother's influence was gradually weakened, as Nero fell in love with a freedwoman, Acte by name, and took into his confidence Otho[10] and Claudius Senecio,[11] two young men of fashion, the first of whom was descended from a family of consular rank, while Senecio's father was one of the Emperor's freedmen. Without the mother's knowledge, then in spite of her opposition, they had crept into his favor by debaucheries and equivocal secrets, and even the prince's older friends did not thwart him, for here was a girl who without harm to anyone gratified his desires, when he loathed his wife Octavia, highborn as she was, and of approved virtue, either from some fatality, or because vice is overpoweringly attractive. It was feared too that he might rush into outrages on noble ladies, were he debarred from this indulgence.

13. Agrippina, however, raved with a woman's fury about having a freedwoman for a rival, a slave girl for a daughter-in-law, with like expressions. Nor would she wait till her son repented or wearied of his passion. The fouler her reproaches, the more powerfully did they inflame him, till completely mastered by the strength of his desire, he threw off all respect for his mother, and put himself under the guidance of Seneca, one of whose friends, Annæus Serenus,[12] had veiled the young prince's intrigue in its beginning by pretending to be in love with the same woman, and had lent his name as the ostensible giver of the presents secretly sent by the Emperor to the girl. Then Agrippina, changing her tactics, plied the lad with various blandishments, and even offered the seclusion of her chamber for the concealment of indulgences which youth and the highest rank might claim. She went further; she pleaded guilty to an ill-timed strictness, and handed over to him the abundance of her wealth, which nearly approached the imperial treasures, and from having been of late extreme in her restraint of her son, became now, on the other hand, lax to excess. The change did not escape Nero; his most intimate friends dreaded it, and begged him to beware of

the arts of a woman who would at all times stop at nothing and was now insincere into the bargain.

It happened at this time that the Emperor, after inspecting the apparel in which wives and mothers of the imperial house had been seen to glitter, selected a jeweled robe and sent it as a gift to his mother, with the unsparing liberality of one who was bestowing by preference on her a choice and much coveted present. Agrippina, however, publicly declared that so far from her wardrobe being furnished by these gifts, she was really kept out of the remainder, and that her son was merely dividing with her what he derived wholly from herself.

14. There were some who put even a worse meaning on her words. And so Nero, furious with those who abetted such arrogance in a woman, removed Pallas from the charge of the business with which he had been entrusted by Claudius, and in which he acted, so to say, as the controller of the throne. The story went that as he was departing with a great retinue of attendants, the Emperor rather wittily remarked that Pallas was going to swear himself out of office.[13] Pallas had in truth stipulated that he should not be questioned for anything he had done in the past, and that his accounts with the state were to be considered as balanced. Thereupon, with instant fury, Agrippina rushed into frightful menaces, sparing not the prince's ears her solemn protest that "Britannicus was now of full age, he who was the true and worthy heir of his father's sovereignty, which a son by mere admission and adoption was abusing in outrages on his mother. She shrank not from an utter exposure of the wickedness of that ill-starred house, of her own marriage, to begin with, and of her poisoner's craft. All that the gods and she herself had taken care of was that her stepson was yet alive; with him she would go to the camp, where on one side should be heard the daughter of Germanicus, on the other, the crippled Burrus and the exile Seneca, claiming, one with his one hand and the other with a pedant's tongue, the government of the world." As she spoke, she raised her hand in menace and heaped insults on him, as she

appealed to the deified Claudius, to the infernal shades of the Silani, and to those many crimes, now all in vain.

15. Nero was confounded at this, and as the day was near on which Britannicus would complete his fourteenth year, he reflected, now on the domineering temper of his mother, and now again on the character of the young prince, which a trifling circumstance had lately tested, sufficient, however, to gain for him wide popularity. During the Saturnalia, amid other pastimes of his playmates, at a game of lot-drawing for king, the lot fell to Nero, upon which he gave all his other companions different orders, and such as would not put them to the blush; but when he told Britannicus to step forward and begin a song, hoping for a laugh at the expense of a boy who knew nothing of sober, much less of riotous society, the lad with perfect coolness commenced some verses which hinted at his expulsion from his father's house and from supreme power. This procured him pity, which was the more conspicuous, as night with its merriment had stripped off all disguise. Nero saw the reproach and redoubled his hate. Pressed by Agrippina's menaces, having no charge against his brother and not daring openly to order his murder, he meditated a secret device and directed poison to be prepared through the agency of Julius Pollio, tribune of one of the prætorian cohorts, who had in his custody a woman under sentence for poisoning, Locusta by name, with a vast reputation for crime. That everyone about the person of Britannicus should care nothing for right or honor had long ago been provided for. He actually received his first dose of poison from his tutors and passed it off in his bowels, as it was either rather weak or so qualified as not at once to prove deadly. But Nero, impatient at such slow progress in crime, threatened the tribune and ordered the poisoner to execution for prolonging his anxiety while they were thinking of the popular talk and planning their own defense. Then they promised that death should be as sudden as if it were the hurried work of the dagger, and a rapid poison of previously tested ingredients was prepared close to the Emperor's chamber.

16. It was customary for the imperial princes to sit during their meals with other nobles of the same age, in the sight of their kinsfolk, at a table of their own, furnished somewhat frugally. There Britannicus was dining, and as what he ate and drank was always tested by the taste of a select attendant, the following device was contrived that the usage might not be dropped or the crime betrayed by the death of both prince and attendant. A cup as yet harmless, but extremely hot and already tasted, was handed to Britannicus; then, on his refusing it because it was too hot, poison was poured in with some cold water, and this so penetrated his entire frame that he lost alike voice and breath. There was a stir among the company; some, taken by surprise, ran hither and thither, while those whose discernment was keener remained motionless, with their eyes fixed on Nero, who, as he still reclined in seeming unconsciousness, said that this was a common occurrence, from a periodical epilepsy, with which Britannicus had been afflicted from his earliest infancy, and that his sight and senses would gradually return. As for Agrippina, her terror and confusion, though her countenance struggled to hide it, so visibly appeared that she was clearly just as ignorant as was Octavia, Britannicus' own sister. She saw, in fact, that she was robbed of her only remaining refuge, and that here was a precedent for matricide. Even Octavia, notwithstanding her youthful inexperience, had learned to hide her grief, her affection, and indeed every emotion.

17. And so after a brief pause the company resumed its mirth. One and the same night witnessed Britannicus' death and funeral, preparations having been already made for his obsequies, which were on a humble scale. He was, however, buried in the Campus Martius, amid storms so violent that in the popular belief they portended the wrath of heaven against a crime which many were even inclined to forgive when they remembered the immemorial feuds of brothers and the impossibility of a divided throne. It is related by several writers of the period that on many successive days before the murder, Nero had offered the worst insult to the boyhood of

Britannicus; so that his death could no longer seem a
premature or dreadful event, though it happened at the
sacred board, without even a moment for the embraces
of his sisters, hurried on too, as it was, under the eyes
of an enemy, on the sole surviving offspring of the
Claudii, the victim first of dishonor, then of poison. The
Emperor apologized for the hasty funeral by reminding
people that it was the practice of our ancestors to withdraw from view any grievously untimely death, and not
to dwell on it with panegyrics or display. For himself, he
said that as he had now lost a brother's help, his remaining hopes centered in the state, and all the more tender-
ness ought to be shown by the Senate and people toward a prince who was the only survivor of a family
born to the highest greatness.

18. He then enriched his most powerful friends with
liberal presents. Some there were who reproached men
of austere professions with having on such an occasion
divided houses and estates among themselves, like so
much spoil. It was the belief of others that a pressure
had been put on them by the Emperor, who, conscious
as he was of guilt, hoped for merciful consideration, if
he could secure the most important men by wholesale
bribery. But his mother's rage no lavish bounty could al-
lay. She would clasp Octavia to her arms, and have
many a secret interview with her friends; with more
than her natural rapacity, she clutched at money everywhere, seemingly for a reserve, and courteously received
tribunes and centurions. She honored the names and
virtues of the nobles who still were left, seeking apparently a party and a leader. Of this Nero became aware,
and he ordered the departure of the military guard now
kept for the Emperor's mother, as it had formerly been
for the imperial consort, along with some German troops,
added as a further honor. He also gave her a separate
establishment, that throngs of visitors might no longer
wait on her, and removed her to what had been Antonia's house;[14] and whenever he went there himself,
he was surrounded by a crowd of centurions, and used
to leave her after a hurried kiss.

19. Of all things human the most precarious and tran-

sitory is a reputation for power which has no strong support of its own. In a moment Agrippina's doors were deserted; there was no one to comfort or to go near her, except a few ladies, whether out of love or malice was doubtful. One of these was Junia Silana, whom Messallina had driven from her husband, Gaius Silius, as I have already related.[15] Conspicuous for her birth, her beauty, and her wantonness, she had long been a special favorite of Agrippina, till after a while there were secret mutual dislikes, because Sextius Africanus,[16] a young nobleman, had been deterred from marrying Silana by Agrippina, who repeatedly spoke of her as an immodest woman in the decline of life, not to secure Africanus for herself, but to keep the childless and wealthy widow out of a husband's control. Silana having now a prospect of vengeance, suborned as accusers two of her creatures, Iturius and Calvisius, not with the old and often-repeated charges about Agrippina's mourning the death of Britannicus or publishing the wrongs of Octavia, but with a hint that it was her purpose to encourage in revolutionary designs Rubellius Plautus,[17] who on his mother's side was as nearly connected as Nero with the divine Augustus; and then, by marrying him and making him Emperor, again seize the control of the state. All this Iturius and Calvisius divulged to Atimetus, a freedman of Domitia,[18] Nero's aunt. Exulting in the opportunity, for Agrippina and Domitia were in bitter rivalry, Atimetus urged Paris, who was himself also a freedman of Domitia, to go at once and put the charge in the most dreadful form.

20. Night was far advanced and Nero was still sitting over his cups when Paris[19] entered, who was generally wont at such times to heighten the Emperor's enjoyments, but who now wore a gloomy expression. He went through the whole evidence in order, and so frightened his hearer as to make him resolve not only on the destruction of his mother and of Plautus, but also on the removal of Burrus from the command of the guards, as a man who had been promoted by Agrippina's interest, and was now showing his gratitude. We have it on the authority of Fabius Rusticus[20] that a note was written

to Cæcina Tuscus,[21] entrusting to him the charge of the prætorian cohorts, but that through Seneca's influence that distinguished post was retained for Burrus. According to Plinius[22] and Cluvius,[23] no doubt was felt about the commander's loyalty. Fabius certainly inclines to the praise of Seneca, through whose friendship he rose to honor. Proposing as I do to follow the consentient testimony of historians, I shall give the differences in their narratives under the writers' names. Nero, in his bewilderment and impatience to destroy his mother, could not be put off till Burrus answered for her death, should she be convicted of the crime, but "anyone," he said, "much more a parent, must be allowed a defense. Accusers there were none forthcoming; they had before them only the word of a single person from an enemy's house, and this the night, with its darkness and prolonged festivity and everything savoring of recklessness and folly, was enough to refute."

21. Having thus allayed the prince's fears, they went at daybreak to Agrippina, that she might know the charges against her, and either rebut them or suffer the penalty. Burrus fulfilled his instructions in Seneca's presence, and some of the freedmen were present to witness the interview. Then Burrus, when he had fully explained the charges with the authors' names, assumed an air of menace. Instantly Agrippina, calling up all her high spirit, exclaimed, "I wonder not that Silana, who has never borne offspring, knows nothing of a mother's feelings. Parents do not change their children as lightly as a shameless woman does her paramours. And if Iturius and Calvisius, after having wasted their whole fortunes, are now, as their last resource, repaying an old hag for their hire by undertaking to be informers, it does not follow that I am to incur the infamy of plotting a son's murder, or that a Cæsar is to have the consciousness of like guilt. As for Domitia's enmity, I should be thankful for it, were she to vie with me in goodwill toward my Nero. Now through her paramour, Atimetus, and the actor, Paris, she is, so to say, concocting a drama for the stage. She at her villa at Baiæ was increasing the magnificence of her fishponds, when I was planning in

196

my counsels his adoption with a proconsul's powers and a consul-elect's rank and every other step to empire. Only let the man come forward who can charge me with having tampered with the prætorian cohorts in the capital, with having sapped the loyalty of the provinces, or, in a word, with having bribed slaves and freedmen into any wickedness. Could I have lived with Britannicus in the possession of power? And if Plautus or any other were to become master of the state so as to sit in judgment on me, accusers, I think, would not be lacking to charge me not merely with a few incautious expressions prompted by the eagerness of affection, but with guilt from which a son alone could absolve me."

There was profound excitement among those present, and they even tried to soothe her agitation, but she insisted on an interview with her son. Then, instead of pleading her innocence, as though she lacked confidence, or her claims on him by way of reproach, she obtained vengeance on her accusers and rewards for her friends.

22. The superintendence of the corn supply was given to Fænius Rufus,[24] the direction of the games which the Emperor was preparing to Arruntius Stella,[25] and the province of Egypt to Tiberius Balbillus.[26] Syria was to be assigned to Publius Anteius,[27] but he was soon put off by various artifices and finally detained at Rome. Silana was banished; Calvisius and Iturius exiled for a time; Atimetus was capitally punished, while Paris was too serviceable to the Emperor's profligacy to allow of his suffering any penalty. Plautus for the present was silently passed over.

23. Next Pallas and Burrus were accused of having conspired to raise Cornelius Sulla[28] to the throne, because of his noble birth and connection with Claudius, whose son-in-law he was by his marriage with Antonia. The promoter of the prosecution was one Pætus, who had become notorious by frequent purchases of property confiscated to the exchequer and was now convicted clearly of imposture. But the proved innocence of Pallas did not please men so much as his arrogance offended them. When his freedmen, his alleged accomplices, were called, he replied that at home he signified his wishes only by

a nod or a gesture, or, if further explanation was required, he used writing, so as not to degrade his voice in such company. Burrus, though accused, gave his verdict as one of the judges. The prosecutor was sentenced to exile, and the account books in which he was reviving forgotten claims of the exchequer were burned.

24. At the end of the year the cohort usually on guard during the games was withdrawn, that there might be a greater show of freedom, that the soldiery too might be less demoralized when no longer in contact with the license of the theater, and that it might be tested whether the populace, in the absence of a guard, would maintain their self-control. The Emperor, on the advice of the augurs, purified Rome by a lustration, as the temples of Jupiter and Minerva had been struck by lightning.

25. In the consulship of Quintus Volusius and Publius Scipio,[29] there was peace abroad, but a disgusting licentiousness at home on the part of Nero, who in a slave's disguise, so as to be unrecognized, would wander through the streets of Rome to brothels and taverns with comrades, who seized on goods exposed for sale and inflicted wounds on any whom they encountered, some of these last knowing him so little that he even received blows himself, and showed the marks of them in his face. When it was notorious that the Emperor was the assailant, and the insults on men and women of distinction were multiplied, other persons too, on the strength of a license once granted under Nero's name, ventured with impunity on the same practices, and had gangs of their own, till night presented the scenes of a captured city. Julius Montanus, a senator, but one who had not yet held any office, happened to encounter the prince in the darkness, and because he fiercely repulsed his attack and then on recognizing him begged for mercy, as though this was a reproach, was forced to destroy himself. Nero was for the future more timid, and surrounded himself with soldiers and a number of gladiators, who, when a fray began on a small scale and seemed a private affair, were to let it alone, but, if the injured persons resisted stoutly, they rushed in with their swords. He also turned the license of the games and the en-

thusiasm for the actors into something like a battle by
the impunity he allowed, and the rewards he offered,
and especially by looking on himself, sometimes concealed, but often in public view, till, with the people at
strife and the fear of a worse commotion, the only remedy which could be devised was the expulsion of the
offending actors from Italy, and the presence once more
of the soldiery in the theater.

26. During the same time there was a discussion in
the Senate on the misconduct of freedmen, and a strong
demand was made that, as a check on the undeserving,
former owners should have the right of revoking freedom. There were several who supported this. But the
consuls did not venture to put the motion without the
Emperor's knowledge, though they recorded the Senate's
general opinion, to see whether he would sanction the
arrangement, considering that only a few were opposed
to it, while some loudly complained that the irreverent
spirit which freedom had fostered had broken into such
excess that freedmen would ask their former owners'
advice as to whether they should treat them with violence, or, as legally, their equals, and would actually
threaten them with blows, at the same time recommending them not to punish. "What right," it was asked, "was
conceded to an injured patron but that of temporarily
banishing the freedman a hundred miles off to the shores
of Campania? In everything else, legal proceedings were
equal and the same for both. Some weapon ought to be
given to the patrons which could not be despised. It
would be no grievance for the enfranchised to have to
keep their freedom by the same respectful behavior
which had procured it for them. But, as for notorious
offenders, they deserved to be dragged back into slavery,
that fear might be a restraint where kindness had had
no effect."

27. It was argued in reply that, though the guilt of a
few ought to be the ruin of the men themselves, there
should be no diminution of the rights of the entire
class. "For it was," they contended, "a widely diffused
body; from it, the city tribes, the various public func-
tionaries, the establishments of the magistrates and

199

priests were for the most part supplied, as well as the cohorts of the city guard; very many too of the knights and several of the senators derived their origin from no other source. If freedmen were to be a separate class, the paucity of the freeborn would be conspicuously apparent. Not without good reason had our ancestors, in distinguishing the position of the different orders, thrown freedom open to all. Again, two kinds of enfranchisement had been instituted, so as to leave room for retracting the boon, or for a fresh act of grace. Those whom the patron had not emancipated with the freedom-giving rod were still held, as it were, by the bonds of slavery. Every master should carefully consider the merits of each case, and be slow to grant what once given could not be taken away."

This view prevailed, and the Emperor replied to the Senate that, whenever freedmen were accused by their patrons, they were to investigate each case separately and not to annul any right to their common injury. Soon afterward, his aunt Domitia had her freedman Paris taken from her, avowedly by civil law, much to the disgrace of the Emperor, by whose direction a decision that he was freeborn was obtained.

28. Still there yet remained some shadow of a free state. A contest arose between Vibullius, the prætor, and Antistius, a tribune of the people; for the tribune had ordered the release of some disorderly applauders of certain actors, whom the prætor had imprisoned. The Senate approved the imprisonment, and censured the presumption of Antistius. Tribunes were also forbidden to usurp the authority of prætors and consuls, or to summon from any part of Italy persons liable to legal proceedings. It was further proposed by Lucius Piso,[30] consul-elect, that tribunes were not to try any case in their own houses, that a fine imposed by them was not to be entered on the public books by the officials of the exchequer till four months had expired, and that in the meantime appeals were to be allowed, which the consuls were to decide.

Restrictions were also put on the powers of the ædiles and a limit fixed to the amount of bail or penalty which

curule and plebeian ædiles could respectively exact.[31]
On this, Helvidius Priscus, a tribune of the people,[32] followed up a personal quarrel he had with Obultronius
Sabinus, one of the quæstors of the exchequer,[33] by insinuating that he stretched his right of confiscation with
merciless rigor against the poor. The Emperor then transferred the charge of the public accounts from these officers to the prefects of the treasury.

29. The arrangement of this business had been variously and frequently altered. Augustus allowed the Senate to appoint prefects; then, when corrupt practices
were suspected in the voting, men were chosen by lot
for the office out of the whole number of prætors. This
did not last long, as the lot strayed away to unfit persons. Claudius then again appointed quæstors, and that
they might not be too lax in their duties from fear of
offending, he promised them promotion out of the usual
course. But what they lacked was the firmness of mature
age, entering, as they did, on this office as their first
step, and so Nero appointed ex-prætors of approved competency.

30. During the same consulship, Vipsanius Lænas was
condemned for rapacity in his administration of the
province of Sardinia.[34] Cestius Proculus was acquitted
of extortion, his accusers, the people of Crete,[35] dropping the charge. Clodius Quirinalis, having, when in
command of the crews at Ravenna, caused grievous distress to Italy by his profligacy and cruelty, just as if it
was the most contemptible of countries, forestalled his
doom by poison. Caninius Rebilus, one of the first men
in legal knowledge and vastness of wealth,[36] escaped
the miseries of an old age of broken health by letting
the blood trickle from his veins, though men did not
credit him with sufficient resolution for a self-inflicted
death, because of his infamous effeminacy. Lucius Volusius on the other hand died with a glorious name.[37]
There was his long life of ninety-three years, his conspicuous wealth, honorably acquired, and his wise avoidance of the malignity of so many emperors.

31. During Nero's second consulship with Lucius Piso
for his colleague,[38] little occurred deserving mention, un-

less one were to take pleasure in filling volumes with the praise of the foundations and timber work on which the Emperor piled the immense amphitheater in the Field of Mars. But custom prescribes that it suits the dignity of the Roman people to reserve history for great achievements, and to leave such details to the city's daily register. I may mention that the colonies of Nuceria and Capua[39] were strengthened by an addition of veterans; to every member of the city populace four hundred sesterces were given, and forty million paid into the exchequer to maintain the credit of the citizens.

A tax also of four per cent on the sale of slaves was remitted, an apparent more than a real boon, for as the seller was ordered to pay it, purchasers found that it was added as part of the price. The Emperor by an edict forbade any magistrate or procurator in the government of a province to exhibit a show of gladiators, or of wild beasts, or indeed any other public entertainment; for hitherto our subjects had been as much oppressed by such bribery as by actual extortion, while governors sought to screen by corruption the guilty deeds of arbitrary caprice.

32. The Senate next passed a decree providing alike for punishment and safety. If a master were murdered by his slaves, all those who were enfranchised by his will and lived under the same roof were to suffer the capital penalty with his other slaves.[40] Lurius Varius, an ex-consul, who had been crushed in the past under charges of extortion, was restored to his rank as a senator. Pomponia Græcina, a distinguished lady, wife of the Plautius[41] who returned from Britain with an ovation, was accused of some foreign superstition and handed over to her husband's judicial decision. Following ancient precedent, he heard his wife's cause in the presence of kinsfolk, involving as it did her legal status and character, and he reported that she was innocent. This Pomponia lived a long life of unbroken melancholy. After the murder of Julia, Drusus' daughter,[42] by Messallina's treachery, for forty years she wore only the attire of a mourner, with a heart ever sorrowful. For this, during

Claudius' reign, she escaped unpunished, and it was afterward counted a glory to her.

33. The same year saw many impeached. One of these, Publius Celer,[43] prosecuted by the province of Asia, the Emperor could not acquit, and so he put off the case till the man died of old age. Celer, as I have related, had murdered Silanus, the proconsul, and the magnitude of this crime veiled his other enormities. Cossutianus Capito[44] was accused by the people of Cilicia; he was a man stained with the foulest guilt, and had actually imagined that his audacious wickedness had the same rights in a province as he had claimed for it at Rome. But he had to confront a determined prosecution, and at last abandoned his defense. Eprius Marcellus,[45] from whom Lycia demanded compensation, was so powerfully supported by corrupt influence that some of his accusers were punished with exile, as though they had imperiled an innocent man.

34. Nero entered on his third consulship with Valerius Messalla,[46] whose great-grandfather, the orator Corvinus, was still remembered by a few old men, as having been the colleague of the divine Augustus, Nero's great-grandfather, in the same office. But the honor of a noble house was further increased by an annual grant of five hundred thousand sesterces on which Messalla might support virtuous poverty. Aurelius Cotta[47] too and Haterius Antoninus had yearly stipends assigned them by the Emperor, though they had squandered their ancestral wealth in profligacy.

[*The last part of Chapter 34 and Chapters 35-41, which deal with Corbulo's victories over the Parthians, are omitted.*]

42. A man who had struggled with various calamities and earned the hate of many was then impeached and condemned, but not without angry feelings toward Seneca. This was Publius Suillius.[48] He had been terrible and venal while Claudius reigned, and when times were changed, he was not so much humbled as his enemies wished, and was one who would rather seem a criminal

than a suppliant. With the intent of crushing him, so men believed, a decree of the Senate was revived, along with the penalty of the Cincian Law[49] against persons who had pleaded for hire. Suillius spared not complaint or indignant remonstrance; freespoken because of his extreme age as well as from his insolent temper, he taunted Seneca with his savage enmity against the friends of Claudius, under whose reign he had endured a most righteously deserved exile. "The man," he said, "familiar as he was only with useless studies, and with the ignorance of boyhood, envied those who employed a lively and genuine eloquence in the defense of their fellow citizens. *He* had been Germanicus' quæstor, while Seneca had seduced his daughter.[50] Was it to be thought a worse offense to obtain a reward for honest service with the litigant's consent, than to penetrate the bedrooms of princesses? By what kind of wisdom or maxims of philosophy had Seneca within four years of royal favor amassed three hundred million sesterces? At Rome the wills of the childless were, so to say, caught in his snare, while Italy and the provinces were drained by a boundless usury. His own money, on the other hand, had been plundered when Suillius governed the province He would suffer prosecutions, perils, anything indeed rather than make an old and self-earned position of honor to bow before an upstart prosperity."

43. Persons were not wanting to report all this to Seneca, in the exact words, or with a worse sense put on it. Accusers were also found who alleged that our allies had been plundered when Suillius governed the province of Asia, and that there had been embezzlement of public monies. Then, as an entire year had been granted to them for inquiries, it seemed a shorter plan to begin with his crimes at Rome, the witnesses of which were on the spot. These men charged Suillius with having driven Quintus Pomponius[51] by a relentless prosecution into the extremity of civil war, with having forced Julia, Drusus' daughter, and Poppæa Sabina[52] to suicide, with having treacherously ruined Valerius Asiaticus, Lusius Saturninus,[53] and Cornelius Lupus,[54] in fact, with the wholesale conviction of troops of Roman knights,[55] and

with all the cruelty of Claudius. His defense was that of all this he had done nothing on his own responsibility but had simply obeyed the Emperor, till Nero stopped such pleadings by stating that he had ascertained from his father's notebooks that he had never compelled the prosecution of a single person.

Suillius then sheltered himself under Messallina's orders, and the defense began to collapse. "Why," it was asked, "was no one else chosen to put his tongue at the service of that savage harlot? We must punish the instruments used to perform atrocious acts, when, having gained the rewards of wickedness, they delegate the actual crimes to others."

And so, with the loss of half his property, his son and granddaughter being allowed to retain the other half, and what they had inherited under their mother's or grandmother's will being also exempted from confiscation, Suillius was banished to the Balearic Isles. Neither in the crisis of his peril nor after his condemnation did he quail in spirit. Rumor said that he supported that lonely exile by a life of ease and plenty. When the accusers attacked his son Nerullinus[56] on the strength of men's hatred of the father and of some charges of extortion, the Emperor interposed, as if implying that vengeance was fully satisfied.

44. About the same time Octavius Sagitta,[57] a tribune of the people, who was madly in love with Pontia, a married woman, bribed her by most costly presents into an intrigue and then into abandoning her husband. He had offered her marriage and had won her consent. But as soon as she was free, she devised delays, pretended that her father's wishes were against it, and having secured the prospect of a richer husband, she repudiated her promises. Octavius, on the other hand, now remonstrated, now threatened; his good name, he protested, was lost, his means exhausted, and as for his life, which was all that was left to him, he surrendered it to her mercy. When she spurned him, he asked the solace of one night, with which to soothe his passion, that he might set bounds to it for the future. A night was fixed, and Pontia entrusted the charge of her chamber to a

female slave acquainted with her secret. Octavius, attended by one freedman, entered, with a dagger concealed under his dress. Then, as usual in lovers' quarrels, there were chidings, entreaties, reproaches, excuses, and some period of the darkness was given up to passion; then, when seemingly about to go, and she was fearing nothing, he stabbed her with the steel, and having wounded and scared away the slave girl who was hurrying to her, rushed out of the chamber. Next day the murder became known, and there was no question as to the murderer, for it was proved that he had passed some time with her. The freedman, however, declared the deed was his, that he had, in fact, avenged his patron's wrongs. He had made some impression by the nobleness of his example, when the slave girl recovered and revealed the truth. Octavius, when he ceased to be tribune, was prosecuted before the consuls by the father of the murdered woman, and was condemned by the sentence of the Senate under the law concerning assassins.

45. A profligacy equally notorious in that same year proved the beginning of great evils to the state. There was at Rome one Poppæa Sabina; her father was Titus Ollius, but she had assumed the name of her maternal grandfather, Poppæus Sabinus,[58] a man of illustrious memory and pre-eminently distinguished by the honors of a consulship and a triumph. As for Ollius, before he attained promotion, the friendship of Sejanus was his ruin. This Poppæa had everything but a right mind. Her mother, who surpassed in personal attractions all the ladies of her day, had bequeathed to her alike fame and beauty. Her fortune adequately corresponded to the nobility of her descent. Her conversation was charming and her wit anything but dull. She professed virtue, while she practiced laxity. Seldom did she appear in public, and it was always with her face partly veiled, either to disappoint men's gaze or to set off her beauty. Her character she never spared, making no distinction between a husband and a paramour, while she was never a slave to her own passion or to that of her lover. Wherever there was a prospect of advantage, there she transferred her favors. And so while she was living as the

wife of Rufrius Crispinus, a Roman knight,[59] by whom
she had a son, she was attracted by the youth and fashionable elegance of Otho,[60] and by the fact too that he
was reputed to have Nero's most ardent friendship. Without any delay the intrigue was followed by marriage.

46. Otho now began to praise his wife's beauty and
accomplishments to the Emperor, either from a lover's
thoughtlessness or to inflame Nero's passion in the hope
of adding to his own influence by the further tie which
would arise out of possession of the same woman. Often,
as he rose from the Emperor's table, was he heard repeatedly to say that he was going to her, to the high
birth and beauty which had fallen to his lot, to that
which all men pray for, the joy of the fortunate. These
and like incitements allowed but of brief delay. Once
having gained admission, Poppæa won her way by artful
blandishments, pretending that she could not resist her
passion and that she was captivated by Nero's person.
Soon, as the Emperor's love grew ardent, she would
change and be supercilious, and, if she were detained
more than one or two nights, would say again and again
that she was a married woman and could not give up
her husband, attached as she was to Otho by a manner
of life which no one equaled. "His ideas and his style
were grand; at his house everything worthy of the highest fortune was ever before her eyes. Nero, on the contrary, with his slave-girl mistress, tied down by his attachment to Acte, had derived nothing from his slavish
associations but what was low and degrading."

Otho was now cut off from Nero's usual familiar intercourse, and then even from interviews and from the
royal suite, and at last was appointed governor of the
province of Lusitania,[61] that he might not be the Emperor's rival at Rome. There he lived up to the time of
the civil wars, not in the fashion of his disgraceful past,
but uprightly and virtuously, a pleasure-loving man when
idle, and self-restrained when in power.

47. Hitherto Nero had sought a veil for his abominations and wickedness. He was particularly suspicious of
Cornelius Sulla,[62] whose apathetic temper he interpreted
as really the reverse, inferring that he was, in fact, an

artful dissembler. Graptus, one of the Emperor's freedmen, whose age and experience had made him thoroughly acquainted with the imperial household from the time
of Tiberius, quickened these apprehensions by the following falsehood. The Mulvian Bridge[63] was then a famous haunt of nightly profligacy, and Nero used to go
there that he might take his pleasures more freely outside the city. So Graptus, taking advantage of an idle
panic into which the royal attendants had chanced to
have been thrown on their return by one of those youthful frolics which were then everywhere practiced, invented a story that a treacherous attack had been
planned on the Emperor, should he go back by the
Flaminian road, and that through the favor of destiny
he had escaped it, as he went home by a different way
to the Gardens of Sallust.[64] Sulla, he said, was the author
of this plot. Not one, however, of Sulla's slaves or clients
was recognized, and his character, despicable as it was
and incapable of a daring act, was utterly at variance
with the charge. Still, just as if he had been found guilty,
he was ordered to leave his country, and confine himself
within the walls of Massilia.[65]

48. During the same consulship a hearing was given
to two conflicting deputations from Puteoli,[66] sent to the
Senate by the town council and by the populace. The
first spoke bitterly of the violence of the multitude; the
second, of the rapacity of the magistrates and of all the
chief citizens. That the disturbance, which had gone as
far as stoning and threats of fire, might not lead on to
bloodshed and armed fighting, Gaius Cassius was appointed to apply some remedy. As they would not endure
his rigor, the charge of the affair was at his own request
transferred to the brothers Scribonii,[67] to whom was
given a prætorian cohort, the terror of which, coupled
with the execution of a few persons, restored peace to
the townspeople.

49. I should not mention a very trivial decree of the
Senate which allowed the city of Syracuse to exceed the
prescribed number in their gladiatorial show,[68] had not
Thrasea Pætus[69] spoken against it and furnished his tra-
ducers with a ground for censuring his motion. "Why,"

it was asked, "if he thought that the public welfare required freedom of speech in the Senate, did he pursue such trifling abuses? Why should he not speak for or against peace and war, or on the taxes and laws and other matters involving Roman interests? The senators, as often as they received the privilege of stating an opinion, were at liberty to say out what they pleased, and to claim that it should be put to the vote. Was it the only worthy object of reform to provide that the Syracusans should not give shows on a larger scale? Were all other matters in every department of the Empire as admirable as if Thrasea and not Nero had the direction of them? But if the highest affairs were passed by and ignored, how much more ought there to be no meddling with things wholly insignificant!"

Thrasea in reply, when his friends asked an explanation, said that "it was not in ignorance of Rome's actual condition that he sought to correct such decrees, but that he was giving what was due to the honor of the senators, in making it evident that those who attended even to the merest trifles would not disguise their responsibility for important affairs."

50. That same year, repeated demands on the part of the people, who denounced the excessive greed of the revenue collectors,[70] made Nero doubt whether he should not order the repeal of all indirect taxes, and so confer a most splendid boon on the human race. But this sudden impulse was checked by the senators, who, having first heartily praised the grandeur of his conception, pointed out that "the dissolution of the Empire must ensue if the revenues which supported the state were to be diminished; for as soon as the customs were swept away, there would follow a demand for the abolition of the direct taxes. Many companies for the collection of the indirect taxes had been formed by consuls and tribunes, when the freedom of the Roman people was still in its vigor, and arrangements were subsequently made to ensure an exact correspondence between the amount of income and the necessary disbursements. Certainly some restraint, they admitted, must be put on the cupidity of the publicans, that they might not by new oppres-

sions bring into odium what for so many years had been endured without a complaint."

51. Accordingly the Emperor issued an edict that the regulations about every branch of the public revenue, which had hitherto been kept secret, should be published; that claims which had been dropped should not be revived after a year; that the prætor at Rome, the proprætor or proconsul in the provinces, should give judicial precedence to all cases against the publicans; that the soldiers should retain their immunities except when they traded for profit, with other very equitable arrangements, which for a short time were maintained and were subsequently disregarded. However, the repeal of the two-per-cent and two-and-a-half-per-cent taxes remained in force, as well as that of others bearing names invented by the collectors to cover their illegal exactions. In our transmarine provinces the conveyance of corn was rendered less costly, and it was decided that merchant ships should not be assessed with their owners' property, and that no tax should be paid on them.

52. Two men under prosecution from Africa, in which province they had held proconsular authority, Sulpicius Camerinus[71] and Pompeius Silvanus,[72] were acquitted by the Emperor. Camerinus had against him a few private persons who charged him with cruelty rather than with extortion. Silvanus was beset by a host of accusers, who demanded time for summoning their witnesses, while the defendant insisted on being at once put on his defense. And he was successful, through his wealth, his childlessness, and his old age, which he prolonged beyond the life of those by whose corrupt influence he had escaped.

[Chapters 53-58, *which deal with affairs in Germany, are omitted.*]

BOOK XIV   *59-62 A.D.*

1. In the year of the consulship of Gaius Vipstanus and Gaius Fonteius,[1] Nero deferred no more a long-

meditated crime. Length of power had matured his daring, and his passion for Poppæa daily grew more ardent. As the woman had no hope of marriage for herself or of Octavia's divorce while Agrippina lived, she would reproach the Emperor with incessant vituperation and sometimes call him in jest a mere ward who was under the rule of others, and was so far from having empire that he had not even his liberty. "Why," she asked, "was her marriage put off? Was it her beauty and her ancestors, with their triumphal honors,[2] that failed to please, or her being a mother, and her sincere heart? No; the fear was that as a wife at least she would divulge the wrongs of the Senate, and the wrath of the people at the arrogance and rapacity of his mother. If the only daughter-in-law Agrippina could bear was one who wished evil to her son, let her be restored to her union with Otho. She would go anywhere in the world, where she might hear of the insults heaped on the Emperor, rather than witness them, and be also involved in his perils."

These and the like complaints, rendered impressive by tears and by the cunning of an adulteress, no one checked, as all longed to see the mother's power broken, while not a person believed that the son's hatred would steel his heart to her murder.

2. Cluvius relates that Agrippina in her eagerness to retain her influence went so far that more than once at midday, when Nero, even at that hour, was flushed with wine and feasting, she presented herself attractively attired to her half-intoxicated son and offered him her person, and that when kinsfolk observed wanton kisses and caresses, portending infamy, it was Seneca who sought a female's aid against a woman's fascinations, and hurried in Acte, the freedwoman, who, alarmed at her own peril and at Nero's disgrace, told him that the rumor of their incest had circulated widely, as his mother boasted of it, and that the soldiers would never endure the rule of a sacrilegious sovereign. Fabius Rusticus tells us that it was not Agrippina, but Nero, who lusted for the crime, and that it was frustrated by the adroitness of that same freedwoman. Cluvius' account, however, is also that of all other authors, and popular belief inclines to

it, whether it was that Agrippina really conceived such a monstrous wickedness in her heart, or perhaps because the thought of a strange passion seemed comparatively crédible in a woman who in her girlish years had allowed herself to be seduced by Lepidus[3] in the hope of winning power, had stooped with a like ambition to the lust of Pallas, and had trained herself for every infamy by her marriage with her uncle.

3. Nero accordingly avoided secret interviews with her, and when she withdrew to her gardens or to her estates at Tusculum[4] and Antium,[5] he praised her for courting repose. At last, convinced that she would be too formidable, wherever she might dwell, he resolved to destroy her, merely deliberating whether it was to be accomplished by poison, or by the sword, or by any other violent means. Poison at first seemed best, but, were it to be administered at the imperial table, the result could not be referred to chance after the recent circumstances of the death of Britannicus. Again, to tamper with the servants of a woman who, from her familiarity with crime, was on her guard against treachery appeared to be extremely difficult, and then too, she had fortified her constitution by the use of antidotes. How again the dagger and its work were to be kept secret, no one could suggest, and it was feared too that whoever might be chosen to execute such a crime would spurn the order.

An ingenious suggestion was offered by Anicetus, a freedman, commander of the fleet at Misenum,[6] who had been tutor to Nero in boyhood and had a hatred of Agrippina which she reciprocated. He explained that a vessel could be constructed, from which a part might by a contrivance be detached, when out at sea, so as to plunge her unawares into the water. "Nothing," he said, "allowed of accidents so much as the sea, and should she be overtaken by shipwreck, who would be so unfair as to impute to crime an offense committed by the winds and waves? The Emperor would add the honor of a temple and of shrines to the deceased lady, with every other display of filial affection."

4. Nero liked the device, favored as it also was by the particular time, for he was celebrating Minerva's five-

day festival at Baiæ. Thither he enticed his mother by repeated assurances that children ought to bear with the irritability of parents and to soothe their tempers, wishing thus to spread a rumor of reconciliation and to secure Agrippina's acceptance through feminine credulity, which easily believes what gives joy. As she approached, he went to the shore to meet her (she was coming from Antium), welcomed her with outstretched hand and embrace, and conducted her to Bauli. This was the name of a country house, washed by a bay of the sea, between the promontory of Misenum and the lake of Baiæ. Here was a vessel distinguished from others by its equipment, seemingly meant, among other things, to do honor to his mother; for she had been accustomed to sail in a trireme, with a crew of marines. And now she was invited to a banquet, that night might serve to conceal the crime. It was well known that somebody had been found to betray it, that Agrippina had heard of the plot, and in doubt whether she was to believe it, was conveyed to Baiæ in her litter. There some soothing words allayed her fear; she was graciously received, and seated at table above the Emperor. Nero prolonged the banquet with various conversation, passing from a boy's playful familiarity to an air of constraint, which seemed to indicate serious thought; and then, after protracted festivity, escorted her on her departure, clinging with kisses to her eyes and bosom, either to crown his hypocrisy or because the last sight of a mother on the eve of destruction caused a lingering even in that brutal heart.

5. A night of brilliant starlight with the calm of a tranquil sea was granted by heaven, seemingly, to convict the crime. The vessel had not gone far—Agrippina having with her two of her intimate attendants, one of whom, Crepereius Gallus, stood near the helm, while Acerronia,[7] reclining at Agrippina's feet as she reposed herself, spoke joyfully of her son's repentance and of the recovery of the mother's influence—when at a given signal the ceiling of the place, which was loaded with a quantity of lead, fell in, and Crepereius was crushed and instantly killed. Agrippina and Acerronia were protected by the projecting sides of the couch, which hap-

pened to be too strong to yield under the weight. But this was not followed by the breaking up of the vessel; for all were bewildered, and those too who were in the plot were hindered by the unconscious majority. The crew then thought it best to throw the vessel on one side and so sink it, but they could not themselves promptly unite to face the emergency, and others, by counteracting the attempt, gave an opportunity of a gentler fall into the sea. Acerronia, however, thoughtlessly exclaiming that she was Agrippina, and imploring help for the Emperor's mother, was dispatched with poles and oars, and such naval implements as chance offered. Agrippina was silent and was thus the less recognized; still, she received a wound in her shoulder. She swam, then met with some small boats which conveyed her to the Lucrine lake, and so entered her house.

6. There she reflected how for this very purpose she had been invited by a lying letter and treated with conspicuous honor, how also it was near the shore, not from being driven by winds or dashed on rocks, that the vessel had in its upper part collapsed, like a mechanism anything but nautical. She pondered too the death of Acerronia; she looked at her own wound, and saw that her only safeguard against treachery was to ignore it. Then she sent her freedman Agerinus to tell her son how by heaven's favor and his good fortune she had escaped a terrible disaster; that she begged him, alarmed as he might be by his mother's peril, to put off the duty of a visit, as for the present she needed repose. Meanwhile, pretending that she felt secure, she applied remedies to her wound, and fomentations to her person. She then ordered a search to be made for the will of Acerronia, and her property to be sealed, in this alone throwing off disguise.

7. Nero, meantime, as he waited for tidings of the consummation of the deed, received information that she had escaped with the injury of a slight wound, after having so far encountered the peril that there could be no question as to its author. Then, paralyzed with terror and protesting that she would show herself the next moment eager for vengeance, either arming the slaves or

stirring up the soldiery, or hastening to the Senate and the people, to charge him with the wreck, with her wound, and with the destruction of her friends, he asked what resource he had against all this, unless something could be at once devised by Burrus and Seneca. He had instantly summoned both of them, and possibly they were already in the secret. There was a long silence on their part; they feared they might remonstrate in vain, or believed the crisis to be such that Nero must perish, unless Agrippina were at once crushed. Thereupon Seneca was so far the more prompt as to glance back on Burrus, as if to ask him whether the bloody deed must be required of the soldiers. Burrus replied that "the prætorians were attached to the whole family of the Cæsars, and remembering Germanicus would not dare a savage deed on his offspring. It was for Anicetus to accomplish his promise."

Anicetus, without a pause, claimed for himself the consummation of the crime. At those words, Nero declared that that day gave him empire, and that a freedman was the author of this mighty boon. "Go," he said, "with all speed and take with you the men readiest to execute your orders." He himself, when he had heard of the arrival of Agrippina's messenger, Agerinus, contrived a theatrical mode of accusation, and, while the man was repeating his message, threw down a sword at his feet, then ordered him to be put in irons, as a detected criminal, so that he might invent a story how his mother had plotted the Emperor's destruction and in the shame of discovered guilt had by her own choice sought death.

8. Meantime, Agrippina's peril being universally known and taken to be an accidental occurrence, everybody, the moment he heard of it, hurried down to the beach. Some climbed projecting piers; some the nearest vessels; others, as far as their stature allowed, went into the sea; some, again, stood with outstretched arms, while the whole shore rang with wailings, with prayers and cries, as different questions were asked and uncertain answers given. A vast multitude streamed to the spot with torches, and as soon as all knew that she was safe,

they at once prepared to wish her joy, till the sight of an armed and threatening force scared them away. Anicetus then surrounded the house with a guard, and having burst open the gates, dragged off the slaves who met him, till he came to the door of her chamber, where a few still stood, after the rest had fled in terror at the attack. A small lamp was in the room, and one slave girl with Agrippina, who grew more and more anxious, as no messenger came from her son, not even Agerinus, while the appearance of the shore was changed, a solitude one moment, then sudden bustle and tokens of the worst catastrophe. As the girl rose to depart, she exclaimed, "Do you too forsake me?" and looking round saw Anicetus, who had with him the captain of the trireme, Herculeius, and Obaritus, a centurion of marines. "If," said she, "you have come to see me, take back word that I have recovered, but if you are here to commit a crime, I believe nothing about my son; he has not ordered his mother's murder."

The assassins closed in round her couch, and the captain of the trireme first struck her head violently with a club. Then, as the centurion bared his sword for the fatal deed, presenting her person she exclaimed, "Smite my womb," and with many wounds she was slain.

9. So far our accounts agree. That Nero gazed on his mother after her death and praised her beauty, some have related, while others deny it. Her body was burned that same night on a dining couch, with a mean funeral; nor, as long as Nero was in power, was the earth raised into a mound, or even decently closed. Subsequently she received from the solicitude of her domestics a humble sepulcher on the road to Misenum, near the country house of Cæsar the dictator, which from a great height commands a view of the bay beneath. As soon as the funeral pile was lighted, one of her freedmen, surnamed Mnester, ran himself through with a sword, either from love of his mistress or from the fear of destruction.

Many years before, Agrippina had anticipated this end for herself and had spurned the thought. For when she consulted the astrologers about Nero, they replied that he would be Emperor and kill his mother. "Let him kill her," she said, "provided he is Emperor."[8]

10. But the Emperor, when the crime was at last accomplished, realized its portentous guilt. The rest of the night, now silent and stupified, now and still oftener starting up in terror, bereft of reason, he awaited the dawn as if it would bring with it his doom. He was first encouraged to hope by the flattery addressed to him, at the prompting of Burrus, by the centurions and tribunes, who again and again pressed his hand and congratulated him on his having escaped an unforeseen danger and his mother's daring crime. Then his friends went to the temples, and, an example having once been set, the neighboring towns of Campania testified their joy with sacrifices and deputations. He himself, with an opposite phase of hypocrisy, seemed sad, and almost angry at his own deliverance, and shed tears over his mother's death. But as the aspects of places change not, as do the looks of men, and as he had ever before his eyes the dreadful sight of that sea with its shores (some too believed that the notes of a funereal trumpet were heard from the surrounding heights, and wailings from the mother's grave), he retired to Neapolis[9] and sent a letter to the Senate, the drift of which was that Agerinus, one of Agrippina's confidential freedmen, had been detected with the dagger of an assassin, and that in the consciousness of having planned the crime she had paid its penalty.

11. He even revived the charges of a period long past, how she had aimed at a share of empire, and at inducing the prætorian cohorts to swear obedience to a woman, to the disgrace of the Senate and people; how, when she was disappointed, in her fury with the soldiers, the Senate, and the populace, she opposed the usual largess, and organized perilous prosecutions against distinguished citizens. What efforts had it cost him to hinder her from bursting into the Senate House and giving answers to foreign nations! He glanced too with indirect censure at the days of Claudius, and ascribed all the abominations of that reign to his mother, thus seeking to show that it was the state's good fortune which had destroyed

her. For he actually told the story of the shipwreck; but who could be so stupid as to believe that it was accidental, or that a shipwrecked woman had sent one man with a weapon to break through an Emperor's guards and fleets? So now it was not Nero, whose brutality was far beyond any remonstrance, but Seneca who was in ill repute, for having written a confession in such a style.

12. Still there was a marvelous rivalry among the nobles in decreeing thanksgivings at all the shrines, and the celebration with annual games of Minerva's festival, as the day on which the plot had been discovered; also, that a golden image of Minerva with a statue of the Emperor by its side should be set up in the Senate House, and that Agrippina's birthday should be classed among the inauspicious days. Thrasea Pætus,[10] who had been used to pass over previous flatteries in silence or with brief assent, then walked out of the Senate, thereby imperiling himself, without communicating to the other senators any impulse toward freedom.·

There occurred too a thick succession of portents, which meant nothing. A woman gave birth to a snake, and another was killed by a thunderbolt in her husband's embrace. Then the sun was suddenly darkened and the fourteen districts of the city were struck by lightning. All this happened quite without any providential design; so much so, that for many subsequent years Nero prolonged his reign and his crimes. Still, to deepen the popular hatred toward his mother, and prove that since her removal his clemency had increased, he restored to their ancestral homes two distinguished ladies, Junia and Calpurnia, with two ex-prætors, Valerius Capito and Licinius Gabolus, whom Agrippina had formerly banished. He also allowed the ashes of Lollia Paulina[11] to be brought back and a tomb to be built over them. Iturius and Calvisius, whom he had himself temporarily exiled, he now released from their penalty. Silana indeed had died a natural death at Tarentum,[12] whither she had returned from her distant exile when the power of Agrippina, to whose enmity she owed her fall, began to totter, or her wrath was at last appeased.

13. While Nero was lingering in the towns of Campania, doubting how he should enter Rome, whether he would find the Senate submissive and the populace enthusiastic, all the vilest courtiers, and of these never had a court a more abundant crop, argued against his hesitation by assuring him that Agrippina's name was hated and that her death had heightened his popularity. "He might go without a fear," they said, "and experience in his person men's veneration for him." They insisted at the same time on preceding him. They found greater enthusiasm than they had promised, the tribes coming forth to meet him, the Senate in holiday attire, troops of their children and wives according to sex and age, tiers of seats raised for the spectacle where he was to pass, as a triumph is witnessed. Thus elated and exulting over his people's slavery, he proceeded to the Capitol, performed the thanksgiving, and then plunged into all the excesses which, though ill-restrained, some sort of respect for his mother had for a while delayed.

14. He had long had a fancy for driving a four-horse chariot, and a no less degrading taste for singing to the harp, in a theatrical fashion, when he was at dinner.[13] This he would remind people was a royal custom, and had been the practice of ancient chiefs; it was celebrated too in the praises of poets and was meant to show honor to the gods. Songs indeed, he said, were sacred to Apollo, and it was in the dress of a singer that that great and prophetic deity was seen in Roman temples as well as in Greek cities. He could no longer be restrained, when Seneca and Burrus thought it best to concede one point that he might not persist in both. A space was enclosed in the Vatican valley where he might manage his horses, without the spectacle being public. Soon, he actually invited all the people of Rome, who extolled him in their praises, like a mob which craves for amusements and rejoices when a prince draws them the same way. However, the public exposure of his shame acted on him as an incentive instead of sickening him, as men expected. Imagining that he mitigated the scandal by disgracing many others, he brought on the stage descendants of noble families, who sold themselves because

they were paupers. As they have ended their days, I
think it due to their ancestors not to hand down their
names. And indeed the infamy is his who gave them
wealth to reward their degradation rather than to deter
them from degrading themselves. He prevailed too on
some well-known Roman knights, by immense presents,
to offer their services in the amphitheater; only pay from
one who is able to command carries with it the force of
compulsion.

15. Still, not yet wishing to disgrace himself on a
public stage, he instituted some games under the title
of Juvenilia,[14] for which people of every class gave in
their names. Neither rank nor age nor previous high
promotion hindered anyone from practicing the art of a
Greek or Latin actor and even stooping to gestures and
songs unfit for a man. Noble ladies too actually played
disgusting parts, and in the grove with which Augustus
had surrounded the lake for the naval fight,[15] there
were erected places for meeting and refreshment, and
every incentive to excess was offered for sale. Money too
was distributed, which the respectable had to spend
under sheer compulsion and which the profligate gloried
in squandering. Hence a rank growth of abominations
and of all infamy. Never did a more filthy rabble add a
worse licentiousness to our long-corrupted morals. Even
with virtuous training, purity is not easily upheld; far
less amid rivalries in vice could modesty or propriety or
any trace of good manners be preserved. Last of all, the
Emperor himself came on the stage, tuning his lute
with elaborate care and trying his voice with his attendants. There were also present, to complete the show,
a guard of soldiers with centurions and tribunes, and
Burrus, who grieved and yet applauded. Then it was that
Roman knights were first enrolled under the title of
Augustiani, men in their prime and remarkable for their
strength, some from a natural frivolity, others from the
hope of promotion. Day and night they kept up a thunder
of applause, and applied to the Emperor's person and
voice the epithets of deities. Thus they lived in fame
and honor, as if on the strength of their merits.

16. Nero, however, that he might not be known only

for his accomplishments as an actor, also affected a taste
for poetry, and drew round him persons who had some
skill in such compositions, but not yet generally recognized. They used to sit with him, stringing together
verses prepared at home, or extemporized on the spot,
and fill up his own expressions, such as they were, just
as he threw them off. This is plainly shown by the very
character of the poems, which have no vigor or inspiration, or unity in their flow.

He would also bestow some leisure after his banquets
on the teachers of philosophy, for he enjoyed the wran-
gles of opposing dogmatists. And some there were who
liked to exhibit their gloomy faces and looks as one of
the amusements of the court.

17. About the same time a trifling beginning led to
frightful bloodshed between the inhabitants of Nuceria[16]
and Pompeii,[17] at a gladiatorial show exhibited by Livineius Regulus, who had been, as I have related, expelled
from the Senate.[18] With the unruly spirit of townsfolk,
they began with abusive language toward each other;
then they took up stones and at last weapons, the advantage resting with the populace of Pompeii, where the
show was being exhibited. And so there were brought
to Rome a number of the people of Nuceria, with their
bodies mutilated by wounds, and many lamented the
deaths of children or of parents. The Emperor entrusted
the trial of the case to the Senate, and the Senate to the
consuls, and then the matter again being referred back
to the Senators, the inhabitants of Pompeii were forbidden to have any such public gathering for ten years,
and all associations they had formed in defiance of the
laws were dissolved. Livineius and the others who had
excited the disturbance, were punished with exile.

18. Pedius Blæsus was also expelled from the Senate
on the accusation of the people of Cyrene, that he had
violated the treasury of Æsculapius and had tampered
with a military levy by bribery and corruption. This
same people prosecuted Acilius Strabo, who had held the
office of prætor, and had been sent by Claudius to ad-
judicate on some lands which were bequeathed by King
Apion,[19] their former possessor, together with his king-

dom to the Roman people, and which had since been seized by the neighboring proprietors, who trusted to a long-continued license in wrong, as if it constituted right and justice. Consequently, when the adjudication was against them, there arose a bitter feeling toward the judge, but the Senate replied that they knew nothing of the instructions given by Claudius, and that the Emperor must be consulted. Nero, though he approved Strabo's decision, wrote word that nevertheless he was for relieving the allies, and that he waived all claim to what had been taken into possession.

19. Then followed the deaths of two illustrious men, Domitius Afer[20] and Marcus Servilius, who had flourished through a career of the highest honors and great eloquence. The first was a pleader; Servilius,[21] after long practice in the courts, distinguished himself by his history of Rome and by the refinement of his life, which the contrast of his character to that of Afer, whom he equaled in genius, rendered the more conspicuous.

20. In Nero's fourth consulship with Cornelius Cossus for his colleague,[22] a theatrical entertainment to be repeated every four years was established at Rome in imitation of the Greek festival.[23] Like all novelties, it was variously canvassed. There were some who declared that even Cnæus Pompeius[24] was censured by the older men of the day for having set up a fixed and permanent theater. "Formerly," they said, "the games were usually exhibited with hastily erected tiers of benches and a temporary stage, and the people stood to witness them, that they might not, by having the chance of sitting down, spend a succession of entire days in idleness. Let the ancient character of these shows be retained, whenever the prætors exhibited them, and let no citizen be under the necessity of competing. As it was, the morality of their fathers, which had by degrees been forgotten, was utterly subverted by the introduction of a lax tone, so that all which could suffer or produce corruption was to be seen at Rome, and a degeneracy bred by foreign tastes was infecting the youth who devoted themselves to athletic sports, to idle loungings and low intrigues, with the encouragement of the Emperor and Senate,

who not only granted license to vice, but even applied a
compulsion to drive Roman nobles into disgracing themselves on the stage, under the pretense of being orators
and poets. What remained for them but to strip themselves naked, put on the boxing glove, and practice such
battles instead of the arms of legitimate warfare? Would
justice be promoted, or would they serve on the knights'
commissions for the honorable office of a judge, because
they had listened with critical sagacity to effeminate
strains of music and sweet voices? Night too was given
up to infamy, so that virtue had not a moment left to
her, but all the vilest of that promiscuous throng dared
to do in the darkness anything they had lusted for in
the day."

21. Many people liked this very license, but they
screened it under respectable names. "Our ancestors,"
they said, "were not averse to the attractions of shows on
a scale suited to the wealth of their day, and so they introduced actors from the Etruscans[25] and horse races
from Thuria.[26] When we had possessed ourselves of
Achæa and Asia, games were exhibited with greater
elaboration, and yet no one at Rome of good family
had stooped to the theatrical profession during the two
hundred years following the triumph of Lucius Mum-
mius,[27] who first displayed this kind of show in the
capital. Besides, even economy had been consulted,
when a permanent edifice was erected for a theater in
preference to a structure raised and fitted up yearly at
vast expense. Nor would the magistrates, as hitherto,
exhaust their substance, nor would the populace have the
same motive for demanding of them the Greek contests,
when once the state undertakes the expenditure. The victories won by orators and poets would furnish a stimulus
to genius, and it could not be a burden for any judge
to bestow his attention on graceful pursuits or on legitimate recreations. It was to mirth rather than to profligacy that a few nights every four years were devoted,
and in these amid such a blaze of illumination no lawless conduct could be concealed."

This entertainment, it is true, passed off without any
notorious scandal. The enthusiasm too of the populace

was not even slightly kindled, for the pantomimic actors, though permitted to return to the stage, were excluded from the sacred contests. No one gained the first prize for eloquence, but it was publicly announced that the Emperor was victorious. Greek dresses, in which most people showed themselves during this festival, had then gone out of fashion.

22. A comet meantime blazed in the sky, which in popular opinion always portends revolution to kingdoms. So people began to ask, as if Nero were already dethroned, who was to be elected. In everyone's mouth was the name of Rubellius Plautus,[28] who inherited through his mother the high nobility of the Julian family. He was himself attached to the ideas of our ancestors; his manners were austere, his home was one of purity and seclusion, and the more he lived in retirement from fear, the more fame did he acquire. Popular talk was confirmed by an interpretation put with similar credulity on a flash of lightning. While Nero was reclining at dinner in his house named Sublaqueum[29] on the Simbruine lake, the table with the banquet was struck and shattered, and as this happened close to Tibur,[30] from which town Plautus derived his origin on his father's side, people believed him to be the man marked out by divine providence; and he was encouraged by that numerous class whose eager and often mistaken ambition it is to attach themselves prematurely to some new and hazardous cause. This alarmed Nero, and he wrote a letter to Plautus, bidding him "consider the tranquillity of Rome and withdraw himself from mischievous gossip. He had ancestral possessions in Asia, where he might enjoy his youth safely and quietly." And so thither Plautus retired with his wife, Antistia,[31] and a few intimate friends.

About the same time an excessive love of luxurious gratification involved Nero in disgrace and danger. He had plunged for a swim into the source of the Aqua Marcia,[32] and it was thought that, by thus immersing his person in it, he had polluted the sacred waters and the sanctity of the spot. A fit of illness which followed convinced people of the divine displeasure.

[*Chapters 23-26, which deal with Armenian affairs, are omitted.*]

27. One of the famous cities of Asia, Laodicea,[33] was that same year overthrown by an earthquake, and, without any relief from us, recovered itself by its own resources. In Italy meanwhile the old town of Puteoli[34] obtained from Nero the privileges of a colony with an additional name. A further enrollment of veterans in Tarentum[35] and Antium[36] did but little for those thinly peopled places; for most scattered themselves in the provinces where they had completed their military service. Not being accustomed to tie themselves by marriage and rear children, they left behind them homes without families. For whole legions were no longer transplanted, as in former days, with tribunes and centurions and soldiers of every grade, so as to form a state by their unity and mutual attachment, but strangers to one another from different companies, without a head or any community of sentiment, were suddenly gathered together, as it might be out of any other class of human beings, and became a mere crowd rather than a colony.

28. As at the elections for prætors, now generally under the Senate's control, there was the excitement of a particularly keen competition, the Emperor quieted matters by promoting the three supernumerary candidates to legionary commands. He also raised the dignity of the Senate by deciding that all who appealed from private judges to its house were to incur the same pecuniary risk as those who referred their cause to the Emperor. Hitherto such an appeal had been perfectly open, and free from penalty.

At the close of the year Vibius Secundus, a Roman knight, on the accusation of the Moors, was convicted of extortion, and banished from Italy, contriving through the influence of his brother Vibius Crispus[37] to escape heavier punishment.

29. In the consulship of Cæsennius Pætus and Petronius Turpilianus,[38] a serious disaster was sustained in Britain, where Aulus Didus, the Emperor's legate,[39] had merely retained our existing possessions, and his

TACITUS

successor, Veranius,[40] after having ravaged the Silures
in some trifling raids, was prevented by death from
extending the war. While he lived, he had a great name
for manly independence, though, in his will's final
words, he betrayed a flatterer's weakness; for, after heaping adulation on Nero, he added that he should have
conquered the province for him, had he lived for the
next two years. Now, however, Britain was in the hands
of Suetonius Paullinus,[41] who in military knowledge and
in popular favor, which allows no one to be without a
rival, vied with Corbulo, and aspired to equal the glory
of the recovery of Armenia by the subjugation of
Rome's enemies. He therefore prepared to attack the
island of Mona,[42] which had a powerful population and
was a refuge for fugitives. He built flat-bottomed vessels
to cope with the shallows and uncertain depths of the
sea. Thus the infantry crossed, while the cavalry followed by fording, or, where the water was deep, swam
by the side of their horses.

30. On the shore stood the opposing army with its
dense array of armed warriors, while between the ranks
dashed women, in black attire like the Furies, with hair
disheveled, waving brands. All around, the Druids, lifting up their hands to heaven, and pouring forth dreadful imprecations, scared our soldiers by the unfamiliar
sight, so that, as if their limbs were paralyzed, they stood
motionless, and exposed to wounds. Then, urged by their
general's appeals and mutual encouragements not to
quail before a troop of frenzied women, they bore the
standards onward, smote down all resistance, and
wrapped the foe in the flames of his own brands. A force
was next set over the conquered, and their groves, devoted to inhuman superstitions, were destroyed. They
thought it a religious duty to cover their altars with the
blood of captives and to consult their deities by inspecting human livers.

31. Suetonius while thus occupied received tidings of
the sudden revolt of the province. Prasutagus, king of
the Iceni,[43] famed for his long prosperity, had made the
Emperor his heir along with his two daughters, under
the impression that this token of submission would put

226

his kingdom and his house out of the reach of wrong. But the reverse was the result, so much so that his kingdom was plundered by centurions, his house by slaves, as if they were the spoils of war. First, his wife, Boudicca, was scourged and his daughters outraged. All the chief men of the Iceni, as if Rome had received the whole country as a gift, were stripped of their ancestral possessions, and the king's relatives were made slaves. Roused by these insults and the dread of worse, reduced as they now were into the condition of a province, they flew to arms and stirred to revolt the Trinobantes[44] and others who, not yet cowed by slavery, had agreed in secret conspiracy to reclaim their freedom. It was against the veterans that their hatred was most intense. For these new settlers in the colony of Camulodunum[45] drove people out of their houses, ejected them from their farms, called them captives and slaves, and the lawlessness of the veterans was encouraged by the soldiers, who lived a similar life and hoped for similar license. A temple, also, erected to the divine Claudius was ever before their eyes, a citadel, as it seemed, of perpetual tyranny. Men chosen as priests had to squander their whole fortunes under the pretense of a religious ceremonial. It appeared too no difficult matter to destroy the colony, undefended as it was by fortifications, a precaution neglected by our generals, while they thought more of what was agreeable than of what was expedient.

32. Meanwhile, without any evident cause, the statue of victory at Camulodunum fell prostrate and turned its back to the enemy, as though it fled before them. Women excited to frenzy prophesied impending destruction; ravings in a strange tongue, it was said, were heard in their Senate House; their theater resounded with wailings, and in the estuary of the Tamesa[46] had been seen the appearance of an overthrown town; even the ocean had worn the aspect of blood, and when the tide ebbed, there had been left the likenesses of human forms, marvels interpreted by the Britons as hopeful, by the veterans as alarming. But as Suetonius was far away, they implored aid from the procurator, Catus Decianus. All he did was to send two hundred men, and

no more, without regular arms, and there was in the
place but a small military force. Trusting to the protection of the temple, hindered too by secret accomplices
in the revolt, who embarrassed their plans, they had
constructed neither fosse nor rampart; nor had they
removed their old men and women, leaving their youth
alone to face the foe. Surprised, as it were, in the midst
of peace, they were surrounded by an immense host of
the barbarians. All else was plundered or fired in the
onslaught; the temple where the soldiers had assembled
was stormed after a two-day siege. The victorious enemy
met Petilius Cerialis,[47] commander of the ninth legion,
as he was coming to the rescue, routed his troops, and
destroyed all his infantry. Cerialis escaped with some
cavalry into the camp, and was saved by its fortifications. Alarmed by this disaster and by the fury of the
province which he had goaded into war by his rapacity,
the procurator Catus crossed over into Gaul.

33. Suetonius, however, with wonderful resolution,
marched amidst a hostile population to Londinium,[48]
which, though undistinguished by the name of a colony,
was much frequented by a number of merchants and
trading vessels. Uncertain whether he should choose it as
a seat of war, as he looked round on his scanty force of
soldiers and remembered with what a serious warning
the rashness of Petilius had been punished, he resolved
to save the province at the cost of a single town. Nor
did the tears and weeping of the people, as they implored
his aid, deter him from giving the signal of departure
and receiving into his army all who would go with him.
Those who were chained to the spot by the weakness
of their sex, or the infirmity of age, or the attractions of
the place, were cut off by the enemy. Like ruin fell on
the town of Verulamium,[49] for the barbarians, who delighted in plunder and were indifferent to all else, passed
by the fortresses with military garrisons, and attacked
whatever offered most wealth to the spoiler, and was
unsafe for defense. About seventy thousand citizens and
allies, it appeared, fell in the places which I have mentioned. For it was not on making prisoners and selling
them, or on any of the barter of war, that the enemy

was bent, but on slaughter, on the gibbet, the fire and the cross, like men soon about to pay the penalty and meanwhile snatching at instant vengeance.

34. Suetonius had the fourteenth legion with the veterans of the twentieth, and auxiliaries from the neighborhood, to the number of about ten thousand armed men, when he prepared to break off delay and fight a battle. He chose a position approached by a narrow defile, closed in at the rear by a forest, having first ascertained that there was not a soldier of the enemy except in his front, where an open plain extended without any danger from ambuscades. His legions were in close array; round them, the light-armed troops, and the cavalry in dense array on the wings. On the other side, the army of the Britons, with its masses of infantry and cavalry, was confidently exulting, a vaster host than ever had assembled, and so fierce in spirit that they actually brought with them, to witness the victory, their wives riding in wagons, which they had placed on the extreme border of the plain.

35. Boudicca, with her daughters before her in a chariot, went up to tribe after tribe, protesting that it was indeed usual for Britons to fight under the leadership of women. "But now," she said, "it is not as a woman descended from noble ancestry, but as one of the people that I am avenging lost freedom, my scourged body, the outraged chastity of my daughters. Roman lust has gone so far that not our very persons, nor even age or virginity, are left unpolluted. But heaven is on the side of a righteous vengeance; a legion which dared to fight has perished; the rest are hiding themselves in their camp, or are thinking anxiously of flight. They will not sustain even the din and the shout of so many thousands, much less our charge and our blows. If you weigh well the strength of the armies, and the causes of the war, you will see that in this battle you must conquer or die. This is a woman's resolve; as for men, they may live and be slaves."

36. Nor was Suetonius silent at such a crisis. Though he confided in the valor of his men, he yet mingled encouragements and entreaties to disdain the clamors and

TACITUS

empty threats of the barbarians. "There," he said, "you see more women than warriors. Unwarlike, unarmed, they will give way the moment they have recognized that sword and that courage of their conquerors, which have so often routed them. Even among many legions, it is a few who really decide the battle, and it will enhance their glory that a small force should earn the renown of an entire army. Only close up the ranks, and having discharged your javelins, then with shields and swords continue the work of bloodshed and destruction, without a thought of plunder. When once the victory has been won, everything will be in your power."

Such was the enthusiasm which followed the general's address, and so promptly did the veteran soldiery, with their long experience of battles, prepare for the hurling of the javelins, that it was with confidence in the result that Suetonius gave the signal of battle.

37. At the first, the legion kept its position, clinging to the narrow defile as a defense; when they had exhausted their missiles, which they discharged with unerring aim on the closely approaching foe, they rushed out in a wedgelike column. Similar was the onset of the auxiliaries, while the cavalry with extended lances broke through all who offered a strong resistance. The rest turned their back in flight, and flight proved difficult, because the surrounding wagons had blocked retreat. Our soldiers spared not to slay even the women, while the very beasts of burden, transfixed by the missiles, swelled the piles of bodies. Great glory, equal to that of our old victories, was won on that day. Some indeed say that there fell little less than eighty thousand of the Britons, with a loss to our soldiers of about four hundred, and only as many wounded. Boudicca put an end to her life by poison.[50] Pœnius Postumus too, camp prefect of the second legion, when he knew of the success of the men of the fourteenth and twentieth, feeling that he had cheated his legion out of like glory, and had contrary to all military usage disregarded the general's orders, threw himself on his sword.

38. The whole army was then brought together and kept under canvas to finish the remainder of the war.

230

The Emperor strengthened the forces by sending from Germany two thousand legionaries, eight cohorts of auxiliaries, and a thousand cavalry. On their arrival the men of the ninth had their number made up with legionary soldiers. The allied infantry and cavalry were placed in new winter quarters, and whatever tribes still wavered or were hostile were ravaged with fire and sword. Nothing, however, distressed the enemy so much as famine, for they had been careless about sowing corn, people of every age having gone to the war, while they reckoned on our supplies as their own. Nations, too, so high-spirited inclined the more slowly to peace, because Julius Classicianus, who had been sent as successor to Catus and was at variance with Suetonius, let private animosities interfere with the public interest, and had spread an idea that they ought to wait for a new governor, who, having neither the anger of an enemy nor the pride of a conqueror, would deal mercifully with those who had surrendered. At the same time he stated in a dispatch to Rome that no cessation of fighting must be expected, unless Suetonius were superseded, attributing that general's disasters to perverseness and his successes to good luck.

39. Accordingly one of the imperial freedmen, Polyclitus, was sent to survey the state of Britain, Nero having great hopes that his influence would be able not only to establish a good understanding between the governor and the procurator, but also to pacify the rebellious spirit of the barbarians. And Polyclitus, who with his enormous suite had been a burden to Italy and Gaul, did not fail, as soon as he had crossed the ocean, to make his progresses a terror even to our soldiers. But to the enemy he was a laughingstock, for they still retained some of the fire of liberty, knowing nothing yet of the power of freedmen, and so they marveled to see a general and an army who had finished such a war cringing to slaves. Everything, however, was softened down for the Emperor's ears, and Suetonius was retained in the government; but as he subsequently lost a few vessels on the shore with the crews, he was ordered, as though the war continued, to hand over his army to Petronius Tur-

pilianus, who had just resigned his consulship. Petronius neither challanged the enemy nor was himself molested, and veiled this tame inaction under the honorable name of peace.

40. That same year two remarkable crimes were committed at Rome, one by a senator, the other by the daring of a slave. Domitius Balbus, an ex-prætor, from his prolonged old age, his childlessness and his wealth, was exposed to many plots. His kinsman Valerius Fabianus,[51] who was intending to stand for public office, forged a will in his name with Vinicius Rufinus and Terentius Lentinus, Roman knights, for his accomplices. These men had associated with them Antonius Primus[52] and Asinius Marcellus.[53] Antonius was a man of ready audacity; Marcellus had the glory of being the great-grandson of Asinius Pollio, and bore a character far from contemptible, except that he thought poverty the greatest of all evils. So Fabianus, with the persons whom I have named and some others less distinguished, executed the will. The crime was proved against them before the Senate, and Fabianus and Antonius with Rufinus and Terentius were condemned under the Cornelian Law.[54] Marcellus was saved from punishment rather than from disgrace by the memory of his ancestors and the intercessions of the Emperor.

41. That same day was fatal also to Pompeius Ælianus, a young ex-quæstor, suspected of complicity in the villainies of Fabianus. He was outlawed from Italy, and from Spain, where he was born. Valerius Pontius[55] suffered the same degradation for having indicted the defendants before the prætor to save them from being prosecuted in the court of the city-prefect, purposing meanwhile to defeat justice on some legal pretext and subsequently by collusion. A clause was added to the Senate's decree, that whoever bought or sold such a service was to be just as liable to punishment as if he had been publicly convicted of false accusation.

42. Soon afterward one of his own slaves murdered the city prefect, Pedanius Secundus, either because he had been refused his freedom, for which he had made a bargain, or in the jealousy of a love in which he could

not brook his master's rivalry. Ancient custom required that the whole slave establishment which had dwelled under the same roof should be dragged to execution,[56] when a sudden gathering of the populace, which was for saving so many innocent lives, brought matters to actual insurrection. Even in the Senate there was a strong feeling on the part of those who shrank from extreme rigor, though the majority were opposed to any innovation. Of these, Gaius Cassius,[57] in giving his vote, argued to the following effect:

43. "Often have I been present, senators, in this assembly when new decrees were demanded from us contrary to the customs and laws of our ancestors, and I have refrained from opposition, not because I doubted but that in all matters the arrangements of the past were better and fairer and that all changes were for the worse, but that I might not seem to be exalting my own profession[58] out of an excessive partiality for ancient precedent. At the same time I thought that any influence I possess ought not to be destroyed by incessant protests, wishing that it might remain unimpaired, should the state ever need my counsels. Today this has come to pass, since an ex-consul has been murdered in his house by the treachery of slaves, which not one hindered or divulged, though the Senate's decree, which threatens the entire slave establishment with execution, had been till now unshaken. Vote impunity, in heaven's name, and then who will be protected by his rank, when the prefecture of the capital has been of no avail to its holder? Who will be kept safe by the number of his slaves when four hundred have not protected Pedanius Secundus? Which of us will be rescued by his domestics, who, even with the dread of punishment before them, regard not our dangers? Was the murderer, as some do not blush to pretend, avenging his wrongs because he had bargained about money from his father or because a family slave was taken from him? Let us actually decide that the master was justly slain.

44. "Is it your pleasure to search for arguments in a matter already weighed in the deliberations of wiser men than ourselves? Even if we had now for the first

time to come to a decision, do you believe that a slave took courage to murder his master without letting fall a threatening word or uttering a rash syllable? Granted that he concealed his purpose, that he procured his weapon without his fellows' knowledge. Could he pass the night guard, could he open the doors of the chamber, carry in a light, and accomplish the murder, while all were in ignorance? There are many preliminaries to guilt; if these are divulged by slaves, we may live singly amid numbers, safe among a trembling throng; lastly, if we must perish, it will be with vengeance on the guilty. Our ancestors always suspected the temper of their slaves, even when they were born on the same estates, or in the same houses with themselves and thus inherited from their birth an affection for their masters. But now that we have in our households nations with different customs to our own, with a foreign worship or none at all, it is only by terror you can hold in such a motley rabble. But, it will be said, the innocent will perish. Well, even in a beaten army when every tenth man is felled by the club, the lot falls also on the brave.[59] There is some injustice in every great precedent, which, though injurious to individuals, has its compensation in the public advantage."

45. No one indeed dared singly to oppose the opinion of Cassius, but clamorous voices rose in reply from all who pitied the number, age, or sex as well as the undoubted innocence of the great majority. Still, the party which voted for their execution prevailed. But the sentence could not be obeyed in the face of a dense and threatening mob, with stones and firebrands. Then the Emperor reprimanded the people by edict, and lined with a force of soldiers the entire route by which the condemned had to be dragged to execution. Cingonius Varro[60] had proposed that even all the freedmen under the same roof should be transported from Italy. This the Emperor forbade, as he did not wish an ancient custom, which mercy had not relaxed, to be strained with cruel rigor.

46. During the same consulship, Tarquitius Priscus[61] was convicted of extortion on the prosecution of the

234

Bithynians, to the great joy of the senators, who remembered that he had impeached Statilius, his own proconsul. An assessment was made of Gaul by Quintus Volusius, Sextius Africanus, and Trebellius Maximus. There was a rivalry, on the score of rank, between Volusius and Africanus. While they both disdained Trebellius, they raised him above themselves.[62]

47. In that year died Memmius Regulus,[63] who from his solid worth and consistency was as distinguished as it is possible to be under the shadow of an emperor's grandeur, so much so, in fact, that Nero when he was ill, with flatterers round him who said that if aught befell him in the course of destiny there must be an end of the Empire, replied that the state had a resource, and on their asking where it was specially to be found, he added, "in Memmius Regulus." Yet Regulus lived after this, protected by his retiring habits, and by the fact that he was a man of newly risen family and of wealth which did not provoke envy. Nero, the same year, established a gymnasium, where oil was furnished to knights and senators after the lax fashion of the Greeks.

48. In the consulship of Publius Marius and Lucius Afinius,[64] Antistius,[65] the prætor, whose lawless behavior as tribune of the people I have mentioned, composed some libelous verses on the Emperor, which he openly recited at a large gathering, when he was dining at the house of Ostorius Scapula.[66] He was upon this impeached of high treason by Cossutianus Capito,[67] who had lately been restored to a senator's rank on the intercession of his father-in-law, Tigellinus.[68] This was the first occasion on which the law of treason was revived, and men thought that it was not so much the ruin of Antistius which was aimed at, as the glory of the Emperor, whose veto as tribune might save from death one whom the Senate had condemned. Though Ostorius had stated that he had heard nothing as evidence, the adverse witnesses were believed, and Junius Marullus, consul-elect, proposed that the accused should be deprived of his prætorship, and be put to death in the ancient manner. The rest assented, and then Thrasea Pætus, after much eulogy of Cæsar, and most bitter censure of Antistius,

urged that it was not what a guilty prisoner might deserve to suffer, which ought to be decreed against him, under so excellent a prince, and by a Senate bound by no compulsion. "The executioner and the halter," he said, "we have long ago abolished; still, there are punishments ordained by the laws, which prescribe penalties, without judicial cruelty and disgrace to our age. Rather send him to some island, after confiscating his property; there, the longer he drags on his guilty life, the more wretched will he be personally, and the more conspicuous as an example of public clemency."

49. Thrasea's freespokenness broke through the servility of the other senators. As soon as the consul allowed a division, they voted with him, with but few exceptions. Among these, the most enthusiastic in his flattery was Aulus Vitellius,[69] who attacked all the best men with abuse, and was silent when they replied, the usual way of a cowardly temper. The consuls, however, did not dare to ratify the Senate's vote, and simply communicated their unanimous resolution to the Emperor. Hesitating for a while between shame and rage, he at last wrote to them in reply that "Antistius, without having been provoked by any wrong, had uttered outrageous insults against the sovereign; that a demand for punishment had been submitted to the Senate, and that it was right that a penalty should be decreed proportioned to the offense; that for himself, inasmuch as he would have opposed severity in the sentence, he would not be an obstacle to leniency. They might determine as they pleased, and they had free liberty to acquit."

This and more to the same effect having been read out, clearly showing his displeasure, the consuls did not for that reason alter the terms of the motion, nor did Thrasea withdraw his proposal, nor the Senate reject what it had once approved. Some were afraid of seeming to expose the Emperor to odium; the majority felt safe in numbers, while Thrasea was supported by his usual firmness of spirit, and a determination not to let his fame perish.

50. A similar accusation caused the downfall of Fabricius Veiento. He had composed many libels on senators

and pontiffs in a work to which he gave the title of *Codicils*. Tullius Geminus,[70] the prosecutor, further stated that he had habitually trafficked in the Emperor's favors and in the right of promotion. This was Nero's reason for himself undertaking the trial and having convicted Veiento, he banished him from Italy,[71] and ordered the burning of his books, which, while it was dangerous to procure them, were anxiously sought and much read. Soon full freedom for their possession caused their oblivion.

51. But while the miseries of the state were daily growing worse, its supports were becoming weaker. Burrus died, whether from illness or from poison was a question. It was supposed to be illness from the fact that from the gradual swelling of his throat inwardly and the closing up of the passage he ceased to breathe. Many positively asserted that by Nero's order his throat was smeared with some poisonous drug under the pretense of the application of a remedy, and that Burrus, who saw through the crime, when the Emperor paid him a visit, recoiled with horror from his gaze, and merely replied to his question, "I indeed am well." Rome felt for him a deep and lasting regret, because of the remembrance of his worth, because too of the merely passive virtue of one of his successors and the very flagrant iniquities of the other. For the Emperor had appointed two men to the command of the prætorian cohorts: Fænius Rufus,[72] for a vulgar popularity, which he owed to his administration of the corn supplies without profit to himself; and Ofonius Tigellinus, whose inveterate shamelessness and infamy were an attraction to him. As might have been expected from their known characters, Tigellinus had the greater influence with the prince, and was the associate of his most secret profligacy, while Rufus enjoyed the favor of the people and of the soldiers, and this, he found, prejudiced him with Nero.

52. The death of Burrus was a blow to Seneca's power, for virtue had not the same strength when one of its champions, so to say, was removed, and Nero too began to lean on worse advisers. They assailed Seneca with various charges, representing that he continued to increase a wealth which was already so vast as to be be-

yond the scale of a subject, and was drawing to himself the attachment of the citizens, while in the picturesqueness of his gardens and the magnificence of his country houses he almost surpassed the Emperor. They further alleged against him that he claimed for himself alone the honors of eloquence, and composed poetry more assiduously, as soon as a passion for it had seized on Nero. "Openly inimical to the prince's amusements, he disparaged his ability in driving horses, and ridiculed his voice whenever he sang. When was there to be an end of nothing being publicly admired but what Seneca was thought to have originated? Surely Nero's boyhood was over, and he was all but in the prime of youthful manhood. He ought to shake off a tutor, furnished as he was with sufficiently noble instructors in his own ancestors."

53. Seneca meanwhile, aware of these slanders, which were revealed to him by those who had some respect for merit, coupled with the fact that the Emperor more and more shunned his intimacy, besought the opportunity of an interview. This was granted, and he spoke as follows:

"It is fourteen years ago, Cæsar, that I was first associated with your prospects, and eight years since you have been Emperor. In the interval you have heaped on me such honors and riches that nothing is wanting to my happiness but a right use of it. I will refer to great examples taken not from my own but from your position. Your great-grandfather Augustus granted to Marcus Agrippa the calm repose of Mytilene,[73] to Gaius Mæcenas what was nearly equivalent to a foreign retreat in the capital itself. One of these men shared his wars; the other struggled with many laborious duties at Rome; both received rewards which were indeed splendid, but only proportioned to their great merits. For myself, what other recompense had I for your munificence than a culture nursed, so to speak, in the shade of retirement, and to which a glory attaches itself, because I thus seem to have helped on the early training of your youth, an ample reward for the service.

"You on the other hand have surrounded me with vast

influence and boundless wealth, so that I often think within myself: Am I, who am but of an equestrian and provincial family, numbered among the chief men of Rome? Among nobles who can show a long succession of glories, has my new name become famous? Where is the mind once content with a humble lot? Is this the man who is building up his garden terraces, who paces grandly through these suburban parks, and revels in the affluence of such broad lands and such widely spread investments? Only one apology occurs to me, that it would not have been right in me to have thwarted your bounty.

54. "And yet we have both filled up our respective measures, you in giving as much as a prince can bestow on a friend, and I in receiving as much as a friend can receive from a prince. All else only fosters envy, which, like all things human, sinks powerless beneath your greatness, though on me it weighs heavily. To me relief is a necessity. Just as I should implore support if exhausted by warfare or travel, so in this journey of life, old as I am and unequal even to the lightest cares, since I cannot any longer bear the burden of my wealth, I crave assistance. Order my property to be managed by your agents and to be included in your estate. Still I shall not sink myself into poverty, but having surrendered the splendors which dazzle me, I will henceforth again devote to my mind all the leisure and attention now reserved for my gardens and country houses. You have yet before you a vigorous prime, and that on which for so many years your eyes were fixed, supreme power. We, your older friends, can answer for our quiet behavior. It will likewise redound to your honor that you have raised to the highest places men who could also bear moderate fortune."

55. Nero's reply was substantially this: "My being able to meet your elaborate speech with an instant rejoinder is, I consider, primarily your gift, for you taught me how to express myself not only after reflection but at a moment's notice. My great-grandfather Augustus allowed Agrippina and Mæcenas to enjoy rest after their labors, but he did it at an age carrying with it an authority sufficient to justify any boon, of any sort, he might have

239

bestowed. But neither of them did he strip of the rewards he had given. It was by war and its perils they had earned them; for in these the youth of Augustus was spent. And if I had passed my years in arms, your sword and right hand would not have failed me. But, as my actual condition required, you watched over my boyhood, then over my youth, with wisdom, counsel, and advice. And indeed your gifts to me will, as long as life holds out, be lasting possessions; those which you owe to me, your parks, investments, your country houses, are liable to accidents. Though they seem much, many far inferior to you in merit have obtained more.[74] I am ashamed to quote the names of freedmen who parade a greater wealth. Hence I actually blush to think that, standing as you do first in my affections, you do not as yet surpass all in fortune.

56. "Yours too is a still vigorous manhood, quite equal to the labors of business and to the fruit of those labors; and, as for myself, I am but treading the threshold of empire. But perhaps you count yourself inferior to Vitellius, three times a consul,[75] and me to Claudius. Such wealth as long thrift has procured for Volusius,[76] my bounty, you think, cannot fully make up to you. Why not rather, if the frailty of my youth goes in any respect astray, call me back and guide yet more zealously with your help the manhood which you have instructed? It will not be your moderation, if you restore me your wealth, not your love of quiet, if you forsake your Emperor, but my avarice, the fear of my cruelty, which will be in all men's mouths. Even if your self-control were praised to the utmost, still it would not be seemly in a wise man to get glory for himself in the very act of bringing disgrace on his friend."[77]

To these words the Emperor added embraces and kisses; for he was formed by nature and trained by habit to veil his hatred under delusive flattery. Seneca thanked him, the usual end of an interview with a despot. But he entirely altered the practices of his former greatness; he kept the crowds of his visitors at a distance, avoided trains of followers, seldom appeared in Rome, as though weak health or philosophical studies detained him at home.

57. When Seneca had fallen, it was easy to shake the position of Fænius Rufus by making Agrippina's friendship a charge against him. Tigellinus, who was daily becoming more powerful and who thought that the wicked schemings which alone gave him strength would be better liked if he could secure the Emperor's complicity in guilt, dived into Nero's most secret apprehensions, and, as soon as he had ascertained that Plautus and Sulla were the men he most dreaded, Plautus having been lately sent away to Asia, Sulla to Gallia Narbonensis, he spoke much of their noble rank and of their respective proximity to the armies of the East and of Germany. "I have no eye," he said, "like Burrus, to two conflicting aims, but only to Nero's safety, which is at least secured against treachery in Rome by my presence. As for distant commotions, how can they be checked? Gaul is roused at the name of the great dictator, and I distrust no less the nations of Asia, because of the renown of such a grandfather as Drusus.[78] Sulla is poor, and hence comes his surpassing audacity; he shams apathy, while he is seeking an opening for his reckless ambition. Plautus again, with his great wealth, does not so much as affect a love of repose, but he flaunts before us his imitations of the old Romans, and assumes the self-consciousness of the Stoics along with a philosophy which makes men restless, and eager for a busy life."

There was not a moment's delay. Sulla, six days afterward, was murdered by assassins brought over to Massilia, while he was reclining at the dinner table, before he feared or heard of his danger. The head was taken to Rome, and Nero scoffed at its premature gray hairs as if they were a disfigurement.

58. It was less of a secret that there was a design to murder Plautus, as his life was dear to many. The distance too by land and sea, and the interval of time, had given rise to rumors, and the popular story was that he had tampered with Corbulo, who was then at the head of great armies, and would be a special mark for danger, if illustrious and innocent men were to be destroyed.

241

Again Asia, it was said, from its partiality for the young man, had taken up arms, and the soldiers sent to do the crime, not being sufficient in number or decided in purpose, and finding themselves unable to execute their orders, had gone over to the new cause. These absurdities, like all popular gossip, gathered strength from the idle leisure of a credulous society.

As it was, one of Plautus' freedmen, thanks to swift winds, arrived before the centurion and brought him a message from his father-in-law, Lucius Antistius.[79] "He should avoid the obvious refuge of a coward's death, and in the pity felt for a noble name he would soon find good men to help him, and daring spirits would rally round him. Meantime no resource was to be rejected. If he did but repel sixty soldiers (this was the number on the way), while tidings were being carried back to Nero, while another force was on its march, many events would follow which would ripen into war. Finally, by this plan he either secured safety, or he would suffer nothing worse by daring than by cowardice."

59. But all this had no effect on Plautus. Either he saw no resource before him, an unarmed exile as he was, or he was weary of an uncertain hope, or was swayed by his love of his wife and of his children, to whom he thought the Emperor, if harassed by no anxiety, would be more merciful. Some say that another message came to him from his father-in-law, representing that no dreadful peril hung over him, and that two teachers of philosophy, Cœranus from Greece and Musonius[80] from Etruria, advised him to await death with firmness rather than lead a precarious and anxious life. At all events, he was surprised at midday, when stripped for exercise. In that state the centurion slew him in the presence of Pelago, a eunuch, whom Nero had set over the centurion and his company, like a despot's minister over his satellites.

The head of the murdered man was brought to Rome. At its sight the Emperor exclaimed, "I never realized he had such a large nose." Then, casting off all fear, he prepared to hurry on his marriage with Poppæa, hitherto deferred because of such alarms as I have described, and to divorce his wife, Octavia, notwithstanding her virtuous life, because her father's name and the people's affection for her made her an offense to him. He wrote, however, a letter to the Senate, confessing nothing about the murders of Sulla and Plautus, but merely hinting that both had a restless temper, and that he gave the most anxious thought to the safety of the state. On this pretext a thanksgiving was decreed, and also the expulsion from the Senate of Sulla and Plautus, more grievous, however, as a farce than as an actual calamity.

60. Nero, on receiving this decree of the Senate and seeing that every piece of his wickedness was regarded as a conspicuous merit, drove Octavia from him, alleging that she was barren, and then married Poppæa. The woman who had long been Nero's mistress and ruled him first as a paramour, then as her husband, instigated one of Octavia's servants to accuse her of an intrigue with a slave. The man fixed on as the guilty lover was one by name Eucærus, an Alexandrine by birth, skilled in singing to the flute. As a consequence, her slave girls were examined under torture, and though some were forced by the intensity of agony into admitting falsehoods, most of them persisted in upholding the virtue of their mistress. One of them said, in answer to the furious menaces of Tigellinus, that Octavia's private parts were purer than his mouth. Octavia, however, was dismissed under the form of an ordinary divorce, and received possession of the house of Burrus and of the estates of Plautus, an ill-starred gift. She was soon afterward banished to Campania under military surveillance. This led to incessant and outspoken remonstrances among the common people, who have less discretion and are exposed to fewer dangers than others from the insignificance of their position. A rumor now arose that Nero had recalled Octavia.

61. Then people in their joy went up to the Capitol and, at last, gave thanks to the gods. They threw down the statues of Poppæa; they bore on their shoulders the images of Octavia, covering them with flowers, and setting them up in the forum and in the temples. There was even a burst of applause for the Emperor, men hail-

ing the recalled Octavia. And now they were pouring into the palace in crowds, with loud shoutings, when some companies of soldiers rushed out and dispersed the tumultuous throng with blows, and at the point of the sword. Whatever changes had been made in the riot were reversed, and Poppæa's honors restored. Ever relentless in her hatred, she was now enraged by the fear that either the violence of the mob would burst on her with yet fiercer fury, or that Nero would be swayed by the popular bias, and so, flinging herself at his knees, she exclaimed that she was not in the position of a rival fighting for marriage, though that was dearer to her than life, but that her very life was brought into jeopardy by the dependants and slaves of Octavia, who had assumed the name of the people, and dared in peace what could hardly happen in war. "Those arms," she said, "have been taken up against the Emperor; a leader only is wanting, and he will easily be found in a commotion. Only let her whose mere beck, though she is far away, stirs up tumult quit Campania, and make her way in person to Rome. And, again, what is my sin? What offense have I caused anyone? Is it that I am about to give to the house of the Cæsars a lawful heir? Do the people of Rome prefer that the offspring of an Egyptian flute player should be raised to the imperial throne? In a word, if it be expedient, Nero should of his own choice rather than on compulsion send for her who ruled him, or else secure his safety by a righteous vengeance. The beginning of a commotion has often been quieted by slight precautions; but if people once despair of Octavia being Nero's wife, they will soon find her a husband."

62. Her various arguments, tending both to frighten and to enrage, at once alarmed and incensed her listener. But the suspicion about the slave was of little weight, and the torture of the slave girls exposed its absurdity. Consequently it was decided to procure a confession from someone on whom could also be fastened a charge of revolutionary designs. Fittest for this seemed the perpetrator of the mother's murder, Anicetus, commander, as I have already mentioned, of the fleet at Misenum,

The Annals

who got but scant gratitude after that atrocious deed, and subsequently all the more vehement hatred, inasmuch as men look on their instruments in crime as a sort of standing reproach to them.

The Emperor accordingly sent for Anicetus, and reminded him of his former service. "He alone," he said, "had come to the rescue of the prince's life against a plotting mother. Close at hand was a chance of winning no less gratitude by ridding him of a malignant wife. No violence or weapons were needed; only let him confess to an intrigue with Octavia." Nero then promised him a secret but ample immediate recompense, and some delightful retreat, while he threatened him with death in case of refusal. Anicetus, with the moral insensibility of his nature and a promptness inspired by previous atrocities, invented even more than was required of him, and confessed before friends whom the prince had called in, as a sort of judicial council. He was then banished to Sardinia, where he endured exile without poverty, and died a natural death.

63. Nero meanwhile declared by edict that the prefect had been corrupted into a design of gaining over the fleet, and added, in forgetfulness of his late charge of barrenness against Octavia, that, conscious of her profligacies, she had procured abortion, a fact he had himself ascertained. Then he confined her in the island of Pandateria.[81] No exile ever filled the eyes of beholders with tears of greater compassion. Some still remembered Agrippina, banished by Tiberius,[82] and the yet fresher memory of Julia, whom Claudius exiled,[83] was present to men's thoughts. But they had life's prime for their stay; they had seen some happiness, and the horror of the moment was alleviated by recollections of a better lot in the past. For Octavia, from the first, her marriage day was a kind of funeral, brought, as she was, into a house where she had nothing but scenes of mourning, her father and, an instant afterward, her brother having been snatched from her by poison; then, a slave girl[84] raised above the mistress; Poppæa married only to ensure a wife's ruin, and, to end all, an accusation more horrible than any death.

245

64. And now the girl, in her twentieth year, with centurions and soldiers around her, already removed from among the living by the forecast of doom, still could not reconcile herself to death. After an interval of a few days, she received an order that she was to die, although she protested that she was now a widow and only a sister, and appealed to their common ancestors, the Germanici,[85] and finally to the name of Agrippina, during whose life she had endured a marriage, which was miserable enough indeed, but not fatal. She was then tightly bound with cords, and the veins of every limb were opened; but as her blood was congealed by terror and flowed too slowly, she was killed outright by the steam of an intensely hot bath. To this was added the yet more appalling horror of Poppæa looking on the severed head, which was conveyed to Rome.

And for all this offerings were voted to the temples. I record the fact with a special object. Whoever would study the calamities of that period in my pages or those of other authors is to take it for granted that as often as the Emperor directed banishments or executions, so often was there a thanksgiving to the gods, and what formerly commemorated some prosperous event, was then a token of public disaster. Still, if any decree of the Senate was marked by some new flattery, or by the lowest servility, I shall not pass it over in silence.

65. That same year Nero was believed to have destroyed by poison two of his most powerful freedmen, Doryphorus[86] on the pretext of his having opposed the marriage with Poppæa, Pallas for still keeping his boundless wealth by a prolonged old age. Romanus had accused Seneca, in stealthy calumnies, of having been an accomplice of Gaius Piso, but he was himself crushed more effectually by Seneca on the same charge. This alarmed Piso, and gave rise to a huge fabric of unsuccessful conspiracies against Nero.

BOOK XV   *62-65 A.D.*

[*Chapters 1-17, which deal with the war in Armenia, are omitted.*]

18. At Rome meanwhile, trophies for the Parthian War and arches were erected in the center of the Capitoline Hill; these had been decreed by the Senate while the war was yet undecided, and even now they were not given up, appearances being consulted, in disregard of known facts. And to hide his anxious fears about foreign affairs, Nero threw the people's corn,[1] which was so old as to be spoiled, into the Tiber, with the view of keeping up a sense of security about the supplies. There was no addition to the price, although about two hundred ships were destroyed in the very harbor by a violent storm, and one hundred more, which had sailed up the Tiber, by an accidental fire. Nero next appointed three ex-consuls, Lucius Piso, Ducenius Geminus, and Pompeius Paullinus, to the management of the public revenues, and inveighed at the same time against former emperors whose heavy expenditure had exceeded their legitimate income. He himself, he said, made the state an annual present of sixty million sesterces.[2]

19. A very demoralizing custom had at this time become rife, of fictitious adoptions of children, on the eve of the elections or of the assignment of the provinces, by a number of childless persons, who, after obtaining along with real fathers prætorships and provinces, forthwith dismissed from paternal control the sons whom they had adopted.[3] An appeal was made to the Senate under a keen sense of wrong. Parents pleaded natural rights and the anxieties of nurture against fraudulent evasions and the brief ceremony of adoption. "It was," they argued, "sufficient reward for the childless to have influence and distinction, everything, in short, easy and open to them, without a care and without a burden. For themselves, they found that the promises held out by the laws, for which they had long waited, were turned into mockery,

when one who knew nothing of a parent's solicitude or of the sorrows of bereavement could rise in a moment to the level of a father's long deferred hopes."

On this, a decree of the Senate was passed that a fictitious adoption should be of no avail in any department of the public service, or even hold good for acquiring an inheritance.[4]

20. Next came the prosecution of Claudius Timarchus of Crete, on such charges as often fall on very influential provincials, whom immense wealth has emboldened to the oppression of the weak.[5] But one speech of his had gone to the extremity of a gross insult to the Senate; for he had repeatedly declared that it was in his power to decide whether the proconsuls who had governed Crete should receive the thanks of the province. Thrasea Pætus, turning the occasion to public advantage, after having stated his opinion that the accused ought to be expelled from Crete, further spoke as follows:

"It is found by experience, senators, that admirable laws and right precedents among the good have their origin in the misdeeds of others. Thus the license of advocates resulted in the Cincian Bill;[6] the corrupt practices of candidates, in the Julian Laws;[7] the rapacity of magistrates, in the Calpurnian enactments.[8] For, in point of time, guilt comes before punishment, and correction follows after delinquency. And therefore, to meet the new insolence of provincials, let us adopt a measure worthy of Roman good faith and resolution, whereby our allies may lose nothing of our protection, while among ourselves people may cease to think that the estimate of a man's character is to be found anywhere rather than in the judgment of our citizens.

21. "Formerly, it was not only prætors or consuls, but private persons also, who were sent to inspect the provinces, and to report what they thought about each man's loyalty. And nations were timidly sensitive to the opinion of individual Romans. But now we court foreigners and flatter them, and just as there is a vote of thanks at anyone's pleasure, so even more eagerly is a prosecution decided on. Well; let it be decided on, and let the provincials retain the right of showing their power in this

248

fashion, but as for false praise which has been extorted by entreaties, let it be as much checked as fraud or tyranny. More faults are often committed while we are trying to oblige than while we are giving offense. Why, some virtues are actually hated; inflexible strictness, for example, and a temper proof against partiality. Consequently, our magistrate's early career is generally better than its close, which deteriorates, when we are anxiously seeking votes, like candidates. If such practices are stopped, our provinces will be ruled more equitably and more steadily. For as the dread of a charge of extortion has been a check to rapacity, so, by prohibiting the vote of thanks, will the pursuit of popularity be restrained."

22. This opinion was hailed with great unanimity, but the Senate's resolution could not be finally passed, as the consuls decided that there had been no formal motion on the subject. Then, at the Emperor's suggestion, they decreed that no one was to propose to any provincial diet[9] of our allies that a vote of thanks ought to be given in the Senate to propraetors or proconsuls, and that no one was to discharge such a mission.

During the same consulship a gymnasium was wholly consumed by a stroke of lightning, and a statue of Nero within it was melted down to a shapeless mass of bronze.[10] Also, an earthquake demolished a large part of Pompeii, a populous town in Campania.[11] And one of the Vestal Virgins, Lælia, died, and in her place was chosen Cornelia, of the family of the Cossi.[12]

23. During the consulship of Memmius Regulus and Verginius Rufus,[13] Nero welcomed with something more than mortal joy the birth of a daughter by Poppæa, whom he called Augusta, the same title having also been given to Poppæa. The place of her confinement was the colony of Antium, where the Emperor himself was born. Already the Senate had commended Poppæa's safety to the gods, and had made vows in the state's name, which were repeated again and again and duly discharged. To these was added a public thanksgiving, and a temple was decreed to the goddess of fecundity, as well as games and contests after the type of the ceremonies commemorative of Actium, and golden images of the two For-

tunes[14] were to be set up on the throne of Jupiter of the Capitol. Shows of the circus were also to be exhibited in honor of the Claudian and Domitian families at Antium, like those at Bovillæ in commemoration of the Julii.[15] Transient distinctions all of them, as within four months the infant died. Again there was an outburst of flattery, men voting the honors of deification, of a shrine, a temple, and a priest.

The Emperor, too, was as excessive in his grief as he had been in his joy. It was observed that when all the Senate rushed out to Antium to honor the recent birth, Thrasea was forbidden to go, and received with fearless spirit an affront which foreboded his doom. They say that soon afterward the Emperor boasted to Seneca of his reconciliation with Thrasea, on which Seneca congratulated him. And now henceforth the glory and the peril of these illustrious men grew greater.

[*Chapters 24-31, which deal with the Parthian War, are omitted.*]

32. That same year the Emperor put into possession of Latin rights the tribes of the Maritime Alps.[16] To the Roman knights he assigned places in the circus in front of the seats of the people, for up to that time they used to enter in a promiscuous throng, as the Roscian Law extended only to fourteen rows in the theater.[17] The same year witnessed shows of gladiators as magnificent as those of the past. Many ladies of distinction, however, and senators disgraced themselves by appearing in the amphitheater.

33. In the year of the consulship of Gaius Læcanius and Marcus Licinius[18] a yet keener impulse urged Nero to show himself frequently on the public stage. Hitherto he had sung in private houses or gardens, during the Juvenilia,[19] but these he now despised, as being but little frequented, and on too small a scale for so fine a voice. As, however, he did not venture to make a beginning at Rome, he chose Neapolis,[20] because it was a Greek city. From this as his starting point he might cross into Achæa, and there, winning the well-known and sacred

garlands of antiquity,[21] evoke, with increased fame, the enthusiasm of the citizens. Accordingly, a rabble of the townsfolk was brought together, with those whom the excitement of such an event had attracted from the neighboring towns and colonies, and such as followed in the Emperor's train to pay him honor or for various objects. All these, with some companies of soldiers, filled the theater at Neapolis.

34. There an incident occurred which many thought unlucky, though to the Emperor it seemed due to the province of auspicious deities. The people who had been present had quitted the theater, and the empty building then fell in without harm to anyone. Thereupon Nero in an elaborate ode thanked the gods, celebrating the good luck which attended the late downfall, and as he was on his way to cross the sea of Hadria, he rested a while at Beneventum,[22] where a crowded gladiatorial show was being exhibited by Vatinius.[23] The man was one of the most conspicuously infamous sights in the imperial court, bred, as he had been, in a shoemaker's shop, of a deformed person and vulgar wit, originally introduced as a butt. After a time he grew so powerful by accusing all the best men, that in influence, wealth, and ability to injure he was pre-eminent even in that bad company.

35. While Nero was frequently visiting the show, even amid his pleasures there was no cessation to his crimes. For during the very same period Torquatus Silanus was forced to die, because over and above his illustrious rank as one of the Junian family he claimed to be the great-grandson of Augustus. Accusers were ordered to charge him with prodigality in lavishing gifts, and with having no hope but in revolution. They said further that he had freedmen whom he had designated as *ab epistulis, a libellis,* and *a rationibus,* titles that suggested preparation to undertake the highest duties.[24] Then the most intimate of his freedmen were taken away in chains; and finally knowing the doom which impended, Torquatus cut the arteries in his arms. A speech from Nero followed, as usual, which stated that though he was guilty and with good reason distrusted his defense, his life

251

would yet have been spared, had he awaited the clemency of the judge.

36. Soon afterward, giving up Achæa for the present (his reasons were not certainly known), he returned to Rome, there dwelling in his secret imaginations on the provinces of the East, especially Egypt. Then, having declared in a public proclamation that his absence would not be long and that all things in the state would remain unchanged and prosperous, he visited the temple of the Capitol for advice about his departure. There he adored the gods; then he entered also the temple of Vesta,[25] and there, feeling a sudden trembling throughout his limbs, either from terror inspired by the deity or because, from the remembrance of his crimes, he was never free from fear, he relinquished his purpose, repeatedly saying that all his plans were of less account than his love of his country. "He had seen the sad countenances of the citizens, he heard their secret complainings at the prospect of his entering on so long a journey, when they could not bear so much as his brief excursions, accustomed as they were to cheer themselves under mischances by the sight of the Emperor. Hence, as in private relationships the closest ties were the strongest, so the people of Rome had the most powerful claims and must be obeyed in their wish to retain him."

These and the like sentiments suited the people, who craved amusement, and feared, always their chief anxiety, scarcity of corn, should he be absent. The Senate and leading citizens were in doubt whether to regard him as more terrible at a distance or among them. After a while, as is the way with great terrors, they thought what actually happened the worse alternative.

37. Nero, to win credit for himself of enjoying nothing so much as the capital, prepared banquets in the public places, and used the whole city, so to say, as his private house. Of these entertainments the most famous for their notorious profligacy were those furnished by Tigellinus, which I will describe as an example so as not to have to narrate similar extravagance again and again. He had a raft constructed on Agrippa's lake,[26] put the guests on board, and set it in motion by other vessels

towing it. These vessels glittered with gold and ivory; the crews were arranged according to age and experience in vice. Birds and beasts had been procured from remote countries, and sea monsters from the ocean. On the margin of the lake were set up brothels crowded with noble ladies, and on the opposite bank were seen naked prostitutes with obscene gestures and movements. As darkness approached, all the adjacent grove and surrounding buildings resounded with song, and shone brilliantly with lights. Nero, who polluted himself by every lawful or lawless indulgence, had not omitted a single abomination which could heighten his depravity, till a few days afterward he stooped to marry himself to one of that filthy herd, by name Pythagoras, with all the forms of regular wedlock. The bridal veil was put over the Emperor; people saw the witnesses of the ceremony, the wedding dower, the couch, and the nuptial torches; everything in a word was plainly visible which even when a woman weds darkness hides.

38. A disaster followed, whether accidental or treacherously contrived by the Emperor is uncertain, as authors have given both acounts; worse, however, and more dreadful than any which have ever happened to this city by the violence of fire. It had its beginning in that part of the circus which adjoins the Palatine and Cælian hills, where, amid the shops containing inflammable wares, the conflagration both broke out and instantly became so fierce and so rapid from the wind that it seized in its grasp the entire length of the circus. For here there were no houses fenced in by solid masonry, or temples surrounded by walls, or any other obstacle to interpose delay. The blaze in its fury ran first through the level portions of the city, then rising to the hills, while it again devastated every place below them, it outstripped all preventive measures; so rapid was the mischief and so completely at its mercy the city, with those narrow winding passages and irregular streets, which characterized old Rome. Added to this were the wailings of terror-stricken women, the feebleness of age, the helpless inexperience of childhood, the crowds who sought to save themselves or others, dragging out the infirm or

waiting for them, and by their hurry in the one case, by their delay in the other, aggravating the confusion. Often, while they looked behind them, they were intercepted by flames on their side or in their face. Or if they reached a refuge close at hand, when this too was seized by the fire, they found that even places which they had imagined to be remote were involved in the same calamity. At last, doubting what place they should avoid or what place they should make for, they crowded the streets or flung themselves down in the fields, while some who had lost their all, even their very daily bread, and others out of love for their kinsfolk, whom they had been unable to rescue, perished though escape was open to them. And no one dared to stop the mischief, because of incessant menaces from a number of persons who forbade the extinguishing of the flames, because again others openly hurled brands, and kept shouting that there was one who gave them authority, either seeking to plunder more freely, or obeying orders.

39. Nero at this time was at Antium, and did not return to Rome until the fire approached his house, which he had built to connect the Palatine with the gardens of Mæcenas.[27] It could not, however, be stopped from devouring the palace, the house, and everything around it. However, to relieve the people, driven out homeless as they were, he threw open to them the Campus Martius and the public buildings of Agrippa,[28] and even his own gardens, and raised temporary structures to receive the destitute multitude. Supplies of food were brought up from Ostia and the neighboring towns, and the price of corn was reduced to three sesterces a peck. These acts, though popular, produced no effect, since a rumor had gone forth everywhere that at the very time when the city was in flames, the Emperor appeared on a private stage and sang of the destruction of Troy, comparing present misfortunes with the calamities of antiquity.

40. At last, after five days, an end was put to the conflagration at the foot of the Esquiline Hill, by the destruction of all buildings on a vast space, so that the violence of the fire was met by clear ground and an open sky. But before people had laid aside their fears, the

flames returned, with no less fury this second time, and especially in the spacious districts of the city. Consequently, though there was less loss of life, the temples of the gods and the porticoes which were devoted to enjoyment fell in a yet more widespread ruin. And to this conflagration there attached the greater infamy because it broke out on the property of Tigellinus in the Æmiliana,[29] and it seemed that Nero was aiming at the glory of founding a new city and calling it by his name. Rome, indeed, is divided into fourteen districts, of which four remained uninjured, three were leveled to the ground, while in the other seven were left only a few shattered, half-burned relics of houses.

41. It would not be easy to enter into a computation of the private mansions, the blocks of tenements, and of the temples which were lost. Those with the oldest ceremonial, as that dedicated by Servius Tullius[30] to the Moon, the great altar and shrine raised by the Arcadian Evander[31] to Hercules in the hero's very presence, the temple of Jupiter Stator,[32] which was vowed by Romulus, Numa's royal palace,[33] and the sanctuary of Vesta, with the tutelary deities of the Roman people, were burned. So too were the riches acquired by our many victories, various beauties of Greek art, then again the ancient and genuine historical monuments of men of genius, and, notwithstanding the striking splendor of the restored city, old men will remember many things which could not be replaced. Some persons observed that the beginning of this conflagration was on the 19th of July, the day on which the Senones captured and fired Rome.[34] Others have pushed a curious inquiry so far as to reduce the interval between these two conflagrations into equal numbers of years, months, and days.

42. Nero meanwhile availed himself of his country's desolation, and erected a mansion in which the jewels and gold, long familiar objects, quite vulgarized by our extravagance, were not so marvelous as the fields and lakes, with woods on one side to resemble a real landscape, and, on the other, open spaces and extensive views. The directors and contrivers of the work were Severus and Celer, who had the genius and the audacity

to attempt by art even what nature had refused, and to fool away an Emperor's resources. They-had actually undertaken to sink a navigable canal from Lake Avernus[35] to the mouths of the Tiber along a barren shore or through the face of hills, where one meets with no moisture which could supply water, except the Pomptine marshes. The rest of the country is broken rock and perfectly dry. Even if it could be cut through, the labor would be intolerable, and there would be no adequate result. Nero, however, with his love of the impossible, endeavored to dig through the hills nearest to Avernus, and there still remain the traces of his disappointed hope.

43. Of Rome meanwhile, so much as was left unoccupied by his mansion was not built up, as it had been after its burning by the Gauls, without any regularity or in any fashion, but with rows of streets according to measurement, with broad thoroughfares, with a restriction on the height of houses, with open spaces, and the further addition of colonnades, as a protection to the frontage of the blocks of tenements. These colonnades Nero promised to erect at his own expense, and to hand over the open spaces, when cleared of the debris, to the ground landlords. He also offered rewards proportioned to each person's position and property, and prescribed a period within which they were to obtain them on the completion of so many houses or blocks of building. He fixed on the marshes of Ostia for the reception of the rubbish, and arranged that the ships which had brought up corn by the Tiber should sail down the river with cargoes of this rubbish. The buildings themselves, to a certain height, were to be solidly constructed, without wooden beams, of stone from Gabii[36] or Alba,[37] that material being impervious to fire. And to provide that the water which individual license had illegally appropriated might flow in greater abundance in several places for the public use, officers were appointed, and everyone was to have in the open court the means of stopping a fire. Every building too was to be enclosed by its own proper wall, not by one common to others. These changes, which were liked for their utility, also added beauty to the new city. Some, however, thought that its old arrangement

had been more conducive to health, inasmuch as the narrow streets with the elevation of the roofs were not equally penetrated by the sun's heat, while now the open space, unsheltered by any shade, was scorched by a fiercer glow.

44. Such indeed were the precautions of human wisdom. The next thing was to seek means of propitiating the gods, and recourse was had to the Sibylline Books, by the direction of which prayers were offered to Vulcan, Ceres, and Proserpine. Juno too was entreated by the matrons, first in the Capitol, then on the nearest part of the coast, from where water was fetched to sprinkle the fane and image of the goddess. And there were sacred banquets and nightly vigils celebrated by married women. But all human efforts, all the lavish gifts of the Emperor, and the propitiations of the gods, did not banish the sinister belief that the conflagration was the result of an order. Consequently, to get rid of the report, Nero fastened the guilt and inflicted the most exquisite tortures on a class hated for their abominations, called Christians by the populace. Christus, from whom the name had its origin,[38] suffered the extreme penalty during the reign of Tiberius at the hands of one of our procurators, Pontius Pilatus,[39] and a most mischievous superstition, thus checked for the moment, again broke out not only in Judæa, the first source of the evil, but even in Rome, where all things hideous and shameful from every part of the world find their center and become popular. Accordingly, they first arrested all who pleaded guilty; then, upon their information, an immense multitude was convicted, not so much of the crime of firing the city, as of hatred against mankind. Mockery of every sort was added to their deaths. Covered with the skins of beasts, they were torn by dogs and perished, or were nailed to crosses, or were doomed to the flames and burned, to serve as a nightly illumination, when daylight had expired.

Nero offered his gardens for the spectacle, and was exhibiting a show in the circus, while he mingled with the people in the dress of a charioteer or stood aloft on a car. Hence, even for criminals who deserved extreme and exemplary punishment, there arose a feeling of compassion; for it was not, as it seemed, for the public good, but to glut one man's cruelty, that they were being destroyed.[40]

45. Meanwhile Italy was thoroughly exhausted by contributions of money, the provinces were ruined, as also the allied nations and the free states, as they were called. Even the gods fell victims to this plunder; for the temples in Rome were despoiled and the gold carried off, which, for a triumph or a vow, the Roman people in every age had consecrated in their prosperity or their alarm. Throughout Asia and Achæa not only votive gifts, but the images of deities were seized, Acratus and Carrinas Secundus having been sent into those provinces. The first was a freedman ready for any wickedness; the latter, as far as speech went; was thoroughly trained in Greek learning, but he had not imbued his heart with sound principles. Seneca, it was said, to avert from himself the obloquy of sacrilege, begged for the seclusion of a remote rural retreat, and, when it was refused, feigning ill health, as though he had a nervous ailment, would not quit his chamber. According to some writers, poison was prepared for him at Nero's command by his own freedman, whose name was Cleonicus. This Seneca avoided through the freedman's disclosure, or his own apprehension, while he supported life on the very simple diet of wild fruits, with water from a running stream when thirst prompted.

46. During the same time some gladiators in the town of Præneste,[41] who attempted to break loose, were put down by a military guard stationed on the spot to watch them, and the people, ever desirous and yet fearful of change, began at once to talk of Spartacus,[42] and of bygone calamities. Soon afterward, tidings of a naval disaster was received, but not from war, for never had there been so profound a peace. Nero, however, had ordered the fleet to return to Campania on a fixed day, without making any allowance for the dangers of the sea. Consequently the pilots, in spite of the fury of the waves, started from Formiæ,[43] and while they were struggling to double the promontory of Misenum,[44] they were dashed

by a violent southwest wind on the shores of Cumæ,[45] and lost, in all directions, a number of their triremes with some smaller vessels.

47. At the close of the year people talked much about prodigies presaging impending evils. Never were lightning flashes more frequent, and a comet too appeared, for which Nero always made propitiation with noble blood. Human and other births with two heads were exposed to public view, or were discovered in those sacrifices in which it is usual to immolate victims in a pregnant condition. And in the district of Placentia,[46] close to the road, a calf was born with its head attached to its leg. Then followed an explanation of the diviners, that another head was preparing for the world, which, however, would be neither mighty nor hidden, as its growth had been checked in the womb, and it had been born by the wayside.

48. Silius Nerva and Atticus Vestinus[47] then entered on the consulship, and now a conspiracy was planned, and at once became formidable, for which senators, knights, soldiers, even women, had given their names with eager rivalry, out of hatred of Nero as well as a liking for Gaius Piso.[48] A descendant of the Calpurnian house, and embracing in his connections through his father's noble rank many illustrious families, Piso had a splendid reputation with the people from his virtue or semblance of virtue. His eloquence he exercised in the defense of fellow citizens, his generosity toward friends, while even for strangers he had a courteous address and demeanor. He had too the fortuitous advantages of tall stature and a handsome face. But solidity of character and moderation in pleasure were wholly alien to him. He indulged in laxity, in display, and occasionally in excess. This suited the taste of that numerous class who, when the attractions of vice are so powerful, do not wish for strictness or special severity on the throne.

49. The origin of the conspiracy was not in Piso's personal ambition. But I could not easily narrate who first planned it, or whose prompting inspired a scheme into which so many entered. That the leading spirits were Subrius Flavus, tribune of a prætorian cohort, and

Sulpicius Asper, a centurion, was proved by the fearlessness of their death. Annæus Lucanus,[49] too, and Plautius Lateranus,[50] imported into it an intensely keen resentment. Lucanus had the stimulus of personal motives, for Nero tried to disparage the fame of his poems and, with the foolish vanity of a rival, had forbidden him to publish them. As for Lateranus, a consul-elect, it was no wrong, but love of the republic which linked him with the others. Flavius Scævinus and Afranius Quintianus, on the other hand, both of senatorial rank, contrary to what was expected of them undertook the beginning of this daring crime. Scævinus, indeed, had enfeebled his mind by excess, and his life, accordingly, was one of sleepy languor. Quintianus, infamous for his effeminate vice, had been satirized by Nero in a lampoon, and was bent on avenging the insult.

50. So, while they dropped hints among themselves or among their friends about the Emperor's crimes, the approaching end of Empire, and the importance of choosing someone to rescue the state in its distress, they associated with them Claudius Senecio,[51] Cervarius Proculus, Vulcatius Araricus, Julius Augurinus, Munatius Gratus, Antonius Natalis, and Marcius Festus, all Roman knights. Of these, Senecio, one of those who was specially intimate with Nero, still kept up a show of friendship, and had consequently to struggle with all the more dangers. Natalis shared with Piso all his secret plans. The rest built their hopes on revolution. Besides Subrius and Sulpicius, whom I have already mentioned, they invited the aid of military strength—of Gavius Silvanus and Statius Proximus, tribunes of prætorian cohorts, and of two centurions, Maximus Scaurus and Venetus Paullus. But their mainstay, it was thought, was Fænius Rufus,[52] the commander of the guard, a man of esteemed life and character, to whom Tigellinus with his brutality and shamelessness was superior in the Emperor's regard. He harassed him with calumnies, and had often put him in terror by hinting that he had been Agrippina's paramour, and from sorrow at her loss was intent on vengeance. And so, when the conspirators were assured by his own repeated language that the com-

mander of the prætorian guard had come over to their side, they once more eagerly discussed the time and place of the fatal deed. It was said that Subrius Flavus had formed a sudden resolution to attack Nero when singing on the stage, or when his house was in flames and he was running hither and thither, unattended, in the darkness. In the one case was the opportunity of solitude; in the other, the very crowd which would witness so glorious a deed was a stimulus to his courage; it was only the desire of escape, that foe to all great enterprises, which held him back.

51. Meanwhile, as they hesitated in prolonged suspense between hope and fear, a certain Epicharis (how she informed herself is uncertain, as she had never before had a thought of anything noble) began to stir and upbraid the conspirators. Wearied at last of their long delay, she endeavored, when staying in Campania, to shake the loyalty of the officers of the fleet at Misenum, and to entangle them in a guilty complicity. She began thus. There was a captain in the fleet, Volusius Proculus, who had been one of Nero's instruments in his mother's murder, and had not, as he thought, been promoted in proportion to the greatness of his crime. Either as an old acquaintance of the woman or on the strength of a recent intimacy, he divulged to her his services to Nero and their barren result to himself, adding complaints and his determination to have vengeance, should the chance arise. He thus inspired the hope that he could be persuaded, and could secure many others. No small help was to be found in the fleet, and there would be numerous opportunities, as Nero delighted in frequent enjoyment of the sea off Puteoli and Misenum.

Epicharis accordingly said more, and began the history of all the Emperor's crimes. "The Senate," she affirmed, "had no power left it; yet means had been provided whereby he might pay the penalty of having destroyed the state. Only let Proculus gird himself to do his part and bring over to their side his bravest soldiers, and then look for an adequate recompense." The conspirators' names, however, she withheld. Consequently the information of Proculus was useless, even though he reported what he had heard to Nero. For Epicharis, being summoned and confronted with the informer, easily silenced him, unsupported as he was by a single witness. But she was herself detained in custody, for Nero suspected that even what was not proved to be true was not wholly false.

52. The conspirators, however, alarmed by the fear of disclosure, resolved to hurry on the assassination at Baiæ, in Piso's villa, whither the Emperor, charmed by its loveliness, often went, and where, unguarded and without the cumbrous grandeur of his rank, he would enjoy the bath and the banquet. But Piso refused, alleging the odium of an act which would stain with an Emperor's blood, however bad he might be, the sanctity of the hospitable board and the deities who preside over it. "Better," he said, "in the capital, in that hateful mansion which was piled up with the plunder of the citizens, or in public, to accomplish what on the state's behalf they had undertaken."

So he said openly, with, however, a secret apprehension that Lucius Silanus[53] might, on the strength of his distinguished rank and the teachings of Gaius Cassius, under whom he had been trained, aspire to any greatness and seize on empire, which would be promptly offered him by all who had no part in the conspiracy, and who would pity Nero as the victim of a crime. Many thought that Piso shunned also the enterprising spirit of Vestinus, the consul, who might, he feared, rise up in the cause of freedom, or, by choosing another emperor, make the republic his own gift. Vestinus, indeed, had no share in the conspiracy, though Nero on that charge gratified an old resentment against an innocent man.

53. At last they decided to carry out their design on that day of the circus games which is celebrated in honor of Ceres,[54] as the Emperor, who seldom went out, and shut himself up in his house or gardens, used to go to the entertainments of the circus, and access to him was the easier from his keen enjoyment of the spectacle. They had so arranged the order of the plot that Lateranus was to throw himself at the prince's knees in earnest entreaty,[55] apparently craving relief for his private ne-

cessities, and, being a man of strong nerve and huge frame, hurl him to the ground and hold him down. When he was prostrate and powerless, the tribunes and centurions and all the others who had sufficient daring were to rush up and do the murder, the first blow being claimed by Scævinus, who had taken a dagger from the Temple of Safety, or, according to another account, from that of Fortune,[56] in the town of Ferentinum,[57] and used to wear the weapon as though dedicated to some noble deed. Piso, meanwhile, was to wait in the sanctuary of Ceres,[58] whence he was to be summoned by Fænius, the commander of the guard, and by the others, and then conveyed into the camp, accompanied by Antonia, the daughter of Claudius Cæsar,[59] with a view to evoke the people's enthusiasm. So it is related by Gaius Plinius.[60] Handed down from whatever source, I had no intention of suppressing it, however absurd it may seem, either that Antonia should have lent her name at her life's peril to a hopeless project, or that Piso, with his well-known affection for his wife,[61] should have pledged himself to another marriage, but for the fact that the lust of dominion inflames the heart more than any other passion.

54. It was, however, wonderful how among people of different class, rank, age, sex, among rich and poor, everything was kept in secrecy till betrayal began from the house of Scævinus. The day before the treacherous attempt, after a long conversation with Antonius Natalis, Scævinus returned home, sealed his will, and drawing from its sheath the dagger of which I have already spoken, and complaining that it was blunted from long disuse, he ordered it to be sharpened on a stone to a keen and bright point. This task he assigned to his freedman Milichus. At the same time he sat down to a more than usually sumptuous banquet, and gave his favorite slaves their freedom, and money to others. He was himself depressed, and evidently in profound thought, though he affected gaiety in desultory conversation. Last of all, he directed ligatures for wounds and the means of stanching blood to be prepared by the same Milichus, who either knew of the conspiracy and

263

was faithful up to this point, or was in complete ignorance and then first caught suspicions, as most authors have inferred from what followed. For when his servile imagination dwelled on the rewards of perfidy, and he saw before him at the same moment boundless wealth and power, conscience and care for his patron's life, together with the remembrance of the freedom he had received, fled from him. From his wife too he had adopted a womanly and yet baser suggestion; for she even held over him a dreadful thought, that many had been present, both freedmen and slaves, who had seen what he had; that one man's silence would be useless, whereas the rewards would be for him alone who was first with the information.

55. Accordingly at daybreak Milichus went to the Servilian Gardens,[62] and finding the doors shut against him, said again and again that he was the bearer of important and alarming news. Upon this he was conducted by the gatekeepers to one of Nero's freedmen, Epaphroditus,[63] and by him to Nero, whom he informed of the urgent danger, of the formidable conspiracy, and of all else which he had heard or inferred. He showed him too the weapon prepared for his destruction, and bade him summon the accused.

Scævinus on being arrested by the soldiers began his defense with the reply that the dagger about which he was accused had of old been regarded with a religious sentiment by his ancestors, that it had been kept in his chamber, and been stolen by a trick of his freedman. He had often, he said, signed his will without heeding the observance of particular days, and had previously given presents of money as well as freedom to some of his slaves, only on this occasion he gave more freely, because, as his means were now impoverished and his creditors were pressing him, he distrusted the validity of his will. Certainly his table had always been profusely furnished, and his life luxurious, such as rigid censors would hardly approve. As to the bandages for wounds, none had been prepared at his order, but as all the man's other charges were absurd, he added an accusation in which he might make himself alike informer and witness.

He backed up his words by an air of resolution. Turning on his accuser, he denounced him as an infamous and depraved wretch, with so fearless a voice and look that the information was beginning to collapse, when Milichus was reminded by his wife that Antonius Natalis had had a long secret conversation with Scævinus, and that both were Piso's intimate friends.

56. Natalis was therefore summoned, and they were separately asked what the conversation was, and what was its subject. Then a suspicion arose because their answers did not agree, and they were both put in irons. They could not endure the sight and the threat of torture.[64] Natalis, however, taking the initiative, knowing as he did more of the whole conspiracy, and being also more practiced in accusing, first confessed about Piso, next added the name of Seneca, either as having been a messenger between him and Piso, or to win the favor of Nero, who hated Seneca and sought every means for his ruin. Then Scævinus too, when he knew the disclosure of Natalis, with like pusillanimity, or under the impression that everything was now divulged, and that there could be no advantage in silence, revealed the other conspirators. Of these, Lucanus, Quintianus, and Senecio long persisted in denial; after a time, when bribed by the promise of impunity, anxious to excuse their reluctance, Lucanus named his mother, Acilia; Quintianus and Senecio their chief friends, respectively, Glitius Gallus and Annius Pollio.[65]

57. Nero, meanwhile, remembering that Epicharis was in custody on the information of Volusius Proculus, and assuming that a woman's frame must be unequal to the agony, ordered her to be torn on the rack. But neither the scourge nor fire, nor the fury of the men as they increased the torture that they might not be despised by a woman, overcame her positive denial of the charge. Thus the first day's inquiry was futile. On the morrow, as she was being dragged back on a chair to the same torments (for with her limbs all dislocated she could not stand), she tied a band, which she had stripped off

her bosom, in a sort of noose to the arched back of the
chair, put her neck in it, and then straining with the
whole weight of her body, wrung out of her frame its
little remaining breath. All the nobler was the example
set by a freedwoman at such a crisis in screening strangers and those whom she hardly knew, when freeborn
men, Roman knights, and senators, yet unscathed by
torture, betrayed, everyone, his dearest kinsfolk. For even
Lucanus and Senecio and Quintianus failed not to reveal their accomplices indiscriminately, and Nero was
more and more alarmed, though he had fenced his person with a largely augmented guard.

58. Even Rome itself he put, so to say, under custody, garrisoning its walls with companies of soldiers
and occupying with troops the coast and the river banks.
Incessantly were there flying through the public places,
through private houses, country fields, and the neighboring villages, horse and foot soldiers, mixed with Germans, whom the Emperor trusted as being foreigners.
In long succession, troops of prisoners in chains were
dragged along and stood at the gates of his gardens.
When they entered to plead their cause, a smile of joy
on any of the conspirators, a casual conversation, a sudden meeting, or the fact of having entered a banquet or
a public show in company, was construed into a crime,
while to the savage questionings of Nero and Tigellinus
were added the violent menaces of Fænius Rufus, who
had not yet been named by the informers, but who, to
get the credit of complete ignorance, frowned fiercely
on his accomplices. When Subrius Flavus at his side
asked him by a sign whether he should draw his sword
in the middle of the trial and perpetrate the fatal deed,
Rufus refused, and checked the man's impulse as he was
putting his hand to his sword hilt.

59. Some there were who, as soon as the conspiracy
was betrayed, urged Piso, while Milichus' story was being heard, and Scævinus was hesitating, to go to the
camp or mount the Rostra and test the feelings of the
soldiers and of the people. "If," said they, "your accomplices join your enterprise, those also who are yet undecided will follow, and great will be the fame of the

movement once started, and this in any new scheme is all-powerful. Against it Nero has taken no precaution. Even brave men are dismayed by sudden perils; far less will that stage player, with Tigellinus and his concubines in his train, raise arms against you. Many things which cowards think impossible are accomplished by those who dare. It is vain to expect secrecy and fidelity from the varying tempers and bodily constitutions of such a host of accomplices. Torture or reward can overcome everything. Men will soon come to put you also in chains and inflict on you an ignominious death. How much more gloriously will you die while you cling to the state and invoke aid for liberty. Rather let the soldiers fail, the people be traitors, provided that you, if prematurely robbed of life, justify your death to your ancestors and descendants."

Unmoved by these considerations, Piso showed himself a few moments in public, then sought the retirement of his house, and there fortified his spirit against the worst, till a troop of soldiers arrived, raw recruits, or men recently enlisted, whom Nero had selected, because he was afraid of the veterans, imbued though they were with a liking for him. Piso expired by having the veins in his arms severed. His will, full of loathsome flatteries of Nero, was a concession to his love of his wife, a degenerate woman, with only a beautiful person to recommend her, whom he had taken away from her husband, one of his friends. Her name was Satria Galla; that of her former husband, Domitius Silus. The tame spirit of the man, the profligacy of the woman, blazoned Piso's infamy.

60. In quick succession Nero added the murder of Plautius Lateranus, consul-elect, so promptly that he did not allow him to embrace his children or to have the brief choice of his own death. He was dragged off to a place set apart for the execution of slaves, and butchered by the hand of the tribune Statius, maintaining a resolute silence, and not reproaching the tribune with complicity in the plot.

Then followed the destruction of Seneca, a special joy to the Emperor, not because he had convicted him of the conspiracy, but anxious to accomplish with the sword what poison had failed to do. It was, in fact, Natalis alone who divulged Seneca's name, to this extent, that he had been sent to Seneca when ailing, to see him and remonstrate with him for excluding Piso from his presence, when it would have been better to have kept up their friendship by familiar intercourse; that Seneca's reply was that mutual conversations and frequent interviews were to the advantage of neither, but still that his own life depended on Piso's safety. Gavius Silvanus, tribune of a prætorian cohort, was ordered to report this to Seneca and to ask him whether he acknowledged what Natalis said and his own answer. Either by chance or purposely, Seneca had returned on that day from Campania, and had stopped at a country house four miles from Rome. Thither the tribune came next evening, surrounded the house with troops of soldiers, and then made known the Emperor's message to Seneca as he was at dinner with his wife, Pompeia Paullina, and two friends.

61. Seneca replied that Natalis had been sent to him and had complained to him in Piso's name because of his refusal to see Piso, upon which he excused himself on the ground of failing health and the desire of rest. "He had no reason," he said, "for preferring the interest of any private citizen to his own safety, and he had no natural aptitude for flattery. No one knew this better than Nero, who had oftener experienced Seneca's free-spokenness than his servility." When the tribune reported this answer in the presence of Poppæa and Tigellinus, the Emperor's most confidential advisers in his moments of rage, he asked whether Seneca was meditating suicide. Upon this the tribune asserted that he saw no signs of fear, and perceived no sadness in his words or in his looks. He was accordingly ordered to go back and to announce sentence of death. Fabius Rusticus tells us that he did not return the way he came, but went out of his course to Fænius, the commander of the guard, and having explained to him the Emperor's orders, and asked whether he was to obey them, was by him admonished to carry them out, for a fatal spell of coward-

ice was on them all. For this very Silvanus was one of the conspirators, and he was now abetting the crimes which he had united with them to avenge. But he spared himself the anguish of a word or of a look, and merely sent in to Seneca one of his centurions, who was to announce to him his last doom.

62. Seneca, quite unmoved, asked for tablets on which to inscribe his will, and on the centurion's refusal, turned to his friends, protesting that as he was forbidden to requite them, he bequeathed to them the only, but still the noblest possession yet remaining to him, the pattern of his life, and that, if they remembered it, they would win a name for moral worth and steadfast friendship. At the same time he called them back from their tears to manly resolution, now with friendly talk and now with the sterner language of rebuke. "Where," he asked again and again, "are your maxims of philosophy, or the preparation of so many years' study against evils to come? Who was ignorant of Nero's cruelty? After a mother's and a brother's murder, nothing remains but to add the destruction of a guardian and a tutor."

63. Having spoken these and like words, meant, so to say, for all, he embraced his wife; then softening a while from the stern resolution of the hour, he begged and implored her to spare herself the burden of perpetual sorrow, and, in the contemplation of a life virtuously spent, to endure a husband's loss with honorable consolations. She declared, in answer, that she too had decided to die, and claimed for herself the blow of the executioner. Thereupon Seneca, not to thwart her noble ambition, from an affection too which would not leave behind him for insult one whom he dearly loved, replied, "I have shown you ways of smoothing life; you prefer the glory of dying. I will not grudge you such a noble example. Let the fortitude of so courageous an end be alike in both of us, but let there be more in your decease to win fame."

Then by one and the same stroke they sundered with a dagger the arteries of their arms. Seneca, as his aged frame, attenuated by frugal diet, allowed the blood to escape but slowly, severed also the veins of his legs and knees. Worn out by cruel anguish, afraid too that his sufferings might break his wife's spirit, and that, as he looked on her tortures, he might himself sink into ir- resolution, he persuaded her to retire into another cham- ber. Even at the last moment his eloquence failed him not; he summoned his secretaries, and dictated much to them which, as it has been published for all readers in his own words, I forbear to paraphrase.

64. Nero meanwhile, having no personal hatred against Paullina and not wishing to heighten the odium of his cruelty, forbade her death. At the soldiers' prompt- ing, her slaves and freedmen bound up her arms and stanched the bleeding, whether with her knowledge is doubtful. For as the vulgar are ever ready to think the worst, there were persons who believed that, as long as she dreaded Nero's relentlessness, she sought the glory of sharing her husband's death, but that after a time, when a more soothing prospect presented itself, she yielded to the charms of life. To this she added a few subsequent years, with a most praiseworthy remem- brance of her husband, and with a countenance and frame white to a degree of pallor which denoted a loss of much vital energy.

Seneca meantime, as the tedious process of death still lingered on, begged Annæus Statius,[66] whom he had long esteemed for his faithful friendship and medical skill, to produce a poison with which he had some time before provided himself, the same drug which extin- guished the life of those who were condemned by a pub- lic sentence of the people of Athens.[67] It was brought to him and he drank it in vain, chilled as he was throughout his limbs, and his frame closed against the efficacy of the poison. At last he entered a pool of heated water, from which he sprinkled the nearest of his slaves, adding the exclamation, "I offer this liquid as a libation to Jupiter the Deliverer." He was then carried into a bath, with the steam of which he was suffocated, and he was burned without any of the usual funeral rites. So he had directed in a codicil of his will, when even in the height of his wealth and power he was thinking of his life's close.

270

65. There was a rumor that Sabrius Flavus had held a secret consultation with the centurions, and had planned, not without Seneca's knowledge, that when Nero had been slain by Piso's instrumentality, Piso also was to be murdered, and the Empire handed over to Seneca, as a man singled out for his splendid virtues by all persons of integrity. Even a saying of Flavus was popularly current: "that it made no difference as to the disgrace if a harp player were removed and a tragic actor succeeded him." For as Nero used to sing to the harp, so did Piso assume the dress of a tragedian.

66. The soldiers' part too in the conspiracy no longer escaped discovery, some in their rage becoming informers to betray Fænius Rufus, whom they could not endure to be both an accomplice and a judge. Accordingly Scævinus, in answer to his browbeating and menaces, said with a smile that no one knew more than he did, and actually urged him to show gratitude to so good a prince. Fænius could not meet this with either speech or silence. Halting in his words and visibly terror-stricken, while the rest, especially Cervarius Proculus, a Roman knight, did their utmost to convict him, he was, at the Emperor's bidding, seized and bound by Cassius, a soldier who was in attendance, because of his well-known strength of limb.

67. Shortly afterward, the information of the same men proved fatal to Subrius Flavus. At first he grounded his defense on his moral contrast to the others, implying that an armed soldier, like himself, would never have shared such an attempt with unarmed and effeminate associates. Then, when he was pressed, he embraced the glory of a full confession. Questioned by Nero as to the motives which had led him on to forget his oath of allegiance: "I once loved you," he replied, "and no soldier was more loyal to you while you deserved to be loved. I began to hate you when you became the murderer of your mother and your wife, a charioteer, an actor, and an incendiary." I have given the man's very words, because they were not, like those of Seneca, generally published, though the rough and vigorous sentiments of a soldier are no less deserving to be known.

Throughout the conspiracy nothing, it was certain, fell with more terror on the ears of Nero, who was as unused to be told of the crimes he perpetrated as he was eager in their perpetration. The punishment of Flavus was entrusted to Veianius Niger, a tribune. At his direction a pit was dug in a neighboring field. Flavus, on seeing it, censured it as too shallow and confined, saying to the soldiers around him, "Even this is not according to military rule." When bidden to offer his neck resolutely, "I wish," said he, "that your stroke may be as resolute." The tribune trembled greatly, and having only just severed his head at two blows, vaunted his brutality to Nero, saying that he had slain him with a blow and a half.

68. Sulpicius Asper, a centurion, exhibited the next example of fortitude. To Nero's question why he had conspired to murder him, he briefly replied that it was the only way of stopping his career of crime. He then underwent the prescribed penalty. Nor did the remaining centurions forget their courage in suffering their punishment. But Fænius Rufus had not equal spirit; he even put his laments into his will.

Nero waited in the hope that Vestinus also, the consul, whom he thought an impetuous and deeply disaffected man, would be involved in the charge. None, however, of the conspirators had shared their counsels with him, some from old feuds against him, most because they considered him a reckless and dangerous associate. Nero's hatred of him had had its origin in intimate companionship, Vestinus seeing through and despising the Emperor's cowardice, while Nero feared the high spirit of his friend, who often bantered him with that rough humor which, when it draws largely on facts, leaves a bitter memory behind it. There was too a recent aggravation in the circumstance of Vestinus having married Statilia Messallina,[68] without being ignorant that the Emperor was one of her paramours.

69. As neither crime nor accuser appeared, Nero, being thus unable to assume the semblance of a judge, had recourse to the sheer might of despotism, and dispatched Gerellanus, a tribune, with a cohort of soldiers, and with

orders to forestall the designs of the consul, to seize what he might call his fortress, and crush his train of chosen youths. For Vestinus had a house towering over the forum, and a host of handsome slaves of the same age. On that day he had performed all his duties as consul, and was entertaining some guests, fearless of danger, or perhaps by way of hiding his fears, when the soldiers entered and announced to him the tribune's summons. He rose without a moment's delay, and every preparation was at once made. He shut himself into his chamber; a physician was at his side; his veins were opened; with life still strong in him, he was carried into a bath, and plunged into warm water, without uttering a word of pity for himself. Meanwhile the guards surrounded those who had sat at his table, and it was only at a late hour of the night that they were dismissed, when Nero, having pictured to himself and laughed over their terror at the expectation of a fatal end to their banquet, said that they had suffered enough punishment for the consul's entertainment.

70. Next he ordered the destruction of Marcus Annæus Lucanus. As the blood flowed freely from him, and he felt a chill creeping through his feet and hands, and the life gradually ebbing from his extremities, though the heart was still warm and he retained his mental power, Lucanus recalled some poetry he had composed in which he had told the story of a wounded soldier dying a similar kind of death, and he recited the very lines. These were his last words.[69] After him, Senecio, Quintianus, and Scævinus perished, not in the manner expected from the past effeminacy of their life, and then the remaining conspirators, without deed or word deserving record.

71. Rome all this time was thronged with funerals, the Capitol with sacrificial victims. One after another, on the destruction of a brother, a kinsman, or a friend, would return thanks to the gods, deck his house with laurels, prostrate himself at the knees of the Emperor, and weary his hand with kisses. He, in the belief that this was rejoicing, rewarded with impunity the prompt informations of Antonius Natalis and Cervarius Procu-

lus. Milichus was enriched with gifts and assumed in its Greek equivalent the name of Saviour.[70] Of the tribunes, Gavius Silvanus, though acquitted, perished by his own hand; Statius Proximus threw away the benefit of the pardon he had accepted from the Emperor by the folly of his end. Cornelius Martialis, Flavius Nepos, Statius Domitius were then deprived of the tribuneship, on the ground, not of actually hating the Emperor, but of having the credit of it. Novius Priscus, as Seneca's friend, Glitius Gallus, and Annius Pollio, as men disgraced rather than convicted, escaped with sentences of banishment. Priscus and Gallus were accompanied respectively by their wives, Artoria Flaccilla and Egnatia Maximilla. The latter possessed at first a great fortune, still unimpaired, and was subsequently deprived of it, both of which circumstances enhanced her reputation.

Rufrius Crispinus[71] too was banished, on the opportune pretext of the conspiracy, but he was in fact hated by Nero, because he had once been Poppæa's husband. It was the splendor of their name which drove Verginius Flavus and Musonius Rufus into exile. Verginius[72] encouraged the studies of our youth by his eloquence; Rufus[73] by the teachings of philosophy. Cluvidienus Quietus, Julius Agrippa, Blitius Catulinus, Petronius Priscus, Julius Altinus, mere rank and file, so to say, had islands in the Ægean Sea assigned to them. Cædicia, the wife of Scævinus, and Cæsonius Maximus were forbidden to live in Italy, their penalty being the only proof they had of having been accused. Acilia, the mother of Annæus Lucanus, without either acquittal or punishment, was simply ignored.

72. All this having been completed, Nero assembled the troops and distributed two thousand sesterces to every common soldier, with an addition of as much corn without payment as they had previously the use of at the market price. Then, as if he was going to describe successes in war, he summoned the Senate, and awarded triumphal honors to Petronius Turpilianus,[74] an ex-consul, to Cocceius Nerva,[75] prætor-elect, and to Tigellinus, commander of the prætorians. Tigellinus and Nerva he so distinguished as to place busts of them in the

palace in addition to triumphal statues in the forum. He granted a consul's decorations to Nymphidius,[76] on whose origin, as he now appears for the first time, I will briefly touch. For he too was to be a part of Rome's calamities.

The son of a freedwoman who had prostituted a handsome person among the slaves and freedmen of the Emperors, he gave out that he was the offspring of Gaius Cæsar, for he happened to be of tall stature and to have a fierce look. In addition to his other tastes, Gaius Cæsar was partial to harlots, and this man's mother may have been one of those who enjoyed his favors.

73. Nero meanwhile summoned the Senate, addressed them in a speech, and further added a proclamation to the people, with the evidence which had been entered on records, and the confessions of the condemned. He was indeed perpetually under the lash of popular talk, which said that he had destroyed men perfectly innocent out of jealousy or fear. However, that a conspiracy was begun, matured, and conclusively proved was not doubted at the time by those who took pains to ascertain the truth, and is admitted by those who after Nero's death returned to the capital. When everyone in the Senate, those especially who had most cause to mourn, abased himself in flattery, Salienus Clemens denounced Junius Gallio,[77] who was terror-stricken at his brother Seneca's death and was pleading for his life. He called him an enemy and traitor to the state, till the unanimous voice of the senators deterred him from perverting public miseries into an occasion for a personal resentment, and thus importing fresh bitterness into what by the prince's clemency had been hushed up or forgotten.

74. Then offerings and thanksgivings to the gods were decreed, with special honors to the Sun, who has an ancient temple in the circus where the crime was planned, as having revealed by his power the secrets of the conspiracy. Also, the games of Ceres in the circus were to be celebrated with more horse races, and the month of April was to be called after the name of Nero. A temple also was to be erected to Safety, on the spot

whence Scævinus had taken his dagger. The Emperor himself dedicated the weapon in the temple of the Capitol, and inscribed on it "To Jupiter Vindex." This passed without notice at the moment, but after the war of Julius Vindex[78] it was construed as an omen and presage of impending vengeance. I find in the registers of the Senate that Anicius Cerialis, consul-elect, proposed a motion that a temple should as soon as possible be built at the public expense to the divine Nero. He implied indeed by this proposal that the prince had transcended all mortal grandeur and deserved the adoration of mankind. But Nero himself forbade it, fearing it might be taken as an omen of his death, seeing that divine honors are not paid to an emperor till he has ceased to live among men.

BOOK XVI *65-66 A.D.*

1. FORTUNE soon afterward made a dupe of Nero through his own credulity and the promises of Cæsellius Bassus, a Carthaginian by birth and a man of a crazed imagination, who twisted a vision seen in the slumber of night into a confident expectation. He sailed to Rome, and having purchased admission to the Emperor, he explained how he had discovered on his land a cave of immense depth, which contained a vast quantity of gold, not in the form of coin but in the shapeless and ponderous masses of ancient days. In fact, he said, ingots of great weight lay there, with bars standing near them in another part of the cave, a treasure hidden for so many ages to increase the wealth of the present. Phœnician Dido, as he sought to show by inference, after fleeing from Tyre and founding Carthage, had concealed these riches in the fear that a new people might be demoralized by a superabundance of money, or that the Numidian kings, already for other reasons hostile, might by lust of gold be provoked to war.[1]

2. Nero upon this, without sufficiently examining the credibility of the author of the story, or of the matter itself, or sending persons through whom he might ascertain whether the intelligence was true, himself actually

encouraged the report and dispatched men to bring the spoil, as if it were already acquired. They had triremes assigned them and crews specially selected to promote speed. Nothing else at the time was the subject of the credulous gossip of the people, and of the very different conversation of thinking persons. It happened too that the quinquennial games were being celebrated for the second time, and the orators took from this same incident their chief materials for eulogies on the Emperor. "Not only," they said, "were there the usual harvests, and the gold of the mine with its alloy, but the earth now teemed with a new abundance, and wealth was thrust on them by the bounty of the gods." These and other servile flatteries they invented, with consummate eloquence and equal sycophancy, confidently counting on the facility of his belief.

3. Extravagance meanwhile increased, on the strength of a chimerical hope, and ancient wealth was wasted, as apparently the Emperor had lighted on treasures he might squander for many a year. He even gave away profusely from this source, and the expectation of riches was one of the causes of the poverty of the state. Bassus indeed dug up his land and extensive plains in the neighborhood, while he persisted that this or that was the place of the promised cave, and was followed not only by our soldiers but by the rustic population who were engaged to execute the work, till at last he threw off his infatuation, and expressing wonder that his dreams had never before been false, and that now for the first time he had been deluded, he escaped disgrace and danger by a voluntary death. Some have said that he was imprisoned and soon released, his property having been taken from him as a substitute for the royal treasure.

4. Meanwhile the Senate, as they were now on the eve of the quinquennial contest,[2] wishing to avert scandal, offered the Emperor the "victory in song," and added the "crown of eloquence," that thus a veil might be thrown over a shameful exposure on the stage. Nero, however, repeatedly declared that he wanted neither favor nor the Senate's influence, as he was a match for his rivals,

and was certain, in the conscientious opinion of the judges, to win the honor by merit. First he recited a poem on the stage; then, at the importunate request of the rabble that he would make public property of all his accomplishments (these were their words), he entered the theater, and conformed to all the laws of harp playing, not sitting down when tired, nor wiping off the perspiration with anything but the garment he wore, nor letting himself be seen to spit or clear his nostrils. Last of all, on bended knee he saluted the assembly with a motion of the hand, and awaited the verdict of the judges with pretended anxiety. And then the city populace, who were used to encouraging every gesture even of actors, made the place ring with measured strains of elaborate applause. One would have thought they were rejoicing, and perhaps they did rejoice, in their indifference to the public disgrace.

5. All, however, who were present from remote towns and the parts of Italy that still retained strict morals and primitive ways; all too who had come on embassies or on private business from distant provinces, where they had been unused to such wantonness, were unable to endure the spectacle or sustain the degrading fatigue, which wearied their unpracticed hands, while they disturbed those who knew their part, and were often struck by soldiers stationed in the seats to see that not a moment of time passed with less vigorous applause or in the silence of indifference. It was a known fact that several knights, in struggling through the narrow approaches and the pressure of the crowd, were trampled to death, and that others while keeping their seats day and night were seized with some fatal malady. For it was a still worse danger to be absent from the show, as many openly and many more secretly made it their business to scrutinize names and faces, and to note the delight or the disgust of the company. Hence came cruel severities, immediately exercised on the humble, and resentments, concealed for the moment, but subsequently paid off, toward men of distinction. There was a story that Vespasianus[3] was insulted by Phœbus, a freedman, for closing his eyes in a doze, and that having

with difficulty been screened by the intercessions of the well disposed, he escaped imminent destruction through his grander destiny.

6. After the conclusion of the games Poppæa died from a casual outburst of rage in her husband, who felled her with a kick when she was pregnant. That there was poison I cannot believe, though some writers so relate, from hatred rather than from belief, for the Emperor was desirous of children, and wholly swayed by love of his wife. Her body was not consumed by fire according to Roman usage, but after the custom of foreign princes was filled with fragrant spices and embalmed, and then consigned to the sepulcher of the Julii. She had, however, a public funeral, and Nero himself from the Rostra eulogized her beauty, her lot in having been the mother of a deified child, and fortune's other gifts, as though they were virtues.

7. To the death of Poppæa, which, though a public grief, was a delight to those who recalling the past thought of her shamelessness and cruelty, Nero added fresh and greater odium by forbidding Gaius Cassius[4] to attend the funeral. This was the first token of mischief. Nor was it long delayed. Silanus[5] was coupled with Cassius, no crime being alleged, but that Cassius was eminent for his ancestral wealth and dignity of character, Silanus for the nobility of his birth and the quiet demeanor of his youth. The Emperor accordingly sent the Senate a speech in which he argued that both ought to be removed from the state, and made it a reproach against Cassius that among his ancestors' busts he had specially revered that of Gaius Cassius,[6] which bore the inscription "To the Party Leader." In fact, he had thereby sought to sow the seeds of civil war and revolt from the house of the Cæsars. And that he might not merely avail himself of the memory of a hated name to stir up strife, he had associated with him Lucius Silanus, a youth of noble birth and reckless spirit, to whom he might point as an instrument of revolution.

8. Nero next denounced Silanus himself in the same terms as he had his uncle Torquatus,[7] implying that he was already arranging the details of imperial business,

and setting freedmen to manage his accounts, papers, and correspondence, imputations utterly groundless and false. Silanus, in truth, was intensely apprehensive, and had been frightened into caution by his uncle's destruction. Nero then procured persons, under the name of informers, to invent against Lepida,[8] the wife of Cassius and aunt of Silanus, a charge of incest with her brother's son, and of some sinister religious ceremonial. Vulcatius Tullinus and Cornelius Marcellus, senators, and Calpurnius Fabatus,[9] a Roman knight, were drawn in as accomplices. By an appeal to the Emperor these men eluded an impending doom and subsequently, as being too insignificant, escaped from Nero, who was busy with crimes on a far greater scale.

9. The Senate was then consulted and sentences of exile were passed on Cassius and Silanus. As to Lepida, the Emperor was to decide. Cassius was transported to the island of Sardinia, and he was quietly left to old age. Silanus was removed to Ostia, whence, it was pretended, he was to be conveyed to Naxos.[10] ·He was afterward confined in a town of Apulia named Barium.[11] There, as he was calmly enduring a most undeserved calamity, he was suddenly seized by a centurion sent to slay him. When the man advised him to sever his veins, he replied that though he had resolved in his heart to die, he would not let a cutthroat have the glory of the service. The centurion, seeing that, unarmed as he was, he was very powerful, and more like an enraged than a frightened man, ordered his soldiers to overpower him. And Silanus failed not to resist and to strike blows, as well as he could with his bare hands, till he was cut down by the centurion, as though in battle, with wounds in his breast.

10. With equal courage Lucius Vetus,[12] his mother-in-law, Sextia, and his daughter, Pollitta,[13] submitted to death. They were hated by the Emperor because they seemed a living reproach to him for the murder of Rubellius Plautus,[14] son-in-law of Lucius Vetus. But the first opportunity of unmasking his savage wrath was furnished by Fortunatus, a freedman, who, having embezzled his patron's property, deserted him to become

his accuser. He had as his accomplice Claudius Demia-
nus, whom Vetus, when proconsul of Asia, had imprisoned for his gross misdeeds, and whom Nero now
released as a recompense for the accusation.

When the accused knew this and saw that he and
his freedman were pitted against each other on an equal
footing, he retired to his estate at Formiæ. There he was
put under the secret surveillance of soldiers. With him
was his daughter, who, to say nothing of the now imminent peril, had all the fury of a long grief ever since
she had seen the murderers of her husband Plautus. She
had clasped his bleeding neck, and still kept by her the
bloodstained apparel, clinging in her widowhood to
perpetual sorrow, and taking only such nourishment as
might suffice to avert starvation. Then at her father's
bidding she went to Neapolis. And as she was forbidden
to approach Nero, she would haunt his doors and implore him to hear an innocent man, and not surrender to
a freedman one who had once been his colleague in
the consulship, now pleading with the cries of a woman,
now again forgetting her sex and lifting up her voice in
a tone of menace, till the Emperor showed himself unmoved alike by entreaty and reproach.

11. She therefore told her father by message that she
cast hope aside and yielded to necessity. He was at the
same time informed that judicial proceedings in the
Senate and a dreadful sentence were hanging over him.
Some there were who advised him to name the Emperor
as his chief heir, and so secure the remainder for his
grandchildren. But he spurned the notion, and unwilling
to disgrace a life which had clung to freedom by a
final act of servility, he bestowed on his slaves all his
ready money, and ordered each to convey away for
himself whatever he could carry, leaving only three
couches for the last scene. Then in the same chamber,
with the same weapon, they sundered their veins, and
speedily hurried into a bath, covered each, as delicacy
required, with a single garment, the father gazing intently on his daughter, the grandmother on her grandchild, she again on both, while with rival earnestness
they prayed that the ebbing life might have a quick

departure, each wishing to leave a relative still surviving, but just on the verge of death. Fortune preserved the due order; the oldest died first, then the others according to priority of age. They were prosecuted after their burial, and the sentence was that "they should be punished in ancient fashion." But Nero interposed his veto, allowing them to die without his interference. Such were the mockeries added to murders already perpetrated.

12. Publius Gallus, a Roman knight, was outlawed for having been intimate with Fænius Rufus[15] and somewhat acquainted with Vetus. To the freedman who was the accuser was given, as a reward for his service, a seat in the theater among the tribune's officers. Also, the month following April, or Neroneus, was changed from Maius into the name of Claudius, and Junius into that of Germanicus, Cornelius Orfitus, the proposer of the motion, publicly declaring that the month Junius had been passed over because the execution of the two Torquati for their crimes had now rendered its name inauspicious.[16]

13. A year of shame and of so many evil deeds heaven also marked by storms and pestilence. Campania was devastated by a hurricane, which destroyed everywhere country houses, plantations, and crops, and carried its fury to the neighborhood of Rome, where a terrible plague was sweeping away all classes of human beings without any such derangement of the atmosphere as to be visibly apparent. Yet the houses were filled with lifeless forms and the streets with funerals. Neither age nor sex was exempt from peril. Slaves and the freeborn populace alike were suddenly cut off, amid the wailings of wife and children, who were often consumed on the very funeral pile of friends by whom they had been sitting and shedding tears. Knights and senators perished indiscriminately, and yet their deaths were less deplored because they seemed to forestall the Emperor's cruelty by an ordinary death. That same year levies of troops were held in Narbonese Gaul, Africa, and Asia, to fill up the legions of Illyricum, all soldiers in which, worn out by age or ill health, were receiving their dis-

charge. Lugdunum[17] was consoled by the prince for a ruinous disaster by a gift of four million sesterces, so that what was lost to the city might be replaced. Its people had previously offered this same amount for the distresses of Rome.

14. In the consulship of Gaius Suetonius and Luccius Telesinus,[18] Antistius Sosianus, who, as I have stated, had been punished with exile for repeated satires on Nero;[19] having heard that there was such honor for informers and that the Emperor was so partial to bloodshed, being himself too of a restless temper and quick to seize opportunities, made a friend of a man in like condition with himself, one Pammenes, an exile in the same place, noted for his skill as an astrologer, and consequently bound to many in close intimacy. He thought there must be a meaning in the frequent messages and the consultations, and he learned at the same time that an annual payment was furnished him by Publius Anteius.[20] He knew too that Anteius was hated by Nero for his love of Agrippina, and that his wealth was sufficiently conspicuous to provoke cupidity, and that this was the cause of the destruction of many. Accordingly he intercepted a letter from Anteius, and having also stolen some notes about the day of his nativity and his future career, which were hidden away among Pammenes' secret papers, and having further discovered some remarks on the birth and life of Ostorius Scapula,[21] he wrote to the Emperor that he would communicate important news which would contribute to his safety, if he could but obtain a brief reprieve of his exile. Anteius and Ostorius were, he hinted, grasping at empire and prying into the destinies of themselves and of the prince. Some swift galleys were then dispatched and Socianus speedily arrived. On the disclosure of his information, Anteius and Ostorius were classed with condemned criminals rather than with men on their trial, so completely, indeed, that no one would attest the will of Anteius till Tigellinus interposed to sanction it. Anteius had been previously advised by him not to delay this final document. Then he drank

poison, but disgusted at its slowness, he hastened death by severing his veins.

15. Ostorius was living at the time on a remote estate on the Ligurian frontier;[22] and a centurion was sent there to hurry on his destruction. There was a motive for promptitude, since Ostorius, with his great military fame and the civic crown he had won in Britain, and possessed too as he was of huge bodily strength and skill in arms, had made Nero, who was always timid and now more frightened than ever by the lately discovered conspiracy, fearful of a sudden attack. So the centurion, having barred every exit from the house, disclosed the Emperor's orders to Ostorius. That fortitude which he had often shown in fighting the enemy Ostorius now turned against himself. And as his veins, though severed, allowed but a scanty flow of blood, he used the help of a slave, simply to hold up a dagger firmly, and then pressing the man's hand toward him, he met the point with his throat.

16. Even if I had to relate foreign wars and deaths encountered in the service of the state with such a monotony of disaster, I should myself have been overcome by disgust, while I should look for weariness in my readers, sickened as they would be by the melancholy and continuous destruction of our citizens, however glorious to themselves. But now a servile submissiveness and so much wanton bloodshed at home fatigue the mind and paralyze it with grief. The only indulgence I would ask from those who will acquaint themselves with these horrors is that I be not thought to hate men who perished so tamely. Such was the wrath of heaven against the Roman state that one may not pass over it with a single mention, as one might the defeat of armies and the capture of cities. Let us grant this privilege to the posterity of illustrious men, that just as in their funeral obsequies such men are not confounded in a common burial, so in the record of their end they may receive and retain a special memorial.

17. Within a few days, in quick succession, Annæus Mela, Anicius Cerialis,[23] Rufrius Crispinus,[24] and Gaius Petronius[25] fell, Mela and Crispinus being Roman knights

with senatorial rank. The latter had once commanded
the prætorians and had been rewarded with the decorations of the consulate. He had lately been banished to
Sardinia on a charge of conspiracy, and on receiving
a message that he was doomed to die had destroyed
himself. Mela, son of the same parents as Gallio[26] and
Seneca, had refrained from seeking promotion out of a
perverse vanity which wished to raise a Roman knight
to an equality with ex-consuls. He also thought that
there was a shorter road to the acquisition of wealth
through offices connected with the administration of
the Emperor's private business. He had too in his son
Annæus Lucanus[27] a powerful aid in rising to distinction.
After the death of Lucanus, he rigorously called in the
debts due to his estate, and thereby provoked an accuser
in the person of Fabius Romanus, one of the intimate
friends of Lucanus. A story was invented that the father
and son shared between them a knowledge of the conspiracy, and a letter was forged in Lucanus' name. This
Nero examined, and ordered it to be conveyed to Mela,
whose wealth he ravenously desired. Mela meanwhile,
adopting the easiest mode of death then in fashion,
opened his veins, after adding a codicil to his will bequeathing an immense amount to Tigellinus and his
son-in-law Cossutianus Capito,[28] in order to save the
remainder. In this codicil he is also said to have written,
by way of remonstrance against the injustice of his
death, that he died without any cause for punishment,
while Rufrius Crispinus and Anicius Cerialis still enjoyed life, though bitter foes to the prince. It was
thought that he had invented this about Crispinus, because the man had been already murdered; about Cerialis, with the object of procuring his murder. Soon
afterward Cerialis laid violent hands on himself, and
received less pity than the others, because men remembered that he had betrayed a conspiracy to Gaius Cæsar.

18. With regard to Gaius Petronius, I ought to dwell a
little on his antecedents. His days he passed in sleep, his
nights in the business and pleasures of life. Indolence
had raised him to fame, as energy raises others, and he
was reckoned not a debauchee and spendthrift, like most

of those who squander their substance, but a man of
refined luxury. And indeed his talk and his doings, the
freer they were and the more show of carelessness they
exhibited, were the better liked, for their look of a natural
simplicity. Yet as proconsul of Bithynia and soon afterward as consul, he showed himself a man of vigor and
equal to business. Then falling back into vice or affecting
vice, he was chosen by Nero to be one of his few intimate
associates, as a critic in matters of taste, while the Emperor thought nothing charming or elegant in luxury
unless Petronius had expressed to him his approval of
it. Hence jealousy on the part of Tigellinus, who looked
on him as a rival and even his superior in the science of
pleasure. And so he worked on the prince's cruelty, which
dominated every other passion, charging Petronius with
having been the friend of Scævinus,[29] bribing a slave to
become informer, robbing him of the means of defense,
and hurrying into prison the greater part of his domestics.

19. It happened at the time that the Emperor was on
his way to Campania and that Petronius, after going as
far as Cumæ,[30] was there detained. He bore no longer
the suspense of fear or of hope. Yet he did not fling away
life with precipitate haste, but having made an incision
in his veins and then, according to his humor, bound
them up, he again opened them, while he conversed with
his friends, not in a serious strain or on topics that might
win for him the glory of courage. And he listened to them
as they repeated, not thoughts on the immortality of the
soul or on the theories of philosophers, but light poetry
and playful verses. To some of his slaves he gave liberal
presents, a flogging to others. He dined, indulged himself
in sleep, that death, though forced on him, might have a
natural appearance. Even in his will he did not, as did
many in their last moments, flatter Nero or Tigellinus or
any other of the men in power. On the contrary, he described fully the prince's shameful excesses, with the
names of his male and female companions and their
novelties in debauchery, and sent the account under seal
to Nero. Then he broke his signet ring, that it might not
be subsequently available for imperiling others.

20. When Nero was in doubt how the ingenious varieties of his nightly revels became notorious, Silia came into his mind, who, as a senator's wife, was a conspicuous person, and who had been his chosen associate in all his profligacy and was very intimate with Petronius. She was banished for not having, as was suspected, kept secret what she had seen and endured, a sacrifice to his personal resentment. Minucius Thermus,[31] an ex-prætor, he surrendered to the hate of Tigellinus, because a freedman of Thermus had brought criminal charges against Tigellinus, such that the man had to atone for them himself by the torture of the rack, his patron by an undeserved death.

21. Nero, after having butchered so many illustrious men, at last aspired to extirpate virtue itself by murdering Thrasea Pætus[32] and Barea Soranus.[33] Both men he had hated of old, Thrasea on additional grounds, because he had walked out of the Senate when Agrippina's case was under discussion, as I have already related,[34] and had not given the Juvenilia any conspicuous encouragement. Nero's displeasure at this was the deeper, since this same Thrasea had sung in a tragedian's dress at Patavium,[35] his birthplace, in some games instituted by the Trojan Antenor. On the day, too, on which the prætor Antistius was being sentenced to death for libels on Nero,[36] Thrasea proposed and carried a more merciful decision. Again, when divine honors were decreed to Poppæa, he was purposely absent and did not attend her funeral. All this Cossutianus Capito would not allow to be forgotten. He had a heart eager for the worst wickedness, and he also bore ill will to Thrasea, the weight of whose influence had crushed him, while envoys from Cilicia, supported by Thrasea's advocacy, were accusing him of extortion.[37]

22. He alleged, too, against him the following charges: "Thrasea," he said, "at the beginning of the year always avoided the usual oath of allegiance; he was not present at the recital of the public prayers, though he had been promoted to the priesthood of the Fifteen; he had never offered a sacrifice for the safety of the prince or for his heavenly voice. Though formerly he had been assiduous

and unwearied in showing himself a supporter or an
opponent even of the most ordinary motions of senators,
he had not entered the Senate House for three years, and
very lately, when all were rushing thither with rival
eagerness to put down Silanus and Vetus,[38] he had
attended by preference to the private business of his
clients. This was political schism, and, should many dare
to do the like, it was actual war."

Capito further added, "The country in its eagerness for
discord is now talking of you, Nero, and of Thrasea, as
it talked once of Julius Cæsar and Marcus Cato. Thrasea
has his followers, or rather his satellites, who copy, not
indeed as yet the audacious tone of his sentiments, but
only his manners and his looks, a sour and gloomy set,
bent on making your mirthfulness a reproach to you. He
is the only man who cares not for your safety, honors not
your accomplishments. The prince's prosperity he de-
spises. Can it be that he is not satisfied with your sorrows
and griefs? It shows the same spirit not to believe in
Poppæa's divinity as to refuse to swear obedience to the
acts of the divine Augustus and the divine Julius. He
contemns religious rites; he annuls laws. The daily
records of the Roman people are read attentively in the
provinces and the armies that they may know what
Thrasea has not done.

"Either let us go over to his system, if it is better than
ours, or let those who desire change have their leader
and adviser taken from them. That sect of his gave birth
to men like Tubero and Favonius,[39] names hateful even
to the old republic. They make a show of freedom, to
overturn the Empire; should they destroy it, they will
attack freedom itself. In vain have you banished Cassius,[40] so if you are going to allow imitators of the Bruti[41]
to multiply and flourish. Finally, write nothing yourself
about Thrasea; leave the Senate to decide for us." Nero
further stimulated the eager wrath of Cossutianus, and
associated with him the pungent eloquence of Eprius
Marcellus.[42]

23. As for the impeachment of Barea Soranus, Ostorius Sabinus, a Roman knight, had already claimed it for
himself. It arose out of his proconsulate in Asia,[43] where

he increased the prince's animosity by his uprightness and diligence, as well as by having bestowed pains on opening the port of Ephesus and passed over without punishment the violence of the citizens of Pergamum in their efforts to hinder Acratus,[44] one of the Emperor's freedmen, from carrying off statues and pictures. But the crime imputed to him was friendship with Rubellius Plautus and intrigues to lure the province into thoughts of revolt. The time chosen for the fatal sentence was that at which Tiridates was on his way to receive the sovereignty of Armenia, so that crime at home might be partially veiled amid rumors on foreign affairs, or that Nero might display his imperial grandeur by the murder of illustrious men, as though it were a kingly exploit.

24. Accordingly, when all Rome rushed out to welcome the Emperor and see the king, Thrasea, though forbidden to appear, did not let his spirit be cast down, but wrote a note to Nero, in which he demanded to know the charges against him, and asserted that he would clear himself, if he were informed of the crimes alleged and had an opportunity of refuting them. This note Nero received with eagerness, in the hope that Thrasea in dismay had written something to enhance the Emperor's glory and to tarnish his own honor. When it turned out otherwise, and he himself, on the contrary, dreaded the glance and the defiant independence of the guiltless man, he ordered the Senate to be summoned.

25. Thrasea then consulted his most intimate friends whether he should attempt or spurn defense. Conflicting advice was offered. Those who thought it best for him to enter the Senate House said that they counted confidently on his courage, and were sure that he would say nothing but what would heighten his renown. "It was for the feeble and timid to invest their last moments with secrecy. Let the people behold a man who could meet death. Let the Senate hear words, almost of divine inspiration, more than human. It was possible that the very miracle might impress even a Nero. But should he persist in his cruelty, posterity would at least distinguish between the memory of an honorable death and the cowardice of those who perished in silence."

26. Those, on the other hand, who thought that he ought to wait at home, though their opinion of him was the same, hinted that mockeries and insults were in store for him. "Spare your ears," they said, "taunts and revilings. Not only are Cossutianus and Eprius eagerly bent on crime; there are numbers more, daring enough, perchance, to raise the hand of violence in their brutality. Even good men through fear do the like. Better save the Senate which you have adorned to the last the infamy of such an outrage, and leave it a matter of doubt what the senators would have decided, had they seen Thrasea on his trial. It is with a vain hope we are aiming to touch Nero with shame for his abominations, and we have far more cause to fear that he will vent his fury on your wife, your household, on all others dear to you. And therefore, while you are yet stainless and undisgraced, seek to close life with the glory of those in whose track and pursuits you have passed it."

Present at this deliberation was Arulenus Rusticus,[45] an enthusiastic youth, who in his ardor for renown offered, as he was tribune of the people, to protest against the sentence of the Senate. Thrasea checked his impetuous temper, not wishing him to attempt what would be as futile, and useless to the accused, as it would be fatal to the protester. "My days," he said, "are ended, and I must not now abandon a scheme of life in which for so many years I have persevered. You are at the beginning of a career of office, and your future is yet clear. Weigh thoroughly with yourself beforehand, at such a crisis as this, the path of political life on which you enter." He then reserved for his own consideration the question whether it became him to enter the Senate.

27. Next day, however, two prætorian cohorts under arms occupied the temple of Venus Genetrix.[46] A group of ordinary citizens with swords which they did not conceal had blocked the approach to the Senate. Through the squares and colonnades were scattered bodies of soldiers, amid whose looks of menace the senators entered their house. A speech from the Emperor was read by his quæstor. Without adressing anyone by name, he censured the senators for neglecting their public duties, and draw-

ing by their example the Roman knights into idleness.
"For what wonder is it," he asked, "that men do not
come from remote provinces when many, after obtaining
the consulate or some sacred office, give all their thoughts
by choice to the beauty of their gardens?" Here was, so
to say, a weapon for the accusers, on which they fastened.

28. Cossutianus made a beginning, and then Marcellus in more violent tones exclaimed that the whole
commonwealth was at stake. "It is," he said, "the stub-
bornness of inferiors which lessens the clemency of our
ruler. We senators have hitherto been too lenient in
allowing him to be mocked with impunity by Thrasea
throwing off allegiance, by his son-in-law Helvidius Priscus[47] indulging similar frenzies, by Paconius Agrippinus,[48] the inheritor of his father's hatred toward emperors, and by Curtius Montanus,[49] the habitual composer
of abominable verses. I miss the presence of an ex-
consul in the Senate, of a priest when we offer our vows,
of a citizen when we swear obedience, unless indeed, in
defiance of the manners and rites of our ancestors,
Thrasea has openly assumed the part of a traitor and an
enemy. In a word, let the man accustomed to act the
senator and to screen those who disparage the prince
come among us; let him propose any reform or change
he may desire. We shall more readily endure his censure
of details than we can now bear the silence by which he
condemns everything. Is it the peace throughout the
world or victories won without loss to our armies which
vex him? A man who grieves at the country's prosperity,
who treats our public places, theaters, and temples as if
they were a desert, and who is ever threatening us with
exile, let us not enable such a one to gratify his perverse
vanity. To him the decrees of this house, the offices of
state, the city of Rome seem as nothing. Let him sever
his life from a country all love for which he has long
lost and the very sight of which he has now put from
him."

29. While Marcellus, with the savage and menacing
look he usually wore, spoke these and like words with
rising fury in his voice, countenance, and eye, that famil-

291

iar grief to which a thick succession of perils had habituated the Senate gave way to a new and profounder
panic, as they saw the soldiers' hands on their weapons.
At the same moment the venerable form of Thrasea rose
before their imagination, and some there were who pitied
Helvidius too, doomed as he was to suffer for an innocent alliance. "What again," they asked, "was the charge
against Agrippinus except his father's sad fate, since he
too, though guiltless as his son, fell beneath the cruelty
of Tiberius? As for Montanus, a youth without a blemish,
author of no libelous poem, he was positively driven out
because he had given proof of literary gifts."

30. And meanwhile Ostorius Sabinus, the accuser of
Soranus, entered, and began by speaking of his friendship with Rubellius Plautus and of his proconsulate in
Asia, which he had, he said, adapted to his own glory
rather than to the public welfare, by fostering seditious
movements in the various states. These were bygones, but
there was a fresh charge involving the daughter in the
peril of the father, to the effect that she had lavished
money on astrologers. This indeed had really occurred
through the filial affection of Servilia[50] (that was the
girl's name), who, out of love for her father and the
thoughtlessness of youth, had consulted them, only, however, about the safety of her family, whether Nero could
be appeased, and the trial before the Senate have no
dreadful result.

She was accordingly summoned before the Senate, and
there they stood facing one another before the consuls'
tribunal, the aged parent, and opposite to him the
daughter, in the twentieth year of her age, alone and
forlorn, her husband, Annius Pollio, having lately been
driven into banishment, without so much as a glance at
her father, whose peril she seemed to have aggravated.

31. Then on the accuser asking her whether she had
sold her bridal presents or stripped her neck of its ornaments to raise money for the performance of magical
rites, she at first flung herself on the ground and wept
long in silence. After a while, clasping the altar steps and
altar, she exclaimed, "I have invoked no impious deities,
no enchantments, nor any other power in my unhappy

prayers, but only that you, Cæsar, and you, senators, might preserve unharmed this best of fathers. My jewels, my apparel, and the signs of my rank I gave up, as I would have given up my lifeblood had they demanded it. They must have seen this, those men before unknown to me, both as to the name they bear and the arts they practice. No mention was made by me of the Emperor, except as one of the divinities. But my most unhappy father knows nothing, and if it is a crime, I alone am guilty."

32. While she was yet speaking, Soranus caught up her words, and exclaimed that she had not gone with him into the province; that, from her youth, she could not have been known to Plautus, and that she was not involved in the charges against her husband. "Treat separately," he said, "the case of one who is guilty only of an exaggerated filial piety, and as for myself, let me undergo any fate." He was rushing, as he spoke, into the embraces of his daughter, who hurried toward him, but the lictors interposed and stopped them both. Place was then given to the witnesses, and the appearance among them of Publius Egnatius[51] provoked as much indignation as the cruelty of the prosecution had excited pity. A client of Soranus, and now hired to ruin his friend, he professed the dignified character of a Stoic, and had trained himself in demeanor and language to exhibit an ideal of virtue. In his heart, however, treacherous and cunning, he concealed greed and sensuality. As soon as money had brought these vices to light, he became an example, warning us to beware just as much of those who under the guise of virtuous tastes are false and deceitful in friendship, as of men wholly entangled in falsehoods and stained with every infamy.

33. That same day brought with it a noble pattern in Cassius Asclepiodotus, whose vast wealth made him a foremost man in Bithynia. He had honored Soranus in his prosperity with a respect which he did not cast off in his fall, and he was now stripped of all his property and driven into exile; so impartially indifferent is heaven to examples of virtue and vice. Thrasea, Soranus, and Servilia were allowed the choice of death. Helvidius[52] and

Paconius were banished from Italy. Montanus was spared to his father's intercessions on the understanding that he was not to be admitted to political life. The prosecutors, Eprius and Cossutianus, received each five million sesterces, Ostorius twelve hundred thousand, with the decorations of the quæstorship.

34. Then, as evening approached, the consul's quæstor was sent to Thrasea, who was passing his time in his garden. He had had a crowded gathering of distinguished men and women, giving special attention to Demetrius,[53] a professor of the Cynic philosophy. With him, as might be inferred from his earnest expression of face and from words heard when they raised their voices, he was speculating on the nature of the soul and on the separation of the spirit from the body, till Domitius Cæcilianus, one of his intimate friends, came to him and told him in detail what the Senate had decided. When all who were present wept and complained bitterly, Thrasea urged them to hasten their departure and not mingle their own perils with the fate of a doomed man. Arria,[54] too, who aspired to follow her husband's end and the example of Arria, her mother, he counseled to preserve her life, and not rob their beloved daughter of her only stay.

35. Then he went out into a colonnade, where he was found by the quæstor, joyful rather than otherwise, as he had learned that Helvidius, his son-in-law, was merely excluded from Italy. When he heard the Senate's decision, he led Helvidius and Demetrius into a chamber, and having laid bare the arteries of each arm, he let the blood flow freely, and, as he sprinkled it on the ground, he called the quæstor to his side and said, "We pour out a libation to Jupiter the Deliverer.[55] Behold, young man, and may the gods avert the omen, but you have been born into times in which it is well to fortify the spirit with examples of courage." Then as the slowness of his end brought with it grievous anguish, turning his eyes on Demetrius. . .

The Histories

BOOK I

1. I BEGIN my work with the time when Servius Galba[1] was consul for the second time with Titus Vinius[2] for his colleague. Of the former period, the 820 years dating from the founding of the city, many authors have treated; and while they had to record the transactions of the Roman people, they wrote with equal eloquence and freedom. After the conflict at Actium, and when it became essential to peace that all power should be centered in one man, these great intellects passed away. Then too the truthfulness of history was impaired in many ways; at first, through men's ignorance of public affairs, which were now wholly strange to them; then, through their passion for flattery, or, on the other hand, their hatred of their masters. And so between the enmity of the one and the servility of the other, neither had any regard for posterity. But while we instinctively shrink from a writer's adulation, we lend a ready ear to detraction and spite, because flattery involves the shameful imputation of servility, whereas malignity wears the false appearance of honesty. I myself knew nothing of Galba, of Otho, or of Vitellius, either from benefits or from injuries. I would not deny that my elevation was begun by Vespasianus, augmented by Titus, and still further advanced by Domitian;[3] but those who profess inviolable truthfulness must speak of all without partiality and without hatred. I have reserved as an employment for my old age, should my life be long enough, a subject at once more fruitful and less anxious in the reign of the divine Nerva and the Empire of Trajan, enjoying the rare happiness of times when we may think what we please, and express what we think.

2. I am entering on the history of a period rich in disasters, frightful in its wars, torn by civil strife, and even in peace full of horrors. Four emperors perished by the sword.[4] There were three civil wars,[5] there were more with foreign enemies;[6] there were often wars that had both characters at once.[7] There was success in the East,

and disaster in the West. There were disturbances in
Illyricum; Gaul wavered in its allegiance; Britain was
thoroughly subdued and immediately abandoned;[8] the
tribes of the Suebi and the Sarmatæ[9] rose in concert
against us; the Dacians[10] had the glory of inflicting as
well as suffering defeat; the armies of Parthia were all
but set in motion by the cheat of a counterfeit Nero.[11]
Now too Italy was prostrated by disasters either entirely
novel, or that recurred only after a long succession of
ages; cities in Campania's richest plains were swallowed
up and overwhelmed;[12] Rome was wasted by conflagrations,[13] its oldest temples consumed, and the Capitol itself fired by the hands of citizens. Sacred rites were profaned;[14] there was profligacy in the highest ranks; the
sea was crowded with exiles, and its rocks polluted with
bloody deeds. In the capital there were yet worse horrors.
Nobility, wealth, the refusal or the acceptance of office
were grounds for accusation, and virtue ensured destruction. The rewards of the informers were no less odious
than their crimes; for while some seized on consulships
and priesthoods as their share of the spoil, others on
procuratorships and posts of more confidential authority,
they robbed and ruined in every direction amid universal
hatred and terror. Slaves were bribed to turn against
their masters, and freedmen to betray their patrons; and
those who had not an enemy were destroyed by friends.

3. Yet the age was not so barren in noble qualities as
not also to exhibit examples of virtue. Mothers accompanied the flight of their sons; wives followed their
husbands into exile; there were brave kinsmen and faithful sons-in-law; there were slaves whose fidelity defied
even torture; there were illustrious men driven to the
last necessity, and enduring it with fortitude; there were
closing scenes that equaled the famous deaths of antiquity. Besides the manifold vicissitudes of human
affairs, there were prodigies in heaven and earth, the
warning voices of the thunder, and other intimations of
the future, auspicious or gloomy, doubtful or not to be
mistaken. Never surely did more terrible calamities of
the Roman people, or evidence more conclusive, prove

that the gods take no thought for our happiness, but only for our punishment.

4. I think it proper, however, before I commence my purposed work, to pass under review the condition of the capital, the temper of the armies, the attitude of the provinces, and the elements of weakness and strength which existed throughout the whole Empire, that so we may become acquainted, not only with the vicissitudes and the issues of events, which are often matters of chance, but also with their relations and their causes. Welcome as the death of Nero had been in the first burst of joy, yet it had not only roused various emotions in Rome, among the senators, the people, or the soldiery of the capital, it had also excited all the legions and their generals; for now had been divulged that secret of the Empire, that emperors could be made elsewhere than at Rome. The senators enjoyed the first exercise of freedom with the less restraint, because the Emperor was new to power, and absent from the capital. The leading men of the equestrian order sympathized most closely with the joy of the senators. The respectable portion of the people, which was connected with the great families, as well as the dependents and freedmen of condemned and banished persons, were high in hope. The degraded populace, frequenters of the arena and the theater, the most worthless of the slaves, and those who, having wasted their property, were supported by the infamous excesses of Nero, caught eagerly in their dejection at every rumor.

5. The soldiery of the capital, who were imbued with the spirit of an old allegiance to the Cæsars, and who had been led to desert Nero by intrigues and influences from without rather than by their own feelings, were inclined for change when they found that the donative promised in Galba's name was withheld, and reflected that for great services and great rewards there was not the same room in peace as in war, and that the favor of an Emperor created by the legions must be already preoccupied. They were further excited by the treason of Nymphidius Sabinus,[15] their prefect, who himself aimed at the throne. Nymphidius indeed perished in the attempt, but though the head of the mutiny was thus

TACITUS

removed, there yet remained in many of the soldiers the consciousness of guilt. There were even men who talked in angry terms of the feebleness and avarice of Galba. The strictness once so commended, and celebrated in the praises of the army, was galling to troops who rebelled against the old discipline, and who had been accustomed by fourteen years' service under Nero to love the vices of their emperors, as much as they had once respected their virtues. To all this was added Galba's own expression: "I choose my soldiers, I do not buy them," noble words for the commonwealth, but fraught with peril for himself. His other acts were not after this pattern.

6. Titus Vinius and Cornelius Laco,[16] one the most worthless, the other the most spiritless of mankind, were ruining the weak old Emperor, who had to bear the odium of such crimes and the scorn felt for such cowardice. Galba's progress had been slow and bloodstained. Cingonius Varro,[17] consul-elect, and Petronius Turpilianus,[18] a man of consular rank, were put to death; the former as an accomplice of Nymphidius, the latter as one of Nero's generals. Both had perished without hearing or defense, just as if they had been innocent. His entry into the capital, made after the slaughter of thousands of unarmed soldiers, was most ill-omened, and was terrible even to the executioners. As he brought into the city his Spanish legion, while that which Nero had levied from the fleet still remained, Rome was full of strange troops. There were also many detachments from Germany, Britain, and Illyria, selected by Nero, and sent on by him to the Caspian Gates, for service in the expedition which he was preparing against the Albani,[19] but afterward recalled to crush the insurrection of Vindex. Here there were vast materials for a revolution, without indeed a decided bias toward any one man, but ready to a daring hand.

7. At this juncture it happened that tidings of the deaths of Clodius Macer[20] and Fonteius Capito[21] reached the capital. Macer was executed in Africa, where he was undoubtedly fomenting sedition, by Trebonius Garutianus, the procurator, who acted on Galba's authority; Capito fell in Germany, while he was making similar at-

tempts, by the hands of Cornelius Aquinus and Fabius
Valens, legates of legions, who did not wait for an order.
There were, however, some who believed that Capito,
though foully stained with avarice and profligacy, had yet
abstained from all thought of revolution, that this was a
treacherous accusation invented by the commanders
themselves, who had urged him to take up arms, when
they found themselves unable to prevail, and that Galba
had approved of the deed, either from weakness of character, or to avoid investigation into the circumstances of
acts which could not be altered. Both executions, however, were unfavorably regarded; indeed, when a ruler
once becomes unpopular, all his acts, be they good or
bad, tell against him. The freedmen in their excessive
power were now putting up everything for sale; the slaves
caught with greedy hands at immediate gain, and, reflecting on their master's age, hastened to be rich. The
new court had the same abuses as the old, abuses as
grievous as ever, but not so readily excused. Even the age
of Galba caused ridicule and disgust among those whose
associations were with the youth of Nero, and who were
accustomed, as is the fashion of the vulgar, to value their
emperors by the beauty and grace of their persons.

8. Such, as far as one can speak of so vast a multitude, was the state of feeling at Rome. Among the provinces, Spain was under the government of Cluvius
Rufus,[22] an eloquent man, who had all the accomplishments of civil life, but who was without experience in
war. Gaul, besides remembering Vindex, was bound to
Galba by the recently conceded privileges of citizenship,
and by the diminution of its future tribute. Those Gallic
states, however, which were nearest to the armies of
Germany had not been treated with the same respect, and
had even in some cases been deprived of their territory;
and these were reckoning the gains of others and their
own losses with equal indignation. The armies of Germany were at once alarmed and angry, a most dangerous
temper when allied with such strength; while elated by
their recent victory, they feared because they might seem
to have supported an unsuccessful party. They had been
slow to revolt from Nero, and Verginius[23] had not imme-

diately declared for Galba; it was doubtful whether he had himself wished to be Emperor, but all agreed that the Empire had been offered to him by the soldiery. Again, the execution of Capito was a subject of indignation, even with those who could not complain of its injustice. They had no leader, for Verginius had been withdrawn on the pretext of his friendship with the Emperor. That he was not sent back, and that he was even impeached, they regarded as an accusation against themselves.

9. The army of Upper Germany despised their legate, Hordeonius Flaccus, who, disabled by age and lameness, had no strength of character and no authority; even when the soldiery were quiet, he could not control them, and in their fits of frenzy they were irritated by the very feebleness of his restraint. The legions of Lower Germany had long been without any general of consular rank, until, by the appointment of Galba, Aulus Vitellius[24] took the command. He was the son of that Vitellius who was censor and three times consul;[25] this was thought sufficient recommendation. In the army of Britain there was no angry feeling; indeed, no troops behaved more blamelessly throughout all the troubles of these civil wars, either because they were far away and separated by the ocean from the rest of the Empire, or because continual warfare had taught them to concentrate their hatred on the enemy. Illyricum too was quiet, though the legions drawn from that province by Nero had, while lingering in Italy, sent deputations to Verginius. But separated as these armies were by long distances, a thing of all others the most favorable for keeping troops to their duty, they could neither communicate their vices, nor combine their strength.

10. In the East there was as yet no movement. Syria and its four legions were under the command of Licinius Mucianus,[26] a man whose good and bad fortune were equally famous. In his youth he had cultivated with many intrigues the friendship of the great. His resources soon failed, and his position became precarious, and as he also suspected that Claudius had taken some offense, he withdrew into a retired part of Asia, and was as near

to being an exile, as he was afterward as near to being
an emperor. He was a compound of dissipation and energy, of arrogance and courtesy, of good and bad qualities. His self-indulgence was excessive, when he had
leisure, yet whenever he had served he had shown great
qualities. In his public capacity he might be praised;
his private life was in bad repute. Yet over subjects,
friends, and colleagues, he exercised the influence of
many fascinations. He was a man who would find it
easier to transfer the imperial power to another than to
hold it for himself. Flavius Vespasianus,[27] a general of
Nero's appointment, was carrying on the war in Judæa
with three legions, and he had no wish or feeling adverse
to Galba. He had in fact sent his son Titus to acknowledge his authority and bespeak his favor, as in its proper
place I shall relate. As for the hidden decrees of fate,
the omens and the oracles that marked out Vespasianus
and his sons for imperial power, we believed in them
only after his success.

11. Ever since the time of the divine Augustus Roman
knights have ruled Egypt as kings, with the forces by
which it has to be kept in subjection. It has been thought
expedient thus to keep under home control a province so
difficult of access, so productive of corn, ever distracted,
excitable, and restless through the superstition and
licentiousness of its inhabitants, knowing nothing of
laws, and unused to civil rule. Its governor was at this
time Tiberius Alexander, a native of the country.[28] Africa
and its legions, now that Clodius Macer was dead, were
disposed to be content with any emperor, after having
experienced the rule of a smaller tyrant. The two divisions of Mauritania, Rhætia, Noricum, and Thrace, and
the other provinces governed by procurators, as they
were near this or that army, were driven by the presence
of such powerful neighbors into friendship or hostility.
The unarmed provinces with Italy at their head were
exposed to any kind of slavery, and were ready to become
the prize of victory. Such was the state of the Roman
world, when Servius Galba, consul for the second time,
with Titus Vinius for his colleague, entered upon a year

which was to be the last of their lives, and which almost proved the last of the republic.

12. A few days after the 1st of January, there arrived from Belgica dispatches of Pompeius Propinquus, the procurator, to this effect: that the legions of Upper Germany had broken through the obligation of their military oath, and were demanding another emperor, but conceded the power of choice to the Senate and people of Rome, in the hope that a more lenient view might be taken of their revolt. These tidings hastened the plans of Galba, who had been long debating the subject of adoption with himself and with his intimate friends. There was indeed no more frequent subject of conversation during these months, at first because men had libetry and inclination to talk of such matters, afterward because the feebleness of Galba was notorious. Few had any discrimination or patriotism, many had foolish hopes for themselves, and spread interested reports, in which they named this or that person to whom they might be related as friend or dependant. They were also moved by hatred of Titus Vinius, who grew daily more powerful, and in the same proportion more unpopular. The very easiness of Galba's temper stimulated the greedy cupidity which great advancement had excited in his friends, because with one so weak and so credulous, wrong might be done with less risk and greater gain.

13. The real power of the Empire was divided between Titus Vinius, the consul, and Cornelius Laco, prefect of the prætorian guard. Icelus, a freedman of Galba, was in equal favor; he had been presented with the rings of knighthood, and bore the equestrian name of Martianus. These men, being at variance, and in smaller matters pursuing their own aims, were divided in the affair of choosing a successor, into two opposing factions. Titus Vinius was for Marcus Otho;[29] Laco and Icelus agreed, not indeed in supporting any particular individual, but in striving for someone else. Galba indeed was aware of the friendship between Vinius and Otho; the gossip of those who allow nothing to pass in silence had named them as father-in-law and son-in-law, for Vinius had a widowed daughter, and Otho was unmarried. I believe that he had

also at heart some care for the commonwealth, in vain, he would think, rescued from Nero, if it was to be left with Otho. For Otho's had been a careless boyhood and a riotous youth, and he had made himself agreeable to Nero by emulating his profligacy. For this reason the Emperor had entrusted to him, as being the confidant of his amours, Poppæa Sabina, the imperial favorite, until he could rid himself of his wife Octavia. Soon suspecting him with regard to this same Poppæa, he sent him out of the way to the province of Lusitania, ostensibly to be its governor. Otho ruled the province with mildness, and as he was the first to join Galba's party, was not without energy, and while the war lasted was the most conspicuous of the Emperor's followers, he was led to cherish more and more passionately every day those hopes of adoption which he had entertained from the first. Many of the soldiers favored him, and the court was biased in his favor because he resembled Nero.

14. When Galba heard of the mutiny in Germany, though nothing was as yet known about Vitellius, he felt anxious as to the direction which the violence of the legions might take, while he could not trust even the soldiery of the capital. He therefore resorted to what he supposed to be the only remedy, and held a council for the election of an emperor. To this he summoned, besides Vinius and Laco, Marius Celsus,[30] consul-elect, and Ducenius Geminus,[31] prefect of the city. Having first said a few words about his advanced years, he ordered Piso Licinianus to be summoned. It is uncertain whether he acted on his own free choice, or, as believed by some, under the influence of Laco, who through Rubellius Plautus had cultivated the friendship of Piso. But, cunningly enough, it was as a stranger that Laco supported him, and the high character of Piso gave weight to his advice. Piso, who was the son of Marcus Crassus and Scribonia, and thus of noble descent on both sides, was in look and manner a man of the old type. Rightly judged, he seemed a stern man, morose to those who estimated him less favorably. This point in his character pleased his adopted father in proportion as it raised the anxious suspicions of others.

15. We are told that Galba, taking hold of Piso's hand, spoke to this effect: "If I were a private man, and were now adopting you by a formal act before the pontiffs, as our custom is, it would be a high honor to me to introduce into my family a descendant of Cnæus Pompeius and Marcus Crassus; it would be a distinction to you to add to the nobility of your race the honors of the Sulpician and Lutatian[32] houses. As it is, I, who have been called to the throne by the unanimous consent of gods and men, am moved by your splendid endowments and by my own patriotism to offer to you, a man of peace, that power, for which our ancestors fought, and which I myself obtained by war. I am following the precedent of the divine Augustus, who placed on an eminence next to his own, first his nephew Marcellus, then his son-in-law Agrippa, afterward his grandsons, and finally Tiberius Nero, his stepson.[33] But Augustus looked for a successor in his own family, I look for one in the state, not because I have no relatives or companions of my campaigns, but because it was not by any private favor that I myself received the imperial power. Let the principle of my choice be shown not only by my connections which I have set aside for you, but by your own. You have a brother, noble as yourself, and older, who would be well worthy of this dignity, were you not worthier. Your age is such as to be now free from the passions of youth, and such your life that in the past you have nothing to excuse. Hitherto you have only borne adversity; prosperity tries the heart with keener temptations; for hardships may be endured, whereas we are spoiled by success. You indeed will cling with the same constancy to honor, freedom, friendship, the best possessions of the human spirit, but others will seek to weaken them with their servility. You will be fiercely assailed by adulation, by flattery, that worst poison of the true heart, and by the selfish interests of individuals. You and I speak together today with perfect frankness, but others will be more ready to address us as emperors than as men. For to urge his duty upon a prince is indeed a hard matter; to flatter him, whatever his character, is a mere routine gone through without any heart.

16. "Could the vast frame of this Empire have stood and preserved its balance without a directing spirit, I was not unworthy of inaugurating a republic. As it is, we have been long reduced to a position in which my age can confer no greater boon on the Roman people than a good successor, your youth no greater than a good emperor. Under Tiberius, Gaius, and Claudius, we were, so to speak, the inheritance of a single family. The choice which begins with us will be a substitute for freedom. Now that the family of the Julii and the Claudii has come to an end, adoption will discover the worthiest successor. To be begotten and born of a princely race is a mere accident, and is only valued as such. In adoption there is nothing that need bias the judgment, and if you wish to make a choice, a unanimous opinion points out the man. Let Nero be ever before your eyes, swollen with the pride of a long line of Cæsars; it was not Vindex with his unarmed province, it was not myself with my single legion, that shook his yoke from our necks. It was his own profligacy, his own brutality, and that though there had been before no precedent of an emperor condemned by his own people. We, who have been called to power by the issues of war, and by the deliberate judgment of others, shall incur unpopularity, however illustrious our character. Do not, however, be alarmed if, after a movement which has shaken the world, two legions are not yet quiet. I did not myself succeed to a throne without anxiety; and when men shall hear of your adoption I shall no longer be thought old, and this is the only objection which is now made against me. Nero will always be regretted by the thoroughly depraved; it is for you and me to take care that he be not regretted also by the good. To prolong such advice suits not this occasion, and all my purpose is fulfilled if I have made a good choice in you. The most practical and the shortest method of distinguishing between good and bad measures is to think what you yourself would or would not like under another emperor. It is not here, as it is among nations despotically ruled, that there is a distinct governing family, while all the rest are slaves. You have to reign over men who cannot

bear either absolute slavery or absolute freedom." This, with more to the same effect, was said by Galba; he spoke to Piso as if he were creating an emperor; the others addressed him as if he were an emperor already.

17. It is said of Piso that he betrayed no discomposure or excessive joy, either to the gaze to which he was immediately subjected, or afterward when all eyes were turned upon him. His language to the Emperor, his father, was reverential; his language about himself was modest. He showed no change in look or manner; he seemed like one who had the power rather than the wish to rule. It was next discussed whether the adoption should be publicly pronounced in front of the Rostra, in the Senate, or in the camp. It was thought best to go to the camp. This would be a compliment to the soldiery, and their favor, base as it was to purchase it by bribery or intrigue, was not to be despised if it could be obtained by honorable means. Meanwhile the expectant people had surrounded the palace, impatient to learn the great secret, and those who sought to stifle the ill-concealed rumor did but spread it the more.

18. The 10th of January was a gloomy, stormy day, unusually disturbed by thunder, lightning, and all bad omens from heaven. Though this had from ancient time been made a reason for dissolving an assembly, it did not deter Galba from proceeding to the camp; either because he despised such things as being mere matters of chance, or because the decrees of fate, though they be foreshown, are not escaped. Addressing a crowded assembly of the soldiers he announced, with imperial brevity, that he adopted Piso, following the precedent of the divine Augustus, and the military custom by which a soldier chooses his comrade. Fearing that to conceal the mutiny would be to make them think it greater than it really was, he spontaneously declared that the 4th and 18th legions, led by a few factious persons, had been insubordinate, but had not gone beyond certain words and cries, and that they would soon return to their duty. To this speech he added no word of flattery, no hint of a bribe. Yet the tribunes, the centurions, and such of the soldiers as stood near made an encouraging response.

A gloomy silence prevailed among the rest, who seemed to think that they had lost by war that right to a donative which they had made good even in peace. It is certain that their feelings might have been conciliated by the very smallest liberality on the part of the parsimonious old man. He was ruined by his old-fashioned inflexibility, and by an excessive sternness, which we are no longer equal to enduring.

19. Then followed Galba's speech in the Senate, which was as plain and brief as his speech to the soldiery. Piso delivered a graceful oration and was supported by the feeling of the Senate. Many who wished him well spoke with enthusiasm; those who had opposed him, in moderate terms; the majority met him with an officious homage, having aims of their own and no thought for the state. Piso neither said nor did anything else in public in the following four days which intervened between his adoption and his death. As tidings of the mutiny in Germany were arriving with daily-increasing frequency, while the country was ready to receive and to credit all intelligence that had an unfavorable character, the Senate came to a resolution to send deputies to the German armies. It was privately discussed whether Piso should go with them to give them a more imposing appearance; they, it was said, would bring with them the authority of the Senate, he the majesty of the Cæsar. It was thought expedient to send with them Cornelius Laco, prefect of the prætorian guard, but he vetoed the design. In nominating, excusing, and changing the deputies, the Senate having entrusted the selection to Galba, the Emperor showed a disgraceful want of firmness, yielding to individuals, who made interest to stay or to go as their fears or their hopes prompted.

20. Next came the question of money. On a general inquiry it seemed the fairest course to demand restitution from those who had caused the public poverty. Nero had squandered in presents two thousand two hundred million sesterces. It was ordered that each recipient should be sued, but should be permitted to retain a tenth part of the bounty. They had, however, barely a tenth part left, having wasted the property of others in the

same extravagances in which they had squandered their own, till the most rapacious and profligate among them had neither capital nor land remaining, nothing in fact but the appliances of their vices. Thirty Roman knights were appointed to conduct the process of recovery, a novel office, and made burdensome by the number and intriguing practices of those with whom it had to deal. Everywhere were sales and brokers, and Rome was in an uproar with auctions. Yet great was the joy to think that the men whom Nero had enriched would be as poor as those whom he had robbed. About this time were cashiered two tribunes of the prætorian guard, Antonius Taurus and Antonius Naso, an officer of the city cohorts, Æmilius Pacensis, and one of the watch, Julius Fronto. This led to no amendment with the rest, but only started the apprehension that a crafty and timid policy was getting rid of individuals, while all were suspected.

21. Otho, meanwhile, who had nothing to hope while the state was tranquil, and whose whole plan depended on revolution, was being roused to action by a combination of many motives, by a luxury that would have embarrassed even an emperor, by a poverty that a subject could hardly endure, by his rage against Galba, by his envy of Piso. He even pretended to fear to make himself keener in desire. "I was," said he, "too formidable to Nero, and I must not look for another Lusitania, another honorable exile. Rulers always suspect and hate the man who has been named for the succession. This has injured me with the aged Emperor, and will injure me yet more with a young man whose temper, naturally savage, has been rendered ferocious by prolonged exile. How easy to put Otho to death! I must therefore do and dare now while Galba's authority is still unsettled, and before that of Piso is consolidated. Periods of transition suit great attempts, and delay is useless where inaction is more hurtful than temerity. Death, which nature ordains for all alike, yet admits of the distinction of being either forgotten, or remembered with honor by posterity; and, if the same lot awaits the innocent and

the guilty, the man of spirit will at least deserve his fate."

22. The soul of Otho was not effeminate like his person. His confidential freedmen and slaves, who enjoyed a license unknown in private families, brought the debaucheries of Nero's court, its intrigues, its easy marriages, and the other indulgences of despotic power before a mind passionately fond of such things, dwelled upon them as his if he dared to seize them, and reproached the inaction that would leave them to others. The astrologers also urged him to action, predicting from their observation of the heavens' revolutions, and a year of glory for Otho. This is a class of men whom the powerful cannot trust, and who deceive the aspiring, a class which will always be proscribed in this country, and yet always retained. Many of these men were attached to the secret councils of Poppæa and were the vilest tools in the employ of the imperial household. One of them, Ptolemæus, had attended Otho in Spain, and had there foretold that his patron would survive Nero. Gaining credit by the result, and arguing from his own conjectures and from the common talk of those who compared Galba's age with Otho's youth, he had persuaded the latter that he would be called to the throne. Otho, however, received the prediction as the words of wisdom and the intimation of destiny, with that inclination so natural to the human mind readily to believe in the mysterious.

23. Nor did Ptolemæus fail to play his part; he now even prompted to crime, to which from such wishes it is easy to pass. Whether indeed these thoughts of crime were suddenly conceived is doubtful. Otho had long been courting the affections of the soldiery, either in the hope of succeeding to the throne, or in preparation for some desperate act. On the march, on parade, and in their quarters, he would address all the oldest soldiers by name, and remembering the progresses of Nero would call them his messmates. Some he would recognize, he would inquire after others, and would help them with his money and interest. He would often intersperse his conversation with complaints and insinuations against

Galba and anything else that might excite the vulgar mind. Laborious marches, a scanty commissariat, and the rigor of military discipline were especially distasteful, when men accustomed to sail to the lakes of Campania and the cities of Greece had painfully to struggle under the weight of their arms over the Pyrenees, the Alps, and vast distances of road.

24. The minds of the soldiery were already on fire, when Mævius Pudens, a near relative of Tigellinus, added, so to speak, fuel to the flames. In his endeavor to win over all who were particularly weak in character, or who wanted money and were ready to plunge into revolution, he gradually went so far as to distribute, whenever Galba dined with Otho, one hundred sesterces to each soldier of the cohort on duty, under pretext of treating them. This, which we may almost call a public bounty, Otho followed up by presents more privately bestowed on individuals; nay, he bribed with such spirit that, finding there was a dispute between Cocceius Proculus, a soldier of the bodyguard, and one of his neighbors, about some part of their boundaries, he purchased with his own money the neighbor's entire estate, and made a present of it to the soldier. He took advantage of the lazy indifference of the prefect, who overlooked alike notorious facts and secret practices.

25. He then entrusted the conduct of his meditated treason to Onomastus, one of his freedmen, who brought over to his views Barbius Proculus, officer of the watchword to the bodyguard, and Veturius, a deputy centurion in the same force. Having assured himself by various conversations with these men that they were cunning and bold, he loaded them with presents and promises, and furnished them with money with which to tempt the cupidity of others. Thus two soldiers from the ranks undertook to transfer the Empire of Rome, and actually transferred it. Only a few were admitted to be accomplices in the plot, but they worked by various devices on the wavering minds of the remainder: on the more distinguished soldiers, by hinting that the favors of Nymphidius had brought them under suspicion; on the vulgar herd, by the anger and despair with which the repeated

postponement of the donative had inspired them. Some were fired by their recollections of Nero and their longing regrets for their old license. All felt a common alarm at the idea of having to serve elsewhere.

26. The contagion spread to the legions and the auxiliary troops, already excited by the news of the wavering loyalty of the army of Germany. So ripe were the disaffected for mutiny and so close the secrecy preserved by the loyal, that they could actually have seized Otho on the 14th of January, as he was returning from dinner, had they not been deterred by the risks of darkness, the inconvenient dispersion of the troops over the whole city, and the difficulty of concerted action among a half-intoxicated crowd. It was no care for the state, which they deliberately meditated polluting with the blood of their Emperor; it was a fear lest in the darkness of night anyone who presented himself to the soldiers of the Pannonian or German army might be fixed on instead of Otho, whom few of them knew. Many symptoms of the approaching outburst were repressed by those who were in the secret. Some hints, which had reached Galba's ears, were turned into ridicule by Laco the prefect, who knew nothing of the temper of the soldiery, and who, inimical to all measures, however excellent, which he did not originate, obstinately thwarted men wiser than himself.

27. On the 15th of January, as Galba was sacrificing in front of the temple of Apollo, the haruspex[34] Umbricius announced to him that the entrails had a sinister aspect, that treachery threatened him, that he had an enemy at home. Otho heard, for he had taken his place close by, and interpreted it by contraries in a favorable sense, as promising success to his designs. Not long after, his freedman Onomastus informed him that the architect and the contractors were waiting for him. It had been arranged thus to indicate that the soldiers were assembling, and that the preparations of the conspiracy were complete. To those who inquired the reason of his departure, Otho pretended that he was purchasing certain farm buildings, which from their age he suspected to be unsound, and which had therefore to be first sur-

veyed. Leaning on his freedman's arm, he proceeded through the palace of Tiberius to the Velabrum,[35] and thence to the golden milestone near the temple of Saturn. There twenty-three soldiers of the bodyguard saluted him as Emperor, and, while he trembled at their scanty number, put him hastily into a chair, drew their swords, and hurried him onward. About as many more soldiers joined them on their way, some because they were in the plot, many from mere surprise; some shouted and brandished their swords, others proceeded in silence, intending to let the issue determine their sentiments.

28. Julius Martialis was the tribune on guard in the camp. Appalled by the enormity and suddenness of the crime, or perhaps fearing that the troops were very extensively corrupted and that it would be destruction to oppose them, he made many suspect him of complicity. The rest of the tribunes and centurions preferred immediate safety to danger and duty. Such was the temper of men's minds that, while there were few to venture on so atrocious a treason, many wished it done, and all were ready to acquiesce.

29. Meanwhile the unconscious Galba, busy with his sacrifice, was importuning the gods of an empire that was now another's. A rumor reached him that some unknown senator was being hurried into the camp; before long it was affirmed that this senator was Otho. At the same time came messengers from all parts of the city, where they had chanced to meet the procession, some exaggerating the danger, some, who could not even then forget to flatter, representing it as less than the reality. On deliberation it was determined to sound the feeling of the cohort on guard in the palace, but not through Galba in person, whose authority was to be kept unimpaired to meet greater emergencies. They were accordingly collected before the steps of the palace, and Piso addressed them as follows: "Comrades, this is the sixth day since I became a Cæsar by adoption, not knowing what was to happen, whether this title was to be desired, or dreaded. It rests with you to determine what will be the result to my family and to the state. It is not that I dread on my own account the gloomier issue;

for I have known adversity, and I am learning at this very moment that prosperity is fully as dangerous. It is the lot of my father, of the Senate, of the Empire itself, that I deplore, if we have either to fall this day, or to do what is equally abhorrent to the good, to put others to death. In the late troubles we had this consolation, a capital unstained by bloodshed, and power transferred without strife. It was thought that by my adoption provision was made against the possibility of war, even after Galba's death.

30. "I will lay no claim to nobleness, or moderation, for indeed, to count up virtues in comparing oneself with Otho is needless. The vices, of which alone he boasts, overthrew the Empire, even when he was but the Emperor's friend. Shall he earn that Empire now by his manner and his gait, or by those womanish adornments? They are deceived on whom luxury imposes by its false show of liberality; he will know how to squander, he will not know how to give. Already he is thinking of debaucheries, of revels, of tribes of mistresses. These things he holds to be the prizes of princely power, things in which the wanton enjoyment will be for him alone, the shame and the disgrace for all. Never yet has anyone exercised for good ends the power obtained by crime. The unanimous will of mankind gave to Galba the title of Cæsar, and you consented when he gave it to me. Were the Senate, the country, the people but empty names, yet, comrades, it is your interest that the most worthless of men should not create an emperor. We have occasionally heard of legions mutinying against their generals, but your loyalty, your character, stand unimpeached up to this time. Even with Nero, it was he that deserted you, not you that deserted him. Shall less than thirty runaways and deserters whom no one would allow to choose a tribune or centurion for themselves assign the Empire at their pleasure? Do you tolerate the precedent? Do you by your inaction make the crime your own? This lawless spirit will pass into the provinces, and though we shall suffer from this treason, you will suffer from the wars that will follow. Again, no more is offered you for murdering your prince than you will have if you

shun such guilt. We shall give you a donative for your loyalty, as surely as others can give it for your treason."

31. The soldiers of the bodyguard dispersed, but the rest of the cohort, who showed no disrespect to the speaker, displayed their standards, acting, as often happens in a disturbance, on mere impulse and without any settled plan, rather than, as was afterward believed, with treachery and an intention to deceive. Marius Celsus was sent to the picked troops from the army of Illyricum, then encamped in the Porticus Vipsania.[36] Instructions were also given to Amullius Serenus and Domitius Sabinus, centurions of the first rank, to bring up the German soldiers from the Atrium Libertatis.[37] No confidence was placed in the legion levied from the fleet, which had been enraged by the massacre of their comrades, whom Galba had slaughtered immediately on his entry into the capital. Meanwhile Cetrius Severus, Subrius Dexter, and Pompeius Longinus, all three military tribunes, proceeded to the prætorian camp, in the hope that a sedition, which was but just· commencing, and not yet fully matured, might be swayed by better counsels. Two of these tribunes, Subrius and Cetrius, the soldiers assailed with menaces; Longinus they seized and disarmed; it was not his rank as an officer but his friendship with Galba that bound him to the Emperor, and roused a stronger suspicion in the mutineers. The legion levied from the fleet joined the prætorians without any hesitation. The Illyrian detachments drove Celsus away with a shower of javelins. The German veterans wavered long. Their frames were still enfeebled by sickness, and their minds were favorably disposed toward Galba, who, finding them exhausted by their long return voyage from Alexandria, where they had been sent on by Nero, had supplied their wants with a most unsparing attention.

32. The whole populace and the slaves with them were now crowding the palace, clamoring with discordant shouts for the death of Otho and the destruction of the conspirators, just as if they were demanding some spectacle in the circus or amphitheater. They had not indeed any discrimination or sincerity, for on that same

day they would raise with equal zeal a wholly different cry. It was their traditional custom to flatter any ruler with reckless applause and meaningless zeal. Meanwhile two suggestions were keeping Galba in doubt. Titus Vinius thought that he should remain within the palace, array the slaves against the foe, secure the approaches, and not go out to the enraged soldiers. "You should," he said, "give the disaffected time to repent, the loyal time to unite. Crimes gain by hasty action, better counsels by delay. At all events, you will still have the same facilities of going out, if need be, whereas your retreat, should you repent of having gone, will be in the power of another."

33. The rest were for speedy action, "before," they said, "the yet feeble treason of this handful of men can gather strength. Otho himself will be alarmed, Otho, who stole away to be introduced to a few strangers, but who now, thanks to the hesitation and inaction in which we waste our time, is learning how to play the Emperor. We must not wait till, having arranged matters in the camp, he bursts into the forum, and under Galba's very eyes makes his way to the Capitol, while our noble Emperor with his brave friends barricades the doors of his palace. We are to stand a siege forsooth, and truly we shall have an admirable resource in the slaves, if the unanimous feeling of this vast multitude, and that which can do so much, the first burst of indignation, be suffered to subside. Moreover, that cannot be safe which is not honorable. If we must fall, let us go to meet the danger. This will bring more odium upon Otho, and will be more becoming to ourselves." Vinius opposing this advice, Laco assailed him with threats, encouraged by Icelus, who persisted in his private animosities to the public ruin.

34. Without further delay Galba sided with these more plausible advisers. Piso was sent on into the camp, as being a young man of noble name, whose popularity was of recent date, and who was a bitter enemy to Titus Vinius; that is, either he was so in reality, or these angry partisans would have it so, and belief in hatred is but too ready. Piso had hardly gone forth when there

came a rumor, at first vague and needing confirmation, that Otho had been slain in the camp; soon, as happens in the case of monstrous lies, men asserted that they had been present, and had seen the deed; and between the delight of some and the indifference of others, the report was easily believed. Many thought the rumor had been invented and circulated by the Othonians, who were now mingling with the crowd, and who disseminated these false tidings of success to draw Galba out of the palace.

35. Upon this not only did the people and the ignorant rabble break out into applause and vehement expressions of zeal, but many of the knights and senators, losing their caution as they laid aside their fear, burst open the doors of the palace, rushed in, and displayed themselves to Galba, complaining that their revenge had been snatched from them. The most arrant coward, the man who, as the event proved, would dare nothing in the moment of danger, was the most voluble and fierce of speech. No one knew anything, yet all were confident in assertion, till at length Galba in the dearth of all true intelligence, and overborne by the universal delusion, assumed his cuirass, and as, from age and bodily weakness, he could not stand up against the crowd that was still rushing in, he was elevated on a chair. He was met in the palace by Julius Atticus, a soldier of the bodyguard, who, displaying a bloody sword, cried "I have slain Otho." "Comrade," replied Galba, "who gave the order?" So singularly resolute was his spirit in curbing the license of the soldiery; threats did not dismay him, nor flatteries seduce.

36. There was now no doubt about the feeling of all the troops in the camp. So great was their zeal that, not content with surrounding Otho with their persons in close array, they elevated him to the pedestal on which a short time before had stood the gilt statue of Galba, and there, amid the standards, encircled him with their colors. Neither tribunes nor centurions could approach. The common soldiers even insisted that all the officers should be watched. Everything was in an uproar with their tumultuous cries and their appeals to each other,

which were not, like those of a popular assembly or a mob, the discordant expressions of an idle flattery; on the contrary, as soon as they caught sight of any of the soldiers who were flocking in, they seized him, gave him the military embrace, placed him close to Otho, dictated to him the oath of allegiance, commending sometimes the Emperor to his soldiers, sometimes the soldiers to their Emperor. Otho did not fail to play his part; he stretched out his arms, and bowed to the crowd, and kissed his hands, and altogether acted the slave, to make himself the master. It was when the whole legion from the fleet had taken the oath to him that, feeling confidence in his strength, and thinking that the men, on whose individual feeling he had been working, should be roused by a general appeal, he stood before the rampart of the camp, and spoke as follows:

37. "Comrades, I cannot say in what character I have presented myself to you; I refuse to call myself a subject, now that you have named me Emperor, or Emperor, while another reigns. Your title also will be equally uncertain, so long as it shall be a question whether it is the Emperor of the Roman people or a public enemy whom you have in your camp. Mark you, how in one breath they cry for my punishment and for your execution. So evident it is that we can neither perish, nor be saved, except together. Perhaps, with his usual clemency, Galba has already promised that we should die, like the man who, though no one demanded it, massacred so many thousands of perfectly guiltless soldiers. A shudder comes over my soul whenever I call to mind that ghastly entry, Galba's solitary victory, when, before the eyes of the capital he gave orders to decimate the prisoners, the suppliants, whom he had admitted to surrender. These were the auspices with which he entered the city. What is the glory that he has brought to the throne? None but that he has murdered Obultronius Sabinus and Cornelius Marcellus[38] in Spain, Betuus Chilo in Gaul, Fonteius Capito in Germany, Clodius Macer in Africa, Cingonius on the high road, Turpilianus in the city, Nymphidius in the camp. What province, what camp in the world, but is stained with blood and foul with crime,

319

or, as he expresses it himself, purified and chastened? For what others call crimes he calls reforms, and, by similar misnomers, he speaks of strictness instead of barbarity, of economy instead of avarice, while the cruelties and affronts inflicted upon you he calls discipline. Seven months only have passed since Nero fell, and already Icelus has seized more than the Polycliti,[39] the Vatinii,[40] and the Ægiali amassed. Vinius would not have gone so far with his rapacity and lawlessness had he been emperor himself; as it is, he had lorded it over us as if we had been his own subjects, has held us as cheap as if we had been another's. That one house would furnish the donative, which is never given you, but with which you are daily upbraided.

38. "Again, that we might have nothing to hope even from his successor, Galba fetches out of exile the man in whose ill humor and avarice he considers that he has found the best resemblance to himself. You witnessed, comrades, how by a remarkable storm even the gods discountenanced that ill-starred adoption; and the feeling of the Senate, of the people of Rome, is the same. It is to your valor that they look, in you these better counsels find all their support; without you, noble as they may be, they are powerless. It is not to war or to danger that I invite you; the swords of all Roman soldiers are with us. At this moment Galba has but one half-armed cohort, which is detaining, not defending him. Let it once behold you, let it receive my signal, and the only strife will be, who shall oblige me most. There is no room for delay in a business which can only be approved when it is done." He then ordered the armory to be opened. The soldiers immediately seized the arms without regard to rule or military order, no distinction being observed between prætorians and legionaries, both of whom again indiscriminately assumed the shields and helmets of the auxiliary troops. No tribune or centurion encouraged them, every man acted on his own impulse and guidance, and the vilest found their chief incitement in the dejection of the good.

39. Meanwhile, appalled by the roar of the increasing sedition and by the shouts which reached the city, Piso

had overtaken Galba, who in the interval had quitted the palace, and was approaching the forum. Already Marius Celsus had brought back discouraging tidings. And now some advised that the Emperor should return to the palace, others that he should make for the Capitol, many again that he should occupy the Rostra, though most did but oppose the opinions of others, while, as ever happens in these ill-starred counsels, plans for which the opportunity had slipped away seemed the best. It is said that Laco, without Galba's knowledge, meditated the death of Vinius, either hoping by this execution to appease the fury of the soldiers, or believing him to be an accomplice of Otho, or, it may be, out of mere hatred. The time and the place, however, made him hesitate; he knew that a massacre once begun is not easily checked. His plan too was disconcerted by a succession of alarming tidings, and the desertion of immediate adherents. So languid was now the zeal of those who had at first been eager to display their fidelity and courage.

40. Galba was hurried to and fro with every movement of the surging crowd; the halls and temples all around were thronged with spectators of this mournful sight. Not a voice was heard from the people or even from the rabble. Everywhere were terror-stricken countenances, and ears turned to catch every sound. It was a scene neither of agitation nor of repose, but there reigned the silence of profound alarm and profound indignation. Otho, however, was told that they were arming the mob. He ordered his men to hurry on at full speed, and to anticipate the danger. Then did Roman soldiers rush forward like men who had to drive a Vologeses or Pacorus[41] from the ancestral throne of the Arsacidæ, not as though they were hastening to murder their aged and defenseless Emperor. In all the terror of their arms, and at the full speed of their horses, they burst into the forum, thrusting aside the crowd and trampling on the Senate. Neither the sight of the Capitol, nor the sanctity of the overhanging temples, nor the thought of rulers past or future, could deter them from committing a crime which anyone succeeding to power must avenge.

41. When this armed array was seen to approach, the standard bearer of the cohort that escorted Galba (he is said to have been one Atilius Vergilio) tore off and dashed upon the ground Galba's effigy. At this signal the feeling of all the troops declared itself plainly for Otho. The forum was deserted by the flying populace. Weapons were pointed against all who hesitated. Near the Lacus Curtius,[42] Galba was thrown out of his litter and fell to the ground, through the alarm of his bearers. His last words have been variously reported according as men hated or admired him. Some have said that he asked in a tone of entreaty what wrong he had done, and begged a few days for the payment of the donative. The more general account is that he voluntarily offered his neck to the murderers, and bade them haste and strike, if it seemed to be for the good of the commonwealth. To those who slew him it mattered not what he said. About the actual murderer nothing is clearly known. Some have recorded the name of Terentius, an enrolled pensioner, others that of Læcanius; but it is the current report that one Camurius, a soldier of the 15th legion, completely severed his throat by driving his sword through it. The rest of the soldiers foully mutilated his arms and legs, for his breast was protected, and in their savage ferocity inflicted many wounds even on the headless trunk.

42. They next fell on Titus Vinius; and in his case also it is not known whether the fear of instant death choked his utterance, or whether he cried out that Otho had not given orders to slay him. Either he invented this in his terror, or he thus confessed his share in the conspiracy. His life and character incline us rather to believe that he was an accomplice in the crime which he certainly caused. He fell in front of the temple of the divine Julius,[43] and at the first blow, which struck him on the back of the knee; immediately afterward Julius Carus, a legionary, ran him through the body.

43. A noble example of manhood was on that day witnessed by our age in Sempronius Densus. He was a centurion in a cohort of the prætorian guard, and had been appointed by Galba to escort Piso. Rushing, dagger in hand, to meet the armed men, and upbraiding them with

their crime, he drew the attention of the murderers on himself by his exclamations and gestures, and thus gave Piso, wounded as he was, an opportunity of escape. Piso made his way to the temple of Vesta,⁴⁴ where he was admitted by the compassion of one of the public slaves, who concealed him in his chamber. There, not indeed through the sanctity of the place or its worship, but through the obscurity of his hiding place, he obtained a respite from instant destruction, till there came, by Otho's direction and specially eager to slay him, Sulpicius Florus, of the British auxiliary infantry, to whom Galba had lately given the citizenship, and Statius Murcus, one of the bodyguard. Piso was dragged out by these men and slaughtered in the entrance of the temple.

44. There was, we are told, no death of which Otho heard with greater joy, no head which he surveyed with so insatiable a gaze. Perhaps it was that his mind was then for the first time relieved from all anxiety, and so had leisure to rejoice; perhaps there was with Galba something to recall departed majesty, with Vinius some thought of old friendship, which troubled with mournful images even that ruthless heart; Piso's death, as that of an enemy and a rival, he felt to be a right and lawful subject of rejoicing. The heads were fixed upon poles and carried about among the standards of the cohorts, close to the eagle of the legion, while those who had struck the blow, those who had been present, those who whether truly or falsely boasted of the act, as of some great and memorable achievement, vied in displaying their bloodstained hands. Vitellius afterward found more than one hundred twenty memorials from persons who claimed a reward for some notable service on that day. All these persons he ordered to be sought out and slain, not to honor Galba, but to comply with the traditional policy of rulers, who thus provide protection for the present and vengeance for the future.

45. One would have thought it a different Senate, a different people. All rushed to the camp, outran those who were close to them, and struggled with those who were before, inveighed against Galba, praised the wisdom of the soldiers, covered the hand of Otho with

kisses; the more insincere their demonstrations, the more they multiplied them. Nor did Otho repulse the advances of individuals, while he checked the greed and ferocity of the soldiers by word and look. They demanded that Marius Celsus, consul-elect, Galba's faithful friend to the very last moment, should be led to execution, loathing his energy and integrity as if they were vices. It was evident that they were seeking to begin massacre and plunder, and the proscription of all the most virtuous citizens, and Otho had not yet sufficient authority to prevent crime, though he could command it. He feigned anger, and ordered him to be loaded with chains, declaring that he was to suffer more signal punishment, and thus he rescued him from immediate destruction.

46. Everything was then ordered according to the will of the soldiery. The prætorians chose their own prefects. One was Plotius Firmus, who had once been in the ranks, had afterward commanded the watch, and who, while Galba was yet alive, had embraced the cause of Otho. With him was associated Licinius Proculus, Otho's intimate friend, and consequently suspected of having encouraged his schemes. Flavius Sabinus[45] they appointed prefect of the city, thus adopting Nero's choice, in whose reign he had held the same office, though many in choosing him had an eye to his brother Vespasianus. A demand was then made that the fees for furloughs usually paid to the centurions should be abolished. These the common soldiers paid as a kind of annual tribute. A fourth part of every company might be scattered on furlough, or might even loiter about the camp, provided that they paid the fees to the centurions. No one cared about the amount of the tax, or the way in which it was raised. It was by robbery, plunder, or the most servile occupations that the soldiers' holiday was purchased. The man with the fullest purse was worn out with toil and cruel usage till he bought his furlough. His means exhausted by this outlay, and his energies utterly relaxed by idleness, the once rich and vigorous soldier returned to his company a poor and spiritless man. One after another was ruined by the same poverty and license, and rushed into mutiny and dissension, and finally into civil war.

Otho, however, not to alienate the affections of the centurions by an act of bounty to the ranks, promised that his own purse should pay these annual sums. It was undoubtedly a salutary reform, and was afterward under good emperors established as a permanent rule of the service. Laco, prefect of the city, who had been ostensibly banished to an island, was assassinated by an enrolled pensioner, sent on by Otho to do the deed. Icelus Martianus, being but a freedman, was publicly executed.

47. A day spent in crime found its last horror in the rejoicing that concluded it. The prætor Urbanus summoned the Senate; the rest of the magistrates vied with each other in their flatteries. The senators hastily assembled and conferred by decree upon Otho the tribunicial office, the name of Augustus, and every imperial honor. All strove to extinguish the remembrance of those taunts and invectives which had been thrown out at random, and which no one supposed were rankling in his heart. Whether he had forgotten or only postponed his resentment the shortness of his reign left undecided. The forum yet streamed with blood, when he was borne in a litter over heaps of dead to the Capitol, and thence to the palace. He suffered the bodies to be given up for burial, and to be burned. For Piso, the last rites were performed by his wife, Verania, and his brother Scribonianus; for Vinius, by his daughter Crispina, their heads having been discovered and purchased from the murderers, who had reserved them for sale.

48. Piso, who was then completing his thirty-first year, had enjoyed more fame than good fortune. His brothers, Magnus[46] and Crassus, had been put to death by Claudius and Nero respectively. He was himself for many years an exile, for four days a Cæsar, and Galba's hurried adoption of him only gave him this privilege over his elder brother—that he perished first. Vinius had lived to the age of fifty-seven, with many changes of character. His father was of a prætorian family, his maternal grandfather was one of the proscribed. He had disgraced himself in his first campaign when he served under the legate Calvisius Sabinus. That officer's wife,

urged by a perverse curiosity to view the camp, entered
it by night in the disguise of a soldier, and after extending the insulting frolic to the watches and the general
arrangements of the army, actually dared to commit the
act of adultery in the headquarters. Vinius was charged
with having participated in her guilt, and by order of
Gaius was loaded with irons. The altered times soon
restored him to liberty. He then enjoyed an uninterrupted succession of honors, first filling the prætorship, and
then commanding a legion with general satisfaction, but
he subsequently incurred the degrading imputation of
having pilfered a gold cup at the table of Claudius, who
the next day directed that he alone should be served on
earthenware. Yet as proconsul of Narbonese Gaul he
administered the government with strict integrity. When
forced by his friendship with Galba to a dangerous elevation, he showed himself bold, crafty, and enterprising;
and whether he applied his powers to vice or virtue, was
always equally energetic. His will was made void by his
vast wealth; that of Piso owed its validity to his poverty.

49. The body of Galba lay for a long time neglected,
and subjected, through the license which the darkness
permitted, to a thousand indignities, till Argius, his stew-
ard, who had been one of his slaves, gave it a humble
burial in his master's private gardens. His head, which
the sutlers and camp followers had fixed on a pole and
mangled, was found only the next day in front of the
tomb of Patrobius, a freedman of Nero's, whom Galba
had executed. It was put with the body, which had by
that time been reduced to ashes. Such was the end of
Servius Galba, who in his seventy-three years had lived
prosperously through the reigns of five emperors, and
had been more fortunate under the rule of others than
he was in his own. His family could boast an ancient
nobility, his wealth was great. His character was of an
average kind, rather free from vices than distinguished
by virtues. He was not regardless of fame, nor yet vainly
fond of it. Other men's money he did not covet; with
his own he was parsimonious, with that of the state
avaricious. To his freedmen and friends he showed a
forbearance which, when he had fallen into worthy

hands, could not be blamed; when, however, these persons were worthless, he was even culpably blind. The nobility of his birth and the perils of the times made what was really indolence pass for wisdom. While in the vigor of life, he enjoyed a high military reputation in Germany; as proconsul he ruled Africa with moderation, and when advanced in years showed the same integrity in eastern Spain. He seemed greater than a subject while he was yet in a subject's rank, and by common consent would have been equal to empire, had he never been Emperor.

50. The alarm of the capital, which trembled to see the atrocity of these recent crimes, and to think of the old character of Otho, was heightened into terror by fresh news about Vitellius, news which had been suppressed before the murder of Galba, in order to make it appear that only the army of Upper Germany had revolted. That two men, who for shamelessness, indolence, and profligacy, were the most worthless of mortals, had been selected, it would seem, by some fatality to ruin the Empire, became the open complaint, not only of the Senate and the knights, who had some stake and interest in the country, but even of the common people. It was no longer to the late horrors of a dreadful peace, but to the recollections of the civil wars, that men recurred, speaking of how the capital had been taken by Roman armies, how Italy had been wasted and the provinces spoiled, of Pharsalia, Philippi,[47] Perusia,[48] and Mutina,[49] and all the familiar names of great public disasters. "The world," they said, "was almost turned upside down when the struggle for empire was between worthy competitors, yet the Empire continued to exist after the victories of Gaius Julius and Cæsar Augustus; the Republic would have continued to exist under Pompey and Brutus. And is it for Otho or for Vitellius that we are now to repair to the temples? Prayers for either would be impious, vows for either a blasphemy, when from their conflict you can only learn that the conqueror must be the worse of the two." Some were speculating on Vespasianus and the armies of the East. Vespasianus was indeed preferable to either, yet they shuddered at the

idea of another war, of other massacres. Even about Vespasianus there were doubtful rumors, and he, unlike any of his predecessors, was changed for the better by power.

[Chapters 51-90 are omitted. They describe how the armies of the two Germanies, which had crushed the revolt of Julius Vindex, were infuriated by the favor shown by Galba to Gaul, which had supported it. On the 1st of January the army of Upper Germany refused to swear the oath of allegiance to Galba; the feeble governor, Hordeonius Flaccus (see above, I, 9), failed to check the mutiny, and with the active support of the ambitious legates of legions, A. Cæcina Alienus and C. Fabius Valens, the governor of Lower Germany, Aulus Vitellius, raised the standard of revolt. Not only the armies of the two Germanies, but that of Britain gave him support. Valens with 40,000 troops from Lower Germany marched through Gaul to Lyons and then down the Rhone and over the western Alps into the Plain of Lombardy; Cæcina with 30,000 troops from Upper Germany marched through Switzerland and crossed the Alps by the Great St. Bernard Pass. Both armies acted brutally toward the peoples through whose territory they passed; Valens' men perpetrated a massacre at Metz and were only with difficulty bribed into sparing Vienne, the center of Vindex's revolt, and Cæcina's men slaughtered thousands of the Helvetii and came near to sacking their capital, Avenches. Cæcina gained a great advantage when a cavalry force stationed in North Italy deserted Otho and secured for him Milan and the other principal places north of the Po; by early March he had occupied Cremona, not far from an Othonian force under Vestricius Spurinna which had occupied Placenza, while another under Annius Gallus lay at Mantua.

Spain, Narbonese Gaul, and Aquitaine all declared for Vitellius; but Dalmatia, Mœsia and Pannonia declared for Otho, a fact which had an important bearing on the war now impending in the north of Italy. Otho had now begun to show himself aware of the danger of his position; he forced Tigellinus to commit suicide (see Book XIV, note 68), brought back from exile some of Nero's victims, and gave offices and honors to several deserving persons. After appeasing, by oratory and bribery, a tumult among the prætorian guard, and dispatching an expedition to deal with the revolt in Gaul, he left Rome in mid-March to take command in the north of Italy.]

BOOK II

1. In a distant part of the world fortune was now preparing the origin and rise of a new dynasty, whose varied destinies brought happiness or misery on the state, prosperity or destruction on the princes of its line. Titus Vespasianus had been sent from Judæa by his father while Galba still lived, and alleged as a reason for his journey the homage due to the Emperor, and his age, which now qualified him to compete for office. But the vulgar, ever eager to invent, had spread the report that he was sent for to be adopted. The advanced years and childless condition of the Emperor furnished matter for such gossip, and the country never can refrain from naming many persons until one be chosen. The report gained the more credit from the genius of Titus himself, equal as it was to the most exalted fortune, from the mingled beauty and majesty of his countenance, from the prosperous fortunes of Vespasianus, from the prophetic responses of oracles, and even from accidental occurrences which, in the general disposition to belief, were accepted as omens. At Corinth, the capital of Achæa, he received positive information of the death of Galba, and found men who spoke confidently of the revolt of Vitellius and of the fact of war. In the anxiety of his mind, he sent for a few of his friends, and carefully surveyed his position from both points of view. He considered that if he should proceed to Rome, he should get no thanks for a civility intended for another, while his person would be a hostage in the hands either of Vitellius or of Otho; that should he turn back, the conqueror would certainly be offended, but with the issue of the struggle still doubtful, and the father joining the party, the son would be excused; on the other hand, if Vespasianus should assume the direction of the state, men who had to think of war would have to forget such causes of offense.

2. These and like thoughts made him waver between hope and fear; but hope triumphed. Some supposed that he retraced his steps for love of the Princess Berenice,[1] nor was his young heart averse to her charms, but this affection occasioned no hindrance to action. He passed, it is true, a youth enlivened by pleasure, and practiced more self-restraint in his own than in his father's reign. So, after coasting Achæa and Asia, leaving the land on his left, he made for the islands of Rhodes and Cyprus, and then by a bolder course for Syria. Here he conceived a desire to visit and inspect the temple of the Paphian Aphrodite, a place of celebrity both among natives and foreigners. It will not be a tedious digression to record briefly the origin of the worship, the ceremonial of the temple, and the form under which the goddess is adored, a form found in no other place.

3. The founder of the temple,[2] according to old tradition, was King Aerias, though some represent this as the name of the goddess herself. Later accounts tell us that the temple was consecrated by Cinyras, and that the goddess herself after her birth from the sea was wafted to this spot, but that the wisdom and craft of the diviners was a foreign importation introduced by Tamiras of Cilicia; and that it was agreed that the descendants of both families should preside over the worship. Afterward, that the royal family might not be without some superiority over the foreign stock, the strangers relinquished the craft which they had themselves introduced. The priest of the line of Cinyras is alone consulted. The victims are such as each worshiper has vowed, but males are selected; the surest prognostics are seen in the entrails of kids. It is forbidden to pour blood on the altar; the place of sacrifice is served only with prayers and pure flame, and though it stands in the open air, it is never wet with rain. The image of the goddess does not bear the human shape; it is a rounded mass rising like a cone from a broad base to a small circumference. The meaning of this is doubtful.

4. Titus, after surveying the treasures, the royal presents, and the other objects which the antiquarian tendencies of the Greek arbitrarily connect with some uncertain past, first consulted the oracle about his voyage. Receiving an answer that the way was open and the sea propitious, he then, after sacrificing a number of victims, asked some question in ambiguous phrase concerning himself. Sostratus (that was the name of the priest), seeing that the entrails presented a uniformly favorable appearance, and that the goddess signified her favor to some great enterprise, returned at the moment a brief and ordinary answer, but afterward soliciting a private interview, disclosed the future. His spirits raised, Titus rejoined his father, and was received as a mighty pledge of success by the wavering minds of the provincials and the troops. Vespasianus had all but completed the Jewish war, and only the siege of Jerusalem now remained, an operation the difficulty and arduousness of which was due rather to the character of its mountain citadel and the perverse obstinacy of the national superstition than to any sufficient means of enduring extremities left to the besieged. As we have mentioned above, Vespasianus himself had three legions inured to war. Mucianus had four under his command in his peaceful province. Emulation, however, and the glory won by the neighboring army had banished all tendency to sloth, and unbroken rest and exemption from the hardships of war had given them a vigor equivalent to the hardihood which the others had gained by their perils and their toils. Each had auxiliary forces of infantry and cavalry, each had fleets and tributary kings, and each, though their renown was of a different kind, had a celebrated name.

5. Vespasianus was an energetic soldier; he could march at the head of his army, choose the place for his camp, and bring by night and day his skill or, if the occasion required, his personal courage to oppose the foe. His food was such as chance offered; his dress and appearance hardly distinguished him from the common soldier; in short, but for his avarice, he was equal to the generals of old. Mucianus, on the contrary, was eminent

for his magnificence, for his wealth, and for a greatness
that transcended in all respects the condition of a subject; readier of speech than the other, he thoroughly understood the arrangement and direction of civil business.
It would have been a rare combination of princely
qualities if, with their respective faults removed, their
virtues only could have been united in one man. Mucianus was governor of Syria, Vespasianus of Judæa. In
the administration of these neighboring provinces jealousy had produced discord between them, but on Nero's
fall they had dropped their animosities and associated
their counsels. At first they communicated through
friends, till Titus, who was the great bond of union between them, by representing their common interests had
terminated their mischievous feud. He was indeed a man
formed both by nature and by education to attract even
such a character as that of Mucianus. The tribunes, the
centurions, and the common soldiers were brought over
to the cause by appeals to their energy of their love of
license, to their virtues or to their vices, according to
their different dispositions.

6. Long before the arrival of Titus, both armies had
taken the oath of allegiance to Otho. The news had
come, as is usual, with great speed, while there was
much to delay the gigantic undertaking of a civil war,
for which the East after a long period of repose was
then for the first time preparing. In former times the
mightiest civil conflicts had been begun in Gaul or Italy
with the resources of the West. Pompeius, Brutus, Cassius,
and Antonius, all of whom had been followed across the
sea by civil war, had met with a disastrous end,[3] and the
emperors had been oftener heard of than seen in Syria
and Judæa. There had been no mutiny among the legions, nothing indeed but some demonstrations against
the Parthians, attended with various success. In the last
civil war, though other provinces had been disturbed,
peace had been here unshaken. Then had followed a
loyal adherence to Galba. But when it became notorious
that Otho and Vitellius, opposed in impious strife, were
ready to make a spoil of the Empire, the thought that
others would engross the rewards of power, while they

would have nothing left for themselves but a compulsory submission, made the soldiers murmur and take a survey of their own strength. There were close at hand seven legions; there were Syria and Judæa, with a vast number of auxiliaries. Then, without any interval of separation, there was Egypt and its two legions, and on the other side Cappadocia, Pontus, and all the garrisons along the frontier of Armenia. There was Asia Minor; there were the other provinces, not without a military population, and well furnished with money. There were all the islands of the Mediterranean. And there was the sea itself, which during the interval of preparation for war would be both a convenience and a protection.

7. The ardor of the troops was not unknown to their generals; but it was judged advisable to wait for the issue of the struggle which others were carrying on. The conquerors and the conquered, it was said, never unite with a genuine good faith. It matters not whether fortune make Otho or Vitellius to be the victor. Even great generals grow insolent in prosperity; these men are quarrelsome, indolent, and profligate, and their own faults will make war fatal to the one, and success to the other. They therefore postponed the war until a more fitting opportunity, and though Vespasianus and Mucianus had but lately resolved on concerted action, the others had done so long before. The worthiest among them were moved by patriotism; many were wrought upon by the attractions of plunder; some by their private embarrassments. And so, good and bad, from different motives, but with equal zeal, were all eager for war.

8. About this time Achæa and Asia Minor were terrified by a false report that Nero was at hand. Various rumors were current about his death; and so there were many who pretended and believed that he was still alive. The adventures and enterprises of the other pretenders I shall relate in the regular course of my work. The pretender in this case was a slave from Pontus, or, according to some accounts, a freedman from Italy, a skillful harp player and singer, accomplishments which, added to a resemblance in the face, gave a very deceptive plausibility to his pretensions. After attaching to

himself some deserters, needy vagrants whom he bribed with great offers, he put to sea. Driven by stress of weather to the island of Cythnus,[4] he induced certain soldiers, who were on their way from the East, to join him, and ordered others, who refused, to be executed. He also robbed the traders and armed all the most able-bodied of the slaves. The centurion Sisenna, who was the bearer of the clasped right hands, the usual emblems of friendship, from the armies of Syria to the prætorians, was assailed by him with various artifices, till he left the island secretly, and, fearing actual violence, made his escape with all haste. Thence the alarm spread far and wide, and many roused themselves at the well-known name, eager for change, and detesting the present state of things. The report was daily gaining credit when an accident put an end to it.

9. Galba had entrusted the government of Galatia and Pamphylia to Calpurnius Asprenas. Two triremes from the fleet of Misenum were given him to pursue the adventurer; with these he reached the island of Cythnus. Persons were found to summon the captains in the name of Nero. The pretender himself, assuming a studied appearance of sorrow, and appealing to their fidelity as old soldiers of his own, besought them to land him in Egypt or Syria. The captains, perhaps wavering, perhaps intending to deceive, declared that they must address their soldiers, and that they would return when the minds of all had been prepared. Everything, however, was faithfully reported to Asprenas, and at his bidding the ship was boarded and taken, and the man, whoever he was, killed. The body, in which the eyes, the hair, and the savage countenance were remarkable features, was conveyed to Asia, and thence to Rome.

10. In a state that was distracted by strife, and that from frequent changes in its rulers trembled on the verge between liberty and license, even little matters were attended with great excitement. Vibius Crispus,[5] whose wealth, power, and ability made him rank among men of distinction rather than among men of worth, demanded that Annius Faustus, of the equestrian order, who in the days of Nero had practiced the trade of the

informer, should be brought to trial before the Senate. The senators indeed had recently, during the reign of Galba, passed a resolution that cognizance should be taken of the cases of the informers. This decree was variously carried out, and, while retained as law, was powerless or effectual, according as the person who happened to be accused was influential or helpless. Besides the terror of the law, Crispus had exerted his own power to the utmost to destroy the man who had informed against his brother. He had prevailed upon a great part of the Senate to demand that he should be consigned to destruction, undefended and unheard. But, on the other hand, there were some with whom nothing helped the accused person so much as the excessive power of the accuser. They gave it as their opinion that time ought to be allowed, that the charges ought to be specified, that, odious and guilty as the man might be, he yet ought to be heard, as precedent required. At first they carried their point, and the trial was postponed for a few days, but before long Faustus was condemned, but by no means with that unanimity on the part of the people which his detestable character had deserved. Men remembered that Crispus had followed the same profession with profit; nor was it the penalty but the prosecutor that they disliked.

11. Meanwhile the campaign had opened favorably for Otho, at whose bidding the armies of Dalmatia and Pannonia had begun to move. These comprised four legions, from each of which two thousand troops were sent on in advance. The 7th had been raised by Galba; the 11th, 13th, and 14th were veteran soldiers, the 14th having particularly distinguished itself by quelling the revolt in Britain. Nero had added to their reputation by selecting them as his most effective troops. This had made them long faithful to Nero, and kindled their zeal for Otho. But their self-confidence induced a tardiness of movement proportionate to their strength and solidity. The auxiliary infantry and cavalry moved in advance of the main body of the legions. The capital itself contributed no contemptible force, namely five prætorian cohorts, some troops of cavalry, and the first legion, and

together with these, two thousand gladiators, a disreputable kind of auxiliaries, but employed throughout the civil wars even by strict disciplinarians. Annius Gallus was put at the head of this force, and was sent on with Vestricius Spurinna[6] to occupy the banks of the Po, the original plan of the campaign having fallen to the ground, now that Cæcina, who they had hoped might have been kept within the limits of Gaul, had crossed the Alps. Otho himself was accompanied by some picked men of the bodyguard, with whom were the rest of the prætorian cohorts, the veteran troops from the prætorian camp, and a vast number of the levies raised from the fleet. No indolence or riot disgraced his march. He wore a cuirass of iron, and was to be seen in front of the standards, on foot, rough and negligent in dress, and utterly unlike what common report had pictured him.

12. Fortune seemed to smile on his efforts. Through his fleets, which commanded the sea, he held the greater part of Italy, even as far as where the chain of the Maritime Alps begins.[7] The task of attempting the passage of this chain, and of advancing into Narbonese Gaul, he had entrusted to three generals, Suedius Clemens, Antonius Novellus, and Æmilius Pacensis. Pacensis, however, was put in irons by his insubordinate troops, Antonius possessed no kind of authority, and Clemens commanded only for popularity, and was as reckless in transgressing the good order of military discipline as he was eager to fight. One would not have thought that it was Italy, the fields and the habitations of their native country, that they were passing through. They burned, spoiled, and plundered as if they were among the lands of the foreigner and the cities of a hostile people, and all with the more frightful effect as nowhere had there been made any provision against the danger. The fields were full of rural wealth, the houses stood with open doors; and the owners, as with their wives and children they came forth to meet the army, found themselves surrounded, in the midst of the security of peace, with all the horrors of war. Marius Maturus was then governing as procurator the province of the Maritime Alps. Raising the population, in which is no lack

of able-bodied men, he resolved to drive back the Othonians from the borders of his province; but the mountaineers were cut down and broken by the first charge, as might be expected of men who had been hastily collected, who were not familiar with camps or with regular command, who saw no glory in victory, no infamy in flight.

13. Exasperated by this conflict, the troops of Otho vented their rage on the town of Albintimilium.[8] In the field indeed they had secured no plunder; their rustic adversaries were poor, and their arms worthless; nor could they be taken prisoners, for they were swift of foot, and knew the country well. But the rapacity of the troops glutted itself in the ruin of an innocent population. The horror of these acts was aggravated by a noble display of fortitude in a Ligurian woman; she had concealed her son, and when the soldiers, who believed that some money had been hidden with him, questioned her with torture as to where she was hiding him, she pointed to her bosom, and replied, "It is here that he is concealed"; nor could any subsequent threats or even death itself make her falter in this courageous and noble answer.

14. Messengers now came in haste and alarm to inform Fabius Valens how Otho's fleet was threatening the province of Narbonese Gaul, which had sworn allegiance to Vitellius. Envoys from the colonies were already on the spot praying for aid. He dispatched two cohorts of Tungrian[9] infantry, four squadrons of horse, and all the cavalry of the Treviri under the command of Julius Classicus. Part of these troops were retained for the defense of the colony of Forum Julii,[10] for it was feared that if the whole army were sent by the route through the interior, the enemy's fleet might make a rapid movement on the unprotected coast. Twelve squadrons of cavalry and some picked infantry advanced against the enemy; they were reinforced by a cohort of Ligurians, an auxiliary local force of long standing, and five hundred Pannonians, not yet regularly enrolled. The conflict began without delay, the enemy's line of battle being so arranged that part of the levies from the fleet, who

337

had a number of rustics among their ranks, were posted
on the slope of the hills which border on the coast, the
prætorians fully occupying the level ground between the
hills and the shore, while on the sea was the fleet,
moored to the land and ready for action, drawn up in
line so as to present a formidable front. The Vitellians,
whose infantry was inferior, but who were strong in
cavalry, stationed the mountaineers on the neighboring
heights, and their infantry in close ranks behind the
cavalry. The squadrons of the Treviri charged the enemy
incautiously, and found themselves encountered in front
by the veteran troops, while on the flanks they were also
annoyed by showers of stones from the rustic band, who
were skillful throwers, and who, mixed up as they were
among the regular soldiers, whether cowardly or brave,
were all equally bold in the moment of victory. The general consternation of the Vitellians was increased by a
new alarm as the fleet attacked the rear of the combatants. By this movement they were hemmed in on all
sides, and the whole force would have perished, had not
the shades of night checked the advance of the victorious army, and covered the retreat of the vanquished.

15. The Vitellians, however, though beaten, did not
remain inactive. They brought up reinforcements and attacked the enemy, who felt themselves secure, and whose
vigilance was relaxed by success. The sentinels were cut
down, the camp stormed, and the panic reached the
ships, till, as the alarm gradually subsided, they again
assumed the offensive under the protection of some
neighboring heights which they had occupied. A terrible
slaughter ensued, and the prefects of the Tungrian cohorts, after having long maintained their line unbroken,
fell beneath a shower of missiles. The Othonians, however, did not achieve a bloodless victory, as the enemy's
cavalry wheeled round, and cut off some who had imprudently prolonged the pursuit. And then, as if a sort
of armistice had been concluded to provide against any
sudden panic that the cavalry of the one party or the
fleet of the other might cause, the Vitellians retreated
to Antipolis,[11] a town of Narbonese Gaul, the Othonians
to Albingaunum,[12] in Upper Liguria.

16. Corsica, Sardinia, and the other islands of the neighboring seas were retained in the interests of Otho by the fame of these naval successes. Corsica, however, all but suffered fatal injury from the rash proceedings of Pacarius Decumus, the procurator, proceedings which in so gigantic a war could contribute nothing to the general result, and which only brought destruction upon their author. In his hatred of Otho he resolved to support Vitellius with the whole strength of Corsica, an insignificant assistance even had the design succeeded. He collected the chief men of the island, and explained his plans. Claudius Pyrrhicus, captain of the Liburnian[13] ships stationed in the place, and Quintius Certus, a Roman knight, who ventured to offer opposition, he ordered to execution. All who were present were terrified at their death, and, with the ignorant populace, which ever blindly shares in the fears of others, took the oath of allegiance to Vitellius. But when Pacarius began to enlist troops, and to weary with military duties an undisciplined population, disgusted with the unusual toil, they began to reflect upon their own weakness. "The country which we inhabit," they said to themselves, "is an island: Germany and its mighty legions are far from us, and we know that even countries protected by infantry and cavalry have been plundered and ravaged by the fleet." Their feelings underwent a sudden change; they did not, however, resort to open violence, but chose an opportunity for a treacherous attack. When the persons who usually surrounded Pacarius had left him, and he was naked and helpless in the bath, they slew him. His associates were slaughtered with him. The perpetrators of the deed carried the heads of the slain to Otho, as being the heads of public enemies; but, lost among the crowd of greater criminals, in the vast confusion of events, they were neither rewarded by Otho nor punished by Vitellius.

17. Silius' horse had now, as I have already related, opened the way into Italy, and transferred the war across the borders. No one entertained any attachment to Otho, yet it was not because they preferred Vitellius: long years of peace had subdued them to any kind of servi-

tude, had made them ready to submit to the first comer
and careless about the better cause. The wealthiest district of Italy, the broad plains and cities which lie between the Po and the Alps, was now held by the troops
of Vitellius; for by this time the infantry sent on in advance by Cæcina had also arrived. A cohort of Pannonians had been taken prisoners at Cremona, a hundred cavalry, and a thousand of the levies from the fleet
intercepted between Placentia[14] and Ticinum.[15] Elated
by these successes, the troops of Vitellius would no
longer be restrained by the boundaries of the river's
bank. The very sight of the Po excited the men from Ba-
tavia and the Transrhenane provinces. Crossing the
stream by a sudden movement, they advanced on Placentia, and seizing some reconnoiterers, so terrified the
rest that, deceived by their alarm, they announced that
the whole army of Cæcina was at hand.

18. Spurinna, who now held Placentia, was sure that
Cæcina had not yet arrived, and that, even were he approaching, he ought to keep his men within their fortifications, and not confront a veteran army with three
prætorian cohorts, a thousand veterans, and a handful
of cavalry. But the undisciplined and inexperienced soldiery seized their standards and colors, and rushed to the
attack, brandishing their weapons in the face of their
general when he sought to restrain them, and spurning
from them the tribunes and centurions, and even crying out that Otho was betrayed and that Cæcina had
come by invitation. Spurinna associated himself with
the rash movement which others had originated, at first
acting under compulsion, but afterward pretending to
consent, in the hope that his counsels might have more
influence should the mutinous spirit abate.

19. When the Po was in sight and night began to fall,
they judged it expedient to entrench a camp. The labor,
new as it was to the soldiery of the capital, broke their
spirits. All the oldest among them began to inveigh
against their own credulity, and to point out the difficulty and danger of their position, if on those open
plains Cæcina and his army were to surround their
scanty forces. By this time more temperate language

was heard throughout the camp, and the tribunes and centurions, mixing with the troops, suggested commendations of the prudence of their general in selecting for the rallying point and basis of his operations a colony rich in military strength and resources. Finally, Spurinna himself, not so much reproaching them with their error as exposing it by his arguments, conducted them all back to Placentia, except some scouts whom he left, in a less turbulent temper and more amenable to command. The walls were strengthened, battlements were added, and the towers were raised in height. It was not only of the implements of war that provision and preparation were made, but of the spirit of subordination and the love of obedience. This was all that was wanting to the party, for they had no reason to be dissatisfied with their courage.

20. Cæcina, who seemed to have left his cruelty and profligacy on the other side of the Alps, advanced through Italy with his army under excellent discipline. The towns and colonies, however, found indications of a haughty spirit in the general's dress, when they saw the cloak of various colors, and the trousers, a garment of foreign fashion, which he wore when speaking to their toga-clad citizens. And they resented, as if with a sense of personal wrong, the conduct of his wife, Salonina, though it injured no one that she presented a conspicuous figure as she rode through their towns on horseback in a purple habit. They were acting on the instincts of human nature, which prompt men to scrutinize with keen eyes the recent elevation of their fellows, and to demand a temperate use of prosperity from none more rigorously than from those whom they have seen on a level with themselves. Cæcina, after crossing the Po, sought to tamper with the loyalty of the Othonians at a conference in which he held out hopes of reward, and he was himself assailed with the same arts. After the specious but meaningless names of peace and concord had been thus bandied to and fro, Cæcina turned all his thoughts and plans on the capture of Placentia, making a formidable show of preparation, as he knew that according to the success

of his opening operations would be the subsequent prestige of his arms.

21. The first day, however, was spent in a furious onset rather than in the skillful approaches of a veteran army. Exposed and reckless, the troops came close under the walls, stupefied by excess in food and wine. In this struggle the amphitheater, a most beautiful building, situated outside the walls, was burned to the ground, possibly set on fire by the assailants while they showered brands, fireballs, and ignited missiles on the besieged, possibly by the besieged themselves while they discharged incessant volleys in return. The populace of the town, always inclined to be suspicious, believed that combustibles had been purposely introduced into the building by certain persons from the neighboring colonies, who viewed it with envious and jealous eyes, because there was not in Italy another building so capacious. Whatever the cause of the accident, it was thought of but little moment as long as more terrible disasters were apprehended; but as soon as they again felt secure, they lamented it as though they could not have endured a heavier calamity. In the end Cæcina was repulsed with great slaughter among his troops, and the night was spent in the preparation of siege works. The Vitellians constructed mantlets, hurdles, and sheds, for undermining the walls and screening the assailants; the Othonians busied themselves in preparing stakes and huge masses of stone and of lead and brass, with which to break and overwhelm the hostile ranks. The shame of failure, the hope of renown, wrought on both armies; both were appealed to by different arguments; on the one side they extolled the strength of the legions and of the army of Germany; on the other, the distinctions of the soldiery of the capital and the prætorian cohorts; the one reviled their foes as slothful and indolent soldiers, demoralized by the circus and the theaters; the others retorted with the names of foreigner and barbarian. At the same time they lauded or vituperated Otho and Vitellius, but found indeed a more fruitful source of mutual provocation in invective than in praise.

22. Almost before dawn of day the walls were crowd-

ed with combatants, and the plains glittered with masses of armed men. The close array of the legions and the skirmishing parties of auxiliaries assailed with showers of arrows and stones the loftier parts of the walls, attacking them at close quarters, where they were undefended, or old and decayed. The Othonians, who could take a more deliberate and certain aim, poured down their javelins on the German cohorts as they recklessly advanced to the attack with fierce war cries, brandishing their shields above their shoulders after the manner of their country, and leaving their bodies unprotected. The soldiers of the legions, working under cover of mantlets and hurdles, undermined the walls, threw up earthworks, and endeavored to burst open the gates. The prætorians opposed them by rolling down with a tremendous crash ponderous masses of rock, placed for the purpose. Beneath these many of the assailants were buried, and many, as the slaughter increased with the confusion, and the attack from the walls became fiercer, retreated wounded, fainting, and mangled, with serious damage to the prestige of the party. Cæcina, ashamed of the assault on which he had so rashly ventured, and unwilling, ridiculed and baffled as he was, to remain in the same position, again crossed the Po, and resolved on marching to Cremona. As he was going, Turullius Cerialis with a great number of the levies from the fleet, and Julius Briganticus[16] with a few troopers, gave themselves up to him. Julius commanded a squadron of horse; he was a Batavian. Turullius was a centurion of the first rank, not unfriendly to Cæcina, as he had commanded a company in Germany.

23. Spurinna, on discovering the enemy's route, informed Annius Gallus by letter of the successful defense of Placentia, of what had happened, and of what Cæcina intended to do. Gallus was then bringing up the first legion to the relief of Placentia; he hardly dared trust so few cohorts, fearing that they could not sustain a prolonged siege or the formidable attack of the German army. On hearing that Cæcina had been repulsed, and was making his way to Cremona, though the legion could hardly be restrained, and in its eagerness for action

343

even went to the length of open mutiny, he halted at Bedriacum.[17] This is a village situated between Verona and Cremona, and has now acquired an ill-omened celebrity by two great days of disaster to Rome. About the same time Martius Macer fought a successful battle not far from Cremona. Martius, who was a man of energy, conveyed his gladiators in boats across the Po, and suddenly threw them upon the opposite bank. The Vitellian auxiliaries on the spot were routed; those who made a stand were cut to pieces, the rest directing their flight to Cremona. But the impetuosity of the victors was checked; for it was feared that the enemy might be strengthened by reinforcements, and change the fortune of the day. This policy excited the suspicions of the Othonians, who put a sinister construction on all the acts of their generals. Vying with each other in an insolence of language proportioned to their cowardice of heart, they assailed with various accusations Annius Gallus, Suetonius Paullinus, and Marius Celsus. The murderers of Galba were the most ardent promoters of mutiny and discord. Frenzied with fear and guilt, they sought to plunge everything into confusion, resorting now to openly seditious language, now to secret letters to Otho; and he, ever ready to believe the meanest of men and suspicious of the good, irresolute in prosperity, but rising higher under reverses, was in perpetual alarm. The end of it was that he sent for his brother Titianus, and entrusted him with the direction of the campaign.

24. Meanwhile, brilliant successes were gained under the command of Celsus and Paullinus. Cæcina was greatly annoyed by the fruitlessness of all his undertakings, and by the waning reputation of his army. He had been repulsed from Placentia; his auxiliaries had been recently cut up, and even when the skirmishers had met in a series of actions, frequent indeed but not worth relating, he had been worsted; and now that Valens was coming up, fearful that all the distinctions of the campaign would center in that general, he made a hasty attempt to retrieve his credit, but with more impetuosity than prudence. Twelve miles from Cremona (at a place called Ad Castores) he posted some of the bravest of his

auxiliaries, concealed in the woods that there overhang the road. The cavalry were ordered to move forward, and after provoking a battle, voluntarily to retreat, and draw on the enemy in hasty pursuit, till the ambuscade could make a simultaneous attack. The scheme was betrayed to the Othonian generals, and Paullinus assumed the command of the infantry, Celsus of the cavalry. The veterans of the 13th legion, four cohorts of auxiliaries, and five hundred cavalry were drawn up on the left side of the road; the raised causeway was occupied by three prætorian cohorts, ranged in deep columns; on the right front stood the first legion with two cohorts of auxiliaries and five hundred cavalry. Besides these, a thousand cavalry, belonging to the prætorian guard and to the auxiliaries, were brought up to complete a victory or to retrieve a repulse.

25. Before the hostile lines engaged, the Vitellians began to retreat, but Celsus, aware of the stratagem, kept his men back. The Vitellians rashly left their position, and seeing Celsus gradually give way, followed too far in pursuit, and themselves fell into an ambuscade. The auxiliaries assailed them on either flank, the legions were opposed to them in front, and the cavalry, by a sudden movement, had surrounded their rear. Suetonius Paullinus did not at once give the infantry the signal to engage. He was a man naturally tardy in action, and one who preferred a cautious and scientific plan of operations to any success which was the result of accident. He ordered the trenches to be filled up, the plain to be cleared, and the line to be extended, holding that it would be time enough to begin his victory when he had provided against being vanquished. This delay gave the Vitellians time to retreat into some vineyards, which were obstructed by the interlacing layers of the vines, and close to which was a small wood. From this place they again ventured to emerge, slaughtering the foremost of the prætorian cavalry. The prince Epiphanes[18] was wounded, while he was zealously cheering on the troops for Otho.

26. Then the Othonian infantry charged. The enemy's line was completely crushed, and the reinforcements

who were coming up to their aid were also put to flight. Cæcina indeed had not brought up his cohorts in a body, but one by one; as this was done during the battle, it increased the general confusion, because the troops who were thus divided, not being strong at any one point, were borne away by the panic of the fugitives. Besides this, a mutiny broke out in the camp because the whole army was not led into action. Julius Gratus, prefect of the camp, was put in irons, on a suspicion of a treacherous understanding with his brother, who was serving with Otho's army, at the very time that the Othonians had done the same thing and on the same grounds to that brother, Julius Fronto,[19] a tribune. In fact such was the panic everywhere, among the fugitives and among the troops coming up, in the lines and in front of the entrenchments, that it was very commonly said on both sides that Cæcina and his whole army might have been destroyed, had not Suetonius Paullinus given the signal of recall. Paullinus alleged that he feared the effects of so much additional toil and so long a .march, apprehending that the Vitellians might issue fresh from their camp, and attack his wearied troops, who, once thrown into confusion, would have no reserves to fall back upon. A few approved the general's policy, but it was unfavorably canvassed by the army at large.

27. The effect of this disaster on the Vitellians was not so much to drive them to fear as to draw them to obedience. Nor was this the case only among the troops of Cæcina, who indeed laid all the blame upon his soldiers, more ready, as he said, for mutiny than for battle. The forces also of Fabius Valens, who had now reached Ticinum, laid aside their contempt for the enemy and, anxious to retrieve their credit, began to yield a more respectful and uniform obedience to their general. A serious mutiny, however, had raged among them, of which, as it was not convenient to interrupt the orderly narrative of Cæcina's operations, I shall take up the history at an earlier period. I have already described how the Batavian cohorts who separated from the 14th legion during the Neronian war, hearing on their way to Britain of the rising of Vitellius, joined Fabius Valens

346

in the country of the Lingones. They behaved themselves insolently, boasting, as they visited the quarters of the several legions, that they had mastered the men of the 14th, that they had taken Italy from Nero, that the whole destiny of the war lay in their hands. Such language was insulting to the soldiers, and offensive to the general. The discipline of the army was relaxed by the brawls and quarrels which ensued. At last Valens began to suspect that insolence would end in actual treachery.

28. When, therefore, intelligence reached him that the cavalry of the Treviri and the Tungrian infantry had been defeated by Otho's fleet, and that Narbonese Gaul was blockaded, anxious at once to protect a friendly population, and, like a skillful soldier, to separate cohorts so turbulent and, while they remained united, so inconveniently strong, he directed a detachment of the Batavians to proceed to the relief of the province. This having been heard and become generally known, the allies were discontented and the legions murmured. "We are being deprived," they said, "of the help of our bravest men. Those veteran troops victorious in so many campaigns, now that the enemy is in sight, are withdrawn, so to speak, from the very field of battle. If indeed a province be of more importance than the capital and the safety of the Empire, let us all follow them thither, but if the reality, the support, the mainstay of success, center in Italy, you must not tear, as it were, from a body its very strongest limbs."

29. In the midst of these fierce exclamations, Valens, sending his lictors into the crowd, attempted to quell the mutiny. On this they attacked the general himself, hurled stones at him, and, when he fled, pursued him. Crying out that he was concealing the spoil of Gaul, the gold of the men of Vienna, the hire of their own toils, they ransacked his baggage, and probed with javelins and lances the walls of the general's tent and the very ground beneath. Valens, disguised in the garb of a slave, found concealment with a subaltern officer of cavalry. After this, Alfenus Varus, prefect of the camp, seeing that the mutiny was gradually subsiding, promoted the reaction by the following device. He forbade the centurions to

visit the sentinels, and discontinued the trumpet calls
by which the troops are summoned to their usual military duties. Thereupon all stood paralyzed, and gazed
at each other in amazement, panic-stricken by the very
fact that there was no one to direct them. By their silence, by their submission, finally by their tears and
entreaties, they craved forgiveness. But when Valens,
thus unexpectedly preserved, came forward in sad plight,
shedding tears, they were moved to joy, to pity, even to
affection. Their revulsion to delight was just that of a
mob, always extreme in either emotion. They greeted
him with praises and congratulations, and surrounding
him with the eagles and standards, carried him to the
tribunal. With a politic prudence he refrained from demanding capital punishment in any case; yet, fearing
that he might lay himself more open to suspicion by
concealment of his feelings, he censured a few persons,
well aware that in civil wars the soldiers have more
license than the generals.

30. While they were fortifying a camp at Ticinum, the
news of Cæcina's defeat reached them, and the mutiny
nearly broke out afresh from an impression that under-
hand dealing and delay on the part of Valens had kept
them away from the battle. They refused all rest; they
would not wait for their general; they advanced in front
of the standards, and hurried on the standard bearers.
After a rapid march they joined Cæcina. The character
of Valens did not stand well with Cæcina's army. They
complained that, though so much weaker in numbers,
they had been exposed to the whole force of the enemy,
thus at once excusing themselves, and extolling, in the
implied flattery, the strength of the new arrivals, who
might, they feared, despise them as beaten and spiritless
soldiers. Though Valens had the stronger army, nearly
double the number of legions and auxiliaries, yet the
partialities of the soldiers inclined to Cæcina, not only
from the geniality of heart, which he was thought more
ready to display, but even from his vigorous age, his
commanding person, and a certain superficial attractive-
ness which he possessed. The result was a jealousy between the two generals. Cæcina ridiculed his colleague

348

as a man of foul and infamous character; Valens retorted with charges of emptiness and vanity. But concealing their enmity, they devoted themselves to their
common interest, and in frequent letters, without any
thought of pardon, heaped all manner of charges upon
Otho, while the Othonian generals, though they had the
most abundant materials for invective against Vitellius,
refrained from employing them.

31. In fact, before the death of these two men (and
it was by his death that Otho gained high renown, as
Vitellius incurred by his the foulest infamy), Vitellius
with his indolent luxury was less dreaded than Otho
with his ardent passions. The murder of Galba had made
the one terrible and odious, while no one reckoned
against the other the guilt of having begun the war.
Vitellius with his sensuality and gluttony was his own
enemy; Otho, with his profligacy, his cruelty, and his
recklessness, was held to be more dangerous to the commonwealth. When Cæcina and Valens had united their
forces, the Vitellians had no longer any reason to delay
giving battle with their whole strength. Otho deliberated
as to whether protracting the war or risking an engagement were the better course.

32. Then Suetonius Paullinus, thinking that it befitted his reputation—which was such that no one at
that period was looked upon as a more skillful soldier—
to give an opinion on the whole conduct of the war,
contended that impatience would benefit the enemy,
while delay would serve their own cause.

"The entire army of Vitellius," he said, "has already
arrived. Nor have they much strength in their rear, since
Gaul is ready to rise, and to abandon the banks of the
Rhine, when such hostile tribes are ready to burst in,
would not answer his purpose. A hostile people and an
intervening sea keep from him the army of Britain;
Spain is not overfull of troops; Narbonese Gaul has
been cowed by the attack of our ships and by a defeat;
Italy beyond the Po is shut in by the Alps, cannot be
relieved from the sea, and has been exhausted by the
passage of his army. For that army there is nowhere
any corn, and without supplies an army cannot be kept

together. Then the Germans, the most formidable part of the enemy's forces, should the war be protracted into the summer, will sink with enfeebled frames under the change of country and climate. Many a war, formidable in its first impetuosity, has passed into nothing through the weariness of delay. We, on the other hand, have on all sides abundant resources and loyal adherents. We have Pannonia, Mœsia, Dalmatia, the East with its armies yet intact, we have Italy and Rome, the capital of the Empire, the Senate, and the people, names that never lose their splendor, though they may sometimes be eclipsed. We have the wealth of the state and of private individuals. We have a vast supply of money, which in a civil war is a mightier weapon than the sword. Our soldiers are inured to the climate of Italy or to yet greater heat. We have the river Po on our front, and cities strongly garrisoned and fortified, none of which will surrender to the enemy, as the defense of Placentia has proved. Let Otho therefore protract the war. In a few days the 14th legion, itself highly renowned, will arrive with the troops from Mœsia. He may then again consider the question, and should a battle be resolved on, we shall fight with increased strength."

33. Marius Celsus acquiesced in the opinion of Paullinus; and Annius Gallus, who a few days before had been seriously injured by the fall of his horse, was reported to agree by those who had been sent to ascertain his opinion. Otho was inclined to risk a decisive battle. His brother Titianus, and Proculus, the prefect of the prætorian guard, ignorant and therefore impatient, declared that fortune, the gods, and the genius of Otho were with their counsels, and would be with their enterprises. That no one might dare to oppose their views, they had taken refuge in flattery. It having been resolved to give battle, it became a question whether it would be better for the Emperor to be present in person, or to withdraw. Paullinus and Celsus no longer opposed, for they would not seem to put the Emperor in the way of peril, and these same men who suggested the worse policy prevailed on him to retire to Brixellum,[20] and thus secure from the hazards of the field, to reserve himself

for the administration of empire. That day first gave
the death blow to the party of Otho. Not only did a
strong detachment of the prætorian cohorts, of the bodyguard, and of the cavalry depart with him, but the spirit
of those who remained was broken, for the men suspected their generals, and Otho, who alone had the confidence of the soldiers, while he himself trusted in
none but them, had left the generals' authority on a
doubtful footing.

34. Nothing of this escaped the Vitellians, for, as is
usual in civil wars, there were many deserters, and the
spies, while busy in inquiring into the plans of the
enemy, failed to conceal their own. Meanwhile Cæcina
and Valens remained quiet, and watched intently for the
moment when the enemy in his blindness should rush
upon destruction, and found the usual substitute for
wisdom in waiting for the folly of others. They began to
form a bridge, making a feint of crossing the Po, in
the face of an opposing force of gladiators; they wished
also to keep their own soldiers from passing their unoccupied time in idleness. Boats were ranged at equal
distances from each other, connected at both ends by
strong beams, and with their heads turned against the
current, while anchors were thrown out above to keep
the bridge firm. The cables, however, instead of being
taut, hung loose in the water, in order that as the
stream rose, the vessels might rise without their arrangement being disturbed. On the end of the bridge was
placed a turret; it was built out on the last boat, and
from it engines and machines might be worked to repel
the enemy. The soldiers of Otho also raised a turret
on the opposite bank, and hurled from it stones and
flaming missiles.

35. In the middle of the river was an island. While
the gladiators were making their way to it in boats, the
Germans swam and outstripped them. A considerable
number, as it chanced, had effected the passage, when
Macer, having manned some light galleys, attacked them
with the most active of his gladiators. But the gladiator
has not in battle the firmness of the regular soldier,
and now, as they stood on rocking vessels, they could

not direct their blows like men who had a sure footing on land. As the men in their alarm made confused movements, rowers and combatants were mingled together in disorder; upon this, the Germans themselves leaped into the shallows, laid hold of the boats, climbed over the gunwales, or sank them with their hands. All this passed in the sight of both armies, and the more it delighted the Vitellians, the more vehemently did the Othonians curse the cause and author of the disaster.

36. The conflict was terminated by the flight of the vanquished, who carried off what boats were left. Then they cried out for the execution of Macer. He had been wounded by a javelin thrown from a distance, and the soldiers had made a rush upon him with drawn swords, when he was saved by the interference of the tribunes and centurions. Soon after, Vestricius Spurinna, having received orders to that effect from Otho, joined with his cohorts, leaving but a moderate force in garrison at Placentia. After this Otho sent Flavius Sabinus,[21] consul-elect, to take the command of the troops which had been under Macer; the soldiers were delighted by this change of generals, while the generals were led by these continual outbreaks to regard with disgust so hateful a service.

37. I find it stated by some authors that either the dread of war or the disgust felt for both Emperors, whose wickedness and infamy were coming out every day into more open notoriety, made the two armies hesitate whether they should not cease their strife, and either themselves consult together, or allow the Senate to choose an emperor; and that, for this reason, Otho's generals recommended a certain measure of delay, Paullinus especially entertaining hopes for himself, on the ground that he was the senior among the men of consular rank, that he was well known as a soldier, and had attained great distinction and fame by his campaigns in Britain. Though I would allow that there were some few who in their secret wishes prayed for peace instead of disorder, for a worthy and blameless emperor in the room of men utterly worthless and wicked, yet I cannot suppose that Paullinus, wise as he was, could have hoped in an age thoroughly depraved to find such

moderation in the common herd, that men who in their passion for war had trampled peace underfoot should now in their affection for peace renounce the charms of war; nor can I think that armies differing in language and in character could have united in such an agreement; or that lieutenants and generals, who were for the most part burdened by the consciousness of profligacy, of poverty, and of crime, could have endured any emperor who was not himself stained by vice, as well as bound by obligation to themselves.

38. That old passion for power which has been ever innate in man increased and broke out as the Empire grew in greatness. In a state of moderate dimensions equality was easily preserved; but when the world had been subdued, when all rival kings and cities had been destroyed, and men had leisure to covet wealth which they might enjoy in security, the early conflicts between the patricians and the people were kindled into flame. At one time the tribunes were factious, at another the consuls had unconstitutional power; it was in the capital and the forum that we first essayed civil wars. Then rose Gaius Marius, sprung from the very dregs of the populace, and Lucius Sulla, the most ruthless of the patricians, who perverted into absolute dominion the liberty which had yielded to their arms. After them came Cnæus Pompeius, with a character more disguised but no way better. Henceforth men's sole object was supreme power. Legions formed of Roman citizens did not lay down their arms at Pharsalia and Philippi; much less were the armies of Otho and Vitellius likely of their own accord to abandon their strife. They were driven into civil war by the same wrath from heaven, the same madness among men, the same incentives to crime. That these wars were terminated by what we may call single blows was owing to want of energy in the chiefs. But these reflections on the character of ancient and modern times have carried me too far from my subject. I now return to the course of events.

39. Otho having started for Brixellum, the honors of supreme command devolved on his brother Titianus, while the real power and control were in the hands of

the prefect Proculus. Celsus and Paullinus, as no one
made any use of their skill, did but screeñ with their
idle title of general the blunders of others. The tribunes
and centurions were perplexed to see that better men
were despised, and that the most worthless carried the
day. The common soldiers were full of eagerness, but
liked to criticize rather than to obey the orders of their
officers. It was resolved to move the camp forward to
the fourth milestone from Bedriacum, but it was done so
unskillfully that though it was spring, and there were
so many rivers in the neighborhood, the troops were distressed for want of water. Then the subject of giving
battle was discussed, Otho in his dispatches ever urging
them to make haste, and the soldiers demanding that the
Emperor should be present at the conflict; many begged
that the troops quartered beyond the Po should be
brought up. It is not so easy to determine what was best
to be done, as it is to be sure that what was done was
the very worst.

40. They started for a campaign rather than for a
battle, making for the confluence of the Po and Arda,[22]
a distance of sixteen miles from their position. Celsus
and Paullinus remonstrated against exposing troops
wearied with a march and encumbered with baggage to
any enemy, who, being himself ready for action and
having marched barely four miles, would not fail to attack them, either when they were in the confusion of
an advance, or when they were dispersed and busy with
the work of entrenchment. Titianus and Proculus, overcome in argument, fell back on the imperial authority.
It was true that a Numidian had arrived at full gallop
with an angry message from Otho, in which the Emperor, sick of delay and impatient of suspense, sharply
rebuked the inactivity of the generals, and commanded
that matters should be brought to an issue.

41. The same day, while Cæcina was engaged on the
construction of a bridge, two tribunes of the prætorian
guard came to him and begged an interview. He was on
the point of hearing their proposals and sending back
his own, when the scouts arrived at headlong speed with
the news that the enemy was close at hand. The address

of the tribunes was thus abruptly terminated. Thus it remained uncertain whether deception, or treason, or some honorable arrangement had been in their thoughts. Cæcina dismissed the tribunes and rode back to the camp. There he found that Fabius Valens had given the signal for battle, and that the troops were under arms. While the legions were casting lots for the order of march, the cavalry charged and, strange to say, were kept only by the courage of the Italian legion from being driven back on the entrenchments by an inferior force of Othonians. These men, at sword's point, compelled the beaten squadron to wheel round and resume the conflict. The line of the Vitellians was formed without hurry, for though the enemy was close at hand, the sight of their arms was intercepted by the thick brushwood. In Otho's army the generals were full of fear, and the soldiers hated their officers; the baggage wagons and the camp followers were mingled with the troops; and as there were steep ditches on both sides of the road, it would have been found too narrow even for an undisturbed advance. Some were gathering round their standards; others were seeking them; everywhere was heard the confused shouting of men who were joining the ranks, or calling to their comrades, and each, as he was prompted by courage or by cowardice, rushed on to the front, or slunk back to the rear.

42. From the consternation of panic their feelings passed under the influence of a groundless joy into languid indifference, some persons spreading the lie that Vitellius' army had revolted. Whether this rumor was circulated by the spies of Vitellius, or originated in treachery or in accident among the partisans of Otho, has never been clearly ascertained. Forgetting their warlike ardor, the Othonians at once greeted the foe; as they were answered by an angry murmur, they caused apprehensions of treachery in many of their own side, who did not know what the greeting meant. Then the enemy's line charged with its ranks unbroken, in strength and in numbers superior; the Othonians, scattered and weary as they were, met the attack with spirit. The ground was so entangled with trees and vineyards that

the battle assumed many forms. They met in close and in distant conflict, in line and in column. On the raised road they stood foot to foot, they pushed with their bodies and their shields, and ceasing to throw their javelins, they struck through helmets and breastplates with swords and battle-axes. Recognizing each other and distinctly seen by the rest of the combatants, they were fighting to decide the whole issue of the war.

43. In an open plain between the Po and the road, two legions happened to meet. On the side of Vitellius was the 21st, called the Rapax, a corps of old and distinguished renown. On that of Otho was the 1st, called Adjutrix, which had never before been brought into the field, but was high-spirited, and eager to gain its first triumph. The men of the 1st, overthrowing the foremost ranks of the 21st, carried off the eagle. The 21st, infuriated by this loss, not only repulsed the 1st, and slew the legate, Orfidius Benignus, but captured many colors and standards from the enemy. In another quarter the 13th legion was put to flight by a charge of the 5th. The 14th was surrounded by a superior force. Otho's generals had long since fled, and Cæcina and Valens strengthened their army with the reserves. New reinforcements were supplied by Alfenus Varus with his Batavians. They had routed the band of gladiators, which had been ferried across the river, and which had been cut to pieces by the opposing cohorts while they were actually in the water. Thus flushed with victory, they charged the flank of the enemy.

44. The center of their line had been penetrated, and the Othonians fled on all sides in the direction of Bedriacum. The distance was very great, and the roads were blocked up with heaps of corpses; thus the slaughter was the greater, for captives taken in civil war can be turned to no profit. Suetonius Paullinus and Licinius Proculus, taking different roads, avoided the camp. Vedius Aquila, legate of the 13th legion, in the blindness of fear, fell in the way of the furious soldiery. Late in the day he entered the entrenchments, and found himself the center of a mob of clamorous and mutinous fugitives. They did not refrain from abuse or actual violence; they

reviled him as a deserter and traitor, not having any specific charge against him, but all, after the fashion of the mob, imputing to him their own crimes. Titianus and Celsus were favored by the darkness. By that time the sentries had been posted, and the soldiers reduced to order. Annius Gallus had prevailed upon them by his prayers, his advice, and his personal influence, not to aggravate the disaster of their defeat by mutual slaughter. Whether the war was at an end, or whether they might choose to resume the conflict, the vanquished would find in union the sole mitigation of their lot. The spirit of the rest of the army was broken, but the prætorians angrily complained that they had been vanquished not by valor, but by treachery. "The Vitellians indeed," they said, "gained no bloodless victory; their cavalry was defeated, a legion lost its eagle. We have still the troops beyond the Po, and Otho himself. The legions of Mœsia are coming; a great part of the army remained at Bedriacum; these certainly were never vanquished; and if it must be so, it is on the battlefield that we shall fall with most honor." Amid all the exasperation or terror of these thoughts, the extremity of despair yet roused them to fury rather than to fear.

45. The army of Vitellius bivouacked at the fifth milestone from Bedriacum. The generals did not venture an assault on the enemy's camp that same day; besides, a capitulation was expected. Though they were without baggage, and had marched out only to fight, it was sufficient protection to them that they had arms, and were victorious. On the following day, as the feeling of Otho's army was evident, and those who had been most furious were inclined to repent, envoys were sent, nor did the generals of Vitellius hesitate to grant conditions of peace. The envoys indeed were detained for some little time, and this circumstance caused some doubt, as it was not known whether they had obtained their object; before long, however, they returned, and the camp was thrown open. Both victors and vanquished melted into tears, and cursed the fatality of civil strife with a melancholy joy. There in the same tents did they dress the wounds of brothers or of kinsmen. Their hopes, their

rewards, were all uncertain; death and sorrow were sure. And no one had so escaped misfortune as to have no bereavement to lament. Search was made for the body of the legate Orfidius, and it was burned with the customary honors. A few were buried by their friends; the multitude that remained were left above ground.

46. Otho was awaiting news of the battle free from alarm and resolved in purpose. First came gloomy tidings, and then fugitives from the field, making known that all was lost. The zeal of the soldiers did not wait for the Emperor to speak. They bade him be of good cheer, telling him that he had still fresh forces, and that they would themselves endure and dare to the last. This was no flattery; they were fired by a furious impulse to seek the battlefield, and raise again the fallen fortunes of their party. Those who stood at a distance stretched out their arms, those who were near clasped the Emperor's knees, and Plotius Firmus[23] was the most zealous of them all. This man, who was prefect of the prætorian guard, repeatedly besought Otho not to desert an army so loyal and soldiers so deserving; "there was more courage in bearing trouble," he said, "than in escaping from it; the brave and the energetic cling to hope, even in spite of fortune; the cowardly and the indolent are hurried into despair by their fears." While he was thus speaking, as Otho assumed a relenting or a stern expression, the soldiers cheered or groaned. Nor was it only the prætorians, who were peculiarly Otho's troops, that thus acted; those who had been sent on from Mœsia declared that the approaching army was as firmly resolved, and that the legions had entered Aquileia. No one therefore can doubt that the war might have been renewed with its terrible disasters, and its uncertainties both for victors and vanquished.

47. Otho himself was opposed to all thoughts of war. He said, "I hold that to expose such a spirit, such a courage as yours to any further risk is to put too high a value on my life. The more hope you hold out to me, should I choose to live, the more glorious will be my death. Fortune and I now know each other; you need not reckon for how long, for it is peculiarly difficult to be

moderate with that prosperity which you think you will not long enjoy. The civil war began with Vitellius; he was the first cause of our contending in arms for the throne; the example of not contending more than once shall belong to me. By this let posterity judge of Otho. Vitellius is welcome to his brother, his wife, his children. I need neither revenge nor consolation. Others may have held the throne for a longer time, but no one can have left it with such fortitude. Shall I suffer so large a portion of the youth of Rome and so many noble armies to be again laid low and to be lost to the state? Let this thought go with me, that you were willing to die for me. But live, and let us no longer delay, lest I interfere with your safety, you with my firmness. To say too much about one's end is a mark of cowardice. Take as the strongest proof of my determination the fact that I complain of no one. To accuse either gods or men is only for him who wishes to live."

48. After having thus spoken, he courteously entreated all in terms befitting their age and rank to go at once, and not exasperate the anger of the conqueror by staying. With the young he used his authority, with the old his prayers, and still his look was calm, his speech collected, as he checked the unseasonable tears of his friends. He gave orders that those who were departing should be furnished with boats and carriages; he destroyed all memorials and letters remarkable for their expressions of zeal for himself or their abuse of Vitellius. He distributed some gratuities, but sparingly, and not like a man who was soon to die. Then he even administered consolation to Salvius Cocceianus, his brother's son, a very young man, who was anxious and sorrowful, praising his affection while he rebuked his fear. "Do you think," he said, "that Vitellius will show so ruthless a temper that he will not make even this return for the preservation of his whole family? By hastening my end I earn the clemency of the conqueror. It is not in the extremity of despair, but while my army yet cries for battle, that I have sacrificed to the state my last chance. I have obtained enough reputation for myself, enough nobility for my family. Successor to the

Julii, the Claudii, the Servii,[24] I have been the first to
bring the imperial dignity into a new family. Enter then
on life with a brave heart, and never entirely forget, or
remember too vividly, that Otho was your uncle."

49. After this he dismissed everyone, and took some
repose. He was now pondering in his heart the last
cares of life, when his attention was distracted by a sudden tumult and he was told of the confusion and outrageous conduct of the soldiers. They were threatening
with death all who attempted to depart, and were extreme in their violence against Verginius, whose house
they had blockaded and were besieging. After rebuking
the ringleaders of the tumult, he returned and employed
himself in granting interviews to those who were departing, till all had left in safety. Toward evening he
quenched his thirst with a draught of cold water. Two
daggers were brought to him; he tried the edge of each,
and then put one under his head. After satisfying himself that his friends had set out, he passed a tranquil
night, and it is even said that he slept. At dawn he fell
with his breast upon the steel. Hearing a groan from
the dying man, his freedmen and slaves, and Plotius
Firmus, prefect of the prætorian guard, came in. They
found but one wound. His funeral was hastily performed. He had made this the subject of earnest entreaties, anxious that his head might not be cut off and
subjected to indignities. The prætorian cohorts carried
his body with praises and tears, covering his wound and
his hands with kisses. Some of the soldiers killed themselves near the funeral pile, not moved by remorse or
by fear, but by the desire to emulate his glory, and by
love of their Emperor. Afterward this kind of death
became a common practice among all ranks at Bedriacum, at Placentia, and in the other camps. Over Otho
was built a tomb that was unpretentious and therefore
likely to stand.

50. Thus Otho ended his life in the thirty-seventh
year of his age. He came from the municipal town of
Ferentinum.[25] His father was of consular, his grandfather of prætorian rank. His family on the mother's
side was of less distinction, but yet respectable. What

his boyhood and his youth had been, we have already
shown. By two daring acts, one most atrocious, the other
singularly noble, he earned in the eyes of posterity about
an equal share of infamy and of glory. I should think
it unbecoming the dignity of the task which I have
undertaken to collect fabulous marvels, and to amuse
with fiction the tastes of my readers; at the same time
I would not venture to impugn the credit of common
report and tradition. The natives of these parts relate
that on the day when the battle was being fought at
Bedriacum, a bird of unfamiliar appearance settled in
a much frequented grove near Regium Lepidum,[26] and
was not frightened or driven away by the concourse of
people, or by the multitude of birds that flocked round
it, until Otho killed himself; then it vanished. When
they came to compute the time, it was found that the
commencement and the end of this strange occurrence
tallied with the last scenes of Otho's life.

[*Chapters 51-78 are omitted. The march through Italy
of the victorious Vitellian armies was marked by further
brutalities, Cæcina and Valens doing little to restrain
their followers. Vitellius himself at length followed his
triumphant generals to Rome, where he disgraced himself by giving full rein to his accustomed greed and
indolence. Meanwhile in the East, Mucianus was egging
on his colleague, Vespasianus, to make a bid for empire.*]

79. The initiative in transferring the Empire to Vespasianus was taken at Alexandria under the prompt direction of Tiberius Alexander, who on the 1st of July made
the legions swear allegiance to him. That day was ever
after celebrated as the first of his reign, though the
army of Judæa on July 3rd took the oath to Vespasianus
in person with such eager alacrity that they would not
wait for the return of his son Titus, who was then on
his way back from Syria, acting as the medium between
Mucianus and his father for the communication of their
plans. All this was done by the impulsive action of the
soldiers without the preliminary of a formal harangue
or any concentration of the legions.

80. While they were seeking a suitable time and place, and for that which in such an affair is the great difficulty—the first man to speak—while hope, fear, the chances of success or of disaster were present to their minds, one day, on Vespasianus quitting his chamber, a few soldiers who stood near, in the usual form in which they would salute their legate, suddenly saluted him as Emperor. Then all the rest hurried up, called him Cæsar and Augustus, and heaped on him all the titles of imperial rank. Their minds had passed from apprehension to confidence of success. In Vespasianus there appeared no sign of elation or arrogance, or of any change arising from his changed fortunes. As soon as he had dispelled the mist with which so astonishing a vicissitude had clouded his vision, he addressed the troops in a soldierlike style, and listened to the joyful intelligence that came pouring in from all quarters. This was the very opportunity for which Mucianus had been waiting. He now at once administered to the eager soldiers the oath of allegiance to Vespasianus. Then he entered the theater at Antioch, where it is customary for the citizens to hold their public deliberations, and as they crowded together with profuse expressions of flattery, he addressed them. He could speak Greek with considerable grace, and in all that he did and said he had the art of displaying himself to advantage. Nothing excited the provincials and the army so much as the assertion of Mucianus that Vitellius had determined to remove the legions of Germany to Syria, to an easy and lucrative service, while the armies of Syria were to have given them in exchange the encampments of Germany with their inclement climate and their harassing toils. On the one hand, the provincials from long use felt a pleasure in the companionship of the soldiers, with whom many of them were connected by friendship or relationship; on the other, the soldiers from the long duration of their service loved the well-known and familiar camp as a home.

81. Before the 15th of July the whole of Syria had adopted the same allegiance. There joined him, each with his entire kingdom, Sohemus,[27] who had no con-

temptible army, and Antiochus,[28] who possessed vast ancestral wealth, and was the richest of all the subject kings. Before long Agrippa, who had been summoned from the capital by secret dispatches from his friends, while as yet Vitellius knew nothing, was crossing the sea with all speed. The princess Berenice[29] too, who was then in the prime of youth and beauty, and who had charmed even the old Vespasianus by the splendor of her presents, promoted his cause with equal zeal. All the provinces washed by the sea, as far as Asia and Achæa, and the whole expanse of country inland toward Pontus and Armenia, took the oath of allegiance. The legates of these provinces were without troops, however, Cappadocia as yet having had no legions assigned to it. A council was held at Berytus[30] to deliberate on the general conduct of the war. Mucianus came then with the legates and tribunes and all the most distinguished centurions and soldiers, and there also the picked troops of the army of Judæa. Such a vast assemblage of cavalry and infantry, and the pomp of the kings that strove to rival each other in magnificence, presented an appearance of imperial splendor.

82. The first business of the campaign was to levy troops and recall the veterans to service. The strong cities were set apart for the manufacture of arms; at Antioch gold and silver money was coined, everything being vigorously carried on in its appointed place by properly qualified agents. Vespasianus himself went everywhere, urged to exertion, encouraged the industrious by praise, and with the indolent used the stimulus of example rather than of compulsion, and chose to be blind to the faults rather than to the merits of his friends. Many among them he distinguished with prefectures and governments, and several with the honors of senatorial rank; all these were men of eminence who soon reached the highest positions. In some cases good fortune served instead of merit. Of a donative to the troops Mucianus in his first speech had held out only moderate hopes, and even Vespasianus offered no more in the civil war than others had done in times of peace, thus making a noble stand against all bribery of the soldiery, and possessing

in consequence a better army. Envoys were sent to
Parthia and Armenia, and precautions were taken that,
when the legions were engaged in the civil war, the
country in their rear might not be exposed to attack. It
was arranged that Titus should pursue the war in Judæa,
while Vespasianus should secure the passes into Egypt. To
cope with Vitellius, a portion of the army, the generalship of Mucianus, the prestige of Vespasianus' name, and
the destiny before which all difficulties vanish, seemed
sufficient. To all the armies and legates letters were dispatched, and instructions were given to them that they
were to attach the prætorians, who hated Vitellius, by
the inducement of renewed military service.

83. Mucianus, who acted more as a colleague than as
a servant of the Emperor, moved on with some light-
armed troops, not indeed at a tardy pace so as to give the
appearance of delay, yet not with extraordinary speed.
Thus he allowed rumor to gather fresh strength by distance, well aware that his force was but small, and that
exaggerated notions are formed about what is not seen.
Behind him, however, came in a vast body the 6th legion
and thirteen thousand veterans. He had given directions
that the fleet from the Pontus should be brought up to
Byzantium,[31] not having yet made up his mind whether,
avoiding Mœsia, he should move on Dyrrachium[32] with
his infantry and cavalry, and at the same time blockade
the sea on the side of Italy with his ships of war, thus
leaving Asia and Achæa safe in his rear, which, being
bare of troops, would be left at the mercy of Vitellius,
unless they were occupied with proper garrisons. And
thus too Vitellius himself, finding Brundisium,[33] Tarentum,[34] and the shores of Calabria and Lucania menaced
by hostile fleets, would be in utter perplexity as to which
part of Italy he should protect.

84. Thus the provinces echoed with the bustle of preparing fleets, armies, and the implements of war. Nothing, however, was so vexatious as the raising of money.
Mucianus, with the perpetual assertion that money was
the sinews of civil war, looked in all questions not to
right or truth, but only to the extent of a man's fortune.
Information abounded, and all the richest men were

fastened on for plunder. These intolerable oppressions, which yet found some excuse in the necessities of war, were continued even in peace. Indeed Vespasian himself at the beginning of his reign was not so bent on enforcing these iniquitous measures, till, spoiled by prosperity and evil counselors, he learned this policy and ventured to use it. Mucianus contributed to the war even from his own purse, liberal with his private means because he helped himself without scruple from the wealth of the state. The rest followed his example in contributing their money; very few enjoyed the same license in reimbursing themselves.

85. Meanwhile the operations of Vespasianus were hastened by the zeal of the army of Illyricum, which had come over to his side. The 3rd legion set the example to the other legions of Mœsia. These were the 8th and 7th (Claudius'), who were possessed with a strong liking for Otho, though they had not been present at the battle of Bedriacum. They had advanced to Aquileia, and by roughly repulsing the messengers who brought the tidings of Otho's defeat, by tearing the colors which displayed the name of Vitellius, by finally seizing on the military chest and dividing it among themselves, had assumed a hostile attitude. Then they began to fear; fear suggested a new thought, that acts might be made a merit of with Vespasianus which would have to be excused to Vitellius. Accordingly, the three legions of Mœsia sought by letter to win over the army of Pannonia, and prepared to use force if they refused. During this commotion, Aponius Saturninus, governor of Mœsia, ventured on a most atrocious act. He dispatched a centurion to murder Tettius Julianus, the legate of the 7th legion, to gratify a private pique, which he concealed beneath the appearance of party zeal. Julianus, having discovered his danger, and procured some guides who were acquainted with the country, fled through the pathless wastes of Mœsia beyond Mount Hæmus,[35] nor did he afterward take any part in the civil war. He set out to join Vespasianus, but contrived to protract his journey by various pretexts, lingering or hastening on his way, according to the intelligence he received.

86. In Pannonia, however, the 13th legion and the 7th (Galba's), which still retained their vexation and rage at the defeat of Bedriacum, joined Vespasianus without hesitation, mainly under the influence of Antonius Primus.[36] This man, though an offender against the law, and convicted of fraud in the reign of Nero, had, among the other calamities of war, recovered his rank as a senator. Having been appointed by Galba to command the 7th legion, he was commonly believed to have often written to Otho, offering the party his services as a general. Being slighted, however, by that Emperor, he found no employment during the war. When the fortunes of Vitellius began to totter, he attached himself to Vespasianus, and brought a vast accession of strength to his party. He was brave in battle, ready of speech, dexterous in bringing odium upon other men, powerful amidst civil strife and rebellion, rapacious, prodigal, the worst of citizens in peace, but in war no contemptible ally. United by these means, the armies of Mœsia and Pannonia drew with them the soldiery of Dalmatia, though the consular legates took no part in the movement. Tampius Flavianus was the governor of Pannonia, Pompeius Silvanus[37] of Dalmatia. They were both rich and advanced in years. The imperial procurator, however, was Cornelius Fuscus,[38] a man in the prime of life and of illustrious birth. Though in early youth the desire of repose had led him to resign his senatorial rank, he afterward put himself at the head of his colony in fighting for Galba, and by this service he obtained his procuratorship. Subsequently embracing the cause of Vespasianus, he lent the movement the stimulus of a fiery zeal. Finding his pleasure not so much in the rewards of peril as in peril itself, to assured and long acquired possession he preferred novelty, uncertainty, and risk. Accordingly, both he and Antonius strove to agitate and disturb wherever there was any weak point. Dispatches were sent to the 14th legion in Britain and to the 1st in Spain, for both these legions had been on the side of Otho against Vitellius. Letters too were scattered through every part of Gaul, and in a moment a mighty war burst into flame, for the armies of

Illyricum were already in open revolt, and the rest were waiting only the signal of success.

87. While Vespasianus and the generals of his party were thus occupied in the provinces, Vitellius was daily becoming more contemptible and indolent, halting to enjoy the pleasures of every town and villa in his way, as with his cumbrous host he advanced toward the capital. He was followed by sixty thousand armed soldiers demoralized by license. Still larger was the number of camp followers; and of all slaves, the slaves of soldiers are the most unruly. So numerous a retinue of officers and personal friends would have been difficult to keep under restraint, even if controlled by the strictest discipline. The crowd was made more unwieldy by senators and knights who came to meet him from the capital, some moved by fear, many by a spirit of adulation, others, and by degrees all, that they might not be left behind while the rest were going. From the dregs of the people there thronged buffoons, players, and charioteers, known to Vitellius from their infamous compliance with his vices; for in such disgraceful friendships he felt a strange pleasure. And now not only were the colonies and town exhausted by having to furnish supplies, but the very cultivator of the soil and his lands, on which the harvests were now ripe, were plundered like an enemy's territory.

88. There were many sanguinary encounters between the soldiers; for ever since the mutiny which broke out at Ticinum there had lingered a spirit of dissension between the legions and the auxiliary troops, though they could unite whenever they had to fight with the rustic population. The most terrible massacre took place at the seventh milestone from Rome. Vitellius was distributing to each soldier provisions ready dressed on the same abundant scale as the gladiators' rations, and the populace had poured forth, and spread themselves throughout the entire camp. Some with the frolicsome humor of slaves robbed the careless soldiers by slyly cutting their belts, and then asked them whether they were armed. Unused to insult, the spirit of the soldiers resented the jest. Sword in hand, they fell upon the unarmed people. Among the

367

slain was the father of a soldier, who was with his son. He was afterward recognized, and his murder becoming generally known, they spared the innocent crowd. Yet there was a panic at Rome, as the soldiers pressed on in all directions. It was to the forum that they chiefly directed their steps, anxious to behold the spot where Galba had fallen. Nor were the men themselves a less frightful spectacle, bristling as they were with the skins of wild beasts, and armed with huge lances, while in their strangeness to the place they were embarrassed by the crowds of people, or tumbling down in the slippery streets or from the shock of some casual encounter, they fell to quarreling, and then had recourse to blows and the use of their swords. Besides, the tribunes and prefects were hurrying to and fro with formidable bodies of armed men.

89. Vitellius himself, mounted on a splendid charger, with military cloak and sword, advanced from the Mulvian Bridge, driving the Senate and people before him; but deterred by the advice of his friends from marching into Rome as if it were a captured city, he assumed a civil garb, and proceeded with his army in orderly array. The eagles of four legions were borne in front, and an equal number of colors from other legions on either side, then came the standards of twelve auxiliary squadrons, and the cavalry behind the ranks of the infantry. Next came thirty-four auxiliary cohorts, distinguished according to the names or various equipments of the nations. Before each eagle were the prefects of the camp, the tribunes, and the centurions of highest rank, in white robes, and the other officers by the side of their respective companies, glittering with arms and decorations. The ornaments and chains of the soldiers presented a brilliant appearance. It was a glorious sight, and the army was worthy of a better emperor than Vitellius. Thus he entered the capital, and he there embraced his mother and honored her with the title of Augusta.

90. The next day, as if he were addressing the senate and people of another state, he pronounced a high panegyric on himself, extolling his own energy and moderation, though his enormities were known both to those

who happened to be present and to the whole of Italy, his progress through which had been disgraced by sloth and profligacy. Yet the mob, who had no patriotic anxieties, and who, without distinguishing between truth and falsehood, had learned the lesson of habitual flattery, applauded him with shouts and acclamations, and, reluctant as he was to assume the name of Augustus, extorted from him a compliance as idle as his previous refusal.

91. The country, ready to find a meaning in every circumstance, regarded it as an omen of gloomy import that Vitellius, on obtaining the office of supreme pontiff, should have issued a proclamation concerning the public religious ceremonial on the 18th of July, a day which from old times the disasters of Cremera[39] and Allia had marked as unlucky. Thus, utterly regardless of all law human and divine, with freedmen and friends as reckless as himself, he lived as if he were among a set of drunkards. Still, at the consular elections he was present in company with the candidates like an ordinary citizen, and by showing himself as a spectator in the theater, as a partisan in the circus, he courted every breath of applause from the lowest rabble. Agreeable and popular as this conduct would have been had it been prompted by noble qualities, it was looked upon as undignified and contemptible from the remembrance of his past life. He habitually appeared in the Senate even when unimportant matters were under discussion; and it once happened that Helvidius Priscus,[40] the prætor-elect, had spoken against his wishes. Though at the moment provoked, he only called on the tribunes of the people to support his insulted authority, and then, when his friends, who feared that his resentment was deeper than it appeared, sought to appease him, he replied that it was nothing strange that two senators in a commonwealth should disagree: he had himself been in the habit of opposing even Thrasea. Most of them laughed at the effrontery of such a comparison, though some were pleased at the very circumstance of his having selected, not one of the most influential men of the time, but Thrasea, as his model of true glory.

92. He had advanced to the command of the prætorian

guard, Publilius Sabinus, a prefect of a cohort, and Julius Priscus, then only a centurion. It was through the influence of Cæcina and Valens respectively that they rose to power. Though always at variance, these two men left no authority to Vitellius. The functions of empire were discharged by Cæcina and Valens. They had long before been led to suspect each other by animosities scarcely concealed amid the cares of the campaign and the camp, and aggravated by unprincipled friends and a state of society calculated to produce such feuds. In their struggles for popularity, in their long retinues, and in the vast crowds at their levées, they vied with each other and challenged comparison, while the favor of Vitellius inclined first to one, and then to the other. There can never be complete confidence in a power which is excessive. Vitellius himself, who was ever varying between sudden irritation and unseasonable fondness, they at once despised and feared. Still this had not made them less keen to seize on palaces and gardens and all the wealth of the Empire, while a sad and needy throng of nobles, whom with their children Galba had restored to their country, received no relief from the compassion of the Emperor. By an edict which gratified the leading men of the state, while it approved itself even to the populace, Vitellius gave back to the returned exiles their rights over their freedmen, although servile ingenuity sought in every way to neutralize the boon, concealing money in quarters which either obscurity or rank rendered secure. Some freedmen had made their way into the palace of the Emperor, and thus became more powerful even than their patrons.

93. Meanwhile the soldiers, as their numbers overflowed the crowded camp, dispersed throughout the porticoes, the temples, and the whole capital, did not know their own headquarters, kept no watch, and ceased to brace themselves by toil. Amidst the allurements of the city and all shameful excesses, they wasted their strength in idleness, and their energies in riot. At last, reckless even of health, a large portion of them quartered themselves in the notoriously pestilential neighborhood of the

Vatican; hence ensued a great mortality in the ranks. The Tiber was close at hand, and their extreme eagerness for the water and their impatience of the heat weakened the constitutions of the Germans and Gauls, always liable to disease. To make matters worse, the organization of the service was deranged by unprincipled intrigue and favor. Sixteen prætorian and four city cohorts were being raised, each to consist of a thousand men. In this levy Valens ventured to do more than his rival on the pretense of his having rescued Cæcina himself from peril. Doubtless his arrival had restored the fortunes of the party, and his victory had reversed the unfavorable rumors occasioned by his tardy advance. The entire army too of Lower Germany was attached to him; this circumstance, it is thought, first made the allegiance of Cæcina waver.

94. Much, however, as Vitellius indulged his generals, his soldiers enjoyed yet greater license. Everyone chose his own service. However unfit, he might, if he preferred it, be enrolled among the soldiers of the capital. Soldiers again of good character were allowed, if they so wished, to remain with the legions, or in the cavalry; and this was the choice of many who were worn out with disease, or who shrank from the unhealthiness of the climate. But the main strength of the legions and cavalry was drafted from them, while the old glory of the prætorian camp was destroyed by these twenty thousand men indiscriminately taken rather than chosen out of the whole army. While Vitellius was haranguing the troops, the men called out for the execution of Asiaticus,[41] Flavius, and Rufinus, the Gallic chieftains, because they had fought for Vindex. He never checked these cries; for to say nothing of the cowardice natural to that feeble soul, he was aware that he would soon have to distribute a donative and, having no money, he lavished everything else on the soldiers. A contribution in the form of a tax was exacted from the freedmen of former emperors in proportion to the number of their slaves. Vitellius himself, thinking only how to squander, was building a stable for his charioteers, was filling the circus with

shows of gladiators and wild beasts, and fooling away
his money as if he had the most abundant supplies.

95. Moreover, Cæcina and Valens celebrated the birthday of Vitellius by exhibiting in every quarter of the city
shows of gladiators on a vast and hitherto unparalleled
scale. He pleased the most infamous characters, but
utterly disgusted all the respectable citizens, by building
altars in the Campus Martius, and performing funeral
rites to Nero. Victims were slaughtered and burned in the
name of the state; the pile was kindled by the Augustales,
an order of priesthood dedicated by the Emperor Tiberius
to the Julian family, just as Romulus had dedicated one
to King Tatius.[42] Within four months from the victory
of Bedriacum, Asiaticus, the Emperor's freedman, was
rivaling the Polycleti,[43] the Patrobii,[44] and all the old
hateful names. No one sought promotion in that court
by integrity or diligence; the sole road to power was to
glut the insatiable appetites of Vitellius by prodigal
entertainments, extravagance, and riot. The Emperor
himself, thinking it enough to enjoy the present, and
without a thought for the future, is believed to have
squandered nine hundred million sesterces in a very few
months. Rome, as miserable as she was great, afflicted in
one year by an Otho and a Vitellius, what with the Vinii,
the Fabii,[45] the Iceli,[46] and the Asiatici, passed through
all vicissitudes of infamy, till there came Mucianus and
Marcellus,[47] and different men rather than a different
morality.

96. The first revolt of which Vitellius received tidings
was that of the 3rd legion, dispatches having been sent
by Aponius Saturninus before he too attached himself to
the party of Vespasianus. Aponius, however, agitated by
the unexpected occurrence, had not written all the particulars, and flattering friends softened down its import.
"It was," they said, "a mutiny of only a single legion; the
loyalty of the other armies was unshaken." Vitellius in
addressing the soldiers spoke to the same effect. He
inveighed against the lately disbanded prætorians, and
asserted that false rumors were circulated by them, and
that there was no fear of a civil war. The name of
Vespasianus he suppressed, and soldiers were dispersed

through the city to check the popular gossip. This more than anything else kept these rumors alive.

97. Nevertheless Vitellius summoned auxiliary troops from Germany, Britain, and Spain, tardily, however, and with an attempt to conceal his necessities. The legates and the provinces were equally slow. Hordeonius Flaccus, who was beginning to suspect the Batavians, feared that he should have a war on his own hands, and Vettius Bolanus had in Britain a province never very quiet; and both these officers were wavering in their allegiance. Spain too, which then was without a governor of consular rank, showed no alacrity. The legates of the three legions, equal in authority, and ready, while Vitellius was prosperous, to vie in obedience, stood aloof with one consent from his falling fortunes. In Africa, the legion, and the auxiliary infantry levied by Clodius Macer and soon after disbanded by Galba, again entered the service at the order of Vitellius, while all the rest of the youth promptly gave in their names. Vitellius had ruled that province as proconsul with integrity and popularity; Vespasianus' government had been infamous and odious. The allies formed conjectures accordingly as to the manner in which each would reign, but the result contradicted them.

98. At first Valerius Festus, the legate, loyally seconded the zeal of the provincials. Soon he began to waver, supporting Vitellius in his public dispatches and edicts, Vespasianus in his secret correspondence, and intending to hold by the one or the other according as they might succeed. Some soldiers and centurions, coming through Rhætia and Gaul, were seized with letters and edicts from Vespasianus and on being sent to Vitellius were put to death. More, however, eluded discovery, escaping either through the faithful protection of friends or by their own tact. Thus the preparations of Vitellius became known, while the plans of Vespasianus were for the most part kept secret. At first the supineness of Vitellius was in fault; afterward the occupation of the Pannonian Alps with troops stopped all intelligence. And on the sea the prevalent trade winds favored an eastward voyage, but hindered all return.

99. At length Vitellius, appalled by the irruption of the enemy and by the menacing intelligence from every quarter, ordered Cæcina and Valens to take the field. Cæcina was sent on in advance; Valens, who was just recovering from a severe illness, was delayed by weakness. Far different was the appearance of the German army as it marched out of the capital. All strength had departed from their bodies, all energy from their spirits. Slowly, and with thin ranks, the column moved along, their weapons feebly grasped, their horses spiritless. The soldiers, impatient of the heat, the dust, and the weather, in proportion as they were less capable of enduring toil were more ready for mutiny. All this was aggravated by the old vanity of Cæcina, and by the indolence that had of late crept over him; presuming on the excessive favor of fortune, he had abandoned himself to luxury. Perhaps he meditated perfidy, and it was part of his policy to enervate the courage of the army. Many believe that his fidelity had been shaken by the suggestions of Flavius Sabinus, who employed Rubrius Gallus as the bearer of communications intimating that the conditions of desertion would be held binding by Vespasianus. At the same time he was reminded of his hatred and jealousy of Fabius Valens. Being inferior to his rival in influence with Vitellius, he should seek to secure favor and power with the new Emperor.

100. Cæcina, having embraced Vitellius and received tokens of high distinction, left him, and sent a detachment of cavalry to occupy Cremona. It was followed by the veteran troops of the 4th, 10th, and 16th legions, by the 5th and 22nd legions, and the rear was brought up by the 21st Rapax and the 1st Italica with the veteran troops of three British legions, and a chosen body of auxiliaries. After the departure of Cæcina, Valens sent a dispatch to the army which had been under his own command with directions that it should wait for him on the road; such, he said, was his arrangement with Cæcina. Cæcina, however, being with the army in person, and consequently having greater influence, pretended that this plan had been changed, so that the gathering forces of the enemy might be met with their

whole strength. Orders were therefore given to the legions
to advance with all speed upon Cremona, while a portion
of the force was to proceed to Hostilia.⁴⁸ Cæcina himself
turned aside to Ravenna, on the pretext that he wished
to address the fleet. Soon, however, he sought the retirement of Patavium,⁴⁹ there to concert his treachery.
Lucilius Bassus, who had been promoted by Vitellius
from the command of a squadron of cavalry to be ad-
miral of the fleets at Ravenna and Misenum, failing
immediately to obtain the command of the prætorian
guard, sought to gratify his unreasonable resentment by
an atrocious act of perfidy. It cannot be certainly known
whether he carried Cæcina with him, or whether (as is
often the case, with bad men, that they are like each
other) both were actuated by the same evil motives.⁵⁰

101. The historians of the period, who during the
ascendancy of the Flavian family composed the chron-
icles of this war, have in the distorted representations of
flattery assigned as the motives of these men a regard
for peace and a love of their country. For my own part I
believe that, to say nothing of a natural fickleness and
an honor which they must have held cheap after the
betrayal of Galba, feelings of rivalry, and jealousy lest
others should outstrip them in the favor of Vitellius,
made them accomplish his ruin. Cæcina, having overtaken the legions, strove by every species of artifice to
undermine the fidelity of the centurions and soldiers,
who were devoted to Vitellius. Bassus, in making the
same attempt, experienced less difficulty, for the fleet,
remembering how recently it had served in the cause of
Otho, was ready to change its allegiance.

BOOK III

1. UNDER happier auspices and in a more loyal spirit
the Flavian leaders were discussing the plans of the campaign. They had assembled at Pœtovio,¹ the winter
quarters of the 13th legion. There they debated whether
they should blockade the passes of the Pannonian Alps
till the whole strength of their party should be gathered

in their rear, or whether it would be the more vigorous policy to close with the enemy, and to contend for the possession of Italy. Those who thought it advisable to wait for reinforcements, and to protract the campaign, dwelled on the strength and reputation of the German legion. "Vitellius," they said, "has now joined them with the flower of the British army. Our numbers are not even equal to those of the legions whom they lately defeated; and the conquered, let them talk as fiercely as they will, lose something of their courage. But if we occupy meanwhile the passes of the Alps, Mucianus will come up with the forces of the East. Vespasianus has in addition the command of the sea, his fleets, and provinces loyal to his cause, in which he may collect the vast materials for what may be called another war. A salutary delay will bring us new forces, while we shall lose nothing of what we have."

2. In answer to this, Antonius Primus, who was the most energetic promoter of the war, declared that prompt action would be advantageous to themselves, and fatal to Vitellius. "Supineness," he said, "rather than confidence has grown upon the conquerors. They are not even kept under arms or within camps. In every town of Italy, sunk in sloth, formidable only to their entertainers, they have drunk of unaccustomed pleasures with an eagerness equal to the rudeness of their former life. They have been emasculated by the circus, the theater, and the allurements of the capital, or they are worn out with sickness. Yet even to these men, if you give them time, their old vigor will return with the preparation for war. Germany, whence their strength is drawn, is not far away; Britain is separated only by a strait; the provinces of Gaul and Spain are near; on either side they can find troops, horses, tribute; they have Italy itself, and the resources of the capital, and, should they choose themselves to take the offensive, they have two fleets, and the Illyrian Sea open to them. What good then will our mountain passes do us? What will be the use of having protracted the war into another summer? Where are we to find money and supplies meanwhile? Why not rather avail ourselves of the fact that the legions of

Pannonia, which were cheated rather than vanquished, are hastening to rise again for vengeance, and that the armies of Mœsia have brought us their unimpaired strength? If you reckon the number of soldiers rather than that of legions, we have greater strength, and no vices, for our very humiliation has been most helpful to our discipline. As for the cavalry, they were not vanquished even on that day; though the fortune of war was against them, they penetrated the Vitellian lines. Two squadrons of Mœsian and Pannonian cavalry then broke through the enemy; now the united standards of sixteen squadrons will bury and overwhelm with the crash and din and storm of their onset these horses and horsemen that have forgotten how to fight. Unless anyone hinders me, I who suggest will execute the plan. You, whose fortune never suffered a reverse, may keep back the legions; the light cohorts will be enough for me. Before long you will hear that Italy has been opened, and the power of Vitellius shaken. You will be delighted to follow, and to tread in the footsteps of victory."

3. With flashing eyes, and in the fierce tones that might be most widely heard (for the centurions and some of the common soldiers had intruded themselves into the deliberations), he poured out such a torrent of these and similar words that he carried away even the cautious and prudent, while the general voice of the multitude extolled him as the one man, the one general in the army, and spurned the inaction of the others. He had raised this reputation for himself at the very first assembly, when, after Vespasian's letters had been read, he had not, like many, used ambiguous language, on which he might put this or that construction as might serve his purpose. It was seen that he openly committed himself to the cause, and he had therefore greater weight with the soldiers, as being associated with them in what was either their crime or their glory.

4. Next to Primus in influence was Cornelius Fuscus, the procurator. He also had been accustomed to inveigh mercilessly against Vitellius, and had thus left himself no hope in the event of defeat. Tampius Flavianus, disposed to caution by natural temperament and advanced

years, excited in the soldiers a suspicion that he still remembered his relationship to Vitellius; and as he had fled when the movement in the legions began, and had then voluntarily returned, it was believed that he had sought an opportunity for treachery. Flavianus indeed had left Pannonia, and had entered Italy, and was out of the way of danger, when his desire for revolution urged him to resume the title of legate, and to take part in the civil strife. Cornelius Fuscus had advised him to this course, not that he needed the talents of Flavianus, but wishing that a consular name might clothe with its high prestige the very first movements of the party.

5. Still, that the passage into Italy might be safe and advantageous, directions were sent to Aponius Saturninus to hasten up with the armies of Mœsia. That the provinces might not be exposed without defense to the barbarian tribes, the princes of the Sarmatæ Iazyges,[2] who had in their hands the government of that nation, were enrolled in the army. These chiefs also offered the service of their people, and its force of cavalry, their only effective troops; but the offer was declined, lest in the midst of civil strife they should attempt some hostile enterprise, or, influenced by higher offers from other quarters, should cast off all sense of right and duty. Sido and Italicus, kings of the Suebi, were brought over to the cause. Their loyalty to the Roman people was of long standing, and their nation was more faithful than the other to any trust reposed in them. On the flank of the army were posted some auxiliaries, for Rhætia was hostile, Porcius Septiminus, the procurator, remaining incorruptibly faithful to Vitellius. Accordingly, Sextilius Felix, with Aurius' horse, eight cohorts, and the native levies of Noricum, was sent to occupy the bank of the river Ænus,[3] which flows between Rhætia and Noricum. Neither hazarded an engagement, and the fate of the two parties was decided elsewhere.

6. Antonius, as he hurried with the veteran soldiers of the cohorts and part of the cavalry to invade Italy, was accompanied by Arrius Varus, an energetic soldier. Service under Corbulo, and successes in Armenia, had gained for him this reputation; yet it was generally said

that in secret conversations with Nero he had calumniated Corbulo's high qualities. The favor thus infamously acquired made him a centurion of the first rank, yet the illgotten prosperity of the moment afterward turned to his destruction. Primus and Varus, having occupied Aquileia, were joyfully welcomed in the neighborhood, and in the towns of Opitergium[4] and Altinum.[5] At Altinum a force was left to oppose the Ravenna fleet, the defection of which from Vitellius was not yet known. They next attached to their party Patavium[6] and Ateste.[7] There they learned that three cohorts belonging to Vitellius, and the Sebonian horse had taken up a position at the Forum Alieni,[8] where they had thrown a bridge across the river. It was determined to seize the opportunity of attacking this force, unprepared as it was; for this fact had likewise been communicated. Coming upon them at dawn, they killed many before they could arm. Orders had been given to slay but few, and to constrain the rest by fear to transfer their allegiance. Some indeed at once surrendered, but the greater part broke down the bridge, and thus cut off the advance of the pursuing enemy.

7. When this success became known, two legions, the 7th (Galba's) and the 18th (the Gemina), finding the campaign opening in favor of the Flavians, repaired with alacrity to Patavium under the command of Vedius Aquila the legate.[9] A few days were there taken for rest, and Minucius Justus, prefect of the camp in the 7th legion, who ruled with more strictness than a civil war will permit, was withdrawn from the exasperated soldiery, and sent to Vespasianus. An act that had been long desired was taken by a flattering construction for more than it was worth, when Antonius gave orders that the statues of Galba, which had been thrown down during the troubles of the times, should be restored in all the towns. It would, he supposed, reflect honor on the cause if it were thought that they had been friendly to Galba's rule, and that his party was again rising into strength.

8. The next question was, what place should be selected as the seat of war. Verona seemed the most eligible, surrounded as it was with open plains, suitable for the action of cavalry, in which they were very

strong. At the same time it was thought that in wresting from Vitellius a colony so rich in resources there would be both profit and glory. They secured Vicetia,[10] by simply passing through it. Though in itself a small gain, for the town is but of moderate strength, it was considered an important advantage when they reflected that in this town Cæcina was born, and that the general of the enemy had lost his native place. The people of Verona were a valuable aid; they served the cause by the example of their zeal and by their wealth, and the army thus occupied a position between Rhætia and the Julian Alps. It was to cut off all passage at this point from the armies of Germany that they had barred this route. All this was done either without the knowledge, or against the commands of Vespasianus. He gave orders that the army should halt at Aquileia and there await Mucianus; and these orders he supported by the argument, that as Egypt, which commanded the corn supplies, and the revenues of the wealthiest provinces were in his hands, the army of Vitellius would be compelled to capitulate from the want of pay and provisions. Mucianus in frequent letters advised the same policy; a victory that should cost neither blood nor tears, and other objects of the kind, were his pretexts; but in truth he was greedy of glory, and anxious to keep the whole credit of the war to himself. Owing, however, to the vast distances, the advice came only after the matter was decided.

9. Then Antonius by a sudden movement fell upon the outposts of the enemy, and made trial of their courage in a slight skirmish, the combatants separating on equal terms. Soon afterward, Cæcina strongly fortified a camp between Hostilia, a village belonging to Verona, and the marshes of the river Tartarus,[11] where his position was secure, as his rear was covered by the river, and his flank by intervening marshes. Had he only been loyal, those two legions, which had not been joined by the army of Mœsia, might have been crushed by the united strength of the Vitellians, or driven back and compelled to evacuate Italy in a disgraceful retreat. Cæcina, however, by various delays betrayed to the enemy

the early opportunities of the campaign, assailing by
letters those whom it was easy to drive out by force of
arms, until by his envoys he settled the conditions of
his treachery. In this interval Aponius Saturninus came
up with the 7th legion (Claudius'). This legion was
commanded by the tribune Vipstanus Messalla, a man
of illustrious family,¹² himself highly distinguished, the
only man who had brought into that conflict an honest
purpose. To this army, which was far from equaling the
forces of Vitellius (it in fact consisted of three legions),
Cæcina dispatched a letter reproaching them with rashness in again drawing the sword in a vanquished cause.
At the same time he extolled the valor of the German
army; of Vitellius he made but some slight and common-
place mention without any abuse of Vespasianus. Certainly he said nothing which could either seduce or terrify
the enemy. The leaders of the Flavian party, omitting all
apology for their former fortune, at once took up a tone
of high praise of Vespasianus, of confidence in their
cause, of security as to their army, and of hostility to
Vitellius, while hopes were held out to the tribunes and
centurions of retaining the privileges which Vitellius had
granted them, and Cæcina was himself encouraged in
no ambiguous terms to change sides. These letters read
to the assembled army increased their confidence; for
Cæcina had written in a humble strain, as if he feared
to offend Vespasianus, while their own generals had used
contemptuous language, meant, it would seem, to insult
Vitellius.

10. On the subsequent arrival of two legions, the 3rd
commanded by Dillius Aponianus, the 8th by Numisius
Lupus, it was resolved to make a demonstration of
their strength, and to surround Verona with military
lines. It so happened that Galba's legion had had their
work allotted to them on that side of the lines which
faced the enemy, and that some of the allied cavalry
appearing in the distance were taken for the enemy,
and excited a groundless panic. They flew to arms, and
as the rage of the soldiers at the supposed treachery fell
upon Tampius Flavianus, not from any proof of his guilt,
but because he had been long unpopular, they clamored

TACITUS

for his death in a very whirlwind of passion, vociferating
that he was the kinsman of Vitellius, that he had betrayed Otho, that he had embezzled the donative. He
could get no opportunity of defending himself, even
though he stretched out his hands in entreaty, repeatedly
prostrating himself on the ground, his garments torn, his
breast and features convulsed with sobs. This very conduct provoked afresh these furious men, for fear so excessive seemed to argue a consciousness of guilt. Aponius
was clamored down by the shouts of the soldiers, when
he attempted to address them; everyone else was repulsed with noisy cries. To Antonius alone the soldiers'
ears were open; for he had eloquence, the art of soothing an angry crowd, and personal influence. As the
mutiny grew fiercer, and the soldiers went on from abuse
and taunts to use their hands and their weapons, he
ordered that Flavianus should be put in irons. The soldiers saw what a mockery it was, and pushing aside
those who were guarding the tribunal, were about to
commit the most outrageous violence. Antonius threw
himself in the way with his sword drawn, protesting that
he would die either by the soldiers' hands or by his own;
whenever he saw anyone who was known to him, or
who was distinguished by any military decoration, he
summoned him by name to his assistance. Then he
turned to the standards, and prayed to the gods of war,
that they would inspire the armies of the enemy, rather
than his own, with such madness and such strife. So the
mutiny began to abate, and at the close of the day the
men dispersed to their tents. The same night Flavianus
set out, and being met by letters from Vespasianus, was
relieved from his perilous position.

11. The legions had caught the infection of mutiny,
and next assailed Aponius Saturninus, legate of the army
of Mœsia,[13] this time the more furiously because their
rage broke out, not as before, when they were wearied
with labor and military toils, but at midday. Some letters had been published, which Saturninus was believed
to have written to Vitellius. If once they had emulated
each other in valor and obedience, so now there was a
rivalry in insubordination and insolence, till they clam-

ored as violently for the execution of Aponius as they had for that of Flavianus. The legions of Mœsia recalled how they had aided the vengeance of the Pannonian army, while the soldiers of Pannonia, as if they were absolved by the mutiny of others, took a delight in repeating their fault. They hastened to the gardens in which Saturninus was passing his time, and it was not the efforts of Antonius Primus, Aponianus, and Messalla, though they exerted themselves to the uttermost, that saved him, so much as the obscurity of the hiding place in which he concealed himself, for he was hidden in the furnace of some baths that happened to be out of use. In a short time he gave up his lictors, and retired to Patavium. After the departure of the two men of consular rank, all power and authority over the two armies centered in Antonius alone, his colleagues giving way to him, and the soldiers being strongly biased in his favor. There were those who believed that both these mutinies were set on foot by the intrigues of Antonius, in order that he might engross all the prizes of the war.

12. Nor indeed was there less restlessness among the partisans of Vitellius, who were distracted by yet more fatal dissensions, springing, not from the suspicions of the common men, but from the treachery of the generals. Lucilius Bassus,[14] prefect of the Ravenna fleet, finding that the troops wavered in purpose, from the fact that many were natives of Dalmatia and Pannonia, provinces held for Vespasianus, had attached them to the Flavian party. Nighttime was chosen for accomplishing the treason, because then, unknown to all the rest, the ringleaders alone might assemble at headquarters. Bassus, moved by shame, or perhaps by fear, awaited the issue in his house. The captains of the triremes rushed with a great outcry on the images of Vitellius; a few, who attempted to resist, were cut down; the great majority, with the usual love of change, were ready to join Vespasianus. Then Bassus came forward and openly sanctioned the movement. The fleet appointed Cornelius Fuscus to be prefect, and he hastened to join them. Lucilius was put under honorable arrest, and conveyed as far as Atria[15] by the Liburnian ships; there he was thrown in-

to prison by Vibennius Rufinus, prefect of a squadron of cavalry, which was there in garrison. His chains, however, were immediately struck off on the interference of Hormus, one of the Emperor's freedmen, for he too ranked among the generals.

13. On the revolt of the fleet becoming known, Cæcina called together to headquarters, which he purposely selected as being the most retired part of the camp, the chief centurions and some few soldiers, while the rest were dispersed on various military duties. Then he extolled the valor of Vespasianus, and the strength of his party; he told them that the fleet had changed sides, that they were straitened for supplies, that Gaul and Spain were against them, that in the capital there was nothing on which to rely, thus making the worst of everything that concerned Vitellius. Then, the conspirators present setting the example, and the rest being paralyzed by the strangeness of the proceeding, he made them swear allegiance to Vespasianus. At the same time the images of Vitellius were torn down, and persons were dispatched to convey the intelligence to Antonius. But when this treason became noised abroad throughout the camp, when the soldiers, hurrying back to headquarters, saw the name of Vespasianus written on the colors, and the images of Vitellius thrown upon the ground, first there was a gloomy silence, then all their rage burst out at once. "What," they cried, "has the glory of the army of Germany fallen so low that without a battle, even without a wound, they should yield up hands ready bound and arms resigned to surrender? What legions indeed are these against us? Only the conquered. The 1st and the 12th, the sole strength of the Othonian army, are not there, and even them we routed and crushed on these very plains, only that so many thousands of armed men, like a herd of slaves for sale, might be given as a present to the exile Antonius. As though the adhesion of one fleet could be worth eight legions! So it pleases Bassus and Cæcina, after robbing the Emperor of palaces, gardens, and money, to rob the soldiers of their Emperor. But we, who have seen nothing of toil and bloodshed, we, who must be contemptible

even to the Flavians, what shall we answer to those who shall ask us of our victories and our defeats?"

14. Joining one and all in these cries, by which each expressed his own vexation, they proceeded, following the lead of the 5th legion, to replace the images of Vitellius, and to put Cæcina in irons. They elected to the command Fabius Fabullus, legate of the 5th legion, and Cassius Longus, prefect of the camp; they massacred the soldiers from three Liburnian ships, who happened to fall in their way, but who were perfectly ignorant and innocent of these proceedings; they then abandoned the camp, and, after breaking down the bridge, fell back on Hostilia, and thence on Cremona, in order to effect a junction with the two legions, the 1st Italica and the 21st Rapax, which, with a portion of the cavalry, Cæcina had sent on to occupy Cremona.

15. On this becoming known to Antonius, he determined to attack the hostile armies, while they were still distracted in feeling and divided in strength, before the generals could recover their authority, and the soldiers their subordination along with that confidence which would spring from the junction of the legions. He concluded indeed that Fabius Valens had left the capital, and would hasten his march, on hearing of the treason of Cæcina; and Fabius was loyal to Vitellius, and not without some military skill. At the same time he dreaded the approach of a vast body of Germans by way of Rhætia. Vitellius had also summoned reinforcements from Britain, Gaul, and Spain, whose arms would have wasted like a widespread pestilence, had not Antonius, fearful of this very danger, hurried on an engagement, and thus secured his victory. He reached Bedriacum with his whole army in two days' march from Verona. The next day, keeping the legions to fortify the position, he sent the auxiliary infantry into the territories of Cremona, ostensibly to collect supplies, really to imbue the soldiery with a taste for the spoils of civil war. He himself advanced with four thousand cavalry as far as the eighth milestone from Bedriacum, in order that they might plunder with greater freedom. The scouts, as usual, took a wider range.

385

16. It was almost eleven o'clock, when a horseman arrived at full speed with the news that the enemy was approaching, that a small body was moving in front, but that the stir and noise could be heard far and wide. While Antonius was deliberating as to what was to be done, Arrius Varus, eager to do his best, charged with the bravest of the cavalry, and drove back the Vitellians, inflicting upon them some slight loss; as more came up, the fortune of the day changed, and those who had been most eager in the pursuit found themselves last in the flight. This rash act did not originate with Antonius; he anticipated in fact what actually happened. He now urged his soldiers to enter on the battle with a good heart; he then drew off the squadrons of his cavalry to the two flanks, leaving in the midst an open space in which to receive Varus and his troopers; the legions were ordered to arm themselves, signals were made over the country that every man should leave plundering, and join the battle at the nearest point. Meanwhile the terror-stricken Varus plunged into the disordered ranks of his friends, and brought a panic with him. The fresh troops were driven back along with the wounded fugitives, confused by their own alarm and by the difficulties of the road.

17. In the midst of this panic Antonius omitted nothing that a self-possessed commander or a most intrepid soldier could do. He threw himself before the terrified fugitives, he held back those who were giving way, and wherever the struggle was hardest, wherever there was a gleam of hope, there he was with his ready skill, his bold hand, his encouraging voice, easily recognized by the enemy, and a conspicuous object to his own men. At last he was carried to such a pitch of excitement that he transfixed with a lance a fleeing standard bearer, and then, seizing the standard, turned it toward the enemy. Touched by the reproach, a few troopers, not more than a hundred in number, made a stand. The locality favored them, for the road was at that point particularly narrow, while the bridge over the stream which crossed it had been broken down, and the stream itself, with its varying channel and its precipitous banks, checked

their flight. It was this necessity, or a happy chance, that restored the fallen fortunes of the party. Forming themselves into strong and close ranks, they received the attack of the Vitellians, who were now imprudently scattered. These were at once overthrown. Antonius pursued those that fled, and crushed those that encountered him. Then came the rest of his troops, who, as they were severally disposed, plundered, made prisoners, or seized on weapons and horses. Roused by the shouts of triumph, those who had lately been scattered in flight over the fields hastened to share in the victory.

18. At the fourth milestone from Cremona glittered the standards of two legions, the Italica and the Rapax, which had been advanced as far as that point during the success achieved by the first movement of their cavalry. But when fortune changed, they would not open their ranks, nor receive the fugitives, nor advance and themselves attack an enemy now exhausted by so protracted a pursuit and conflict. Vanquished by accident, these men had never in their success valued their general as much as they now in disaster felt his absence. The victorious cavalry charged the wavering line; the tribune Vipstanus Messalla followed with the auxiliary troops from Mœsia, whom, though hurriedly brought up, long service had made as good soldiers as the legionaries. The horse and foot, thus mixed together, broke through the line of the legions. The near neighborhood of the fortifications of Cremona, while it gave more hope of escape, diminished the vigor of their resistance.

19. Antonius did not press forward, for he thought of the fatigue and the wounds with which a battle so hard fought, notwithstanding its successful termination, must have disabled his cavalry and their horses. As the shadows of evening deepened the whole strength of the Flavian army came up. They advanced amid heaps of dead and the traces of recent slaughter, and, as if the war was over, demanded that they should advance to Cremona, and receive the capitulation of the vanquished party or take the place by storm. This was the motive alleged, and it sounded well, but what everyone said to himself was this: "The colony, situated as it is on

level ground, may be taken by assault. If we attack under cover of darkness, we shall be at least as bold, and shall enjoy more license in plunder. If we wait for the light, we shall be met with entreaties for peace, and in return for our toil and our wounds shall receive only the empty satisfaction of clemency and praise, but the wealth of Cremona will go into the purses of the legates and the prefects. The soldiers have the plunder of a city that is stormed, the generals of one which capitulates." The centurions and tribunes were spurned away; that no man's voice might be heard, the troops clashed their weapons together, ready to break through all discipline, unless they were led as they wished.

20. Antonius then made his way into the companies. When his presence and personal authority had restored silence, he declared, "I would not snatch their glory or their reward from those who have deserved them so well. Yet there is a division of duties between the army and its generals. Eagerness for battle becomes the soldiers, but generals serve the cause by forethought, by counsel, by delay oftener than by temerity. As I promoted your victory to the utmost of my power by my sword and by my personal exertions, so now I must help you by prudence and by counsel, the qualities which belong peculiarly to a general. What you will have to encounter is indeed perfectly plain. There will be the darkness, the strange localities of the town, the enemy inside the walls, and all possible facilities for ambuscades. Even if the gates were wide open, we ought not to enter the place, except we had first reconnoitered it, and in the daytime. Shall we set about storming the town when we have no means of seeing where the ground is level, what is the height of the walls, whether the city is to be assailed by our artillery and javelins, or by siege works and covered approaches?" He then turned to individual soldiers, asking them whether they had brought with them their axes and spades and whatever else is used when towns are to be stormed. On their admitting that they had not done so, "Can any hands," he answered, "break through and undermine walls with swords and lances? And if it should be found necessary to throw up an embankment

and to shelter ourselves under mantlets and hurdles, shall we stand baffled like a thoughtless mob, marveling at the height of the towers and at the enemy's defenses? Shall we not rather, by delaying one night, till our artillery and engines come up, take with us a strength that must prevail?" At the same time he sent the sutlers and camp followers with the freshest of the cavalry to Bedriacum to fetch supplies and whatever else they needed.

21. The soldiers, however, were impatient, and a mutiny had almost broken out, when some cavalry, who had advanced to the very walls of Cremona, seized some stragglers from the town, from whose information it was ascertained that the six legions of Vitellius and the entire army which had been quartered at Hostilia had on that very day marched a distance of thirty miles, and having heard of the defeat of their comrades, were preparing for battle, and would soon be coming up. This alarm opened the ears that had before been deaf to their general's advice. The 13th legion was ordered to take up its position on the raised causeway of the Via Postumia, supported on the left by the 7th (Galba's) which was posted in the plain, next came the 7th (Claudius'), defended in front by a field ditch, such being the character of the ground. On the right was the 8th legion, drawn up in an open space, and then the 3rd, whose ranks were divided by some thick brushwood. Such was the arrangement of the eagles and the standards. The soldiers were mingled in the darkness as accident had determined. The prætorian colors were close to the 3rd legion; the auxiliary infantry were stationed on the wings; the cavalry covered the flanks and the rear. Sido and Italicus, the Suebian chieftains, with a picked body of their countrymen, maneuvered in the van.

22. It would have been the best policy for the army of Vitellius to rest at Cremona, and, with strength recruited by food and repose, to attack and crush the next day an enemy exhausted by cold and hunger; but now, in need of a leader, and having no settled plan, they came into collision about nine o'clock at night with the Flavian troops, who stood ready, and in order of battle. Respect-

ing the disposition of the Vitellian army, disordered as
it was by its fury and by the darkness, I would not venture to speak positively. Some, however, have related
that on the right wing was the 4th legion (the Macedonian); that the 5th and 15th, with the veterans of
three British legions (the 9th, 2nd, and 20th), formed
the center, while the left wing was made up of the 1st,
the 16th, and the 22nd. Men of the legions Rapax and
Italica were mingled with all the companies. The cavalry
and the auxiliaries chose their position themselves.
Throughout the night the battle raged in many forms,
indecisive and fierce, destructive first to one side, then
to the other. Courage, strength, even the eye with its
keenest sight, were of no avail. Both armies fought with
the same weapons; the watchword, continually asked,
became known; the colors were confused together, as
parties of combatants snatched them from the enemy,
and hurried them in this or that direction. The 7th legion, recently levied by Galba, was the hardest pressed.
Six centurions of the first rank were killed, and some of
the standards taken; but the eagle was saved by Atilius
Verus, the centurion of the first company, who, after
making a great slaughter among the enemy, at last fell.

23. The line was supported, as it began to waver, by
Antonius, who brought up the prætorians. They took up
the conflict, repulsed the enemy, and were then themselves repulsed. The troops of Vitellius had collected their
artillery on the raised causeway, where there was a free
and open space for the discharge of the missiles, which
at first had been scattered at random, and had struck
against the trees without injury to the enemy. An engine
of remarkable size, belonging to the 15th legion, was
crushing the hostile ranks with huge stones, and would
have spread destruction far and wide, had not two soldiers ventured on a deed of surpassing bravery. Disguis-
ing themselves with shields snatched from the midst
of the carnage, they cut the ropes and springs of the
engine. They were instantly slain, and their names have
consequently been lost; but the fact is undoubted. Fortune favored neither side, till at a late hour of the night
the moon rose and showed, but showed deceptively, both

390

armies. The light, however, shining from behind, favored the Flavians. With them a lengthened shadow fell from men and horses, and the enemy's missiles, incorrectly aimed at what seemed the substance, fell short, while the Vitellians, who had the light shining on their faces, were unconsciously exposed to an enemy who were, so to speak, concealed while they aimed.

24. As soon as Antonius could recognize his men and be recognized by them, he sought to kindle their courage, striving to shame some with his reproaches, stirring many with praise and encouragement, and all with hopes and promises. "Why," he demanded of the legions of Pannonia, "have you again taken up arms? There is the field where you may wipe out the stain of past disgrace, and redeem your honor." Then turning to the troops of Mœsia, he appealed to them as the authors and originators of the war. "Idly," he said "have you challenged the Vitellians with threatening words, if you cannot abide their attack or even their looks." So he spoke to each as he approached them. The 3rd legion he addressed at greater length, reminding them of old and recent achievements, how under Marcus Antonius they had defeated the Parthians, under Corbulo the Armenians, and had lately discomfited the Sarmatians. Then angrily turning to the prætorians, "Clowns," said he, "unless you are victorious, what other general, what other camp will receive you? There are your colors and your arms; defeat is death, for disgrace you have exhausted." A shout was raised on all sides, and the soldiers of the 3rd legion saluted, as is the custom in Syria, the rising sun.

25. A vague rumor thus arose, or was intentionally suggested by the general, that Mucianus had arrived, and that the two armies had exchanged salutations. The men then charged as confidently as if they had been strengthened by fresh reinforcements, while the enemy's array was now less compact; for, as there was no one to command, it was now contracted, now extended, as the courage or fear of individual soldiers might prompt. Antonius, seeing that they gave way, charged them with a heavy column; the loose ranks were at once broken, and,

entangled as they were among their wagons and artillery, could not be reformed. The conquerors, in the eagerness of pursuit, dispersed themselves over the entire line of road. The slaughter that followed was made particularly memorable through the killing of a father by his son. I will record the incident with the names, on the authority of Vipstanus Messalla. Julius Mansuetus, a Spaniard, enlisting in the legion Rapax, had left at home a son of tender age. The lad grew up to manhood, and was enrolled by Galba in the 7th legion. Now chancing to meet his father, he brought him to the ground with a wound, and, as he rifled his dying foe, recognized him, and was himself recognized. Clasping the expiring man in his arms, in piteous accents he implored the spirit of his father to be propitious to him, and not to turn from him with loathing as from a parricide. "This guilt," he said, "is shared by all; how small a part of a civil war is a single soldier!" With these words he raised the body, opened a grave, and discharged the last duties for his father. This was noticed by those who were on the spot, then by many others; astonishment and indignation ran through the whole army, and they cursed this most horrible war. Yet as eagerly as ever they stripped the bodies of slaughtered kinsfolk, connections, and brothers. They talk of an impious act having been done, and they do it themselves.

26. When they reached Cremona, a fresh work of vast difficulty presented itself. During the war with Otho the legions of Germany had formed their camp round the walls of the city, round this camp had drawn an entrenchment, and had again strengthened these defenses. At this sight the victorious army hesitated, while the generals doubted what orders they should give. To attempt an assault with troops exhausted by the toil of a day and a night would be difficult, and with no proper reserves might be perilous. Should they return to Bedriacum, the fatigue of so long a march would be insupportable, and their victory would result in nothing. To entrench a camp with the enemy so close at hand would be dangerous, as by a sudden sortie they might cause confusion among them while dispersed and busied with

the work. Above all, they were afraid of their own soldiers, who were more patient of danger than delay. Cautious measures they disliked; their rashness inspired them with hope, and eagerness for plunder outweighed all the horrors of carnage, wounds, and bloodshed.

27. Antonius himself was this way inclined, and he ordered the entrenched camp to be invested. At first they fought from a distance with arrows and stones, the Flavians suffering most, as the enemy's missiles were aimed at them from a superior height. Antonius then assigned to each legion the attack on some portion of the entrenchments, and on one particular gate, seeking by this division of labor to distinguish the cowardly from the brave, and to stimulate his men by an honorable rivalry. The 3rd and 7th legions took up a position close to the road from Bedriacum; more to the right of the entrenchments were stationed the 8th and the 7th (Claudius'). The 13th were carried by the impetuosity of their attack as far as the gate looking toward Brixia.[16] There ensued a little delay, while from the neighboring fields some were collecting spades and pickaxes, others hooks and ladders. Then raising their shields over their heads, they advanced to the rampart in a dense *testudo*.[17] Both used the arts of Roman warfare; the Vitellians rolled down ponderous stones, and drove spears and long poles into the broken and tottering *testudo*, till the dense array of shields was loosened, and the ground was strewn with a vast number of lifeless and mangled bodies.

28. Some hesitation had shown itself, when the generals, seeing that the weary troops would not listen to what seemed to them unmeaning encouragement, pointed to Cremona. Whether this was, as Messalla relates, the device of Hormus, or whether Gaius Plinius[18] is the better authority when he charges it upon Antonius, I cannot easily determine. All I can say is this, that neither in Antonius nor in Hormus would this foulest of crimes have been a degeneracy from the character of their former lives. Wounds or bloodshed no longer kept the men back from undermining the rampart and battering the gates. Supported on the shoulders of comrades, and forming a second *testudo*, they clambered up and seized

the weapons and even the hands of the enemy. The unhurt and the wounded, the half-dead and the dying, were mingled together with every incident of slaughter and death in every form.

29. The fiercest struggle was maintained by the 3rd and 7th legions, and Antonius in person with some chosen auxiliaries concentrated his efforts on the same point. The Vitellians, unable to resist the combined and resolute attack, and finding that their missiles glided off the *testudo*, at last threw the engine itself on the assailants; for a moment it broke and overwhelmed those on whom it fell, but it drew after it in its fall the battlements and upper part of the rampart. At the same time an adjoining tower yielded to the volleys of stones, and, while the 7th legion in wedgelike array was endeavoring to force an entrance, the 3rd broke down the gate with axes and swords. All authors are agreed that Gaius Volusius, a soldier of the 3rd legion, entered first. Beating down all who opposed him, he mounted the rampart, waved his hand, and shouted aloud that the camp was taken. The rest of the legion burst in, while the troops of Vitellius were seized with panic, and threw themselves from the rampart. The entire space between the camp and the walls of Cremona was filled with slain.

30. Difficulties of another kind presented themselves in the lofty walls of the town, its stone towers, its iron-barred gates, in the garrison who stood brandishing their weapons, in its numerous population devoted to the interests of Vitellius, and in the vast conflux from all parts of Italy which had assembled at the fair regularly held at that time. The besieged found a source of strength in these large numbers; the assailants an incentive in the prospect of booty. Antonius gave orders that fire should instantly be set to the finest buildings without the city, to see whether the inhabitants of Cremona might not be induced by the loss of their property to transfer their allegiance. Some houses near the walls, which overtopped the fortifications, he filled with the bravest of his soldiers, who, by hurling beams, tiles, and flaming missiles, dislodged the defenders from the ramparts

31. The legions now began to form themselves into a

testudo, and the other troops to discharge volleys of stones and darts, when the courage of the Vitellians began to flag. The higher their rank, the more readily they succumbed to fortune, fearing that when Cremona had fallen quarter could no longer be expected, and that all the fury of the conqueror would be turned, not on the penniless crowd, but on the tribunes and centurions, by whose slaughter something was to be gained. The common soldiers, careless of the future and safer in their obscurity, still held out. Roaming through the streets or concealed in the houses, they would not sue for peace even when they had abandoned the contest. The principal officers of the camp removed the name and images of Vitellius; Cæcina, who was still in confinement, they released from his chains, imploring him to plead their cause. When he haughtily rejected their suit, they entreated him with tears; and it was indeed the last aggravation of misery that many valiant men should invoke the aid of a traitor. Then they displayed from the walls the olive branches and chaplets of suppliants, and when Antonius had ordered that the discharge of missiles should cease, they brought out the eagles and standards. Then followed, with eyes bent on the ground, a dismal array of unarmed men. The conquerors had gathered round; at first they heaped reproaches on them and pointed at them their weapons; then seeing how they offered their cheeks to insulting blows, how, with all their high spirit departed, they submitted, as vanquished men, to every indignity, it suddenly occurred to their recollection that these were the very soldiers who but shortly before had used with moderation their victory at Bedriacum. Yet, when Cæcina the consul, conspicuous in his robes of state and with his train of lictors, came forward thrusting aside the crowd, the victors were fired with indignation, and reproached him with his tyranny, his cruelty, and, so hateful are such crimes, even with his treason. Antonius checked them, gave him an escort, and sent him to Vespasianus.

32. Meanwhile the population of Cremona was roughly handled by the soldiers, who were just beginning a massacre, when their fury was mitigated by the en-

treaties of the generals. Antonius summoned them to an
assembly, extolled the conquerors, spoke kindly to the
conquered, but said nothing either way of Cremona.
Over and above the innate love of plunder, there was an
old feud which made the army bent on the destruction
of the inhabitants. It was generally believed that in the
war with Otho, as well as in the present, they had supported the cause of Vitellius. Afterward, when the 13th
legion had been left to build an amphitheater, with the
characteristic insolence of a city population, they had
wantonly provoked and insulted them. The ill feeling
had been aggravated by the gladiatorial show exhibited
there by Cæcina, by the circumstance that their city was
now for the second time the seat of war, and by the fact
that they had supplied the Vitellians with provisions in
the field, and that some of their women, taken by party
zeal into the battle, had there been slain. The occurrence
of the fair filled the colony, rich as it always was, with
an appearance of still greater wealth. The other generals
were unnoticed; Antonius from his success and high
reputation was observed of all. He had hastened to the
baths to wash off the blood; and when he found fault
with the temperature of the water, an answer was heard,
"that it would soon be warm enough." Thus the words
of a slave brought on him the whole odium of having
given the signal for firing the town, which was indeed
already in flames.

33. Forty thousand armed men burst into Cremona,
and with them a body of sutlers and camp followers,
yet more numerous and yet more abandoned to lust and
cruelty. Neither age nor rank were any protection from
indiscriminate slaughter and violation. Aged men and
women past their prime, worthless as booty, were
dragged about in wanton insult. Did a grown-up maiden
or boy of marked beauty fall in their way, they were
torn in pieces by the violent hands of ravishers; and in
the end the destroyers themselves were provoked into
mutual slaughter. Men, as they carried off for themselves
coin or temple offerings of massive gold, were cut down
by others of superior strength. Some, scorning what met
the eye, searched for hidden wealth, and dug up buried

treasures, applying the scourge and the torture to the owners. In their hands were flaming torches, which, as soon as they had carried out the spoil, they wantonly hurled into the gutted houses and plundered temples. In an army which included such varieties of language and character, an army comprising Roman citizens, allies, and foreigners, there was every kind of lust, each man had a law of his own, and nothing was forbidden. For four days Cremona satisfied the plunderers. When all things else, sacred and profane, were settling down into the flames, the temple of Mefitis[19] outside the walls alone remained standing, saved by its situation or by divine interposition.

34. Such was the end of Cremona, 286 years after its foundation. It was built in the consulship of Tiberius Sempronius Gracchus and Publius Cornelius Scipio,[20] when Hannibal was threatening Italy, as a protection against the Gauls from beyond the Po, or against any other sudden invader from the Alps. From the number of settlers, the conveniences afforded by the rivers, the fertility of the soil, and the many connections and intermarriages formed with neighboring nations, it grew and flourished, unharmed by foreign enemies, though most unfortunate in civil wars. Ashamed of the atrocious deed, and aware of the detestation which it was inspiring, Antonius issued a proclamation that no one should detain in captivity a citizen of Cremona. The spoil indeed had been rendered valueless to the soldiers by a general agreement throughout Italy, which rejected with loathing the purchase of such slaves. A massacre then began; when this was known, the prisoners were secretly ransomed by their friends and relatives. The remaining inhabitants soon returned to Cremona; the temples and squares were restored by the munificence of the burghers, and Vespasianus gave his exhortations.

35. The soil poisoned with blood forbade the enemy to remain long by the ruins of the buried city. They advanced to the third milestone, and gathered the dispersed and panic-stricken Vitellians round their proper standards. The vanquished legions were then scattered throughout Illyricum; for civil war was not over, and

they might play a doubtful part. Messengers carrying news of the victory were then dispatched to Britain and to Spain. Julius Calenus, a tribune, was sent to Gaul, and Alpinius Montanus, prefect of a cohort, to Germany; as the one was an Æduan, the other a Trever, and both had been Vitellians, they would be a proof of the success. At the same time the passes of the Alps were occupied with troops, for it was suspected that Germany was arming itself to support Vitellius.

36. A few days after the departure of Cæcina, Vitellius had hurried Fabius Valens to the seat of war, and was now seeking to hide his apprehensions from himself by indulgence. He made no military preparation; he did not seek to invigorate the soldiers by encouraging speeches or warlike exercises; he did not keep himself before the eyes of the people. Buried in the shades of his gardens, like those sluggish animals which, if you supply them with food, lie motionless and torpid, he had dismissed with the same forgetfulness the past, the present, and the future. While he thus lay wasting his powers in sloth among the woods of Aricia,[21] he was startled by the treachery of Lucilius Bassus and the defection of the fleet at Ravenna. Then came the news about Cæcina, and he heard with a satisfaction mingled with distress, first, that he had revolted, and then, that he had been put in irons by the army. In the dull soul joy was more powerful than apprehension. In great exultation he returned to Rome, and before a crowded assembly of the people heaped praises on the dutiful obedience of the soldiers. He ordered Publilius Sabinus, prefect of the prætorian guard, to be thrown into prison because of his friendship with Cæcina, and substituted in his place Alfenus Varus.[22]

37. He then addressed the Senate in a speech of studied grandiloquence, and was extolled by the senators with elaborate adulation. A savage resolution against Cæcina was moved by Lucius Vitellius; the rest affected indignation at the idea that a consul had betrayed the state, a general his Emperor, a man loaded with wealth so vast and honors so numerous his benefactor, and seemed to deplore the wrongs of Vitellius, while they ut-

tered their private griefs. Not a word from any one of them disparaged the Flavian leaders; they censured the delusion and recklessness of the armies, and with a prudent circumlocution avoided the name of Vespasianus. A man was found who, while all regarded with great contempt both giver and receiver, wormed himself by flattery into the one day of office which remained to complete the consulate of Cæcina. On the last day of October Rosius Regulus both assumed and resigned the office. The learned remarked that never before had a new consul been elected without a formal act of deprivation and the passing of a law. Before this indeed Caninius Rebilus had been consul for a single day during the dictatorship of, Gaius Cæsar,[23] when the prizes of the civil war had to be enjoyed in haste.

38. At this time the murder of Junius Blæsus[24] obtained an infamous notoriety. Of this act I have heard the following account. Vitellius, who was suffering from severe illness, observed from the Servilian Gardens[25] a neighboring turret brilliantly illuminated throughout the night. Inquiring the cause, he was told that Cæcina Tuscus[26] was entertaining a large party, of whom Junius Blæsus was the most distinguished. Other particulars were given with much exaggeration about the splendor of the banquet and the unrestrained gaiety of the guests. There were persons who charged Tuscus and his guests, and Blæsus more vindictively than any, with passing their days in merriment while the Emperor was sick. As soon as it was sufficiently clear to those who keenly watch the angry moods of princes that Vitellius was exasperated, and that Blæsus might be destroyed, the part of the informer was entrusted to Lucius Vitellius. An unworthy jealousy made him the enemy of Blæsus, whose illustrious character raised him far above one who was stained with every infamy; he burst into the imperial chamber, and clasping to his bosom the Emperor's son, fell at his knees. When Vitellius inquired the cause of his emotion, he replied, "It is not from any private apprehension, or because I am anxious for myself; it is for a brother and for a brother's children that I have come hither with my prayers and tears. It is idle to fear

Vespasianus, when there are so many legions of Germany, so many provinces with their valor and their loyalty, and lastly, so vast an extent of sea and land with enormous distances to keep him from us. In the capital, in the very bosom of the Empire, there is the foe of whom we must beware, a foe who boasts of Junii and Antonii[27] among his ancestors, and who, claiming an imperial descent, displays to the soldiers his condescension and his magnificence. On him all thoughts are fixed, while Vitellius, regardless alike of friends and foes, is cherishing a rival who from his banqueting table gazes at the sufferings of his sovereign. For such ill-timed mirth let him be recompensed with a night of sorrow and of death, that he may know and feel that Vitellius still lives and reigns, and has a son, if in the course of destiny anything should happen to himself."

39. Vitellius, after wavering between his guilty purpose and his fears, dreading lest to postpone the murder of Blæsus might hasten his own ruin, while openly to order it might provoke terrible odium, determined to destroy him by poison. He gave a proof of his guilt by his marked joy when he visited Blæsus. He was even heard to utter a most brutal speech, in which (I will relate the very words) he boasted that he had feasted his eyes on the spectacle of his enemy's death. Besides his noble birth and refinement of character, Blæsus was a man of resolute loyalty. In the flourishing days of the party, when canvassed by Cæcina and the leading men, who were beginning to despise Vitellius, he persevered in rejecting their solicitations. A righteous man and a lover of peace, who coveted no sudden elevation, much less the throne, he could not escape being thought to deserve it.

40. Meanwhile Fabius Valens, who was moving along with a vast and luxurious train of concubines and eunuchs too tardily for a general about to take the field, received speedy intelligence of the betrayal of the Ravenna fleet by Lucilius Bassus. Had he hastened the march which he had then begun, he might have come up with Cæcina while still undecided, or have reached the legions previous to the decisive action. Some advised

him to take a few of his most devoted soldiers, and, avoiding Ravenna, to hurry on by unfrequented paths to Hostilia or Cremona. Others thought that he should summon the prætorian cohorts from Rome, and then force his way with a strong body of troops. But with a ruinous delay he wasted in deliberation the opportunities of action. Eventually he rejected both plans, and did what is the very worst thing in circumstances of peril, attempted a middle course, and was neither bold enough on the one hand, nor cautious enough on the other.

41. He wrote to Vitellius asking for aid. Three cohorts with some British cavalry arrived, a force too numerous to elude observation, too small to force its way. Even amidst such perils Valens could not keep himself clear of the infamous reputation of grasping at unlawful gratifications, and of polluting the houses of his hosts with intrigue and violation. He had power, he had money, and he indulged the lusts that are the last solace of desperate fortunes. At length on the arrival of the infantry and cavalry the folly of his plans became evident. With so small a force, even had it been thoroughly loyal, he could not have made his way through the enemy, and the loyalty they had brought with them was not beyond suspicion. Yet shame and respect for the presence of their general held them in check, no lasting restraint with men who loved danger and were careless of disgrace. Moved by this apprehension, Valens, while he retained a few attendants whom adversity had not changed, sent on the infantry to Ariminum[28] and ordered the cavalry to cover his rear. He then himself made his way to Umbria, and thence to Etruria, where, having learned the issue of the battle of Cremona, he conceived a plan not wanting in vigor, and which, had it succeeded, would have had terrible results. This was to seize some ships, to land on some part of Narbonese Gaul, to rouse Gaul with its armies as well as the tribes of Germany, and so to kindle a fresh war.

42. The garrison of Ariminum were discouraged by the departure of Valens, and Cornelius Fuscus, bringing up his army and disposing his Liburnian ships at the nearest points of the shore, invested the place by sea and

land. His troops occupied the plains of Umbria and that
portion of the Picentine territory that is washed by the
Adriatic, and now the whole of Italy was divided by the
range of the Apennines between Vespasianus and Vitellius. Valens, having started from the Bay of Pisa, was
compelled, by either a calm or a contrary wind, to put in
at the port of Hercules Monœcus.[29] Near this place was
stationed Marius Maturus,[30] procurator of the Maritime
Alps, who was loyal to Vitellius, and who, though everything around him was hostile, had not yet thrown off
his allegiance. While courteously receiving Valens, he
deterred him by his advice from rashly invading Narbonese Gaul. And now the fidelity of the rest of the party was weakened by their fears. In fact the procurator
Valerius Paullinus, an enterprising officer, who had been
a friend of Vespasianus before his elevation to the throne,
had made the neighboring states swear allegiance to
that Emperor.

43. Paullinus had collected all the troops who, having
been disbanded by Vitellius, were now spontaneously
taking up arms, and was holding with this force the
colony of Forum Julii,[31] which commanded the sea. His
influence was all the greater because Forum Julii was his
native place, and because he was respected by the prætorians, in which force he had once been a tribune. The
inhabitants themselves, favoring a fellow townsman, and
anticipating his future greatness, did their best to promote the cause. When these preparations, which were
really formidable and were exaggerated by report, became known among the now distracted Vitellians, Fabius
Valens returned to his ships with four soldiers of the
bodyguard, three personal friends, and as many centurions, while Maturus and the rest chose to remain behind and swear allegiance to Vespasianus. For Valens indeed the open sea was safer than the coast or the towns,
yet, all uncertain about the future, and knowing rather
what he must avoid than what he could trust, he was
thrown by adverse weather on the Stœchades,[32] islands
off Massilia.[33] There he was captured by some Liburnian
ships, dispatched by Paullinus.

44. Valens once captured, everything turned to swell

the resources of the conqueror; the lead was taken in Spain by the 1st legion (the Adjutrix), whose recollections of Otho made them hate Vitellius; they drew with them the 6th and 10th. Gaul did not hesitate to follow. A partiality long felt in Britain for Vespasianus, who had there commanded the 2nd legion by the appointment of Claudius, and had served with distinction, attached that province to his cause, though not without some commotion among the other legions, in which were many centurions and soldiers promoted by Vitellius, who felt uneasy in exchanging for another ruler one whom they knew already.

45. These dissensions, and the continual rumors of civil war, raised the courage of the Britons. They were led by one Venutius, who, besides being naturally high spirited, and hating the name of Rome, was fired by his private animosity against Queen Cartimandua.[34] Cartimandua ruled the Brigantes in virtue of her illustrious birth; and she strengthened her throne when, by the treacherous capture of King Caratacus, she was regarded as having given its chief distinction to the triumph of Claudius Cæsar. Then followed wealth and the self-indulgence of prosperity. Spurning her husband, Venutius, she made Vellocatus, his armor bearer, the partner of her bed and throne. By this enormity the power of her house was at once shaken to its base. On the side of the husband were the affections of the people, on that of the adulterer, the lust and savage temper of the queen. Accordingly Venutius collected some auxiliaries, and, aided at the same time by a revolt of the Brigantes, brought Cartimandua into the utmost peril. She asked for some Roman troops, and our auxiliary infantry and cavalry, after fighting with various success, contrived to rescue the queen from her peril. Venutius retained the kingdom, and we had the war on our hands.

46. About the same time, Germany suffered from the supineness of our generals and the mutinous conduct of our legions; the assaults of enemies and the perfidy of allies all but overthrew the power of Rome. Of this war, its origin and its issue, for it lasted long, I shall hereafter speak. The Dacians also were in motion, a peo-

ple which never can be trusted, and which, now that our legions were withdrawn from Mœsia, had nothing to fear. They quietly watched the opening of the campaign, but when they heard that Italy was in a blaze of war, and that the whole Empire was divided against itself, they stormed the winter quarters of the auxiliary infantry and cavalry, and occupied both banks of the Danube. They were then preparing to destroy the camp of the legions, but Mucianus sent the 6th legion against them, for he knew of the victory of Cremona, and he feared this double pressure of barbarian power with Dacians and Germans invading Italy from opposite sides. We were helped, as often before, by the good fortune of the Roman people, which brought to the spot Mucianus with the armies of the East, and by the decisive settlement which in the meantime was effected at Cremona. Fonteius Agrippa was removed from Asia (which province he had governed as proconsul for a year) to Mœsia, and had some troops given him from the army of Vitellius. That this army should be dispersed through the provinces and closely occupied with foreign wars was sound policy and essential to peace.

47. All other nations were equally restless. A sudden outbreak had been excited in Pontus by a barbarian slave, who had before commanded the royal fleet. This was Anicetus, a freedman of Polemon,[35] once a very powerful personage, who, when the kingdom was converted into a Roman province, ill brooked the change. Accordingly he raised in the name of Vitellius the tribes that border on Pontus, bribed a number of very needy adventurers by the hope of plunder, and, at the head of a force by no means contemptible, made a sudden attack on the old and famous city of Trapezus,[36] founded by the Greeks on the furthest shore of the Pontus. There he destroyed a cohort, once a part of the royal contingent. They had afterward received the privileges of citizenship, and while they carried their arms and banners in Roman fashion, they still retained the indolence and license of the Greek. Anicetus also set fire to the fleet, and, as the sea was not guarded, escaped, for Mucianus had brought up to Byzantium the best of the Liburnian[37]

ships and all the troops. The barbarians even insolently scoured the sea in hastily constructed vessels of their own called *camaræ*, built with narrow sides and broad bottoms, and joined together without fastenings of brass or iron. Whenever the water is rough, they raise the bulwarks with additional planks according to the increasing height of the waves, till the vessel is covered in like a house. Thus they roll about amid the billows, and, as they have a prow at both extremities alike and a convertible arrangement of oars, they may be paddled in one direction or another indifferently and without risk.

48. The matter attracted the attention of Vespasianus, and induced him to dispatch some veterans from the legions under Yirdius Geminus, a tried soldier. Finding the enemy in disorder and dispersed in the eager pursuit of plunder, he attacked them, and drove them to their ships. Hastily fitting out a fleet of Liburnian ships, he pursued Anicetus, and overtook him at the mouth of the river Chobus,[38] where he was protected by the king of the Sedochezi, whose alliance he had secured by a sum of money and other presents. This prince at first endeavored to protect the suppliant by a threat of hostilities; when, however, the choice was presented to him between war and the profit to be derived from treachery, he consented, with the characteristic perfidy of barbarians, to the destruction of Anicetus, and delivered up the refugees. So ended this servile war. Amidst the joy of this success, while everything was prosperous beyond his hopes, tidings of the victory of Cremona reached Vespasianus in Egypt. This made him hasten his advance to Alexandria, for now that the army of Vitellius was shattered, he sought to apply the pressure of famine to the capital, which is always dependent on foreign supplies. He was indeed also preparing to invade by sea and land the province of Africa, which lies on the same line of coast, intending by thus closing the supplies of corn to cause famine and dissension among the enemy.

49. While with this worldwide convulsion the imperial power was changing hands, the conduct of Antonius Primus, after the fall of Cremona, was by no means as blameless as before. Either he believed that

the necessities of the war had been satisfied, and that all
else would follow easily, or, perhaps, success, working
on such a temperament, developed his latent pride, rapacity, and other vices. He swept through Italy as if it
were a conquered country, and caressed the legions as
if they were his own; by all his words and acts he sought
to pave for himself the way to power. To imbue the
army with a spirit of license, he offered to the legions
the commissions of the centurions killed in the war. By
their vote the most turbulent men were elected. The soldiers in fact were not under the control of the generals,
but the generals were themselves constrained to follow
the furious impulses of the soldiers. These mutinous
proceedings, so ruinous to discipline, Antonius soon
turned to his own profit, regardless of the near approach
of Mucianus, a neglect more fatal than any contempt
for Vespasianus.

50. As winter was approaching, and the low country
was flooded by the Po, the army marched on without its
heavy baggage. The standards and eagles of the victorious legions, the old and wounded soldiers, and even
many effective men, were left at Verona. The auxiliary
infantry and cavalry, with some picked troops from the
legions, appeared sufficient for a war that was all but
finished. They had been joined by the 11th legion,
which at first had hesitated, but now in the hour of success felt alarm at having stood aloof. A recent levy of
six thousand Dalmatians was attached to the legion.
They were under the command of Pompeius Silvanus, a
man of consular rank; the real direction of affairs was
in the hands of Annius Bassus, the legate of the legion.
This officer contrived, under an appearance of submission, to govern Silvanus, a leader without vigor, and apt
to waste in words the opportunities of action. Bassus,
with his unobtrusive energy, was ready for everything
that had to be done. To these forces were added the elite
of the marines of the Ravenna fleet, who demanded permission to serve in the legions. The crews were made up
with Dalmatians. The army and generals halted at the
temple of Fortune,[39] undecided as to their line of action.
They had heard that the prætorian guard had marched

out of Rome, and they supposed that the Apennines were occupied with troops. The generals, finding themselves in a country utterly impoverished by war, were terrified by the scarcity of provisions and the mutinous clamors of the soldiery, who incessantly demanded the *clavarium,* as the donative was called. They had provided neither money nor corn, and they were embarrassed by the general impatience and rapacity; for what they might have obtained was plundered.

51. I have the very highest authority for asserting that there was among the conquerors such an impious disregard of right and wrong that a private cavalry soldier declared he had slain his brother in the late battle, and claimed a reward from the generals. The common law of humanity on the one hand forbade them to reward this act of blood, the necessities of the war on the other forbade them to punish it. They put him off, on the ground that the obligation was too great to be immediately discharged. Nothing more is recorded. In the earlier civil wars indeed a similar horror had occurred. In the battle with Cinna at the Janiculum,⁴⁰ a soldier in Pompeius' army, as Sisenna⁴¹ tells us, slew his own brother and, on discovering the horrible deed he had committed, destroyed himself. So much more earnest among our ancestors was the honor paid to virtue, and the remorse that waited on crime. These and like instances, drawn from the recollections of the past, I shall mention not irrelevantly, whenever the subject and the occasion shall call for some example of goodness or some solace in the presence of evil.

52. Antonius and the other generals of the party judged it expedient to send forward the cavalry and explore the whole of Umbria for some point where the Apennines presented a more gentle ascent, and also to bring up the eagles and standards and all the troops at Verona, while they were to cover the Po and the sea with convoys. Some there were among the generals who were contriving delays, for Antonius in fact was now becoming too great a man, and their hopes from Mucianus were more definite. That commander, troubled at so speedy a success, and imagining that unless he occupied

Rome in person he should lose all share in the glory of
the war, continued to write in ambiguous terms to Varus
and Antonius, enlarging at one time on the necessity of
following up their operations, at another on the advantage of delay, and with expressions so worded that he
could, according to the event, repudiate a disastrous, or
claim a successful policy. To Plotius Griphus, who had
lately been raised by Vespasianus to the senatorial rank
and appointed to command a legion, as well as to all
others on whom he could fully rely, he gave plainer instructions. All these men sent replies reflecting unfavorably on the precipitancy of Varus and Antonius, and
suiting the wishes of Mucianus. By forwarding these
letters to Vespasianus he had accomplished this much,
that the measures and achievements of Antonius were not
valued according to his hopes.

53. Antonius was indignant, and blamed Mucianus,
whose calumnies had depreciated his own hazardous
achievements. Nor was he temperate in his expressions,
for he was habitually violent in language, and was unaccustomed to obey. He wrote a letter to Vespasianus in
terms more arrogant than should be addressed to an
emperor, and not without implied reproach against Mucianus. "It was I," he said, "who brought into the field
the legions of Pannonia; my instigations roused the generals in Mœsia; my courageous resolution forced a passage through the Alps, seized on Italy, and cut off the
succors from Germany and Rhætia. The discomfiture
of the disunited and scattered legions of Vitellius by a
fierce charge of cavalry, and afterward by the steady
strength of the infantry in a conflict that lasted for a
day and a night, was indeed a most glorious achievement, and it was my work. For the destruction of Cremona the war must be answerable; the civil strifes of
former days cost the state more terrible loss and the
overthrow of many cities. Not with messages and letters, but with my arm and my sword, have I served my
Emperor. I would not seek to hinder the renown of
those who in the meanwhile have reduced Asia to tranquillity. They had at heart the peace of Mœsia, I the
safety and security of Italy. By my earnest representa-

tions Gaul and Spain, the most powerful region of the world, have been won for Vespasianus. But all my efforts have been wasted, if they alone who have not shared the peril obtain its rewards." The meaning of all this did not escape Mucianus, and there thus arose a deadly feud, cherished by Antonius with frankness, by Mucianus with reserve, and therefore with the greater bitterness.

54. Vitellius, after his power had been shattered at Cremona, endeavored to suppress the tidings of the disaster, and by this foolish attempt at concealment he put off, not indeed his troubles, but only the application of the remedy. Had he avowed and discussed his position, he had some chance, some strength, left; whereas, on the contrary, when he pretended that all was prosperous, he aggravated his perils by falsehood. A strange silence was observed in his presence as to the war; throughout the country all discussion was prohibited, and so, many who would have told the truth had it been allowed, finding it forbidden, spread rumors exaggerating the calamity. The generals of the enemy failed not to magnify the report of their strength, for they sent back any spies of Vitellius whom they captured, after conducting them round the camp in order that they might learn the force of the victorious army. All of these persons Vitellius questioned in secret, and then ordered that they should be put to death. Singular bravery was displayed by a centurion, Julius Agrestis, who, after several interviews, in which he had in vain endeavored to rouse Vitellius to courage, prevailed on the Emperor to send him in person to see what was the strength of the enemy's resources, and what had happened at Cremona. He did not seek to escape the notice of Antonius by making his observations in secret, but avowed the Emperor's instructions and his own purpose, and asked leave to see everything. Persons were sent to show him the field of battle, the remains of Cremona, and the captured legions. He then made his way back to Vitellius, and when the Emperor denied the truth of the intelligence which he brought, and even charged him with having been bribed, he replied, "Since you require some de-

cisive proof, and I can no longer serve you in any other way either by my life or death, I will give you a proof which you can believe." So he departed, and confirmed his statement by a voluntary death. Some say that he was slain by order of Vitellius, but they bear the same testimony to his loyalty and courage.

55. Vitellius, who seemed like a man roused from slumber, ordered Julius Priscus and Alfenus Varus, with fourteen of the prætorian cohorts and the entire force of cavalry, to occupy the Apennines. A legion of troops drafted from the fleet followed. So many thousand troops, comprising the picked men and horses of the army, had they been under the direction of a different general would have been quite equal even to aggressive operations. The rest of the prætorian cohorts were entrusted to Lucius Vitellius, brother of the Emperor, for the defense of the capital. Vitellius, while he abated nothing of his habitual indulgence, with a precipitancy prompted by alarm anticipated the elections, at which he appointed consuls for several years. With a profuse liberality, he granted treaties to allies, and the rights of Latin citizenship to foreigners; some he relieved by the remission of tribute, others by exemptions; in a word, utterly careless of the future, he mutilated the resources of the Empire. But the mob was attracted by the magnificence of his bounties. The most foolish bought these favors with money; the wise held that to be invalid which could neither be given nor received without ruin to the state. Yielding at length to the importunity of the army, which had taken up its position at Mevania,[42] and accompanied by a numerous train of senators, into which many were brought by ambition and more by fear, he entered the camp, undecided in purpose and at the mercy of faithless counsels.

56. While he was haranguing his troops—marvelous to relate—such a multitude of ill-omened birds flew over him as to obscure with a dark cloud the light of day. There occurred another terrible presage. A bull escaped from the altar, scattered the preparations for sacrifice, and was finally slain far from the spot where the victims are usually struck down. But the most portentous

spectacle of all was Vitellius himself, ignorant of military matters and without forethought in his plans, even asking others about the order of march, about the business of reconnoitering, and the discretion to be used in pushing on or protracting the campaign, betraying in his countenance and gait his alarm at every fresh piece of intelligence, and finally drinking to intoxication. At last, weary of the camp, and having received tidings of the defection of the fleet at Misenum, he returned to Rome, trembling at every new disaster, but reckless of the final result. For though it was open to him to have crossed the Apennines with an army in unimpaired vigor, and to have attacked in the field an enemy suffering from cold and scant supplies, yet, by dividing his forces, he abandoned to destruction or captivity troops of the keenest courage and faithful to the last, against the judgment of the most experienced among the centurions, who, had they been consulted, would have told him the truth. They were all kept at a distance by the intimate friends of Vitellius; for the Emperor's ears were so formed that all profitable counsels were offensive to him, and that he would hear nothing but what would please and ruin.

57. The fleet at Misenum—so much can be done in times of civil discord by the daring of even a single man—was drawn into revolt by Claudius Faventinus, a centurion cashiered by Galba, who forged letters in the name of Vespasianus offering a reward for treachery. The fleet was under the command of Claudius Apollinaris, a man neither firm in his loyalty nor energetic in his treason. Apinius Tiro, who had filled the office of prætor, and who then happened to be at Minturnæ,[43] offered to head the revolt. By these men the colonies and municipal towns were drawn into the movement, and as Puteoli[44] was particularly zealous for Vespasianus, while Capua on the other hand remained loyal to Vitellius, they introduced their municipal jealousy into the civil war. Claudius Julianus, who had lately exercised an indulgent rule over the fleet at Misenum, was selected by Vitellius to soothe the irritation of the soldiery. He was supported by a city cohort and a troop of gladiators whose chief officer he was. As soon as the two camps were pitched,

Julianus, without much hesitation, went over to the side of Vespasianus, and they then occupied -Tarracina,[45] which was protected by its fortifications and position rather than by any ability of theirs.

58. Vitellius, when informed of these events, left a portion of his army at Narnia[46] under the command of the prefect of the prætorian guard and deputed his brother Lucius with six cohorts of infantry and five hundred cavalry to encounter the danger that now threatened him on the side of Campania. Sick at heart, he found relief in the zeal of the soldiers and in the shouts with which the people clamored for arms, while he gave the delusive name of an army and of Roman legions to a cowardly mob that would not venture on anything beyond words. At the instance of his freedmen (for his friends were the less faithful the more distinguished their rank) he ordered the tribes to be convoked, and to those who gave in their names administered the oath of service. As the numbers were excessive, he divided the business of enrollment between the consuls. He required the senators to furnish a prescribed number of slaves and a certain weight of silver. The Roman knights offered their services and money, and even the freedmen voluntarily sought the privilege of doing the same. This pretense of loyalty, dictated at first by fear, passed into enthusiasm, and many expressed compassion, not so much for Vitellius as for the fallen condition of the imperial power. Vitellius himself did not fail to draw out their sympathies by his pitiable looks, his voice, and his tears; he was liberal in his promises and even extravagant, as men in their alarm naturally are. He even expressed a wish to be saluted as Cæsar, a title which he had formerly rejected. But now he had a superstitious feeling about the name; and it is a fact that in the moment of terror the counsels of the wise and the voice of the rabble are listened to with equal respect. But as all movements that originate in thoughtless impulse, however vigorous in their beginnings, become feeble after a time, the throng of senators and knights gradually melted away, dispersing at first tardily and during the absence of the Emperor, but before long with

a contemptuous indifference to his presence, till, ashamed of the failure of his efforts, Vitellius waived his claims to services which were not offered.

59. As the occupation of Mevania, and the apparent revival of the war with new vigor, had struck terror into Italy, so now did the timorous retreat of Vitellius give an unequivocal bias in favor of the Flavians. The Samnites, the Peligni, and the Marsi[47] roused themselves, jealous at having been anticipated by Campania, and, as men who serve a new master, were energetic in all the duties of war. The army, however, was much distressed by bad weather in its passage over the Apennines, and since they could hardly struggle through the snow, though their march was unmolested, they perceived what danger they would have had to encounter, had not Vitellius been made to turn back by that good fortune which, not less often than the wisdom of their counsels, helped the Flavian generals. Here they fell in with Petilus Cerialis,[48] who had escaped the sentries of Vitellius by a rustic disguise and by his knowledge of the country. There was a near relationship between Cerialis and Vespasianus, and he was not without reputation as a soldier. He was therefore admitted to rank among the generals. It has been said by many that the means of escape were likewise open to Flavius Sabinus and to Domitian,[49] and indeed messengers, dispatched by Antonius, contrived under various disguises to make their way to them, offering them a place of refuge and a protecting force. Sabinus pleaded his ill health, unsuited to toil and adventure. Domitian did not want the courage, but he feared that the guards whom Vitellius had set over him, though they offered to accompany him in his flight, had treacherous designs. And Vitellius himself, out of a regard for his own connections, did not meditate any cruelty against Domitian.

60. The Flavian generals on their arrival at Carsulæ[50] took a few days for repose, while the eagles and standards of the legions were coming up. Carsulæ appeared a good position for an encampment, for it commanded an extensive prospect, provisions could be safely brought up, and there were in its rear several very wealthy

towns. They also calculated on interviews with the Vitellians, who were only ten miles distant, and on the chance of defection. The soldiers were dissatisfied with this prospect, and wished for victory rather than for peace. They would not even await the arrival of their own legions, whom they looked upon as sharers in the spoil rather than in the dangers of the compaign. Antonius summoned them to an assembly, and explained to them that Vitellius still had forces, which would waver in their loyalty if they had time to reflect, but would be fierce foes if driven to despair. "The opening of a civil war must," he said, "be left to chance; the final triumph is perfected by wise counsels and skill. The fleet of Misenum and the fairest portion of Campania have already revolted, and out of the whole world Vitellius has nothing left but the country between Tarracina and Narnia. From our victory at Cremona sufficient glory has accrued to us, and from the destruction of that city only too much disgrace. Let us not be eager to capture rather than to preserve the capital. Greater will be our reward, far higher our reputation, if we secure without bloodshed the safety of the Senate and of the people of Rome." By this and similar language their impatience was allayed.

61. Soon after, the legions arrived. Alarmed by the report of this increase to the army, the Vitellian cohorts began to waver; no one urged them to fight, many urged them to change sides, each more eager than the other to hand over his company or troop, a present to the conqueror, and a source of future advantage to himself. From these men it was ascertained that Interamna,[51] situated in the adjoining plain, was occupied by a garrison of four hundred cavalry. Varus was at once dispatched with a lightly equipped force, and cut to pieces a few who attempted to resist; the greater number threw down their arms, and begged for quarter. Some fled back into the camp, and spread panic everywhere by exaggerated reports of the courage and strength of the enemy, seeking thus to mitigate the disgrace of having lost the position. Among the Vitellians treason went unpunished; all loyalty was subverted by the rewards of

desertion, and nothing was left but emulation in perfidy. There were numerous desertions among the tribunes and centurions; the common soldiers remained obstinately faithful to Vitellius, till Priscus and Alfenus, deserting the camp and returning to Vitellius, relieved all from any shame they might feel at being traitors.

62. About the same time Fabius Valens was put to death while in confinement at Urbinum.[52] His head was displayed to the Vitellian cohorts, that they might not cherish any further hope, for they generally believed that Valens had made his way into Germany, and was there bringing into the field veteran as well as newly levied armies. The bloody spectacle reduced them to despair, and it was amazing how the army of Vespasianus welcomed in their hearts the destruction of Valens as the termination of the war. Valens was a native of Anagnia,[53] and belonged to an equestrian family; he was a man of loose character, but of no small ability, who sought to gain by profligacy a reputation for elegance. In the theatricals performed by young men during the reign of Nero, at first apparently from compulsion, afterward of his own free choice, he repeatedly acted in the farces, with more cleverness than propriety. While legate of a legion, he first supported, then slandered, Verginius. Fonteius Capito he murdered, either after he had corrupted him, or because he had failed to do so. Though a traitor to Galba he was loyal to Vitellius, and gained a luster from the perfidy of others.

63. Finding all their hopes cut off, the troops of Vitellius, intending to pass over to the side of the conqueror, but to do so with honor, marched down with their standards and colors into the plains beneath Narnia. The army of Vespasianus, prepared and equipped as if for action, was drawn up in dense array on both sides of the road. The Vitellians were received between the two columns; when they were thus surrounded, Antonius addressed them kindly. One division was ordered to remain at Narnia, another at Interamna; with them were left some of the victorious legions, which would not be formidable to them if they remained quiet, but were strong enough to crush all turbulence. At the same

time Primus and Varus did not neglect to forward continual messages to Vitellius, offering him personal safety, the enjoyment of wealth, and a quiet retreat in Campania, provided he would lay down his arms and surrender himself and his children to Vespasianus. Mucianus also wrote to him to the same effect, and Vitellius was often disposed to trust these overtures, and even discussed the number of his household and the choice of a residence on the coast. Such a lethargy had come over his spirit that, had not others remembered he was an emperor, he would have himself forgotten it.

64. The leading men in the state had secret conferences with Flavius Sabinus, prefect of the city, urging him to secure a share in the credit of the victory. "You have," they said, "a force of your own in the city cohorts; the cohorts of the watch will not fail you, and there are also our own slaves, there is the prestige of the party, there is the fact that to the victorious everything is easy. You should not yield the glory of the war to Antonius and Varus. Vitellius has but a few cohorts, and they are alarmed by gloomy tidings from every quarter. The feelings of the people are easily swayed, and if you put yourself at their head, there will soon be the same flatteries ready for Vespasianus. Vitellius even in prosperity was unequal to his position, and he is proportionately unnerved by disaster. The merit of having finished the war will belong to him who may have possessed himself of the capital. It would well become Sabinus to keep the Empire for his brother, and Vespasianus equally well to count his other adherents inferior to Sabinus."

65. Old and infirm as he was, it was with anything but eagerness that he listened to these suggestions. Some indeed assailed him with dark insinuations, implying that from motives of envy and rivalry he was seeking to retard the elevation of his brother. It was true that while both were in a private station, Flavius Sabinus, who was the elder, was the superior of Vespasianus in influence and in wealth. He was believed indeed to have sustained the failing credit of his brother, while taking a mortgage of his house and lands; and hence, though the outward appearance of harmony was preserved, some secret

grudge was feared. It is more charitable to suppose that the mild temper of the man shrank from bloodshed and slaughter, and that for this reason he had held frequent conferences with Vitellius to discuss the question of peace and the cessation of hostilities upon certain conditions. After many private interviews, they finally, so report said, ratified an agreement in the temple of Apollo. The words of their conversation had two witnesses in Cluvius Rufus[54] and Silius Italicus.[55] Their looks were noted by the more distant spectators; the expression of Vitellius was abject and mean, that of Sabinus not triumphant, but rather akin to pity.

66. Could Vitellius have swayed the feelings of his partisans as easily as he had himself yielded, the army of Vespasianus might have entered the capital without bloodshed. But the more loyal his adherents, the more did they protest against peace and negotiation. They pointed out the danger and disgrace of submission in which the caprice of the conqueror would be their sole guarantee. "And Vespasianus," they said, "is not so arrogant as to tolerate such a subject as Vitellius. Even the vanquished would not endure it. Their pity would be dangerous to him. You certainly are an old man, and have had enough both of prosperity and of adversity, but think what a name, what a position, you will leave to your son Germanicus. Now indeed they promise you wealth, and a large establishment, and a luxurious retreat in Campania; but when Vespasianus has once seized the throne, neither he, nor his friends, nor even his armies, will feel themselves secure till all rivalry has been extinguished. Fabius Valens, captive as he was, and reserved against the chance of disaster, was yet too formidable to them; and certainly Primus, Fuscus, and Mucianus, who exhibits the temper of his party, will not be allowed power over Vitellius except to put him to death. Cæsar did not leave Pompeius, Augustus did not leave Antonius in safety; and will Vespasianus show a more lofty spirit—Vespasianus, who was a dependent of Vitellius when Vitellius was the colleague of Claudius? If you would act as becomes the censorship, the thrice-repeated consulate of your father, and all the honors of

417

your illustrious house, let despair at any rate arm you to courageous action. The troops are still firm, and among the people there is abundant zeal. Lastly, nothing can happen to us more terrible than that upon which we are voluntarily rushing. If we are conquered, we must die; we must die if we capitulate. All that concerns us is this; shall we draw our last breath amidst scorn and insult, or in a valiant struggle?"

67. The ears of Vitellius were deaf to manly counsels. His whole soul was overwhelmed by a tender anxiety, lest by an obstinate resistance he might leave the conqueror less mercifully disposed to his wife and children. He had also a mother old and feeble, but she, expiring a few days before, escaped by her opportune death the ruin of her house, having gained from the imperial dignity of her son nothing but sorrow and a good name. On the 18th of December, after hearing of the defection of the legion and the auxiliary infantry which had surrendered at Narnia, he left the palace, clad in mourning robes, and surrounded by his weeping household. With him went his little son, carried in a litter, as though in a funeral procession. The greetings of the people were flattering, but ill-suited to the time; the soldiers preserved an ominous silence.

68. There could hardly be a man so careless of human interests as not to be affected by this spectacle. There was the Roman Emperor, lord but a few days before of the whole human race, leaving the seat of his power, and passing through the midst of his people and his capital, to abdicate his throne. Men had never before seen or heard of such an event. Cæsar the dictator had fallen by sudden violence, Caligula by secret treason. The shades of night and the obscurity of a rural hiding place had veiled the flight of Nero. Piso and Galba had, it might be said, fallen in battle. In an assembly of his own people, and in the midst of his own soldiers, with the very women of his family looking on, Vitellius stood and spoke a few words suitable to the sad conjuncture. "He gave way," he said, "for the sake of peace, for the sake of his country; let them only remember him, and think with compassion of his brother, of his wife, of his young

and innocent children." At the same time he held out his son, commending him first to individual bystanders, then to the whole assembly. At last, unable to speak for weeping, he unfastened the dagger from his side, and offered it to the consul Cæcilius Simplex, who was standing by him, as if to indicate that he surrendered the power of life and death over the citizens. The consul rejecting it, and those who were standing by in the assembly shouting remonstrance, he departed, as if with the intention of laying aside the emblems of imperial power in the temple of Concord,[56] and of betaking himself to his brother's house. Louder shouts here met him from the crowd, which hindered him from entering a private house, and invited him to return to the palace. Every other route was closed, and the only one open was one which led into the Sacred Way. Then in utter perplexity he returned to the palace. The rumor that he had renounced the imperial dignity had preceded him thither, and Flavius Sabinus had sent written orders to the tribunes of the cohorts to keep their soldiers under restraint.

69. Then, as if the whole state had passed into the hands of Vespasianus, the leading men of the Senate, many of the equestrian order, with all the city soldiery and the watch thronged the dwelling of Sabinus. Intelligence was there brought to him of the enthusiasm of the populace and of the threatening attitude of the German cohorts. He had now gone too far to be able to retreat, and everyone, fearing for himself, should the Vitellians come upon them while they were scattered and comparatively weak, urged him, in spite of his reluctance, to hostilities. As usually happens, however, in such cases, all gave the advice, but few shared the risk. The armed retinue which was escorting Sabinus was met, as it was coming down by Lake Fundanus,[57] by some of the most determined of the Vitellians. From this unforeseen collision resulted an encounter slight indeed, but terminating favorably for the Vitellians. In the hurry of the moment Sabinus adopted the safest course open to him, and occupied the Capitol with a miscellaneous body of soldiery, and some senators and

knights. It is not easy to give the names of these persons, since after the triumph of Vespasianus many pretended to have rendered this service to his party. There were even women who braved the dangers of the siege; the most conspicuous among them being Verulana Gratilla, who was taken thither not by the love of children or kindred, but by the fascination of war. The Vitellians kept but a careless watch over the besieged, and thus at the dead of night Sabinus was able to bring into the Capitol his own children and Domitian, his brother's son, and to send by an unguarded route a messenger to the generals of the Flavian party, with information that they were besieged, and that, unless succor arrived, they must be reduced to distress. The night passed so quietly that he might have quitted the place without loss; for, brave as were the soldiers of Vitellius in encountering danger, they were far from attentive to the laborious duties of watching. Besides this, the sudden fall of a winter storm baffled both sight and hearing.

70. At dawn, before either side commenced hostilities, Sabinus sent Cornelius Martialis, a centurion of the first rank, to Vitellius, with instructions to complain of the infraction of the stipulated terms. "There has evidently," he said, "been a mere show and pretense of abdicating the Empire, with the view of deceiving a number of distinguished men. If not, why, when leaving the Rostra, had he gone to the house of his brother, looking as it did over the forum, and certain to provoke the gaze of the multitude, rather than to the Aventine, and the family house of his wife?" This would have befitted a private individual anxious to shun all appearance of imperial power. But on the contrary, Vitellius retraced his steps to the palace, the very stronghold of Empire; thence issued a band of armed men. One of the most frequented parts of the city was strewed with the corpses of innocent persons. The Capitol itself had not been spared. "I," said Sabinus, "was only a civilian and a member of the Senate, while the rivalry of Vitellius and Vespasianus was being settled by conflicts between legions, by the capture of cities, by the capitulation of cohorts; with Spain, Germany, and Britain in revolt, the brother

of Vespasianus still remained firm to his allegiance, till actually invited to discuss terms of agreement. Peace and harmony bring advantage to the conquered, but only credit to the conqueror. If you repent of your compact, it is not against me, whom you treacherously deceived, that you must draw the sword, nor is it against the son of Vespasianus, who is yet of tender age. What would be gained by the slaughter of one old man and one boy? You should go and meet the legions, and fight there for empire; everything else will follow the issue of that struggle." To these representations the embarrassed Vitellius answered a few words in his own exculpation, throwing all the blame upon the soldiers, with whose excessive zeal his moderation was, he said, unable to cope. He advised Martialis to depart unobserved through a concealed part of the palace, in case he should be killed by the soldiers, as the negotiator of this abhorred convention. Vitellius had not now the power either to command or to forbid. He was no longer emperor, he was merely the pretext of the war.

71. Martialis had hardly returned to the Capitol, when the infuriated soldiery arrived, without any leader, every man acting on his own impulse. They hurried at quick march past the forum and the temples which hang over it, and advanced their line up the opposite hill as far as the outer gates of the Capitol. There were formerly certain colonnades on the right side of the slope as one went up; the defenders, issuing forth on the roof of these buildings, showered tiles and stones on the Vitellians. The assailants were not armed with anything but swords, and it seemed too tedious to send for machines and missiles. They threw lighted brands on a projecting colonnade, and following the track of the fire would have burst through the half-burned gates of the Capitol, had not Sabinus, tearing down on all sides the statues, the glories of former generations, formed them into a barricade across the opening. They then assailed the opposite approaches to the Capitol, near the grove of the Asylum,[58] and where the Tarpeian Rock[59] is mounted by a hundred steps. Both these attacks were unexpected; the closer and fiercer of the two threatened the Asylum.

The assailants could not be checked as they mounted the continuous line of buildings, which, as was natural in a time of profound peace, had grown up to such a height as to be on a level with the soil of the Capitol. A doubt arises at this point, whether it was the assailants who threw lighted brands onto the roofs, or whether, as the more general account has it, the besieged thus sought to repel the assailants, who were now making vigorous progress. From them the fire passed to the colonnades adjoining the temples; the eagles supporting the pediment, which were of old timber, caught the flames. And so the Capitol, with its gates shut, neither defended by friends, nor spoiled by a foe, was burned to the ground.

72. This was the most deplorable and disgraceful event that had happened to the commonwealth of Rome since the foundation of the city; for now, assailed by no foreign enemy, with heaven ready to be propitious, had our vices only allowed, the seat of Jupiter Supremely Good and Great,[60] founded by our ancestors with solemn auspices to be the pledge of empire, the seat which neither Porsenna, when the city was surrendered,[61] nor the Gauls, when it was captured, had been able to violate, was destroyed by the madness of our emperors. Once before indeed during civil war the Capitol had been consumed by fire, but then only through the crime of individuals; now it was openly besieged, and openly set on fire. And what were the motives of this conflict; what the compensation for so great a disaster? Was it for our country we were fighting? King Tarquinius Priscus[62] had vowed its erection in his war with the Sabines, and had laid the foundations on a scale which suited the hopes of future greatness rather than what the yet moderate resources of Rome could achieve. After him, Servius Tullius,[63] heartily assisted by the allies, and Tarquinius Superbus, employing the spoils of war from the conquered Suessa Pometia,[64] raised the superstructure. But the glory of its completion was reserved for the days of liberty. After the expulsion of the kings, Horatius Pulvillus, in his second consulate,[65] dedicated

it, a building so magnificent that the vast wealth afterward acquired by the people of Rome served to embellish rather than increase it. It was rebuilt on the same site when, after an interval of 415 years, it was burned to the ground in the consulate of Lucius Scipio and Gaius Norbanus.[66] Sulla, after his final triumph, undertook the charge of restoring it, but did not live to dedicate it, the one thing denied to his uniform good fortune. The name of Lutatius Catulus, the dedicator,[67] remained among all the vast erections of the emperors, down to the days of Vitellius. This was the building that was now on fire.

73. The catastrophe, however, caused more panic among the besieged than among the besiegers. In fact, the troops of Vitellius lacked neither skill nor courage in the midst of peril. Opposed to them were soldiers without self-possession, and a spiritless and, so to speak, infatuated commander, who had not the use of his tongue or his ears, who would not be guided by other men's counsels, and could not carry out his own, who, hurried to and fro by the shouts of the enemy, forbade what he had just ordered, and ordered what he had just forbidden. Then, as usually happens when everything is lost, all gave orders, and no one obeyed. At last, they threw away their arms, and began to look about for ways of escape and means of concealment. The Vitellians burst in, carrying everywhere with indiscriminate ferocity the firebrand and the sword. A few of the military men, among whom the most conspicuous were Cornelius Martialis, Æmilius Pacensis, Casperius Niger, and Didius Scæva, ventured to resist, and were cut down. Flavius Sabinus, who was unarmed, and who did not attempt to fly, was surrounded, and with him the consul Quintius Atticus, marked out by his clinging to the shadow of office, and by his folly in having scattered among the people edicts highly eulogistic of Vespasianus and insulting to Vitellius. The rest escaped by various chances, some disguised as slaves, others concealed by the fidelity of dependents, and hiding among the baggage. Some caught the watchword by which the Vitellians recognized each other, and, themselves challenging

others and giving it when challenged, found in their
audacity an effectual disguise.

74. When the enemy first burst in, Domitian concealed himself in the house of a servant of the temple.
At the ingenious suggestion of a freedman, he assumed
a linen vestment, and passing unnoticed among a crowd
of acolytes, found a refuge with Cornelius Primus, one
of his father's dependents, in a house near the Velabrum.[68] When his father mounted the throne, he pulled
down the chamber of the temple servant, and built a
small chapel, dedicated to Jupiter the Preserver,[69] with
an altar on which his own adventures were represented
in marble. Afterward, on his own accession to the imperial power, he consecrated a vast temple to Jupiter the
Guardian,[70] with an effigy of himself in the arms of
the god. Sabinus and Atticus were loaded with chains,
and conducted to Vitellius, who received them with anything but anger in his words and looks, amidst the murmurs of those who demanded the privilege of slaying
them and their pay for the work they had done. Those
who were standing near began the clamor, and the degraded rabble cried out for the execution of Sabinus, and
mingled threats with their flatteries. Vitellius, who was
standing before the steps of the palace, and was preparing to intercede, was induced to desist. The body of
Sabinus, pierced and mutilated and with the head
severed from it, was dragged to the Gemonian Stairs.[71]

75. Such was the end of a man in no wise contemptible. In thirty-five campaigns he had served the state, and
had gained distinction both at home and abroad. His
blamelessness and integrity no one could question. He
was somewhat boastful; this was the only fault of
which rumor accused him in the seven years during
which he had governed Mœsia, and the twelve during
which he was prefect of the city. In the closing scene
of his life some have seen pusillanimity, many a moderate temper, sparing of the blood of his countrymen.
One thing is allowed by all, that before the accession of
Vespasianus, the distinction of the family was centered
in Sabinus. I have heard that his death gratified Mucianus, and many indeed asserted that the interests of

peace were promoted by the removal of the rivalry
between these two men, one of whom felt himself to
be the brother of the Emperor, while the other thought
himself his colleague. Vitellius resisted the demands of
the people for the execution of the consul; he was now
pacified, and wished, it would seem, to recompense
Atticus, who, when asked who had set fire to the Capitol,
had confessed his own guilt, and by this confession,
which may indeed have been an opportune falsehood,
was thought to have taken upon himself the odium of
the crime, and to have acquitted the Vitellian party.

76. Meanwhile Lucius Vitellius, who was encamped
near Feronia,[72] was threatening Tarracina with destruction. There were shut up in the place a few gladiators
and seamen, who dared not leave the walls and risk an
engagement in the plain. I have mentioned before that
Julianus was in command of the gladiators, Apollinaris
of the seamen, two men whose profligacy and indolence
made them resemble gladiators rather than generals.
They kept no watch; they did not strengthen the weak
points of the fortifications; but, making each pleasant
spot ring with the noise of their daily and nightly dissipation, they dispersed their soldiers on errands which
were to minister to their luxury, and never spoke of
war, except at their banquets. Apinius Tiro had quitted
the place a few days before, and was now, by the harsh
exaction of presents and contributions from the towns,
adding to the unpopularity rather than to the resources
of his party.

77. Meanwhile a slave belonging to Vergilius Capito[73]
deserted to Lucius Vitellius, and having engaged, on being furnished with a force, to put him in possession of
the unoccupied citadel, proceeded at a late hour of
the night to place some light-armed cohorts on the
summit of a range of hills which commanded the
enemy's position. From this place the troops descended
to what was more a massacre than a conflict. Many
whom they slew were unarmed or in the act of arming
themselves, some were just awaking from sleep, amid
the confusion of darkness and panic, the braying of
trumpets, and the shouts of the foe. A few of the

425

gladiators resisted, and fell not altogether unavenged. The rest made a rush for the ships, where everything was involved in a general panic, the troops being mingled with country people, whom the Vitellians slaughtered indiscriminately. Six Liburnian ships with Apollinaris, prefect of the fleet, escaped in the first confusion. The rest were either seized upon the beach, or were swamped by the weight of the crowds that rushed on board. Julianus was brought before Lucius Vitellius, and, after being ignominiously scourged, was put to death in his presence. Some persons accused Triaria, the wife of Lucius Vitellius, of having armed herself with a soldier's sword, and of having behaved with arrogance and cruelty amid the horrors and massacres of the storm of Tarracina. Lucius himself sent to his brother a laureled dispatch with an account of his success, and asked whether he wished him at once to return in Rome, or to complete the subjugation of Campania. This circumstance was advantageous to the state as well as to the cause of Vespasian. Had the army, fresh from victory, and with all the pride of success added to its natural obstinacy, marched upon Rome, a conflict of no slight magnitude, and involving the destruction of the capital, must have ensued. Lucius Vitellius, infamous as he was, had yet some energy, but it was not through his virtues, as is the case with the good, but through his vices, that he, like the worst of villains, was formidable.

78. While these successes were being achieved on the side of Vitellius, the army of Vespasianus had left Narnia, and was passing the holiday of the Saturnalia[74] in idleness at Ocriculum.[75] The reason alleged for so injurious a delay was that they might wait for Mucianus. Some persons indeed there were who assailed Antonius with insinuations, that he lingered with treacherous intent, after receiving private letters from Vitellius, which conveyed to him the offer of the consulship and of the Emperor's daughter in marriage with a vast dowry, as the price of treason. Others asserted that this was all a fiction, invented to please Mucianus. Some again alleged that the policy agreed upon by all the generals was to

threaten rather than actually to attack the capital, as Vitellius' strongest cohorts had revolted from him, and it seemed likely that, deprived of all support, he would abdicate the throne, but that the whole plan was ruined by the impatience and subsequent cowardice of Sabinus, who, after rashly taking up arms, had not been able to defend against three cohorts the great stronghold of the Capitol, which might have defied even the mightiest armies. One cannot, however, easily fix upon one man the blame which belongs to all. Mucianus did in fact delay the conquerors by ambiguously worded dispatches; Antonius, by a perverse acquiescence, or by an attempt to throw the odium upon another, laid himself open to blame; the other generals, by imagining that the war was over, contrived a distinction for its closing scene. Even Petilius Cerialis, though he had been sent on with a thousand cavalry by crossroads through the Sabine district so as to enter Rome by the Via Salaria,[76] had not been sufficiently prompt in his movements, when the report of the siege of the Capitol put all alike on the alert.

79. Antonius marched by the Via Flaminia,[77] and arrived at Saxa Rubra,[78] when the night was far spent, too late to give any help. There he received nothing but gloomy intelligence, that Sabinus was dead, that the Capitol had been burned to the ground, that Rome was in consternation, and also that the populace and the slaves were arming themselves for Vitellius. And Petilius Cerialis had been defeated in a cavalry skirmish. While he was hurrying on without caution, as against a vanquished enemy, the Vitellians, who had disposed some infantry among their cavalry, met him. The conflict took place not far from the city among buildings, gardens, and winding lanes, which were well known to the Vitellians, but disconcerting to their opponents, to whom they were strange. Nor indeed were all the cavalry one in heart, for there were with them some who had lately capitulated at Narnia, and who were anxiously watching the fortunes of the rival parties. Julius Flavianus, commanding a squadron, was taken prisoner; the rest fled

in disgraceful confusion, but the victors did not continue
the pursuit beyond Fidenæ.[79]

80. By this success the zeal of the people was increased. The mob of the city armed itself. Some few
had military shields, the greater part seized such arms
as came to hand, and loudly demanded the signal of
battle. Vitellius expressed his thanks to them, and bade
them sally forth to defend the capital. Then the Senate
was called together, and envoys were selected to meet
the armies and urge them in the name of the commonwealth to union and peace. The reception of these
envoys was not everywhere the same. Those who fell
in with Petilius Cerialis were exposed to extreme peril,
for the troops disdained all offers of peace. The prætor
Arulenus Rusticus[80] was wounded. This deed seemed all
the more atrocious when, over and above the insult
offered to the dignity of the envoy and prætor, men
considered the personal excellence of the man. His companions were dispersed, and the lictor that stood next to
him, venturing to push aside the crowd, was killed. Had
they not been protected by an escort provided by the
general, the dignity of the ambassador, respected even
by foreign nations, would have been profaned with fatal
violence by the madness of Roman citizens before the
very walls of their country. The envoys who met Antonius were more favorably received, not because the
troops were of quieter temper, but because the general
had more authority.

81. One Musonius Rufus,[81] a man of equestrian rank,
strongly attached to the pursuit of philosophy and to
the tenets of the Stoics, had joined the envoys. He
mingled with the troops, and, enlarging on the blessings of peace and the perils of war, began to admonish
the armed crowd. Many thought it ridiculous; more
thought it tiresome; some were ready to throw him down
and trample him underfoot, and had he not yielded to the
warnings of the more orderly and the threats of others,
and ceased to display his ill-timed wisdom. The Vestal
Virgins also presented themselves with a letter from
Vitellius to Antonius. He asked for one day of truce
before the final struggle, and said that if they would

permit some delay to intervene, everything might be more easily arranged. The sacred virgins were sent back with honor, but the answer returned to Vitellius was that all ordinary intercourse of war had been broken off by the murder of Sabinus and the conflagration of the Capitol.

82. Antonius, however, summoned the legions to an assembly, and endeavored to calm them, proposing that they should encamp near the Mulvian Bridge,[82] and enter the capital on the following day. His reason for delay was the fear that the soldiers, once exasperated by conflict, would respect neither the people nor the Senate, nor even the shrines and temples of the gods. They, however, looked with dislike on all procrastination as inimical to victory. At the same time the colors that glittered among the hills, though followed by an unwarlike population, presented the appearance of a hostile array. They advanced in three divisions, one column straight from where they had halted along the Via Flaminia, another along the bank of the Tiber, a third moved on the Colline Gate by the Via Salaria. The mob was routed by a charge of the cavalry. Then the Vitellian troops, themselves also drawn up in three columns of defense, met the foe. Numerous engagements with various issues took place before the walls, but they generally ended in favor of the Flavians, who had the advantage of more skillful generalship. Only that division suffered which had wound its way along narrow and slippery roads to the left quarter of the city as far as the gardens of Sallust. The Vitellians, taking their stand on the garden walls, kept off the assailants with stone and javelins till late in the day, when they were taken in the rear by the cavalry, which had then forced an entrance by the Colline Gate. In the Campus Martius also the hostile armies met, the Flavians with all the prestige of fortune and repeated victory, the Vitellians rushing on in sheer despair. Though defeated, they rallied again in the city.

83. The populace stood by and watched the combatants; and, as though it had been a mimic conflict, encouraged first one party and then the other by their shouts and

plaudits. Whenever either side gave way, they cried out that those who concealed themselves in the shops, or took refuge in any private house, should be dragged out and butchered, and they secured the larger share of the booty; for, while the soldiers were busy with bloodshed and massacre, the spoils fell to the crowd. It was a terrible and hideous sight that presented itself throughout the city. Here raged battle and death; there the bath and the tavern were crowded. In one spot were pools of blood and heaps of corpses, and close by prostitutes and men of character as infamous; there were all the debaucheries of luxurious peace, all the horrors of a city most cruelly sacked, till one was ready to believe the country to be mad at once with rage and lust. It was not indeed the first time that armed troops had fought within the city; they had done so twice when Sulla, once when Cinna triumphed.[83] The bloodshed then had not been less, but now there was an unnatural recklessness, and men's pleasures were not interrupted even for a moment. As if it were a new delight added to their holidays, they exulted in and enjoyed the scene, indifferent to parties, and rejoicing over the sufferings of the commonwealth.

84. The most arduous struggle was the storming of the camp, which the bravest of the enemy still held as a last hope. It was, therefore, with peculiar energy that the conquerors, among whom the veteran cohorts were especially forward, brought to bear upon it at once all the appliances which have been discovered in reducing the strongest cities—the *testudo*, the catapult, the earthwork, and the firebrand. They repeatedly shouted that "all the toil and danger they had endured in so many conflicts would be crowned by this achievement. The capital has been restored to the Senate and people of Rome, and their temples to the gods; but the soldier's peculiar distinction is in the camp; this is his country, and this his home; unless this be recovered forthwith, the night must be passed under arms." On the other hand the Vitellians, though unequal in numbers and doomed to defeat, could yet disturb the victory, delay the conclusion of peace, and pollute both hearth and altar

with blood; and they clung to these last consolations of the vanquished. Many, desperately wounded, breathed their last on the towers and ramparts. When the gates were torn down, the survivors threw themselves in a body on the conquerors, and fell to a man, with their wounds in front and their faces turned toward the foe, so anxious were they even in their last hours to die with honor.

When the city had been taken, Vitellius caused himself to be carried in a litter through the back of the palace to the Aventine, to his wife's dwelling, intending, if by any concealment he could escape for that day, to make his way to his brother's cohorts at Tarracina. Then, with characteristic weakness, and following the instincts of fear, which, dreading everything, shrinks most from what is immediately before it, he retraced his steps to the desolate and forsaken palace, whence even the meanest slaves had fled, or where they avoided his presence. The solitude and silence of the place scared him; he tried the closed doors, he shuddered in the empty chambers, till, wearied out with his miserable wanderings, he concealed himself in an unseemly hiding place, from which he was dragged out by the tribune Julius Placidus. His hands were bound behind his back, and he was led along with tattered robes, a revolting spectacle, amidst the invectives of many, the tears of none. The degradation of his end had extinguished all pity. One of the German soldiers met the party, and aimed a deadly blow at Vitellius, perhaps in anger, perhaps wishing to release him the sooner from insult. Possibly the blow was meant for the tribune. He struck off that officer's ear, and was immediately dispatched.

85. Vitellius, compelled by threatening swords first to raise his face and offer it to insulting blows, then to behold his own statues falling round him, and more than once to look at the Rostra and the spot where Galba was slain, was then driven along till they reached the Gemonian Stairs, the place where the corpse of Flavius Sabinus had lain. One speech was heard from him showing a spirit not utterly degraded, when to the insults of a tribune he answered, "Yet I was your Emperor." Then

431

he fell under a shower of blows, and the mob reviled the dead man with the same heartlessness with which they had flattered him when he was alive.

86. Luceria[84] was his native place; he had nearly completed his fifty-seventh year. His consulate, his priesthood, his high reputation, his place among the first men of the state, he owed not to any energy of his own, but to the renown of his father. The throne was offered him by men who did not know him. Seldom have the affections of the army attached themselves to any man who sought to gain them by his virtues as firmly as they did to him from the indolence of his character. Yet he had a certain frankness and generosity, qualities indeed which turn to a man's ruin, unless tempered with discretion. Believing that friendship may be retained by munificent gifts rather than by consistency of character, he deserved more of it than he secured. Doubtless it was good for the state that Vitellius should be overthrown, but they who betrayed Vitellius to Vespasianus cannot make a merit of their treachery, since they had themselves revolted from Galba. The day was now fast drawing to a close, and the Senate could not be convened, owing to the panic of the magistrates and senators, who had stolen out of the city, or were concealing themselves in the houses of dependants. When nothing more was to be feared from the enemy, Domitian came forward to meet the leaders of the party; he was universally saluted by the title of Cæsar, and the troops, in great numbers, armed as they were, conducted him to his father's house.

BOOK IV

1. WHEN Vitellius was dead, the war had indeed come to an end, but peace had yet to begin. Sword in hand, throughout the capital, the conquerors hunted down the conquered with merciless hatred. The streets were choked with carnage, the squares and temples reeked with blood, for men were massacred everywhere as chance threw them in the way. Soon, as their license

increased, they began to search for and drag forth hidden foes. Whenever they saw a young and tall man they cut him down, making no distinction between soldiers and civilians. But the ferocity which in the first impulse of hatred could be gratified only by blood, soon passed into the greed of gain. They let nothing be kept secret, nothing be closed; Vitellians, they pretended, might be thus concealed. Here was the first step to breaking open private houses; here, if resistance were made, a pretext for slaughter. The most needy of the populace and the most worthless of the slaves did not fail to come forward and betray their wealthy masters; others were denounced by friends. Everywhere were lamentations, and wailings, and all the miseries of a captured city, till the license of the Vitellian and Othonian soldiery, once so odious, was remembered with regret. The leaders of the party, so energetic in kindling civil strife, were incapable of checking the abuse of victory. In stirring up tumult and strife the worst men can do the most, but peace and quiet cannot be established without virtue.

2. Domitian had entered into possession of the title and residence of Cæsar, but not yet applying himself to business, was playing the part of a son of the throne with debauchery and intrigue. The office of prefect of the prætorian guard was held by Arrius Varus,[1] but the supreme power was in the hands of Antonius Primus, who carried off money and slaves from the establishment of the Emperor, as if they were the spoils of Cremona. The other generals, whose moderation or insignificance had shut them out from distinction in the war, had accordingly no share in its prizes. The country, terror-stricken and ready to acquiesce in servitude, urgently demanded that Lucius Vitellius with his cohorts should be intercepted on his way from Tarracina, and that the last sparks of war should be trodden out. The cavalry were sent on to Aricia[2] the main body of the legions halted on this side of Bovillæ.[3] Without hesitation Vitellius surrendered himself and his cohorts to the discretion of the conqueror, and the soldiers threw down their ill-starred arms in rage quite as much as in alarm. The long train of prisoners, closely guarded by armed

men, passed through the capital. Not one of them wore the look of a suppliant; sullen and savage, they were unmoved by the shouts and jests of the insulting rabble. A few who ventured to break away were overpowered by the force that hemmed them in; the rest were thrown into prison. Not one of them uttered an unworthy word; even in disaster the honor of the soldier was preserved. After this Lucius Vitellius was executed. Equally vicious with his brother, he had yet shown greater vigilance during that brother's reign, and may be said not so much to have shared his elevation, as to have been dragged down by his fall.

3. About the same time Lucilius Bassus was sent with some light cavalry to establish order in Campania, where the towns were still disturbed, but by mutual animosities rather than by any spirit of opposition to the new Emperor. The sight of the soldiery restored quiet, and the smaller colonies escaped unpunished. At Capua, however, the third legion was stationed to pass the winter, and the noble families suffered severely. Tarracina, on the other hand, received no relief; so much more inclined are we to requite an injury than an obligation. Gratitude is a burden, while there seems to be a profit in revenge. They were consoled by seeing the slave of Vergilius Capito,[4] whom I have mentioned as the betrayer of Tarracina, gibbeted in the very rings of knighthood, the gift of Vitellius, which they had seen him wear. At Rome the Senate, delighted and full of confident hope, decreed to Vespasianus all the honors customarily bestowed on the emperors. And indeed the civil war which, beginning in Gaul and Spain, and afterward drawing into the struggle first Germany and then Illyricum, had traversed Egypt, Judæa, and Syria, every province, and every army—this war, now that the whole earth was, as it were, purged from guilt, seemed to have reached its close. Their alacrity was increased by a letter from Vespasianus, written while the war was still in progress. Such indeed was its character at first sight; the writer, however, expressed himself as an Emperor, speaking modestly about himself, in admirable language about the state. There was no want of deference on the part of the

Senate. On the Emperor and his son Titus the consulship was bestowed by decree; on Domitian the office of prætor with consular authority.

4. Mucianus had also forwarded to the Senate certain letters which furnished matter for talk. It was said, "Why, if he is a private citizen, does he speak like a public man? In a few days' time he might have said the very same words in his place as a senator. And even the invective against Vitellius comes too late, and is ungenerous; while certainly it is arrogance to the state and an insult to the Emperor to boast that he had the imperial power in his hands, and made a present of it to Vespasianus." Their dislike, however, was concealed; their adulation was open enough. In most flattering language they voted a triumph to Mucianus, a triumph for a civil war, though the expedition against the Sarmatæ was the pretext. On Antonius Primus were bestowed the insignia of consular rank, on Arrius Varus and Cornelius Fuscus prætorian honors. Then they remembered the gods. It was determined that the Capitol should be restored. All these motions Valerius Asiaticus,[5] consulelect, proposed. Most of the senators signified their assent by their looks, or by raising the hand; but a few, who either held a distinguished rank, or had a practiced talent for flattery, declared their acquiescence in studied speeches. When it came to the turn of Helvidius Priscus,[6] prætor-elect, to vote, he delivered an opinion full of respect indeed to a worthy Emperor, and yet wholly free from insincerity; and he was strongly supported by the sympathies of the Senate. To Priscus indeed this day was in an especial manner the beginning of a great quarrel and a great renown.

5. As I have again happened to mention a man of whom I shall often have to speak, the subject seems to demand that I should give a brief account of his life and pursuits, and of his fortunes. Helvidius Priscus was a native of the town of Cluviæ;[7] his father had been a centurion of the first rank. In early youth he devoted his distinguished talents to the loftiest pursuits, not wishing, as do many, to cloak under an imposing name a life of indolence, but to be able to enter upon public life with

435

a spirit fortified against the chances of fortune. He followed those teachers of philosophy who hold nothing to be good but what is honorable, nothing evil but what is base, and who refuse to count either among things good or evil, power, rank, or indeed anything not belonging to the mind. While still holding the quæstorship, he was selected by Thrasea Pætus to be his son-in-law, and from the example of his father-in-law imbibed with peculiar eagerness a love of liberty. As a citizen and as a senator, as a husband, as a son-in-law, as a friend, and in all the relations of life, he was ever the same, despising wealth, steadily tenacious of right, and undaunted by danger.

6. There were some who thought him too eager for fame, and indeed the desire of glory is the last infirmity cast off even by the wise.[8] The fall of his father-in-law drove him into exile, but he returned when Galba mounted the throne, and proceeded to impeach Eprius Marcellus, who had been the informer against Thrasea. This retribution, as great as it was .just, had divided the Senate into two parties; for, if Marcellus fell, a whole army of fellow culprits was struck down. At first there was a fierce struggle, as is proved by the great speeches delivered by both men. But afterward, as the feelings of Galba were doubtful, and many senators interceded, Priscus dropped the charge, amidst comments varying with the tempers of men, some praising his moderation, and others deploring a lack of courage. On the day, however, that the Senate was voting about the imperial dignities of Vespasianus, it had been resolved that envoys should be sent to the new Emperor. Hence arose a sharp altercation between Helvidius and Eprius. Priscus proposed that they should be chosen by name by the magistrates on oath. Marcellus demanded the ballot; and this had been the opinion expressed by the consul-elect.

7. It was the dread of personal humiliation that made Marcellus so earnest, for he feared that, if others were chosen, he should himself appear slighted. From an angry conversation they passed by degrees to long and bitter speeches. Helvidius asked, "Why should Marcellus

436

be so afraid of the judgment of the magistrates? He
has wealth and eloquence, which might make him superior to many, were he not oppressed by the consciousness
of guilt. The chances of the ballot do not discriminate
men's characters; the voting and the judgment of the
Senate were devised to reach the lives and reputations of
individuals. It concerns the interests of the commonwealth, it concerns the honor due to Vespasianus, that he
should be met by those whom the Senate counts to be
peculiarly blameless, and who may fill the Emperor's
ear with honorable counsels. Vespasianus was the friend
of Thrasea, Soranus, and Sentius;[9] and the accusers of
these men, though it may not be expedient to punish
them, ought not to be paraded before him. By this selection on the part of the Senate the Emperor will, so to
speak, he advised whom he should mark with approval,
and from whom he should shrink. There can be no more
effectual instrument of good government than good
friends. Let Marcellus be satisfied with having urged
Nero to destroy so many innocent victims; let him enjoy
the wages of his crimes and his impunity, but let him
leave Vespasianus to worthier advisers."

8. Marcellus declared, "It is not my opinion that is
assailed; the consul-elect has made a motion in ac-
cordance with old precedents, which directed the use
of the ballot in the appointment of envoys, in order that
there might be no room for intrigue or private animosities. Nothing has happened why customs of long standing should fall into disuse, or why the honor due to
the Emperor should be turned into an insult to any
man. All senators are competent to pay their homage.
What we have rather to avoid is this, that a mind unsettled by the novelty of power, and which will keenly
watch the very looks and language of all, should be irritated by the obstinacy of certain persons. I do not forget the times in which I have been born, or the form
of government which our fathers and grandfathers established. I may regard with admiration an earlier period,
but I acquiesce in the present, and, while I pray for
good emperors, I can endure whomsoever we may have.
It was not through my speech any more than it was

through the judgment of the Senate that Thrasea fell. The savage temper of Nero amused itself under these forms, and I found the friendship of such a prince as harassing as others found their exile. Finally, Helvidius may rival the Catos and the Bruti of old in constancy and courage; I am but one of the Senate which bows to the same yoke. Besides, I would advise Priscus not to climb higher than the throne, or to impose his counsels on Vespasianus, an old man, who has won the honors of a triumph, and has two sons grown to manhood. For as the worst emperors love an unlimited despotism, so the noblest like some check on liberty." These speeches, which were delivered with much vehemence on both sides, were heard with much diversity of feeling. That party prevailed which preferred that the envoys should be taken by lot, as even the neutral section in the Senate exerted themselves to retain the old practice, while the more conspicuous members inclined to the same view, dreading jealousy, should the choice fall on themselves.

9. Another struggle ensued. The prætors of the treasury (the treasury was at this time managed by prætors)[10] complained of the poverty of the state, and demanded a retrenchment of expenditure. The consul-elect, considering how great was the evil and how difficult the remedy, was for reserving the matter for the Emperor. Helvidius gave it as his opinion that measures should be taken at the discretion of the Senate. When the consuls came to take the votes, Vulcacius Tertullinus, tribune of the people, put his veto on any resolution being adopted in so important a matter in the absence of the Emperor. Helvidius had moved that the Capitol should be restored at the public expense, and that Vespasianus should give his aid. All the more moderate of the senators let this opinion pass in silence, and in time forgot it; but there were some who remembered it.

10. Musonius Rufus[11] then made a violent attack on Publius Celer,[12] accusing him of having brought about the destruction of Barea Soranus by perjury. By this impeachment all the hatreds of the days of the in-

formers seemed to be revived; but the accused person
was so worthless and so guilty that he could not be
protected. For indeed the memory of Soranus was held
in reverence; Celer had been a professor of philosophy,
and had then given evidence against Barea, thus betraying and profaning the friendship of which he claimed
to be a teacher. The next day was fixed for the trial. But
it was not of Musonius or Publius, it was of Priscus, of
Marcellus, and his brother informers that men were
thinking, now that their hearts were once roused to
vengeance.

11. While things were in this state, while there was
division in the Senate, resentment among the conquered,
no real authority in the conquerors, and in the country
at large no laws and no Emperor, Mucianus entered the
capital, and at once drew all power into his own hands.
The influence of Antonius Primus and Arrius Varus was
destroyed; for the irritation of Mucianus against them,
though not revealed in his looks, was but ill-concealed,
and the country, keen to discover such dislikes, had
changed its tone and transferred its homage. He alone
was canvassed and courted, and he, surrounding himself with armed men, and bargaining for palaces and
gardens, ceased not, what with his magnificence, his
proud bearing, and his guards, to grasp at the power,
while he waived the titles of empire. The murder of Calpurnius Galerianus caused the utmost consternation. He
was a son of Gaius Piso,[13] and had done nothing, but
a noble name and his own youthful beauty made him
the theme of common talk; and while the country was
still unquiet and delighted in novel topics, there were
persons who associated him with idle rumors of imperial honors. By order of Mucianus he was surrounded
with a guard of soldiers. So that his execution in the
capital should not excite too much notice, they conducted him to the fortieth milestone from Rome on the
Appian Way, and there put him to death by opening his
veins. Julius Priscus,[14] who had been prefect of the
prætorian guard under Vitellius, killed himself rather
out of shame than by compulsion. Alfenus Varus survived the disgrace of his cowardice. Asiaticus,[15] who was

only a freedman, expiated by the death of a slave his evil exercise of power.

[*Chapters 12-37, which describe the beginning of the revolt of the Batavi under Civilis, are omitted.*]

38. Meanwhile Vespasianus (now consul for the second time) and Titus entered upon their office,[16] both being absent from Rome. People were gloomy and anxious under the pressure of manifold fears, for over and above immediate perils they had taken groundless alarm under the impression that Africa was in rebellion through the revolutionary movements of Lucius Piso.[17] He was governor of that province, and was far from being a man of turbulent disposition. The fact was that the wheat ships were detained by the severity of the weather, and the lower orders, who were accustomed to buy their provisions from day to day, and to whom cheap corn was the sole subject of public interest, feared and believed that the ports had been closed and the supplies stopped, the Vitellians, who had not yet given up their party feelings, helping to spread the report, which was not displeasing even to the conquerors. Their ambition, which even foreign campaigns could not fill to the full, was not satisfied by any triumphs that civil war could furnish.

39. On the 1st of January, at a meeting of the Senate, convoked for the purpose by Julius Frontinus,[18] prætor of the city, votes of thanks were passed to the legates, to the armies, and to the allied kings. The office of prætor was taken away from Tettius Julianus, as having deserted his legion when it passed over to the party of Vespasianus,[19] with a view to its being transferred to Plotius Grypus. Equestrian rank was conferred on Hormus.[20] Then, on the resignation of Frontinus, Domitian assumed the office of prætor of the city. His name was put at the head of dispatches and edicts, but the real authority was in the hands of Mucianus, with this exception, that Domitian ventured on several acts of power, at the instigation of his friends, or at his own caprice. But Mucianus found his principal cause of apprehension in

Antonius Primus and Arrius Varus, who, in the freshness of their fame, while distinguished by great achievements and by the attachment of the soldiery, were also
supported by the people, because in no case had they
extended their severities beyond the battlefield. It was
also reported that Antonius had urged Crassus Scribonianus,[21] whom an illustrious descent added to the honors
of his brother made a conspicuous person, to assume the
supreme power; and it was understood that a number
of accomplices would not have failed to support him,
had not the proposal been rejected by Scribonianus, who
was a man not easily to be tempted even by a certainty,
and was proportionately apprehensive of risk. Mucianus,
seeing that Antonius could not be openly crushed, heaped
many praises upon him in the Senate, and loaded him
with promises in secret, holding out as a prize the government of eastern Spain, then vacant in consequence
of the departure of Cluvius Rufus. At the same time he
lavished on his friends tribuneships and prefectures; and
then, when he had filled the vain heart of the man with
hope and ambition, he destroyed his power by sending
into winter quarters the 7th legion, whose affection for
Antonius was particularly vehement. The 3rd legion, old
troops of Arrius Varus, were sent back to Syria. Part of
the army was on its way to Germany. Thus, all elements
of disturbance being removed, the usual appearance of
the capital, the laws, and the jurisdiction of the magistrates were once more restored.

40. Domitian, on the day of his taking his seat in
the Senate, made a brief and measured speech in reference to the absence of his father and brother, and to his
own youth. He was graceful in his bearing, and, his
real character being yet unknown, the frequent blush
on his countenance passed for modesty. On his proposing the restoration of the imperial honors of Galba,
Curtius Montanus[22] moved that respect should also be
paid to the memory of Piso. The Senate passed both
motions, but that which referred to Piso was not carried
out. Certain commissioners were then appointed by lot,
who were to see to the restitution of property plundered
during the war, to examine and restore to their place

the brazen tables of the laws, which had fallen down
through age, to free the calendar from the additions
with which the adulatory spirit of the time had disfigured it, and to put a check on the public expenditure.
The office of prætor was restored to Tettius Julianus, as
soon as it was known that he had fled for refuge to
Vespasianus. Grypus still retained his rank. It was then
determined that the cause of Musonius Rufus[23] against
Publius Celer should be again brought on. Publius was
condemned, and thus expiation was made to the shade
of Soranus. The day thus marked by an example of
public justice was not barren of distinction to individuals. Musonius was thought to have fulfilled the righteous
duty of an accuser, but men spoke very differently of
Demetrius,[24] a disciple of the Cynical school of philosophy, who pleaded the cause of a notorious criminal by
appeals to corrupt influences rather than by fair argument. Publius himself, in his peril, had neither spirit
nor power of speech left. The signal for vengeance on
the informers having been thus given, Junius Mauricus[25]
asked Domitian to give the Senate access to the imperial registers, from which they might learn what im-
peachments the several informers had proposed. Domitian answered that in a matter of such importance the
Emperor must be consulted.

41. The Senate, led by its principal members, then
framed a form of oath, which was eagerly taken by all
the magistrates and by the other senators in the order
in which they voted. They called the gods to witness,
that nothing had been done by their instrumentality to
prejudice the safety of any person, and that they had
gained no distinction or advantage by the ruin of Roman
citizens. Great was the alarm, and various the devices
for altering the words of the oath, among those who felt
the consciousness of guilt. The Senate appreciated the
scruple, but denounced the perjury. This public censure,
as it might be called, fell with especial severity on three
men, Sariolenus Vocula, Nonius Attianus, and Cestius
Severus, all of them infamous for having practiced the
trade of the informer in the days of Nero. Sariolenus indeed labored under an imputation of recent date. It

was said that he had attempted the same practices during the reign of Vitellius. The senators did not desist from threatening gestures till he quitted the chamber; then, passing to Paccius Africanus, they assailed him in the same way. It was he, they said, who had singled out as victims for Nero the brothers Scribonius,[26] renowned for their mutual affection and for their wealth. Africanus dared not confess his guilt, and could not deny it; but he himself turned on Vibius Crispus, who was pressing him with questions, and complicating a charge which he could not rebut, shifted the blame from himself by associating another with his guilt.

42. Great was the reputation for brotherly affection, as well as for eloquence, which Vipstanus Messalla[27] earned for himself on that day, by venturing, though not yet of senatorial age, to plead for his brother Aquilius Regulus.[28] The fall of the families of the Crassi and Orfitus had brought Regulus into the utmost odium. Of his own free will, as it seemed, and while still a young man, he had undertaken the prosecution, not to ward off any peril from himself, but in the hope of gaining power. The wife of Crassus, Sulpicia Prætextata, and her four children were ready, should the Senate take cognizance of the cause, to demand vengeance. Accordingly, Messalla, without attempting to defend the case or the person accused, had simply thrown himself in the way of the perils that threatened his brother, and had thus wrought upon the feelings of several senators. On this Curtius Montanus met him with a fierce speech, in which he went to the length of asserting that after the death of Galba money had been given by Regulus to the murderer of Piso, and that he had even fastened his teeth in the murdered man's head. "Certainly," he said, "Nero did not compel this act; you did not secure by this piece of barbarity either your rank or your life. We may bear with the defense put forward by men who thought it better to destroy others than to come into peril themselves. As for you, the exile of your father, and the division of his property among his creditors, had left you perfectly safe, besides that your youth incapacitated you for office; there was nothing in you

443

which Nero could either covet or dread. It was from sheer lust of slaughter and greed of gain that you, unknown as you were, you, who had never pleaded in any man's defense, steeped your soul in noble blood, when, though you had snatched from the very grace of your country the spoils of a man of consular rank, had been fed to the full with seven million sesterces, and shone with all sacerdotal honors, you yet overwhelmed in one common ruin innocent boys, old men of illustrious name, and noble ladies, when you actually blamed the tardy movements of Nero in wearying himself and his informers with the overthrow of single families, and declared that the whole Senate might be destroyed by one word. Keep, Conscript Fathers, preserve a man of such ready counsels, that every age may be furnished with its teacher, and that our young men may imitate Regulus, just as our old men imitate Marcellus and Crispus.[29] Even unsuccessful villainy finds some to emulate it: what will happen if it flourish and be strong? And the man whom we dare not offend when he holds only quæstor's rank—are we to see him rise to the dignities of prætor and consul? Do you suppose that Nero will be the last of the tyrants? Those who survived Tiberius, those who survived Caligula, thought the same; and yet after each there arose another ruler yet more detestable and more cruel. We are not afraid of Vespasian; the age and moderation of the new Emperor reassure us. But the influence of an example outlives the individual character. We have lost our vigor, Conscript Fathers; we are no longer that Senate which, when Nero had fallen, demanded that the informers and ministers of the tyrant should be punished according to ancient custom. The first day after the downfall of a wicked emperor is the best of opportunities."

43. Montanus was heard with such approval on the part of the Senate that Helvidius conceived a hope that Marcellus also might be overthrown. He therefore began with a panegyric on Cluvius Rufus, who, though not less rich nor less renowned for eloquence, had never imperiled a single life in the days of Nero. By this comparison, as well as by direct accusations, he pressed

Eprius hard, and stirred the indignation of the senators. When Marcellus perceived this, he made as if he would leave the House, exclaiming, "We go, Priscus, and leave you your Senate; act the king, though Cæsar himself be present." Crispus followed. Both were enraged, but their looks were different; Marcellus cast furious glances about him, while Crispus smiled. They were drawn back, however, into the Senate by the hasty interference of friends. The contest grew fiercer, while the well-disposed majority on the one side, and a powerful minority on the other, fought out their obstinate quarrel, and thus the day was spent in altercation.

44. At the next meeting of the Senate Domitian began by recommending that the wrongs, the resentments, and the terrible necessities of former times should be forgotten, and Mucianus spoke at great length in favor of the informers. At the same time he admonished in gentle terms and in a tone of entreaty those who were reviving indictments which they had before commenced and afterward dropped. The senators, when they found themselves opposed, relinquished the liberty which they had begun to exercise. That it might not be thought that the opinion of the Senate was disregarded, or that impunity was accorded to all acts done in the days of Nero, Mucianus sent back to their islands two men of senatorial rank, Octavius Sagitta and Antistius Sosianus, who had quitted their places of banishment. Octavius had seduced one Pontia Postumia, and on her refusing to marry him, in the frenzy of passion had murdered her.[30] Sosianus by his depravity had brought many to ruin.[31] Both had been condemned and banished by a solemn decision of the Senate, and, though others were permitted to return, were kept under the same penalty. But this did not mitigate the hatred felt against Mucianus. Sosianus and Sagitta were utterly insignificant, even if they did return; but men dreaded the abilities of the informers, their wealth, and the power which they exercised in many sinister ways.

45. A trial conducted in the Senate according to ancient precedents brought into harmony for a time the feelings of its members. Manlius Patruitus, a senator,

laid a complaint that he had been beaten by a mob in
the colony of Sena,[32] and by order of the magistrates;
that the wrong had not stopped here, but that lamentations and wailings, in fact a representation of funeral
obsequies, had been enacted in his presence, accompanied with contemptuous and insulting expressions
leveled against the whole Senate. The persons accused
were summoned to appear, and after the case had been
investigated, punishment was inflicted on those who
were found guilty. A resolution of the Senate was also
passed, recommending more orderly behavior to the people of Sena. About the same time Antonius Flamma was
condemned under the law against extortion, at the suit
of the people of Cyrene, and was banished for cruel
practices.

[*The rest of Book IV (46-86) is omitted; it is mainly occupied with the rebellion of Civilis.*]

BOOK V

1. EARLY in this year Titus Cæsar, who had been selected by his father to complete the subjugation of
Judæa, and who had gained distinction as a soldier while
both were still subjects, began to rise in power and
reputation, as armies and provinces emulated each other
in their attachment to him. The young man himself,
anxious to be thought not to owe everything to fortune,
was ever displaying his gracefulness and his energy in
war. By his courtesy and affability he called forth a
willing obedience, and he often mixed with the common
soldiers, while working or marching, without impairing
his dignity as general. He found in Judæa three legions,
the 5th, the 10th, and the 15th, all old troops of Vespasianus'. To these he added the 12th from Syria, and
some men belonging to the 18th and 3rd, whom he had
withdrawn from Alexandria. This force was accompanied by twenty cohorts of allied troops and eight squadrons of cavalry, by the two kings Agrippa and Sohemus,[1]
by the auxiliary forces of King Antiochus, by a strong

446

contingent of Arabs, who hated the Jews with the usual hatred of neighbors, and, lastly, by many persons brought from the capital and from Italy by private hopes of securing the yet unengaged affections of the prince. With this force Titus entered the enemy's territory, preserving strict order on his march, reconnoitering every spot, and always ready to give battle. At last he encamped near Jerusalem.

2. As I am about to relate the last days of a famous city, it seems appropriate to throw some light on its origin.

Some say that the Jews were fugitives from the island of Crete, who settled on the nearest coast of Africa about the time when Saturn was driven from his throne by the power of Jupiter. Evidence of this is sought in the name. There is a famous mountain in Crete called Ida; the neighboring tribe, the Idæi, came to be called Judæi by a barbarous lengthening of the national name.[2] Others assert that in the reign of Isis the overflowing population of Egypt, led by Hierosolymus and Judas, discharged itself into the neighboring countries. Many, again, say that they were a race of Ethiopian origin, who in the time of King Cepheus[3] were driven by fear and hatred of their neighbors to seek a new dwelling place. Others describe them as an Assyrian horde who, not having sufficient territory, took possession of part of Egypt, and founded cities of their own in what is called the Hebrew country, lying on the borders of Syria. Others, again, assign a very distinguished origin to the Jews, alleging that they were the Solymi, a nation celebrated in the poems of Homer, who called the city which they founded Hierosolyma after their own name.[4]

3. Most writers, however, agree in stating that once a disease, which horribly disfigured the body, broke out over Egypt; that King Bocchoris,[5] seeking a remedy, consulted the oracle of Hammon,[6] and was bidden to cleanse his realm, and to convey into some foreign land this race detested by the gods. The people, who had been collected after diligent search, finding themselves left in a desert, sat for the most part in a stupor of grief, till one of the

exiles, Moses[7] by name, warned them not to look for
any relief from god or man, forsaken as they were of
both, but to trust to themselves, taking for their heaven-
sent leader that man who should first help them to be
quit of their present misery. They agreed, and in utter
ignorance began to advance at random. Nothing, however, distressed them so much as the scarcity of water,
and they had sunk ready to perish in all directions over
the plain, when a herd of wild asses was seen to retire
from their pasture to a rock shaded by trees. Moses followed them, and, guided by the appearance of a grassy
spot, discovered an abundant spring of water. This furnished relief. After a continuous journey for six days,
on the seventh they possessed themselves of a country,
from which they expelled the inhabitants, and in which
they founded a city and a temple.

4. Moses, wishing to secure for the future his authority over the nation, gave them a novel form of worship,
opposed to all that is practiced by other men. Things
sacred with us, with them have no sanctity, while they
allow what with us is forbidden. In their holy place
they have consecrated an image of the animal by whose
guidance they found deliverance from their long and
thirsty wanderings. They slay the ram, seemingly in
derision of Hammon, and they sacrifice the ox, because
the Egyptians worship it as Apis.[8] They abstain from
swine's flesh, in consideration of what they suffered when
they were infected by the leprosy to which this animal
is liable. By their frequent fasts they still bear witness
to the long hunger of former days, and the Jewish bread,
made without leaven, is retained as a memorial of their
hurried seizure of corn. We are told that the rest of the
seventh day was adopted because this day brought with
it a termination of their toils; after a while the charm of
indolence beguiled them into giving up the seventh year
also to inaction. But others say that it is an observance
in honor of Saturn, either from the primitive elements
of their faith having been transmitted from the Idæi,
who are said to have shared the flight of that god, and
to have founded the race, or from the circumstance that

of the seven stars which rule the destinies of men Saturn moves in the highest orbit and with the mightiest power, and that many of the heavenly bodies complete their revolutions and courses in multiples of seven.

5. This worship, however introduced, is upheld by its antiquity; all their other customs, which are at once perverse and disgusting, owe their strength to their very badness. The most degraded out of other races, scorning their own national beliefs, brought to them their contributions and presents. This augmented the wealth of the Jews, as also did the fact that among themselves they are inflexibly honest and ever ready to show compassion, though they regard the rest of mankind with all the hatred of enemies. They sit apart at meals, they sleep apart, and though, as a nation, they are singularly prone to lust, they abstain from intercourse with foreign women; among themselves nothing is unlawful. Circumcision was adopted by them as a mark of difference from other men. Those who come over to their religion adopt the practice, and have this lesson first instilled into them, to despise all gods, to disown their country, and set at nought parents, children, and brethren. Still they provide for the increase of their numbers. It is a crime among them to kill any of their own kin. They hold that the souls of all who perish in battle or by the hands of the executioner are immortal. Hence a passion for propagating their race and a contempt for death. They bury rather than burn their dead, following in this the Egyptian custom; they bestow the same care on the dead, and they hold the same belief about the lower world. Quite different is their faith about things divine. The Egyptians worship many animals and images of monstrous form; the Jews have purely mental conceptions of deity, as one in essence. They call those profane who make representations of God in human shape out of perishable materials. They believe that Being to be supreme and eternal, capable neither of representation, nor of decay. They therefore do not allow any images to stand in their cities, much less in their temples. This flattery is not paid to their kings, nor this

honor to our emperors. From the fact, however, that
their priests used to chant to the music of flutes and
cymbals, and to wear garlands of ivy, and that a golden
vine was found in the temple, some have thought that
they worshiped Father Liber,[9] the conqueror of the East,
though their institutions do not by any means harmonize
with the theory; for Liber established a festive and
cheerful worship, while the Jewish religion is tasteless
and squalid.

6. Eastward the country is bounded by Arabia; to the
south lies Egypt; on the west are Phœnicia and the
Mediterranean. Northward it commands an extensive
prospect over Syria. The inhabitants are healthy and
able to bear fatigue. Rain is uncommon, but the soil is
fertile. Its products resemble our own. They have, besides, the balsam tree[10] and the palm. The palm groves
are tall and graceful. The balsam is a shrub; each
branch, as it fills with sap, may be pierced with a
fragment of stone or pottery. If steel is employed, the
veins shrink up. The sap is used by physicians. Libanus
is the principal mountain, and has, strange to say,
amidst these burning heats, a summit shaded with trees
and never deserted by its snows. The same range supplies and sends forth the stream of the Jordan.[11] This
river does not discharge itself into the sea, but flows
entire through two lakes, and is lost in the third.[12] This
is a lake of vast circumference; it resembles the sea, but
is more nauseous in taste; it breeds pestilence among
those who live near by its noisome odor; it cannot be
moved by the wind, and it affords no home either to fish
or water birds. These strange waters support what is
thrown upon them, as on a solid surface, and all persons,
whether they can swim or no, are equally buoyed up by
the waves. At a certain season of the year the lake
throws up bitumen, and the method of collecting it has
been taught by that experience which teaches all other
arts. It is naturally a fluid of dark color; when vinegar
is sprinkled upon it, it coagulates and floats upon the
surface. Those whose business it is take it with the hand,
and draw it onto the deck of the boat; it then continues

of itself to flow in and lade the vessel till the stream is cut off. Nor can this be done by any instrument of brass or iron. It shrinks from blood or any cloth stained by the menstrual discharge of women. Such is the account of old authors; but those who know the country say that the bitumen moves in heaving masses on the water, that it is drawn by hand to the shore, and that there, when dried by the evaporation of the earth and the power of the sun, it is cut into pieces with axes and wedges just as timber or stone would be.

7. Not far from this lake lies a plain, once fertile, they say, and the site of great cities, but afterward struck by lightning and consumed.[13] Of this event, they declare, traces still remain, for the soil, which is scorched in appearance, has lost its productive power. Everything that grows spontaneously, as well as what is planted by hand, either when the leaf or flower have been developed, or after maturing in the usual form, becomes black and rotten, and crumbles into a kind of dust. I am ready to allow, on the one hand, that cities, once famous, may have been consumed by fire from heaven, while, on the other, I imagine that the earth is infected by the exhalations of the lake, that the surrounding air is tainted, and that thus the growth of harvest and the fruits of autumn decay under the equally noxious influences of soil and climate. The river Belus[14] also flows into the Jewish sea. About its mouth is a kind of sand which is collected, mixed with niter, and fused into glass. This shore is of limited extent, but furnishes an inexhaustible supply to the exporter.

8. A great part of Judæa consists of scattered villages. They have also towns. Jerusalem is the capital. There stood a temple of immense wealth. First came the city with its fortifications, then the royal palace, then, within the innermost defenses, the temple itself. Only the Jew might approach the gates; all but priests were forbidden to pass the threshold. While the East was under the sway of the Assyrians, the Medes, and the Persians, Jews were the most contemptible of the subject tribes. When the Macedonians became supreme, King Anti-

ochus[15] strove to destroy the national superstition, and
to introduce Greek civilization, but was prevented by
his war with the Parthians from at all improving this
vilest of nations; for at this time the revolt of Arsaces[16]
had taken place. The Macedonian power was now weak,
while the Parthian had not yet reached its full strength,
and, as the Romans were still far off, the Jews chose
kings for themselves.[17] Expelled by the fickle populace,
and regaining their throne by force of arms, these
princes, while they ventured on the wholesale banishment of their subjects, on the destruction of cities, on
the murder of brothers, wives, and parents, and the other
usual atrocities of despots, fostered the national superstition by appropriating the dignity of the priesthood
as the support of their political power.

9. Cnæus Pompeius was the first of our countrymen
to subdue the Jews. Availing himself of the right of conquest, he entered the temple.[18] Thus it became commonly known that the place stood empty with no similitude
of gods within, and that the shrine had nothing to reveal. The walls of Jerusalem were destroyed, the temple
was left standing. After these provinces had fallen, in
the course of our civil wars, into the hands of Marcus
Antonius, Pacorus, prince of the Parthians, seized Judæa. He was slain by Publius Ventidius, and the Parthians were driven back over the Euphrates.[19] Gaius
Sosius reduced the Jews to subjection. The royal power,
which had been bestowed by Antonius on Herod, was augmented by the victorious Augustus. On Herod's death,
one Simon, without waiting for the approbation of the
Emperor, usurped the title of king. He was punished by
Quintilius Varus,[20] then governor of Syria, and the nation, with its liberties curtailed, was divided into three
provinces under the sons of Herod.[21] Under Tiberius all
was quiet. But when the Jews were ordered by Caligula
to set up his statue in the temple, they preferred the
alternative of war.[22] The death of the Emperor put an
end to the disturbance. The kings were either dead, or
reduced to insignificance, when Claudius entrusted the
province of Judæa to Roman knights or to his own

freedmen, one of whom, Antonius Felix,[23] indulging in every kind of barbarity and lust, exercised the power of a king in the spirit of a slave. He had married Drusilla, the granddaughter of Antonius and Cleopatra, and so was the grandson-in-law, as Claudius was the grandson, of Antonius.[24]

10. Yet the endurance of the Jews lasted till Gessius Florus[25] was procurator. In his time the war broke out. Cestius Gallus,[26] legate of Syria, who attempted to crush it, had to fight several battles, generally with ill success. Cestius dying, either in the course of nature or from vexation, Vespasianus was sent by Nero, and by help of his good fortune, his high reputation, and his excellent subordinates, succeeded within the space of two summers in occupying with his victorious army the whole of the level country and all the cities, except Jerusalem. The following year had been wholly taken up with civil strife, and had passed, as far as the Jews were concerned, in inaction. Peace having been established in Italy, foreign affairs were once more remembered. Our indignation was heightened by the circumstance that the Jews alone had not submitted. At the same time it was held to be more expedient, in reference to the possible results and contingencies of the new reign, that Titus should remain with the army.

Accordingly he pitched his camp, as I have related, before the walls of Jerusalem, and displayed his legions in order of battle.

11. The Jews formed their line close under their walls, whence, if successful, they might venture to advance, and where, if repulsed, they had a refuge at hand. The cavalry with some light infantry was sent to attack them, and fought without any decisive result. Shortly afterward the enemy retreated. During the following days they fought a series of engagements in front of the gates, till they were driven within the walls by continual defeats. The Romans then began to prepare for an assault. It seemed beneath them to await the result of famine. The army demanded the more perilous alternative, some prompted by courage, many by sheer ferocity

and greed of gain. Titus himself had Rome with all its wealth and pleasures before his eyes. Jerusalem must fall at once, or it would delay his enjoyment of them. But the commanding situation of the city had been strengthened by enormous works which would have been a thorough defense even for level ground. Two hills of great height were fenced in by walls which had been skillfully obliqued or bent inward, in such a manner that the flank of an assailant was exposed to missiles. The rock terminated in a precipice; the towers were raised to a height of sixty feet, where the hill lent its aid to the fortifications, where the ground fell, to a height of one hundred and twenty. They had a marvelous appearance, and to a distant spectator seemed to be of uniform elevation. Within were other walls surrounding the palace, ar 1, rising to a conspicuous height, the tower Antonia, so called by Herod in honor of Marcus Antonius.

12. The temple resembled a citadel, and had its own walls, which were more laboriously constructed than the others. Even the colonnades with which it was surrounded formed an admirable outwork. It contained an inexhaustible spring; there were subterranean excavations in the hill, and tanks and cisterns for holding rain water. The founders of the state had foreseen that frequent wars would result from the singularity of its customs, and so had made every provision against the most protracted siege. After the capture of their city by Pompeius, experience and apprehension taught them much. Availing themselves of the sordid policy of the Claudian era to purchase the right of fortification, they raised in time of peace such walls as were suited for war. Their numbers were increased by a vast rabble collected from the overthrow of the other cities. All the most obstinate rebels had escaped into the place, and perpetual seditions were the consequence. There were three generals, and as many armies. Simon held the outer and larger circuit of walls. John, also called Bargioras, occupied the middle city. Eleazar had fortified the temple. John and Simon were strong in numbers and equipment,

Eleazar in position.[27] There were continual skirmishes, surprises, and incendiary fires, and a vast quantity of corn was burned. Before long John sent some emissaries, who, under pretense of sacrificing, slaughtered Eleazar and his partisans, and gained possession of the temple. The city was thus divided between two factions, till, as the Romans approached, war with the foreigner brought about a reconciliation.

13. Prodigies had occurred, which this nation, prone to superstition but hating all religious rites, did not think it lawful to expiate by offering and sacrifice. There had been seen hosts joining battle in the skies, the fiery gleam of arms, the temple illuminated by a sudden radiance from the clouds. The doors of the inner shrine were suddenly thrown open, and a voice of more than mortal tone was heard to cry that the gods were departing. At the same instant there was a mighty stir as of departure. Some few put a fearful meaning on these events, but in most there was a firm persuasion that in the ancient records of their priests was contained a prediction of how at this very time the East was to grow powerful, and rulers, coming from Judæa, were to acquire universal empire. These mysterious prophecies had pointed to Vespasian and Titus, but the common people, with the usual blindness of ambition, had interpreted these mighty destinies of themselves, and could not be brought even by disasters to believe the truth. I have heard that the total number of the besieged, of every age and both sexes, amounted to six hundred thousand. All who were able bore arms, and a number, more than proportionate to the population, had the courage to do so. Men and women showed equal resolution, and life seemed more terrible than death, if they were to be forced to leave their country. Such was this city and nation; and Titus Cæsar, seeing that the position forbade an assault or any of the more rapid operations of war, determined to proceed by earthworks and covered approaches. The legions had their respective duties assigned to them, and there was a cessation from fighting, till all the inventions used in ancient warfare or de-

vised by modern ingenuity for the reduction o
were constructed.

*[Chapters 14-26, which deal with the rebellion
are omitted.]*

Notes

Book I

1. Supposed to have been one of the first pair of consuls, 509 B.C.

2. A commission of ten, appointed to prepare a new constitution, it was supposed to have supreme power from 451 to 449 B.C. but had to resign it because of the tyrannical behavior of its leading member, Appius Claudius.

3. Cinna was consul every year from 87 to 84 B.C.; Sulla was dictator from 82 to 79 B.C.

4. Brutus and Cassius killed themselves at the battle of Philippi in 42 B.C.

5. Sextus Pompeius, son of the great Pompey, carried on naval warfare for a time against the triumvirs, but lost his fleet at Naulochus in 36 B.C.; Lepidus lost his triumviral powers the same year. Antony killed himself after the battle of Actium in 31 B.C.

6. See III, 56.

7. Marcus Claudius Marcellus (42-23 B.C.).

8. Marcus Vipsanius Agrippa (63-12 B.C.), Augustus' right-hand man from the first, married his daughter Julia, the widow of Marcellus, in 21 B.C. He was consul in 37, 28, and 27, and from 18 B.C. held special powers that seemed to mark him out as Augustus' successor.

9. Tiberius Claudius Nero, born 42 B.C., eventually succeeded Augustus. Nero Claudius Drusus (39-9 B.C.) married the younger Antonia, daughter of Mark Antony by Augustus' sister, and was the father of Germanicus and of the Emperor Claudius.

10. Gaius Cæsar (20 B.C.-4 A.D.) and Lucius Cæsar (17 B.C.-2 A.D.) were Agrippa's sons by Julia.

11. Now Planosa. Agrippa Postumus (12 B.C.-14 A.D.) was the younger brother of Gaius and Lucius.

12. Germanicus (15 B.C.-19 A.D.) went to the Rhine in 13 A.D.

13. Drusus (13 B.C.-23 A.D.).

14. P. Quintilius Varus commanded three legions that were annihilated by the Germans under Arminius in the Teutoburger Wald in 2 A.D.

15. He and his brother Drusus had carried on important operations in Illyricum and Germany between 15 and 6 B.C.

16. He had been at Rhodes from 6 B.C. to 4 A.D.

17. Paullus Fabius Maximus (consul 11 B.C).

18. In Campania.

19. Gaius Sallustius Crispus, great-nephew of the historian Sallust, was Mæcenas' successor as Augustus' man of confidence in matters of this kind; see III, 30.

20. The year was 14 A.D.

21. Gaius Asinius Gallus (consul 8 B.C.) was the son of the statesman, orator, and historian Gaius Asinius Pollio (consul 40 B.C.).

22. Consul in 6 A.D.

23. Marcus Valerius Messalla (consul 3 B.C.) was son of the statesman and orator Messalla Corvinus (consul 31 B.C.). See III, 34.

24. $6+7=13$.

25. 23 B.C. to 14 A.D.

26. In 43 B.C. he had fought on the side of the Senate against Mark Antony at the battle of Mutina. When the two consuls of the year (Aulus Hirtius and Gaius Vibius Pansa) died in the battle, he got himself made consul, and soon after made an agreement with Antony, joining him and Lepidus in the proscription of their enemies.

27. See above, notes 4 and 5.

28. Marcus Lollius (consul 21 B.C.) when governing Gaul suffered a defeat from raiding Germans; see III, 48. On Varus, see above, note 14.

29. Aulus Terentius Varro Murena, the brother-in-law of Augustus' man of confidence, Mæcenas, was executed in the year of his consulship (23 B.C.) for conspiring against Augustus. Egnatius Rufus won popularity as ædile by organizing a private fire brigade; in 19 B.C. he

stood unsuccessfully for the consulship, and was soon after executed for conspiracy. Iullus Antonius (consul 10 B.C.), son of Mark Antony, was executed for adultery with Augustus' daughter Julia in 2 B.C.

30. Livia had been pregnant by her first husband, Tiberius Claudius Nero, when she was divorced and married Augustus in 38 B.C.

31. Publius Vedius Pollio, the son of a freedman, seems to have exercised authority in the province of Asia soon after Actium. He was said to feed his lampreys with live slaves in order to improve their taste.

32. Tiberius had been made to divorce this lady, to whom he was devoted, in order to marry Augustus' daughter Julia after she had been left a widow by the death of Agrippa. Vipsania was Agrippa's daughter by his first wife, Pomponia, the daughter of Cicero's great friend Titus Pomponius Atticus.

33. Marcus Æmilius Lepidus (consul 6 A.D.) was a nephew of the triumvir; see I, 1.

34. Cnæus Piso (consul 7 B.C.).

35. Quintus Haterius (suffect consul 5 B.C.) had been born as early as 63 B.C.

36. Mamercus Æmilius Scaurus (suffect consul 21 A.D.).

37. While the Republic lasted, the election of magistrates had been a jealousy guarded right of the Roman people. They took place in the Campus Martius, and voters had to be registered as members of one of the thirty-five citizen tribes. The people now had from the Emperor all that they had formerly got from the candidates for office who had competed for their favors. A law of 5 A.D., recorded on a bronze tablet lately found in Spain known as the Tabula Hebana, shows that in that year the senators, together with those Roman knights who were liable for jury service, were formed into ten centuries, which were to choose candidates whom the people would then elect. This may represent an earlier stage in a process that culminated in 14 A.D.; but it is likelier that Tacitus is wrong about the nature of the change.

38. Under the Republic the games had been paid for by the magistrates; they were now paid for by the state, that is, the Emperor.

39. Vandotena, a little north of the Bay of Naples.

40. Reggio di Calabria.

41. As a tragic poet he may have brought special skill to the composition of this letter. Karkenah, in Syrtis Minor, will have been not less uncomfortable than Vandotena.

42. Lucius Nonius Asprenas (suffect consul 6 A.D.).

43. The title had been given by acclamation to Cicero for his part in suppressing Catiline's conspiracy in 63 B.C. In 45 B.C. it was given to Julius Cæsar and in 2 B.C. to Augustus. Cf. II, 87.

44. Just as under the Republic the magistrates had sworn to keep the laws, so in 45 B.C. the magistrates had had to swear to do nothing contrary to the acts of Julius Cæsar. Augustus exacted the same oath in 29 B.C., after his return to Italy for the first time after the defeat of Antony.

45. See Introduction.

46. This great orator was banished by Augustus probably in 12 A.D.; see IV, 21 and VI, 18.

47. Consul in 9 A.D., grandfather of Nero's beautiful and wicked wife; see VI, 39.

48. The province of Mœsia extended along the lower Danube from the Drin to the Black Sea. Achæa comprised mainland Greece apart from Macedonia.

49. See I, 15.

Book II

1. She was the mother of his only child, Julia.

2. Suffect consul in 31 A.D.

3. Brindisi; the Appian Way from Rome to Brundisium by way of Capua, Beneventum, Venusia, and Tarentum was begun by the censor Appius Claudius the Blind in 312 and finished about 244 B.C.

4. See III, 48.

5. Consul in 20 A.D., brother of the man mentioned at I, 8.

6. Consul in 17 A.D., later governor of Mœsia and Syria.

7. Suffect consul in 9 A.D.

8. Suffect consul in 8 A.D., later governor of Lower Germany.

9. See I, 13.

10. Gaius Fabricius (consul in 282 and 278, censor in 275 B.C.), famous for heroic conduct in the war with Pyrrhus of Epirus, was known especially for his incorruptibility. The elder Scipio Africanus defeated Hannibal at Zama in 202 B.C.; but the speaker probably has in mind the younger Scipio Africanus, who destroyed Carthage in 146 B.C.

11. Lucius Calpurnius Piso, consul in 1 B.C.; see IV, 21.

12. Her granddaughter and namesake was the first wife of the Emperor Claudius.

13. See I, 13.

14. Quintus Hortensius Hortalus (consul in 69 B.C.) had been after Cicero the greatest orator of the last age of the Republic.

15. Monte Argentaro.

16. See I, 6.

17. In the forum, near the foot of the Capitoline Hill.

18. In Latium, eleven miles from Rome.

19. 17 A.D.

20. See I, 3.

21. Marcus Cæcilius Metellus Creticus Silanus (consul 7 A.D.).

22. See I, 13.

23. Her grandfather Lucius Munatius Plancus (consul 42 B.C.) was famous for changing sides at the right moment more than once during the civil wars.

24. Drusus' mother was Vipsania; see Book I, note 32.

25. Germanicus was the son of Tiberius' brother Drusus by Antonia, younger daughter of Mark Antony by Augustus' sister, Octavia.

26. But Atticus (see Book I, note 32) was not only highly cultivated but immensely rich.

27. Maroboduus, king of the Marcomanni (a branch of the Suebi) had in 9 B.C. obliged his tribe to move from southern Germany to Bohemia; from here they had extended their rule over Saxony and Silesia. The Semnones lived in Brandenburg and Lausitz, between the middle Elbe and the Oder, and the Langobardi (later famous as the Lombards) on both banks of the lower Elbe.

28. A general term for the range of wooded mountains that runs from the Rhine to the Carpathians, encloses Bohemia, and cuts off the north German plain from southern Germany.

29. The Marcomanni with the Quadi had migrated from Franconia to Bohemia after a defeat by Drusus in 9 B.C.

30. The Goths lived at this time on the lower Vistula; their own belief was that they had come there from Scandinavia.

31. The province of Noricum lay in the Alps, south of the Danube, between Rætia and Pannonia.

32. Philip II of Macedonia (359-336 B.C.).

33. Pyrrhus of Epirus (297-272 B.C.), defeated by the Romans at Beneventum in 275.

34. Antiochus III of Syria (223-187 B.C.), defeated by the Romans at Magnesia in 190.

35. They extended from the neighborhood of Regensburg on the Danube northward through Franconia into Thuringia, and were on friendly terms with Rome.

36. Fréjus.

37. The March and the Waag.

38. See above, note 29.

39. Built by Augustus to commemorate his revenge upon the murderers of Julius Cæsar, it stood in the middle of the forum of Augustus.

40. They extended along the east side of the Carpathians from Galicia onward.

41. The inhabitants of the northern Black Sea coast.

42. See II, 32.

43. Marcus Æmilius Lepidus (consul in 187 B.C.) was sent to Egypt on the death of Ptolemy Epiphanes in 180 B.C.

44. The port of Antioch.

45. Suffect consul in 17 A.D.; see VI, 47.

46. Suffect consul in 4 A.D.

47. In the eastern Ægean, north of Rhodes.

48. Latakia, on the coast opposite Cyprus.

49. Kilindri.

50. An ancient brotherhood of priests of Mars, who during their ritual chanted a hymn of great antiquity, fragments of which survive.

51. See I, 54.

52. The name *flamen* was applied to the holders of fifteen priesthoods of special importance.

53. The augurs were the official diviners of the state; membership in their college of Sixteen was a high honor.

54. The mountain horseshoe of Elma Dagh above Alexandretta.

55. A suburb of Antioch.

56. An aunt of this lady, also called Vistilia, had six husbands; it has been suggested that the niece's application may have been a protest against the aunt's career.

57. A small island in the Ægean.

58. We learn from the Jewish historian Josephus what provoked this discussion. A Roman knight wished to obtain the favors of a lady much addicted to the mysteries of Isis, and succeeded by bribing the priest of Isis to tell her that the god Osiris wished to spend a night with her and to allow him to impersonate the god. Another lady had been persuaded to make an offering to the temple at Jerusalem, which the people who persuaded her then embezzled. The four thousand deported were in fact Jews; since the conquest of Judæa by Pompeius in 63 B.C., Jews had become numerous at Rome.

59. There were six Vestals, and the period of service was thirty years.

60. Gaius Fabricius (see Book II, note 10) had refused a similar offer.

Book III

1. Corfu.
2. Brindisi.
3. Terracina.
4. For 20 A.D.
5. Pavia.
6. Julia, who married Pompey, and died in 54 B.C.
7. Games in honor of Cybele, the Anatolian mother of the gods, had been celebrated at Rome every fourth of April since 204 B.C.
8. The part of the Adriatic coast between Ancona and the river Sangro.
9. Built in 220 B.C., it ran from Rome to the Adriatic coast at Ariminum (Rimini).
10. Narni, on the Nera.
11. See II, 28.
12. See I, 8, etc.
13. Consul 2 A.D., father of the consul of 30 and 45.
14. Prætor in 19 A.D., and nephew of Asinius Gallus.
15. See I, 7.
16. See I, 13.
17. See II, 34.
18. Also of consular rank.
19. Down which the bodies of criminals were dragged with a hook.
20. See Book I, note 29.
21. See I, 8.
22. See Book II, note 39.
23. See I, 12.
24. See I, 3 (Gaius and Lucius); I, 6 (Agrippa Postumus); IV, 71 (the younger Julia); VI, 25 (Agrippina).
25. She had been betrothed to Lucius Cæsar (see I, 3); the Æmilii Lepidi were a patrician house of great distinction.
26. See II, 30; III, 48.
27. See I, 13, etc.
28. Consul in 3 A.D.
29. The theater of Pompey was built by Pompeius Magnus during his second consulship in 55 B.C.

30. Suffect consul in 18 A.D.

31. See I, 13; Scaurus too was a descendant of an old and noble family.

32. Decimus Junius Silanus had been in exile since 8 A.D.

33. The elder Julia; see I, 53.

34. The younger Julia, daughter of the elder Julia by Agrippa and wife of Lucius Æmilius Paullus (consul 1 A.D.), was exiled in 8 A.D.; her husband was executed for conspiracy, apparently at the same time.

35. Suffect consul in 15 A.D.; his daughter was one of the wives of the Emperor Gaius (see VI, 20).

36. This law, carried in 9 A.D., supplemented the Julian Laws of 18 B.C., which were intended to strengthen the institution of marriage by repressing adultery and encouraging procreation.

37. Crete and Sparta in classical times both had severe constitutions of an aristocratic type, much admired by Plato. The Cretans claimed to have inherited this from their Minoan predecessors, as Aristotle states and as the mention of Minos here implies; more probably this type of constitution is common to Crete and Sparta because both were inhabited in classical times by Dorians. Very different dates are given for Lycurgus, who may be a legendary figure.

38. Statesman and poet, archon at Athens in 594-593 B.C., and reformer of the Athenian constitution.

39. Legendary founder and first king of Rome, supposed to have lived in the middle of the eighth century B.C.

40. Successor to Romulus.

41. Tullus Hostilius and Ancus Martius, third and fourth kings of Rome.

42. Sixth king, traditionally from 578 to 535 B.C.

43. Tarquin the Proud (534-510 B.C.).

44. See I, 1, with notes.

45. The earliest Roman legal code, supposed to have been drawn up by the decemvirs in the middle of the fifth century B.C.

46. Tiberius Sempronius Gracchus, tribune in 133

B.C.; his brother, Gaius Sempronius Gracchus, tribune in 123-122 B.C.; and Lucius Appuleius Saturninus, tribune in 103 and 100 B.C., were all authors of reforming legislation who relied on popular support. "As flagrant a corruptor in the Senate's name" suggests that the Drusus meant is Marcus Livius Drusus (tribune in 122 B.C.), who tried to outbid Gaius Gracchus in the interest of the Senate; but the mention of the Italian allies just after suggests that it is his son and namesake (tribune in 91 B.C.), who tried to get the franchise for the Italian allies in defiance of the majority of senators. It seems that Tacitus has confused the two. See Introduction.

47. Marcus Æmilius Lepidus as consul in 78 B.C. began the attack upon Sulla's settlement of the constitution.

48. In 70 B.C., when Pompey and Crassus were consuls together the first time.

49. In 52 B.C., when he was consul without a colleague.

50. 28 B.C.

51. This son of Claudius died as a child.

52. Suffect consul in 12 B.C.; for his son, see XIII, 30.

53. See I, 6, with note.

54. Gaius Sallustius Crispus (86-34 B.C.); we possess his monographs on the conspiracy of Catiline and the war against Jugurtha, but only fragments of his five books of histories. See Introduction.

55. 21 A.D.

56. Father of the great general of that name.

57. Consul in 33 A.D.; doubtless descended from the dictator.

58. See I, 8, with note.

59. His wife afterward poisoned him.

60. Consul in 35 A.D.

61. See II, 30; III, 22-23. Publius Sulpicius Quirinius was consul in 12 B.C.; as governor of Syria in 6 A.D. he conducted the census referred to in St. Luke's Gospel, 2:2.

62. In the Alban hills.

63. See I, 10, with note.

64. See III, 22.

65. Suffect consul in 19 A.D., married to a daughter of Aulus Plautius (suffect consul in 1 B.C.); he later governed Syria.

66. 22 A.D. Sulpicius was an elder brother of the Emperor Galba.

67. I.e., from 31 B.C. to 69 A.D.

68. Emperor from 69 to 79 A.D.

69. See I, 3, with notes.

70. Servius Cornelius Lentulus Maluginensis was consul in 10 A.D.; his priestly title was *flamen Dialis*; see II, 83, with note.

71. Quirinus was the name under which Romulus (see III, 26, with note) had been deified.

72. He was among those massacred by Marius in 87 B.C.

73. All emperors held the office of Pontifex Maximus, head of the state religion; the title was later assumed by the popes.

74. Dedicated by Augustus in 11 B.C.; see I, 3.

75. They had charge of the Sibylline Books.

76. Also called *epulones,* from their duty of supervising a banquet (*epula*) supposed to be given to Jupiter.

77. See I, 54.

78. Roman priestly officials who had charge of observances connected with the making of treaties and the declaration of war.

79. Consul in 10 A.D.

80. In about 130 B.C.

81. In 149 B.C.

82. In 92 B.C. Marcus Æmilius Scaurus (consul in 115 B.C.) was the the most famous ancestor of this Scaurus. It is significant that Cotta and Galba, who seem to have been guilty, were acquitted, while Rutilius, who was innocent, was condemned. The irony is hardly unintentional.

83. See Juvenal, X, 82 f., a passage which suggests that Bruttedius may have fallen with Sejanus.

84. Consul in 40 A.D.

85. Consul in 5 A.D., and supposed to have executed 300 people in one day.

86. A small island in the Cyclades.

87. The mother of Augustus also came of this family.

88. Not far from Gyarus, but larger.

89. See III, 75.

90. Anzio.

91. Consul in 119 B.C.

92. Begun by his grandfather in 50 B.C., finished by his father in 34 B.C., and restored in 14 B.C.

93. Titus Statilius Taurus (suffect consul in 37 B.C.) built a theater after his triumph in 34 B.C.; Lucius Philippus (suffect consul in 38 B.C.) repaired the temple of Hercules after his triumph in 33 B.C.; Lucius Cornelius Balbus (consul in 19 B.C.) built a theater in 13 B.C. Balbus came from Gades (Cadiz) in Spain, the first provincial to reach the consulship.

94. See III, 23.

95. The son of Asinius Gallus (see I, 8, with note) by Vipsania (see I, 12); had been betrothed to a daughter of Germanicus.

96. See III, 70.

97. This Junia's mother was Servilia, sister of Marcus Cato, reputed mistress of Julius Cæsar and mother of his murderer, Marcus Brutus, by her second husband, Decimus Junius Silanus (consul in 62 B.C.).

98. See I, 2, with note.

Book IV

1. 23 A.D.

2. In Etruria.

3. Lucius Seius Strabo exchanged the prefectship of the prætorian guard for the prefectship of Egypt in 15 A.D. Seius Strabo was the son of a sister of Mæcenas' wife (see Book I, note 29) and himself married into the aristocratic family of the Lentuli.

4. See I, 3, with note.

5. Perhaps the famous epicure under whose name a Roman cookbook survives; but there were two other gourmands of this name.

6. See II, 43, 84.

7. See Introduction.

8. Miseno, on the northern headland of the Bay of Naples.

9. Fréjus.

10. First king of Numidia, then from 25 B.C. king of Mauretania; his wife was a daughter of Antony and Cleopatra.

11. Iberia lay south of the Caucasus and north of Armenia.

12. See II, 68, with note.

13. See II, 67 f.

14. The Roman province south and west of the Danube.

15. See Book I, note 48.

16. The country on the east coast of the Adriatic south of Epirus, forming the southern part of the province of Illyricum.

17. The state farmed out to associations of publicans the right to collect taxes up to a certain sum in particular areas.

18. The Julii traced their descent from the Trojan hero Æneas, ancestor of the kings of Rome and hero of Virgil's *Æneid*.

19. The kings of Alba Longa were descendants of Æneas and ancestors of the kings of Rome.

20. The legendary ancestor of the Claudii, supposed to have been of Sabine origin.

21. Probably wife of Gaius Fufius Geminus, consul in 29 A.D.; see V, 2.

22. In southwestern Phrygia.

23. On the gulf of Corinth.

24. See II, 30.

25. Further Spain had been divided by Augustus into Lusitania (Portugal) and Bætica, the civilized area in the south and center; the name came to be applied to Bætica alone.

26. One of the Cyclades, east of Naxos.

27. See I, 53.

28. Herodotus (II, 148; III, 60) calls the temple of Hera on Samos the greatest temple known to him.

TACITUS

29. Cos, an island of the Dodecanese, had been from early times the home of a school of physicians who claimed descent from Asclepius, god of medicine; the great Hippocrates was one of them.

30. The most famous Amphictyonic Council was the league of Greek cities centering upon Delphi; but the one mentioned here was probably a less celebrated one which centered upon Delos.

31. The ancient Atellane farce, originally performed by amateurs, but now taken over by the pantomimes (see I, 54, with note); they took their name from Atella, in Campania, and at one time the ancient Italic dialect called Oscan had been used in them.

32. Suffect consul in 7 A.D.

33. A public funeral; the term arose either because such matters came within the province of the censors or because such a funeral was customarily given to those who had held the censorship, the most dignified of Roman magistracies.

34. A procurator was a fiscal official appointed by the Emperor; his trial before the Senate could therefore be regarded as a proof of the Senate's continued importance.

35. The primitive form of marriage made divorce more difficult.

36. 24 A.D.

37. See I, 13, etc.

38. See II, 32, etc.

39. See II, 34.

40. The name in the manuscript is corrupt. It may have been "Quintus Veranius" (see II, 74).

41. See I, 72, with note.

42. See Book II, note 60.

43. See II, 34.

44. Suffect consul in 44 A.D.; see XI, 1 f.; XIII, 42-43.

45. See II, 27 f.

46. 25 A.D.

47. It is clear from other sources, including the consolation addressed by Seneca to Cremutius' daughter Marcia, that this was not the only charge; Cremutius

perished mainly in consequence of a quarrel with Sejanus.

48. The famous historian Livy (59 B.C.-17 A.D.).

49. Quintus Cæcilius Metellus Pius Scipio, consul in 52 B.C. and father of Pompey's last wife; he killed himself after Cæsar's victory at Thapsus in 46 B.C.

50. Lucius Afranius, consul in 60 B.C., who fought against Cæsar in Spain in 49 B.C and was killed after Thapsus.

51. See Book I, note 21.

52. Cæsar replied to Cicero's encomium on Marcus Porcius Cato (95-46 B.C.) in an Anticato.

53. See Suetonius' life of Augustus, Ch. 69, for some entertaining extracts from this correspondence.

54. Marcus Furius Bibaculus (born 103 B.C.), epic poet, elegist, and epigrammatist.

55. The great poet Gaius Valerius Catullus (84-54 B.C.); see the poems numbered 29, 54, 57, 93. Cæsar's response was to invite Catullus to dinner.

56. The ancient festival of the Latin League was held in January, just after the new consuls for the year took office. In their absence the magistrates were represented by a "city prefect," whose office was purely honorific and quite distinct from the important post created by the emperors under that name (see VI, 11). To give notice of a prosecution at this time was an act of ill omen, and therefore bound to offend Tiberius, with his scrupulous concern for the observances of the official cult.

57. Sextus Marius was the richest man in Spain (see VI, 19), and his accuser also was of Spanish origin.

58. On the Bosporus, near Byzantium; it had been attacked by Mithridates in 74 B.C., and was relieved in the following year by the great Roman general Lucius Licinius Lucullus.

59. Consul in 12 A.D., son of a friend of Mark Antony (suffect consul in 33 B.C.).

60. In Mysia, in the valley of the Caicus; this was in 29 B.C.

61. These precedents are part of the regular stock-in-

trade of emperor-worship. If Tiberius had granted the request, would Tacitus have praised him for doing so?

62. The person Sejanus had in mind is Gaius Proculeius, the half-brother of Mæcenas' wife, Terentia (see I, 10, with note), who was considered by Augustus as a possible husband for Julia (see Book I, note 8).

63. See I, 3.

64. Cnæus Cornelius Lentulus Gætulicus, consul in 26 A.D., governed Upper Germany from 30 to 39, when he was executed for alleged conspiracy by the Emperor Gaius; cf. VI, 30.

65. Lucius Domitius Ahenobarbus (consul in 16 B.C.) had crossed the Elbe with an army in 2 B.C.; he had married the elder, not the younger Antonia, and had by her a son who became father of the Emperor Nero. His grandfather, consul in 54 B.C., had died fighting fiercely against Julius Cæsar; his father, consul in 32 B.C., is the original of Shakespeare's Enobarbus in *Antony and Cleopatra*.

66. See I, 10, with note 30.

67. Marseilles.

68. His father had been son of Mark Antony by Octavia, sister of Augustus.

69. They lived near the sources of the Douro. This is not the Lucius Piso of II, 34, etc.

70. Daughter of Marcus Valerius Messalla Barbatus (consul in 12 B.C.) by Claudia Marcella, niece of Augustus, and widow of Varus (see I, 3).

71. Suffect consul in 39, a great orator and a notorious prosecutor. See IV, 66; XIV, 19.

72. See IV, 19.

73. Marcus Cocceius Nerva (suffect consul in 21 or 22), jurist, grandfather of the Emperor Nerva.

74. Near Sperlonga, between Gaieta and Terracina.

75. Fondi.

76. See IV, 52.

77. Capri.

78. Sorrento.

79. In 79 A.D.

80. They are said to have come there from the islands off the coast of Acarnania in western Greece.

81. 28 A.D.
82. See IV, 18-19.
83. See VI, 4. But most of this part of the work is lost.
84. See III, 24. The island is now called San Domenico.

Book V

1. 29 A.D.
2. She was eighty-six. Her father, Marcus Livius Drusus Claudianus, a Claudius adopted into the Livian family, fought under Brutus and Cassius at Philippi and killed himself after the battle.
3. He fought against Augustus on the side of Lucius Antonius and Fulvia, brother and wife of Mark Antony, at Perusia in 42 B.C. and returned to Rome in 36 B.C.
4. Gaius Fufius Geminus.

[Book VI]

1. As the widow of Tiberius' adopted son Germanicus, Livia could be called his daughter.
2. Sejanus' uncle; cf. *Histories* III, 39.
3. See III, 13, etc.
4. Publius Pomponius Secundus (suffect consul in 44 A.D. and later governor of Upper Germany) was the most celebrated tragic poet of this period.
5. Now the gulfs of Cassandra and Salonika, on the coast of Thrace.
6. The port of Athens.
7. See III, 24, 57.
8. Fulcinius Trio (see II, 28) had become suffect consul on July 1; Publius Memmius Regulus had become his colleague on October 1. For Regulus' obituary, see XIV, 47.

Book VI

1. 32 A.D.
2. See III, 74.
3. See III, 24.
4. Probably Lucius Cassius Longinus (consul in 30 A.D.); cf. VI, 15. All these men came of noble families, whereas the mere name of Togonius proclaimed his alien origin.
5. Cf. IV, 68 f.
6. Suffect consul in 23 A.D. and again in 39; died as governor of Lower Germany in 47.
7. The Gaius meant is the one who was later Emperor.
8. In the original, "Tiberiolus meus." English cannot convey the force of the Latin diminutive.
9. Plato; see *Gorgias* 524 E, a passage often quoted in antiquity.
10. See III, 36.
11. The name survives in that of the district of Saintonge, north of the lower Garonne, and that of its chief town, Saintes. This man was the father of the famous orator mentioned in Tacitus' *Dialogue* Ch. 15.
12. See IV, 34; VI, 47. Nothing is known of this Pomponius.
13. All except Vinicianus were of consular rank.
14. See II, 28.
15. Consul in 15 B.C., son of Cicero's enemy, the consul of 58 B.C., and so brother of Julius Cæsar's last wife, Calpurnia.
16. See Book III, notes 41-45.
17. See IV, 36.
18. See I, 54.
19. See I, 8.
20. See III, 72.
21. See Book III, note 77. Lucius Caninius Gallus was consul in 2 B.C.
22. The great scholar Varro recognized ten distinct Sibyls, those of Persia, Libya, Delphi, Cimmeria, Erythræ, Samos, Cumæ, the Hellespont, Phrygia, and Tibur.

23. 33 A.D. Servius Sulpicius Galba was Emperor in 68-69. On Sulla, see III, 31.

24. See Book VI, note 4.

25. Consul in 30 and again in 45.

26. In 49 or 48 B.C.

27. Book III, note 47.

28. See [V, 8].

29. Cnæus Pompeius Theophanes of Mytilene on Lesbos, a historian and influential adviser of the great Pompey. His son, Pompeius Macer, was procurator in Asia; another son entered the Senate under Augustus, and was probably Macrina's father; a later member of this distinguished Greek family was suffect consul in 100 or 101. Gaius Julius Laco was a relation of Gaius Julius Eurycles, dynast of Sparta under Augustus.

30. See IV, 36.

31. See III, 24, with note 37.

32. Suffect consul in 27 A.D., consul in 44 A.D.; he was the heir of Gaius Sallustius Crispus (see I, 6); famous for wit and eloquence as well as wealth, he was at one time married to the younger Agrippina, the Emperor Nero's mother.

33. Cf. IV, 58. Besides being an astrologer, Thrasyllus was a Platonic philosopher of some distinction.

34. The Epicureans.

35. The Stoics.

36. Belief in astral determinism was at this time common even among educated people; see F. Cumont, *Astrology and Religion Among the Greeks and Romans* (paperback edition, Dover Books, 1960). See Introduction.

37. This part of the narrative is lost.

38. By blood Drusus was his great-nephew; but by virtue of his adoption of Germanicus, he counted as his grandson.

39. See IV, 58.

40. See Introduction.

41. See III, 23.

42. Consul in 3 A.D.

43. See IV, 20.

44. 34 A.D. Lucius Vitellius, consul for the third time

in 47 A.D., was censor, favorite, and flatterer of Claudius and father of Aulus Vitellius, Emperor in 69.

45. The legend of the phœnix seems to have spread from Egypt over a wide area. Herodotus (II, 73) describes it in connection with Heliopolis; but it is mentioned in a poem ascribed to Hesiod, and is perhaps as old as the seventh century B.C.

46. Sesosis is another form of the name of Sesostris, to whom Herodotus assigns the conquests of Ramses. Amasis reigned during the sixth century and Ptolemy III during the third century B.C.

47. See I, 13, with note, etc.

48. See IV, 42.

49. See IV, 13; VI, 16.

50. See II, 67.

51. See VI, 3.

52. See I, 80, etc.

53. 36 A.D.

54. See VI, 7.

55. See III, 52.

56. Probably the sons of Sejanus' uncle.

57. Somewhere in the lost part; she was a daughter of Marcus Lepidus (I, 13; IV, 20, etc.). This Drusus was the son of Germanicus and Agrippina.

58. One of the Seven Hills of Rome; the Circus Maximus lay in the valley between it and the Palatine Hill.

59. See IV, 75.

60. See VI, 15.

61. See VI, 27.

62. See III, 49.

63. 37 A.D.

64. See VI, 20.

65. Perhaps granddaughter of Thrasyllus (see VI, 21).

66. The survivor of the twin sons born to Drusus and Livia (II, 84), known as Tiberius Gemellus, and now in his eighteenth year.

67. Now in his forty-sixth year; Gaius was twenty-four.

68. Perhaps son of the prætor of 22 A.D. (III, 66).

69. See IV, 34; VI, 8.

70. See IV, 75.

71. See II, 74, etc.

72. See I, 8, 13, etc.
73. Cf. VI, 40.
74. See IV, 5, with note.
75. Consul in 73 B.C.; see Book IV, n. 56.
76. See V, 1.
77. See I, 3.
78. See I, 4; 53.

Book XI

1. Decimus Valerius Asiaticus (consul in 35 and again in 46) was a native of Vienna (now Vienne) in Narbonese Gaul. He was married to a sister of the beautiful Lollia Paulina (see XII, 1).

2. See IV, 36; VI, 50.

3. See IV, 31.

4. A Greek freedman, later executed at Agrippina's insistence.

5. Rufrius Crispinus, at this time joint prefect of the prætorian guard (cf. XII, 42).

6. On the Bay of Naples, near Puteoli.

7. See VI, 28, with note.

8. Publius Cornelius Scipio, consul in 56 A.D.

9. In this way Crispinus, who as prætorian prefect was necessarily a Roman knight and not a senator, was given the status conferred by an office which he could not hold. The first knight thus honored had been Sejanus.

10. No doubt Suillius brought a charge against Samius, took a bribe to drop it, and then went ahead with it.

11. Carried by Marcus Cincius Alimentus in 204 B.C.; revived by Augustus in 17 B.C., but systematically evaded.

12. Gaius Silius, already designated to be consul in the following year, 48 A.D.

13. See I, 8, etc.

14. See III, 11.

15. Cossutianus Capito was a notorious informer, who in Nero's reign prosecuted Thrasea Pætus (XVI, 28).

16. Publius Clodius Pulcher (d. 52 B.C.) and Gaius Scribonius Curio were two turbulent tribunes of the

Ciceronian age, both notorious for taking bribes for political services of a disreputable kind.

17. With the passing of every *sæculum*, a period supposed to represent the extreme limit of a human life, secular games were supposed to be held at Rome. Some authorities held the period to be 110, some 100 years, and the discrepancy made it easy for an emperor who wished to hold secular games to make a case for doing so. Augustus had held them in 17 B.C., only 64 years before Claudius, and Domitian, who professed to follow Augustus' reckoning, held them in 88 A.D., 105 years after the games of Augustus and not 110 years after, as according to his own theory he should have done.

18. In the lost part of the *Histories*.

19. See III, 64.

20. A kind of mock battle between teams of boys on horseback, revived by Augustus, and described by Virgil as being held by Æneas and his Trojans (*Æneid* V, 545 f.).

21. See IV, 75. Nero was nine and Britannicus, Claudius' son by Messallina, six years of age.

22. Alexander the Great was supposed to have been conceived by a god in the form of a snake.

23. Daughter of Germanicus and the elder Agrippina.

24. See [V, 8].

25. This great aqueduct had been begun by Gaius in 38 A.D.; of its two parts, the Aqua was 35 and the Anio Novus 62 miles long. Considerable remains of it can still be seen.

26. One of his letters, Ⅎ, used to express the Latin semiconsonantal V, was useful; the other two were pedantic encumbrances.

27. Both the hieratic and demotic Egyptian scripts are cursive forms deriving from the hieroglyphics. The Phœnician alphabet does not really derive from the Egyptian; but the belief that the Greek derives from the Phœnician, held by the ancients themselves (see Herodotus V, 58), is generally accepted. See D. Diringer, *Writing* (London, 1962).

28. The legendary founder of Thebes, said to be son of a king of Tyre.

29. The first legendary king of Athens.

30. A legendary musician, said to have taught Hercules.

31. A Greek hero who fought in the Trojan War, famous for his skill as an inventor.

32. Greek lyric poet (556-468 B.C.). No author earlier than the elder Pliny (d. 79 A.D.) tells this story, which is patently absurd.

33. Said by Livy to have been father of Tarquinius Priscus, king of Rome. The Roman alphabet derives from the Greek, which may have come to the Romans by way of Etruria. Probably the alphabet was known to both Etruscans and Romans from a very early date.

34. This is the name given in the Roman tradition to the primitive population of Latium.

35. An Arcadian hero, the mythical founder of Pallanteum, on the site of the Palatine Hill; according to Virgil he helped Æneas in his war against the Rutulian prince, Turnus.

36. The haruspices were diviners of a type originally introduced from Etruria. They existed at Rome as early as the time of the last king, according to Livy, and though they were long despised as barbarous and had had no official recognition before this time, they had for long successfully encroached on the territory of the augurs (see Book II, note 56). Claudius as an authority on the Etruscans would have felt a special interest in them.

37. The quæstorship was the most junior office to form part of the Roman *cursus honorum*; its duties were for the most part financial. Other authorities date its establishment to the republican period.

38. A fixed age for the holders of the various magistracies was laid down by the Lex Villia Annalis of 180 B.C.

39. The law by which authority was conferred on the elected magistrates of each year.

40. 447 B.C.

41. 48 A.D. Aulus Vitellius, Emperor in 69 A.D., was the son of Lucius Vitellius (see VI, 28).

481

42. A general term for the whole of Gaul apart from
the long-Romanized *provincia*, Gallia Narbonensis (Narbonese Gaul). Gallia Comata was divided into Aquitania,
Lugdunum, and Belgica.

43. The Veneti lived in the district of Padua, the
Insubres in that of Milan; both had received the citizenship when Julius Cæsar gave it to the Transpadane Gauls
(the inhabitants of Italy north of the Po) in 49 B.C.

44. The capital of the Mandubii, where the Gauls
under Vercingetorix besieged Julius Cæsar in 52 B.C.;
probably Alise Ste. Reine, west of Dijon.

45. A Gallic tribe called the Senones took Rome in
390 B.C.

46. See IV, 9.

47. The first eminent member of this family, the jurist
Tiberius Coruncanius, was consul in 280 B.C.

48. The first eminent Porcius was the famous censor
Cato (consul in 195 B.C.).

49. See III, 72.

50. Claudius' actual speech tactlessly mentions Valerius Asiaticus, Messallina's victim (XI, 1 f.).

51. The Tarquins were Etruscan.

52. Irony; these were neighboring peoples in Latium
who fought fierce wars against the Romans in the early
republican period.

53. Rome was taken by the Etruscan Lars Porsenna
(see *Histories* III, 72); and the Samnites, who lived in
the southern Apennines, captured an entire Roman army
at the Caudine Forks in 433 B.C. and made it pass under
a yoke in token of subjection.

54. Plebeians became eligible to hold the consulship
in 367 B.C., the censorship in 351, and the prætorship
in 337.

55. The original patricians were the hundred original
senators of Romulus (Livy, XVIII, 7). Their families
were the "greater houses"; the "lesser houses" were the
families of the hundred senators added by Brutus (or,
according to Livy, by Tarquinius Priscus). The early
republican period was marked by the struggle of the
plebeians to break down the privilege of patrician priv-

ilege; but well before the Ciceronian age the distinction between the patricians and the more important plebeian families had ceased to be more than formal.

56. The Cassian Law was passed in 45 B.C., the Sænian Law in 29 B.C.

57. See I, 72.

58. A lustrum was a period of five years; every five years censors were elected, and after reviewing the roll of senators and expelling the unworthy, they "closed the lustrum" with a special sacrifice.

59. The port of Rome, at the mouth of the Tiber, 16 miles from the city.

60. Mnester; see XI, 4; 36.

61. Callistus, Narcissus, and Pallas were all freedmen who had great power under Claudius and became vastly rich. Callistus, who was in charge of petitions addressed to the Emperor (*a libellis*), had been important under Gaius, and had been privy to his murder. Narcissus was in charge of the Emperor's correspondence (*ab epistulis*). Pallas was Claudius' treasurer (*a rationibus*); a freedman of Antonia (see I, 3), he had been employed by her to warn Tiberius against Sejanus.

62. For Vettius, see the next chapter; for Plautius, see Ch. 36.

63. See I, 7; he held office till over ninety years old. Geta was the colleague of Rufrius Crispinus (XI, 1); both were friendly to Messallina.

64. A celebrated physician, according to the elder Pliny.

65. See XI, 1, with note.

66. Daughter of Claudius and Messallina, born about 40 A.D.

67. Consul in 42 A.D.

68. Son of the informer (see XI, 2).

69. Later executed by Nero for complicity in Piso's conspiracy; a nephew of Aulus Plautius Lateranus, commander in the invasion of Britain.

70. Domitia Lepida, daughter of Lucius Domitius and the elder Antonia. See Book IV, note 63. So Messallina and Nero were first cousins.

Book XII

1. She was rather the granddaughter of the consul of
21 B.C. (see I, 10), and was equally famous for her
beauty and her wealth. She had been married first to
Publius Memmius Regulus (see [V, 11]) and later, briefly,
to the Emperor Gaius. Cf. XII, 22.

2. See IV, 75.

3. Daughter of a consular, whose family contained
several eminent jurists, she had already been married
and divorced by Claudius, and had by him a daughter
called Antonia.

4. Lucius Junius Silanus Torquatus, son of the consul
of 19 A.D. by Æmilia Lepida. This Æmilia Lepida was
the daughter of Julia, granddaughter of Augustus (see
IV, 71); so Silanus was a great-great-grandson of
Augustus.

5. Seneca in his satire on Claudius calls her "the most
delightful girl in the world."

6. See XI, 25.

7. Titus Eprius Marcellus (suffect consul in 62, again
consul in 74), a notorious informer.

8. 49 A.D.

9. He had been married first to Urgulania, the granddaughter of Livia's friend (see II, 34; IV, 21-22); then to
Ælia Pætina; then to Valeria Messallina.

10. The last sentence of this masterly oration is surely
a parody of the last sentence of Claudius' speech at
XI, 24.

11. She returned ten years later (XIV, 12), and seems
to have been still alive under Vespasian.

12. See III, 26.

13. Lucius Annæus Seneca (suffect consul in 55 or
56 A.D.), the leading writer of the age. Born at Corduba
(Cordova), Spain, in 5 or 4 B.C., he was the son of a
well-known writer on rhetoric, two of whose treatises
have survived. In 41 A.D. he was banished to Corsica on
a charge of adultery with Julia, daughter of Germanicus
and sister of Agrippina. Eminent as a Stoic philosopher,
orator, and tragic poet, he wrote in a concise, pointed,

antithetic style which had an immense influence on his contemporaries; his tragedies greatly influenced Renaissance writers, including Shakespeare. Soon after Claudius died and was deified, Seneca ridiculed him in a satire, still extant, called "The Pumpkinification of the Divine Claudius."

14. Nero was twelve, Octavia nine.

15. See XII, 1.

16. See III, 30; XIII, 30.

17. See II, 32, etc.

18. Long before this date Gallia Narbonensis had been completely Romanized; the elder Pliny says it was "more like part of Italy than a province."

19. The Ituræans were an Arab people, conquered by Pompeius Magnus in 63 B.C. and later subject to Herod the Great and his son the tetrarch Philip. In 39 A.D. Gaius had made Sohæmus king over them.

20. Herod Agrippa, grandson of Herod the Great, had been given the tetrarchies of his uncles, Philip and Herod Antipas, by Gaius; Claudius had added Judæa and Samaria. He died suddenly in 44 A.D. (see Acts 12:23).

21. This meant that the augurs resorted to divination to discover whether the gods were willing that they should pray for the public safety. This could only be done if the state were involved in no kind of war, a very rare occurrence.

22. It seems that only the addition of Italian territory justified such an extension; so it is probably the incorporation of the Anauni near Trent rather than the conquest of Britain that led Claudius to perform this ceremony.

23. The Ox Market (*Forum Boarium*) was near San Giorgio in Velabro; so the line must have run between the Palatine and the Aventine, and then between the Palatine and Cælian past the Arch of Titus and so to the *Forum Romanum*.

24. The *Ara Maxima* (Great Altar); see XV, 41.

25. Near the winning point of the Circus; Consus was an ancient god of counsel.

26. The Lares were the gods of the crossroads, worshiped privately in each house as well as in this temple.

27. 50 A.D.

28. Nero was born on December 15, 37; Britannicus on February 12 or 13, 41.

29. See Book IV, note 18.

30. Nero was a name belonging to the Claudian house.

31. Colonia Agrippinensis=Cologne.

32. In 38 B.C.

33. See V, 8, etc. The Vangiones centered upon Worms, the Nemetes upon Speyer.

34. Probably Hochst.

35. Publius Ostorius Scapula (suffect consul about 44 A.D.). The following narrative carries events in Britain down to the end of Claudius' reign in 54.

36. They lived in Norfolk, Suffolk, and Cambridgeshire. The move provoked them because it cut them off from the Brigantes, who held the country from the Mersey and the Humber as far north as the Solway and the Tyne.

37. Perhaps in Flintshire (in Wales).

38. Ireland.

39. They held South Wales, with Monmouthshire and Herefordshire.

40. Colchester, surprisingly far east of the Silures.

41. They occupied most of central and northern Wales.

42. This claim is mere rhetoric; Cæsar came only to make a demonstration.

43. Syphax, king of Numidia, was according to one account led in the triumph of Scipio Africanus the Elder after the defeat of Hannibal at Zama in 202 B.C.

44. Perseus, king of Macedonia (179-168 B.C.), was defeated by Æmilius Paulus at Pydna in 168.

45. Aulus Didius Gallus (suffect consul in 36 A.D.) was probably appointed in 52, and held the appointment for rather more than five years.

46. 51 A.D.

47. He came from Vasio in Narbonese Gaul, now Vaison-la-Romaine; he had only been a military tribune, and most of his service had been financial, for he had been procurator to Livia, Tiberius, and Claudius.

48. The mention of prodigies is a regular feature of Roman annalistic history. This is the first instance of it

in the *Annals*, but from this point on they are regularly noticed.

49. 52 A.D. Sulla was married to Claudius' daughter Antonia; Otho was the brother of the future emperor.

50. The consul of 8 A.D. was his grandfather; his father was consul in 32 A.D. and killed himself after his revolt in 42 A.D.

51. Suffect consul in 52 A.D.; later executed by Nero.

52. See III, 74, etc. Tacitus clearly felt intense disgust that the bearer of such a name should be capable of such an utterance.

53. See Acts 24:4. Felix married three Oriental princesses in succession; one was Drusilla, daughter of Herod Agrippa (see XII, 23).

54. Gaius' order that his effigy be erected in the Holy of Holies in the temple at Jerusalem had provoked a threat of serious trouble, which was averted by his assassination in 41 A.D.

55. Gaius Ummidius Quadratus (suffect consul in 40 A.D.) governed Syria from 51 till his death in 60. Josephus gives a different account of this affair. In his version Felix was not sent out till after Cumanus had been recalled in 52. Cumanus, he says, was sent to Rome for trial, and would have been acquitted through the influence of the freedmen had not the young Herod Agrippa II persuaded Agrippina to have him exiled.

56. They had been reduced by Lucius Vitellius in 36 A.D.

57. Lago di Celano.

58. The Garigliano. The work employed 30,000 men for eleven years; it was done to increase the cultivable area and to make the river more navigable.

59. His candidate for Messallina's place had been Ælia Pætina (XII, 2).

60. 53 A.D.

61. See IV, 9.

62. Bologna; a Roman colony in Cisalpine Gaul, founded in 189 B.C.

63. They had been punished for their equivocal attitude in the Third Macedonian War by the making of Delos into a free port (167 B.C.), which struck a severe

blow at Rhodian trade. They had lost their freedom in 44 B.C., and were to lose it again under Vespasian and regain it under Domitian.

64. In Phrygia, near Celænæ (now Denier, near Ishekli), not to be confused with Syrian Apamea on the Orontes.

65. Consul in 44 A.D., son of the consul of 16 A.D., and grandson of a general of Augustus (III, 72).

66. But later he returned (see XIV, 46).

67. The imperial provinces were governed by senators, but their revenues were administered by Roman knights with the title of procurators. The great offices of prefect of Egypt and prætorian prefect could be held only by knights; their holders were far more powerful than most senators.

68. The Sempronian Laws were carried by Gaius Gracchus in 122 B.C.; in 106 B.C. the Servilian Laws of Quintus Cæpio restored the juries to the senators. Only a year or two afterward the knights recovered them; but Sulla restored them to the Senate in 81 B.C.

69. Oppius, a rich banker, was an important agent of Julius Cæsar; for Balbus, who was influential through Cæsar long before he entered the Senate (see III, 72).

70. Gaius Matius, banker and poet, was another friend of Cæsar; for Vedius Pollio, see I, 10.

71. 54 A.D.

72. See XI, 37. Lepida's mother was really the elder Antonia.

73. Mandragone, near the mouth of the Volturno.

74. Other writers say Lucusta.

Book XIII

1. Marcus Junius Silanus (consul 46 A.D.) was the elder brother of Decimus (see XII, 58) and Lucius Silanus (see XII, 3 f.). Compare this opening sentence with that of I, 6.

2. Left in charge of Rome and Italy by Nero when he was in Greece in 67-69; executed by Galba.

3. See Book IV, note 31.

488

4. For this feature of Claudius' rule, see, for example, XI, 1 f.

5. This sentence glances at Claudius' freedmen, the next one at his wives.

6. See XI, 5-7.

7. See XI, 22.

8. 55 A.D. Lucius Antistius Vetus, probably cousin of the consul of 50 A.D. (see XII, 25); he governed Upper Germany and then Asia, and was executed by Nero in 65 (see XVI, 10-11).

9. See XI, 36. Seneca's treatise *On Clemency* gives a notion of the nature of his influence over Nero at this time.

10. Marcus Salvius Otho, brother of the consul of 52 A.D. (see XII, 52); later Emperor; for his family, see *Histories* II, 50.

11. A Roman knight, later involved in Piso's conspiracy (see XV, 50 f.).

12. He held the office of prefect of the watch. Seneca dedicated two treatises to him, and bitterly mourned his death.

13. Magistrates swore an oath on leaving office.

14. The younger Antonia, wife of Drusus; see I, 3.

15. See XI, 12.

16. Titus Sextius Africanus (suffect consul 59 A.D.); see XIV, 46.

17. Son of Rubellius Blandus by Julia, granddaughter of Tiberius; see VI, 27.

18. Domitia Lepida; XII, 64-65.

19. Since the death of Mnester, Paris had been the leading pantomimist of the time; he was executed by Nero as a rival in 67.

20. A historian of the time.

21. Son of Nero's nurse, later prefect of Egypt.

22. The elder Pliny.

23. See *Histories* I, 8.

24. Later prefect of the prætorian guard.

25. Probably the father of Lucius Arruntius Stella (suffect consul 101 A.D.?), the poet, to whom Statius dedicated the first book of his *Silvæ*.

26. Tiberius Claudius Balbillus, probably identical

with the celebrated astrologer of Greek birth, who had accompanied Claudius on the expedition to Britain.

27. Publius Anteius Rufus (suffect consul, year unknown); see XVI, 14.

28. See XII, 52.

29. 56 A.D.

30. Lucius Calpurnius Piso, son of the consul of 27 A.D. (see *Histories* IV, 38).

31. Four ædiles were elected annually, two curule and two plebeian ædiles; they were in charge of the care of the streets, the maintenance of public order, the supervision of weights and measures, etc.

32. Helvidius Priscus (prætor 70 A.D.), son-in-law of Thrasea Pætus, can hardly have been tribune at this date; see Book XVI, note 47.

33. See XI, 22.

34. Corsica together with Sardinia was governed by a procurator.

35. Crete together with Cyrene was a senatorial province.

36. Gaius Caninius Rebilus (suffect consul in 37, son of the consul of 12 B.C.), a man of infamous life.

37. For many years prefect of the city; see III, 30; XII, 22.

38. 57 A.D.

39. The great Campanian city of Capua had lost its political rights and most of its territory as a punishment for having revolted to Hannibal during the Second 'Punic War; later, Julius Cæsar had settled 20,000 colonists on the site. Nuceria (now Nocera) was another of Cæsar's Campanian colonies.

40. See XIV, 42 f.; the slaves would normally be executed in such a case.

41. See Book XI, note 69. Pomponia was probably a daughter of Ovid's friend Pomponius Græcinus (suffect consul in 16 A.D.). She lived on until about 83 A.D.

42. Wife of Rubellius Blandus (see VI, 27) and mother of Rubellius Plautus (see XIII, 19), executed in 43 A.D. through the influence of Messallina, who was jealous of her. Suillius was the prosecutor; see XIII, 43.

43. See XIII, 1.

44. See Book XI, note 15.

45. See Book XII, note 7.

46. 58 A.D. Valerius Messalla was probably son of the consul of 20 A.D. (see III, 2); for his grandfather and great-grandfather, see Book I, note 23. Corvinus had been consul with Augustus in 31 B.C., the year of Actium.

47. Probably the son or grandson of Cotta Messallinus (see Book II, note 5), who had himself become impoverished (see VI, 7), and so another descendant of Corvinus.

48. See IV, 31; XI, 1, etc.

49. See XI, 5.

50. See Book XII, note 13.

51. See VI, 18; as suffect consul soon after the murder of Gaius, he had proposed the restoration of the Republic, and had then become involved in the conspiracy of Camillus Scribonianus (see XII, 52).

52. See XI, 1 f.

53. Suffect consul late in Tiberius' reign; we do not know the details of his end.

54. Suffect consul in 42 A.D., after governing Crete and Cyrene under Tiberius; again the details of his end are unknown.

55. More than 300, according to Suetonius (life of Claudius, 29).

56. On Suillius' sons, see XI, 2, 36.

57. The episode is mentioned, I suspect, only because of the circumstances of Sagitta's return (see *Histories* IV, 44).

58. For her grandfather, see I, 80, etc.; for her mother, see XI, 1, with note.

59. See Book XI, note 5.

60. See XIII, 12.

61. Portugal.

62. See XII, 52; XIII, 23.

63. The Ponte Molle, on the Flaminian Way, two miles outside Rome; for the Flaminian Way, see Book III, note 9.

64. In the valley between the Pincian and the Quirinal. Laid out by the historian Sallust, they had passed

to his nephew Gaius Sallustius Crispus (see I, 6; III, 30), and from him probably to Tiberius.

65. Marseille.

66. Pozzuoli; near Baiæ, on the Bay of Naples.

67. Scribonius Proculus and Scribonius Rufus; for some time one governed Lower and the other Upper Germany; they were made to commit suicide by Nero in 67 A.D.

68. Augustus had limited the shows in Rome to two a year in 22 B.C.; how many were allowed in other towns is not known.

69. Thrasea Pætus (suffect consul in 56 A.D.), leader of the Stoic opposition; see Book XIII, note 32.

70. The right to collect taxes up to a certain amount was sold to companies, whose members were called publicans.

71. Quintus Sulpicius Camerinus (suffect consul in 46 A.D.), later executed during Nero's Greek tour of 67-69.

72. Marcus Pompeius Silvanus (suffect consul in 45 A.D.), was governor of Dalmatia at the time of Nero's death; he had governed Africa in 53-54; see *Histories* II, 86.

Book XIV

1. 59 A.D.

2. Rhetorical plural; Poppæus Sabinus (see I, 80, etc.) was the only one she had.

3. Marcus Æmilius Lepidus, husband of Agrippina's sister, Drusilla; executed by Gaius in 39 A.D. for complicity in the conspiracy of Cnæus Cornelius Lentulus Gætulicus (see Book IV, note 62).

4. Fifteen miles southeast of Rome, near the modern Frascati.

5. Now Anzio.

6. See Book IV, note 7.

7. Probably daughter of the consul of 37 A.D. (see VI, 45).

8. Agrippina's words are more effective in the original Latin: *"occidat, dum imperet."*

9. Naples.

10. See XIII, 49.

11. See XII, 22.

12. See XI, 12; XIII, 19.

13. To a Greek there would have been nothing degrading in either practice; to a noble Roman, both appeared degrading in the extreme.

14. The name implies that only young men competed.

15. See XII, 56.

16. See Book XIII, note 39.

17. Five and a quarter miles southeast of Vesuvius, and destroyed by its eruption in 79 A.D.

18. For his father, see III, 11; his expulsion from the Senate must have been referred to in the lost part of the work.

19. Ptolemy Apion, the last king of Cyrene, had died in 96 B.C., leaving his kingdom to the Roman people; but the province was constituted only in 74 B.C.

20. See IV, 52.

21. Marcus Servilius Nonianus, consul in 35 A.D. and a distinguished historian, used as a source by Tacitus.

22. 60 A.D.

23. This was called the Neronia, and was suggested by the model of the great games of Greece.

24. See III, 23.

25. In 364 B.C., according to Livy (VII, 2).

26. Thuria was founded on the site of Sybaris near the Gulf of Taranto as a Panhellenic enterprise under the auspices of Pericles in 443 B.C. Livy (I, 35) says that horse racing came in from Etruria under Tarquinius Priscus.

27. Consul in 146 B.C.; he sacked Corinth after his victory over the Achæan League that year.

28. See XIII, 19.

29. Now Subiaco.

30. Now Tivoli.

31. Daughter of Lucius Antistius Vetus (see XIII, 11).

32. The Aqua Marcia was an aqueduct beginning from the 36th milestone on the Via Valeria, which runs

from Rome to Aternum on the Adriatic; it was built by Lucius Marcius Rex in 149 B.C. Several of its arches still stand.

33. On the Lycus, a tributary of the Mæander, on the borders of Phrygia and Caria.

34. Pozzuoli.

35. Taranto.

36. Anzio.

37. Quintus Vibius Crispus (suffect consul for the third time about 83 A.D.), famous as an orator and wit, contrived to keep the favor of successive emperors; he held the important post of curator of the water supply for many years, besides governing Africa and Tarraconensis. See Juvenal, IV, 81-93.

38. 61 A.D.

39. See XII, 40.

40. See III, 10, etc.

41. Gaius Suetonius Paullinus (suffect consul about 43, and again in 66) had put down a rebellion in Mauretania in 41-42; he later commanded for Otho in 69. His memoirs may have been one of Tacitus' sources.

42. Anglesey.

43. See XII, 31-32.

44. They lived in Suffolk and Essex, just south of the Iceni.

45. See XII, 32.

46. The Thames.

47. Quintus Petilius Cerialis (suffect consul in 70, and again in 74) afterward suppressed the revolt of the Gauls and Germans under Civilis in 70.

48. London.

49. St. Albans.

50. She is commemorated by a statue on Westminster Bridge in London.

51. Domitius Balbus and Valerius Fabianus were probably Romans from Spain.

52. Marcus Antonius Primus later played an important part in the war between Vitellius and Vespasian in 69 on the side of Vespasian.

53. Consul in 54 A.D.

54. A law of Sulla, carried in 81, to punish forgery of wills.

55. Ælianus and Pontius, like Balbus and Fabianus, probably came from Spain.

56. See XIII, 32.

57. See XIII, 48, with note.

58. He was a famous jurist.

59. The reference is to the military punishment of mutinous or cowardly troops by "decimation," inflicted by Lucius Apronius during his operations against Tacfarinas as late as 20 A.D. (see III, 21).

60. Executed without trial by Galba when consul designate in 68 A.D.

61. See XII, 59.

62. Volusius was consul in 56 A.D.; Africanus suffect consul in 59; Trebellius suffect consul in 56 (he later governed Britain).

63. See [V, 11]; VI, 4, etc.

64. 62 A.D.

65. See XIII, 28.

66. Marcus Ostorius Scapula, son of Publius Ostorius Scapula (see XII, 31).

67. See XI, 6; XIII, 33.

68. Sofonius Tigellinus, later notorious as prefect of the prætorian guard (XIV, 57, etc.).

69. Later Emperor; see XI, 23.

70. Possibly the author of some epigrams in the Greek Anthology.

71. Fabricius Veiento, returning from exile, received one consulate from Vespasian (date unknown), a second from Titus (suffect consul in 80), and a third from Domitian (82 or 83). Though a notorious informer and sycophant, he comfortably survived the murder of Domitian, enjoyed intimate friendship with Nerva, and lived into Trajan's reign.

72. See XIII, 22.

73. Mytilene is in the island of Lesbos.

74. Pallas, in particular, must have been in Nero's mind.

75. See Book VI, note 45.

76. See XIII, 30.

77. Nero's speech exactly catches the tone of Seneca's moralizing writings.

78. The son of Tiberius; see VI, 27.

79. See XIII, 11, with note.

80. Gaius Musonius Rufus, a Roman knight and a distinguished Stoic philosopher, who taught Epictetus.

81. See I, 53.

82. See VI, 25.

83. See note on XII, 8; Julia, daughter of Germanicus and sister of Agrippina, was banished at Messallina's insistence in 41 A.D. and soon afterward put to death.

84. Acte; see XIII, 12, etc.

85. The elder Drusus (see I, 3) had had this title; he was Octavia's grandfather and, through his son Germanicus, Nero's great-grandfather.

86. He had succeeded Callistus in charge of petitions to the Emperor, and had received from Nero a gift of ten million sesterces. For Pallas, see XI, 29, etc. It is not known who Romanus was.

Book XV

1. The corn had been stored for sale at a low price.

2. Nero was probably referring to his transference of the cost of corn distribution from the state treasury to the privy purse.

3. The Lex Papia Poppæa of 9 A.D. gave preference to candidates who had children; for this law, see III, 25, with note.

4. The same law restricted the right of unmarried persons to receive legacies.

5. "Magnates in the eastern cities had a bad name for pride and oppression."—Sir Ronald Syme, *Tacitus* (2 vols., Oxford University Press, 1958), p. 467.

6. See XI, 5; XIII, 42.

7. Augustus twice took action against this offense, in 18 and in 8 B.C.; a law (Lex Julia) seems to have been passed only on the latter occasion.

8. Carried by Lucius Calpurnius Piso (consul in 133 B.C.) when he was tribune in 149 B.C.

9. At these provincial diets representatives of the different communities of the province met once a year.

10. This might be regarded as a bad omen.

11. Pompeii and Herculaneum were destroyed by a much worse earthquake sixteen years later; see Book XIV, note 17.

12. Perhaps daughter of the consul of 60 A.D. (see XIV, 20); perhaps the same Vestal Virgin of this name who was executed on a charge of adultery on the order of Domitian, as recorded by Pliny, *Letters* IV, 11.

13. 63 A.D. Lucius Verginius Rufus as governor of Upper Germany in 68 A.D. crushed the rebellion of Vindex in Gaul and declined the invitation of his troops to become a candidate for the Empire. He was suffect consul again in 69 and consul for the third time in 97 A.D. when he was eighty-three years old. Dying that year, he was succeeded in the consulship by Tacitus, who spoke his funeral oration.

14. Antium was the site of a celebrated cult of Fortune, who was represented there by two statues, supposed to be of Fortune in peace and Fortune in war.

15. See II, 41.

16. The inland district drained by the Var (including part of the modern departments of the Basses Alpes and Nice) had been made into a small province by Augustus in 14 B.C. Latin rights constituted a halfway stage between subordinate status and full citizenship.

17. Other authorities say that both senators and knights had had special seats in the Circus reserved from a much earlier date. The Roscian Law of 67 B.C. had given the knights special seats (in the fourteen rows above the orchestra) at the theater only.

18. 64 B.C.

19. See XIV, 15.

20. Now Naples; it had been founded from the Greek colony of Cumæ in about 600 B.C.

21. The garlands given to winners at the great games of Greece.

22. Now Benevento; on the Appian Way leading to Brundisium (Brindisi).

23. He gave his name to a kind of cheap drinking

TACITUS

cup (Juvenal, V, 46). Byron in a letter (No. 308 in Moore's *Life*) describes Porson when drunk as having been in a rage because no one present knew the name of the "Cobbler of Messina." "Messina" was probably Byron's mistake for "Beneventum."

24. See Book XI, note 61; XII, n. 60.

25. Goddess of the hearth, attended by the Vestal Virgins.

26. An artificial lake, probably near the Pantheon, itself built by Marcus Agrippa (see Book I, note 8).

27. The gardens of Mæcenas were on the Esquiline Hill, on the site later occupied by the baths of Titus.

28. Several splendid buildings erected by Agripps stood on the other side of the Campus Martius.

29. The name of a locality near Trajan's Forum.

30. See III, 26, with note 44; the temple was on the Aventine.

31. See XI, 14, with note 35.

32. This temple to Jupiter, the "Stayer of Flight," had been vowed by Romulus when in danger of defeat by the Sabines; it was on the Palatine near where the arch of Titus now stands.

33. Numa's palace, the Regia, had long been the official residence of the Pontifex Maximus (see Book III, note 75); both buildings stood close together, near the forum. On the temple of Vesta, see XV, 36.

34. See Book XI, note 45.

35. Lago d'Averno.

36. Halfway between Rome and Præneste (see note 41 below).

37. The quarry is near Marino.

38. The name is said in Acts 11:26 to have originated at Antioch.

39. Procurator in Judæa from 27 to 37 A.D., according to Josephus.

40. The Neronian persecution is also mentioned by Suetonius (life of Nero, 16). In the tradition of the Church it is associated with the martyrdom of St. Peter and St. Paul. There is little doubt that the Beast of the Apocalypse symbolizes Nero.

41. Now Palestrina, 23 miles east of Rome.

42. The slave revolt of 73-71 B.C., led by Spartacus, had begun with the escape of seventy-four gladiators from a gladiatorial school near Capua.

43. Now Mola di Gæta, on the coast of Latium.

44. See IV, 5.

45. Cumæ lay six miles north of the Cape of Misenum.

46. Piacenza.

47. 65 A.D.

48. See XIV, 65.

49. The poet Lucan (Marcus Annæus Lucanus), nephew of Seneca and author of the *Pharsalia,* a celebrated epic poem on the civil war between Julius Cæsar and Pompeius Magnus, still extant.

50. See XI, 36; XIII, 11.

51. See XIII, 12.

52. See XIII, 22, with note; XIV, 51, ᵛ.

53. Lucius Junius Silanus Torquatus ᵥ ᵛ probably the son of Marcus Junius Silanus (consul in 46 A.D.; see XIII, 1), and therefore descended from Augustus; his aunt, Junia Lepida, was married to Cassius (see XIII, 48; XIV, 42, 45).

54. These games began on April 12.

55. Lucius Tillius Cimber played a similar part in the assassination of Julius Cæsar.

56. The same goddess is meant by both names, for both are applied to Nortia, the Etruscan goddess of Fortune.

57. An Etrurian town, now Ferento, near Viterbo.

58. Near the Circus Maximus.

59. See XII, 2, etc.

60. The elder Pliny.

61. For Piso's wife, see 59 above.

62. Between the Palatine and the Porta Ostiensis, probably on the site of the bastion San Gallo.

63. He succeeded Doryphorus (see XIV, 65) in charge of petitions to the Emperor. He helped Nero to kill himself, and was later executed by Domitian for this act. He was a friend of the Jewish historian Josephus, and the philosopher Epictetus was among his slaves.

64. The torture of Roman citizens was of course illegal; but it seems to have been allowed in cases touching the safety of the Emperor as early as the time of Tiberius.

65. Grandson of the man mentioned in VI 9; son-in-law of Barea Soranus (XII, 53).

66. Clearly a client, who bore his patron's name (Annæus).

67. Hemlock. There is a Latin word for it, *cicuta*, which Tacitus carefully avoids using, presumably because he thought it beneath the dignity of the grand style.

68. For her father, see XII, 59; she was rich, beautiful, and clever, had had three husbands before Vestinus, and after Poppæa's death she married Nero.

69. The passage Lucan recited is thought by some to be from his *Pharsalia*, Book 3, lines 635-646; but it may have been from some other work, not now extant.

70. The Greek word is *Soter;* Tacitus avoids Greek words.

71. See XI, 1, etc.

72. He is praised by Quintilian, and was the teacher of the poet Persius.

73. See XIV, 59; he was sent to Gyarus (see III, 68).

74. See XIV, 29.

75. Marcus Cocceius Nerva, later Emperor; he was consul with Vespasian in 71 and with Domitian in 90. He was remarkably successful in keeping the favor of successive emperors. Grandson of the Nerva mentioned in IV, 58.

76. Gaius Nymphidius Sabinus became prefect of the prætorian guard as successor to Fænius Rufus and as Tigellinus' colleague in 65. In 68 he induced the guard to declare for Galba, and then perished in an attempt to get the Empire for himself.

77. Lucius Annæus Junius Gallio; as proconsul of Achæa in 52, he encountered St. Paul (Acts 18:12). He was made to commit suicide in the following year.

78. *Vindex* means "avenger"; and the revolt of Gaius Julius Vindex, governor of Gallia Lugdunensis, in 68 later led to the fall of Nero.

Book XVI

1. Dido, widow of Sychæus, king of Tyre, was the legendary founder of Carthage; in the *Æneid* she is threatened by the Numidian King Iarbas (IV, 36, etc.).
2. See XIV, 20, with note.
3. Later Emperor; see III, 55.
4. See Book XVI, n. 5. Gaius Cassius Longinus (suffect consul in 30 A.D.), jurist, formerly governor of Syria, where he maintained discipline among his troops with antique severity; mentioned several times in the ensuing narrative.
5. See XV, 52.
6. See I, 2.
7. XV, 35.
8. See Book XV, note 53.
9. He survived into old age and corresponded with the younger Pliny, who married his granddaughter Calpurnia Hispulla.
10. One of the larger Cyclades.
11. Bari.
12. See XIII, 11; XIV, 58, etc.
13. Antistia Pollitta; see XIV, 22.
14. See XIV, 57-59.
15. See XV, 50, etc.
16. See XV, 74. Naturally the old names were restored after Nero's death. The month of June originally got its name from Lucius Junius Brutus (see I, 1); Junius was also the gentile name of the Torquati (see XV, 35; XVI, 8). For Orfitus, see XII, 41.
17. Lyons.
18. 66 A.D.
19. See XIV, 48-49.
20. See XIII, 22.
21. Marcus Ostorius, the son of Publius. See XII, 31; XIV, 48.
22. Near Genoa.
23. See XV, 74.
24. See XI, 1, etc.

25. Very probably the author of the *Satyricon*. The prænomen Gaius may be wrong; the elder Pliny and Plutarch both call him Titus, and a Titus Petronius was suffect consul in 62.

26. See XV, 73

27. See XV, 49, etc.

28. See XIV, 48.

29. See XV, 49, etc.

30. See XV, 46.

31. For his father, see VI, 7.

32. See XIII, 49, etc.

33. See XII, 53, etc.

34. See XIV, 12.

35. Now Padua; the Trojan refugee Antenor was its legendary founder.

36. See XIV, 48.

37. See XIII, 33.

38. See XVI, 7-10.

39. Quintus Ælius Tubero (tribune 129 B.C.), nephew of the younger Scipio Africanus (see Book III, note 82), an uncompromising Stoic. Marcus Favonius (prætor 49 B.C.), friend and imitator of the younger Cato, put to death after Philippi (see Book I, note 4).

40. See XVI, 7.

41. See I, 1, 2.

42. See XII, 4, etc.

43. He had governed Asia in 61-62.

44. See XV, 45.

45. Quintus Arulenus Junius Rusticus (prætor 69 A.D.; suffect consul in 92 A.D.; see *Histories* III, 80), executed by Domitian in 93. Tribunes still possessed in theory the right of vetoing proposed measures.

46. In the middle of the forum of Julius Cæsar, near the Senate House.

47. Gaius Helvidius Priscus (prætor 70 A.D.), husband of Thrasea's daughter Fannia, executed by Vespasian in 74.

48. For his father, see III, 67.

49. He survived into Vespasian's reign to attack the informer Regulus; see *Histories* IV, 40-42.

50. Wife of Annius Pollio (see XV, 56, 71).

51. Publius Egnatius Celer from Berytus (Beirut); (see *Histories* IV, 10, 40).

52. He returned from exile under Galba.

53. Admired by Seneca. He defended Egnatius Celer (*Histories* IV, 40); but he was exiled by Vespasian in 71, and there are stories of his free speaking to both Nero and Vespasian.

54. Her mother, also called Arria, had voluntarily shared the death of her husband, Aulus Cæcina Pætus (suffect consul in 37 A.D.), executed as an accomplice of Camillus Scribonianus in his conspiracy against Claudius in 42 (see XII, 52). Thrasea's widow was still alive in 97.

55. Compare the words of Seneca at XV, 64. It was the Greek custom to pour the third libation at a banquet to Zeus Soter (Jupiter the Deliverer).

THE HISTORIES

Book I

1. 69 A.D. Galba was born about 3 B.C.; consul for the first time in 33 A.D.; legate of Upper Germany; proconsul of Africa (45 A.D.); governor of Hispania Tarraconensis from 60 A.D. See I, 49.

2. For his character, see I, 48.

3. See Introduction.

4. Galba, Otho, Vitellius, Domitian.

5. Galba against Otho, Otho against Vitellius, Vitellius against Vespasian. But the struggle between Galba and Otho can hardly be called a war; and Tacitus may be referring to the revolt of the German legions against Domitian in 88, which must have been described in the lost parts of the work.

6. Titus suppressed the rebellion of the Jews.

7. The Batavians revolted under Civilis.

8. Much of Britain was subdued by Tacitus' father-in-law, Agricola, who was governor from 77 to 84; Domitian later gave up most of his conquests.

9. Domitian was at war with these peoples from 89 to 92.

10. The Dacian kingdom lay in the loop of the lower Danube; after it had been reunited by Decebalus, Domitian made a preventive attack upon it (86-89 A.D.). Decebalus was later subdued by Trajan.

11. A false Nero was for a time recognized by the Parthians, but then given up.

12. The famous earthquake that destroyed Pompeii and Herculaneum took place in 79 A.D.

13. See III, 71; there was also a great fire in Rome in 80 A.D.

14. Tacitus may be referring to the misconduct of a Vestal Virgin, whom Domitian with his fondness for old Roman ceremonies had buried alive.

15. See *Annals* XV, 72.

16. "Previously a petty law officer, he had only arrogance and obstinacy to supplement his ignorance."—Sir Ronald Syme, *Tacitus* (2 vols., Oxford University Press, 1958), p. 151.

17. See *Annals* XIV, 45.

18. See *Annals* XIV, 29.

19. See *Annals* II, 68.

20. Legate in Africa; he had tried to cut off the Roman corn supply.

21. Consul in 67 A.D.; governor of Lower Germany.

22. See *Annals* XIII, 20.

23. See *Annals* XV, 23.

24. See *Annals* XI, 23.

25. See *Annals* VI, 28.

26. Gaius Licinius Mucianus (consul in 66, 70, 72 A.D.). His family may have come from Spain; he had served in Armenia under Corbulo.

27. See *Annals* XVI, 5.

28. A nephew of the famous Jewish philosopher Philo, but an apostate from his ancestral faith. He had been procurator of Judæa (46-48 A.D.), and had served in Armenia under Corbulo. Later he was with Titus at the siege of Jerusalem, and tried to prevent him from destroying the temple.

29. See *Annals* XIII, 12, 45-46, etc.

30. He had served under Corbulo in Armenia, and seems to have written a history of the campaign.

31. See *Annals* XV, 18.

32. Servius Sulpicius Galba was a relative of the Lutatii, whose family had produced the famous general Quintus Lutatius Catulus (consul in 102 B.C.).

33. See *Annals* I, 3.

34. See *Annals* XI, 15.

35. The temple of Apollo was on the Palatine, near the palace; the Velabrum was a piece of low ground running from the foot of the Palatine toward the forum, where the temple of Saturn was.

36. The Porticus Vipsania was built by Marcus Vipsanius Agrippa (see *Annals* Book I, note 8) and stood in the Campus Martius, near where the Fountain of Trevi now is.

37. This means "Hall of Liberty"; where the building was is unknown.

38. Mentioned at *Annals* XIII, 28 and XVI, 8 respectively; we do not know how they died, nor anything of Betuus Chilo.

39. See *Annals* XIV, 39.

40. See *Annals* XV, 34. Nothing is known of Ægialus; the name is Greek.

41. Names of Parthian kings of the Arsacid dynasty.

42. A pond in the forum, dried up before the time of Augustus. It was supposed to mark the spot where the earth opened to engulf Manius Curtius, who in obedience to an oracle leaped with his horse into the chasm (Livy I, 12).

43. In the forum, on the spot where his body was burned.

44. Near the temple of the divine Julius; a place of extreme sanctity.

45. Titus Flavius Sabinus (suffect consul in 45 A.D.?); he had held a command in Britain. For a character sketch, see III, 75.

46. He had been married to Claudius' daughter Antonia.

47. See *Annals* I, 2.

48. See *Annals* V, 1.

49. The young Cæsar (later Augustus) in alliance with the forces of the Senate defeated Antony near Mutina in 43 B.C.

Book II

1. Daughter of Herod Agrippa (d. 44 A.D.) and sister of his less celebrated son of the same name, together with whom she was present at St. Paul's trial before Festus (Acts 25:13, 23). Suetonius (*Titus* 7) says that Titus sent her away from Rome against his will and hers because of the scandal occasioned by the relation between them, a statement on which Racine's tragedy of *Bérénice* is based.

2. Cinyras was the father of Adonis, and like him a favorite of Aphrodite (Venus). This cult originated from that of the Phœnician goddess Astarte, and retained several un-Greek features.

3. See *Annals* I, 1.

4. One of the western Cyclades, between Ceos and Seriphus.

5. See *Annals* XIV, 28, with note.

6. Titus Vestricius Spurinna (consul for the third time, probably in 100 A.D.) survived to hold important positions under the Flavians, Nerva, and Trajan.

7. See III, 42-43. It was vital for Otho to maintain communications with the armies of Dalmatia, Mœsia, and Pannonia by keeping open the road northeastward to Aquileia, at the head of the Adriatic.

8. Ventimiglia. The mother of the famous general Agricola, Tacitus' father-in-law, was killed by Otho's troops on her family estate in this neighborhood (*Agricola* 7).

9. The Tungri lived in southeast Belgium, in the neighborhood of Spa.

10. Fréjus.

11. Antibes.

12. Now Albenga, on the Italian Riviera.

13. Long, narrow ships originally used by Illyrian

506

pirates (Liburnians) and employed by the Roman navy since the time of Cæsar.

14. Piacenza.

15. Pavia. The Vitellians must have occupied both these places. Cæcina's aim was to prevent Otho from joining forces with troops from Dalmatia, Mœsia, and Pannonia (see II, 11).

16. He was the nephew of Civilis, but fell fighting against him.

17. This is the point where the main artery, the Via Postumia, coming from Verona, was joined by a road from Mantua, along which Annius Gallus' troops advanced.

18. Son of Antiochus, king of Commagene in Asia Minor.

19. See I, 20.

20. Now Bersello; on the south bank of the Po, some way southeast of Bedriacum.

21. Not Vespasian's brother, but the other Flavius Sabinus.

22. Now the Adda, which meets the Po some way west of Cremona. In fact, the confluence is only six or seven miles west of Cremona. Either the Adda has changed its course, or Tacitus thought the confluence was below Cremona near where the battle actually took place.

If Tacitus' figures are reliable, Cæcina and Valens must have had about 100,000 men between them. Otho's forces are hard to estimate, but he must have been outnumbered, and the three legions from Mœsia were still the other side of Aquileia. We do not know how far off were the four legions from Pannonia and Dalmatia; and this ignorance seriously impairs our understanding of the strategy.

23. See I, 46.

24. Servius was a common first name among the Sulpicii, Galba's family. The nephew was executed by Domitian for celebrating his uncle's birthday.

25. In Etruria; now Ferentino. The grandfather owed the rank of senator to Livia's favor; the father, Lucius Salvius Otho (suffect consul in 33 A.D.), governed Africa and was made a patrician by Tiberius.

26. Reggio di Emilia, between Parma and Modena.

27. King of Emesa.

28. King of Commagene with part of Cilicia.

29. See II, 2.

30. Beirut.

31. Later Constantinople, now Istanbul.

32. Durazzo.

33. Brindisi.

34. Taranto.

35. Between Thrace and Mœsia.

36. See *Annals* XIV, 40. He came from Tolosa (now Toulouse).

37. Lucius Tampius Flavianus and Marcus Pompeius Silvanus were consuls together, both for the second time, in 75; see *Annals* XIII, 52.

38. Later prætorian prefect under Domitian, he was killed in Dacia in 86 or 87. We do not know which was his colony; probably one in Narbonese Gaul.

39. Cremera was the scene of the (legendary) destruction of the family of the Fabii by the Gauls in 477 B.C.; Allia that of the defeat of the Romans by the Gauls in 390 B.C.

40. Thrasea's son-in-law; see *Annals* XVI, 28 f.

41. Not to be confused with the son-in-law of Vitellius or with the freedman (II, 95).

42. See *Annals* I, 54.

43. See *Annals* XIV, 39.

44. See I, 49.

45. The allusion is to Fabius Valens.

46. See I, 13, etc.

47. Eprius Marcellus.

48. Ostiglia; on the Po, southeast of Mantua.

49. Padua.

50. Sextus Lucilius Bassus was later rewarded by Vespasian by being made a senator.

Book III

1. In upper Pannonia, near the border of Noricum; now Pettau, in the valley of the Drave, in Styria.

2. They lived between the Danube and the Theiss.

3. The Inn.

4. Oderzo.

5. Altino.

6. Padua.

7. Este.

8. Legnano.

9. See II, 44.

10. Vicenza.

11. See II, 100; the Tartaro flows east of this place. They must have got to Hostilia from Cremona by a march south of the Po.

12. A member of a family of municipal origins, which attained the consulate first only in 18 A.D., but which had evidently allied itself by marriage with the patrician Valerii. Messalla was a friend of Tacitus and is a character in his *Dialogue on Orators*; he wrote a memoir of the civil war, which is twice quoted in the *Histories* (III, 25 and 28). There is no record that Messalla, like his father, Lucius Vipstanus Poplicola Messalla (consul in 48), reached the consulship; he probably died young.

13. The province extended along the Lower Danube from the river Drinus to the Black Sea.

14. See II, 100-101.

15. Adria.

16. Brescia.

17. This word means "tortoise," and is used to describe a mass formation of soldiers, protected by their shields held overhead, that approaches the wall of a besieged city.

18. The elder Pliny, whose history described this war (cf. *Annals* XIII, 20; XV, 53).

19. An ancient Italic goddess of exhalations from the earth; hence we speak of "mephitic" vapors.

20. 218 B.C.

21. In the Alban Hills, 16 miles from Rome.

22. See II, 29, 43.

23. In 45 B.C.

24. Formerly governor of Gallia Lugdunensis.

25. South of the city, near the road to Ostia; a favorite resort of Nero (see *Annals* XV, 55).

26. See *Annals* XIII, 20.

27. Such as Marcus Junius Brutus, Cæsar's murderer, and Marcus Antonius.

28. Rimini.

29. Monaco.

30. See II, 12.

31. Fréjus.

32. Isles d' Hyères.

33. Marseilles.

34. See *Annals* XII, 36.

35. The last king of Pontus, who ceded his kingdom to Rome in 63 A.D.

36. Trebizond.

37. See II, 83.

38. The Kobidzkali, which rises in the Caucasus and flows into the Black Sea northwest of the Rion.

39. Fanum Fortunæ; from this name derives the present name of the place, Fano.

40. The ridge on the west bank of the Tiber. The battle took place in 87 B.C.; for Cinna, see *Annals* I, 1.

41. Lucius Cornelius Sisenna, prætor in 78 B.C., wrote a history of his own times.

42. Bevagna, in Umbria, northwest of Spoleto.

43. On the borders of Latium and Campania, at the mouth of the Liris.

44. Pozzuoli.

45. Terracina, on the Appian Way above the Pontine marshes.

46. In the south of Umbria, nearly two days' march south of Mevania; the passage of the Apennines was now left unopposed.

47. Peoples of central Italy.

48. See *Annals* XIV, 32-33.

49. Brother and son of Vespasian.

50. Casigliano, south of Mevania and ten miles north of Narnia.

51. Now Termini.

52. Urbino.

53. Anagni, in Latium.

54. See I, 8.

55. Tiberius Silius Italicus (consul in 68 A.D.), later

governor of Asia. His epic on the Punic Wars in fourteen books is one of the most tedious ever written; it has survived entire.

56. On the Capitoline Hill, overlooking the forum.

57. Between the Capitol and the Quirinal.

58. This separates the Capitol proper from the Arx ("citadel") to the northeast.

59. On the southwest side of the Capitol proper.

60. Juppiter Optimus Maximus.

61. Livy (II, 13) claims that Rome repulsed the attack of the Etruscan Lars Porsenna in 507 B.C.; Tacitus, no doubt correctly, tells a different story.

62. The fifth king of Rome, whose traditional date is 616-579 B.C.

63. See *Annals* III, 26.

64. See *Annals* III, 27; Suessa Pometia was the capital of the Volsci.

65. 507 B.C.

66. 83 B.C., so the interval should be 424 years.

67. Quintus Lutatius Catulus dedicated it while consul in 69 B.C.; it was renovated by Augustus in 26 and in 9 B.C.

68. See I, 27.

69. Juppiter Conservator.

70. Juppiter Custos.

71. See *Annals* III, 14.

72. Three miles from Terracina.

73. Cnæus Vergilius Capito had been prefect of Egypt under Claudius.

74. Celebrated from December 17 to 23.

75. Otricoli, southwest of Narnia.

76. This ran northeast from Rome through the Sabine country.

77. See *Annals* III, 9.

78. Prima Porta, six or seven miles from Rome.

79. Four or five miles from Rome, on the Via Salaria.

80. See *Annals* XVI, 26.

81. See *Annals* XIV, 59; XV, 71.

82. See *Annals* XIII, 47.

83. See *Annals* I, 1.

84. Now Lucera, in Apulia, west of Arpi.

Book IV

1. See III, 6, etc.
2. See Book III, note 22.
3. See *Annals* II, 41.
4. See III, 77.
5. Son-in-law of Vitellius, lately legate of Belgica.
6. See II, 91.
7. In the Samnite country (see *Annals* XI, 24).
8. When Milton called ambition "that last infirmity of noble mind," he must have had this passage in mind.
9. See *Annals* XVI, 21 f. Nothing is known of Sentius.
10. See *Annals* XIII, 29.
11. See *Annals* XIV, 59, etc.
12. See *Annals* XVI, 32, with note.
13. The leader of the conspiracy against Nero; see *Annals* XV, 48, etc.
14. See II, 92, etc.
15. See II, 95.
16. 70 A.D.
17. Son of the consul of 57 A.D. (see *Annals* XIII, 28 f.), grandson of the consul of 27 A.D.
18. Sextus Julius Frontinus, consul for the third time in 100 A.D.; governor of Britain, curator of the aqueducts, and a man of great influence under Trajan. His works on aqueducts and on stratagems have survived. Tacitus in his *Agricola* calls him "a great man, so far as he was allowed to be."
19. See II, 85.
20. See III, 12, 28.
21. See I, 47.
22. See *Annals* XVI, 28-29, 33. The Piso meant was of course Galba's adopted son.
23. See IV, 10.
24. See *Annals*, XVI, 34.
25. Brother of Junius Rusticus (see *Annals* XVI, 26); exiled by Domitian in 93, recalled by Nerva and favored by him and Trajan.
26. See *Annals* XIII, 48, with note.
27. See III, 9, with note.

28. Marcus Aquilius Regulus, suffect consul in a year unknown, had caused the death of Marcus Crassus (consul in 64 A.D.); of Crassus Scribonianus (see IV, 39); and of Servius Cornelius Orfitus (consul in 51 A.D.).
29. Vibius Crispus; see *Annals* XIV, 28; *Histories* II, 10.
30. See *Annals* XIII, 44.
31. See *Annals* XVI, 14.
32. Siena.

Book V

1. See II, 81.
2. This absurd story, not told by any other writer, seems to derive from the false etymology of "Iudæi" from "Idæi"; the connection with Saturn may have been suggested by the importance of the Jewish Sabbath, which was celebrated on Saturday (Saturn's day).
3. A legendary king of Ethiopia, father of Perseus' wife Andromeda.
4. The Solymi are mentioned three times in Homer (*Iliad* VI, 184, 204; *Odyssey* V, 282); their identification with the Jews goes back to the fifth century B.C. Hierosolyma is the Greek and Latin name for Jerusalem.
5. Bocchoris was a king of the eighth century B.C., and thus too late to be the Pharaoh of the Exodus.
6. Hammon or Ammon was the Egyptian Zeus, whose famous oracle was in the desert, twelve days' march from Memphis.
7. Tacitus calls him "Moyses."
8. The god of Memphis, worshiped in the form of a calf.
9. A name of Bacchus.
10. Josephus says that Solomon received the balsam plant as a present from the Queen of Sheba.
11. The Jordan rises not from the Libanus, but from the Antilibanus.
12. The first two lakes are the Waters of Merom and the Sea of Galilee; the third is the Dead Sea.
13. Sodom and Gomorrah.
14. North of Mount Carmel; it is now the Numan.

15. Antiochus Epiphanes IV of Syria (176-164 B.C.); see the books of Maccabees.

16. A mistake; Arsaces revolted not against Antiochus IV, but against Antiochus II (260-245 B.C.).

17. Aristobulus, son of John Hyrcanus, was the first of the Maccabæan house to take the royal title (107 B.C.).

18. 63 B.C.

19. Pacorus, son of Orodes, king of Parthia, expelled Herod from Judæa in 40 B.C. and was defeated and killed by Antony's general, Publius Ventidius Bassus, in 38. Gaius Sosius, Antony's governor of Syria, occupied Jerusalem and restored Herod the Great to the throne.

20. See *Annals* I, 3; he governed Syria from 6 B.C. The pretender Simon had been a slave of Herod.

21. Herod the Great's kingdom was divided between his sons Archelaus, Antipas, and Philip.

22. In 40 A.D.; the philosopher Philo, who was one of the ambassadors sent by the Jews to try to persuade the Emperor to rescind his order, has left an account of the affair in his *Embassy to Gaius*.

23. Brother of Claudius' powerful freedman Pallas; see *Annals* XII, 54.

24. For Claudius' mother, Antonia, see *Annals* III, 3.

25. A Greek from Clazomenæ in Asia Minor, whose wife Cleopatra was a friend of Poppæa. He took office in 64 A.D. and the war broke out in 66; Josephus says he helped to provoke it by his severity. He was killed early in the rising.

26. Gaius Cestius Gallus (consul in 42 A.D.), who died in 67.

27. Simon, and not John, was called Bargioras. Simon was the leader of the Idumæans, John of Gischala the leader of the Galilean zealots; Eleazer, of the stock of the high priests, was a much abler and more respectable man than these fanatics. He was not actually murdered, as Tacitus says, but was forced to serve under John.

Hugh R. Trevor-Roper, general editor of *The Great Histories Series*, is the distinguished Regius Professor of Modern History at Oxford University. He is probably most well-known to American readers for his book *The Last Days of Hitler*, which is a classic in the field of modern German history and was the result of official investigations carried out by Professor Trevor-Roper at the behest of British Intelligence in an attempt to unshroud the mystery surrounding the dictator's fate. The book has already been translated into nineteen foreign languages. Professor Trevor-Roper is a specialist in sixteenth- and seventeenth-century history and has published several other notable works: *Archbishop Laud, Man and Events*. He has contributed numerous articles on political and historical subjects to the journals and is familiar to American readers of *The New York Times Magazine* and *Horizon*.

Hugh Lloyd-Jones was educated at Westminster School and Christ Church, Oxford. He was a Fellow of Jesus College, Cambridge, from 1948 to 1954, and a Fellow of Corpus Christi College, Oxford, from 1954 to 1960. He has been Regius Professor of Greek and Student of Christ Church, Oxford, since 1960. His published works include an edition of papyrus fragments of Aeschylus in the Loeb Classical Library, the text of a newly discovered play by Menander, *Diskolos*, and a translation of *Greek Metre*, from the German of Paul Maas. He was also editor of *The Greeks* in the New Thinker's Library and has written many articles and reviews, mostly dealing with Greek literature.

Index

517